THE TIMES

Good University Guide 2007

in association with  PRICEWATERHOUSECOOPERS

Edited by
John O'Leary

with
Andrew Hindmarsh
Bernard Kingston

TIMES BOOKS

Acknowledgements

This edition has been produced in association with PricewaterhouseCoopers LLP (PwC). To find out more about undergraduate opportunities with PwC, please visit their website www.pwc.com/uk/eng/careers/main/index.html

The tables and their underlying methodology have been created by Mayfield University Consultants under the guidance of its partners, Bernard Kingston and Andrew Hindmarsh.

We wish to offer our best personal thanks to the many individuals who have helped with this edition of *The Times Good University Guide*. We are indebted to Peter Elias and Kate Purcell for permission to draw on their extensive research into graduate occupations; to Nicola Bright who, once again, has lent her very considerable statistical expertise to the rigour of the tables; to Hannah Brady and Alison Patterson for their assiduous research; to Susannah Attwell, Tabitha Birchall, Mary Brennan, Sharon Burgess*, Kit Campbell, Justin Cole, Sally Dyson*, Carole Finnigan, Geoff Flower, Andy Foster, Anne Gwinnett*, Helen Haydon*, Carole Hobden*, Allan Johnson, Paul Keville*, Ana Kingston, Ann-Marie Martin*, Adrian Pitman, Andrew McKirgan*, Bruce Nelson*, Claire Powell, Anne Reilly, Jon Simmons, Mike Smith*, Patrick Smith, Paul Taylor, Richard Tyler and Zena Wooldridge for sharing professional insights; to Denise Bamford and Jonathan Waller for their technical advice; to Nancy Bailey, Cicely Frew and Christopher Riches for their editorial and publishing expertise, and to Sarah Churchman, Elaine Marron and Zoe Gordon of PricewaterhouseCoopers, our sponsors, for their generous interest and support.

* Members of *The Times Guide* Advisory Group

The publishers wish to thank: BUSA for giving permission to reproduce their championship tables; UNITE, the UK's largest provider of student accommodation, for access to the results of their Student Experience Report 2006 compiled by MORI (to find out more about UNITE visit www.unite-students.com); the Royal Bank of Scotland for permission to reproduce material from the 2005 Student Living Index and to all three for their co-operation in making this information available to the authors.

Please see chapter 2 for a full explanation of the sources of data used in the ranking tables. The data providers do not necessarily agree with the data aggregations or manipulations appearing in this book and are also not responsible for any inference or conclusions thereby derived.

Table of Contents

About the Authors

John O'Leary is the Editor of *The Times Higher Education Supplement*. Until 2002 he was the Education Editor of *The Times*, having joined the paper in 1990 as Higher Education Correspondent and assumed responsibility for the whole range of education coverage in 1992. He has been writing on higher education for nearly 20 years. He has a degree in politics from the University of Sheffield.

Andrew Hindmarsh is Planning Officer at the University of Nottingham, where his responsibilities include providing management information and statistical returns to official bodies. Until 1998 he was head of the Undergraduate Admission Office at the University of Sheffield, where for ten years he worked closely with admissions tutors and UCAS. He has degrees in zoology and animal behaviour from the University of Oxford.

Bernard Kingston is now a university consultant, having been Director of the Careers Advisory Service and latterly Director of International Affairs at the University of Sheffield. He is a past president of the Association of Graduate Careers Advisory Services and has advised governments and universities in Asia, Africa, Australia and the UK. He has degrees in chemistry from the Universities of Leicester and Sussex.

Andrew Hindmarsh and Bernard Kingston are Partners in Mayfield University Consultants, who have compiled the main University League Table and the individual subject tables, as well as contributing ten chapters and the internet resources.

How to Use This Book

The Times Good University Guide 2007 provides a wealth of information to help you select the courses and universities of your choice and to guide you through the whole process of applying to university.

Which are the Best Universities?

The place to start is the main *Times* League Table on pages 39–44. This ranks the universities by assessing their quality not just by their student satisfaction but also through another eight factors, including research assessment, the spending on student facilities and graduate prospects. This table gives an indication of the overall performance of each university. Each measure used in making the assessment is described in the pages that precede the table.

It is also important to read chapter 1, which provides an invaluable introduction to the many aspects of selecting an appropriate university for you.

Which are the Best Universities for Particular Subjects?

Chapter 1 also provides guidance on how to start selecting courses that might interest you. It is a good introduction to chapter 3, which gives detailed information on 61 different subject areas, where universities appear in ranked tables, with our assessment of the top universities for each subject. Background information is given about the subject, along with the latest data on what graduates did on completion of the courses. The notes on pages 35–8 explain the data that is included within these tables.

By using both the subject tables and the main *Times* League Table, you can begin to narrow down your search for appropriate universities.

What is Each University Like?

Chapter 11 devotes two pages to each university, giving a general overview of the institution as well as data on student numbers, how to contact the university, the accommodation provided by the university, and the bursaries and scholarships available. There are also profiles of the main university towns in chapter 12, complete with travel information and websites for further information.

As an International Student, How Do I Choose?

In addition to using all the data on universities and subjects, chapter 9 is devoted to the needs of international students. As well as providing practical advice for students coming to the United Kingdom, this chapter gives details of the most popular subjects and the most popular universities attended by international students, so helping further in the selection of a university.

How Do I Apply?

Chapter 4 outlines the application procedure for university entry. It starts by advising you on how to complete the UCAS application, and then takes you step-by-step through the process that we hope will lead to your university place for autumn 2007.

How Much Will It Cost?

Chapter 7 outlines the costs of studying at university (including the payment of fees) as well as sources of funds (including student loans, grants and bursaries). Chapter 5 provides advice on where to live during the course of your studies, whilst the range of charges for accommodation are given in each university profile in chapter 11.

What Parents Need To Know

Chapter 8 outlines some of the help parents can provide during the process of applying to and preparing for university.

But That's Not All

The whole of chapter 6 is devoted to sport at university, including the first ever systematic ranking of facilities at each institution. If, on the other hand, your concern is personal safety and security then there are hints and hard data in chapter 5.

How Do I Find Out More?

In each university profile (chapter 11) contact details are given (including e-mail addresses and websites), so you can obtain more information on any university you are interested in. More help is provided in the Internet Resources section (pages 520–22) which lists many appropriate websites for students, while a further listing (pages 516–19) provides contact details for Higher Education Institutes and Colleges which are not covered elsewhere within the book.

We hope you find the information presented in the book useful in planning for your university career. If you have any suggestions for further information you would like to see, please send them to:
The Times Good University Guide
Collins Reference
HarperCollins Publishers
77-85 Fulham Palace Road
Hammersmith
London W6 8JB
or contact us through our website, www.collins.co.uk

Introduction

The first year of top-up fees, in 2006, was expected to bring a sea change in English higher education. But, for applicants at least, 2007 may be even trickier. The university edifice did not collapse with the introduction of higher charges – the number of applications dropped by more than 3 per cent, but the comparison was with a boom year when many students were trying to get in ahead of the new fee regime. The total was still higher than for 2005 or any previous year.

Who knows what 2007 will bring? The fees will not change beyond an adjustment for inflation, but universities will have had a year to hone their bursary and scholarship schemes, and applicants will have had the same to get used to the new system. Both sides will be second-guessing whether the initial pattern of demand for degrees was a one-off or the shape of things to come.

Certainly, few would have predicted the full impact at the start of 2006. The trend away from most arts and social sciences towards more obviously job-related courses had been widely forecast, but most believed that it would be the new universities that bore the brunt of any decline in applications. In fact, some of the older and supposedly more prestigious institutions – particularly those away from large centres of population – looked likely to suffer most. It remains to be seen where places will be filled, but initial indications are that more teenagers will stay at home to study and opt for courses that they hope will enable them to repay their debts.

As students and their families adjust to the new system, all this may change. The longstanding preference for studying away from home is likely to reassert itself and some of the non-vocational subjects currently in decline may well recover. For the moment, however, it would appear that fees of £3,000 a year have not dampened the demand for higher education, but they have altered it. In particular, more Scottish and Welsh students are remaining within their borders to escape the higher charges, and that is unlikely to change in the near future.

For those who do not have that choice, it is worth remembering that the fee changes are not all bad news: the requirement to pay fees of £1,000-plus upfront has gone and grants, bursaries and scholarships will be available to bring down the cost for many students. The institutional profiles in this year's *Guide* include a section detailing the (sometimes complex) arrangements at each university.

Competition for places on popular courses is sure to remain intense for the class of 2007. The number of 18-year-olds is still rising, A-level pass rates are improving and the range of qualifications accepted by universities has expanded. In addition, the number of applicants from the accession countries of the European Union is growing and universities have stepped up their efforts to recruit students from other parts of the world, who pay even higher fees. It may well be that the dip in applications in 2006 was a one-off.

That is where this *Guide* comes in. A league table will not identify the most suitable course for any prospective student: that is a matter of personal preference, involving the location and character of a university, and above all the syllabus. But the rankings in this *Guide* will help place those choices in context. They take account of academics' own ratings of the standards of research in each of the 61 subject areas in British higher education, entry standards of undergraduates, and the all-important employment prospects after graduation.

When *The Times Good University Guide* first appeared almost 15 years ago, it helped to explode the myth that any British degree was as good as any other. Although ranking universities proved predictably controversial, the statistics behind the tables confirmed sharp variations in performance within British higher education. Charles Clarke, Labour's former Education Secretary, was prepared to cite this *Guide* as evidence to demolish what he termed the "emperor's clothes idea that all universities are broadly the same".

The changes that Mr Clarke was advocating and that his successors have pursued – chiefly the introduction of variable tuition fees, but also the encouragement of greater specialisation – will create a stark new pecking order in higher education. Employers already distinguish between universities as well as individuals. The need to know the standing of a university, both as an institution and in the various subjects it offers, can only become more important as time goes on.

Unlike most of the rankings that have sprung up in recent years, *The Times Guide* has maintained as much consistency as possible in the methods used to compare universities. But this year's tables contain some big – and unavoidable – changes. The most dated assessments of teaching quality were removed two years ago, but the consensus in the academic community is that the rest are now also too old to represent a fair reflection of any department.

The teaching scores have been replaced (albeit with a lower weighting) by figures from the National Student Satisfaction Survey, which was carried out for the first time throughout England, Wales and Northern Ireland in 2005. To avoid double-counting, only the first four sections of the survey have been included in the calculations. Scores have had to be generated from universities' performance on the other measures in the table where response rates for the satisfaction survey were too low to be published. This was the case for Cambridge, East London, Oxford, London South Bank, Thames Valley and Warwick universities, as well as for all their Scottish counterparts. The change inevitably renders comparisons with the 2006 guide unreliable.

The other big change this year is in the number of universities: nine have been created since the last edition was published. Several appear in relatively advanced positions, Winchester taking the honours among the newcomers in sixty-second place, two ahead of Chichester. None looks out of place in the main ranking and several register good performances in the subject tables. The total would have been higher still if London Metropolitan University had not again blocked the release of data from the Higher Education Statistics Agency. It took this action two years ago because it regarded statistics relating to its two predecessor institutions (London Guildhall and North London) as misleading. Although this objection no longer holds good, the university has maintained its stance and, regrettably for those seeking information on one of the capital's largest universities, it cannot be included in the new table, or in the many subject rankings for which it is eligible. London Met was 98th out of 100 universities in its one appearance in the ranking.

The first *Times* League Table effectively produced a dead heat between Oxford and Cambridge, with the light blues a fraction ahead. After several years of Cambridge domination, changes in methodology saw the roles reversed in the 2003 edition and Oxford subsequently extended its lead. The current table sees the ancient rivals take closer order once more. Cambridge has the better record on research, entry standards, completion rates, graduate destinations and spending on student facilities, but Oxford's lead in staffing levels, degree classifications and spending on libraries and computing makes the difference. Accurate comparisons of the two are difficult because of the mix of college and central university responsibilities, but Oxford appears to include more college spending in its submission. Cambridge remains well clear of Imperial College and the London School of Economics, while Edinburgh remains the top university in Scotland.

For most readers, the scramble over a handful of points at the top of the overall ranking of universities will be literally academic. The key information is contained in the subject tables, which now cover every area of higher education. With the exception of education, which has up-to-date Ofsted scores, these too have had the remaining teaching quality scores removed because of their age.

To compensate for the absence of detailed teaching quality reports, universities are now required to publish particular statistics – some of which were already available nationally – as well as summaries of external examiners' reports. The Teaching Quality Information website (www.tqi.ac.uk) now provides a range of data, including the full results from the National Student Satisfaction survey. The switch has been overwhelmingly popular among academics, who resented the previous system, but it is unlikely to be as effective at pointing up the gems (or duds) in unexpected places.

One of the strengths of this *Guide*, and others like it, has been to highlight the quality of previously underestimated universities such as York and Bath, and to celebrate the achievements of centres of excellence such as the social sciences at Essex. But, far from seeing the end of league tables as the critics of subject assessments intended, the likely impact will be to make them more influential. Universities' own research suggests that well over half of all applicants use newspaper guides and, as the one round of teaching quality reports becomes increasingly dated, more students will look for alternative sources of comparison. University rankings existed before teaching assessments were published and they will continue under the new system.

Any doubt that students would become more selective about the courses they chose has evaporated in recent years. Just as tuition fees and the withdrawal of maintenance grants have added to the financial pressures on students and their families, the winds of change have turned into a gale for some universities. Amid the Government's expansion plans, academics by the score have been made redundant in some institutions, and we have seen the first campus closures. Top-up fees, while promising a financial lifeline for many universities, may bring further institutional casualties if students become even more selective.

The most recent concerns, however, have been in particular subjects where students are in short supply and research costs can only be met with generous funding. Most attention has focused on chemistry, where there have been a number of closures, but other sciences and modern languages have proved vulnerable. The lure of a degree remains strong in some subjects and some universities, but by no means all. The demand for places on new universities' vocational degrees is often buoyant, for example, while applicants are looking elsewhere for traditional academic subjects.

Higher education had already seen important changes with the introduction of incentives to extend access to a wider share of the population, and much more selective allocation of research funds. The Government wants half of all young people to experience higher education by the time they are 30, many of them taking two-year foundation degrees rather than the traditional honours. The result is a gradual return to the hierarchical system that seemed to have been abandoned when the polytechnics acquired university status; only this time there are more than two tiers.

At the top, in terms of funding and prestige, is a group of fewer than 20 universities, which attract 90 per cent of the resources available for research and also take the lion's share of money for teaching, partly because they offer expensive subjects such as medicine and engineering. A middle group, composed mainly of traditional universities, has been recruiting more undergraduates – especially overseas – while trying to compete on research. The remainder are having to survive mainly by expanding, or at least maintaining, student numbers and interacting with local firms.

Universities in the last group have been feeling the squeeze, as several of the most popular institutions have taken advantage of a relaxation in recruitment controls to expand their numbers. But fears have also been expressed for some of those in the middle, which miss out not only on the Government's boost for leading research but also on the rewards for widening access to higher education. Applicants with the necessary qualifications will no doubt continue to migrate towards the more prestigious institutions.

Confusion over sixth–form qualifications continues to complicate matters further for those hoping to begin a course in 2007. Although the Government rejected proposals for an overarching diploma, teenagers and mature applicants would do well to examine the small print in universities' prospectuses and on their websites to gauge their approach to different qualifications. The demand for more than the conventional three A levels and attitudes towards Key Skills, AS levels and vocational qualifications still vary enormously from university to university. Most of the top universities continue to frame their offers in terms of A-level grades, but the majority of others now use the UCAS tariff to set a points requirement.

Whichever system is used, every grade may help in the race for selection. And the right choice of course remains vital. This book should help in the process of choice for, unlike other guides, its emphasis is on the quality of education. As well as the original university rankings, the book contains advice for both home and overseas students on how to choose a suitable course, and there are extended profiles of all the universities in our tables.

Mindful of the competition for graduate jobs, applicants are taking more care than ever over their choice of institution and course. The pattern established in Australia, which began charging for higher education more than a decade ago, is being repeated in Britain. Courses that are perceived to offer a clear career path are seeing a significant rise in applications, while some traditional academic subjects are struggling. There will be a place somewhere in higher education for most of those hoping to start a course in 2007, but such are the uncertainties that candidates would be wise to consider a wide range of options. Some may choose to be more ambitious than they would have been in previous years, while including at least one "insurance" course, for example, where entrance requirements are significantly lower than at the first-choice university.

The University Explosion

At first sight, choosing a university appears to have become simpler over the past decade. The distinction between universities and polytechnics was swept away in 1992 and the number of places expanded to the point where far more young (and not so young) people could benefit from higher education. Although the parties differed in the 2005 election about the scale of expansion, consensus has grown among politicians and business leaders that, quite apart from the benefits to the individual, a modern economy needs mass higher education. Countries such as the United States and Japan reached the same conclusion long ago but a combination of factors – not all of them planned – has seen Britain making up for lost time at a rate that has prompted concerns about the quality of some courses.

More than a third of 18-year-olds are now going on to higher education, compared with one in seven in 1980, while a much higher proportion will take a higher education course at some point in their life. Yet, paradoxically, by ridding Britain of its elite university system, the last Conservative Government sowed the seeds of a different form of elitism. The very process of opening up higher education ensured the creation of a new hierarchy of institutions. The old certainties could not survive in a nation of more than 100 diverse universities and a growing number of degree-providing colleges.

The New Hierarchy

There always was a pecking order of sorts. Oxford and Cambridge were world leaders long before most British universities were established, and parts of London University have always enjoyed a high status in particular fields. But few outside the higher-education world could discriminate between Aberdeen and Exeter, for example. Employers, careers advisers, even academics, had their own ideas of which were the leading universities, but there was little hard evidence to back their conclusions. Often they were based on outdated, inaccurate impressions of distant institutions.

The expanded higher education system has made such judgements more scientific as well as more necessary. Employers of graduates and those who commit their money to student sponsorship or funding research are comparing institutions department by department. This has become possible because of a new transparency in what a former higher-education minister described as the "secret garden of academe". Official demands for more and more published information may have taxed the patience of university administrators, but they have also given outsiders the opportunity to make more meaningful comparisons.

Many see the beginnings of a British Ivy League in the competitive culture that has ensued. Even before the recent upheavals, the lion's share of research cash went to a small group of traditional universities, enabling them to upgrade their facilities and attract many of the top academics. As student numbers have gone through the roof, however, general higher education budgets have been squeezed and the funding gap has widened. Beneath the veneer of a unified higher education system, it was inevitable that greater specialisation would arrive eventually. There is no need for formalised divisions because the market – and now Government policy – are already taking the university system in that direction.

Why University?

Doubtless some will be tempted, once the cost of living has been added to the new fees burden and the attractions of university life balanced against loss of potential earnings, to write off higher education. There are plenty of self-made millionaires who still swear by the University of Life as the only training ground for success. Yet even by narrow financial criteria it would be rash to dismiss higher education. With so many more competing for jobs, a degree will never again be an automatic passport to a fast-track career. But graduates' financial prospects still compare favourably with school leavers'. Indeed, the salary premium enjoyed by UK graduates is among the highest in the world, according to the Organisation of Economic Cooperation and Development. Even for those who cannot or do not wish to afford three or more years of full-time education after leaving school, university remains a possibility. The modular courses adopted by most universities enable students to work through a degree at their own pace, dropping out for a time if necessary, or switching to part-time attendance. Distance learning is another option, and advances in information technology now mean that some nominally full-time courses are delivered mainly via computers.

For many – perhaps most – students, therefore, the university experience is not what it was in their parents' day. There is more assessment, more crowding, more pressure to get the best possible degree while also finding gainful employment for at least part of the year. The proportion of students achieving first-class degrees has risen significantly, while an upper second (rather than the previously ubiquitous 2:2) has become the norm. Research shows that the classification has a real impact in the labour market.

Towards the Future

The 2004 Higher Education Act (and the White Paper that preceded it) ensured that the pace of change will accelerate. There are experiments with two-year degrees and more students are beginning their degrees at further education colleges. Others are taking foundation degrees and deciding later whether to go on to honours. Some predict the rise of the "virtual university" or the demise of the conventional higher-education institution, as companies customise their own courses. However, universities have demonstrated enduring popularity and show every sign of weathering the current turbulence.

Higher education has become a political hot potato, particularly where admission to the top universities is concerned. Those that have tried to broaden their intakes and make allowances for promising students from poor schools have been accused of social engineering. But a change of tack by the Conservatives means that both main parties now acknowledge the value of mass higher education. Places will continue to be plentiful, yet competition is bound to remain intense on many courses. Despite the downturn in applications for places in 2006, for example, the top programmes in most subjects remained oversubscribed.

The new fee regimes in England, Wales and Northern Ireland will take time to bed in, but they (or something like them) are obviously here to stay. Those who opt for an English university may blanch at the thought of future debts, but the new system should reduce the immediate financial problems that students have experienced in recent years. Undergraduates from less-affluent homes will have their pick of bursaries, as well as the possibility of a grant, while middle-class families may be able to offer more financial support when they no longer have to help out with upfront tuition fees. Careful research on the right course will be essential. This guide should be a useful starting point.

Choosing a Course and a University

1

Choosing a course and a university are big decisions which will have an enormous impact on your future life. They will affect the place you live, the friends you make, and quite possibly your future career. They are also very difficult decisions: with tens of thousands of courses and over a hundred universities to choose from (nearer 150 if you include higher education colleges), it can be difficult to know where to start, let alone which to choose. And the problem is likely to get worse as the Government has expressed its desire for more, not less, diversity among universities.

So how do you go about it? There are no easy answers, but it is possible to list a range of factors which need to be looked at. Different people will attach different levels of importance to each one, but most will need at least to think about them all. HERO (www.hero.ac.uk), the national website for higher education in the UK, together with the Teaching Quality Information site (www.tqi.ac.uk) may help you to do this. They publish general information about universities and information about quality of universities, including the results of the National Student Survey, summaries of external examiners' reports and detailed employment statistics. Some guidance on English-speaking alternatives to British universities is given at the end of this chapter. We will start by looking at the choice of course and then the place where you might study.

> **UNITE Student Experience Report 2006**
> 90% of students have a favourable impression of their university.

The Subject

For a few people, choosing a course is simple: they have always wanted to be a brain surgeon or have always had a passion for Tudor England. For most, however, there is a bewildering variety of courses, many of which involve subjects that are not taught in schools or colleges. Somehow you have to narrow down the thousands of courses to just a few.

When it comes to choosing a subject there are several things you need to take into account. First, you must make sure you understand the nature of the subject you are considering, especially if it is one you have not studied before. A course in ecology, for example, sounds as if it might deal with conservation and 'green' issues. However, many ecology courses are about the scientific study of the interaction between living organisms and their environments and may only deal peripherally with conservation issues. Language courses can vary considerably, from those concerned largely with literature to those which concentrate on translation and contemporary area studies. Psychology is another subject which can vary, depending on whether the course focuses on the social or the scientific end of the subject.

Having made sure you understand the nature of the subject, you must be interested in it. You will spend a large proportion of three to six years immersed in the subject and that will be pretty dull if you find it boring. More important, you will probably perform better if you are excited by what you are studying. You are also likely to perform better if you have an aptitude for the subject. A course may be really interesting and lead to a ble is ranked by the sum of the three "positive" (graduate) destinations – Employed in Graduate Jobs, Employed in Graduate Jobs and Studying, and Studying and Not Employed. Source: HESA 2003–04

Times Subject	Employed in Graduate Job	Employed in Graduate Job and Studying	Employed in Non-Graduate Job	Employed in Non-Graduate Job and Studying	Studying and Not Employed	Unemployed
Dentistry	67%	32%	0%	0%	1%	0%
Medicine	85%	5%	0%	0%	9%	0%
Nursing	89%	7%	2%	0%	1%	1%
Veterinary Medicine	77%	2%	2%	0%	16%	3%
Pharmacology and Pharmacy	61%	19%	6%	1%	10%	3%
Architecture	60%	17%	6%	1%	12%	4%
Building	71%	14%	8%	1%	3%	4%
Other Subjects Allied to Medicine	71%	8%	9%	1%	7%	3%
Civil Engineering	68%	10%	9%	1%	7%	5%
Land and Property Management	53%	22%	15%	2%	6%	3%
Chemical Engineering	52%	3%	10%	3%	24%	8%
Education	64%	4%	15%	2%	10%	4%
Social Work	65%	7%	16%	1%	6%	4%
Town and Country Planning and Landscape	49%	12%	18%	2%	14%	4%
Chemistry	35%	4%	18%	2%	35%	6%
Mechanical Engineering	52%	7%	18%	2%	12%	8%
Food Science	53%	4%	20%	2%	15%	7%
Law	19%	6%	19%	6%	44%	5%
Theology and Religious Studies	32%	7%	23%	4%	29%	5%
East and South Asian Studies	38%	10%	17%	5%	21%	10%
Mathematics	31%	11%	23%	3%	25%	7%
Physics and Astronomy	24%	7%	22%	2%	36%	9%
General Engineering	45%	7%	22%	2%	14%	9%
Celtic Studies	22%	5%	23%	6%	39%	4%
Anatomy and Physiology	23%	4%	26%	4%	39%	4%
Aeronautical and Manufacturing Engineering	45%	7%	24%	2%	13%	9%
Economics	35%	12%	26%	4%	16%	7%
Geology	31%	4%	26%	2%	28%	9%
German	38%	5%	28%	4%	20%	5%
Electrical and Electronic Engineering	43%	5%	24%	2%	14%	12%

Times Subject	Employed in Graduate Job	Employed in Graduate Job and Studying	Employed in Non-Graduate Job	Employed in Non-Graduate Job and Studying	Studying and Not Employed	Unemployed
French	35%	6%	30%	3%	20%	5%
Russian	40%	3%	24%	1%	19%	14%
Middle Eastern and African Studies	35%	8%	28%	1%	18%	9%
Biological Sciences	29%	5%	29%	3%	27%	7%
Computer Science	45%	4%	25%	2%	12%	12%
Music	31%	5%	28%	5%	24%	7%
Classics and Ancient History	24%	6%	30%	5%	30%	6%
Italian	40%	3%	30%	5%	15%	7%
Materials Technology	38%	3%	29%	4%	18%	9%
Linguistics	28%	6%	33%	4%	24%	4%
Iberian Languages	35%	6%	33%	3%	17%	6%
Librarianship and Information Management	45%	5%	30%	1%	7%	11%
Anthropology	32%	6%	30%	5%	20%	8%
Accounting and Finance	28%	21%	29%	7%	8%	7%
Politics	30%	5%	32%	5%	21%	7%
Geography	31%	5%	35%	3%	20%	6%
Social Policy	37%	5%	34%	3%	13%	7%
Business Studies	42%	6%	35%	3%	7%	7%
Archaeology	28%	4%	32%	5%	23%	9%
English	28%	4%	34%	5%	22%	7%
Agriculture and Forestry	36%	8%	37%	3%	9%	6%
History	23%	4%	37%	4%	25%	7%
Philosophy	23%	4%	35%	6%	25%	8%
Psychology	28%	6%	38%	5%	17%	6%
History of Art, Architecture and Design	26%	3%	35%	6%	20%	9%
Art and Design	36%	4%	36%	5%	8%	11%
Hospitality, Leisure, Recreation, Sport and Tourism	32%	4%	43%	3%	12%	6%
Sociology	30%	4%	41%	4%	14%	7%
Communication and Media Studies	37%	3%	41%	3%	6%	9%
Drama, Dance and Cinematics	30%	3%	43%	5%	11%	9%
American Studies	25%	3%	45%	5%	14%	8%
All Subjects	**40%**	**6%**	**28%**	**3%**	**16%**	**7%**

guaranteed high-flying career, but if you are no good at it, you may end up performing badly or even failing altogether.

It is also good if you have some aptitude for the subject. Here there are some tests you can do to help you identify subjects you are likely to be good at, such as the free Stamford Test available on the UCAS website (www.ucas.ac.uk).

Career opportunities are another important factor. If you know what you want to do after university, your subject must provide a suitable basis for that career. The choice may be wider than you think, as nearly half of graduate jobs do not specify any particular subject at all. Conversely, a narrowly vocational course could restrict your career options if you subsequently change your mind about the direction you want to go in.

For many professional subjects, such as engineering, psychology or architecture, the course may be accredited by a professional body (such as the Engineering Council). You will usually need to have followed an accredited course if you want to continue with the subject as your chosen career.

Students often refer to employment prospects when they are asked about why they chose their course. However, it is worth looking at the figures. The table on pages 14–15 gives the percentages of graduates in 2004 who, six months after graduation, obtained a graduate job (ie, one which normally recruits graduates), went on to further study,

obtained a job but one that does not normally recruit graduates, or who were unemployed. The unemployment rate varies from 0 per cent (dentistry and medicine) to 14 per cent (Russian) but for most subjects is within the range 4–9 per cent. In other words, for most subjects the chances of getting a job are about the same. Interestingly, business studies, a subject that is often considered to be highly employable, comes out in the middle at 7 per cent.

The picture becomes more varied when you look at the proportions who obtain a graduate-level job. Some subjects, such as dentistry and nursing, do more or less guarantee a graduate-level job with over 95 per cent obtaining one. However, there are a number of subjects where over one third of graduates are in non-graduate jobs after six months. The proportion entering further study also varies considerably, usually because of the normal career paths followed by graduates. Fifty-six per cent of lawyers go on to further study because that is necessary to qualify as a solicitor or barrister and 41 per

Ten Courses You Didn't Know You Could Do		Top Ten Most Popular Subjects		
BA	Adventure recreation	1	Design studies	21,553
BA	Animation	2	Medicine	19,360
BA	Hausa and Arabic	3	Law	19,097
BA	Byzantine studies	4	Psychology	15,847
BSc	Equine science	5	Nursing	14,744
BA	Packaging design	6	Management studies	14,454
BA	Playwork	7	Social work	13,866
BSc	Law and property valuation	8	Computer science	13,650
BSc	Science and football	9	Teacher training	12,698
BA	War studies	10	Business studies	10,654
	available for entry in 2006, UCAS website		applications, entry 2005, UCAS	

cent of chemists do the same because a higher degree is necessary for many chemistry careers.

Of course there will be some variability within these broad subject groups. Some courses may be tailored towards specific careers and so achieve a very high level of employability, but conversely may be seen as too specialised if you try for an alternative career. Also, the longer-term career prospects may be better than the figures for six months after graduation. One study showed that the proportion of graduates in a non-graduate job after four years was one third of that after just six months. Design studies graduates, for example, often take longer to establish their careers than those in some other disciplines.

One reason for some similarity in employment prospects is the point mentioned above, that a significant proportion of job vacancies do not specify any subject at all. You can take the most obscure subject in the UCAS Directory and still have nearly 50 per cent of jobs open to you. Another reason is that class of degree is important: students with first-class honours are very rarely unemployed whatever subject they studied.

Getting a job is one thing, but will it be a well-paid job? Graduate starting salaries also vary between subjects as the table on pages 18–19 shows. The tables are quite highly correlated so that subjects where graduates are likely to find a job are also those which are well paid (at least initially). However, there are some exceptions such as architecture, where graduate jobs seem to be easy to come by but starting salaries are very much in the middle. Do remember that these figures do not reflect your earning prospects as your career develops. For example, nursing graduates receive quite good starting salaries but the longer term earning potential may well be less than that of some other subjects lower down the table.

You also need to consider entry requirements. Some universities have a General Entrance requirement, a basic minimum set of qualifications that all students have to have. For most students this is not a problem as they will meet the requirement easily, but it is worth checking to make sure. It may include an English language requirement and a minimum age. Most universities will also have various escape clauses to enable them to admit good students with unusual backgrounds even if they don't meet the General Entrance requirement.

Each course will also have its entry requirements, both in terms of subjects you must already have studied and the examination grades required for entry. Most mathematics

Top Ten for Average Tariff Score			Bottom Ten for Average Tariff Score	
1	Veterinary medicine	486	1 Social work	222
2	Medicine	470	2 Tourism, transport and travel	225
3	Dentistry	434	3 Information systems	233
4	Mathematics	417	4 Crafts	240
5	Physics	416	5 Human resource management	250
6	Statistics	407	6 Education	252
7	Ophthalmics	394	7 Building	254
8	Astronomy	393	8 Publishing	266
9	Russian	391	9 Agriculture	267
10	Chemical engineering	391	10 Sports science	269

	bject	Graduate Employment or Self Employment	Non-graduate Employment or Self Employment
1	Medicine	£30,740	£11,500
2	Dentistry	£27,169	*
3	Chemical Engineering	£22,068	£13,852
4	Veterinary Medicine	£22,048	*
5	Economics	£21,331	£15,856
6	Social Work	£20,703	£13,430
7	General Engineering	£20,481	£14,637
8	Electrical and Electronic Engineering	£20,387	£14,267
9	Mechanical Engineering	£20,353	£14,470
10	Building	£20,314	£13,135
11	Aeronautical and Manufacturing Engineering	£20,256	£14,327
12	Nursing	£20,174	£15,064
13	Land and Property Management	£19,915	£15,889
14	Theology and Religious Studies	£19,757	£12,058
15	Mathematics	£19,737	£13,814
16	Civil Engineering	£19,711	£13,023
17	Librarianship and Information Management	£19,463	£14,516
18	Computer Science	£19,416	£14,740
19	Physics and Astronomy	£19,339	£13,011
20	East and South Asian Studies	£18,984	£15,113
21	Business Studies	£18,580	£14,398
22	Philosophy	£18,576	£12,816
23	Education	£18,446	£12,607
24	Politics	£18,384	£13,560
25	Food Science	£18,276	£13,806
26	Middle Eastern and African Studies	£18,175	£12,053
27	Classics and Ancient History	£18,115	£14,269
28	Russian	£18,051	£14,747
29	Chemistry	£18,037	£13,373
30	Town & Country Planning and Landscape	£17,950	£14,350
31	Accounting and Finance	£17,918	£14,759
32	Other Subjects Allied to Medicine	£17,903	£12,973
33	Social Policy	£17,862	£12,946
34	French	£17,855	£14,245
35	Italian	£17,798	£14,372
36	German	£17,560	£14,377
37	Law	£17,506	£13,294
38	Materials Technology	£17,478	£15,412
39	Anatomy and Physiology	£17,397	£12,852
40	Sociology	£17,368	£12,975
41	Anthropology	£17,355	£13,700
42	History	£17,286	£13,107

What Do Graduates Earn?

Subject	Graduate Employment or Self Employment	Non-graduate Employment or Self Employment
43 Celtic Studies	£17,242	£11,289
44 Iberian Languages	£17,104	£13,896
45 Geology	£17,023	£12,326
46 Geography	£16,960	£13,209
47 English	£16,534	£12,827
48 Linguistics	£16,466	£12,787
49 Biological Sciences	£16,425	£12,548
50 Hospitality, Leisure, Recreation, Sport, Tourism	£16,213	£13,249
51 Psychology	£16,186	£12,743
52 Music	£16,172	£12,942
53 Pharmacology and Pharmacy	£16,081	£13,257
54 History of Art, Architecture and Design	£16,042	£14,765
55 Agriculture and Forestry	£16,031	£13,823
56 Architecture	£15,836	£12,734
57 American Studies	£15,820	£13,518
58 Communication and Media Studies	£15,707	£13,234
59 Art and Design	£15,557	£12,474
60 Drama, Dance and Cinematics	£15,533	£12,822
61 Archaeology	£15,364	£12,812

*Too few students to calculate a meaningful average.
  Source: HESA 2003–04

courses, for example, will require previous study of mathematics. The UCAS website or the *Official UCAS Guide* are the easiest ways to check this. If you have the right subjects, the grades required will vary between universities and also between subjects. There is little point in applying for medicine unless you are confident of getting As and Bs at A level (or their equivalent in other qualifications) while Ds and Es will get you into a course such as engineering at many less popular universities.

Many universities provide entry profiles on the UCAS website, a more detailed guide to entry requirements and what the university is looking for than can be summarised in a prospectus. This information will also be in course or departmental booklets.

The Qualifications Jungle

The current post-16 curriculum allows universities to express their entry requirements in a wide variety of ways. They have to make choices about the number of units that should be taken, how many A2s or Advanced Highers will be required, whether Key Skills will be compulsory and so on. Inevitably different universities have made different decisions and so you will have to read their websites and prospectuses much more carefully to ensure that you can find your way through the new qualifications jungle.

On some things most universities are in agreement:

- at least two subjects should be taken at A2

- applicants who do not take AS levels in Year 12 will not be disadvantaged.
- applicants with four or five AS levels will not be at an advantage.
- neither Key Skills nor the Advanced Extension Tests will be compulsory

On others, however, there are differences:

- some universities require a total of 21 units, others require 18 units.
- some include Key Skills in offers, others do not.
- some use the UCAS tariff (see *The UCAS Tariff* box, below), others do not.
- some accept General Studies A2, others do not.

Generally speaking, universities that come higher up the ranking in our league table are more likely to require 21 units rather than 18, not to include Key Skills in offers, and not to use the tariff. However, there is a lot of variation so it is important to ensure you read the small print carefully.

In general, the new universities are more likely to accept the more vocationally-oriented A levels for particular courses, and are more likely to use the new UCAS tariff and allow points for Key Skills. However, in all cases you will need to check the university's prospectus and/or the *Official UCAS Guide* carefully.

Older students, or those with a non-traditional educational background, will generally be treated more flexibly by universities. While you will still be expected to demonstrate your ability and suitability for the course, you will be able to do this

---

The UCAS Tariff

The UCAS tariff allocates a numerical score to a range of qualifications and attainments, establishing an equivalence between them and allowing the aggregation of scores from many different qualifications. It became available in 2002 for universities to use in making their offers of places, but not all universities are using it. Some do not agree with the equivalences and weights determined by UCAS while others simply prefer to make offers based on specific grades in specific subjects. In general, universities that appear higher up *The Times* League Table are less likely to use the UCAS tariff in making their offers. Even those using it are likely to require specific grades in certain key subjects as well as an overall tariff score.

Full details are on the UCAS website (www.ucas.com) but some of the main scores in the new tariff are as follows:

Score	English Qualifications		Scottish Qualifications		Key Skills
	GCE AS	GCE A Level	Advanced Higher	Higher	
120		A	A		
100		B	B		
80		C	C		
72				A	
60	A	D		B	
50	B				
48				C	
40	C	E			
30	D				Level 4
20	E				Level 3

through a wide variety of qualifications or an access course or, in some cases, relevant work experience. The GCSEs you flunked as an unhappy adolescent before diving into the first job that came up will be ignored. The emphasis will be on what you can do now.

Bear in mind that entry standards are essentially market-related. Popular courses at popular universities can afford to be very choosy about whom they admit and so have the highest entry standards. That may not mean the courses are any tougher at those universities (though they could be for other reasons) but it does mean that most of the students on the courses will be very able.

Also, remember that published entry grades are usually the normal levels of offer. A very popular course might make offers of ABB or AAB but in practice only make those offers to applicants expected to get AAA. This is not wilful perversity on the part of universities but an aspect of the market. If they usually made AAA offers and published that, then application rates would plummet as applicants would have to be very confident of getting AAA before they would consider applying. But dropping the offer level means more applicants apply and so, if the actual selection criteria matched the offer level, too many students would be accepted.

In some cases conventional school examinations may not be enough. Many years ago, Oxford and Cambridge ran their own entrance examinations and the idea is being revived (see *Admissions Tests* box, below).

There are also growing calls for the introduction of a general university entrance test, similar to the Scholastic Aptitude Test used in the United States, to enable universities to identify talent among large numbers of applicants.

Admissions Tests

LNAT: entry to Law at Birmingham, Bristol, Cambridge, Durham, East Anglia, Glasgow, King's College London, Manchester Metropolitan, Nottingham, Oxford and University College London.

BMAT: entry to some courses in biomedical sciences, medicine and veterinary science at Bristol, Cambridge, Imperial College, Manchester, Oxford, the Royal Veterinary College and University College London.

MSAT (Medical Schools Admission Test): King's College London, Queen Mary, University of London and Warwick.

GAMSAT: Nottingham, Peninsula, St George's Hospital and Swansea medical courses for graduate entry.

STEP (Sixth Term Examination Paper): mathematics at Cambridge.

MML (Modern and Medieval Languages test): modern languages at Cambridge.

TSA (Thinking Skills Assessment): some interviewees at Cambridge in other subjects may be required to take this test.

HAT (History Aptitude Test): history at Oxford.

UKCAT (UK Clinical Aptitude Test): a new medical and dental entry test from 2007 will be introduced by Aberdeen, Birmingham, Brighton and Sussex, Cardiff, Dundee, Durham, East Anglia, Edinburgh, Glasgow, Hull-York, Keele, King's College London, Leeds, Leicester, Manchester, Newcastle, Nottingham, Oxford (graduate entry), Peninsular, Queen Mary College London, Sheffield, Southampton, St Andrews, St George's Hospital.

Type of Course

Having decided what you want to study, you will be faced with a variety of ways of studying it. The most basic difference is between the levels of the courses. While most higher education courses lead to a degree, some lead to sub-degree qualifications such as a Higher National Diploma (HND) or a Foundation Degree. Foundation Degrees are becoming more common as the Government has decided that future expansion of higher education should largely be through the expansion of this type of course. In general sub-degree courses will be shorter, more vocationally orientated, and have lower entry requirements. Some will be linked to degree courses, giving you the option of progressing to a degree if you perform well enough on the early parts of the course.

Courses can differ markedly in length, varying from two years for most sub-degree courses to six years for a professional course in architecture, and possibly more for some part-time courses. A pilot is running in five universities (Derby, Leeds Metropolitan, Northampton, Staffordshire and the Medway Campus, a partnership between the universities of Greenwich and Kent) to see if some three-year honours degrees can be compressed into two-year "fast track" degrees by the use of the vacations. The majority of full-time courses are three years, but some add a "sandwich" year (usually spent in work experience), most language courses last four years and many science and engineering courses lead to a Master's degree (such as MChem or MEng) after four years. In some cases it is possible to add a foundation year to the beginning of a course, making it a further year in length. These foundation courses vary somewhat in nature and entry requirements. Some are essentially a conversion course for students who have the "wrong" subjects in their examinations and will expect the same or a similar standard for entry as the courses they lead on to (though key subjects for direct entry will not be required). Others are designed to take students who have performed below the normal entry requirements for a course to bring them up to speed. These courses will often have lower entry requirements.

Eleven Things You Didn't Know About Universities

- The oldest university in the country, Oxford, was probably founded in 1096, but no one knows precisely. It was there in 1187, but must have been founded before that.
- There are over 50,000 courses to choose from.
- Fancy a degree in Brewing and Distilling? Go to Heriot-Watt.
- The total income of universities in 2003–04 was £16.9 billion, which is more than that of some countries.
- Women outnumbered men among first-year students in 1996–97 for the first time.
- In his will, the philosopher Jeremy Bentham instructed that his skeleton and head be preserved, clothed and mounted in a seated position. He has sat like that in University College London since 1850.
- There are 300,000 overseas students from 180 countries in the UK.
- At some Scottish universities the Rector is elected by the staff and students. This has sometimes resulted in the election of celebrities rather than distinguished academics.
- The student population in the UK has increased to over 2 million from just 200,000 in the 1960s.
- "University" is a legally controlled title in the UK – only institutions with a Royal Charter or some other legal authority can call themselves a university.
- The total floor area of UK higher education buildings is 24 million square metres.

In some cases the length of a course can be misleading if you intend to go on to a profession in the same subject. Five years of medicine or six of architecture will qualify you to start work as a doctor or an architect (though in both cases there are further hurdles before full qualification). However, three years of law does not qualify you to be a lawyer. You must undertake further training (often at your own expense) before you can work as a barrister or a solicitor. In the case of engineering, a four-year MEng course will give you maximum credit towards the status of Chartered Engineer, but if you take a BEng course you will have to undertake further study after you have finished.

The start of courses may vary, too. While the great majority still start in September or October there are a few that start in the spring. Many of these are nursing courses but some universities are offering a spring start in other subjects, too.

Some differences between courses relate to aspects of the subject itself. Only the very largest academic departments have expertise in all aspects of a subject and so, especially in the later years, the course will focus on the particular expertise of the department. You will need to decide whether a particular course offers the areas of the subject you want to study. Of course you may not know, or may change your mind as you go through the course. If you think this is likely, then a course in a large department with a wide range of options might be best.

Even for courses with a similar content, there may nonetheless be significant differences. Some of the opportunities you may want to consider are:
- spending a year or part of a year in Europe under an ERASMUS programme
- taking time out on a work placement
- extending the course to four years to obtain a Master's degree (common for engineering and some science courses)
- being taught part of your course by a media personality or a Nobel prize-winner who is a member of staff in the department.

Courses also differ in their structure. Some will concentrate on a single subject, some will allow you to combine two subjects in a single course (often called Dual or Joint Honours courses), and others will involve several subjects. Some will have a large proportion of the course fixed in advance, while others will allow you to choose options to make up a substantial part of the course. There are even "pick and mix" courses where you can choose from a wide range of very diverse options.

Some courses are organised on a modular basis, usually with two semesters rather than three terms a year. Each module will require the same amount of study and will

---

Things to Look Out For
- Most degree courses in Scotland last four years, though many students with good A levels can be exempt from the first year.
- Where a university has a split site, check where your course will be based.
- Large adverts in the press usually mean a university is having difficulty filling its places.
- Engineering courses are either MEng or BEng; only the MEng will give maximum credit towards Chartered Engineer status.
- Some courses offer the chance of spending a year or part of a year in Europe or beyond.
- Accommodation might be guaranteed, but check whether it is five miles down the road.
- Courses based in two or more departments can feel as if they are based nowhere – check for a "home" department where you will belong.

usually be assessed separately. This tends to increase the number of examinations and assessments you will have to do. In some cases the courses are organised in this way simply to assist a university with its administration, timetabling and so on. The courses themselves continue to be traditional single or joint honours courses. In some cases the modular courses are advertised as being very flexible, allowing you to choose your options from a very wide range of available modules. However, they may not be as flexible as they appear, as timetable clashes will restrict the real choice available to you. Also, in making your choices you should think about how they will appear to an employer, as they may well prefer to see a coherently structured programme of study rather than an eclectic mix of unrelated modules.

Across the varying course structures, there will be differences in teaching methods and assessment. Some courses will make more use than others of particular teaching methods, such as tutorials (though watch out for groups of 15-20 that are still called tutorials), computer-assisted learning or dissertations. If you seize up in formal examinations, you may want a course with a lot of continuous assessment. Alternatively, if you don't like the continuous pressure that this involves, you may prefer one with an emphasis on final examinations. If that isn't enough variety for you, there are differences between universities in the weight given to second and third-year modules in the final degree classification and there may be different rules about how often you are allowed to re-sit examinations.

Which Subject is Hardest to Get Into?

There is no simple answer to this question. Some courses are very popular – they get a lot of applications – but the standard of those applications may on average be low. For example, teacher training makes the top ten most popular subjects but the average UCAS tariff score of new entrants is one of the lowest for any subject. Similarly, veterinary science only gets 1,400 applications but has the top tariff score. Generally, the hardest subjects to get into will be those which both attract large numbers of applications and attract lots of good applicants and so have high average tariff scores. Having said that, an applicant with AAA (or AAAAA in Highers in Scotland) in the right subjects will find it easy to get into almost any course he or she wants.

For some, the choice of subject and type of course will narrow down the number of possible universities to just a few. If you want to study veterinary science, there are only

Top Ten for Student Satisfaction		Bottom Ten for Student Satisfaction	
1 Loughborough	16.1	1 University of the Arts, London	13.7
2 Lampeter	15.8	2 Middlesex	13.8
3 Leicester	15.7	3 Brunel	14.0
4 East Anglia	15.6	4 Luton	14.1
5 Lancaster	15.6	5 Greenwich	14.2
6 Chichester	15.6	6 Central England	14.2
7 Chester	15.6	7 Westminster	14.3
8 Royal Holloway	15.5	8 Sunderland	14.3
9 York	15.5	9 Leeds Metropolitan	14.3
10 Aberystwyth	15.5	10 Kingston	14.3

seven places you can go. If you want to study Burmese, only one. For many though, particularly if you are interested in one of the major subjects such as English, chemistry, law or mechanical engineering, there may be 30 or more similar courses. Research into the reasons why students leave universities early in the course often finds that choosing the wrong course is important, so it is crucial to do good research and decide carefully.

Now we will look at the choice of university, breaking the decision down into several components: location, type of university, quality and reputation, facilities and cost.

Location

Where do you want to go? Do you really like your parents or do you want to get as far away as possible? Do you want to visit your boyfriend or girlfriend every weekend (or, perhaps, want an excuse not to)? Do you want to find the cheapest way of going to university? One way or another, location is likely to be an important factor. If you want to live at home, the decision might be straightforward, though if you live in London there could easily be half a dozen local universities. If you want to go away from home, then distance or travel time will probably be a factor.

Going away to university and living at home will give you rather different experiences. Going away will be more of an adventure, taking you away from your parents and the town where you live, and any restrictions that implies, to a whole new city or region of the country. You will be free to study and socialise as and when you like, joining in with other students, without having to worry about getting the last bus to your parents' part of town. On the other hand, it will almost certainly be more expensive. You will also have to be much more self-reliant, possibly shopping and cooking for yourself, and generally not having any of the security and comfort of home. Your parents and their central heating can seem very appealing when you are trying to get to sleep in a cold bed-sit.

Incidentally, if you can go away from home it may be to your longer-term advantage to do so. Some recent research has shown that students who move away from home have better job prospects. This is probably because those who stay at home tend to end up with narrower horizons and have less self-confidence in new situations.

If a particular town or city is acceptable, you will need to look at the location of the university itself in relation to that town or city. Is it in the city-centre or several miles outside? The former will be handy for shops and transport but may be noisy and less

Top Ten for Entry Standards			Bottom Ten for Entry Standards		
1	Cambridge	525	1	Bolton	170
2	Oxford	512	2	Luton	186
3	Imperial College	468	3	East London	192
4	London School of Economics	467	4	London South Bank	192
5	Durham	455	5	Wolverhampton	200
6	Warwick	448	6	Middlesex	200
7	York	436	7	Greenwich	201
8	St Andrews	431	8	Thames Valley	203
9	Nottingham	429	9	Kingston	207
10	Edinburgh	415	10	Liverpool John Moores	207

than picturesque. The latter may be a beautiful setting, but if you have to live off-campus there could be high travel costs. Security is another factor: is the university in a well-lit suburban area or in a less desirable and possibly less safe part of town?

The facilities of the town or city may be important for you, too. Your sojourn at university will be a time when you can pursue your interests in a way you may never be able to again. Access to many things, such as sports facilities, will be very cheap and you will have the time to take them seriously. Whether you like to dance the night away, follow the Premier League or haunt the theatre volunteering to design sets, you will want to ensure you can do it.

Prospectuses frequently boast about the attractive surrounding countryside, so much so that it seems that every university is situated in the most picturesque region of the country. However, unless you have a particular interest that takes you there, such as climbing or fell walking, it is doubtful if you will spend much time taking in the sights.

Then, of course, there is cost. Generally, the south of England and London are more expensive places to live than the rest of the country, so if cost is significant for you, you will want to take this into account.

Type of University

Universities are not all the same, and nor is it easy to put them into simple categories. At one extreme is an ancient collegiate university, a world leader in terms of research, offering traditional academic courses, having most students with AAA at A level, and with large numbers of postgraduates, many from overseas. At the other extreme is a very locally-orientated university which does little research, but offers more vocational courses to largely local students, many of whom are mature and do not have A levels. Both universities may be very good at what they do, but what they do is very different and they will feel very different to attend as a student.

UNITE Student Experience Report 2006
46% of students have a very favourable impression of their university. However, more of those attending an old university (58%) report a favourable impression then those attending a new university (34%).

Generally , older universities will do more research, recruit a higher proportion of school leavers and offer more traditional academic courses. Newer universities will be more locally and vocationally orientated and recruit more mature and part-time students.

Top Ten for Library/Computing Spend		Bottom Ten for Library/Computing Spend	
1 Oxford	£1,656	1 Bath Spa	£337
2 Abertay	£1,318	2 Bournemouth	£340
3 Imperial College	£1,230	3 Worcester	£355
4 University College London	£1,152	4 Teesside	£366
5 SOAS	£1,143	5 Northampton	£371
6 Cambridge	£1,129	6 Sunderland	£378
7 London School of Economics	£1,106	7 Lampeter	£383
8 King's College London	£954	8 Oxford Brookes	£393
9 Aston	£921	9 Canterbury Christ Church	£394
10 Edinburgh	£890	10 Thames Valley	£398

Universities also vary greatly in size, from fewer than 2,000 students to over 30,000. A small university will be more personal and cosier but will have fewer facilities and non-academic activities; a big university will be busier and more impersonal (lectures may be to hundreds at a time) but there will be a lot more going on. Student numbers are only a guide to where a university lies on this spectrum. Some large universities are divided into colleges, creating a small university feel within a big university context, while others are on several relatively small sites, but have all the advantages of a large university.

Quality and Reputation

Most people want to go to a good university if they can, and this is where the rankings in this book are helpful. By bringing together a variety of measures they try to give a reasonable basis for deciding how good a university or a subject within a university really is. Differences of a few places in the table are insignificant, but a university in the top ten is doing a lot better than one in the bottom ten or even in the middle.

The subject tables rank universities on the basis of their research quality, the entry standards of their new students and how successful their graduates are.

> **UNITE Student Experience Report 2006**
> 39% of students think the standard of teaching they receive is very good.

A new departure is a series of Centres for Excellence in Teaching and Learning, which will be provided with substantial extra funding. There are 74 of them across the country, based in 54 universities and colleges. Some are focused on particular subjects while others cover broader aspects of teaching, such as enterprise or employability. If the course you are interested in is linked to a centre of excellence, it is likely that at least some aspect of the teaching is a bit special. The HEFCE website will tell you where these are located.

The main university League Table uses a wider range of measures of quality (not all are available at subject level) and ranks the quality of the entire university. However, it is clear from the subject tables that even the best universities vary in quality across subjects. Some universities perform consistently well and appear in the top 20 of many subject tables, while others come low down in the main table but have one or two very good departments that do well in the subject tables. So it is important to look at the main league table alongside the subject tables.

Teaching quality is measured using the outcomes of the National Student Survey (published on the TQI website). This is an annual survey of final-year students asking

Top Ten for Student Facilities Spend			Bottom Ten for Student Facilities Spend		
1	East London	£487	1	Thames Valley	£57
2	Imperial College	£481	2	Canterbury Christ Church	£83
3	Cambridge	£425	3	Bournemouth	£87
4	Bath	£417	4	Glasgow Caledonian	£91
5	Leicester	£395	5	London South Bank	£96
6	UWIC, Cardiff	£395	6	Liverpool Hope	£97
7	Oxford	£364	7	Keele	£100
8	Roehampton	£362	8	Bath Spa	£104
9	Wolverhampton	£362	9	Abertay Dundee	£108
10	Queen's, Belfast	£358	10	De Montfort	£123

about their experiences as a student. It is not a direct measure of quality, but indicates how satisfied students were with the experience they had. As with all satisfaction surveys, it can be influenced by expectations: a student who expects to get a very good experience from a top-quality university may rate it lower than a student who was surprised by the experience they received at a less well-respected university. This needs to be taken into account when you look at the results.

As ever, quality has to be paid for. A Mercedes costs more than a Ford, and Cambridge "costs" more than other universities, though in this case the currency is examination results rather than cash (though see also the cost section below). Look at the entry standards column in the ranking and you will see that it follows the overall ranking fairly closely. In other words, universities high up the table will, in general, ask for higher grades in whatever qualification you are offering than those lower down the table. You will need to make a judgement about how well you are going to do in your school or college examinations and choose universities where you have a realistic chance of meeting the entry requirements. If you are taking A levels and are going to get AAA, there is no problem, but in many subjects CCC will exclude most of the universities near the top of the table.

Facilities

The facilities offered by universities are fairly similar in general terms. All will have a library, a sports hall, a health service, a careers service and so on. But there will be differences and if something is particularly important for you it is worth checking out. Sometimes this will be hard to do – all universities will claim to have a really good careers service, but it is difficult to find out how true those claims are. In other cases, however, it is more straightforward.

Accommodation will be important if you are going away from home. Is there an accommodation guarantee for first-year students? What about later years? If you are a computer geek who spends the early hours on the internet, you will want to know if the rooms are wired up. If you are often out late (and how many students are not?) you may want to know where the accommodation is, how you can get back to it late at night and whether you will feel safe doing so. If you can't live in university accommodation for the whole of your course, where is the private accommodation? Is it all in a city five miles down the road (which could be good for access to shops, night-clubs and maybe the beach, but will probably be bad for travel costs), or in the grotty end of town, or in a leafy suburb by the university? For more detail on the options, see chapter 5, *Where to Live*.

If you have a particular minority interest you want to follow while at university, then this could be a factor. Most universities will have football pitches and a Liberal Democrats Society, but a climbing wall and a deep-sea fishing group may be harder to find. The students' union will be able to tell you.

Students' unions are an increasingly important aspect of student life and have come a long way from the traditional image of providers of cheap beer and student protests. The

UNITE Student Experience Report 2006

87% of students think the availability of IT facilities at their university is very or fairly good.

75% of students think the availability of course books in the library is very or fairly good.

In both cases students at old universities are more likely to rate them very good than those at new universities.

modern entrepreneurial union will have a wide range of services from food and stationery outlets through to comprehensive advice services. Increasingly they are providers of part-time employment for students and are becoming involved in personal skills development. Inevitably, some are more active and innovative than others, so they are worth looking at. The websites of the students' unions are given in chapter 11, *University Profiles*.

As the financial position of students has worsened, universities have responded by setting up employment agencies. These are generally based in careers services or students' unions and use their contacts with employers to identify employment opportunities and their contacts with students to identify suitable employees. The agency will also ensure that rates of pay and hours of work are reasonable. If you think you may be short of cash, a good agency of this type could be vital.

Finally, if you have any particular needs, you will want to know that they can be catered for. Support for students with disabilities has improved greatly in recent years but some universities are particularly good at supporting some kinds of disability, while others have old buildings that make wheelchair access difficult.

Cost

From 2006, cost has become another factor in the decision-making process. The situation is complicated, with different arrangements applying in England, Wales, Scotland and Northern Ireland, and further complicated for students moving from one country in the UK to another. To make it yet more complicated still, most universities

---

Tricks of the Prospectus Trade

The claims made by universities are rarely untrue, but they do need to be read carefully and critically. Here are a few cases where *The Times* League Tables can help you to interpret what the prospectuses and websites are saying. All the quotations were taken from university websites in January 2006.

"Statistics prove that the quality of our teaching and research is amongst the best in UK higher education." No, they don't. According to *The Times* League Table this university was not in the top 30 for either teaching or research.

"We consistently rate within the top ten of all UK universities for graduate employment." Well, that depends on how you measure it. On our measure of graduate employment this university didn't make the top 20.

"The University ... is one of the UK's leading universities. We are renowned for our teaching and research excellence. Our departments and schools are world-class and we have an outstanding reputation for student support." The research record is impressive, but in *The Times* League Table over 30 other universities were more impressive. And while the quality of teaching may have an international reputation, over 40 universities scored higher.

"The University ... is at the cutting edge of teaching and learning, as well as being one of the foremost research-led universities in the UK." The use of the phrase "cutting edge" is presumably designed to suggest a university among the best. In fact this university did not make the top 50 for teaching or the top 20 for research.

have introduced bursary schemes to assist students who are from low-income backgrounds and, in some cases, students who want to study shortage subjects. So, in order to find out how much it will cost to study at a particular university you will have to check their fees and your eligibility for any of their bursary schemes. For further details on all this, see chapter 7, *Managing Your Money*.

Even then, this may not give you the full picture as there will often be a range of costs that you will have to bear but which you are usually not told about in advance. If you want to put an admissions officer on the defensive, try asking about how much it will cost for you to join the sports centre, connect your laptop to the university network, make a photocopy in the library or bring your parents to your graduation ceremony.

Making the Decision

For some, location will be critical and this will immediately narrow down the choice. Others may be keen to go to as prestigious or high quality a university as possible and then the key question will be whether they can meet the entry requirements. Others may be particularly keen to carry on with an obscure martial art and so will want to go to one of the two or three places where they can do this. But for most, a combination of factors such as these will result in the elimination of most universities so that a manageable list of perhaps five or ten emerges. Then the detailed work begins.

The first source of information will probably be the undergraduate prospectus. This is the main recruiting document that universities produce and should include most of what you will need to know, including details of courses, facilities and entry requirements. However, you need to bear in mind that it is not an impartial document; it is a form of advertising designed to make the university seem attractive. Strangely, the sun is always shining in prospectus photographs. They are rarely factually incorrect, though there have been a few legal cases where disappointed students have successfully argued that the course they experienced was not the same as the one advertised in the prospectus and received compensation. However, prospectuses can be incomplete and frequently make generalised claims of quality without any supporting evidence (see box, *Tricks of the Prospectus Trade*, page 29). In addition to the prospectus, many universities will produce a series of departmental booklets, which will give more detail about individual subject areas.

One easy way of obtaining a pile of prospectuses and departmental booklets is to visit a higher education fair where most universities will have a stand to give out information. You may also get an opportunity to talk to someone from the university if you have particular questions you want to ask.

Alternatively, universities usually have prospectuses available on their websites (addresses given in chapter 11, *University Profiles*). This will generally have the most up-to-date module choice and financial details. You can also often take a virtual tour of the university. Departments will usually have their own sites, too, and you can often access student handbooks aimed at current students for all the detail you will ever need about courses, options, teaching methods and assessment.

If you are still unclear about entry requirements, check them out in *University & College Entrance: the Official UCAS Guide* or the entry profiles on the UCAS website. If you want more information about employment or about how happy students are with their courses or about what external examiners have had to say, you can go to the Teaching Quality Information website (www.tqi.ac.uk).

A personal visit can also be very helpful. You can get a feel for the atmosphere of a university and find out just how far you will have to walk between the lecture theatres and the students' union when it is raining. Don't forget that open days are designed to make you want to apply and so you should be critical of what you see and hear, just like when you read a prospectus. If you can't make the date of the open day, many will make arrangements for you to visit more informally during the summer. A few will offer residential visits, which allow a more extended and comprehensive look at the university.

While trawling through all these sources of information, you will no doubt talk to friends, parents, teachers, careers advisers and anyone else who comes within range. While it is good to talk, be critical of what you hear. A parent or teacher may know what they are talking about, but they may be telling you things based on their experiences of 20 or 30 years ago. Universities have changed a lot since then. Alternatively, your next-door neighbour, whom you rarely see, may just happen to work in a university admissions office and be a real source of good advice.

Finally, do a double-check to make sure your chosen university still exists. There are a number of actual and possible mergers around, such as the recent merger of Manchester with UMIST to form, with startling originality, the new University of Manchester. Alternatively, some new universities may have come along, such as Southampton Solent University or the University of Chester.

English–Speaking Alternatives to British Universities

While UK universities have a worldwide reputation, the UK is not the only country with good universities. You may dream of doing your first degree in the USA or a Commonwealth country and every year such dreams become a reality for some students. For example, about 8,400 UK undergraduates are enrolled at US universities. Many more go overseas for further study or employment once they have graduated.

The most common destinations are other English-speaking countries, including Australia, Canada, Ireland and the USA, and plenty of advice and information is available. For example, every October there is a "College Day" in London and another in Edinburgh, organised by the Fulbright Commission, when around 100 US universities come to extol the virtues of an American university education. Interest in these events, and for possible study in other countries, has grown since the introduction of higher fees in the UK from 2006.

The web is the easiest source of information and the following sites are among the more useful:

Association of Commonwealth Universities	www.acu.ac.uk
College Board (USA)	www.collegeboard.com
Education Ireland	www.educationireland.ie
Finaid (USA)	www.finaid.org
Fulbright Commission (USA)	www.fulbright.co.uk
Study in Australia	www.studyinaustralia.gov.au
Study in Canada	www.studyincanada.com

There are also university ranking tables, similar to those found in *The Times Good University Guide*, for each of the major English-speaking countries. Among the more respected are:

Australia	*The Good Universities Guide* (www.thegoodguides.com.au)
Canada	*The Maclean's Guide to Canadian Universities* (www.macleans.ca)
USA	*US News & World Report* (www.usnews.com)

Every course and every university is different, but every student wants different things, so the chances of finding a perfect match is not that high, despite the huge range of courses that are available. You will almost certainly end up having to decide what is most important to you. Do you want the best course or one which is quite good but offers the options you really want? Do you want the ideal work placement or the course with least continuous assessment?

In the end only you can decide. It won't be easy, but after all the reading, visiting, surfing and talking, you have got to do it. You have to decide which six will go on your UCAS application. Good luck!

Checklist

Choosing a course
- [ ] What do you enjoy?
- [ ] What are you good at?
- [ ] Will it lead to the career you want? If you are not sure, will it keep your options open?
- [ ] Are you studying the right subjects?
- [ ] What grades do you expect to get?
- [ ] Will there be an additional university entrance test to take?
- [ ] Do you want to study one subject, two subjects or several subjects?
- [ ] Do you want lots of options?
- [ ] What kinds of assessment do you perform best in?

Choosing a university
- [ ] Which universities offer your chosen subject?
- [ ] Where are they ranked in *The Times* League Table and subject tables?
- [ ] How far away from home do you want to go?
- [ ] Which facilities are important to you?
- [ ] Have you got a copy of the prospectus(es)?
- [ ] Is there an open day you can attend?
- [ ] What are the costs likely to be?

The Top Universities

2

The Times first published a University League Table in October 1992 as a distinctive way of measuring the quality of British universities. Every year since then the Tables have been the subject of vigorous debate among academics. Subsequently, too, a number of other broadsheet newspapers have got in on the act with not dissimilar university tables and this has inevitably led to a certain amount of confusion. Nonetheless, *The Times* League Table retains its position as the most respected and authoritative guide to the quality of UK universities and is frequently used and quoted overseas.

Given that analyses of this type within higher education and elsewhere – in schools, health, etc – have come to be seen as legitimate aids, it is perhaps surprising that many universities remain opposed to the very notion of comparing one with another, and yet that is what applicants have to do all the time. They claim in defence that each is unique, has a distinct mission and serves a different student community. Be that as it may, universities have been known to quote favourable League Table rankings when these assist their cause. Nor will you find tables of the type reproduced in this book in any material published by UCAS or The British Council and yet we remain convinced that comparisons are valid and helpful to students and their mentors when it comes to choosing a university.

Interestingly, the Higher Education Funding Council for England (HEFCE) has itself published sets of performance indicators for each UK university, though these are now published by the Higher Education Statistics Agency (HESA). We have chosen to use one of them, a measure of completion, in *The Times* League Table. This set of "official" performance indicators covers access, completion rates, teaching and learning outcomes, research output and employment. It is in many ways a commentary on how well each university is doing at delivering government policy and, as such, has a different purpose to the measures of quality used in *The Times* League Table.

The raw data for the League Table and other tables in later chapters all come from sources in the public domain. The Higher Education Statistics Agency (HESA) provided data for entry standards, student–staff ratios, library and computer spending, facilities spending, good honours degrees, graduate prospects and overseas student enrolments. HESA is the official agency for the collection, analysis and dissemination of quantitative information about the universities.

The HEFCE, along with the Scottish Higher Education Funding Council (SHEFC) and the Higher Education Funding Council for Wales (HEFCW), are the funding councils whose remit it is to develop policy and allocate public funds to the universities. The 2001 Research Assessment Exercise, conducted by the funding councils, provides the data for the research assessment measure used in the Tables. The funding councils also have a statutory responsibility to assess the quality of learning and teaching in the UK universities they fund. In England, Wales and Northern Ireland the funding councils oversaw the National Student Survey, a major survey of the views of final year students of the quality of the courses they were studying on. We use some of the outcomes of this survey as a measure of teaching quality.

In a few cases the source data were not available and were obtained directly from the individual universities.

All universities were provided with complete sets of their own HESA data well in advance of publication. In addition, where anomalous figures were identified in the 2003–04 HESA data, institutions were given a further opportunity to check for and notify any errors. Similarly, we consulted the universities on methodology. Once a year, an Advisory Group with university representatives meets to discuss the methodology and how it can be improved. Thus, every effort has been made to ensure accuracy, but no responsibility can be taken for errors or omissions. The data providers do not necessarily agree with data aggregations or manipulations appearing in this book and are also not responsible for any inferences or conclusions thereby derived.

A particular feature of The Times Tables is the way the various measures are combined to create a total score. In many other tables each institution's score, for each measure, is expressed as a percentage of the maximum score. Where there is little variation in the scores these percentages are often scaled to spread the variation out and so ensure that the measure contributes something to the overall score in the table. The percentages are then summed to form an overall score.

This approach by other compilers has the advantage that it is possible to see how a particular institution is performing relative to the best performing institution for a particular measure. The main disadvantage is that year-on-year comparisons are not possible. For example, an institution which scored 86 one year (ie, had a score that was 86 per cent of the top score) might perform better the next year but still have a lower score if the top institution happened to perform even better still.

In The Times Tables the scores have undergone a Z-transformation. This is a statistical way of ensuring that each measure contributes the same amount to the overall score and so avoids the need for any scaling. (For the statistically minded, it involves subtracting the mean score from each individual score and then dividing by the standard deviation of the scores.)

Another feature of The Times League Table is that three of the measures have been adjusted to take account of the subject mix at a university. A university with a medical school, for example, will tend to admit students with a higher tariff score than one without simply because it is a medical school. The adjustment removes this subject effect. A side-effect of this is that it is impossible to recalculate the total score in the table using the published data, as you need full access to all the raw data to be able to do this.

Given the various changes and the continuing refinement of the process over the years, you have to be careful when making comparisons between positions in the League Table from year to year. This is particularly important this year as the introduction of the new Student Satisfaction measure is a major change. The Open University and the privately funded Buckingham University, and universities like Cranfield with mainly postgraduate students, are not included.

Apart from noting the overall position of any one university of interest, you can home in on a particular measure of importance to you like entry standards or graduate prospects. But bear in mind that this composite table says nothing about specific subjects at a university and so should be scrutinised in conjunction with the Subject Tables and University Profiles in later chapters.

How the League Table Works

The League Table measures nine key aspects of university activity using the most recent data available at the time of going to press. As we have mentioned a statistical technique called the Z-transformation was applied to each measure to create a score for that measure.

The Z-scores on each measure were then weighted by 1.5 for Student Satisfaction and Research Assessment and 1.0 for the rest and summed to give a total score for the univerity. Finally, these total scores were transformed to a scale where the top score was set at 1000 with the remainder being a proportion of the top score. This scaling does not affect the overall ranking but it avoids giving any university a negative overall score. In addition some measures (Entry Standard, Good Honours, and Graduate Prospects) have been adjusted to take account of the subject mix at the institution. The details of how the measures were compiled, together with some advice about their interpretation, is given below.

If a particular data item is missing for a university, the overall score is based on the remaining data that are available.

Student Satisfaction

What is it? A measure of the view of students of the teaching quality at the university.

Where does it come from? The National Student Survey, a survey of 175,000 final-year students in January/February 2005.

How does it work? The National Student Survey asked questions about a variety of aspects of teaching. The average satisfaction score for the first four question areas, which relate most directly to teaching quality, was calculated.

What should you look out for? The survey is a measure of student opinion, not a direct measure of quality. It may therefore be influenced by a variety of biases, such as the effect of prior expectations. A top-notch university expected to deliver really excellent teaching could score lower than a less good university which, while offering lower quality teaching, nonetheless does better than students expect from it. Scottish universities were not included in the survey and a small number of English ones did not have a sufficiently high response rate to have their outcomes published.

Research Assessment

What is it? A measure of the average quality of the research undertaken in the university.

Where does it come from? The 2001 Research Assessment Exercise undertaken by the funding councils.

How does it work? Each university department entered in the assessment exercise was given a rating of 5* (top), 5, 4, 3a, 3b, 2 or 1 (bottom). These grades were converted to a numerical scale and an average was calculated, weighted according to the number of staff in the department getting each rating. Staff not selected for the exercise were assumed to be conducting research at a level two grades below that of the outcome.

What should you look out for? The rating of 5*, 5, etc, is accompanied by a letter which indicates the proportion of staff included in the assessment. Thus a 5A indicates that most staff were of 5 standard but a 5F indicates that most staff were not included in the return (and so unlikely to be active at that level).

In Scotland, the SHEFC announced in advance that it would not distinguish between 5 and 5*-rated departments for funding purposes. This may have affected the strategies adopted by some Scottish universities with the result that they obtained fewer 5* ratings then they might otherwise have done. The next RAE results will become available in 2008.

Entry Standards
What is it? The average UCAS tariff score of new students under the age of 21.

Where does it come from? HESA data for 2003–04.
How does it work? Each student's examination results were converted to a numerical score (A level A = 120, B = 100 ... E = 40, etc; Scottish Highers A = 72, B = 60, etc) and added up to give a score total. HESA then calculates an average for all students at the university. The results were then adjusted to take account of the subject mix at the university.

What should you look out for? A high average score (it is over 400, or more than three As at A level, at some universities) does not mean that all students score that highly or that you need to take lots of A levels to get in. The actual grades needed will vary by subject and few if any courses will ask for grades in more than three subjects (even if some students do take more). Universities which have a specific policy of accepting students with low grades as part of an access policy will tend to have their average score depressed.

Student–Staff Ratio
What is it? A measure of the average staffing level in the university.

Where does it come from? HESA data for 2003–04.

How does it work? HESA calculated a student–staff ratio, ie, the number of students divided by the number of staff, in a way designed to take account of different patterns of staff employment in different universities.

What should you look out for? A low SSR, ie, a small number of students for each member of staff, does not guarantee good quality of teaching or good access to staff. Universities with a medical school, where SSRs are usually low, will tend to score better.

Library and Computer Spending
What is it? The expenditure per student on library and computing facilities.

Where does it come from? HESA data for 2001–02, 2002–03 and 2003–04.

How does it work? A university's expenditure on library and computing facilities (books, journals, staff, computer hardware and software, but not buildings) was divided by the number of full-time-equivalent students. Expenditure over three years was averaged to allow for uneven expenditure. (For example, a major upgrade of a computer network might cause expenditure to rise sharply in one year but fall back the next.) Libraries and information technology are becoming increasingly integrated (many universities have a single Department of Information Services encompassing both) and so the two areas of expenditure have been taken together.

What should you look out for? Some universities are the location for major national facilities, such as the Bodleian Library in Oxford and national computing facilities in Bath and Manchester. The local and national expenditure is very difficult to separate and so these universities will tend to score more highly on this measure.

Facilities Spending

What is it? The expenditure per student on staff and student facilities.

Where does it come from? HESA data for 2001–02, 2002–03 and 2003–04.

How does it work? A university's expenditure on student facilities (sports, careers services, health, counselling, etc.) was divided by the number of full-time-equivalent students. Expenditure over three years was averaged to allow for uneven expenditure.

What should you look out for? This measure tends to disadvantage some collegiate universities as it mostly includes central university expenditure. In Oxford and Cambridge, for example, a significant amount of facilities expenditure is by the colleges but it has not yet been possible to extract comparable data from the college accounts.

Good Honours

What is it? The percentage of graduates achieving a first or upper second class degree.

Where does it come from? HESA data for 2003–04.

How does it work? The number of graduates with first or upper second class degrees was divided by the total number of graduates with classified degrees. Enhanced first degrees, such as an MEng awarded after a four-year engineering course, were treated as equivalent to a first or upper second for this purpose, while Scottish Ordinary degrees (awarded after three years rather than the usual four in Scotland) were excluded altogether. The results were then adjusted to take account of the subject mix at the university.

What should you look out for? Degree classifications are controlled by the universities themselves, though with some moderation by the external examiner system. It can be argued, therefore, that they are not a very objective measure of quality. However, degree class is the primary measure of individual success in British higher education and will have an impact elsewhere, such as employment prospects.

Graduate Prospects

What is it? A measure of the employability of a university's graduates.

Where does it come from? HESA data for 2003–04.

How does it work? The number of graduates who take up employment or further study divided by the total number of graduates with a known destination expressed as a percentage. Only employment in an area that normally recruits graduates was included. The results were then adjusted to take account of the subject mix at the university.

What should you look out for? A relatively low score on this measure does not mean that many graduates were unemployed. It may be that some had low-level jobs, such as shop assistants, which do not normally recruit graduates. Some universities recruit a high proportion of local students. If they are located in an area where graduate jobs are hard to come by, this can depress the outcome. A measure of the employability of graduates has been included in the HEFCE performance indicators but this is only available at institution level. The HESA data was used so that a subject-mix adjustment could be made.

Completion

What is it? A measure of the completion rate of those studying at the university.

Where does it come from? HESA performance indicators, based on data for 2003–04 and earlier years.

How does it work? HESA calculated the expected outcomes for a cohort of students based on what happened to students in the current year. The figures in the League Table show the percentage of students who were expected to complete their course or transfer to another institution.

What should you look out for? This measure of completion is a projection based upon a snapshot of data. It is therefore vulnerable to statistical fluctuations.

Conclusions

Universities' positions in *The Times* League Table inevitably reflect more than their performance over a single year. Many of those at the top have built their reputations and developed their expertise over many decades or even centuries, while some of those at the bottom are still carving out a niche in the unified higher education system. Perhaps the least surprising conclusions to be drawn from the League Table are that Oxbridge and the University of London remain the dominant forces in British higher education and that, on the measures adopted here, the new universities still have ground to make up on the old. The former polytechnics have different priorities from those of any of their more established counterparts, however, and many can demonstrate strengths in other areas.

Even on the measures adopted here, the table belies the system's reputation for rigidity. For example, a former polytechnic (Northumbria) continues to outperform a number of long-established universities. No doubt others will follow before long. The remarkable rise of universities such as Warwick and Bath, both founded around 40 years ago, shows what can be achieved in a relatively short space of time.

In an exercise such as this, some distortions are inevitable and the main ones have been identified in the *What should you look out for?* sections, above. The use of a variety of indicators is intended to diminish such effects, but they should be borne in mind when making comparisons.

	Max score	Student satisfaction 20.0	Research assessment 7.0	Entry standards n/a	Student–staff ratio n/a	Library/computing spend n/a	Facilities spend n/a	Good honours 100.0	Graduate prospects 100.0	Completion 100.0	Total 1000
1	Oxford	–	6.5	511.7	13	1656	364	88.4	74.8	97.7	1000
2	Cambridge	–	6.6	525.1	11.9	1129	425	84.6	86.9	98.9	973
3	Imperial College	14.4	6.4	468.2	9.4	1230	481	75	83.8	96	878
4	London School of Economics	15.1	6.4	466.9	13.4*	1106*	186*	74.4	81.5	95.5	855
5	University College London	15.3	6	410.8	8.4	1152	172	73.6	78.1	93.4	819
6	Loughborough	16.1	5.1	362.5	18.5	667	355	64.7	70.7	92.5	795
7	Bristol	15.2	5.7	405.9	14.4	768	272	80.8	79.8	95.5	792
8	Warwick	–	6	447.6*	16.4	853	203	78.2	70.2*	94.9	791
9	Bath	15	5.7	403.4	17.3	597	417	75.2	79.8	96.1	786
10	Durham	15.4	5.7	454.9	21.2	747	326	74.6	72.4	95.1	778
11	Edinburgh	–	5.6	414.8	14.2	890	233	77.7	70.7	91.9	774
12	Royal Holloway	15.5	5.7	345.3	14.1	549	311	66.5	67.3	93.8	761
13	Aston	14.9	5	328.3	15	921	356	69.4	76	90.9	758
14	Nottingham	14.9	5.3	429.1	16.2	799	332	75.3	71	95.2	754
15	York	15.5	5.8	435.9	15.8	653	199	69.9	66	95.1	750
16	Cardiff	15.2	5.4	371.1	13	758	238	68.6	73.5	94.8	740
17	King's College London	15.1	5.5	393.7	12	954	156	70.7	81.1	92.9	733
=18	Leicester	15.7	5	351.9	17.1	570	395	64.3	66.2	95.6	732

	Student satisfaction	Research assessment	Entry standards	Student–staff ratio	Library/computing spend	Facilities spend	Good honours	Graduate prospects	Completion	Total
Max score	20.0	7.0	n/a	n/a	n/a	n/a	100.0	100.0	100.0	1000
=18 School of Oriental and African Studies	14.6	5.5	328.6	9.8	1143	175	75.9	74.5	87.4	732
=18 St Andrews	–	5.7	430.5	14.3	587	200	75.1	65.7	97.6	732
21 Lancaster	15.6	5.8	359.2	15.8*	637	254	64.9	54.4	94.6	716
22 Southampton	14.9	5.8	386.5	16	729	252	69.2	70.3	92.3	712
23 East Anglia	15.6	5.4	365.3*	17	604	353	66.9	58.8	86.7	708
24 Sheffield	15.2	5.5	405.3	15.7	613	231	72.4	68.6	90.4	703
25 Newcastle	14.9	5.2	384.6	16.9	774	312	65.8	68	93	699
26 Manchester	14.6	5.7	396.3	14.2	819	263	70	66.8	92.3	694
27 Sussex	14.7	5.5	365.7	12.1	650	296	71.5	59	89.4	689
=28 Exeter	15.3	5.2	369.1	17	608	182*	69.6	61.8	93.8	678
=28 Glasgow	–	5.2	392.6	13.6	688	219	69.6	66.3	85.8	678
30 Essex	15.2	5.6	308.7	14.6	643	307	55.4	62.8	85.7	677
31 Reading	15.4	5.3	341.5	15.9	587	223	64.8	58.9	90.2	671
32 Queen's, Belfast	15.2	4.9	350.4	17.3	473	358	62.9	72.3	87.3	670
33 Birmingham	14.8	5.3	380.3	17.1	701	220	68.9*	68.1	92.8	666
=34 Kent	15.3	4.8	316.4	15.4	648	189	60.3	66.6	86.8	661
=34 Leeds	14.8	5.3	374.7	17.9	635	196	71.5	70.2	91.7	661
36 Aberdeen	–	4.7	348.5	14.1	759	211	65.5	70.1	81.8	653

37	Stirling	–	4.8	341.8	15.3	634	238	67.3	55.8	85.5	647
38	Surrey	14.3	5.4	325.5	16.8	550	275	59.1	79.5	88.5	639
39	Liverpool	14.9	5.2	351.2	16	491	154	63.7	72.7	92.7	627
40	Strathclyde	–	4.7	381.9	18	572	167	68.9	69.3	83	619
41	Queen Mary, London	14.9	5	314.1	12.1	643	173	57.6	71.6	90	615
42	Bangor	15.4	4.7	285.6*	16.6	748	205	54.0*	64.4*	82.9	611
43	Swansea	15.3	4.6	288.1	16.9	520	225	56.8	60.5	89.6	600
44	Dundee	–	5.1	340	15.7*	503	179	61.7	71.9	83.1	596
45	Goldsmiths, London	15.3	5.3	295.5	20.1	530	173	60.9	57.8	82.4	595
46	Aberystwyth	15.5	4.5	299.4	20.8	540	277	59	50.3	89.4	594
47	Bradford	15	4.4	268.2	16.1	542	291	59.9	72.7	81.2	593
48	Heriot–Watt	–	4.7	362.7**	17.3	525	268	60.5	57.9	80.9	588
49	Hull	15.3	4.3	283.7*	18.6	434	177	59.2	64.3	86.7	579
50	Brunel	14	4.3	303.2	18	608	305	66	63.9	86.4	565
51	Ulster	14.9	3.8	262.9	19.5	584	227	61.5	63.4	82.6	550
52	Keele	14.9	4.6	309.3	17.3	431	100	53.2	64.8	90	548
53	City	–	4.4	314.7	22.3	439	154	59.9	74.7	84.5	544
54	Oxford Brookes	14.8	2.8	282.6	16.2	393	306	55.1	67.6	79.8	531
55	Plymouth	14.9	3.2	262.7	17.6	493	235	56	56.4	83.9	520
56	Robert Gordon	–	1.9	305.9	18.6	510*	143*	54.4*	75.9	80.6	513
57	Abertay	–	2	226.2	20.6	1318	108	52.6	74.3	66.9**	512
58	Northumbria	14.7	2.3	272.1*	20.4	673	250	53.3	63.3	82	507
59	Brighton	14.6	2.9	266.1*	18.1	512	193	57.9	65.2*	79.8	504
60	Nottingham Trent	14.6	2.8	275.9	20.5*	611	145*	55.8	63.4	84.1	497
61	UWIC, Cardiff	14.5	2.7	243	20.6	439	395	50.7	57	82.5	490

	Max score	Student satisfaction 20.0	Research assessment 7.0	Entry standards n/a	Student–staff ratio n/a	Library/computing spend n/a	Facilities spend n/a	Good honours 100.0	Graduate prospects 100.0	Completion 100.0	Total 1000
62	Winchester	15.4	2.5	264.4	21.9	476	164	59.2	48.3	86.7	486
63	UCE Birmingham	14.2	2.2	242.2	16.6	536	327	60.4*	62.1	81.6	483
64	Chichester	15.6	2.1	238.9	21.6	452	126	46.3	65	86.2	482
65	Salford	14.5	4.3	249.3	17.9	454	235	52.9	56.4	78.9	479
66	Lampeter	15.8	4.7	245.5	24.6	383	142	59.1	52.1	76.4	478
67	West of England	14.5	2.8	266.5	19.8	503	223	55.2	60.1	84	473
68	Chester	15.6	1.6	251.5	20	441	210	44.9	49.3	84.6	469
69	Bournemouth	14.3	1.9	277	18.3	340	87	61.7	57.2	85.1	465
70	Roehampton	14.6	3.2	229.2	21.2	610	362	50.1	49.7	82.3	463
71	Glasgow Caledonian	–	2.5	306.1	17.6	473	91	58.3	57.9	81.6**	460
72	Central Lancashire	14.9	2.2	252	22.8	406	266	50.8	59.6	80.2	459
73	Bath Spa	15.5	2.5	249.2	24.2	337	104	60	47	87	454
=74	Glamorgan	15.1	2.4	215.1	19.2	496	245	49.7	57.6	73.7**	451
=74	Staffordshire	14.8	2.2	235.8	18.1	671	183	47.7	54.3	77.2	451
=76	Coventry	14.7	2.1	228.8	20.6	527	239	55.2	61.4	79.4	447
=76	Portsmouth	14.6	3.2	247.8	19.3	438	147	45.5	65.2	80.1	447
=78	Gloucestershire	14.7	3	229.4	18.2	419	247	43.9	54.5	81.3	446
=78	Napier	–	2.3	263.8	17.4	512	147	59.2	57.9	70.2	446

=80	UWCN, Newport	14.7	3	216.8	19.7	449	255	54.2	55	76.1	444
=80	Sheffield Hallam	14.3	3	264.3	24.9	451	232	53	61.4	86.4	444
82	Worcester	15.3	1.4	233.1	20.9	355	216	41.8	59.4	81.6	432
83	Liverpool John Moores	14.9	2.6	207.4	17.8	473	154	47.9	60.6	76.2	430
84	University of the Arts, London	13.7	4.7	345.1	26.6	421	123	54.6	47.5	86.9	427
85	Hertfordshire	14.3	2.5	225.4	18.1	522	161	49.9	64.8	80.7	425
86	Canterbury Christ Church	15.4	1.9	239.2	20.7	394	83	46.5	62.8	83.7	420
=87	Anglia Ruskin	14.6	1.5	233.4	19.6	444	161	56.1	61.8	78	418
=87	Bolton	15	1.5	170	18.3	466	345	50.9	63.9	66.6	418
89	Kingston	14.3	2.7	207.2	20.4	547	154	50.4	66.1	81	417
=90	Huddersfield	15	2.4	232.3	20.2	401	126	47.6	57.1	77.9	413
=90	Leeds Metropolitan	14.3	2.2	251.4	23.5	478	134	49.4	62.5	84.6	413
92	Sunderland	14.3	2.8	233.5	17.5	378	203	51.7	61.5	68.3	410
93	East London	–	2.5	191.7	21	614	487	39.6	55.8	67	409
94	Westminster	14.3	2.8	217.8	17.6	457	179	55.8	50.9	74.4	395
95	Teesside	15	1.9	224.3	20.8*	366	125	45.7	61.9	75.2	390
=96	Liverpool Hope	15.2	1.3	208	26	407*	97	48.8*	69.5	76	389
=96	Manchester Metropolitan	14.4	2.9	261.5	22.5	467	131	47.2	57.1	78.8	389
=96	Middlesex	13.8	2.7	200	22.6	726	322	50.5	55.8	73.3	389
=99	De Montfort	14.4	3.1	237.7	20.7	489	123	38.5	61	80	382
=99	Wolverhampton	14.7	2	199.5	22.5	499	362	50	50.9	73.3**	382
101	London South Bank	–	2.9	192.3	19.7	478	96	52.9	65.8	72	370
102	Paisley	–	1.6	265.3	20.2	729	210	45.8	52.1	69.1	367
103	Northampton	14.7	1.7	219	22.2	371	135	53.7	51.8	80.5	359
104	Lincoln	14.5	1.7	249.2	26.4	538	159	49.3	45	81.4	347

	Student satisfaction	Research assessment	Entry standards	Student–staff ratio	Library/computing spend	Facilities spend	Good honours	Graduate prospects	Completion	Total
Max score	20.0	7.0	n/a	n/a	n/a	n/a	100.0	100.0	100.0	1000
105 Derby	14.4	1.5	218.3	22.5	585	137	47	55.6	72.5	336
106 Greenwich	14.2	2.5	200.6	25.8	482	149	47.4	62.7	71.9	325
107 Southampton Solent	–	0.9	224.6	30.2	605	283	41.6	47.9	78.6	321
108 Luton	14.1	1.8	185.7	23.2	606	229	48.4	41.7	74.8	302
109 Thames Valley	–	0.5	202.5	23.7	398	57	48.8	60.1	68.6	281
median	14.9	4.3	282.6	18.0	542	211	58.3	63.3	84.0	520
min	13.7	0.5	170.0	30.2	337	57	38.5	41.7	66.6	281
max	16.1	6.6	525.1	8.4	1656	487	88.4	86.9	98.9	1000

* Institution provided own data
** Data used from previous year
For the third year running, London Metropolitan University refused to allow the release of data. It was ranked 98th out of 100 in the 2004 edition.

The Top Universities by Subject

3

Knowing where a university stands in the pecking order of higher education is a vital piece of information for any prospective student, but the quality of the course is what matters most. The most modest institution may have a centre of specialist excellence and even famous universities have mediocre departments. This section offers some pointers to the leading universities in a wide range of subjects. Expert assessors have produced official ratings for research quality and, for the Education table, teaching quality. The outcomes of the National Student Survey, used in the main League Table, were not available in sufficient detail to use in the Subject Tables. HESA data is used to provide information about students' entry qualifications, as a guide to the calibre of undergraduates on different courses, and the destinations of graduates. The destination information draws a distinction between different types of employment: graduate employment, where a degree is normally required, and non-graduate employment. The tables give the percentage of "positive destinations" by adding those undertaking further study to the total in graduate employment.

To qualify for inclusion in a table, a university had to have data for at least two of the measures.

Cambridge is again by far the most successful university, with 43 top 10 placings including 35 top placings. Oxford has the next highest number of top places with nine, followed Nottingham and Loughborough with three each. The subject rankings demonstrate that there are "horses for courses" in higher education. Thus the London School of Economics is more than a match for its rivals in social science, while Imperial College confirms its reputation in engineering. In their own fields, table-toppers such as Loughborough (sports science; see Hospitality) and Surrey (Food Science) are equally well-known.

In all the tables, the following information is provided when it is available.

Research Quality
This provides a measure of the average quality of research undertaken in the subject area. The first figure gives a quality rating of 5* (top), 5, 4, 3a, 3b, 2 or 1 (bottom). The letter refers to the proportion of staff included in the numerical assessment, with A including virtually everyone and F hardly anyone. These data are from 2001.

Entry Standards
This is the average UCAS tariff score for new students under the age of 21, taken from HESA data for 2003–04. Each student's examination grades were converted to a numerical score (A level A = 120, B = 100, etc; Scottish Highers A = 72, B = 60, etc) and added up to give a total score. HESA then calculated an average score for the university.

Graduate Prospects
This is the percentage of graduates undertaking further study or in graduate job in the annual survey by HESA six months after graduation. Two years of data are aggregated to

make the data more reliable and scores are withheld where the number of students is too small to calculate a reliable percentage. A low number on the measure does not necessarily mean that many graduates were unemployed – some could have obtained jobs that are not usually considered graduate jobs. The averages for each subject are given at the bottom of each subject table in this chapter and in a table in chapter 1 (see pages 14–15).

The Education table uses a fourth measure, teaching quality as measured by the outcomes of Ofsted inspections of teacher training courses.

Who's in the Top Ten for Their Subjects?

		Appearances in Subject Tables	Top Places	Times in Top Ten	Percentage in Top Ten
1	London School of Economics	12	2	12	100.0
2	Oxford	34	9	34	100.0
3	Cambridge	44	35	43	97.7
4	Imperial College	16	2	14	87.5
5	Bristol	40	0	34	85.0
6	University College London	38	1	31	81.6
8	Bath	26	0	20	76.9
7	Warwick	26	1	20	76.9
9	Durham	32	1	23	71.9
10	York	21	0	14	66.7
11	Nottingham	46	3	29	63.0
12	King's College London	29	0	16	55.2
13	Harper Adams UC	2	0	1	50.0
14	Manchester	49	1	24	49.0
17	St Andrews	25	0	12	48.0
15	Surrey	20	1	9	45.0
16	Loughborough	28	3	12	42.9
19	Sheffield	44	0	15	36.4
18	Edinburgh	45	0	16	35.6
20	Queen's, Belfast	40	0	13	32.5

The subjects listed below are covered in the tables in this chapter:

Accounting and finance
Aeronautical and manufacturing engineering
Agriculture and forestry
American studies
Anatomy and physiology
Anthropology
Archaeology
Architecture
Art and design
Biological sciences
Building
Business studies
Celtic studies
Chemical engineering
Chemistry
Civil engineering
Classics and ancient history
Communication and media studies
Computer science
Dentistry
Drama, dance and cinematics
East and South Asian studies
Economics
Education
Electrical and electronic engineering
English
Food science
French
General engineering
Geography
Geology

German
History
History of art, architecture and design
Hospitality, leisure, sport, recreation and tourism
Iberian languages
Italian
Land and property management
Law
Librarianship and information management
Linguistics
Materials technology
Mathematics
Mechanical engineering
Medicine
Middle Eastern and African studies
Music
Nursing
Other subjects allied to medicine
   (see page 137 for included subjects)
Pharmacology and pharmacy
Philosophy
Physics and astronomy
Politics
Psychology
Russian and East European languages
Social policy
Social work
Sociology
Theology and religious studies
Town and country planning and landscape
Veterinary medicine

Accounting and Finance

The LSE remains on top of the accounting and finance table in its second year of publication. Compiled from data extracted from the Business Studies ranking to reflect the growth of accountancy and finance degrees, the table has six new entries since last year despite a 5 per cent drop in applications nationally at the start of 2006. Accounting alone slipped out of the 20 most popular subjects, but still attracted over 26,000 applications. The LSE maintains a clear lead over Warwick, with higher entry standards and better graduate prospects.

Portsmouth, at 31, is the highest-ranking new university, although almost half of the institutions in the ranking are former polytechnics. Edinburgh moves up to third with entry grades bettered only by the top two and a high proportion of academics entered for the last Research Assessment Exercise. Nottingham moves up to fifth, but it is Manchester that makes the most progress, breaking into the top ten for the first time.

Liverpool John Moores has one of the best employment scores, while University of Wales, Newport and Northampton, one of the nine new universities in this year's *Guide*, were among the top scorers in the first national student satisfaction survey. Loughborough was the other favourite for students, but even an outstanding graduate employment record – the best of all the universities – cannot save it from a three-place drop. Only fourth-placed Bristol comes close to Loughborough's record of getting nine out of ten graduates into jobs or further training within six months.

Four universities were considered internationally outstanding for research: the LSE, Warwick, Lancaster and Manchester. Edinburgh has overtaken Glasgow to become the top university in Scotland, while Cardiff is the clear leader in Wales.

Entry scores are quite widely spread among the 73 universities in the table. Nine average more than 400 points, but nine are below 200 points. Employment prospects are better than in many areas of higher education, but in 2004 more than a third of graduates started their careers in low-level jobs. The unemployment rate of 7 per cent was on the average for all subjects.

- **The Chartered Institute of Public Finance and Accountancy:** www.cipfa.org.uk
- **The Institute of Chartered Accountants:** www.icaew.co.uk/students
- **The Association of Chartered Certified Accountants**: www.accaglobal.com

Accounting and Finance	Research quality/5	Entry standards	Graduate prospects %	Overall rating
1 London School of Economics	5*A	468	80	100.0
2 Warwick	5*B	457	74	96.6
3 Edinburgh	5A	443	76	96.1
4 Bristol	5B	382	86	95.4
5 Nottingham	5B	443	74	94.4
6 Loughborough	4C	395	90	93.9
7 Queen's, Belfast	4B	392	84	93.7
8 Glasgow	5C	411	80	93.0
9 Leeds	5C	404	80	92.7
10 Manchester	5*A	414	60	92.2

11 Lancaster	5*B	377	66	91.1
12 Southampton	4B	404	72	90.8
13 Durham	5A	342	70	90.4
14 City	5C	376	74	89.9
15 Sheffield	4B	373	66	87.9
16 Cardiff	5B	359	62	87.7
17 Newcastle	5D	414	68	87.6
18 Aberdeen	4B	362	64	86.8
19 Stirling	5B	358	58	86.5
20 Birmingham	4D	388	70	86.2
21 Dundee	4A	330	62	85.9
22 Strathclyde	5C		66	85.8
23 Kent	3aC	310	76	85.3
24 Exeter	5D	390	58	83.8
25 Essex	5C	281	64	83.3
26 Bradford	4C	252	72	83.1
27 Heriot-Watt	4D	398	56	82.7
28 East Anglia	3aC	329	62	82.1
29 Reading		358	74	81.9
30 Salford	3aB	260	66	81.8
31 Portsmouth	4C	231	70	81.7
=32 Hull	4C	269	64	81.5
=32 Liverpool	3aA	319	54	81.5
34 Robert Gordon		336	74	81.0
35 Nottingham Trent	3bD	276	70	79.9
36 Ulster	3aD	282	62	78.8
37 Bangor	5B	255	44	78.5
38 Liverpool John Moores	3bE	181	82	78.4
39 Aberystwyth	3bC	279	56	77.2
40 Glasgow Caledonian	4F	327	56	76.3
41 Northumbria		301	62	76.2
42 Oxford Brookes		285	64	76.1
43 De Montfort	3aC	244	52	75.9
44 Brighton	3aE	258	60	75.8
45 West of England	5E	273	52	75.3
46 Glamorgan	3bD		58	75.2
47 London South Bank	3aE	175	66	74.2
=48 Napier	3bE	240	58	74.0
=48 Bournemouth		247	62	74.0
=50 Manchester Metropolitan		250	60	73.6
=50 Derby		193	68	73.6
52 Kingston		236	60	73.0
53 Keele		288	52	72.9
54 Southampton Solent		213	62	72.7
55 Paisley	5F	285	48	72.5
56 Staffordshire		250	54	71.9
57 Leeds Metropolitan		245	52	71.2

	Research quality/5	Entry standards	Graduate prospects %	Overall rating
=58 Central Lancashire	3bE	236	48	71.1
=58 Huddersfield	3bE	208	52	71.1
=60 Plymouth	3bE	230	48	70.8
=60 Sheffield Hallam	3aF	223	52	70.8
62 East London		163	62	70.7
63 Hertfordshire		216	52	70.0
64 Middlesex	3aE	178	48	69.3
65 UCE Birmingham		218	48	69.0
66 Gloucestershire		207	46	68.0
67 Northampton		183	48	67.5
68 Greenwich	3bF	184	46	67.4
69 Wolverhampton		202	44	67.2
70 Coventry		183	46	67.0
71 Teesside		242	36	66.6
72 Luton		160	46	66.1
73 Lincoln		211	36	65.3

Average starting salary:	£17,918	Studying and not employed:	8%
Employed in graduate job:	28%	Unemployed:	7%
Employed in graduate job and studying:	21%		
Employed in non-graduate job:	29%	The letters that appear in the Research Quality column indicate the proportion of staff included in the assessment, A showing that almost all staff were included and F showing that hardly any were.	
Employed in non-graduate job and studying:	7%		

Aeronautical and Manufacturing Engineering

Most of the courses under this heading focus on aeronautical or manufacturing engineering, but it includes some with a mechanical title. To add to the confusion, manufacturing degrees often go under the rubric of production engineering (*see* General Engineering and Mechanical Engineering). Although the 43 institutions in the ranking represent an increase on last year, there were 52 in the 2005 *Guide*.

Cambridge holds onto top place with maximum points for research and the best employment record. Imperial College beats Bath to second place with much higher entry grades. Cambridge does not separate its A-level scores for the different branches of engineering, so Imperial registered the highest entry standards, with seventh-placed Bristol next.

Some universities in the ranking had their teaching assessed under a different category, so their other scores are averaged to produce an overall result. Seven universities are top-rated for research, with Liverpool, Southampton and Queen's, Belfast sharing this distinction with the top four in the ranking. Apart from Nottingham, only Kingston, which dropped out of the top ten and almost out of the top 30 this year, was awarded maximum points for teaching. Loughborough and Cambridge were next best in an assessment that produced an unusually wide spread of points.

The subject saw a slight rise in applications at the start of 2006, with more than 9,000 seeking places. This was the third successive rise, bucking the trend in other branches of engineering. Failure rates in first-year exams are high – between 32 and 45 per cent when departments in England were assessed – but most students pass resits. Many graduates go on to further study or training to meet professional requirements and, particularly for aeronautical engineering graduates, employment prospects are bright. The 9 per cent unemployment rate across the whole field is above average for all subjects, but more than half go straight into graduate jobs. Three Cs at A level (and another at AS level) will secure a place on almost any course outside the top ten.

- **The Science, Engineering and Technology Learning Information Portal:** www.elip.info

Aeronautical and Manufacturing Engineering	Research quality/5	Entry standards	Graduate prospects %	Overall rating
1 Cambridge	5*A		96	100.0
2 Imperial College	5*B	484	80	93.8
3 Bath	5*A	415	86	93.5
4 Southampton	5*A	423	70	88.3
5 Nottingham	5B	404	84	87.3
6 Newcastle	4B		92	86.7
7 Bristol	4B	425	82	85.3
8 Loughborough	5B	392	78	84.3
9 Birmingham	4C		94	83.8
10 Liverpool	5*A	299	78	82.9
11 Heriot-Watt	4A	393		82.4
12 Manchester	5A	377	62	79.4
13 Leeds	5*B	302		78.7
14 Sheffield	5A	382	56	77.6
15 Queen's, Belfast	5*B	357	54	75.9
16 Surrey	4B	339		74.6
17 Aston	5C	276	78	73.3
18 Brunel	5C	341	64	72.6
19 Strathclyde	4D	387	68	72.1
20 Glasgow	4A	387	46	71.4
21 Queen Mary	5B	313	56	71.0
22 Salford	3aA	239	64	65.0
23 Brighton	3bC	243	72	62.7
24 City	4D	301	54	61.3
25 Coventry	3aC	229	64	60.9
26 Portsmouth	4D	256	60	60.4
27 Kingston	3aC	256	54	59.1
28 West of England	3bD	237	68	59.0
29 Derby	3aD	203	68	58.2
=30 Hertfordshire	3aD	224	62	57.5
=30 De Montfort	4C	264	42	57.5
32 Buckinghamshire Chilterns UC	2E		66	55.6

Aeronautical and Manufacturing Engineering cont.	Research quality/5	Entry standards	Graduate prospects %	Overall rating
33 Robert Gordon		354	46	54.8
34 London South Bank	3aD		50	53.3
35 Northumbria	3bD	255		53.2
36 Manchester Metropolitan		194	68	52.0
37 Liverpool John Moores	3aE	185	60	51.7
38 UWIC, Cardiff		229	52	48.6
39 Glasgow Caledonian	3aD		38	46.8
40 Sheffield Hallam		210	50	46.6
41 Ulster		206	48	45.6
42 Paisley	2C		36	43.1
43 Plymouth	4E	142	36	41.1

Average starting salary:	£20,256	Studying and not employed:	13%
Employed in graduate job:	45%	Unemployed:	9%
Employed in graduate job and studying:	7%		
Employed in non-graduate job:	24%	The letters that appear in the Research Quality column indicate the proportion of staff included in the assessment, A showing that almost all staff were included and F showing that hardly any were.	
Employed in non-graduate job and studying:	2%		

Agriculture and Forestry

The removal of teaching quality scores shook up the agriculture and forestry ranking last year, but Nottingham retains the leadership. Reading is a close second after overtaking Newcastle. The specialist Harper Adams University College drops from fourth to eighth after losing the benefit of a teaching score matched only by Nottingham, which also shared the top research grade with Reading. Leeds and Bangor also reached grade 5 for research, albeit with a smaller complement of academics entered for assessment.

Queen's, Belfast continues to boast the best employment record, although the proportion finding graduate-level work within six months of graduating has dropped from last year's 90 per cent. Newcastle and fourth-placed Bristol are now close behind. Bristol also has by far the highest average A levels. Greenwich has replaced Plymouth as the only former polytechnic in the top ten.

This is one of the few subject areas in which no university achieved full marks for teaching or research. Scores in both sets of assessments are tightly bunched, covering only three grades in the case of research. However, students appeared generally satisfied with their courses in the first national survey. There was a good response rate and above-average levels of approval.

A quarter of those enrolling for degrees in agriculture and more than a third in forestry do so without A levels, often coming with relevant work experience. Applications for degree places in agriculture were up by 11 per cent at the start of 2005 but this had turned into a decline of almost 9 per cent a year later, with the prospect of top-up fees. As befits a firmly vocational area, employment rates are high, although more than a third of all graduates start in lower-level jobs.

- **The Sector Skills Council for the Environmental and Land-Based Sector (LANTRA):**
  www.lantra.co.uk
- **The Institute of Chartered Foresters:** www.charteredforesters.org

Agriculture and Forestry	Research quality/5	Entry standards	Graduate prospects %	Overall rating
1 Nottingham	5A	292		100.0
2 Reading	5A	292	62	99.1
3 Newcastle	4B	287	72	98.4
4 Bristol		354	72	96.6
5 Queen's, Belfast	4C	264	76	96.1
6 Greenwich	3aD		58	89.6
7 Bangor	5C	261	40	89.5
8 Harper Adams UC	3bE	259	66	89.4
9 Aberdeen	3aC	269	36	87.0
10 Aberystwyth	3aC	255	40	86.8
11 Plymouth	3aE	234	58	86.4
12 Nottingham Trent		237	56	84.4
13 Central Lancashire		210	48	80.7
14 West of England		218	42	80.0

Average starting salary:	£16,031	Studying and not employed:	9%
Employed in graduate job:	36%	Unemployed:	6%
Employed in graduate job and studying:	8%		
Employed in non-graduate job:	37%		
Employed in non-graduate job and studying:	3%		

The letters that appear in the Research Quality column indicate the proportion of staff included in the assessment, A showing that almost all staff were included and F showing that hardly any were.

American Studies

Warwick has lost top place in American Studies after two years of supremacy. Nottingham has lower entry scores, but it is the only university with a 5* research grade and only 14th-placed King's College London has a better graduate employment record. Only the absence of a grade from the 2001 Research Assessment Exercise prevents King's moving further up the table. Sussex, in third place, is not far behind the top two, but has markedly lower entry standards.

Although the top ten places are filled by traditional universities, Central Lancashire shared with East Anglia and Keele the distinction of a maximum 24 points for teaching quality. Teaching scores have been dropped this year because of their age – Warwick was even assessed under the original quality regime, which ended in 1995. Keele was one of six universities to reach grade 5 in the last research assessments.

Students' entry qualifications show wide variation, from 434 at Warwick to little more than 200 at the new universities of Canterbury Christ Church and Northampton. Nine out of ten students taking American Studies have A levels or equivalent qualifications.

American Studies cont.

There is an impressive level of firsts and 2:1s, but the subject has one of the highest proportion of graduates in low-level jobs or still unemployed six months after graduation. Only eight of the 26 universities in this year's table (itself six more than last year's total) saw more than half of leavers go straight into graduate-level jobs or further courses, while the proportion was down to a fifth at De Montfort and Winchester.

The number of places in American studies has been falling gradually. And although applications showed a healthy increase of almost 8 per cent at the start of 2005, there was a catastrophic decline with the arrival of top-up fees a year later. The 2,655 applications represented a 31 per cent drop.

- **The British Association for American Studies:** www.baas.ac.uk

American Studies	Research quality/5	Entry standards	Graduate prospects %	Overall rating
1 Nottingham	5*B	407	60	100.0
2 Warwick	5A	434	50	98.0
3 Sussex	5B	351	60	94.6
4 Manchester	5B	404	45	93.3
5 Sheffield	5B	402	45	93.2
6 Liverpool	5A	303	55	92.9
7 Birmingham	4B	398	50	91.8
8 Lancaster	4A	320	55	90.7
9 Kent	4B	306	60	89.8
10 Keele	5B	308	45	88.6
11 East Anglia	4C	401	35	85.4
12 Swansea	3aA	266	55	85.2
=13 Aberystwyth	4B	292	35	82.6
=13 King's College London		392	65	82.6
=15 Central Lancashire	3bA		45	79.7
=15 Brunel	3aB	285	35	79.7
17 Leicester		323	60	77.9
18 Derby	3aB		30	76.3
19 Reading		313	45	73.5
20 Ulster	4C	219	20	72.5
21 Hull		283	45	72.0
22 Winchester	3aD	252	25	70.9
23 Dundee		304	30	69.2
24 Northampton		214	35	66.0
25 Canterbury Christ Church		212	35	65.9
26 De Montfort		220	20	62.4

Average starting salary:	£15,820	Studying and not employed:	14%
Employed in graduate job:	25%	Unemployed:	8%
Employed in graduate job and studying:	3%		
Employed in non-graduate job:	45%	The letters that appear in the Research Quality column indicate the proportion of staff included in the assessment, A showing that almost all staff were included and F showing that hardly any were.	
Employed in non-graduate job and studying:	5%		

Anatomy and Physiology

Oxford has taken over at the top of the Anatomy and Physiology table, having lost the handicap of an unusually low score by its standards for teaching quality. Indeed, its 21 points out of 24 was the lowest total of any university still offering the subjects, but all teaching scores have been removed this year because of their age. On the remaining measures, Oxford performs consistently well, although it is not actually the top university for any of them.

Second-placed Cambridge has by far the highest entry standards, while Ulster, in 20th place, has the best graduate employment record. Even in research, Bristol, King's College London and Dundee take the honours for anatomy, while Liverpool and Manchester have the top grades for physiology.

Nottingham enjoys the biggest rise this year, from seventh to third, while Loughborough, the leader three years ago, is down to 15th place with one of the lowest employment scores. The number of universities in the ranking is down to 30 this year, with several new universities dropping out. Only Hertfordshire, of the former polytechnics, makes the top 20.

The proportion of graduates going straight into work or further training ranges from under half to more than 90 per cent, with several of the highest scorers languishing in the bottom half of the table. This is because few of them entered the 2001 Research Assessment Exercise.

Twelfth-placed Cardiff is the only Welsh university in the ranking, while Aberdeen is the only Scottish institution in the top ten. The spread of entrance qualifications is wide, with students at Oxford and Cambridge averaging more than 500 points while those at Westminster average less than 200.

Despite awarding generally high marks for teaching, assessors in England found wide variations in some areas. The proportion of students awarded 2:1s, for example, ranged from 30 per cent in one unnamed university to 90 per cent in another. Some equipment was found to be outdated, but students acquired good knowledge of the subjects and skills that are in demand from employers.

There were more than 30,000 applications for anatomy, physiology or pathology by the start of 2006, but this was nearly 6 per cent down on the previous year. Employment prospects are bright, with only 4 per cent out of a job six months after graduation in the latest figures.

- **The Anatomical Society of Great Britain and Ireland:** www.anatsoc.org.uk
- **The Physiological Society:** www.physoc.org

Anatomy and Physiology	Research quality/5 Anatomy	Research quality/5 Physiology	Entry standards	Graduate prospects %	Overall rating
1 Oxford	5B	5A	507	90	100.0
2 Cambridge	5A	4B	550	84	99.0
3 Nottingham		5A	410	86	94.5
4 Bristol	5*A	4A	384	88	92.6

	Research quality/5 Anatomy	Research quality/5 Physiology	Entry standards	Graduate prospects %	Overall rating
5 University College London	5A	4A	410	70	89.0
6 King's College London	5*B		359	72	88.5
7 Liverpool	4A	5*A	340	74	87.8
8 Salford		3aA		90	87.6
9 Aberdeen		5B	343	76	86.8
10 Manchester		5*B	402	58	86.7
11 Newcastle		5A	365	64	86.0
12 Cardiff	5A		357	62	85.0
13 Leeds		5B	350	66	84.3
14 Edinburgh		4A		70	82.5
15 Loughborough		4A	355	58	81.5
16 Southampton			360	88	78.9
17 St Andrews			388	82	78.6
18 Keele			291	92	76.6
19 Hertfordshire		2D	236	92	76.0
20 Ulster			264	94	75.9
21 Sussex			366	66	73.0
22 Queen's, Belfast			314	74	72.7
23 Bradford			218	90	72.4
24 Sheffield			383	56	71.0
25 Dundee	5*B		335	62	70.3
26 Nottingham Trent			226	80	70.0
27 Glasgow			367	54	69.7
28 London South Bank		3aD	202	50	64.8
29 Westminster			190	50	59.7
30 Northampton			214	40	58.1

Average starting salary:	£17,397	Studying and not employed:	39%
Employed in graduate job:	23%	Unemployed:	4%
Employed in graduate job and studying:	4%		
Employed in non-graduate job:	26%	The letters that appear in the Research Quality column indicate the proportion of staff included in the assessment, A showing that almost all staff were included and F showing that hardly any were.	
Employed in non-graduate job and studying:	4%		

Anthropology

Anthropology offers the best chance of a good degree in the social sciences, but the unemployment rate is above average for all subjects, at 8 per cent. One graduate in five goes on to take a higher degree or some form of postgraduate training, but more than a third take non-graduate jobs. Teaching grades were dropped from the table, like all others in this year's *Guide*, because the assessments took place up to a decade ago.

The top three are unchanged for the second successive year, although Cambridge's lead over Oxford has shrunk because Oxford now has the better-qualified students. Cambridge, however, has the best graduate employment record in the table. The third-placed London School of Economics and University College London, in fourth, were the only institutions rated internationally outstanding for research, although all but five of those entering the last assessment exercise reached grade 5.

Anthropology was not assessed separately for teaching quality in Scotland or Wales. Oxford Brookes is the highest-placed of six new universities offering the subject. Outside Oxbridge, entry qualifications are more tightly bunched than for most subjects – only one institution averaged less than 250 points and six more than 400. Although still a minority taste, anthropology's popularity has been growing: there were almost 3,000 applications when the official deadline passed for full-time places on courses beginning in 2006, an increase of 6 per cent to follow a 15 per cent rise the previous year.

- **The Royal Anthropological Institute:** www.therai.org.uk

Anthropology	Research quality/5	Entry standards	Graduate prospects %	Overall rating
1 Cambridge	5A	483	80	100.0
2 Oxford	5A	486	70	97.6
3 London School of Economics	5*A	408	65	96.9
4 University College London	5*B	395	60	92.5
5 St Andrews	5A	386	60	91.3
6 Sussex	5A	365	60	90.5
7 Edinburgh	5B	426	55	89.3
8 Manchester	5B	409	55	88.7
9 Durham	5B	372	60	88.5
10 Goldsmiths, University of London	5A	304	60	88.2
11 School of Asian Studies	5B	358	60	88.0
12 Aberdeen	4A	329	65	86.9
13 Oxford Brookes	4A	298	65	85.7
14 Kent	5B	307	55	84.8
15 Queen's, Belfast	5B	310	50	83.6
16 East London	4B		60	83.4
17 Roehampton	5B	256	40	79.1
18 Lampeter	3aA		55	79.0
19 Hull	3aB	287	55	77.8
20 Teesside		186	70	65.5
21 Southampton		331	45	64.8
22 Nottingham Trent		296	45	63.4
23 Staffordshire		279	25	57.8

Average starting salary:	£17,355	Studying and not employed:	20%
Employed in graduate job:	32%	Unemployed:	8%
Employed in graduate job and studying:	6%		
Employed in non-graduate job:	30%	The letters that appear in the Research Quality column indicate the proportion of staff included in the assessment, A showing that almost all staff were included and F showing that hardly any were.	
Employed in non-graduate job and studying:	5%		

Archaeology

Cambridge again tops the ranking for archaeology, with high entrance qualifications, the best graduate employment score and one of the three 5* research grades. Oxford, one of the other research stars (with tenth-placed Reading) moves up from sixth to second with even higher entry scores and one of the better employment records. Apart from Cambridge, only lowly Glamorgan – 24th out of 30 universities overall – saw more than 70 per cent of leavers go straight into graduate-level work or further training.

The top-rated teaching departments – Leicester, Exeter and York – lose the advantage of their high scores because of the age of the assessments and drop accordingly in the table. Archaeology, which was grouped together with history, produced some of the highest scores in the first national student satisfaction survey. The teaching was rated particularly highly at the Open University and Birkbeck College London.

Glasgow remains the leading Scottish institution in a ranking which includes six new universities, compared with three last year. Winchester is the highest-placed, although still only 23rd out of 30. Cardiff is the leader in Wales. Outside Oxbridge, only Durham and York average more than 400 points on entry. But only two institutions, compared with last year's five, average less than 250 points.

The number of applications was up by more than 8 per cent, to 2,800, at the start of 2005. But uncertain employment prospects may have contributed to a decline of nearly 7 per cent a year later, when top-up fees were being introduced. Assessments of teaching quality generally found high-quality teaching and a broad curriculum. Unemployment six months after graduation was relatively high, at 9 per cent, although none of the universities repeated last year's lowest figures, which saw less than a third of leavers in graduate-level work within six months of finishing a degree.

- **The Council for British Archaeology:** www.britarch.ac.uk

Archaeology	Research quality/5	Entry standards	Graduate prospects %	Overall rating
1 Cambridge	5*A	483	80	100.0
2 Oxford	5*A	493	68	97.2
3 Durham	5A	453	66	93.4
4 University College London	5A	370	60	89.3
5 Sheffield	5A	342	62	89.0
6 Leicester	5A	321	62	88.3
7 Bristol	4B	343	68	87.4
8 Glasgow	4A	372	60	87.3
9 Nottingham	4A	353	62	87.2
10 Reading	5*A	331	48	86.9
11 Southampton	5A	322	56	86.8
12 Manchester	5B	321	60	86.5
=13 Edinburgh	3aA	384	62	86.1
=13 Exeter	5A	319	54	86.1
=13 Queen's, Belfast	5A	283	58	86.1

16 Cardiff	5A	314	54	86.0
17 Bradford	5B	296	60	85.7
18 Liverpool	5A	311	52	85.4
19 York	3aA	422	52	84.7
20 Lampeter	4A	220	60	82.7
21 Birmingham	4B	368	46	82.4
22 Newcastle	3aB	333	48	80.0
23 Winchester	3aA	261	46	78.2
24 Glamorgan		228	74	76.7
25 Kent		294	64	76.0
26 Teesside		252	64	74.8
27 Swansea		281	60	74.6
28 Lincoln		270	58	73.7
29 Liverpool John Moores		214	62	73.1
30 Bournemouth	3aC	178	38	71.2

Average starting salary:	£15,364		Studying and not employed:	23%
Employed in graduate job:	28%		Unemployed:	9%
Employed in graduate job and studying:	4%			
Employed in non-graduate job:	32%			
Employed in non-graduate job and studying:	5%			

The letters that appear in the Research Quality column indicate the proportion of staff included in the assessment, A showing that almost all staff were included and F showing that hardly any were.

Architecture

Cardiff hangs onto the top position in architecture that it wrested away from Cambridge and Nottingham last year, putting an end to their domination of the subject. Cambridge at least moves back above Sheffield in the latest ranking, but Nottingham has slipped out of the top ten for the first time. Meanwhile, Bath has moved to within a whisker of Cambridge to take third place. Cardiff has the best research score and is near the top for both graduate employment and entry qualifications. Cambridge, not surprisingly, has by the far highest average entry grades, while 18th-placed Northumbria has the best employment record.

De Montfort's superior research grade keeps it ahead of Robert Gordon and Oxford Brookes as the top new university. No university was considered internationally outstanding for research, but Sheffield, Bath, Cardiff and Brighton all reached grade 5. Of them, only Cardiff entered a full complement of academics for assessment. Dundee has overtaken Edinburgh as the top department in Scotland.

Architecture was among the first subjects to be assessed for teaching quality, so the grades were dropped last year. A third of all undergraduates enter with qualifications other than A level, Highers or equivalents. There is a wide spread of entrance scores, from more than 500 points at Cambridge to less than 200 at Liverpool John Moores and Wolverhampton. The subject was grouped with building and planning in the first national student satisfaction survey, with Loughborough coming out on top and Cardiff second.

Architecture cont.

Unemployment on graduation is low: only five subjects have more "positive destinations". Nine out of ten graduates go on to complete their professional training, either with further study or within a job. The training is long, but the subject is regaining its popularity: there had been another small rise at the start of 2006, following increases of more than 15 per cent in each of the two previous years.

- **The Royal Institute of British Architects:** www.riba.org

Architecture	Research quality/5	Entry standards	Graduate prospects %	Overall rating
1 Cardiff	5A	432	96	100.0
2 Cambridge	4A	513	90	98.9
3 Bath	5B	438	94	98.5
4 Sheffield	5B	461	88	97.3
5 University College London	4C	434	94	95.4
6 Newcastle	4C	402	96	95.1
7 Dundee	4B	341	92	93.6
8 Manchester	4C	364	94	93.4
9 Liverpool	4B	333	92	93.3
10 Edinburgh	3aB	454	84	93.0
11 Nottingham	4A	419	78	92.5
12 De Montfort	4A	253	90	91.3
13 Strathclyde	4C	392	82	90.5
14 Robert Gordon	3bD	336	96	89.8
15 Oxford Brookes	4D	331	90	89.5
16 Queen's, Belfast	2B	358	90	89.0
17 Westminster	4D	259	94	88.6
18 Northumbria	3bD	259	98	88.1
19 Brighton	5B	280	74	87.8
20 Plymouth		297	96	86.3
21 Sheffield Hallam	3aE	270	92	86.1
=22 East London	4D	278		85.9
=22 Nottingham Trent	3aB	218		85.9
24 Portsmouth	3aD	265	86	85.5
25 Leeds Metropolitan	3bD	237	90	85.1
26 Lincoln	3aD	248	86	85.0
27 West of England		284	90	84.1
28 Huddersfield		229	94	83.7
29 Liverpool John Moores	3bC	192	86	83.6
30 Kingston		234	88	82.0
31 London South Bank	3bD		78	80.8
32 UCE Birmingham	2F	237	80	79.9
33 Glamorgan	3bC		72	79.6
34 Wolverhampton	3aB	192	64	79.3
35 Greenwich	3bE	218	68	76.9

Average starting salary:	£15,836	
Employed in graduate job:	60%	
Employed in graduate job and studying:	17%	
Employed in non-graduate job:	6%	
Employed in non-graduate job and studying:	1%	

Studying and not employed:	12%
Unemployed:	4%

The letters that appear in the Research Quality column indicate the proportion of staff included in the assessment, A showing that almost all staff were included and F showing that hardly any were.

Art and Design

Most courses in art and design are at new universities – often in former art colleges – but it is a clutch of old universities that head the ranking. Oxford remains in first position, with University College London (UCL) moving up one place to second. Oxford has lost the benefit of the only maximum score for teaching quality awarded in England (because all teaching scores have been removed this year) but the A-level entry grades of its students are by far the highest in the table and the employment record of its graduates among the best. Sixty undergraduates take the Fine Art degree at the Ruskin School of Drawing, almost 90 per cent of whom generally achieve a first or upper second. At UCL, students attend the equally famous Slade School of Fine Art.

Art and design was one of the few areas to record poorer research grades in 2001 than in previous assessments – only Salford was rated internationally outstanding. UCL was one of six departments awarded grade 5. Dundee is the top Scottish institution, although it has plunged from fourth to sixteenth place after the removal of the one Excellent teaching grade awarded north of the border. UWIC had secured the same teaching grade in Wales, but ninth-placed Aberystwyth was already ahead in our table and now enjoys a much larger cushion this year.

Brighton remains the best-placed new university and has now broken into the top five. Low entry grades and research scores count against many of the new universities and colleges, although most artists would argue that these are of less significance than in other subjects. Only Kingston joins Brighton in the top ten.

Perhaps inevitably, art and design has one of the highest unemployment rates, at 11 per cent, of all the subjects in these tables. Many graduates are prepared to persevere with part-time or irregular work while pursuing their vocation. The exception this year is at Greenwich, where the 91 per cent of leavers going straight into graduate-level employment or further training produces a bigger lead over the rest of the table than in any other subject. The next best success rate is 68 per cent at Kingston.

Applications for design degrees were down 10 per cent at the start of 2006, but this should be seen in the context of a 30 per cent rise a year earlier. The much smaller foundation degree route saw continued strong growth. Once on courses, art and design students are among the least satisfied, according to the first national survey.

- **The British Institute of Professional Photography:** www.bipp.com
- **Skillfast UK:** www.skillfast-uk.org

Art and Design	Research quality/5	Entry standards	Graduate prospects %	Overall rating
1 Oxford	4A	521	62	100.0
2 University College London	5B	370	60	94.2

	Research quality/5	Entry standards	Graduate prospects %	Overall rating
3 Goldsmiths, University of London	5B	356	56	92.7
4 Loughborough	4C	354	61	91.0
5 Brighton	5B	304	56	90.7
6 Brunel	4A	305	58	90.6
7 Newcastle	4B	374	50	90.5
8 Reading	5A	323	46	90.0
9 Aberystwyth	3aA	349	53	89.5
10 Kingston	4D	300	68	88.9
11 Salford	5*A	213	52	88.8
=12 Bournemouth	5D	283	63	87.8
=12 Leeds	3aA	356	45	87.8
14 Greenwich		218	91	87.4
15 University of the Arts, London	5D	352	48	86.9
16 Dundee	4B	311	42	86.1
17 Southampton	4C	321	46	86.0
18 Oxford Brookes	3bB	313	49	85.0
19 Northumbria	4D	285	52	84.4
20 Hull		188	83	84.3
21 Sheffield Hallam	5C	271	42	84.2
22 Robert Gordon	3aD	317	49	84.1
=23 Sunderland	4C	223	53	83.9
=23 Nottingham Trent	3aE	308	55	83.9
25 Napier	3aD	303	50	83.8
26 Anglia Ruskin	3bA		46	83.3
27 Coventry	3aD	268	53	83.2
=28 Heriot-Watt		315	58	83.1
=28 University College for the Creative Arts	3aD	296	48	83.1
=30 De Montfort	4C	254	44	82.9
=30 Ulster	5D	231	51	82.9
=32 Liverpool Hope	2D	275	57	82.8
=32 Plymouth	3aC	261	47	82.8
34 Edinburgh		460	33	82.7
=35 Kent		289	60	82.6
=35 Middlesex	3aC	249	48	82.6
=37 Leeds Metropolitan	3aD	260	50	82.1
=37 Lancaster	3aC	343	31	82.1
39 Manchester Metropolitan	4E	301	46	81.9
40 Staffordshire	4D	219	52	81.8
41 Chichester	2A	269	46	81.5
42 Westminster	4D	259	44	81.4
=43 Bath Spa	3aD	267	45	81.2
=43 Glamorgan		258	59	81.2
45 UWIC, Cardiff	4D	274	40	81.1

46 Portsmouth	3aD	242	48	81.0
=47 Gloucestershire	3aC	274	37	80.8
=47 Lincoln	3aD	262	44	80.8
49 Southampton Solent	2D	249	52	80.6
50 Falmouth UC	3aE	249	50	80.4
51 West of England	4D	247	41	80.3
=52 Roehampton		287	50	80.1
=52 Buckinghamshire Chilterns UC	3aD	225	47	80.1
54 UCE Birmingham	4E	283	41	80.0
=55 Derby	3bD	261	44	79.9
=55 Hertfordshire	3aD	208	49	79.9
57 Liverpool John Moores	3aC	188	46	79.7
58 University of Wales, Newport	5E	231	45	79.5
59 Central Lancashire	3bE	228	51	79.4
60 Chester	3bD	266	40	79.1
61 East London	4D	173	46	78.6
62 Northampton	2E	227	48	78.1
63 Canterbury Christ Church		276	43	78.0
64 Huddersfield	3bF	223	50	77.9
=65 Teesside		209	51	77.3
=65 Luton		234	47	77.3
67 Glasgow Caledonian		292	37	77.1
=68 Wolverhampton	3aF	198	40	74.7
=68 Bolton	2E	208	37	74.7

Average starting salary:	£15,557	Studying and not employed:	8%
Employed in graduate job:	36%	Unemployed:	11%
Employed in graduate job and studying:	4%		
Employed in non-graduate job:	36%	The letters that appear in the Research Quality column indicate the proportion of staff included in the assessment, A showing that almost all staff were included and F showing that hardly any were.	
Employed in non-graduate job and studying:	5%		

Biological Sciences

Cambridge has opened up a bigger gap over its rivals in the second year of the combined biological sciences table. The highest entry qualifications, the best possible research grade and one of the top employment scores give the university a clear lead over Oxford, with Imperial College, London close behind in third place. Cambridge was one of four English universities with maximum points for teaching and research. Bristol, Newcastle and Sheffield and Newcastle complete the group, while Dundee managed the same feat under the separate Scottish system and has now overtaken Edinburgh as the top university north of the border. Research assessments improved out of all recognition in 2001, with ten universities rated internationally outstanding, compared with only three in the previous exercise.

UWIC again registers easily the best employment score, with 93 per cent of leavers going straight into graduate jobs or further training, but the decision not to enter the last Research Assessment Exercise cost the institute a place in the top 30. Indeed, no new

Biological Sciences cont.

university achieves that feat, and Liverpool Hope, in equal 33rd place, is best placed. The Open University, West of England and Kent were the top performers in the first national student satisfaction survey, which generally showed biology degrees in a good light.

Although entrants to both Cambridge and Oxford average more than 500 points, entry standards elsewhere are more tightly bunched than in many other subjects. Only eight other universities average more than 400 points and the same number dip below 200 points. Graduate prospects nationally are about average for all subjects.

Biology had not suffered the recruitment problems experienced by other sciences until this year. Applications were up by 6 per cent at the start of 2006, and the total of 22,000 is still well ahead of chemistry and physics. Two thirds of all entrants arrive with A levels or their equivalent and more than half of the undergraduates are awarded firsts or 2:1s. More than a third go on to take postgraduate courses, either full or part-time.

- **The Biochemical Society:** www.biology4all.com
- **The Institute of Biology:** www.iob.org

Biological Sciences	Research quality/5	Entry standards	Graduate prospects %	Overall rating
1 Cambridge	5*A	547	85	100.0
2 Oxford	5A	507	72	93.7
3 Imperial College	5*B	464	73	93.0
4 Surrey	5*A	296	85	92.1
5 Bristol	5*A	405	71	91.8
6 Ulster	5*A	232	88	91.0
7 York	5B	446	72	90.7
8 Dundee	5*B	318	80	90.3
9 Bath	5B	397	74	89.7
10 Durham	5B	460	66	89.6
11 Warwick	5B	420	70	89.4
=12 Manchester	5*B	387	68	89.2
=12 Sheffield	5*A	401	62	89.2
14 Newcastle	5*B	355	70	88.7
15 Edinburgh	5A	399	65	88.4
16 St Andrews	5B	400	66	87.7
17 University College London	5B	379	68	87.6
18 Leicester	5*B	346	66	87.4
19 Nottingham	5A	409	60	87.3
20 Queen's, Belfast	4B	313	76	86.3
21 Cardiff	5A	356	62	86.2
22 Birmingham	5B	358	63	85.6
23 Kent	4A	296	70	85.0
=24 Leeds	5B	337	63	84.9
=24 Sussex	5B	346	62	84.9
26 Liverpool	5B	325	64	84.8

27 East Anglia	5B	332	62	84.5
28 Reading	4B	310	66	83.5
29 Southampton	5B	368	53	83.2
30 Glasgow	5B	365	53	83.1
31 Exeter	4B	343	60	82.9
32 Essex	4B	261	68	82.5
=33 Liverpool Hope	3bC		76	82.2
=33 King's College London	3aC	331	68	82.2
35 Royal Holloway	5C	292	64	82.1
36 Lancaster	4B	327	57	81.6
37 Stirling	4A	333	51	81.0
38 UWIC, Cardiff		210	93	80.9
39 Brunel	4C	268	65	80.5
40 Keele	4C	255	66	80.3
41 Portsmouth	5A	222	54	79.9
42 Heriot-Watt	4A	360	43	79.6
43 Kingston	3aC	168	77	79.5
44 Aberdeen	5C	310	52	79.4
45 Bangor	4A	308	47	79.1
=46 Aston	3aC	295	60	78.8
=46 Queen Mary	4B	256	55	78.8
48 Brighton	5C	243	57	78.6
49 Sunderland	3aB	220	62	78.2
50 Napier	4D	236	65	77.9
51 Hertfordshire	3aC	226	64	77.8
52 Salford	3aA	180	62	77.6
53 Oxford Brookes	3aA	230	56	77.5
54 Swansea	3aA	286	49	77.4
55 Nottingham Trent	5D	228	59	76.8
56 Greenwich	3aA	204	56	76.7
57 Aberystwyth	3aA	268	48	76.6
58 Hull	4D	220	61	76.3
59 Wolverhampton	3aC	175	64	76.2
60 Bath Spa	3bE		68	76.1
61 Central Lancashire	3bB	238	57	76.0
62 Robert Gordon		253	68	75.4
63 Chester		246	68	75.2
64 Northumbria	2E	278	58	74.3
65 Staffordshire		273	61	74.2
66 Huddersfield		216	67	74.0
=67 Westminster	3bC	159	60	73.5
=67 Paisley	3bC	262	48	73.5
69 Glasgow Caledonian		289	56	73.3
70 Strathclyde		337	50	73.2
=71 Coventry	2C	224	52	72.2
=71 Bolton		141	69	72.2
73 West of England		257	55	72.0

	Research quality/5	Entry standards	Graduate prospects %	Overall rating
=74 Liverpool John Moores		190	62	71.8
=74 Plymouth	3aE	298	43	71.8
76 East London	2D	162	58	71.3
=77 Manchester Metropolitan	2D	241	48	71.0
=77 Sheffield Hallam		216	56	71.0
79 Leeds Metropolitan		233	53	70.8
80 Derby		183	57	70.3
81 Worcester	2D	206	49	70.2
82 Roehampton		195	53	69.6
83 London South Bank		177	52	68.7

Average starting salary:	£16,425	Studying and not employed:	27%
Employed in graduate job:	29%	Unemployed:	7%
Employed in graduate job and studying:	5%		
Employed in non-graduate job:	29%	The letters that appear in the Research Quality column indicate the proportion of staff included in the assessment, A showing that almost all staff were included and F showing that hardly any were.	
Employed in non-graduate job and studying:	3%		

Building

Nottingham has returned to the top of the building table after dropping out altogether last year because there were not enough students in the relevant year group to compile reliable statistics. Still there were too few to publish a destinations score, but the university's commanding lead in entry standards is enough to reclaim the position it occupied two years ago. Loughborough, last year's leader and one of only two 5* research departments, slips to second, while Salford, the other research star, jumps from tenth to third without the burden of a low teaching quality score. Loughborough was also the most successful university for architecture, planning and building in the first national student satisfaction survey.

Kingston was the only university to be awarded maximum points for teaching – a measure now dropped from all the tables because of the age of the statistics – but low entry grades and the absence of a research score in this category almost cost it a place in the top 20. Nottingham Trent is the top new university, just holding off Oxford Brookes and Wolverhampton. Oxford Brookes was the only institution in this category to see every leaver go straight into graduate-level employment or further training. Employment scores are good throughout the table, with no university dropping below a 74 per cent success rate.

Applications for building showed a small increase at the start of 2006, when top-up fees prompted a decline in most subjects. There had been a 16 per cent increase in 2004 and another 30 per cent in 2005, perhaps because job prospects have been good in recent years. More than 80 per cent of leavers were in graduate jobs within six months, and less than one in 20 was unemployed.

Universities admit 44 per cent of students with qualifications other than A level. Those who do take the A-level route tend not to require the highest grades. No university registered an average of more than 400 points, although only four dropped below 200 – far fewer than last year.

- **The Chartered Institute of Building:** www.ciob.org.uk
- **The Chartered Institute of Building Services Engineers:** www.cibse.org

Building	Research quality/5	Entry standards	Graduate prospects %	Overall rating
1 Nottingham	4A	377		100.0
2 Loughborough	5*B	316	96	98.5
3 Salford	5*A	308	92	97.7
4 Reading	5B	322	88	95.2
=5 Heriot-Watt	5B	337	84	94.5
=5 University College London	4C	319		94.5
7 Manchester	4C	320	90	93.8
8 Ulster	5A	242	90	93.6
9 Nottingham Trent	3aB	236	96	92.6
10 Oxford Brookes	4D	213	100	91.9
11 Wolverhampton	3aB		90	91.8
12 Northampton		285	96	90.7
13 Glamorgan	3bC		90	89.5
14 Sheffield Hallam	3aE	234	94	89.4
15 Robert Gordon	3bD	280	86	88.9
16 Northumbria	3bD	223	92	88.7
17 Anglia Ruskin	2B	256	84	87.7
18 Liverpool John Moores	3bC	194	90	87.6
19 Central Lancashire	3aD	225	86	87.4
20 Kingston		238	90	87.0
21 Brighton	3bC	211	86	87.0
22 Leeds Metropolitan	3bD	242	84	86.9
23 Westminster	3aD	214	84	86.4
24 West of England		235	86	85.7
25 Plymouth	4E	226	82	85.6
26 Napier	3bD	246	78	85.1
27 Glasgow Caledonian	3aD	265	74	85.1
28 Coventry	3bC	203	80	84.8
29 London South Bank	3bD		82	84.7
30 UCE Birmingham	2F	240		84.6
31 Greenwich	3bE	192	80	83.1
32 Teesside	2D	168		81.9
33 Bolton		155	78	80.2

Average starting salary:	£20,314	Studying and not employed:	3%
Employed in graduate job:	71%	Unemployed:	4%
Employed in graduate job and studying:	14%		
Employed in non-graduate job:	8%	The letters that appear in the Research Quality column indicate the proportion of staff included in the assessment, A showing that almost all staff were included and F showing that hardly any were.	
Employed in non-graduate job and studying:	1%		

Business Studies

Oxford retains the top place it has occupied since teaching grades were dropped from the business ranking. But, with the best employment record in the table enabling it to overtake Warwick, the London School of Economics could hardly be closer. Warwick is one of the two universities rated internationally outstanding for research, while eighth-placed Lancaster is the other. St Andrews is the top university in Scotland, despite dropping five places this year, and Cardiff remains the clear the leader in Wales.

Although Oxford's Said Business School is exclusively postgraduate, the colleges offer management in joint honours first-degree courses. London and Manchester business schools, like Cranfield and Cambridge's Judge School of Management, are also absent from the table because they do not offer first degrees.

Both employment rates and especially entrance qualifications vary widely in this, one of the largest tables in the *Guide*. There are more than 100 institutions in this latest edition, over half of them new universities or colleges, but only Portsmouth wins a place in the top 40. More than a dozen have average entry grades of less than 200 points, but at the majority of them fewer than half the leavers were in graduate jobs or post-graduate training within six months. In one case, this proportion falls below 30 per cent.

Applications for degrees in business and management seem to have reached their peak, with student demand and the number of places remaining roughly level in 2004 and 2005. At the start of 2006, management held steady again, while business was down by 3.5 per cent – almost exactly the average for all subjects. However, while job prospects are not what they once were, the two subjects remain among the most popular choices in higher education. Unemployment levels are no higher than average for all subjects, but more than a third of all leavers start off in a non-graduate job. Neither subject emerged particularly well from the first national student satisfaction survey. The Open University achieved the best results for business studies, while Loughborough, Reading and Liverpool Hope were the leaders in management.

- **The Chartered Management Institute:** www.managers.org.uk
- **The Institute of Management Consultancy:** www.imc.co.uk

Business Studies	Research quality/5	Entry standards	Graduate prospects %	Overall rating
1 Oxford	5A	528	78	100.0
2 London School of Economics	5A	464	85	99.7
=3 Warwick	5*B	450	76	97.1
=3 Cambridge	5A		78	97.1
5 Bath	5A	416	81	97.0
6 King's College London	4B	398	79	93.4
7 Nottingham	5B	435	68	93.0
8 Lancaster	5*B	395	67	92.8
9 Aston	5B	358	76	92.6
=10 Manchester	5A	405	65	92.2
=10 St Andrews	4A	434	67	92.2
12 Imperial College	5B	413	65	91.5

=13 Leeds	5C	391	69	90.1
=13 City	5C	351	74	90.1
15 Loughborough	4C	385	70	89.1
=16 Cardiff	5B	362	62	88.9
=16 Surrey	4C	324	77	88.9
18 Southampton	4B	403	61	88.6
19 Royal Holloway	4B	321	69	88.0
=20 Durham	3aD	353	76	87.2
=20 Edinburgh	4B	417	54	87.2
22 Birmingham	4D	375	70	87.1
23 Sheffield	4B	386	57	86.9
=24 Queen's, Belfast	4B	339	61	86.4
=24 Exeter	4C	378	61	86.4
26 Essex	5C	285	68	86.2
27 Newcastle	3aC	387	63	86.1
=28 Strathclyde	4C	430	52	85.7
=28 Stirling	4B	349	57	85.7
30 Bradford	4C	213	79	85.6
31 Leicester	3aB	299	67	85.3
32 Glasgow	4C	379	55	84.8
33 Reading	5C	331	56	84.5
34 Aberdeen	3aB	328	60	84.4
35 York		412	65	83.2
36 Keele	4B	284	55	82.9
37 Heriot-Watt	4D	389	51	82.4
38 East Anglia	3aC	337	55	82.2
=39 Portsmouth	4C	223	64	81.8
=39 Kent	3aC	262	63	81.8
41 Bangor	5B	242	50	81.4
42 Nottingham Trent	3bD	289	65	81.2
43 Brunel	4C	299	51	80.9
44 Hull	4C	240	58	80.8
45 Swansea	3aD	275	60	80.1
46 Northumbria	3bF	290	66	79.6
=47 Bournemouth	3aE	281	60	79.1
=47 Liverpool		331	60	79.1
49 Oxford Brookes	2F	294	64	79.0
50 Hertfordshire	3aC	227	57	78.9
51 University College London		374	53	78.7
52 Ulster	3aD	279	54	78.6
53 Salford	3aB	252	48	78.5
54 Abertay	3bE		61	78.2
55 De Montfort	3aC	231	53	78.0
56 Gloucestershire	3aD	226	58	77.9
57 Robert Gordon	2F	311	57	77.7
=58 Queen Mary		294	59	77.5
=58 West of England	3aD	261	52	77.5

Business Studies cont.

	Research quality/5	Entry standards	Graduate prospects %	Overall rating
60 Central Lancashire	3bE	229	61	77.1
61 Plymouth	3bE	256	57	76.9
62 Brighton	3aE	264	54	76.8
63 Aberystwyth	3bC	259	48	76.5
=64 Manchester Metropolitan	3aE	260	53	76.4
=64 Sheffield Hallam	3bF	259	58	76.4
=66 Queen Margaret College	2C	257	51	76.1
=66 Napier	3bE	256	54	76.1
68 Kingston	3aE	198	59	75.9
=69 Glamorgan	3bD	213	53	75.3
=69 University of the Arts, London		340	45	75.3
71 Lincoln	3bD	213	51	74.8
=72 Derby	2E	202	57	74.6
=72 Leeds Metropolitan	2F	267	51	74.6
74 Glasgow Caledonian	3aE	292	42	74.5
=75 Liverpool Hope		188	61	74.4
=75 UWIC, Cardiff		226	56	74.4
77 Liverpool John Moores	3bE	196	55	74.3
78 Teesside		202	58	74.1
79 Huddersfield	3bE	225	49	73.7
80 Anglia Ruskin	2D	217	49	73.5
81 Sunderland	2F	195	55	73.2
82 Staffordshire	3bE	207	48	72.8
=83 Middlesex	3aE	154	52	72.5
=83 Coventry	2E	205	49	72.5
=85 Chester		243	46	72.2
=85 Westminster	3bE	221	44	72.2
87 London South Bank	3aE	167	48	71.8
88 Bath Spa		206	49	71.7
89 Greenwich	3bF	184	50	71.6
90 UCE Birmingham	2F	209	47	71.5
91 Worcester		195	49	71.4
92 Canterbury Christ Church		202	48	71.3
=93 Paisley	2E	247	39	71.2
=93 Northampton	2E	206	44	71.2
=95 East London	2E	156	50	71.1
=95 Southampton Solent		203	47	71.1
97 Winchester		253	40	70.9
=98 Luton	3aE	177	41	70.3
=98 Roehampton		203	44	70.3
100 Thames Valley		159	49	70.1
101 University of Wales, Newport		200	42	69.6

102 Wolverhampton	3bF	179	40	68.7
103 Buckinghamshire Chilterns UC	2E	184	37	68.5
104 Bolton	1D	170	29	65.7

Average starting salary:	£18,580	Studying and not employed:	7%
Employed in graduate job:	42%	Unemployed:	7%
Employed in graduate job and studying:	6%		
Employed in non-graduate job:	35%	
Employed in non-graduate job and studying:	3%	

The letters that appear in the Research Quality column indicate the proportion of staff included in the assessment, A showing that almost all staff were included and F showing that hardly any were.

Celtic Studies

Cambridge has taken over at the top of the Celtic Studies table, which has one more university (Glasgow) this year. Cambridge does not publish separate destinations data for these subjects but it has by far the highest entry standards and one of the four 5* research grades. Last year's leader, Aberystwyth, slips to second, while the best employment score in the table enables Cardiff to overtake Bangor for third place.

Queen's, Belfast, regains top spot in Irish studies from Ulster by virtue of much higher entry standards, despite Ulster's 5* research grade. Aberystwyth and Bangor are the other research stars. Not surprisingly, universities in Wales, Northern Ireland and Scotland occupy all but one of the places in the table. Aberdeen, which joined the ranking last year, is just ahead of Glasgow as the top centre in Scotland.

The subjects have relatively small enrolments, but both Welsh and Irish studies have been attracting more applicants recently – there were rises of around 10 per cent in both 2004 and 2005. About half of the graduates go on to further study – only law has a higher proportion in this category. Partly as a result, not much more than a quarter go straight into a graduate-level job, but the 4 per cent unemployment rate is one of the lowest.

- **Dalriada Celtic Heritage Trust:** www.dalriada.co.uk
- **CELT:** www.ucc.ie/celt/links.html

Celtic Studies	Research quality/5	Entry standards	Graduate prospects %	Overall rating
1 Cambridge	5*A	471		100.0
2 Aberystwyth	5*A	358	75	94.1
3 Cardiff	5A	360	80	93.6
4 Bangor	5*A	326	75	92.9
5 Queen's, Belfast	5A	333	70	89.9
6 Swansea	5A	277	75	89.2
7 Ulster	5*B	225	70	86.4
8 Aberdeen	4B		60	82.8
9 Glasgow	4A		55	82.3
10 Lampeter	3bC		50	72.2

Celtic Studies cont.

Average starting salary:	£17,242	Studying and not employed:	39%
Employed in graduate job:	22%	Unemployed:	4%
Employed in graduate job and studying:	5%		
Employed in non-graduate job:	23%		
Employed in non-graduate job and studying:	6%		

Chemical Engineering

Cambridge tops the chemical engineering table for the fifth year in a row, but the margin over Imperial College has never been smaller. Cambridge does not publish separate entry data for chemical engineering, but it is again the only university with a 100 per cent graduate employment record. However, Imperial has the better rating for research – 5*, like third-placed Birmingham and University College London, in joint sixth position.

Fourth-placed Bath is the only university to approach Cambridge's employment score, although all but one saw at least 65 per cent of leavers go straight into graduate-level work or further training. Heriot-Watt has the highest entry standards in the table and remains the best-placed Scottish institution. London South Bank and Paisley are the only representatives of the new universities, and both appear at the foot of the ranking.

Chemical engineering is one of the smaller branches of engineering, with little more than 6,000 applications by the start of 2006. But the appeal of the subject seems to be growing: this represented an increase of nearly 9 per cent against the national trend, following an even bigger rise in 2005.

Four out of five students have A levels or equivalent qualifications, and average entry grades are the highest for any engineering subject. This helps produce engineering's largest proportion of firsts and 2:1s. Almost six out of ten students go straight into graduate jobs, but the 8 per cent unemployment rate is slightly higher than the average for all subjects. Teaching quality assessors found the overall standard in English universities to be high in relation to international competition, with most courses offering industrial placements in the final year and leading to Chartered Engineer status.

- **The Royal Society of Chemistry:** www.rsc.org
- **The Institution of Chemical Engineers:** www.icheme.org

Chemical Engineering	Research quality/5	Entry standards	Graduate prospects %	Overall rating
1 Cambridge	5A		100	100.0
2 Imperial College	5*A	457	85	98.4
3 Birmingham	5*A	390	85	94.2
4 Surrey	4B		95	93.6
5 Bath	4A	408	90	92.6
=6 University College London	5*A	353	85	91.9
=6 Manchester	5A	425	75	91.9

	Research Quality			
=8 Swansea	4A		85	91.5
=8 Heriot-Watt	4A	469	70	91.5
10 Queen's, Belfast	4A	376	90	90.6
11 Loughborough	4A	377	85	89.5
12 Newcastle	5B	381	75	88.0
13 Aston	5C		80	87.5
14 Edinburgh	4C	410	70	85.0
15 Sheffield	4B	360	75	84.9
16 Nottingham	4B	391	65	84.4
17 Leeds	5C	261	75	78.4
18 Strathclyde		400	70	77.6
19 London South Bank	3aE		65	73.0
20 Paisley	2C		45	66.2

Average starting salary:	£22,068	Studying and not employed:	24%
Employed in graduate job:	52%	Unemployed:	8%
Employed in graduate job and studying:	3%		
Employed in non-graduate job:	10%		
Employed in non-graduate job and studying:	3%		

The letters that appear in the Research Quality column indicate the proportion of staff included in the assessment, A showing that almost all staff were included and F showing that hardly any were.

Chemistry

The number of universities in the chemistry ranking has dipped below 50 for the first time last year following a much-publicised series of closures that may yet continue. However, applications remain buoyant: the start of 2006 saw the third successive increase of more than 5 per cent at a time when other subjects were in decline. Forensic science has become an attractive alternative to the pure subject but, for many, chemistry remains the classic science.

A much-improved set of research assessments in 2001 produced challengers for Oxford and Cambridge for the first time, but the pair lead the ranking again. Both have the maximum research score and average entry grades of more than four As at A level. Durham, the other top research scorer, remains third, while Imperial College, Bristol and University College London also boast 5* grades. Edinburgh retains top place in Scotland, while Cardiff takes the honours in Wales. However, Queen's, Belfast, is comfortably the top university outside England, thanks partly to the best employment score for the subject.

Chemistry is old university territory, with no former polytechnic in the top 30. Plymouth leads its peer group at 31st. Almost nine out of ten undergraduates have A levels or their equivalent, but entry requirements are not far above the average for all subjects. The unemployment rate, at 6 per cent, is less than the average for higher education as a whole, and three quarters of leavers either undertake further study or go straight into graduate-level jobs. Not a single university in the table had "positive destinations" for fewer than 60 per cent of their graduates.

- **The Royal Society of Chemistry:** www.rsc.org

Chemistry

	Research quality/5	Entry standards	Graduate prospects %	Overall rating
1 Cambridge	5*A	550	84	100.0
2 Oxford	5*A	536	82	99.0
3 Durham	5*A	466	80	96.6
4 Imperial College	5*B	459	80	95.2
5 Queen's, Belfast	4A	361	94	94.9
6 Sussex	5A	382	84	94.0
7 Southampton	5A	440	76	93.0
8 University College London	5*B	354	80	92.5
9 Bristol	5*B	395	76	92.3
=10 York	5A	385	78	92.2
=10 Warwick	5A	383	78	92.2
12 Sheffield	5B	364	82	91.8
13 Edinburgh	5A	387	76	91.7
14 Heriot-Watt	4A	371	82	91.4
15 Bath	4A	381	80	91.0
16 Liverpool	5A	324	78	90.7
17 Reading	4A	314	82	90.0
18 Strathclyde	4A	403	74	89.7
19 Surrey	3aA	268	90	89.6
20 St Andrews	5C	417	76	89.5
=21 Hull	4C	278	90	89.1
=21 Leeds	5B	353	74	89.1
23 Nottingham	5A	422	64	88.8
24 Manchester	5B	336	74	88.6
25 Leicester	4A	313	76	88.1
26 Aberdeen	3aC	379	82	87.9
27 Cardiff	4A	304	76	87.8
28 Loughborough	4B	316	76	87.2
29 East Anglia	5B	299	70	86.5
30 Bradford	4B		74	86.2
31 Plymouth	4C	251	82	85.9
32 Brighton	5C	199	82	85.8
=33 Birmingham	5B	269	70	85.7
=33 Glasgow	4C	365	72	85.7
35 Keele	3aA	310		85.6
36 Kingston	3aC		80	84.8
37 Newcastle	4C	324	68	83.4
38 Bangor	3aA	284	66	82.5
39 Coventry	4C	203	74	82.2
40 Aston	5C	238	66	81.8
41 Manchester Metropolitan	4A	162	68	81.7
42 Liverpool John Moores		168	94	81.6
43 Nottingham Trent	3aD	180	82	81.5

	Research quality/5	Entry standards	Graduate prospects %	Overall rating
44 Northumbria	3bC	268	74	81.4
45 Huddersfield	4C	220	66	80.1
46 Paisley	2C		66	74.6
47 Sheffield Hallam		220	64	73.5

Average starting salary:	£18,037	Studying and not employed:	35%
Employed in graduate job:	35%	Unemployed:	6%
Employed in graduate job and studying:	4%		
Employed in non-graduate job:	18%	The letters that appear in the Research Quality column indicate the proportion of staff included in the assessment, A showing that almost all staff were included and F showing that hardly any were.	
Employed in non-graduate job and studying:	2%		

Civil Engineering

Imperial College has taken over top place in civil engineering after an extended period of dominance by Cardiff. Imperial was one of six universities considered internationally outstanding for research, as well as having the highest entry standards and one of the best employment scores. The other research stars were Cardiff, Southampton and Bristol (in second, third and fourth places respectively), plus more modestly placed Salford and Swansea. Salford was also one of four universities that saw all their leavers go straight into graduate-level employment or further training, but the lowest average A-level entry grades in the entire table relegated the university to outside the top ten. Queen's, Belfast, Loughborough and Exeter were the other employment hotspots.

Nationally, civil engineering has among the best job prospects: the 5 per cent unemployment rate is below average, and three quarters of leavers go straight into graduate jobs.

There is a wide spread of entry scores, from more than 450 points at Imperial to less than 200 at Salford, Kingston and Portsmouth. Almost a third of the universities offering civil engineering are former polytechnics, but only two – Leeds Metropolitan and Nottingham Trent – make the top 30. Nearly four out of ten undergraduates are admitted with A levels or the equivalent, their grades close to the average for all subjects. The subject has been expanding: there were big increases in applications in both 2004 and 2005, while even 2006 saw a 2 per cent rise, despite the imminent arrival of top-up fees.

- **The Institute of Civil Engineers:** www.ice.org.uk

Civil Engineering	Research quality/5	Entry standards	Graduate prospects %	Overall rating
1 Imperial College	5*B	460	95	100.0
2 Cardiff	5*A	380	90	97.1
3 Southampton	5*B	445	85	96.7
4 Bristol	5*C	417	95	96.3
5 Queen's, Belfast	5B	354	100	96.1
6 Loughborough	4B	368	100	95.1
=7 Bath	5B	397	90	94.8
=7 Nottingham	5A	404	85	94.8

	Research Quality/5	Entry Standards	Graduate Prospects %	Overall Rating
9 University College London	5A	342	90	94.0
10 Manchester	5B	403	85	93.6
11 Sheffield	5B	396	85	93.4
12 Swansea	5*B	340	85	93.0
13 Dundee	5A	303	90	92.7
14 Salford	5*A	167	100	92.4
15 Ulster	5A	254	95	92.3
16 Birmingham	5C	336	95	92.2
=17 Liverpool	4A	277	95	91.4
=17 Aberdeen	4C	347	95	91.4
19 Newcastle	5B	334	85	91.2
20 Glasgow	4C	369	90	90.7
21 Surrey	4C	319	95	90.3
22 Strathclyde	4C	371	85	89.4
23 Heriot-Watt	4A	415	70	89.2
=24 Edinburgh	5B	393	70	89.0
=24 Bradford	4B		85	89.0
26 Leeds Metropolitan	3aB		90	88.7
27 Nottingham Trent	3aB	248	95	87.9
28 Leeds	5D	324	85	86.8
29 Exeter		326	100	86.0
30 City	4B	226	85	85.8
31 Paisley	3aC	245	90	85.1
32 Brighton	3bC		90	85.0
33 Napier	4C	279	80	84.7
34 Kingston	3aC	188	95	84.5
35 Plymouth	4E	237	90	82.5
36 East London	2D		90	82.0
37 Portsmouth	3aC	193	85	81.8
38 Coventry	3bC	250	60	75.5
39 Glasgow Caledonian		259	60	72.3

Average starting salary:	£19,711	Studying and not employed:	7%
Employed in graduate job:	68%	Unemployed:	5%
Employed in graduate job and studying:	10%		
Employed in non-graduate job:	9%	The letters that appear in the Research Quality column indicate the proportion of staff included in the assessment, A showing that almost all staff were included and F showing that hardly any were.	
Employed in non-graduate job and studying:	1%		

Classics and Ancient History

Oxford and Cambridge have been locked together at the top of the classics table since it was first published three years ago, when their scores were identical. Cambridge remains ahead in the latest ranking because its lead in graduate destinations was more substantial than Oxford's in entry standards. Like third-placed King's College London, both universities have maximum points for teaching and research.

University College London matched the top three with a 5* research rating and nine of the remaining twenty universities reached grade 5. Bristol shares with Cambridge the best employment record for classics, with 85 per cent of leavers going straight into graduate jobs or postgraduate study, and it has jumped from outside the top ten to fourth place.

The removal of teaching quality scores makes less difference in this table than in many others because six of the eighteen universities in the teaching quality assessment for England achieved perfect scores. No new universities appear in the table, although some offer the subjects as part of a modular degree scheme. A-level grades in classics are among the highest for any group of subjects, but most universities teach the subject from scratch, as well as to more practised students.

The subjects' reputation for attracting analytical high-fliers helps in the jobs market, but relatively few (31 per cent) go directly into graduate jobs. The 6 per cent unemployment rate six months after graduation is just below average for all subjects, but the proportion going on to postgraduate courses is high. Applications were down by more than 8 per cent at the start of 2006.

- **The Classics Pages:** www.classicspage.com

Classics and Ancient History	Research quality/5	Entry standards	Graduate prospects %	Overall rating
1 Cambridge	5*A	505	85	100.0
2 Oxford	5*A	508	70	96.9
3 King's College London	5*A	382	65	89.7
4 Bristol	5B	401	85	89.3
5 Durham	5B	459	60	86.6
6 St Andrews	5B	411	60	84.3
7 Warwick	5A	407	50	84.2
8 University College London	5*B	389	50	84.1
9 Birmingham	5A	361	55	83.0
10 Exeter	5A	380	50	82.9
11 Nottingham	4A	392	60	82.2
12 Manchester	5B	364	55	80.9
=13 Royal Holloway	5A	309	50	79.4
=13 Leeds	4B	350	65	79.4
15 Edinburgh	4B	414	45	78.2
16 Reading	5A	313	35	76.4
17 Liverpool	4A	301	50	75.6
18 Swansea	4A	315	45	75.2
19 Glasgow	4B	413	25	73.8
20 Newcastle	3aA	332	50	73.6
21 Kent		275	60	59.6

Classics and Ancient History cont.

Average starting salary:	£18,115	Studying and not employed:	30%
Employed in graduate job:	24%	Unemployed:	6%
Employed in graduate job and studying:	6%		
Employed in non-graduate job:	30%		
Employed in non-graduate job and studying:	5%		

The letters that appear in the Research Quality column indicate the proportion of staff included in the assessment, A showing that almost all staff were included and F showing that hardly any were.

Communication and Media Studies

Communication and media studies are mainly the preserve of the new universities, but nine of the top ten places are filled by older institutions. East Anglia loses the top place it won last year from Loughborough, largely thanks to higher entry standards. Both score maximum points for research – the only other 5* grade went to Goldsmiths, which entered a much smaller proportion of its academics for assess-ment. Westminster, the best-placed new university for research, was one of six institutions on grade 5.

Stirling is the top university in Scotland, Aberystwyth the leader in Wales, but neither makes the top ten. Entry grades have risen since the last edition of the *Guide*: three universities average more than 400 points at entry, compared with just one last year, while three average less than 200, rather than last year's seven. Warwick has the highest total, the equivalent of three As at A level and another at AS level.

Controversy has raged over the subjects' currency in the employment market, and the division of jobs into graduate and non-graduate hits communication and media studies harder than any other group of subjects. Only two subjects have a lower proportion of "positive destinations". Falmouth University College did best, with three quarters of leavers going straight into graduate jobs or further training. In three institutions the proportion was below a third, sending the subjects to the bottom of the graduate em-ployment table. Academics in the field argue that it is normal for students completing media courses to take "entry level" work that is not classified as a graduate job.

Only at the start of 2006 was there any sign of this affecting the demand for places in media studies. An increase of 19 per cent in 2005 turned into a decline of almost 10 per cent as top-up fees loomed. Teaching quality assessors found that courses varied from conventional academic degrees to advanced vocational training. Their main concern was a shortage of resources in a fast-changing area of study. Media studies recorded below-average results in the first national student satisfaction survey, but Loughborough and the College of St Mark and St John, in Plymouth, did especially well.

- **The Broadcast Journalism Training Council:** www.bjtc.org.uk
- **The Institute of Scientific and Technical Communicators:** www.istc.org.uk

Communication and Media Studies	Research quality/5	Entry standards	Graduate prospects %	Overall rating
1 Loughborough	5*A	384	54	100.0
2 East Anglia	5*A	331		99.9
3 Sheffield	4C	422	64	98.5
4 Leeds	4C	374	71	98.1

5 Cardiff	5B	388	55	97.7
6 Warwick	5B	449	38	96.2
7 Goldsmiths, University of London	5*C	324	61	95.6
8 Sussex	4A	374	50	95.2
9 Royal Holloway	5B	364	49	95.0
10 Central Lancashire	3bC	312	71	92.9
11 Aberystwyth	5B	282		92.3
12 Leicester	3aB	340	50	91.2
13 Westminster	5D	330	54	90.9
14 Stirling	5C	377	34	90.0
15 Ulster	4B	245	56	89.8
=16 Napier	3aD	310	57	89.0
=16 Falmouth UC		268	77	89.0
18 Birmingham	3aC	375	37	88.3
=19 Nottingham Trent	5D	297	48	87.8
=19 Glasgow Caledonian	3aB	305	43	87.8
21 Liverpool		351	57	87.7
=22 Robert Gordon	3bD	297	55	87.0
=22 Leeds Metropolitan	3aD	283	54	87.0
=22 Bournemouth		342	56	87.0
25 City	3bD	269	57	86.3
26 Glasgow		406	40	85.9
27 London South Bank	4B	209	47	85.8
28 Bangor		318	55	85.6
29 West of England	4C	287	37	85.4
30 Staffordshire	4D	264	47	85.2
31 Queen Margaret College	2D	316	45	84.5
32 De Montfort	3aB	251	37	83.7
33 Brunel		286	52	83.4
34 Sunderland	3aD	259	44	83.3
35 Lancaster		342	40	82.9
36 Salford		293	48	82.7
37 University College for the Creative Arts		326	41	82.4
38 UCE Birmingham		278	49	82.2
39 Sheffield Hallam	3aE	285	40	82.1
40 Portsmouth		259	51	81.9
41 Oxford Brookes		282	45	81.4
42 Thames Valley	1A	198	54	81.3
=43 Liverpool John Moores	3bE	243	45	80.9
=43 East London	5D	210	37	80.9
45 Middlesex	3aD	227	40	80.8
46 Greenwich	3bC	215	41	80.7
47 Swansea		259	45	80.4
48 Brighton	3bD	244		80.2
49 Northumbria	4D	204		79.9
50 Southampton Solent		255	43	79.7
=51 Coventry	3bE	223	43	79.5

Communication and Media Studies cont.	Research quality/5	Entry standards	Graduate prospects %	Overall rating
=51 Gloucestershire		258	42	79.5
53 Winchester	3aD	272	26	79.3
54 Teesside	2A	209	36	78.9
55 Queen's, Belfast		305	28	78.1
56 Canterbury Christ Church		204	46	78.0
57 Chester		241	37	77.4
58 Paisley		263	32	77.2
59 Wolverhampton	2E	213	37	77.0
60 Chichester		249	33	76.8
61 Essex		308	21	76.5
62 Buckinghamshire Chilterns UC		190	42	76.4
=63 Northampton		224	35	76.1
=63 Luton	3aE	198		76.1
65 Hertfordshire	1D	206		74.9
66 Worcester		214	24	72.9

Average starting salary:	£15,707	Studying and not employed:		6%
Employed in graduate job:	37%	Unemployed:		9%
Employed in graduate job and studying:	3%			
Employed in non-graduate job:	41%	The letters that appear in the Research Quality column indicate the proportion of staff included in the assessment, A showing that almost all staff were included and F showing that hardly any were.		
Employed in non-graduate job and studying:	3%			

Computer Science

The computing table has got even larger since last year, with more than 100 institutions offering the subject at undergraduate level. However, uncertainty in the dotcom economy has had an effect on what was once seen as a guaranteed career path. Applications were dropping even before top-up fees became a factor – there was a drop of almost 20 per cent at the start of 2004, leading to a 12 per cent cut in full-time degree places. And although demand steadied in 2005, there was another 10 per cent drop at the start of 2006. Only one subject has a higher unemployment rate in the latest figures. The good news for computer scientists is that six out of ten leavers still go straight into graduate jobs or further training. The contrast is reflected in the ranking, which shows 97 per cent graduate employment at the new University of Chichester, but 40 per cent or less at the bottom three institutions.

With teaching grades dropped because of their age, employment has a considerable impact on the ranking. It made the difference between table-topping Cambridge and second-placed Oxford, which had higher average entry scores. Cambridge also has one of eight 5* research grades, although only Edinburgh, Surrey and Salford achieved this distinction while entering a full complement of academics for the 2001 Research Assessment Exercise. York, Manchester, Southampton and Imperial College were the other institutions to reach 5* with a more selective staff entry.

St Andrews and Edinburgh are locked together just outside the top ten as the top Scottish university, while Swansea remains ahead of Cardiff in Wales. Chichester is the best-placed new university, well ahead of Liverpool John Moores and Robert Gordon, the only others in the top half of the table. Entry grades are largely responsible: ten universities in the upper reaches of the table average more than 400 points, while many of the former polytechnics average less than 200. Loughborough and the College of St Mark and St John, in Plymouth, did best in the first national student satisfaction survey.

- **The British Computer Society:** www.bcs.org

Computer Science	Research quality/5	Entry standards	Graduate prospects %	Overall rating
1 Cambridge	5*B	547	91	100.0
2 Oxford	5A	552	83	97.5
3 Imperial College	5*B	487	84	95.9
4 York	5*B	494	76	93.9
5 Bristol	5A	414	82	92.3
6 University College London	5A	398	83	92.0
7 Southampton	5*B	443	74	91.5
8 Bath	4A	421	84	91.4
9 Warwick	5B	470	73	90.6
10 Surrey	5*A	317	79	89.7
=11 St Andrews	5A	392	75	89.5
=11 Edinburgh	5*A	407	67	89.5
13 Durham	4B	451	72	88.2
14 Swansea	5B	330	80	87.7
15 Manchester	5*B	372	69	87.5
16 Lancaster	5A	329	74	87.0
17 Sheffield	5B	372	72	86.9
18 Sussex	5A	345	70	86.5
19 Cardiff	5A	311	74	86.4
20 Nottingham	5B	378	69	86.2
21 King's College London	4B	353	77	86.1
22 Dundee	4A	327	76	85.8
23 Newcastle	5B	337	72	85.6
24 Birmingham	5B	362	68	85.4
25 Royal Holloway	5B	293	76	85.2
26 Kent	4B	326	76	84.9
27 Glasgow	5B	348	66	84.3
28 Aberdeen	4C	324	78	83.8
29 Queen's, Belfast	4A	325	68	83.5
30 Bangor	4B	248	78	82.7
=31 Liverpool	5B	287	67	82.4
=31 Loughborough	3aB	340	71	82.4
33 Aberystwyth	4A	290	68	82.2
34 Leeds	5D	346	71	81.8

Computer Science cont.	Research quality/5	Entry standards	Graduate prospects %	Overall rating
35 Reading	4B	317	65	81.4
36 Heriot-Watt	4A	393	52	81.3
=37 City	4B	271	69	80.9
=37 Exeter	4B	357	58	80.9
39 Chichester		252	97	80.8
40 Leicester	4B	313	63	80.7
41 Brunel	5B	287	60	80.5
42 Salford	5*A	226	56	80.0
43 East Anglia	4B	320	58	79.6
44 Essex	4B	283	61	79.1
45 Aston	5C	265	64	79.0
46 Queen Mary	4B	276	61	78.9
47 Strathclyde	3aD	367	63	78.5
48 Stirling	3bC	308	68	78.0
=49 Hull	3aC	230	70	77.0
=49 Liverpool John Moores	3aB	186	71	77.0
51 Robert Gordon	3aD	272	68	76.6
52 Nottingham Trent	3aE	249	75	76.3
53 Sunderland	3aC	225	64	75.2
54 Keele	3bC	279	61	75.0
55 Glamorgan	4D	222	65	74.8
56 Abertay		268	72	74.3
57 Brighton	4E	232	67	74.0
=58 Bournemouth	2E	241	69	73.3
=58 Paisley	3aC	269	52	73.3
60 Bradford	4E	240	63	73.1
61 De Montfort	4C	190	56	72.8
62 West of England	3aC	211	57	72.7
63 Kingston	3bD	186	67	72.4
=64 Hertfordshire	4C	192	54	72.3
=64 Oxford Brookes	3bD	231	61	72.3
=66 Ulster	4E	251	58	72.1
=66 Goldsmiths, University of London	3bB	171	61	72.1
68 Plymouth	5E	234	58	72.0
69 Napier	3aD	229	57	71.9
=70 Northumbria	3bC	214	58	71.8
=70 Central Lancashire		231	68	71.8
=70 Gloucestershire	3aD	193	61	71.8
73 Huddersfield	3aE	223	60	71.2
74 Manchester Metropolitan	3aD	229	54	71.1
75 Greenwich	4D	171	58	71.0
76 Leeds Metropolitan	3bC	204	56	70.9
=77 Sheffield Hallam	3bE	225	60	70.7

=77 Derby		191	69	70.7
=77 Chester		223	65	70.7
80 Portsmouth		215	64	70.1
81 Liverpool Hope		170	69	70.0
82 Glasgow Caledonian	3bE	282	50	69.9
83 Teesside	2F	227	58	69.0
84 Staffordshire		219	59	68.9
85 London South Bank	4D	144	50	67.8
86 Northampton		208	54	67.1
87 Coventry	2E	189	53	67.0
88 Southampton Solent		182	56	66.7
89 University of Wales, Newport		200	53	66.5
90 Anglia Ruskin		215	51	66.4
91 UCE Birmingham		179	54	66.0
92 UWIC, Cardiff		191	50	65.3
=93 East London	2E	170	49	65.1
=93 Westminster	3aF	154	52	65.1
95 Middlesex	3aE	147	47	64.8
96 Wolverhampton	2F	160	50	64.4
97 Lincoln		230	41	64.1
98 Luton		154	48	63.4
99 Canterbury Christ Church		191	43	63.3
=100 Bolton		146	44	62.0
=100 Worcester		200	37	62.0
102 Buckinghamshire Chilterns UC		170	40	61.7
103 Roehampton		179	38	61.5

Average starting salary:	£19,416	Studying and not employed:	12%
Employed in graduate job:	45%	Unemployed:	12%
Employed in graduate job and studying:	4%		
Employed in non-graduate job:	25%	The letters that appear in the Research Quality column indicate the proportion of staff included in the assessment, A showing that almost all staff were included and F showing that hardly any were.	
Employed in non-graduate job and studying:	2%		

Dentistry

Not even medicine can match dentistry's 99 per cent graduate employment rate. Applications are correspondingly buoyant: a 1 per cent decline at the start of 2006 was less than half the average for all subjects, while the two previous years had seen rises of 14 per cent and 25 per cent. But it is not a subject for academic slouches: entrants to all but one of the thirteen undergraduate schools averaged more than 400 points on the UCAS tariff. Most demand chemistry and may give preference to candidates who also have biology A level.

Leeds takes over the leadership this year, despite registering one of the lowest research grades. Leeds has the highest average entry grades, as well as one of the ten full employment records. Nevertheless, King's College London, last year's leader, could barely be closer. It has one of the two 5* research ratings and was one of four universities

Dentistry cont.

awarded full marks for teaching quality. The removal of teaching grades (because of their age) has had considerable impact on the dentistry ranking: Manchester has dropped from second to eighth, while Leeds has shot up from seventh position last year.

There are surprising variations in dentistry, judging by the indicators in our table. Although it entered a low proportion of academics for assessment, ninth-placed Bristol achieved the other top rating for research. By contrast, Glasgow, which has one of the two lowest grades for research, records the second-highest entry grades, and is the higher of two dental schools in Scotland. Cardiff offers the only dentistry degree in Wales.

Most degrees last five years, although several universities offer a six-year option for those without the necessary scientific qualifications. Shortages of dentists are such that no university has less than 96 per cent of graduates going into employment or further training. The number of places will grow in 2007, partly through the addition of a new dental school at the Peninsula Medical School, in Plymouth and Exeter.

- **The British Dental Association:** www.bda-dentistry.org.uk

Dentistry	Research quality/5	Entry standards	Graduate prospects %	Overall rating
1 Leeds	4C	481	100	100.0
2 King's College London	5*C	440	100	99.8
3 Sheffield	5C	450	100	99.3
=4 Newcastle	5D	451	100	97.5
=4 Queen Mary	5B	389	100	97.5
6 Glasgow	3aD	466	100	96.9
7 Liverpool	4C	423	100	96.7
8 Manchester	4B	429	98	96.1
9 Bristol	5*D	410	100	96.0
10 Queen's, Belfast	3aC	424	100	95.7
11 Dundee	5D	406	100	94.9
12 Birmingham	4D	432	98	93.4
13 Cardiff	4C	420	96	92.0

Average starting salary:	£27,169	Studying and not employed:	1%
Employed in graduate job:	67%	Unemployed:	0%
Employed in graduate job and studying:	32%		
Employed in non-graduate job:	0%	The letters that appear in the Research Quality column indicate the proportion of staff included in the assessment, A showing that almost all staff were included and F showing that hardly any were.	
Employed in non-graduate job and studying:	0%		

Drama, Dance and Cinematics

Warwick takes over the leadership of a ranking that contains some freakish results further down the table. The University of East Anglia jumps from sixteenth place to seventh, while UWIC, this year's equal fifteenth, is the only university ever to register full employment or further training among graduates in these subjects. Bournemouth's 72 per cent success rate is the closest challenger.

The top two demonstrate greater consistency, but also benefit from the only 5* research ratings in this area. Warwick leapfrogs Bristol with higher entrance and employment scores. Fifth-placed Glasgow is the leading institution in Scotland, while Bournemouth is the only new university in the top ten.

This is another table where the gulf in qualifications between entrants to new and old universities is evident, although for drama and dance in particular, this is unlikely to be the main criterion for selection. The new universities occupy most of the places in the table but, while entry standards have risen since last year, there are still 20 where the average was less than 250 points, compared with more than 400 at a number of the old universities. The average tariff score is the lowest in any of the subject tables.

Employment scores also vary widely in a group of subjects where 8 per cent of graduates are without work six months after leaving university and half are in non-graduate jobs. Of the bottom 20 in the ranking, only Portsmouth saw more than half of the leavers go straight into graduate-level jobs or further training, and at three universities the proportion dropped below 30 per cent. Freelancing and periods of temporary employment are common throughout the performing arts, but this does not seem to put off prospective students. Applications for dance were up by over 4 per cent at the start of 2006, following a 34 per cent rise in the previous year. Both drama and cinematics were down by less than the average for all subjects at the official deadline for courses beginning in 2006 and drama was among the 15 most popular choices, with 37,000 applicants.

- **BBC:** www.bbc.co.uk
- **Arts Advice:** www.artsadvice.com
- **SKILLSET:** www.skillset.org
- **The Stage:** www.thestage.co.uk

Drama, Dance and Cinematics	Research quality/5	Entry standards	Graduate prospects %	Overall rating
1 Warwick	5*B	432	68	100.0
2 Bristol	5*A	392	64	98.6
3 Royal Holloway	5B	430	56	94.8
4 Glasgow	4B	398	66	93.8
5 Surrey	4A	386	62	93.3
6 Lancaster	4A	419	44	90.3
7 East Anglia	4A	421	42	89.9
8 Kent	5B	365	50	89.8
9 Bournemouth	3bD	406	72	89.4
10 Manchester	5C	426	40	88.0
11 Loughborough	5C	386	46	87.5
12 Goldsmiths, University of London	4A	361	44	87.3
13 Essex	4B	286	62	87.0
14 Birmingham	4C	387	48	86.5

Drama, Dance and Cinematics cont.

	Research quality/5	Entry standards	Graduate prospects %	Overall rating
=15 UWIC, Cardiff		254	100	85.8
=15 Exeter	4B	355	44	85.8
17 Queen Margaret College	3aD	322	70	85.6
18 Queen's, Belfast	3bA	324	60	85.2
19 Reading	5B	332	38	85.0
20 Nottingham Trent	5C	331	44	84.1
21 University of the Arts, London		448	54	83.7
22 Aberystwyth	5B	304	38	83.5
=23 Brunel	3aB	322	48	83.2
=23 Chichester	3aA	283	52	83.2
25 Brighton	5B	327	32	83.1
26 Hull	4C	316	46	82.3
27 Queen Mary		323	70	81.5
=28 Roehampton	4B	263	42	80.5
=28 Middlesex	3aD	294	56	80.5
=30 Ulster	3aB	234	54	80.2
=30 Southampton		381	54	80.2
32 Leeds		341	58	79.2
33 Northumbria	2C	280	58	79.0
34 Falmouth UC		283	68	78.9
35 Manchester Metropolitan	3aD	290	48	78.1
36 Westminster		286	62	77.4
37 De Montfort	3aC	239	46	76.8
38 Worcester	3aC	249	42	76.2
39 Salford		302	50	75.1
=40 Liverpool John Moores	2E	235	56	74.3
=40 Glamorgan	2C	221	52	74.3
42 Liverpool Hope		221	62	74.1
43 Bangor		298	46	73.8
44 Winchester	3bD	267	40	73.7
45 Kingston		220	60	73.5
46 University College for the Creative Arts		332	38	73.4
47 London South Bank		219	58	72.9
48 Northampton	3bA	217	34	72.8
49 Sunderland	2D	228	48	72.7
=50 West of England		285	44	72.6
=50 Chester		264	48	72.6
52 Portsmouth		239	52	72.4
53 Bath Spa		247	48	71.7
54 Coventry		242	48	71.5
55 Aberdeen		298	36	71.2
56 Canterbury Christ Church		276	38	70.6
57 Huddersfield	3aD	241	28	70.4

58 Plymouth	237	44	70.2
59 Sheffield Hallam	308	28	69.6
60 Central Lancashire	247	38	69.1
61 UCE Birmingham	269	32	68.6
62 Wolverhampton	199	44	68.2
63 Staffordshire	235	36	67.9
64 Lincoln	261	30	67.7
=65 Southampton Solent	279	24	67.0
=65 Buckinghamshire Chilterns UC	196	40	67.0
67 Derby	211	30	65.1
68 Luton	190	28	63.5

Average starting salary: £15,533
Employed in graduate job: 30%
Employed in graduate job and studying: 3%
Employed in non-graduate job: 43%
Employed in non-graduate job and studying: 5%

Studying and not employed: 11%
Unemployed: 9%

The letters that appear in the Research Quality column indicate the proportion of staff included in the assessment, A showing that almost all staff were included and F showing that hardly any were.

East and South Asian Studies

The select group of universities offering East and South Asian Studies is down to seven this year since the removal of teaching scores has left insufficient data to compile a score for Westminster. Student numbers are small – fewer than 2,000 students take the languages as their main subject. Nearly half the leavers go straight into graduate jobs but the unemployment rate is well above average, at 10 per cent.

Burgeoning interest in all things Chinese is beginning to stimulate real growth in the demand for places: almost 64 per cent at the start of 2006, although this still only amounted to 770 applications. It meant that for the first time Chinese overtook Japanese, which saw a 10 per cent drop in applications.

The last research grades were high, with both Oxford and Cambridge rated internationally outstanding. Cambridge retains top spot by virtue higher entry and destinations scores. However, London's School of Oriental and African Studies, in fourth place behind Nottingham, has the best employment record, with 80 per cent of leavers going straight into graduate-level jobs or further training.

Four out of five students enter with tariff scores that are above average for all subjects, so degree classifications are also high. Most undergraduates learn their chosen language from scratch, although universities expect to see evidence of potential in other modern language A levels.

- **The British Association for South Asian Studies:** www.basas.ac.uk
- **The Association of South-East Asian Studies (UK):** http://mercury.soas.ac.uk/aseasuk

East and South Asian Studies	Research quality/5	Entry standards	Graduate prospects %	Overall rating
1 Cambridge	5*B	497	75	100.0
2 Oxford	5*B	477	65	96.6

	Research quality/5	Entry standards	Graduate prospects %	Overall rating
3 Nottingham	5B	421		94.8
4 School of Oriental and African Studies	5B	327	80	93.1
5 Edinburgh	5B	433	55	90.6
6 Leeds	5C	363	60	87.2
7 Sheffield	4D	359	65	85.0

Average starting salary:	£18,984	Studying and not employed:	21%
Employed in graduate job:	38%	Unemployed:	10%
Employed in graduate job and studying:	10%		
Employed in non-graduate job:	17%		
Employed in non-graduate job and studying:	5%		

The letters that appear in the Research Quality column indicate the proportion of staff included in the assessment, A showing that almost all staff were included and F showing that hardly any were.

Economics

Many observers were surprised that the London School of Economics did not occupy a higher position in the early years of this table. Now, however, the LSE has leapfrogged three universities to assume top place for economics. It has one of the five 5* research grades and among the highest entry standards and destinations scores. Second-placed Cambridge and Oxford, in fifth place, are the only universities with higher average A-level scores. Cambridge also saw more leavers than any other university – 90 per cent – go straight into graduate-level jobs or further training.

Of the top-rated research departments, only third-placed University College London entered the maximum proportion of its academics for the last research assessment exercise. Warwick, Essex and Lancaster were the other research stars.

A total of 15 English universities offering economics achieved maximum points for teaching quality – among them the new universities of Leeds Metropolitan, Oxford Brookes and Staffordshire – but all teaching scores have been removed this year because of their age. Portsmouth, in 43rd place, is now the leading new university.

St Andrews is the leading university in Scotland, in equal thirteenth place while Cardiff, at fifteen, is the leader in Wales. In the first national student satisfaction survey, which did not extend to Scotland, Leicester and the Open University were the star performers.

Economics remains a popular option for undergraduates, with almost 34,000 applications at the start of 2006. Although this represented a 2 per cent decline on the figure 12 months earlier, that was a healthier outcome than in most of the social sciences. Employers look favourably because they see it as combining the skills of the sciences and the arts. But economics is not the sure-fire bet for a good job that many assume it to be: although nearly two thirds of leavers are in graduate jobs or on postgraduate courses within six months, the 7 per cent unemployment rate is no better than average.

- **The European Economics Society:** www.eeassoc.org
- **Why Study? Economics:** www.whystudyeconomics.ac.uk

Economics

	Research quality/5	Entry standards	Graduate prospects %	Overall rating
1 London School of Economics	5*A	506	84	100.0
2 Cambridge	5B	537	90	99.3
3 University College London	5*A	447	80	96.9
4 Warwick	5*B	477	78	95.8
5 Oxford	5B	527	76	95.0
6 Nottingham	5A	482	70	93.2
7 Bath	5B	417	82	93.0
8 Bristol	4A	420	82	92.4
9 York	5A	450	68	91.6
=10 Durham	4B	484	72	90.6
=10 Essex	5*B	322	78	90.6
12 Southampton	5A	421	64	89.5
=13 St Andrews	4B	446	66	87.7
=13 Royal Holloway	4B	346	78	87.7
15 Cardiff	5B	373	68	87.6
16 Edinburgh	4B	423	68	87.4
=17 Exeter	5B	378	66	87.2
=17 Lancaster	5*B	389	58	87.2
19 Birmingham	4B	404	68	86.8
20 Leeds	5C	410	68	86.6
21 School of Asian Studies	4B	344	74	86.5
22 Queen Mary	5B	339	64	85.4
23 Loughborough	3aB	349	74	84.8
24 Surrey	3aA	292	76	84.3
=25 Leicester	5B	331	60	84.0
=25 Newcastle	4C	392	66	84.0
27 Manchester	4B	399	58	83.8
28 Queen's, Belfast	4B	322	64	82.9
29 Glasgow	4B	385	56	82.8
30 Reading	5C	335	62	82.4
31 Stirling	4A	303	60	82.3
32 Hull	4C	283	72	82.0
=33 Swansea	4A	258	64	81.9
=33 Kent	4A	290	60	81.9
=35 City	3aB	318	66	81.5
=35 Keele	3aA	291	66	81.5
37 Aberdeen	3aA	338	60	81.4
38 Sussex	4B	372	52	81.2
39 Liverpool	4B	335	56	81.1
40 Sheffield	3aB	368	58	80.9
41 Brunel	4A	314	52	80.4
42 Strathclyde	4C		60	79.5
43 Portsmouth	4C	245	64	78.5

	Research quality/5	Entry standards	Graduate prospects %	Overall rating
44 Ulster	4C	267	60	78.1
45 East Anglia	4B	348	42	77.6
46 Aberystwyth	3bC	249	62	75.1
47 Dundee	3aA	315	40	75.0
48 Bradford	3bD	191	72	74.6
49 Heriot-Watt	4D	328	46	74.1
=50 Manchester Metropolitan	3aC	226	54	73.5
=50 Salford	3aB	264	44	73.5
52 Anglia Ruskin	2D		64	73.2
=53 East London	3aD		54	72.2
=53 Oxford Brookes		273	64	72.2
55 Plymouth	3bE	254	58	71.5
56 Nottingham Trent	3bD	236	54	71.1
=57 Leeds Metropolitan		252	56	69.2
=57 Hertfordshire	3aC	213	40	69.2
59 West of England		224	58	68.9
60 Northumbria	3bE	224	52	68.8
61 Middlesex		157	58	66.6
62 Kingston		175	54	66.1
63 Coventry		214	48	65.7
64 Greenwich	3bE	194	44	65.6
65 Liverpool John Moores		163	46	63.4

Average starting salary:	£21,331		Studying and not employed:	16%
Employed in graduate job:	35%		Unemployed:	7%
Employed in graduate job and studying:	12%			
Employed in non-graduate job:	26%			
Employed in non-graduate job and studying:	4%			

The letters that appear in the Research Quality column indicate the proportion of staff included in the assessment, A showing that almost all staff were included and F showing that hardly any were.

Education

This is the only ranking that still contains teaching scores – because teacher training assessments by Ofsted remain current. Cambridge joins Oxford at the head of the table, moving up one place from last year, after matching its teaching grade. Staffordshire is the only other university with maximum points for teaching quality, but a low research grade relegates it to seventh. Cambridge also has the highest entry standards – Oxford only offers the Post Graduate Certificate in Education.

Third-placed Bristol and Cardiff, which suffers for a low employment score, have the only 5* research grades in the subject. High employment scores are spread throughout the table, with Aberdeen, Stirling, Glasgow and Hertfordshire each recording a 98 per cent success rate among their graduates. Aberdeen remains the top university in

Scotland, with Cardiff taking that title in Wales. Staffordshire is the top new university, with Canterbury Christ Church entering the top 20.

Three of the top five universities – and some further down the table – do not offer undergraduate teacher training, but qualify because they have assessments for both teaching and research. Their positions are a guide to the quality of PGCE courses, which are now the more popular route into teaching, especially for secondary education.

The 4 per cent unemployment level is among the lowest for any subject, and almost 80 per cent of all those completing teacher training courses went into schools or postgraduate study. Education remains one of the biggest subjects at degree level with more than 48,000 applications at the start of 2006 – a small increase at a time when most subjects were in decline. Entry grades have been creeping up – as the Teacher Training Agency has demanded – but the subject is still in the bottom five, with an average of only 250 points.

- **The Training and Development Agency for Schools:** www.tda.gov.uk
- **The General Teaching Council for Scotland:** www.gtcs.org.uk
- **Learn Direct:** www.learndirect-advice.co.uk

Education	Teaching quality/5	Research quality/5	Entry standards	Graduate prospects %	Overall rating
=1 Oxford	4.0	5B			100.0
=1 Cambridge	4.0	5B	404	94	100.0
3 Bristol	3.5	5*A			97.1
4 Aberdeen		5A	326	98	96.0
5 East Anglia	3.6	4B			93.8
6 Stirling		4C	339	98	93.7
7 Staffordshire	4.0	2B			93.3
=8 Manchester	3.5	4C	335		92.5
=8 Warwick	3.2	4B	372	88	92.5
10 Exeter	3.7	5C	287	91	91.9
11 Sheffield	3.2	5A			91.7
12 Sussex	3.3	5B			91.2
=13 King's College London	3.2	5B			90.7
=13 Edinburgh		4D	326	93	90.7
15 Newcastle	3.4	4B			90.6
16 Bath	3.2	5B	322	82	90.5
17 Cardiff		5*A	319	63	90.3
18 Dundee		3aA	284	90	89.7
19 Durham	3.2	5C	326	80	89.3
=20 Glasgow		4F	316	98	88.6
=20 Canterbury Christ Church	3.4	3aE	294	97	88.6
22 Leicester	3.1	4B			87.9
23 Reading	3.2	3aC	265	97	87.7
=24 Leeds	3.2	4B	290	77	87.4
=24 Brunel	3.1	3aC	271	95	87.4
26 Paisley			306	97	87.3

Education cont.

	Teaching quality/5	Research quality/5	Entry standards	Graduate prospects %	Overall rating
27 Brighton	3.3	3bD	268	97	87.1
=28 Northumbria	3.4	3bE		90	86.7
=28 Nottingham	3.2	4C			86.7
30 London South Bank	3.0	4B			86.3
31 Goldsmiths, University of London	3.2	4C	235	89	86.1
32 Keele	3.1	3aB	301	75	86.0
33 Strathclyde		4E	270	90	85.8
=34 Birmingham	3.4	5B	254	61	85.6
=34 Aberystwyth		3aB	261	78	85.6
36 Chester	3.4		255	91	85.4
37 Lancaster	3.4	5B	291	46	85.2
=38 York	3.0	4B	324	59	85.1
=38 Hertfordshire	3.0	3bE	265	98	85.1
40 Manchester Metropolitan	3.3	4E	262	81	84.7
=41 Sunderland	3.3	3aF	248	89	84.0
=41 Oxford Brookes	3.2	3bE	283	79	84.0
=43 Roehampton	3.5	3aE	229	79	83.7
=43 UWIC, Cardiff			257	92	83.7
45 Gloucestershire	3.2	3aE	245	80	83.3
46 West of England	3.1	3aE	253	82	83.1
=47 Winchester	3.1	3bE	260	78	82.5
=47 Chichester	3.0	2D	223	91	82.5
49 Bangor		3aF	258	83	82.4
50 Hull	3.0	3aD	226	85	82.3
51 Nottingham Trent	2.9	3bD	267	77	82.2
52 Liverpool Hope	3.2		231	84	82.1
53 UCE Birmingham	3.2	3bF	238	81	82.0
54 Bath Spa	3.3	2F	255	73	81.9
=55 Middlesex	3.0	2D	214	90	81.7
=55 Kingston	3.0		210	95	81.7
57 Worcester	3.1	3bD	257	68	81.6
58 Plymouth	3.2	3aE	249	69	81.5
59 Liverpool John Moores	3.3	3bF	215	79	81.3
60 Luton	3.2			75	81.1
61 De Montfort	2.9		226	91	81.0
62 Northampton	2.9	3bE	254	76	80.8
63 Sheffield Hallam	3.1	3aE	227	72	80.7
64 Wolverhampton	3.0	2F	235	79	80.5
65 Greenwich	2.9	3aE	201	85	80.1
66 University of Wales, Newport			227	81	80.0
67 Leeds Metropolitan	2.8	3aE	248	70	79.6
68 Southampton	2.8	4C	265	49	79.3
69 Anglia Ruskin	2.1	3bD	269	83	78.0

70 Derby	2.9	3bD	224	60	77.8
71 Huddersfield	2.9	3bE		63	77.3
72 East London	2.8	3bD	197	64	76.9
73 Central Lancashire		3bC	194	56	76.0

Average starting salary:	£18,446	Unemployed:	4%
Employed in graduate job:	64%	Teaching quality assessed 2001	
Employed in graduate job and studying:	4%		
Employed in non-graduate job:	15%		
Employed in non-graduate job and studying:	2%		
Studying and not employed:	10%		

The letters that appear in the Research Quality column indicate the proportion of staff included in the assessment, A showing that almost all staff were included and F showing that hardly any were.

Electrical and Electronic Engineering

Cambridge takes over at the top of the ranking for electrical and electronic engineering, but its lead over Southampton could not be smaller. The pair have two of the seven 5* research grades awarded in 2001, but Cambridge saw 90 per cent of its graduates go straight into employment or further training, compared to Southampton's 88 per cent. Cambridge does not publish separate entrance statistics for the different branches of engineering, but Southampton's average entry grades were bettered only by third-placed Imperial College.

The other universities rated internationally outstanding for research are spread around the top third of the table. Surrey and Sheffield are in the top ten, with Manchester and Edinburgh just outside it, but Leeds, which entered a relatively small proportion of its academics, does not make the top 20. Sixteen institutions achieved maximum points for teaching quality under the separate English, Scottish and Welsh systems, but these scores have been removed because of the age of the assessments.

Edinburgh remains the top university in Scotland, with Cardiff taking the honours in Wales. Robert Gordon and Northumbria are the leading new universities and the only ones in the top 40 of a table where old universities predominate.

Both entry standards and employment rates vary considerably among the 67 universities in the table. While seven institutions saw at least 80 per cent of leavers go straight into graduate jobs or further training, the proportion dropped to 40 per cent at three others. Like computing, the subject has suffered from troubles in high-tech industries: applications were down by almost 19 per cent at the start of 2006. Although almost half of the leavers nationally went straight into graduate jobs, the subjects have the highest unemployment rate of all, at 12 per cent. The gulf in entry standards is equally marked, with Imperial's entrants approaching an average of 500 points and several others well below 200. About half of the students – more in electrical engineering – come with qualifications other than A levels. Yet it is electrical engineering which has the higher proportion of firsts and 2:1s.

Kent, Leeds and Loughborough did best in the first national student satisfaction survey.

- **The Engineering Council (EC UK):** www.engc.org.uk
- **The Institution of Electrical Engineers:** www.iee.org

Electrical and Electronic Engineering

	Research quality/5	Entry standards	Graduate prospects %	Overall rating
1 Cambridge	5*A		90	100.0
2 Southampton	5*A	457	88	99.9
3 Imperial College	5B	479	78	95.1
4 Surrey	5*A	351	86	94.9
5 Bristol	5A	415	82	94.7
6 University College London	5A	424	72	92.5
7 Loughborough	5B	377	80	91.3
8 York	3aA	432	80	91.1
9 Queen's, Belfast	5A	365	76	91.0
10 Sheffield	5*B	377	70	90.5
11 Newcastle	5A	358	74	90.2
=12 Manchester	5*B	358	72	90.1
=12 Edinburgh	5*B	405	64	90.1
14 Warwick	5B	405	70	89.9
15 Strathclyde	5B	385	72	89.6
16 Sussex	5B		72	88.3
17 Cardiff	5A	355	66	88.0
=18 Bath	4C	346	82	87.2
=18 Lancaster	4B	330	78	87.2
20 Nottingham	4A	357	68	86.7
21 Essex	5B	335	68	86.5
22 Liverpool	5A	273	72	86.1
23 Reading	5B	323	68	85.9
24 Leeds	5*D	347	76	85.7
25 Glasgow	5B	349	58	84.5
26 Birmingham	5C	345	66	84.4
27 Heriot-Watt	4B	383	58	84.2
28 Leicester	5A	385	42	83.0
29 Swansea	4C	282	76	82.9
30 Kent	4C	264	76	82.2
31 Brunel	5B	301	56	81.9
32 King's College London	5D	304	70	81.3
33 Aston	5C	248	68	80.8
34 Aberdeen	4C	333	58	80.4
35 Queen Mary	3aB	298	56	78.4
36 Robert Gordon	3bD	289	68	77.3
37 Northumbria	3bC	206	74	76.5
38 Hull	4C	239		76.1
39 Ulster	3bA	236	60	75.8
40 Dundee		347	62	75.5
41 Bangor	4B	263	40	74.5
42 Greenwich	3aB	214	54	74.4
43 City	3aC	198	60	73.9

44 Paisley	3aC	277	46	73.6
45 Bradford	4E	235	62	73.5
46 Nottingham Trent	3aE	244	62	73.3
47 Liverpool John Moores	3aD	166	64	72.1
=48 Plymouth	4E	245	54	71.8
=48 London South Bank	4D		50	71.8
50 Huddersfield	3bF	251	58	70.8
51 Portsmouth	2E	232	54	69.5
52 Glasgow Caledonian	2C	257	42	69.0
53 Westminster	4D	163	48	68.7
=54 Staffordshire	3bA		38	68.4
=54 West of England		278	46	68.4
=56 Teesside		213	56	68.3
=56 Oxford Brookes		237	52	68.3
58 Hertfordshire	3aD	186	46	68.2
59 Bolton		159	64	68.1
60 Anglia Ruskin	2C		48	67.9
=61 Coventry	3aC	134		67.4
=61 Derby		227	50	67.4
63 UCE Birmingham		214	52	67.3
64 Leeds Metropolitan	3bC		40	66.8
65 Sheffield Hallam		207	50	66.5
66 Central Lancashire	3aE	174		65.3
67 East London	2D		34	61.3

Average starting salary:	£20,387	Studying and not employed:	14%
Employed in graduate job:	43%	Unemployed:	12%
Employed in graduate job and studying:	5%		
Employed in non-graduate job:	24%	The letters that appear in the Research Quality column indicate the proportion of staff included in the assessment, A showing that almost all staff were included and F showing that hardly any were.	
Employed in non-graduate job and studying:	2%		

English

Durham is the third different leader of the English ranking in three years, taking over from second-placed Oxford. Durham had one of the best graduate employment records in the table and, perhaps more surprisingly, higher average entry grades than Oxford or Cambridge. All the top eight universities – and five others – have 5* research grades.

By far the best destinations score was at Brighton, where 93 per cent of leavers went straight into graduate jobs or further training and 96 per cent did so last year. However, Brighton did not enter the 2001 Research Assessment Exercise in English, so it only just makes the top 40. Anglia Ruskin is the top new university and the only one in the top 30, thanks to a grade 5 for research and one of the better employment records. Most suffer for the disparity between old and new universities in entry scores and research grades. Although only one new university had average entry points of less than 200, only Oxford Brookes, Northumbria and Sheffield Hallam recorded an average of more than 300 points, which was the norm in the top 40.

English cont.

Cardiff is clearly the leading university in Wales, while Edinburgh has reclaimed top place in Scotland from St Andrews. University College London produced the best results in the first national student satisfaction survey, which showed greater levels of satisfaction generally among English students than in most other subjects. However, although more than had 50,000 applied to read English at the start of 2006, this represented a drop of 4.5 per cent – slightly more than the national average.

The proportion of English students gaining a first or 2:1, at seven out of ten, is among the highest in any subject. Almost a third of all graduates go on to further study, and the 7 per cent unemployment rate is no more than average for all subjects. But the table shows big variations, with a minority of students at 15 universities finding graduate jobs or study places within six months of graduation. Nationally, more than a third of those completing English degrees in 2003 were in non-graduate jobs six months later.

- **Book Careers:** www.bookcareers.com
- **The Publishers' Association:** www.publishers.org.uk
- **Teaching English as a Foreign Language:** www.eflweb.com
- **The Writers' Room:** www.bbc.co.uk/writersroom

English	Research quality/5	Entry standards	Graduate prospects %	Overall rating
1 Durham	5*A	490	73	100.0
2 Oxford	5*A	482	68	98.4
3 University College London	5*A	455	70	98.0
4 Cambridge	5*B	486	70	97.7
5 York	5*A	463	65	96.9
6 Leeds	5*A	430	65	95.8
7 Warwick	5*B	448	63	94.5
8 Edinburgh	5*A	438	56	93.6
9 Nottingham	5A	462	58	93.2
10 Newcastle	5A	412	62	92.6
11 Southampton	5A	425	60	92.5
12 Bristol	5C	425	71	92.4
13 Royal Holloway	5A	386	63	92.1
=14 Leicester	5A	363	65	91.8
=14 Sheffield	5B	438	60	91.8
=16 St Andrews	5*B	437	54	91.7
=16 Cardiff	5*B	395	59	91.7
18 Liverpool	5*B	388	59	91.5
=19 Queen's, Belfast	5A	330	63	90.2
=19 Manchester	5B	423	56	90.2
21 King's College London	4B	423	61	90.0
22 Sussex	5B	402	56	89.5
23 Exeter	5B	416	54	89.4
=24 Queen Mary	5A	338	58	89.1
=24 Anglia Ruskin	5C		67	89.1

26 Glasgow	5*B	385	50	88.9
27 Kent	5B	339	61	88.8
28 Loughborough	5C	367	64	88.6
29 Birmingham	5C	394	58	87.9
30 Reading	5*B	363	48	87.7
31 Lancaster	5A	378	47	87.5
32 De Montfort	5A	242	60	86.5
33 Oxford Brookes	5C	331	60	86.4
34 Keele	5B	326	53	86.2
=35 Aberdeen	4B	326	58	85.9
=35 Essex	4B	306	60	85.9
37 Swansea	4A	308	56	85.8
38 East Anglia	5B	408	41	85.6
=39 Hull	5B	297	54	85.5
=39 Chichester	3aA	271	66	85.5
=39 Strathclyde	5B	362	46	85.5
42 Brighton		258	93	85.4
43 Nottingham Trent	5C	296	59	84.9
44 Dundee	4A	308	51	84.4
=45 Bolton	3aC	197	78	84.3
=45 Goldsmiths, University of London	5A	323	42	84.3
47 Stirling	5B	355	41	83.9
=48 Gloucestershire	4A	240	57	83.8
=48 Lampeter	5B	245	54	83.8
50 Middlesex	4D	207	76	83.5
=51 Sunderland	4C	230	64	82.8
=51 Roehampton	4B	255	55	82.8
=51 Aberystwyth	4B	328	46	82.8
=54 West of England	4B	291	50	82.6
=54 London South Bank	4B		50	82.6
56 Brunel	3aB	302	53	82.2
57 Salford	5A	282	38	81.8
58 Hertfordshire	3aB	244	58	81.7
59 Northumbria	3aC	324	53	81.6
60 Manchester Metropolitan	4C	286	51	81.1
=61 Sheffield Hallam	4B	303	42	80.8
=61 Bath Spa	4B	276	45	80.8
63 Plymouth	3aB	268	50	80.3
64 Worcester	3bC	261	60	80.2
=65 Winchester	3aD	287	57	80.0
=65 Kingston	3aB	225	54	80.0
=67 UCE Birmingham	3aD	235	61	79.4
=67 Central Lancashire	3aC	254	53	79.4
=69 Liverpool John Moores	4C	210	53	79.2
=69 Bangor	4B	301	36	79.2
=71 Glamorgan	4B	230	44	79.0
=71 Liverpool Hope	3bE	224	68	79.0

	Research quality/5	Entry standards	Graduate prospects %	Overall rating
73 Portsmouth	4C	287	41	78.5
74 Ulster	4C	231	47	78.2
75 Falmouth UC	3bB	270		77.9
76 Greenwich		228	68	77.6
77 Northampton	4C	220	43	76.8
78 Teesside		241	61	76.2
79 Chester	2C	276	47	75.9
=80 Staffordshire	3aD	255	45	75.7
=80 Wolverhampton		236	60	75.7
82 Derby		248	57	75.3
83 Leeds Metropolitan		252	55	74.9
84 Westminster	3bD	236	45	74.2
85 Lincoln		253	52	74.1
86 Canterbury Christ Church		243	42	71.0
87 University of Wales, Newport		192	47	70.8

Average starting salary:	£16,534	Studying and not employed:	22%
Employed in graduate job:	28%	Unemployed:	7%
Employed in graduate job and studying:	4%		
Employed in non-graduate job:	34%	The letters that appear in the Research Quality column indicate the proportion of staff included in the assessment, A showing that almost all staff were included and F showing that hardly any were.	
Employed in non-graduate job and studying:	5%		

Food Science

Surrey has knocked Nottingham off top of the food science table for the first time, adding to the best research score in the subject with strong entry qualifications and one of the leading employment scores. Only fourth-placed Leeds can match Surrey's 5* research grade and it entered a much smaller proportion of its academics in the last Research Assessment Exercise. Third placed King's College London has the highest entry standards, while Leeds Metropolitan, in fifth, has the best destinations score, with 95 per cent of leavers going straight into graduate-level employment or further training. Leeds Met is the top new university, although it is joined by Robert Gordon in the top ten.

Most of the institutions offering food science are new universities but, as in other subjects, higher entry scores and research grades give their older counterparts an advantage in our table. Entry standards have been rising: only Liverpool John Moores averages less than 200 points, while eight universities average more than 300. Almost a third of entrants to food science courses arrive with alternative qualifications to A levels. There were almost 1,900 applications at the start of 2006, a rise of 22 per cent following an even bigger increase the previous year. The demand for places has grown substantially in each of the last four years.

Teaching quality assessors in England were concerned at the high drop-out rate on more than half of the courses: more than 20 per cent of students failed to progress to the next stage of their degree. As in other tables, teaching scores have been removed this year because of their age. Career prospects are good in food science, with 72 per cent of graduates going straight into graduate-level work or further study and only the average level of unemployment for all subjects.

- **The Institute of Food Science and Technology:** www.ifst.org

Food Science	Research quality/5	Entry standards	Graduate prospects %	Overall rating
1 Surrey	5*A	335	90	100.0
2 Nottingham	5A	350	85	98.0
3 King's College London	5B	365	80	96.6
4 Leeds	5*C	296	90	94.3
5 Leeds Metropolitan	3bC	307	95	91.7
6 Reading	5A	298	70	90.7
7 Newcastle	4B		75	89.8
8 Coventry		328	95	89.7
9 Queen's, Belfast	4C	280	85	89.6
10 Robert Gordon	3bE	323	90	89.4
11 Nottingham Trent	5D		80	88.4
12 Plymouth	3aE		90	87.9
13 Glasgow Caledonian		340	80	86.5
14 UWIC, Cardiff	3bC	217	85	83.3
15 Sheffield Hallam		309	65	80.5
16 Ulster		258	75	79.9
17 Northumbria	2E	211	80	79.1
18 Manchester Metropolitan		279	65	78.6
19 Huddersfield		242	70	77.6
20 Greenwich	3aA		45	76.7
21 London South Bank	3aE		60	75.9
22 Liverpool John Moores		177	75	74.8
23 Oxford Brookes		232	60	74.3

Average starting salary:	£18,276	Studying and not employed:	15%
Employed in graduate job:	53%	Unemployed:	7%
Employed in graduate job and studying:	4%		
Employed in non-graduate job:	20%	The letters that appear in the Research Quality column indicate the proportion of staff included in the assessment, A showing that almost all staff were included and F showing that hardly any were.	
Employed in non-graduate job and studying:	2%		

French

Cambridge remains the top university for French, with Oxford the only serious challenger. The ancient rivals were among seven universities awarded 5* research grades and have easily the highest entry standards. Only on graduate destinations does third-placed Bristol come to the fore, with 80 per cent of leavers going straight into graduate-level jobs or further training.

French cont.

Aberdeen, Royal Holloway, Southampton, Birmingham and Manchester are the other institutions rated internationally outstanding for research. They are spread about the top half of the table, with Manchester not even making the top 30. The subject still commands high entry grades, with a dozen universities averaging at least 400 points and only one out of 57 less than 200.

French remains the most popular language for a first degree, with almost 4,000 applications at the start of 2006. That represented a small rise at a time when most subjects were in decline and it followed a 13 per cent increase in 2005. Nine out of ten undergraduates enter with A levels or equivalents. Almost two thirds go on to graduate jobs or further study within six months and the 5 per cent unemployment rate is below average for all subjects. Only five universities dipped below the 50 per cent success mark for graduate destinations.

Modern languages generally did well in the first national student satisfaction survey. The University of Wales Bangor and The Open University registered particularly high levels of satisfaction. In our table, however, Cardiff is the clear leader in Wales, while Glasgow emerges as the top university in Scotland.

- **CILT – The National Centre for Languages:** www.cilt.org.uk
- **The Institute of Translation and Interpreting:** www.iti.org.uk

French	Research quality/5	Entry standards	Graduate prospects %	Overall rating
1 Cambridge	5*A	497	78	100.0
2 Oxford	5*A	491	74	98.8
3 Bristol	5A	400	80	95.4
4 Durham	5B	461	72	94.3
5 Nottingham	5A	420	68	93.0
6 King's College London	5A	390	70	92.5
7 Glasgow	5B	418	70	92.3
8 University College London	5A	413	66	92.2
9 Bath	5A	386	66	91.3
10 St Andrews	4B	436	68	90.9
=11 Liverpool	5A	358	68	90.8
=11 Sheffield	5B	403	66	90.8
13 Royal Holloway	5*A	361	60	90.6
14 Warwick	5A	423	58	90.5
15 Cardiff	5A	357	66	90.3
16 Birmingham	5*C	388	68	90.1
17 Queen's, Belfast	4A	353	72	90.0
18 Edinburgh	5C	432	66	89.9
19 Newcastle	4A	396	64	89.4
20 Sussex	4A	367	64	88.4
21 Leeds	4B	391	64	88.3
22 Kent	4A	310	70	88.0
=23 Southampton	5*A	343	52	87.8

	University				
=23	Heriot-Watt	4B	469	52	87.8
25	Exeter	4B	374	64	87.7
26	Queen Mary	5A	306	62	87.5
27	Stirling	5B	337	62	87.4
28	Aberdeen	5*A	338	48	86.6
29	Oxford Brookes	5B	277	66	86.4
30	Aberystwyth	3aA	328	68	86.3
31	Manchester	5*C	379	52	85.6
32	Aston	5C	354	58	85.1
33	Lancaster	5C	377	54	84.8
34	Strathclyde	4C	410	54	84.7
35	Bradford	4D		70	84.6
36	Salford	5A	325	48	84.4
37	Swansea	4A	278	58	83.7
38	Hull	4B	296	58	83.4
39	Reading	5B	306	46	82.1
40	Central Lancashire	3bA		60	81.8
41	East Anglia	3bB	393	48	81.0
42	Leicester	3aB	309	50	80.2
=43	Ulster	4C	256	56	79.9
=43	Kingston	4A	214	52	79.9
45	Nottingham Trent	4B	233	52	79.6
46	Brighton	5E	277	62	79.2
47	Portsmouth	5C	280	44	78.8
48	Plymouth	3bA		50	77.9
49	Keele	2A	319	48	77.3
50	Northumbria	3bE	291	58	77.1
51	Bangor	4D	276	40	74.6
52	Liverpool John Moores		220	62	74.3
53	Leeds Metropolitan		278	50	73.1
54	West of England		234	50	71.6
55	Anglia Ruskin	2C	186	44	70.7
56	Sheffield Hallam		244	44	70.4
57	Manchester Metropolitan		250	42	70.0

Average starting salary:	£17,855	Studying and not employed:	20%
Employed in graduate job:	35%	Unemployed:	5%
Employed in graduate job and studying:	6%		
Employed in non-graduate job:	30%	The letters that appear in the Research Quality column indicate the proportion of staff included in the assessment, A showing that almost all staff were included and F showing that hardly any were.	
Employed in non-graduate job and studying:	3%		

General Engineering

There is no change at the top of the general engineering table, with Cambridge continuing to hold off Oxford, thanks to marginally higher entry standards and a superior graduate employment record. Both have 5* research grades, as does Imperial College, in third place. Southampton is the fourth university considered internationally

General Engineering cont.

outstanding for research, but it has dropped out of the table this year because there is insufficient data on general engineering on entry qualifications or graduate destinations. No new universities reach the top ten, but Leeds Metropolitan and Greenwich only just miss out. Liverpool John Moores has an exceptional grade 5 for research, but the lowest entry grades in the entire ranking relegate it to eighteenth place. Strathclyde just beats Aberdeen to the accolade of top university in Scotland, while Cardiff is top in Wales.

As in the specialist branches of engineering, entry grades vary enormously, from over 500 points at Oxford and Cambridge to less than 200 at five universities More than 7,500 undergraduates take general engineering courses, rather than specialising, but numbers had fallen at the start of 2006. Employment prospects are close to the norm for all engineering courses, with eight out of ten going straight into graduate jobs or further study, but the 9 per cent unemployment rate is above average for all subjects. The assessors of teaching in England found that the courses nurtured the transferable skills required for later specialisation, but they worried about first-year dropout rates.

- **Science, Engineering and Technology Learning Information Portal:** www.elip.info
- **The Engineering Council (EC UK):** www.engc.org.uk

General Engineering	Research quality/5	Entry standards	Graduate prospects %	Overall rating
1 Cambridge	5*A	562	85	100.0
2 Oxford	5*A	540	80	97.2
3 Imperial College	5*B	498		95.7
4 Durham	5B	477	80	90.8
5 Warwick	5B	405	70	84.1
6 Brunel	5B	357	75	84.0
7 Bradford	3bC		90	83.2
8 Strathclyde	5A	414	60	82.2
9 Aberdeen	4C	384		79.3
10 Nottingham	4B	400	60	78.1
11 Leeds Metropolitan	3bC		80	77.5
12 Greenwich	3aB		70	76.9
13 Exeter	4C	315	65	74.4
14 Lancaster	4B	319	55	72.9
15 Liverpool		286	85	72.6
16 Cardiff		352	75	71.6
17 Liverpool John Moores	5A	144	55	69.3
18 West of England	3bD	255	70	69.0
19 Napier	4D	231	65	68.5
20 Derby		225	80	68.2
21 Bournemouth	3bF	244	70	65.8
22 Hull	4C	157		65.3
23 Coventry		280	65	64.9
24 Northumbria	3bC	194	60	64.2
25 Wolverhampton	3aB	197	50	63.9

	Research quality/5	Entry standards	Graduate prospects %	Overall rating
26 Sheffield Hallam	3aF	157	70	62.4
27 Hertfordshire	3aD	186		61.7
28 Queen Mary		198	65	61.5
29 UCE Birmingham	3bF	214	60	60.8
30 Glamorgan		207	55	58.1
31 Central Lancashire	3aE		50	57.4
32 Glasgow Caledonian		260	40	54.7
33 Nottingham Trent		256	40	54.5

Average starting salary:	£20,481	Studying and not employed:	14%
Employed in graduate job:	45%	Unemployed:	9%
Employed in graduate job and studying:	7%		
Employed in non-graduate job:	22%	
Employed in non-graduate job and studying:	2%	

The letters that appear in the Research Quality column indicate the proportion of staff included in the assessment, A showing that almost all staff were included and F showing that hardly any were.

Geography

Cambridge remains on top of the geography ranking, but the London School of Economics has closed the gap somewhat since the last edition of the *Guide*. The LSE has the best employment record, but Cambridge is only just behind and its lead on entry qualifications is more substantial. The 5* research grades went to Bristol, Durham, University College London, Edinburgh, Royal Holloway and Cardiff.

Excellence in research helps Edinburgh retain the top place in Scotland, and Cardiff the same for Wales. While entries to the top eight universities average more than 400 points, even some old universities average less than 300 and the figure dips below 200 at a number of former polytechnics. None of the new universities makes the top 30 but Plymouth is the best-placed, just ahead of Liverpool Hope, which has one of the best employment scores. The Open University, Aberystwyth, Reading and Queen Mary produced the best scores in the first national student satisfaction survey.

Geography and environmental sciences have been benefiting from rising interest in "green" issues among potential students. Applications for physical geography and environmental sciences were up by 9 per cent in 2005, although both human and physical geography were in decline at the start of 2006.

In the latest survey, more than a third of graduates were in low-level jobs six months after completing their courses, but the unemployment rate was still lower than average for all subjects. Universities are more tightly bunched in this table than many others in terms of their graduates' success in the jobs market, but still less than half of those leaving many institutions went straight into graduate work or higher-level courses.

- **The Royal Geographical Society:** www.rgs.org
- **The British Ecological Society:** www.britishecologicalsociety.org

Geography

	Research quality/5	Entry standards	Graduate prospects %	Overall rating
1 Cambridge	5A	492	86	100.0
2 London School of Economics	5A	421	87	97.6

Geography cont.

	Research quality/5	Entry standards	Graduate prospects %	Overall rating
3 Durham	5*A	447	70	95.7
4 Bristol	5*A	412	70	94.4
5 University College London	5*A	408	70	94.2
=6 Nottingham	5B	442	74	93.9
=6 Oxford	4A	491	69	93.9
8 Edinburgh	5*A	396	62	91.7
9 Southampton	5A	398	62	90.2
10 East Anglia	4A	388	69	90.1
11 Newcastle	5A	348	68	89.9
12 Sheffield	5A	401	58	89.2
13 Leeds	5B	376	64	88.9
14 St Andrews	4B	426	62	88.8
15 Royal Holloway	5*A	311	61	88.3
16 Cardiff	5*A	358	54	88.2
17 Loughborough	5B	359	59	86.9
18 King's College London	4A	337	61	86.1
19 Birmingham	4B	371	59	86.0
20 Reading	4A	360	56	85.6
21 Aberystwyth	4A	316	61	85.3
22 Manchester	4B	383	54	85.1
23 Queen's, Belfast	4A	291	63	84.9
24 Exeter	4B	365	55	84.7
25 Dundee	4A	304	59	84.3
26 Aberdeen	4B	309	61	84.2
27 Queen Mary	5A	267	57	84.0
28 Salford	3aA	227	74	83.8
=29 Strathclyde	3aC	379	59	83.7
=29 Glasgow	4C	369	56	83.7
31 Swansea	4A	312	55	83.6
32 Sussex	4B	318	57	83.5
33 Liverpool	4A	331	51	83.2
34 Lancaster	4A	335	50	83.1
=35 Plymouth	4B	288	53	81.3
=35 Hull	5B	271	50	81.3
=35 Leicester	4B	309	50	81.3
38 Liverpool Hope	3bC	194	79	81.0
39 Bangor		283	72	79.2
40 Keele	3aB	302	47	78.9
41 Brunel	3aB	275	49	78.4
42 Bradford	3bD	233	67	78.3
=43 Coventry	3aB	226	55	78.1
=43 Gloucestershire	3aC	235	58	78.1
45 Greenwich	3bE	250	67	78.0

46 Sunderland	3bC	182	68	77.7
=47 Nottingham Trent	3aB	244	50	77.5
=47 Kingston	3bB	197	62	77.5
=49 Brighton	3bB	254	53	77.2
=49 UWIC, Cardiff		227	72	77.2
=51 Manchester Metropolitan	4C	230	50	76.9
=51 Hertfordshire	2B	226	61	76.9
=53 Teesside		227	70	76.6
=53 Portsmouth	3aB	276	42	76.6
55 Bath Spa	2A	264	53	76.5
56 Northumbria	3bD	248	56	76.0
57 Ulster	3bC	221	56	75.9
58 Roehampton		243	61	74.9
59 Chester		268	57	74.7
60 Worcester	2C	245	51	74.4
61 De Montfort		236	60	74.3
62 Huddersfield	2B	233	48	73.7
63 Southampton Solent	3bC	235	45	73.6
64 Northampton	2B	276	41	73.5
65 Bournemouth	2D	230	52	73.4
66 Oxford Brookes		271	49	72.7
67 Derby		225	55	72.6
68 Liverpool John Moores	3bC	209	44	72.4
69 Napier		278	46	72.2
70 Canterbury Christ Church		244	49	71.7
71 West of England	2D	263	40	71.5
72 Wolverhampton		199	54	71.4
=73 Sheffield Hallam		241	47	71.1
=73 Staffordshire	3bC	196	41	71.1
75 Westminster	3aD	171		70.3
=76 Stirling		315	33	70.1
=76 Leeds Metropolitan		206	48	70.1
78 Central Lancashire		248	39	69.3
79 East London	2D		31	64.6

Average starting salary: £16,960
Employed in graduate job: 25%
Employed in non-graduate job: 33%
Studying, not employed: 8%
Employed in graduate job and studying: 17%

Employed in non-graduate job and studying: 9%
Unemployed: 7%

The letters that appear in the Research Quality column indicate the proportion of staff included in the assessment, A showing that almost all staff were included and F showing that hardly any were.

Geology

The top five places in the geology ranking are all unchanged. Higher entry grades and a better graduate employment record continue to keep Cambridge ahead of Oxford. Both are among the four 5* research universities, which again fill the top four places. Bristol and Imperial College, the other research stars, stay well clear of Liverpool and Glasgow.

Geology cont.

Glasgow has the best employment score and is the top university in Scotland. Cardiff has less competition in Wales. Only five new universities appear in the table, but Kingston makes the top 20 with a consistent set of scores. Oxbridge apart, there is less contrast in entry standards than in many other subjects. The average is well above 200 points at every university but one, and above 300 in all but nine.

Six out of ten geology students go on to graduate jobs or further study within six months of graduation, but the unemployment level is above average for all subjects, at 9 per cent. There were almost 6,000 applications to read geology by the start of 2006, but this represented the second successive 2 per cent drop.

- **The Geological Society:** www.geolsoc.org

Geology	Research quality/5	Entry standards	Graduate prospects %	Overall rating
1 Cambridge	5*A	550	84	100.0
2 Oxford	5*A	500	74	95.7
3 Bristol	5*A	375	72	90.8
4 Imperial College	5*A	384	68	90.1
5 Liverpool	5A	344	76	88.5
6 Glasgow	4B	346	88	88.2
7 University College London	5B	362	74	87.1
8 Leeds	5A	366	66	86.6
9 Durham	4B	440	68	86.2
10 Cardiff	5A	328	68	85.9
11 Edinburgh	5A	367	62	85.6
12 Royal Holloway	5B	291	74	84.7
13 St Andrews	4B	403	66	84.4
14 Exeter	4B	251	80	82.8
15 Southampton	5A	344	52	82.2
16 Leicester	4A	326	58	80.9
17 Manchester	5B	335	52	80.4
18 Aberdeen	4C	311	62	78.1
19 Kingston	4B	188	64	76.4
20 Birmingham	3aC	329	56	75.5
21 Keele	3aB	270	56	75.1
22 Plymouth	4C	236	48	71.9
23 Portsmouth	3bA	221	54	71.6
24 Derby		206	76	70.3
25 Aberystwyth		294	48	65.9
26 Staffordshire		221	50	64.0

Average starting salary:	£17,023	Studying and not employed:	28%
Employed in graduate job:	31%	Unemployed:	9%
Employed in graduate job and studying:	4%		
Employed in non-graduate job:	26%	The letters that appear in the Research Quality column indicate the proportion of staff included in the assessment, A showing that almost all staff were included and F showing that hardly any were.	
Employed in non-graduate job and studying:	2%		

German

Cambridge holds onto top place in German after a period in which the leadership has been changing hands annually. Only Oxford has higher entry qualifications and just two universities boast a better employment record. One is second-placed Edinburgh, which has shot up from sixth last year, while the other is Bristol, in seventh. In common with other tables, teaching ratings have been removed this year because of their age. The main casualty is Exeter, last year's runner-up and the only university in England to win full marks, which has dropped out of the top 15 despite being one of the ten universities with 5* research grades. Comparatively low entry grades and graduate destinations score are responsible.

Edinburgh, one of those with a 5* research grade, remains the leader in Scotland. The top two also have maximum research ratings, as do third-placed University College London, Nottingham, King's College London, Manchester, Birmingham, Southampton and Royal Holloway. No new university makes the top 30, but Oxford Brookes is not far away.

More than 50 universities appear in the German table, but only 1,277 degree applications had been made by the official deadline for courses beginning in 2006. There had been signs of a recovery in 2005, when applications were up by almost 20 per cent. But there was a 10 per cent decline as top-up fees became a factor. Nine out of ten enter with A levels or equivalent qualifications, and entry standards are relatively high, especially at the leading universities. Only one of the top 20 averaged less than 350 points.

Employment scores ranged from 85 per cent "positive destinations" to 50 per cent or less at 14 universities. But, as in other modern languages, career prospects are reasonable: although only two thirds of leavers go straight into graduate jobs or further study, the unemployment rate is below average. Assessments in England extend to Dutch and Scandinavian languages. Most universities in the table offer German *ab initio* as part of a languages package.

- CILT – The National Centre for Languages: www.cilt.org.uk
- The Institute of Translation and Interpreting: www.iti.org.uk

German	Research quality/5	Entry standards	Graduate prospects %	Overall rating
1 Cambridge	5*A	497	75	100.0
2 Edinburgh	5*B	436	85	98.8
=3 University College London	5*A	421	75	96.9
=3 Oxford	5A	500	70	96.9
5 Nottingham	5*A	430	70	96.0
6 King's College London	5*A	394	75	95.8
7 Bristol	5B	397	85	95.5
8 Durham	4A	460	70	93.3
9 Birmingham	5*B	396	65	91.8
10 Cardiff	5A	358	70	91.1

German cont.

	Research quality/5	Entry standards	Graduate prospects %	Overall rating
11 Aberystwyth	4A		70	90.7
12 St Andrews	4C	458	70	90.5
13 Bath	5A	369	65	90.2
14 Sheffield	4A	399	65	89.5
15 Southampton	5*A	335	60	89.4
16 Newcastle	4A	389	65	89.1
17 Exeter	5*A	357	55	89.0
18 Warwick	5A	435	50	88.9
19 Manchester	5*B	380	55	88.5
20 Lancaster	5C	407	65	88.4
21 Sussex	4A	361	65	88.0
22 Aberdeen	4A	359	65	87.9
23 Aston	5C	325	75	87.8
24 Liverpool	5A	366	55	87.4
25 Heriot-Watt	4B	469	50	87.3
26 Royal Holloway	5*C	359	60	86.6
27 Queen's, Belfast	4A	349		86.4
28 Queen Mary	5A	300		86.3
29 Salford	5A		50	85.6
30 Swansea	5A	282	60	85.4
31 Leeds	4C	364	60	84.0
32 Glasgow	4C	383	55	83.4
33 Oxford Brookes	4B	271	65	83.3
34 Hull	3aC	330	65	82.6
35 Strathclyde	3bB	436	50	82.5
36 Stirling	4C	344		81.9
=37 East Anglia	3bB	364	55	81.0
=37 Central Lancashire	3bA		60	81.0
39 Kent	4B	292	50	80.1
40 Brighton	5E		65	79.5
41 Reading	4B	321	40	78.7
42 Northumbria	3bE	302	65	77.7
43 Plymouth	3bA		50	77.0
44 Ulster	3aC	256	55	76.9
45 Bangor	3aA	263	45	76.7
46 Portsmouth	5C	280	40	76.6
47 Nottingham Trent	3aB	233	50	76.0
48 Leeds Metropolitan		278	50	71.2
49 West of England		234	50	69.4
50 Sheffield Hallam		244	45	68.5
51 Manchester Metropolitan		250	40	67.4
52 Anglia Ruskin	2C	186	40	67.3

Average starting salary:	£17,560	
Employed in graduate job:	38%	
Employed in graduate job and studying:	5%	
Employed in non-graduate job:	28%	
Employed in non-graduate job and studying:	4%	

Studying and not employed:	20%
Unemployed:	5%

The letters that appear in the Research Quality column indicate the proportion of staff included in the assessment, A showing that almost all staff were included and F showing that hardly any were.

History

Cambridge is top again for history, with the best employment record and entry qualifications, as well as one of eight 5* research ratings. Another of the research stars went to Oxford Brookes, one of the few new universities to achieve this level in any subject in the 2001 Research Assessment Exercise. The accolade almost produces a place in the top 20 and makes Brookes easily the top new university.

Durham holds on to second place, while Oxford moves up to third despite missing out on a 5* research grade. The other research stars were Durham, King's College London, the London School of Economics, the School of Oriental and African Studies, East Anglia and Bradford.

St Andrews remains the top university in Scotland, while Cardiff does the same in Wales. In the national student satisfaction survey, history (which was grouped together with archaeology) produced some of the best results. The Open University and Birkbeck College London did particularly well, and so did Huddersfield, Chester and Hull.

History remains one of the most popular subjects: it was in the top ten again in terms of total applications at the beginning of 2006. But a 9 per cent increase in 2005 had turned into a drop of nearly 8 per cent with top-up fees looming. Entry standards are high: no university's entrants averaged less than 200 points on the UCAS tariff, and 16 averaged more than 400.

Career prospects are mixed: surveys have shown a strong representation of historians among business leaders, celebrities and senior politicians, but more than a third are in non-graduate jobs six months after completing courses. Some universities, like Liverpool Hope, do well on this measure, but scored less than 40 per cent on the proportion of leavers going straight into graduate-level employment or further training. The unemployment rate is average for all subjects, but only law (where the profession requires further training) has a lower proportion of leavers going into non-graduate jobs.

- **The Royal Historical Society:** www.rhs.ac.uk

History	Research quality/5	Entry standards	Graduate prospects %	Overall rating
1 Cambridge	5*A	506	82	100.0
2 Durham	5*A	486	73	97.0
3 Oxford	5A	484	70	94.1
4 King's College London	5*A	432	68	93.9

History cont.

	Research quality/5	Entry standards	Graduate prospects %	Overall rating
5 London School of Economics	5*B	426	75	93.8
=6 Warwick	5A	454	62	91.0
=6 York	5A	473	59	91.0
8 University College London	5A	407	63	89.6
9 Royal Holloway	5A	371	65	88.8
10 Sheffield	5B	435	60	88.5
11 St Andrews	5B	427	61	88.4
12 School of Asian Studies	5*B	315	68	88.1
=13 Leeds	5B	407	62	88.0
=13 Bristol	4A	373	70	88.0
15 Nottingham	4A	442	58	87.5
16 Edinburgh	5B	420	58	87.4
17 Keele	5A	327	65	87.2
18 Exeter	5A	393	55	87.1
19 Southampton	5A	403	52	86.7
20 East Anglia	5*B	380	51	86.2
21 Newcastle	4A	385	59	85.7
22 Cardiff	5A	374	52	85.6
23 Oxford Brookes	5*A	282	56	85.5
24 Manchester	5B	389	53	85.1
25 Bradford	5*A	255		84.9
26 Leicester	5A	347	52	84.7
27 Essex	5A	311	57	84.6
28 Glasgow	5B	395	49	84.3
29 Sussex	4A	376	54	84.1
30 Birmingham	5B	373	51	84.0
31 Hull	5A	298	56	83.9
32 Queen Mary	5B	331	55	83.5
33 Kent	4B	335	60	83.0
=34 Salford	5A	252	57	82.5
=34 Liverpool	5B	339	50	82.5
36 Queen's, Belfast	5B	324	50	82.0
=37 Swansea	4A	299	55	81.6
=37 Aberystwyth	4A	278	58	81.6
39 Roehampton	5B	236	60	81.3
40 Aberdeen	4B	333	53	81.2
41 Strathclyde	4B	356	49	81.0
42 Lancaster	4A	362	43	80.9
43 Dundee	5B	292	47	80.1
44 De Montfort	4B	273	55	79.5
45 Stirling	5A	329	33	79.3
46 Huddersfield	5A	271	38	78.5

47 Lampeter	4A	236	50	78.1
48 Liverpool Hope	3bC	225	76	78.0
49 Reading	4B	321	39	77.3
50 Greenwich	3aA	216	58	77.2
51 Central Lancashire	4A	272	41	77.1
=52 Goldsmiths, University of London	4B	279	43	76.7
=52 Ulster	4B	244	48	76.7
54 Bangor	4B	275	43	76.6
55 Hertfordshire	5B	242	40	76.5
56 Northumbria	3aC	291	53	76.2
57 Sheffield Hallam	5B	274	33	75.9
58 Bolton	3bD		66	75.7
=59 Kingston	4B	227	46	75.6
=59 Brunel	3aB	293	44	75.6
=61 Portsmouth	4C	278	44	75.0
=61 Nottingham Trent	3aB	257	47	75.0
63 Anglia Ruskin	3aC		52	74.8
64 Wolverhampton	4B	234	41	74.6
65 Liverpool John Moores	4B	200	45	74.4
66 Chichester	3aA	251	40	74.0
=67 Canterbury Christ Church	3aA	241	40	73.6
=67 West of England	4B	282	30	73.6
69 Gloucestershire	3aC	250	48	73.5
=70 Manchester Metropolitan	3aC	267	45	73.3
=70 Leeds Metropolitan	3aD	245	55	73.3
=70 Sunderland	4C	230	44	73.3
73 Teesside	5C	216	39	73.1
74 Winchester	4C	249	40	73.0
75 Plymouth	3aC	245	45	72.5
76 Northampton	4B	234	32	72.4
77 Bath Spa	3bA	214	47	72.3
78 Glamorgan	3aC		45	72.1
79 Lincoln		239	66	71.7
80 Worcester	3aC	229	41	71.0
81 Chester	3bC	254	43	70.9
82 Westminster	3aB	255	27	70.0
83 Brighton		245	48	67.5
84 Derby		261	45	67.3
85 Staffordshire	3bC	241	30	67.1

Average starting salary:	£17,286	Studying and not employed:	25%
Employed in graduate job:	23%	Unemployed:	7%
Employed in graduate job and studying:	4%		
Employed in non-graduate job:	37%	The letters that appear in the Research Quality column indicate the proportion of staff included in the assessment, A showing that almost all staff were included and F showing that hardly any were.
Employed in non-graduate job and studying:	4%		

History of Art, Architecture and Design

Cambridge has knocked London's Courtauld Institute off the top of the table in Art History, moving up from fourth last year. Second-placed York has moved up even more, from sixth last year. The Courtauld, now in third place, has the only 5* rating but has lost the benefit of a high teaching score. Cambridge has the highest entry standards and the best employment record.

St Andrews is the top university in Scotland, while Aberystwyth is Wales's only representative. Plymouth has become the top new university and has broken into the top ten. Only six new universities appear in the ranking for a subject that has traditionally been associated with the older institutions.

Nationally, the specialised nature of the jobs market makes for uncertain prospects immediately after graduation: unemployment is above average for all subjects. Even some universities in the top 20 recorded "positive destinations" for only half their graduates in 2004.

Fewer than 4,000 undergraduates take full-time degrees in the history of art, although another 1,000 are registered on part-time courses. The majority of students are female. Outside Cambridge, entry standards range from 423 points at both York and the Courtauld to less than 200 at Sheffield Hallam. Even in the bottom half of the table, however, most universities average around 300 points. Teaching quality assessors in England found that most students were well supported, although about a third of libraries were under pressure.

- **The Gateway to Art, Design, Architecture and Media Information on the Internet (ADAM):** http://adam.ac.uk

History of Art, Architecture and Design	Research quality/5	Entry standards	Graduate prospects %	Overall rating
1 Cambridge	5A	520	75	100.0
2 York	5A	423	70	94.4
3 Courtauld Institute	5*A	423	60	94.3
4 St Andrews	5A	376	65	91.0
5 Birmingham	5A	377		90.9
6 Warwick	5A	389	60	90.4
7 Sussex	5A	382	60	90.1
8 Aberystwyth	3aA		70	87.9
9 Plymouth	5A		50	87.5
10 University College London	5B	401	50	86.9
11 Edinburgh	4B	418	55	86.8
12 Leeds	3aA	358	70	86.7
13 Essex	5B	333	60	86.3
14 Bristol	3aB	391	65	85.9
15 Southampton	4B	381	55	85.1
16 Glasgow	5B	390	40	83.9
17 Brighton	5B	269	60	83.4
18 School of Asian Studies	3aA		55	82.3

19 Leicester	4A	312	50	82.0
20 Manchester	5B	319	45	81.9
21 Goldsmiths, University of London	3bA	299	70	81.7
22 Aberdeen	4C		55	80.7
23 East Anglia	5B	333	35	80.0
24 Kent	3aB	306	55	79.6
25 Reading	4A	334	35	79.2
26 Nottingham	3bC	398	50	79.1
27 Oxford Brookes	3aA	299	50	79.0
28 Manchester Metropolitan	4C	288	50	77.5
29 Loughborough	3aC	268	50	74.9
30 De Montfort	3bC		45	71.9
31 Kingston	4D	222	35	68.4
32 Middlesex	5D		20	65.7
33 Sheffield Hallam		197	40	62.7

Average starting salary:	£16,042	Studying and not employed:	20%
Employed in graduate job:	26%	Unemployed:	9%
Employed in graduate job and studying:	3%		
Employed in non-graduate job:	35%	The letters that appear in the Research Quality column indicate the proportion of staff included in the assessment, A showing that almost all staff were included and F showing that hardly any were.	
Employed in non-graduate job and studying:	6%		

Hospitality, Leisure, Sport, Recreation and Tourism

This is one of the few areas to have seen a big increase in the number of universities offering courses: 11 more institutions qualified for inclusion in last year's table and the total is now up to 68. The removal of teaching scores has cost Liverpool John Moores the leadership and seen it drop to eighth place, although it remains the top new university. It was the only university to register top scores for both teaching and research, but it cannot compete with the entry standards of the universities higher up the ranking.

Loughborough is the new leader, with a consistent set of scores, including one of the four 5* research grades (albeit with a low proportion of academics assessed). Birmingham and Glasgow, in second and third places respectively, and Manchester Metropolitan, in 23rd, are the other universities rated internationally outstanding for research. Durham has the highest entry standards, while East London has by far the best employment record, but is relegated to 25th place with the lowest average entrance qualifications in the entire table.

The category covers a variety of courses, most directed towards management in the leisure and tourism industries. The subjects are offered mainly by new universities, although only JMU now appears in the top ten. Loughborough and fifth-placed Bath – two of the universities with the best sports facilities and largest scholarship programmes – both have average entry scores of more than 400 points. However, less than 200 points were needed to secure a place at 13 other institutions. Brighton, Chichester and Swansea all did well in the first national student satisfaction survey.

Unemployment is below the average for all subjects, but almost half the 2004 leavers were in non-graduate jobs six months after completing their course. Nevertheless, sports

Hospitality, Leisure, Recreation, Sport and Tourism cont.

science, in particular, has been growing in popularity: the number of applications for degree places was up by approaching 2 per cent to more than 40,000 at the start of 2006, when most subjects were in decline. There was a slight increase, too, in demand for the smaller tourism area was also up, which saw an increase of nearly 20 per cent in 2005.

- **Springboard UK Ltd:** www.springboarduk.org.uk
- **English Institute of Sport:** www.eis2win.co.uk
- **British Association of Sport and Exercise Science:** www.bases.org.uk

Hospitality, Leisure, Recreation, Sport and Tourism	Research quality/5	Entry standards	Graduate prospects %	Overall rating
1 Loughborough	5*C	402	64	100.0
2 Birmingham	5*A	368	54	99.1
3 Glasgow	5*A	340	53	97.6
4 Brunel	4B	285	76	96.9
5 Bath	3aC	402	63	96.3
6 Exeter	5C	342	63	95.9
7 Leeds	3aC	343	63	93.6
8 Liverpool John Moores	5*B	246	58	93.4
9 Durham		446	59	92.9
10 Aberdeen	4B	275	61	92.6
11 Edinburgh	3aD	362	57	91.7
12 Brighton	4A	233	61	91.6
13 Surrey	4C	308	56	91.4
14 De Montfort	4B	223	65	91.3
15 Stirling	4B	339	44	91.2
16 Manchester	4C	313	51	90.4
17 Bangor	5A	260	45	90.3
=18 Nottingham Trent	3aC	254	60	88.8
=18 Essex		282	72	88.8
20 Strathclyde	4C	296	44	87.8
21 Ulster	4D	261	54	87.1
22 Chichester	3aC	219	59	87.0
23 Manchester Metropolitan	5*C	219	45	86.8
24 Leeds Metropolitan	3aD	264	53	86.2
25 East London		141	82	84.9
26 UWIC, Cardiff	3aF	240	59	84.1
27 Worcester		210	66	84.0
28 Hull		271	55	83.9
29 Sheffield Hallam	4E	262	47	83.7
30 Hertfordshire	3aC	244	40	83.2
=31 Queen Margaret College		255	54	82.9
=31 Roehampton	3bD	210	53	82.9
=31 Oxford Brookes		266	52	82.9
34 Plymouth	3aE	220	52	82.6

=35 Glamorgan	3bB	171	50	82.2
=35 Robert Gordon		296	44	82.2
37 Napier		259	50	82.1
38 Canterbury Christ Church	3bC	202	47	82.0
39 Swansea		262	48	81.7
=40 Luton	4C	178	40	81.4
=40 Gloucestershire	3bE	215	50	81.4
42 Liverpool Hope		173	62	81.3
43 Kingston		177	61	81.2
44 London South Bank	3aD	188	46	80.9
45 Reading		277	42	80.8
=46 Bournemouth		240	45	79.9
=46 Glasgow Caledonian	3aE	274	32	79.9
48 Chester		226	47	79.8
=49 Coventry		213	48	79.5
=49 Northumbria		275	37	79.5
51 Portsmouth		227	44	79.1
=52 Wolverhampton	3aE	163	47	78.7
=52 Lincoln		212	45	78.7
=52 Staffordshire	3aE	212	38	78.7
55 Bath Spa		233	41	78.6
56 Winchester		242	39	78.5
=57 Central Lancashire		205	45	78.3
=57 Greenwich		192	47	78.3
=59 West of England		237	38	78.0
=59 Westminster	3aD	202	32	78.0
61 Derby		201	43	77.7
62 Northampton		205	41	77.3
63 Thames Valley		183	44	77.1
64 Anglia Ruskin	2B	193	30	76.6
65 Southampton Solent		186	41	76.5
66 Huddersfield		221	33	76.0
67 Salford		196	34	75.1
68 Buckinghamshire Chilterns UC	3bE	189	29	74.8

Average starting salary:	£16,213	Studying and not employed:	12%
Employed in graduate job:	32%	Unemployed:	6%
Employed in graduate job and studying:	4%		
Employed in non-graduate job:	43%	The letters that appear in the Research Quality column indicate the proportion of staff included in the assessment, A showing that almost all staff were included and F showing that hardly any were.	
Employed in non-graduate job and studying:	3%		

Iberian Languages

Cambridge remains well ahead of the field for Iberian languages, with the highest entry standards, the best employment score and one of six 5* ratings for research. The other research stars were King's College London, Manchester, Southampton, Nottingham and

Iberian Languages cont.

Queen Mary, which misses the top 20 because of low entry standards and an exceptionally low graduate employment rate. All of them are beaten to second place by St Andrews, which has a consistent set of scores.

Hull plunges from 4th to 28th place after losing the benefit of the only maximum score for teaching quality in England. Such scores have been removed from all the subject tables because of their age. Durham and Nottingham make the opposite journey, coming from outside the top 20 to share fifth place. No new university makes the top 30, but Oxford Brookes and Central Lancashire come closest. Entry standards are high, with three universities within five points of a 500-point average and only two averaging less than 200.

Spanish is growing in popularity as an alternative to French in schools, and is a common choice as an element of a broader modern languages degree. Applications rose substantially in 2004 and 2005, but there had been a 6 per cent decline by the official deadline for courses starting in 2006. The table also includes Portuguese, which is still offered by about a dozen universities.

Unemployment is slightly below the average for all subjects, at 6 per cent, but the latest figures showed another 36 per cent in non-graduate jobs six months after completing courses. However, employment prospects appear to be more evenly spread than in many subjects: only six universities in the table saw less than half of their leavers go into graduate jobs or further training in 2003.

- **The Association for Contemporary Iberian Studies:** www.bton.ac.uk/languages/acis
- **CILT – The National Centre for Languages:** www.cilt.org.uk
- **The Institute of Translation and Interpreting:** www.iti.org.uk

Iberian Languages	Research quality/5	Entry standards	Graduate prospects %	Overall rating
1 Cambridge	5*A	497	78	100.0
2 St Andrews	5A	435	74	94.8
3 King's College London	5*A	386	72	94.4
4 Oxford	5B	496	68	94.3
5 Durham	4B	460	72	92.4
6 Nottingham	5*A	418	60	92.3
7 Sheffield	5A	403	66	91.5
8 Edinburgh	5A	428	62	91.4
9 Bath	5A	387		90.8
10 Birmingham	5A	394	64	90.7
11 Newcastle	5A	398	62	90.3
12 Queen's, Belfast	4A	340	74	89.5
13 Bristol	4B	392	70	89.4
14 Southampton	5*A	350	58	89.3
15 Manchester	5*A	383	52	88.9
16 Cardiff	5A	358	62	88.8
17 University College London	4A	413	60	88.5
18 Lancaster	5C	371	70	88.3

19 Heriot-Watt	4B	469	52	87.4
=20 Leeds	4B	383	60	86.4
=20 Liverpool	4A	356	60	86.4
22 Kent	4B	338	64	85.8
23 Swansea	5B	284	62	84.9
24 Royal Holloway	4A	357	54	84.8
25 Bradford	4D		72	84.4
26 Glasgow	3aB	399	56	84.3
27 Exeter	4B	359	54	83.9
28 Hull	4A	283	60	83.7
29 Salford	5A	313	48	83.4
30 Strathclyde	4C	411	50	83.1
31 Queen Mary	5*A	290	38	81.8
32 Sussex		357	76	81.7
33 Aberystwyth	3aA	306	54	81.1
34 Oxford Brookes	3aC	272	66	81.0
35 Central Lancashire	3bA		60	80.9
36 Aberdeen	4D	345	54	79.9
37 Portsmouth	5C	280	38	76.4
=38 Roehampton	3aA	220		76.1
=38 East Anglia		364	54	76.1
40 Northumbria	3bE	283	58	75.7
=41 Leicester		309	50	73.0
=41 Stirling		352	44	73.0
43 Plymouth	3bA		40	72.9
44 Leeds Metropolitan		278	50	71.9
45 Ulster		256	52	71.6
46 Nottingham Trent		233	52	70.8
47 Liverpool John Moores		169	60	70.5
48 West of England		234	50	70.3
49 Sheffield Hallam		244	44	69.1
50 Manchester Metropolitan		250	40	68.2
51 Anglia Ruskin	2C	186	34	66.7

Average starting salary:	£17,104		Studying and not employed:	17%
Employed in graduate job:	35%		Unemployed:	6%
Employed in graduate job and studying:	6%			
Employed in non-graduate job:	33%			
Employed in non-graduate job and studying:	3%			

The letters that appear in the Research Quality column indicate the proportion of staff included in the assessment, A showing that almost all staff were included and F showing that hardly any were.

Italian

Cambridge continues to lead a group of 34 universities offering Italian. It has among the best employment records, as well as the highest entry standards, and is one of six universities rated internationally outstanding for research. Oxford is another of them, and it regains second place this year from Swansea, which drops from second place to

Italian cont.

twenty-seventhth after losing the benefit of an Excellent teaching quality grade. All teaching scores have been removed this year because of their age.

Nottingham has the best employment record but, despite high entry grades, the absence of a research assessment condemns the university to fifteenth place. St Andrews is the top university in Scotland, just ahead of Cardiff, the leader in Wales. Most of the table is made up of old universities, but Central Lancashire comes close to a place in the top 20.

The top research grades were widely spread in 2001, after a sharp improvement on the previous assessments. Oxford, Cambridge, Birmingham, University College London, Reading and Leeds were all awarded the 5* grade, although Leeds entered a relatively low proportion of its academic staff.

Fewer than 500 students take the language as a separate subject at degree level, although others include Italian in combined degree programmes. Teaching quality assessors in England found some cases of overcrowding, but they were satisfied with learning resources, which generally included satellite television. Most students have no previous knowledge of the language, but there is a high completion rate. The low numbers can make for mixed messages from the labour market: the unemployment rate is average, at 5 per cent, but over 40 per cent start off in non-graduate jobs.

- **CILT – The National Centre for Languages:** www.cilt.org.u
- **The Institute of Translation and Interpreting:** www.iti.org.uk

Italian	Research quality/5	Entry standards	Graduate prospects %	Overall rating
1 Cambridge	5*A	497	75	100.0
2 Oxford	5*A	476	60	95.1
3 University College London	5*A	403	70	94.8
4 Bristol	5A	382	75	93.3
5 Edinburgh	4A	435	65	90.8
6 St Andrews	4B	445	65	90.1
7 Cardiff	5A	342	65	88.9
8 Warwick	5A	413	50	87.8
=9 Sussex	4A	361	65	87.7
=9 Bath	5A	345	60	87.7
11 Birmingham	5*B	393	50	87.4
12 Royal Holloway	4A	339	65	86.9
13 Strathclyde	4C	436	55	85.3
14 Manchester	5B	379	50	85.1
15 Nottingham		425	80	84.8
16 Salford	5A		45	83.7
17 Durham		460	70	83.5
18 Kent	4B		55	83.3
19 Reading	5*A	318	40	83.1
20 Lancaster	5C		55	82.7

21 Leeds	5*D	353	55	81.9
22 Central Lancashire	3bA		60	81.0
23 Hull	3aC	320	60	80.5
24 Leicester	4A	309	45	80.2
25 Sheffield		396	65	79.5
26 Exeter	4B	349	40	79.4
27 Swansea	4A	255		79.2
28 Glasgow	3bA	378	45	79.1
29 Portsmouth	5C	280	40	76.2
30 Northumbria	3bE	292	60	75.5
31 Nottingham Trent		233	50	68.7
32 Sheffield Hallam		244	45	67.9
33 Manchester Metropolitan		250	40	66.7
34 Anglia Ruskin	2C	186	35	65.4

Average starting salary:	£17,798	Studying and not employed:	15%
Employed in graduate job:	40%	Unemployed:	7%
Employed in graduate job and studying:	3%		
Employed in non-graduate job:	30%	The letters that appear in the Research Quality column indicate the proportion of staff included in the assessment, A showing that almost all staff were included and F showing that hardly any were.	
Employed in non-graduate job and studying:	5%		

Land and Property Management

This year's land and property management table contains only half the number of universities listed in 2005. The removal of teaching quality scores – in common with all the tables – has left too little data to include the others. Most have cohorts that are too small to calculate reliable destinations scores or UCAS tariff averages.

Cambridge maintains its big lead, with by far the highest entry standards and the best graduate employment record. The holder of the only 5* research grade, Salford, is one of those to drop out of the ranking, but the top three all reached grade 5. Others to drop out are Oxford Brookes and Manchester, which were second and third respectively last year.

All but three of the ten universities are former polytechnics – and even third-placed Ulster was created from a merger involving a polytechnic. There is a huge gulf in entry standards between Cambridge, with an average of nearly 500 points and Westminster's 184, but only Sheffield Hallam departs from the norm of high "positive destinations" for graduates. Employment prospects inevitably depend to some extent on the state of the property market, but a higher proportion than in most subjects find graduate-level jobs or take postgraduate courses.

Completion rates tend to be higher at the universities with more demanding entrance requirements. Only about 2,000 students are taking the subject at degree or diploma level, although the subjects are often included in wider environmental programmes.

- **Royal Institution of Chartered Surveyors:** www.rics.org

Land and Property Management

	Research quality/5	Entry standards	Graduate prospects %	Overall rating
1 Cambridge	5B	493	95	100.0
2 Reading	5B	353	80	91.2
3 Ulster	5A	270	85	90.8
4 London South Bank	4D		90	87.0
5 Portsmouth	3aB	230	80	83.5
6 Greenwich	3bE		90	82.4
7 UCE Birmingham	3bE	264	90	82.3
8 Northumbria		364	80	81.7
9 Westminster	3aD	184	85	80.3
10 Sheffield Hallam	4D		45	69.5

Average starting salary:	£19,915	Studying and not employed:	6%
Employed in graduate job:	53%	Unemployed:	3%
Employed in graduate job and studying:	22%		
Employed in non-graduate job:	15%	The letters that appear in the Research Quality column indicate the proportion of staff included in the assessment, A showing that almost all staff were included and F showing that hardly any were.	
Employed in non-graduate job and studying:	2%		

Law

Law attracts more applications than any other single subject – 81,000 at the start of 2006, despite a 7.4 per cent decline. And entry standards reflect the courses' popularity: nine subjects have higher average entry scores, but only in medicine do so many universities make such testing demands. Twenty-four (compared with less than 20 last year) have average entry scores of more than 400 points. However, it is still possible to secure a place at a handful of new universities with less than 200 points.

Oxford and Cambridge continue to head the ranking, but there is movement below them, with University College London not far behind Oxford in third place. Leeds Metropolitan takes over from Oxford Brookes as the best-placed new university.

The top four all achieved 5* research ratings, as did Durham, Keele, Queen Mary University of London and Southampton. Aberdeen, in fifth place, pipped Cambridge for the best destinations score, with 91 per cent of its leavers going into graduate jobs or further training. In most universities, at least 70 per cent of leavers had "positive destinations", even if not necessarily in the legal profession.

Aberdeen overtakes Edinburgh for the top position in Scotland, while Cardiff remains just ahead of Aberystwyth in Wales. In the first national student satisfaction survey, King's College London and Edge Hill College of Higher Education, on Merseyside, registered the best results.

The requirement for further professional training for solicitors and barristers means less than a quarter of students go straight into graduate jobs. Many opt for careers in other areas, but with six out of ten taking additional courses on graduation, the 5 per cent unemployment rate is still well below average.

• **The Bar Council:** www.barcouncil.org

- **The Law Society of England and Wales:** www.lawsociety.org.uk
- **The Law Society of Scotland:** www.lawscot.org.uk

Law	Research quality/5	Entry standards	Graduate prospects %	Overall rating
1 Cambridge	5*A	518	90	100.0
2 Oxford	5*B	504	88	97.9
3 University College London	5*A	478	84	96.9
4 London School of Economics	5*A	474	82	96.1
5 Aberdeen	5B	427	91	95.1
6 Durham	5*A	464	79	94.9
7 Nottingham	5A	465	83	94.8
8 Edinburgh	5B	453	86	94.4
9 King's College London	5A	442	84	94.3
10 Manchester	5A	464	80	93.8
=11 Leeds	5A	449	80	93.3
=11 Warwick	5B	474	80	93.3
13 Glasgow	5B	463	80	92.9
14 Strathclyde	5A	449	78	92.7
15 Queen Mary	5*B	379	84	92.6
16 Dundee	5B	407	83	92.0
17 Queen's, Belfast	5B	398	83	91.7
18 School of Asian Studies	5A	385	81	91.5
19 Bristol	5B	406	81	91.3
20 Kent	5B	348	85	90.7
21 Surrey	5C	350	89	90.5
22 Newcastle	5C	440	79	90.4
=23 Brunel	5A	354	80	90.2
=23 City	5B	372	81	90.2
25 Sheffield	5C	439	78	90.0
26 Hull	5B	351	82	89.8
=27 Leicester	5A	415	71	89.5
=27 Southampton	5*B	433	68	89.5
29 Exeter	5C	408	79	89.3
30 Birmingham	5C	430	76	89.1
31 Keele	5*A	329	73	88.7
32 Reading	5B	381	74	88.4
33 Liverpool	4B	416	74	88.3
34 East Anglia	5B	416	67	87.4
=35 Essex	5B	371	69	86.5
=35 Cardiff	5C	397	71	86.5
37 Sussex	4B	361	71	85.6
38 Aberystwyth	4B	338	73	85.4
39 Lancaster	5B	389	62	85.0

Law cont.

	Research quality/5	Entry standards	Graduate prospects %	Overall rating
=40 Ulster	5C	316	68	82.9
=40 Swansea	3aB	299	73	82.9
42 Leeds Metropolitan	3aE	305	81	82.3
43 Oxford Brookes	4D	334	71	82.1
44 Northumbria		389	75	81.7
45 Nottingham Trent	4F	323	78	81.1
=46 Manchester Metropolitan		332	78	80.8
=46 Central Lancashire	4E	282	77	80.8
48 Bournemouth	3aE	259	78	79.9
=49 Anglia Ruskin	2B	251	75	79.5
=49 Kingston		245	83	79.5
51 Hertfordshire	3aC	235	71	79.3
52 Westminster	5F	271	76	78.9
53 Sheffield Hallam	3aF	300	73	78.6
54 Robert Gordon	3aD	280		78.2
55 West of England	4F	307	69	77.8
56 Huddersfield	3bE	234	74	77.5
=57 Sunderland		248	74	76.8
=57 Teesside		247	74	76.8
59 Napier	3aD	268	62	76.5
60 Liverpool John Moores	3bC	225	66	76.4
=61 Staffordshire	3aF	254	70	76.2
=61 Lincoln		237	73	76.2
63 East London	3aE	181	73	75.8
64 Glamorgan		230	72	75.6
65 Derby		216	73	75.5
66 Glasgow Caledonian	3bE	339	56	75.4
=67 UCE Birmingham		261	66	74.8
=67 De Montfort	4E	248	61	74.8
69 Thames Valley	2F		68	74.4
70 Greenwich	3bF	238	66	74.3
71 Brighton		259	64	74.2
=72 Plymouth	3bE	284	57	73.9
=72 London South Bank		197	70	73.9
74 Middlesex		199	69	73.7
75 Stirling		323	55	73.5
=76 Southampton Solent		209	64	72.5
=76 Coventry		227	62	72.5
=78 Luton		212	62	72.0
=78 Wolverhampton	3aE	202	58	72.0
80 Buckinghamshire Chilterns UC		170	53	67.9
81 Northampton		208	43	66.1
82 Bangor		233	38	65.4

Librarianship and Information Management

Loughborough's lead in librarianship and information management was the biggest in any of the subject tables, but it is down to the smallest possible fraction after the removal of the ageing teaching quality scores. University College London, in second place, has higher entry qualifications and shares with Loughborough the distinction of the best graduate destinations rate, but has a lower research grade. Sheffield, in third, is the only university rated internationally outstanding for research.

There are only nine universities in the ranking – down from 11 last year and 14 the year before because of low student numbers at some of the smaller providers. Fourth-placed Northumbria's high average entry score, just outside 300 points, cements its position as the leading new university. None of them saw more than half of their leavers go straight into graduate-level work or further training, unlike to top three in the table.

As the small size of the table suggests, librarianship and information management are minority interests at degree level, and this makes the subjects vulnerable to swings in employment statistics. The unemployment rate of 11 per cent is marginally down on last year but still one that is exceeded in only two subject categories.

- **The Chartered Institute of Library and Information Professionals:** www.cilip.org.uk/default.cilip

Librarianship and Information Management	Research quality/5	Entry standards	Graduate prospects %	Overall rating
=1 University College London	4A	357	75	100.0
=1 Loughborough	5B	344	75	100.0
3 Sheffield	5*A	316	65	99.3
4 Northumbria	3bC	299		87.2
5 UCE Birmingham	3aB		40	83.8
=6 Manchester Metropolitan	4C	214	45	83.6
=6 Aberystwyth	3aB	233	40	83.6
8 Brighton	3bD	240	45	81.4
9 Leeds Metropolitan	4E	183	50	79.6

Linguistics

Cambridge takes over at the top of the linguistics table after Queen Mary University of London dropped out when the removal of ageing teaching quality scores left it with insufficient data to compile an overall score. Cambridge had one of the four 5* research grades as well as the highest proportion of leavers going straight into graduate-level work or further study. The other research stars were second-placed Oxford, University College London and Queen Mary. The research grades improved dramatically in 2001, with more than half of the universities reaching the top two categories.

Oxford boasts the highest entry qualifications, although Cambridge does not publish separate data for this subject. Edinburgh is Scotland's only representative in the table, while Cardiff outscores Bangor in Wales. Portsmouth is the best-placed new university in a ranking that is dominated by the older foundations. Hertfordshire, Westminster and the West of England are the only other former polytechnics in the ranking.

Fewer than 3,000 students take linguistics at degree level, eight out of ten of them arriving with A levels. Entry standards are relatively high: four of the 21 universities averaged more than 400 points on the UCAS tariff and none fell below 200 points.

Applications were down by 4 per cent at the start of 2006, but this was in the context of a healthy 13 per cent increase in the previous year. Immediate employment prospects are close to the average for all subjects, although the latest figures show almost four out of ten graduates in lower-level jobs six months after completing their courses.

- **The British Association for Applied Linguistics:** www.baal.org.uk

Linguistics	Research quality/5	Entry standards	Graduate prospects %	Overall rating
=1 Oxford	5*A	501		100.0
=1 Cambridge	5*A		80	100.0
3 York	5A	399	65	91.4
4 Newcastle	5A	408	60	90.4
5 Edinburgh	5C	410	65	88.7
6 Sussex	4A	383	60	87.7
7 Manchester	5B	371	55	86.7
8 Essex	5B	331	60	86.6
9 University College London	5*C	372	55	86.1
10 Lancaster	5B	350	55	85.9
11 Leeds	3aC	377	60	83.7
12 Portsmouth	5C	290		81.8
13 King's College London		346	70	80.4
14 Hertfordshire	3aA	220	60	80.3
=15 Reading	3aB	341	45	79.9
=15 Sheffield		406	60	79.9
17 East Anglia	3bB	306	55	79.7
18 Cardiff		366	60	78.5
19 Westminster	5C	214		77.8

20 West of England		277	55	74.2
21 Bangor	3bB	281	35	73.7

Average starting salary:	£16,466	Studying and not employed:	24%
Employed in graduate job:	28%	Unemployed:	4%
Employed in graduate job and studying:	6%		
Employed in non-graduate job:	33%		
Employed in non-graduate job and studying:	4%		

The letters that appear in the Research Quality column indicate the proportion of staff included in the assessment, A showing that almost all staff were included and F showing that hardly any were.

Materials Technology

Oxford overtakes Cambridge at the top of the materials table, but there is precious little between the two. Both have 5* research grades – as do Sheffield, Manchester and Birmingham – but Oxford is five points ahead on entry standards and two percentage points on graduate destinations. Oxford entrants' 555 points average is among the highest score for any subject. Fourth-placed Imperial College was the only institution in England to be awarded full marks for teaching quality, but those scores have been removed because of their age.

Swansea is the only Welsh university in the table, although it has dropped to tenth place despite matching Oxford for the proportion of graduates going straight into work or further training after losing benefit of an Excellent rating for teaching. Heriot-Watt is Scotland's only representative. Manchester Metropolitan is the highest-placed new university, but has lost its place in the top ten. Sheffield Hallam scored a creditable grade 5 for research, although it entered a relatively low proportion of its academics for assessment.

Oxbridge and Imperial apart, there is less variation in entry standards than in many other subjects. Although student numbers are too small to compile scores for three institutions, none of the remainder has an average of less than 200 points.

Courses cover three distinct areas: materials science, mining and engineering; textiles technology and printing; and marine technology. More than three quarters of students go on to further study or graduate jobs within six months of graduating. Nationally, unemployment is above average, at 9 per cent, but more than 40 per cent go straight into graduate jobs.

- **The Institute of Materials, Minerals and Mining:** www.iom3.org
- **Materials Careers:** www.materials-careers.org.uk

Materials Technology	Research quality/5	Entry standards	Graduate prospects %	Overall rating
1 Oxford	5*A	555	86	100.0
2 Cambridge	5*A	550	84	99.1
3 Birmingham	5*A	307	82	86.0
4 Imperial College	5A	383	72	83.5
5 Sheffield	5*A	330	66	81.8

Materials Technology cont.

	Research quality/5	Entry standards	Graduate prospects %	Overall rating
6 Nottingham	5B	342	76	80.7
7 Loughborough	4B	358	74	78.2
8 Manchester	5*B	328	62	78.1
9 Queen Mary	5B	296	74	77.7
10 Swansea	4A	226	86	77.1
11 Manchester Metropolitan	4A	287	66	73.6
12 Leeds	5C	318	60	70.9
13 De Montfort	4A	244	62	70.0
14 Sheffield Hallam	5D		60	65.0
15 Exeter		275	82	63.3
16 Heriot-Watt	3bB		46	56.3
17 Buckinghamshire Chilterns UC	3bB	214	32	51.4
18 University of the Arts, London		211	54	50.7
19 Nottingham Trent	3bD		40	48.0

Average starting salary:	£17,478	Studying and not employed:	18%
Employed in graduate job:	38%	Unemployed:	9%
Employed in graduate job and studying:	3%		
Employed in non-graduate job:	29%	The letters that appear in the Research Quality column indicate the proportion of staff included in the assessment, A showing that almost all staff were included and F showing that hardly any were.	
Employed in non-graduate job and studying:	4%		

Mathematics

Cambridge widens its lead at the top of the mathematics table after the removal of the ageing teaching quality scores. It has the top scores for student qualifications and graduate destinations, and is the only university with 5* research grades in pure and applied maths and statistics. Cambridge's average of 580 points per entrant is the highest in any subject and second-placed Oxford's 558 is next.

The two English universities awarded maximum points for teaching quality in mathematics have tumbled down the ranking. Bath, which once topped the table, drops to eighth, while Birmingham falls from fifth to thirty-third place. Maths had amongst the most satisfied students in the first national satisfaction survey, with the Open University and Queen's University Belfast producing particularly good results.

St Andrews maintains its position as the leader in Scotland, while Cardiff does the same in Wales. The three different research categories meant that 5* grades were sprinkled liberally among the leading universities. Bristol, Oxford, Warwick and Imperial College each achieved two top grades. Even Kent, which shares 40th place with Hertfordshire, the leading new university, has one.

There had been more than 30,000 applications to study maths at the start of 2006, a rise of 11 per cent for the third year in a row despite the imminent introduction of top-up fees. Only medicine, dentistry and veterinary medicine have higher entry standards. No fewer than 19 universities average more than 400 points at entry and only one of those for whom data is available drops below 200.

Although identified as one of the subjects most likely to lead to a high salary, graduate employment rates are not as high as for some vocational areas. Unemployment is average, at 7 per cent and, although more than a quarter take postgraduate courses, only about four leavers in ten go straight into graduate jobs. New universities are among Cambridge's leading challengers for the best employment record: Greenwich saw 84 per cent of its leavers go straight into graduate-level jobs or further training, while Liverpool John Moores, in 62nd place overall, shares the next-best score with the London School of Economics.

- **Math-Jobs:** www.math-jobs.com
- **Maths Careers:** www.mathscareers.org.uk
- **ECM:** www.ecmselection.co.uk

Mathematics

	Research quality/5 Pure	Research quality/5 Applied	Research quality/5 Statistics	Entry standards	Graduate prospects %	Overall rating
1 Cambridge	5*A	5*A	5*B	580	90	100.0
2 Oxford	5*B	5A	5*C	558	78	95.0
3 Durham	5B	5*B	4B	529	76	93.1
4 Warwick	5B	5*A	5*B	507	74	92.8
5 Imperial College	5*B	5*B	5B	482	72	91.8
6 London School of Economics			4B	482	82	91.7
7 University College London	5B	5B	5B	440	80	91.6
8 Bath	5A	5*B	5B	460	74	91.5
9 Bristol	5B	5*A	5*A	447	68	90.7
10 Greenwich			3aA		84	90.4
11 Surrey		5A	5A	356	76	89.5
12 St Andrews	5B	5B	5A	464	68	89.4
13 York	5B	5A		445	66	88.9
14 Nottingham	5B	5B	5A	480	64	88.7
15 Leeds	5B	5B	5B	401	68	87.6
16 Southampton	5C	5B	5A	416	66	87.4
17 Cardiff	5A			367	66	87.3
18 Heriot-Watt		5B	5C	473	60	86.9
=19 Lancaster	4A		5*B	373	64	86.8
=19 Newcastle	5C	4B	5A	389	68	86.8
21 King's College London	5C	5B		387	68	86.7
=22 Dundee		5B		344		86.6
=22 Manchester	5A	5A	4B	408	60	86.6
24 Exeter	4A	5A	4A	380	64	86.2
25 Edinburgh	5*A	5B	4C	437	56	86.1
=26 Loughborough		4B		352	72	86.0
=26 Glasgow	5D	5A	5A	407	64	86.0
28 Swansea	5C			298	78	85.9
=29 Sheffield	5B	4B	5C	385	66	85.7

Mathematics cont.

	Research quality/5 Pure	Research quality/5 Applied	Research quality/5 Statistics	Entry standards	Graduate prospects %	Overall rating
=29 Reading	3aA	5A	4B	361	68	85.7
31 Queen's, Belfast	3aC			379	78	85.6
32 East Anglia	5A	4B		415	56	84.9
33 Birmingham	5C	5B	4B	392	60	84.4
34 Sussex	4A	5B	4A	358	60	84.2
35 Aberdeen	5C	4E	4A	346	66	84.1
36 Leicester	5B	5B		290	64	83.9
37 City		4A	3aC	292	74	83.8
38 Strathclyde		5B	4C	361	58	83.4
39 Keele	2C	5A	3aA	310	64	83.1
=40 Hertfordshire		4C		204	80	82.9
=40 Kent	3aC	5A	5*D	294	66	82.9
42 Aston		5C		323	62	82.5
43 Aberystwyth	3bA	4A		352	58	82.3
=44 Liverpool	5B	5B	4A	328	54	82.2
=44 Brunel		5A	4B	259	62	82.2
46 Royal Holloway	5C			328	60	82.1
47 Essex	3aA	3aA		362	58	82.0
48 Hull	4B	4A		265	62	81.8
=49 Abertay		3aA			60	81.4
=49 Goldsmiths, University of London	3aA		3aA		60	81.4
51 Queen Mary	5A	4B	5A	230	58	81.2
52 Chester		3bA		232	70	80.2
=53 Portsmouth		5C		251	58	79.7
=53 Manchester Metropolitan				294	80	79.7
55 Brighton		3aC		228	68	79.4
56 Oxford Brookes		3aB		260		79.2
57 De Montfort		3bA			60	79.0
58 Plymouth	3bA	3aC	3aE	283	66	78.9
59 West of England		3aC		244	64	78.8
=60 Nottingham Trent		3aC	3aD	292	60	78.3
=60 Stirling	3aA			353	44	78.3
62 Liverpool John Moores				184	82	77.5
63 Ulster		4E		293	62	77.4
64 Coventry		3aC	3aE	232	62	77.3
65 Northumbria		3aD		264	60	77.0
66 Wolverhampton				262	72	76.9
67 Staffordshire		3bC	2D		62	76.0
68 Glasgow Caledonian		3bD		262	58	75.6
69 Sheffield Hallam				237	68	75.3
70 Middlesex	3aF				66	75.1
71 Paisley		2C			38	67.0

Average starting salary:	£19,737
Employed in graduate job:	31%
Employed in graduate job and studying:	11%
Employed in non-graduate job:	23%
Employed in non-graduate job and studying:	3%

| Studying and not employed: | 25% |
| Unemployed: | 7% |

The letters that appear in the Research Quality column indicate the proportion of staff included in the assessment, A showing that almost all staff were included and F showing that hardly any were.

Mechanical Engineering

The top two remain unchanged in the mechanical engineering table but Southampton moves up two places to be the nearest challenger. Imperial has the highest entry scores in the ranking and a slightly better employment rate than second-placed Bath. The top three are among six holders of 5* research grades, the others being Liverpool, Queen's, Belfast and Leeds. Queen's also did well in the first national student satisfaction survey, as did the Open University, Loughborough and Hertfordshire.

Like last year, Hull registers by far the best destinations score, with 96 per cent of leavers finding a graduate job or further training within six months. Unlike last year, this is enough to secure a place in the top 20, although relatively low entry scores restrict the university to nineteenth. Nationally, more than half go straight into graduate jobs, but the 8 per cent unemployment rate is slightly above average.

Cardiff remains the top university in Wales, but Strathclyde hangs onto the leadership in Scotland. The majority of institutions offering mechanical engineering are old universities, which occupy all but one of the top 30 places. The exception is Robert Gordon, at 30th. The open access policies pursued by many of the new universities is reflected in the fact that more than a third of the entrants are admitted without A levels or equivalents. A handful have average entry standards of below 200 points.

Mechanical engineering now attracts more applications than any other branch of the wider discipline. However, although there had been more than 20,000 applications at the start of 2006, this represented a 7 per cent drop. The demand for places had risen by more than 10 per cent in 2004 and there had been another small increase in 2005.

- **The Institute of Mechanical Engineers:** www.imeche.org.uk
- **The Engineering Council (EC UK):** www.engc.org.uk

Mechanical Engineering	Research quality/5	Entry standards	Graduate prospects %	Overall rating
1 Imperial College	5*B	463	84	100.0
2 Bath	5*A	418	82	99.1
3 Southampton	5*A	411	80	98.2
4 Bristol	5A	444	78	97.1
5 Liverpool	5*A	303	86	95.8
6 Nottingham	5B	421	78	95.0
7 Sheffield	5A	400	74	94.2
8 Cardiff	4A	384	82	94.0
9 Queen's, Belfast	5*B	350	78	93.9
10 Strathclyde	5B	419	72	93.2

Mechanical Engineering cont.

	Research quality/5	Entry standards	Graduate prospects %	Overall rating
=11 Leeds	5*B	359	74	93.1
=11 Loughborough	5B	387	76	93.1
=11 Newcastle	4B	386	82	93.1
=14 Aberdeen	4C	360	86	91.5
=14 Manchester	5A	374	68	91.5
=16 Heriot-Watt	4A	404	70	91.3
=16 Surrey	4B	311	86	91.3
18 University College London	5B	349	70	89.9
19 Hull	4C	239	96	89.7
20 Birmingham	4C	363	78	89.4
21 Sussex	5B		68	88.7
22 Glasgow	5B	382	58	87.7
23 Leicester	5A	285	66	87.4
24 Queen Mary	5B	279	70	87.2
25 Bradford	5B	233	76	87.1
=26 Aston	5C	234	82	86.8
=26 King's College London	5C	315		86.8
28 Edinburgh	4C	389	64	86.4
29 Swansea	4A	281	64	84.8
30 Robert Gordon	3bD	303	82	84.4
31 Brunel	5C	321	60	83.9
32 De Montfort	4C		66	82.8
33 Ulster	4A	209	64	82.1
34 Coventry	3aC	260	70	81.7
35 Portsmouth	4D	255	72	81.5
36 Plymouth	4E		76	81.4
37 Staffordshire	3bA		64	80.4
38 Exeter	4C	313	52	79.9
39 Salford	3aA		56	79.7
40 Kingston	3aC	202	62	77.2
41 Nottingham Trent	3bD	219	68	77.1
42 Oxford Brookes		293	66	76.7
43 Northumbria	3bD	204	68	76.5
44 Hertfordshire	3aD	225	60	76.0
45 Brighton	3bC	212	60	75.7
46 Harper Adams UC		278	64	75.6
47 Greenwich	3aB		48	75.1
48 Manchester Metropolitan	3aA	223	44	75.0
=49 Paisley	2C		60	74.2
=49 West of England	3bD	263	52	74.2
51 Dundee		311	52	73.4
52 City	4D	152		72.5
53 Huddersfield	4E	212	50	71.6

54 Sheffield Hallam	3aF	203	58	71.5
55 UCE Birmingham		205	58	71.0
56 Bolton		173	52	68.1
57 Liverpool John Moores	3aE	114		66.5

Average starting salary:	£20,353	Studying and not employed:	12%
Employed in graduate job:	52%	Unemployed:	8%
Employed in graduate job and studying:	7%	
Employed in non-graduate job:	18%	
Employed in non-graduate job and studying:	2%	

The letters that appear in the Research Quality column indicate the proportion of staff included in the assessment, A showing that almost all staff were included and F showing that hardly any were.

Medicine

Medicine is one of the most tightly-bunched tables, with ten percentage points covering all but one of the schools. Cambridge and Oxford swap places at the top this year, with Imperial jumping from tenth place to third. Both of the leaders have 5* research grades in three of the four research categories, but Cambridge has the higher entry grades. Ironically, neither is among the 19 medical schools registering full employment among their graduates, but the deficit is only one percentage point.

The removal of ageing teaching quality scores helps to relegate Southampton and Liverpool from joint third place to joint ninth. They were among four English universities awarded maximum points for teaching, the others being Manchester and Newcastle. Edinburgh takes over from Glasgow as the leader in Scotland, while Cardiff has the field to itself in Wales.

Medical students were generally satisfied with their teaching in the first national satisfaction survey, but were highly critical of standards of feedback and assessment. Overall, Southampton and Newcastle registered the best scores.

The subject is a notoriously difficult one in which to win a place: Government quotas mean that candidates with three or four As at A level are frequently turned away. The establishment of the first new medical schools for more than 20 years was expected to ease this pressure, but the number of applicants has increased and some of the new courses cater for graduates and other mature students. As a result, entry standards have actually risen this year, with no medical school averaging less than 400 points.

Applications for courses beginning in 2006 were up slightly, following a rise of almost 10 per cent in the previous year. Undergraduates have to be prepared to work long hours, particularly towards the end of the course. The latest survey shows no measurable unemployment, with all but five of the schools reporting every student completing training either finding a graduate job or taking on further study.

- **The British Medical Association:** www.bma.org.uk

Medicine	Research quality/5 Clinical Laboratory	Research quality/5 Community	Research quality/5 Hospital	Research quality/5 Pre-Clinical	Entry standards	Graduate prospects %	Overall rating
1 Cambridge	5*A	5*B	5*B		553	99	100.0
2 Oxford	5*A	5*A	5*A		537	99	99.8

	Research quality/5 Clinical Laboratory	Research quality/5 Community	Research quality/5 Hospital	Research quality/5 Pre-Clinical	Entry standards	Graduate prospects %	Overall rating
3 Imperial College	5*B	5B	5*B	5B	477	100	97.8
4 Edinburgh		4B	5*C		499	100	97.4
5 Manchester	4B	5C	5C	5B	485	100	96.5
=6 Glasgow	5B	4C	5C		479	100	96.3
=6 Nottingham	3aB	3aC	4B	5A	499	100	96.3
8 University College London		4B	5B		462	100	96.2
=9 Southampton	5A	3aB	5B		451	100	95.6
=9 Liverpool	5B	4B	4B		459	100	95.6
11 Newcastle	5*D	5C	5C		471	100	95.5
=12 Sheffield		4B	5C	5C	463	100	95.4
=12 Dundee	5*B	4D	5E		471	100	95.4
14 Leicester	4B	3aB	4B		456	100	94.9
15 St George's Hospital	4A	4B	4A	5A	436	100	94.8
16 Birmingham	5*B	4D	5C	5C	478	99	94.6
=17 Cardiff	5C	4B	4B		442	100	94.5
=17 Bristol	5A	5*C	3aB		442	100	94.5
19 King's College London	5C	4C	4B	5C	435	100	94.0
20 Exeter		3aC	5A		439		93.8
21 Aberdeen	4B	5C	4B		459	99	93.7
22 Queen's, Belfast	4C	5E	3aC		443	100	93.1
23 Queen Mary	3aB	3aB	4B		413	100	92.8
24 Hull-York		5A	3aB		428		91.5
25 St Andrews				5B	459	100	90.6
26 Leeds	5C	4C	4C		441	96	87.7

Average starting salary:	£30,740	Studying and not employed:	9%
Employed in graduate job:	85%	Unemployed:	0%
Employed in graduate job and studying:	5%		
Employed in non-graduate job:	0%	The letters that appear in the Research Quality column indicate the proportion of staff included in the assessment, A showing that almost all staff were included and F showing that hardly any were.	
Employed in non-graduate job and studying:	0%		

Middle Eastern and African Studies

Only seven universities remain in the ranking for Middle Eastern and African Studies after the removal of ageing teaching quality scores. Without them, there are insufficient data to compile overall scores for the rest of last year's complement. Among those dropping out is Cambridge, which occupied third place last year.

Oxford takes over from Birmingham at the top, thanks largely to high entry standards. Birmingham is the only university rated internationally outstanding for research, but it has by far the lowest of the four graduate destinations scores. Durham has moved up to second because it shares with Leeds the best of those scores, with three quarters of the leavers going straight into graduate-level employment or further training.

No universities from outside England are left in the table and there are no new universities, Westminster having dropped out. Only Leeds and Durham fell below Grade 5 in the latest Research Assessment Exercise.

Middle Eastern Studies is the larger of two small subjects, in terms of student numbers. Fewer than 100 students were taking African languages, literature or culture at degree level in 1998, when the teaching assessments were carried out, compared with just over 500 for Middle Eastern subjects. The vast majority – all, in the case of African studies – come with A levels or their equivalent.

Completion rates are good, and a high proportion graduate with a first or 2:1. Student numbers are too low to compile valid employment scores at most of the universities in the table. But, while 9 per cent unemployment is relatively high, the overall figures for positive destinations are better than average for all subjects.

- **The African Studies Association of the UK:** www.asauk.net
- **The British Society for Middle Eastern Studies:** www.dur.ac.uk/brismes
- **The European Association for Middle Eastern Studies:** www.eurames.de

Middle Eastern and African Studies	Research quality/5	Entry standards	Graduate prospects %	Overall rating
1 Oxford	5A	483		100.0
2 Durham	4A	403	75	89.0
3 Birmingham	5*A	333	45	84.4
4 Exeter	5B	328		83.3
5 School of Oriental and African Studies	5B	288	70	82.5
6 Manchester	5B	317		82.4
7 Leeds	4C		75	79.2

Average starting salary:	£18,175	Studying and not employed:	18%
Employed in graduate job:	35%	Unemployed:	9%
Employed in graduate job and studying:	8%		
Employed in non-graduate job:	28%	The letters that appear in the Research Quality column indicate the proportion of staff included in the assessment, A showing that almost all staff were included and F showing that hardly any were.	
Employed in non-graduate job and studying:	1%		

Music

Cambridge takes over from Nottingham at the top of the music ranking, moving up for the second year in a row. It has the highest entry standards, the second best employment record and one of the nine 5* research grades. Second-placed King's College London saw marginally more leavers go straight into graduate-level jobs or further study, but is not one of the research stars. Birmingham, Southampton, Manchester, Newcastle, Royal Holloway and City are the remaining 5* departments.

Edinburgh remains the top university in Scotland, while Cardiff does the same in Wales. Huddersfield is the top new university and is joined by Liverpool Hope in the top

Music cont.

30. As in most subjects, the new universities suffer for their lower entry grade, although selection is as much a matter of musical ability as academic achievement.

The 7 per cent unemployment rate in the latest survey was surprisingly low for a subject in which career prospects are notoriously uncertain, although a third of leavers were in non-graduate jobs six months after graduation.

Nevertheless, music had been growing in popularity as a degree subject until the advent of top-up fees. A 6 per cent increase in 2004 was followed by a 21 per cent rise in the following year. But at the start of 2006 the 19,000 applications represented a drop of 11 per cent. Nearly nine out of ten students come with A levels. There can be considerable variation in the character of courses, from the practical and vocational programmes in conservatoires to the more theoretical.

- **The Incorporated Society of Musicians:** www.ism.org
- **The Musicians Union:** www.musiciansunion.org.uk

Music	Research quality/5	Entry standards	Graduate prospects %	Overall rating
1 Cambridge	5*B	472	80	100.0
2 King's College London	5A	434	82	98.3
=3 Nottingham	5*A	450	72	98.2
=3 Oxford	5*A	450	72	98.2
5 Birmingham	5*B	415	74	95.6
6 York	5A	419	72	94.7
7 Southampton	5*A	371	68	93.3
8 Durham	4A	433	70	92.9
9 Bristol	5A	358	74	92.4
10 Manchester	5*B	426	56	91.1
11 Newcastle	5*A	327	64	90.0
=12 Surrey	3aA	362	78	89.6
=12 Sussex	5A	359	64	89.6
=12 Sheffield	5B	373	66	89.6
=12 Goldsmiths, University of London	5A	323	70	89.6
16 Royal Holloway	5*B	357	62	89.4
=17 Lancaster	4A	329	74	88.9
=17 Queen's, Belfast	5B	324	72	88.9
19 Edinburgh	4B	401	64	88.6
20 City	5*C	322	72	88.0
21 Glasgow	4A	385	60	87.7
=22 Cardiff	5C	355	66	86.5
=22 East Anglia	4B	289	76	86.5
24 Leeds	4C	369	66	85.8
25 Liverpool	4A	300	62	84.2
26 Bangor	5C	289	66	83.3
=27 Keele	4A	307	56	82.8
=27 Huddersfield	5C	255	70	82.8

29 Hull	5B	269	56	81.7
30 Liverpool Hope	3bC	221	86	81.4
31 Oxford Brookes	3aA	267	64	81.1
32 UCE Birmingham	3aE	287	78	80.5
33 Roehampton	3aA	243	62	79.4
34 Anglia Ruskin	3bB		64	79.3
35 Thames Valley	2A	278	68	78.8
36 Salford	4A	266	48	78.6
37 Canterbury Christ Church	3bA	254	64	78.5
38 Liverpool John Moores	2D		72	77.7
39 Ulster	3aD	229	72	77.6
40 Bath Spa	3aC	250	58	76.3
41 Westminster	4D	290	52	76.0
42 Kingston	3bC	213	66	75.4
43 Napier	2C	295	56	75.1
44 De Montfort	4A	237	36	73.9
45 Hertfordshire	3bB	238		73.4
46 Brunel		335	52	73.3
47 Middlesex		235	68	72.9
48 Plymouth	3aE		58	72.4
49 Northampton	3bB	209	50	71.8
50 Wolverhampton		171	70	70.4
51 Derby		281	50	70.1
52 Chichester	1A	264	46	69.9
53 Paisley		296	38	67.5
54 Central Lancashire		227	42	65.3
55 Coventry		206	44	64.8
56 Brighton		270	30	64.0
57 Buckinghamshire Chilterns UC		223	26	60.6

Average starting salary:	£16,172		Studying and not employed:	24%
Employed in graduate job:	31%		Unemployed:	7%
Employed in graduate job and studying:	5%			
Employed in non-graduate job:	28%			
Employed in non-graduate job and studying:	5%			

The letters that appear in the Research Quality column indicate the proportion of staff included in the assessment, A showing that almost all staff were included and F showing that hardly any were.

Nursing

Nursing has been one of the main growth points of higher education since becoming a graduate profession. A number of institutions have taken in nursing and midwifery colleges, sometimes at the expense of their normally high research grades. Indeed, the 51,000 applications placed nursing among the five most popular subjects at the start of 2006. This represented a 15 per cent increase, easily the largest among the major subjects, following increases of more than 20 per cent in each of the two preceding years.

In the last assessments, Surrey registered the first 5* nursing grade, which has propelled the university up the ranking following the removal of ageing teaching quality

Nursing cont.

scores. Its teaching score was one of the lowest in the table, keeping the university outside the top 20 until this year's leap to fourth place.

Nottingham has the highest entry standards, while 13 universities tie for the best destinations score after seeing every leaver go straight into work or further study. Only one of the 52 universities in the ranking reported a success rate of less than 90 per cent, while the unemployment rate nationally is only 1 per cent.

Northumbria and Central Lancashire were the only universities in the UK to be awarded full marks for teaching. But it was Bolton and Teesside that came out best in the first national student satisfaction survey. Thames Valley is the leading new university in our ranking.

Entry scores are more closely bunched than in many tables. Only Nottingham and Edinburgh average more than 350 points and only three of the institutions for which scores are available slipped below 200 points.

Almost two thirds of the students arrive without A levels, but there are more than five applicants to every place, mostly female. A quarter of those who join pre-registration programmes drop out, but the wastage rate is nearer 10 per cent thereafter.

- **The Royal College of Nursing:** www.rcn.org.uk

Nursing	Research quality/5	Entry standards	Graduate prospects %	Overall rating
1 Portsmouth	5A		100	100.0
2 Manchester	5B	338	100	99.2
3 Leeds	4A	326	100	98.4
4 Surrey	5*A	286	98	97.8
5 Nottingham	3aC	376	99	97.5
6 King's College London	4A	326	97	96.7
7 Liverpool	3aB	346	98	96.6
8 Sheffield	5D		100	95.7
9 Thames Valley	3bA		100	95.6
10 Bradford	3bB		100	95.2
11 Southampton	3bA	303	99	95.1
12 Cardiff	4D		100	95.0
13 City	4B	248	99	94.6
14 Northumbria	3aC	279	99	94.1
15 De Montfort	3aD	308	98	93.8
=16 Salford	3aA	245	98	93.5
=16 Glamorgan	3bB		98	93.5
=18 Edinburgh	3aB	369	90	93.0
=18 Huddersfield		306	100	93.0
=20 Anglia Ruskin	3aD	248	100	92.8
=20 West of England	3bC	258	99	92.8
22 Robert Gordon	2F	294	100	92.7
=23 Bangor		293	100	92.5
=23 Glasgow	3aD	349	93	92.5

25 Ulster	4D	249	98	92.3
=26 London South Bank	3aE		99	92.2
=26 Brighton	2F	296	99	92.2
=26 Birmingham	3bD	291	97	92.2
29 Plymouth	3bC	240	99	92.1
30 Central Lancashire	3bE	283	98	91.9
=31 Sheffield Hallam		280	99	91.5
=31 Hull	3aE	248	99	91.5
33 Oxford Brookes	3bF	285	98	91.4
34 Swansea	3bB	233	97	91.3
35 Staffordshire		281	98	91.0
36 Hertfordshire	4D	226	97	90.9
37 Queen Margaret College		290	97	90.8
38 Teesside		255	99	90.7
39 Wolverhampton		254	99	90.6
40 Glasgow Caledonian	3aE	300	94	90.5
=41 Liverpool John Moores	3aC	149	100	90.2
=41 Canterbury Christ Church		224	100	90.2
=43 UCE Birmingham	2E	253	97	90.0
=43 Kingston/St George's Hospital	3aA	185		90.0
45 Keele	2E	277		89.8
46 Leeds Metropolitan	3bE	263	95	89.5
47 Coventry		223	98	89.0
48 Northampton		253	95	88.4
49 Greenwich		245	95	88.1
50 Bournemouth	3bF	267	90	86.3
51 Middlesex	3aF	192	90	83.8
52 Luton		214	88	83.2

Average starting salary:	£20,174		Studying and not employed:	1%
Employed in graduate job:	89%		Unemployed:	1%
Employed in graduate job and studying:	7%			
Employed in non-graduate job:	2%			
Employed in non-graduate job and studying:	0%			

The letters that appear in the Research Quality column indicate the proportion of staff included in the assessment, A showing that almost all staff were included and F showing that hardly any were.

Other Subjects Allied to Medicine

The "allied to medicine" category covers audiology, complementary therapies, counselling, health services management, health sciences, nutrition, occupational therapy, optometry, ophthalmology, orthoptics, osteopathy, physiotherapy, podiatry, radiography and speech therapy. Traditional universities monopolise the top ten, but big names such as Durham and Aberdeen find themselves outside the top 40.

Cardiff holds on to top place, with Manchester rising from fourth to become the nearest challenger. The top two are the only universities rated internationally outstanding for research, but Cardiff entered more of its academics for assessment and has a marginally better destinations score. Manchester is one of only four universities to

Other Subjects Allied to Medicine cont.

average 400 points at entry, although it is well behind Cambridge on 550 points. Cambridge did not enter the Research Assessment Exercise in this field and is restricted to equal eighteenth place as a result.

Three universities – Leeds, Bangor and London South Bank – saw every leaver find a graduate job or further study within six months of graduation. Oddly, none of them entered the last RAE either so, while Leeds manages fourteenth place, neither Bangor nor South Bank make the top 40.

Fourth-placed Strathclyde remains the top university in Scotland, just ahead of Queen Margaret University College, while UWIC has the best record in Wales. Queen Margaret has the highest position in the table outside the old universities, but Brighton, Glasgow Caledonian, Portsmouth and Anglia Ruskin all make the top 20.

The Open University and Kent had the best results in the first national student satisfaction survey.

Across the whole range of subjects, almost half of the students arrive without A levels. Applications were up by nearly 9 per cent at the start of 2006. The demand for places is highest on professional courses such as optometry and physiotherapy, where graduate employment prospects are excellent. Nationally, only 3 per cent of graduates were unemployed in the last survey – one of the lowest figures in any set of subjects. Three quarters of those completing courses went straight into graduate jobs.

- **The Chartered Society of Physiotherapists:** www.csp.org.uk
- **The British Association/The College of Occupational Therapists:** www.cot.co.uk
- **The General Chiropractic Council:** www.gcc-uk.org
- **The General Optical Council:** www.optical.org
- **The General Osteopathic Council:** www.osteopathy.org.uk
- **NHS Careers:** www.nhscareers.nhs.uk
- **The Royal College of Speech and Language Therapists:** www.rcslt.org
- **The Society of Chiropodists and Podiatrists:** www.feetforlife.org
- **The Society of Radiographers:** www.sor.org
- **The Health Professions Council:** www.hpc-uk.org

Other Subjects Allied to Medicine	Research quality/5	Entry standards	Graduate prospects %	Overall rating
1 Cardiff	5*A	372	99	100.0
2 Manchester	5*B	400	97	98.9
3 Bradford	5B	377	96	94.4
4 Strathclyde	5A	393	84	93.4
5 Queen Margaret College	4A	375	93	92.2
6 Aston	5C	382	98	92.1
=7 Newcastle	5A	394	79	91.8
=7 City	5C	372	99	91.8
9 University College London	5C	356	94	89.1
10 King's College London	4B	383	83	87.8
11 Brighton	5C	338	93	87.6

12 Glasgow Caledonian	4C	377	91	87.3
13 Liverpool	3aB	343	97	87.1
14 York	5A	375	68	87.0
15 Portsmouth	5A	267	89	86.8
16 Leeds	5D		100	86.6
17 Anglia Ruskin	3bA	398	89	86.4
=18 Southampton	3aA	357	87	86.0
=18 Cambridge		550	84	86.0
20 East Anglia	3bA	349	97	85.8
=21 Nottingham	3aC	376	89	84.5
=21 Robert Gordon	3bC	378	95	84.5
23 Sheffield	4B	370	70	82.7
24 Sheffield Hallam	4D	352	89	82.0
25 West of England	3aB	304	89	81.9
26 Salford	3aA	294	82	80.3
27 Reading		392	96	79.6
28 Teesside	3aC	264	93	78.4
=29 Brunel	3aE	315	95	77.5
=29 Keele		341	100	77.5
31 Plymouth	3bC		89	77.1
32 Ulster	4F	332	94	76.2
33 St George's Hospital	3aE	308	92	76.0
34 Nottingham Trent	5D	261	83	75.5
35 Oxford Brookes		329	95	75.1
36 Hull	4D	257	87	75.0
37 Northampton	2C	251	98	74.9
38 Birmingham		385	83	74.8
39 Coventry	3aE	291	91	74.6
40 UWIC, Cardiff	3bD	271	91	74.2
41 Queen Mary		345	88	73.9
42 Leeds Metropolitan	3aE	305	83	72.9
43 Aberdeen		366	80	72.6
44 Hertfordshire	3bE	273	89	71.8
45 Bangor		247	100	71.4
46 Canterbury Christ Church	2C	193	98	71.1
47 Liverpool John Moores	4A	162	70	70.6
=48 De Montfort	4C	228	69	70.3
=48 Kent		286	89	70.3
50 Central Lancashire	3bA	301	59	70.2
51 Derby		282	87	69.3
52 Chester	3aB	246	62	69.2
53 Northumbria		259	89	68.5
54 UCE Birmingham		262	87	68.0
55 East London	2C	276	71	67.7
56 Manchester Metropolitan	3bD	229	79	67.5
57 Durham		349	67	67.2
58 Kingston	3aC	196	72	67.0

	Research quality/5	Entry standards	Graduate prospects %	Overall rating
59 Westminster	3aC	184	72	66.3
60 Wolverhampton	3aC	215	65	65.9
61 London South Bank		149	100	64.9
62 Napier	4D	255	56	64.7
63 Greenwich	3aA	180	50	62.2
64 Middlesex		233	63	58.2
65 Lincoln		184	70	57.3
66 Liverpool Hope		171	59	52.8
67 Roehampton	2F		54	51.1
68 Worcester		247	37	50.6
69 Bath Spa	2E		35	43.6

Average starting salary:	£17,903	Studying and not employed:	7%
Employed in graduate job:	71%	Unemployed:	3%
Employed in graduate job and studying:	8%		
Employed in non-graduate job:	9%	The letters that appear in the Research Quality column indicate the proportion of staff included in the assessment, A showing that almost all staff were included and F showing that hardly any were.	
Employed in non-graduate job and studying:	1%		

Pharmacology and Pharmacy

Cambridge retains top spot in the pharmacology and pharmacy ranking with by far the highest entrance standards, although it is not one of the universities rated internationally outstanding for research. Neither is second-placed Nottingham, although it has among the highest scores for both entrance and destinations. There were only two 5* research grades in pharmacy, which went to Bath and Manchester, in third and fourth place respectively. The three in pharmacology are much more widely spread through the table: University College London is 11th, Newcastle 21st and Dundee 30th and last, largely because of low graduate employment.

Fifth-placed Cardiff is the only Welsh university in the table, while Strathclyde remains the leader in Scotland. Portsmouth is still the top new university, although it has dropped out of the top ten since the removal of ageing teaching quality grades. Brighton, Robert Gordon, Sunderland and Liverpool John Moores are the other former polytechnics in the top 20.

Departments in England are evenly split between those specialising in pharmacy and pharmacology. Only four cover both. Since 1997, pharmacy degrees have been converted to the four-year MPharm, whereas pharmacology is available either as a three-year BSc or as an extended course. Applications were up by over 20 per cent in 2005 and by another 9.6 per cent at the start of 2006.

Career prospects are excellent, especially in pharmacy, with only 3 per cent unemployment across both subjects in the latest survey. Only medicine, dentistry, nursing and veterinary medicine had a higher proportion of "positive destinations". There was full employment among the graduates of Liverpool John Moores and Robert

Gordon, which managed this feat for the fourth year in a row, and only two universities dropped below a success rate of 60 per cent.

- **The British Pharmacological Society:** www.bps.ac.uk
- **The Royal Pharmaceutical Society of Great Britain:** www.rpsgb.org.uk
- **The National Pharmaceutical Association:** http://npa.co.uk

Pharmacology and Pharmacy	Research quality/5 Pharmacology	Research quality/5 Pharmacy	Entry standards	Graduate prospects %	Overall rating
1 Cambridge	5A		550	84	100.0
2 Nottingham		5A	439	99	97.7
3 Bath		5*A	393	98	96.9
4 Manchester		5*B	416	91	94.7
5 Cardiff		5A	382	96	93.6
=6 Strathclyde		5B	402	91	91.9
=6 Queen's, Belfast		4B	396	99	91.9
8 School of Pharmacy		5A	334	99	91.6
9 King's College London		5B	369	91	90.0
10 Bristol	4A		378	85	88.1
11 University College London	5*A		363	72	88.0
=12 Portsmouth	5A		273	93	86.4
=12 Aston		3aC	365	98	86.4
14 Brighton	5C		318	95	85.9
15 Robert Gordon	3bC		371	100	85.7
=16 Bradford		4B	288	94	84.2
=16 Sunderland		3aB	311	96	84.2
18 Liverpool	5A		301	75	83.1
19 Leeds	5B		325	74	82.8
20 Liverpool John Moores			301	100	77.3
21 Newcastle	5*D		388	80	76.9
22 Edinburgh	4A			55	74.4
23 Nottingham Trent	5D		218	80	73.3
24 De Montfort		4C	272	89	72.6
25 Greenwich	4A			44	69.8
26 Glasgow			320	67	69.4
27 Southampton			349	60	69.2
28 Kingston	3aC		185	71	68.5
29 Hertfordshire	3aC		217	63	68.2
30 Dundee	5*B		315	59	66.9

Average starting salary:	£16,081	Studying and not employed:	10%
Employed in graduate job:	61%	Unemployed:	3%
Employed in graduate job and studying:	19%		
Employed in non-graduate job:	6%	The letters that appear in the Research Quality column indicate the proportion of staff included in the assessment, A showing that almost all staff were included and F showing that hardly any were.	
Employed in non-graduate job and studying:	1%		

Philosophy

Cambridge lost top place in the philosophy ranking for the first time last year and Oxford remains ahead, thanks to the highest entrance qualifications and graduate employment in the table. The top four are all rated internationally outstanding at research, although Oxford entered fewer academics for assessment than the other three. The other research star, Edinburgh, entered a smaller proportion still.

Entry standards are high, even without Oxford's average of 522 points. Another eleven universities averaged more than 400 points and none of the 43 in the ranking dropped below 200. The subject's popularity has been growing. Although applications were down by slightly more than the average for all subjects at the start of 2006, there had been a 14 per cent increase in the previous year.

Sixth-placed St Andrews is the highest-ranked university in Scotland, while Lampeter just pips Cardiff to the leadership in Wales. Brighton was by far the top new university last year, with a grade 5 for research to add to full marks for teaching quality. But it has dropped out of the ranking since the removal of all teaching quality scores because insufficient data remain to compile an overall score. Central Lancashire is now the only new university in the top 30.

An 8 per cent unemployment rate is only just below the average for all subjects, but more than 40 per cent of all philosophers start work in low-level jobs. Barely half of the universities for which employment scores could be compiled saw more than 50 per cent of the leavers go straight into graduate jobs or further study. Only Cambridge and Aberdeen recorded "positive destinations" for more than 70 per cent of graduates.

- **The Philosophical Society of England:**
  http://atschool.eduweb.co.uk/cite/staff/philosopher/philsocindex.htm

Philosophy	Research quality/5	Entry standards	Graduate prospects %	Overall rating
1 Oxford	5*B	522	76	100.0
2 Cambridge	5*A	498	68	98.7
3 London School of Economics	5*A	459	66	96.7
4 King's College London	5*A	417	64	94.5
5 Durham	5B	458	68	93.3
6 St Andrews	5A	431	62	92.2
7 Bristol	5A	398	66	91.9
8 University College London	5B	407	70	91.8
9 Warwick	5B	437	56	89.4
10 York	5B	448	54	89.3
11 Sheffield	5A	424	50	88.8
12 Nottingham	5B	443	52	88.6
13 Edinburgh	5*C	413	56	87.6
14 Stirling	5B	315	66	87.2
15 Southampton	4A	379	56	86.3
16 Sussex	5B	364	52	85.5

17 Aberdeen	3aB	321	72	84.8
18 Essex	5B	308	56	84.3
19 Leeds	5C	397	52	84.2
20 Manchester	4B	395	50	84.1
21 Liverpool	4A	342	50	83.3
22 Kent	4C	298	66	82.3
23 Central Lancashire	3bA		64	82.1
24 Dundee	3aB	329	60	82.0
25 East Anglia	5B	346	40	81.7
=26 Bradford	4B	253	60	81.1
=26 Birmingham	4C	385	48	81.1
28 Reading	5B	343	38	81.0
29 Keele	3aB	318	52	79.5
=30 Hull	4B	273	50	79.3
=30 Glasgow	4C	380	42	79.3
32 Middlesex	5C		44	78.8
33 Lampeter	3aA		44	77.9
34 Cardiff	3aC	357	42	76.7
35 Lancaster	3aB	332	36	75.9
36 Hertfordshire	4B	218	44	75.5
37 Queen's, Belfast	3aD	320	46	74.4
38 Manchester Metropolitan	3aC	249	42	72.5
39 Greenwich	3bC	214	50	71.5
40 Exeter		365	38	69.5
41 Staffordshire	3aC		28	67.6
42 Wolverhampton		244	36	64.3
43 Northampton		239	32	63.0

Average starting salary:	£18,576	Studying and not employed:	25%
Employed in graduate job:	23%	Unemployed:	8%
Employed in graduate job and studying:	4%		
Employed in non-graduate job:	35%		
Employed in non-graduate job and studying:	6%		

The letters that appear in the Research Quality column indicate the proportion of staff included in the assessment, A showing that almost all staff were included and F showing that hardly any were.

Physics and Astronomy

Cambridge takes over from Oxford at the top of the ranking for physics and astronomy with the highest proportion of graduates (86 per cent) starting work or further study within six month of completing the course. Oxford is a single point ahead of Cambridge on average entry scores, both exceeding the equivalent of four As at A level and another A at AS level. Durham, which was top two years ago, also averages more than 500 points per entrant, but is pipped to third place by Imperial College London, which has a better research grade.

All the top three are rated internationally outstanding at research, as are Southampton, in thirteenth place, and Lancaster, which is restricted to twenth-sixth by the lowest graduate prospects score in the entire table. Surrey and Royal Holloway are the nearest challengers to Cambridge on graduate employment rates.

Physics and Astronomy cont.

Glasgow remains ahead of St Andrews as the top university in Scotland, while Cardiff has overtaken Swansea in Wales. Only two new universities appear among the 41 in the top table: Hertfordshire at 34th and Nottingham Trent , which has dropped to 41st after losing the benefit of a perfect teaching quality score.

In spite of the dearth of physicists going into teaching, the subjects command high entry grades. Only four subjects averaged more than the 405 points recorded by physics and astronomy, and only five universities in this year's table averaged less than 300 points. Applications had been declining, but 2005 saw a 12 per cent increase and there was another rise at the start of 2006. The total of almost 17,000 remained ahead of apparently more fashionable subjects such as marketing and journalism.

The profile of undergraduates is among the most traditional: only one in five is female and a similar proportion arrive without A levels or their equivalent. About 5 per cent transfer to other courses or drop out, usually at the end of the first year, but over half of those who remain get firsts or 2:1s. The 9 per cent unemployment rate is above average for all subjects, but two thirds find graduate jobs or go on to higher-level courses.

- **The Institute of Physics:** www.iop.org
- **The Association for Astronomy Education:** www.aae.org.uk

Physics and Astronomy	Research quality/5	Entry standards	Graduate prospects %	Overall rating
1 Cambridge	5*A	550	84	100.0
2 Oxford	5*A	551	78	98.5
3 Imperial College	5*A	495	74	95.6
4 Durham	5A	511	66	91.7
5 Warwick	5A	469	70	91.4
6 Bristol	5A	419	76	91.2
7 Queen's, Belfast	5A	380	80	91.0
8 Leeds	5A	395	76	90.4
9 Surrey	5A	313	82	89.2
10 Royal Holloway	5B	352	82	89.0
11 Nottingham	5A	457	62	88.9
12 Glasgow	5B	388	76	88.7
13 Southampton	5*B	401	64	88.1
=14 Manchester	5A	443	60	87.9
=14 University College London	5B	397	72	87.9
=14 St Andrews	5B	410	70	87.9
=17 Exeter	5A	408	64	87.8
=17 Cardiff	5A	330	74	87.8
19 Sheffield	5B	384	68	86.5
20 Leicester	5A	395	60	86.4
21 Birmingham	5B	393	66	86.3
22 Liverpool	5A	344	64	85.7
23 Swansea	5A	352	62	85.4

24 York	4B	407	68	85.2
25 Edinburgh	5B	425	56	84.8
=26 Lancaster	5*A	359	44	83.4
=26 Strathclyde	4A	331	66	83.4
28 Queen Mary	5B	270	70	83.2
29 Bath	4A	419	52	82.7
30 Sussex	5A	374	48	82.6
31 King's College London	4B	338	66	82.4
32 Heriot-Watt	4A	351	58	82.0
33 Reading	4B	338	60	80.8
34 Hertfordshire	4B	257	70	80.7
35 Aberystwyth	4A	303	52	78.9
36 Kent	3aC	328	66	78.2
37 Hull	4C	258	64	77.0
38 Salford	4A	211	56	76.8
39 Keele	3aB	302		75.9
40 Loughborough	4C	310	50	75.2
41 Nottingham Trent	3aD	237	46	68.1

Average starting salary:	£19,339	Studying and not employed:	36%
Employed in graduate job:	24%	Unemployed:	9%
Employed in graduate job and studying:	7%		
Employed in non-graduate job:	22%		
Employed in non-graduate job and studying:	2%		

The letters that appear in the Research Quality column indicate the proportion of staff included in the assessment, A showing that almost all staff were included and F showing that hardly any were.

Politics

Politics has been enjoying a boom as a degree subject. After four consecutive years of substantial increases, applications held steady at the start of 2006, when other social sciences were struggling to recruit students. Entry scores have been rising as a result, with this year's average up significantly on those in the last edition of the *Guide*. Eleven universities average over 400 points and only two (just) less than 200 points.

Oxford holds onto top place with by far the highest entry scores and one of the five 5* research grades, although it entered a lower proportion of academics for assessment than Aberystwyth, Essex, King's College London or Sheffield. Cambridge, in third place, has the best record for graduate destinations, just ahead of the second-placed London School of Economics, which has shot up the table from eighteenth last year.

St Andrews remains well clear of its rivals in Scotland, while Cardiff pips Aberystwyth for that honour in Wales. No new university appears in the top 40, although Oxford Brookes is not far away. However, Huddersfield produced the best results in the first national student satisfaction survey, with Loughborough, Hull and the Open University not far behind.

Employment prospects varied widely in this ranking. While a handful of universities saw three quarters of their graduates go straight into employment or further study, 19 were below the 50 per cent mark and at four universities the success rate fell below a third. Nationally, the 7 per cent of leavers out of work after six months is on the average

Politics cont.

for all subjects, but more than a third were in low-level employment.

- **The Political Studies Association:** www.psa.ac.uk
- **The Politics Association Online:** www.politicsassociation.com

Politics	Research quality/5	Entry standards	Graduate prospects %	Overall rating
1 Oxford	5*B	515	76	100.0
2 London School of Economics	5A	462	84	99.2
3 Cambridge	4A	489	86	98.2
4 Bristol	5A	389	78	94.6
5 York	5A	451	68	94.5
6 Warwick	5B	440	72	93.4
7 King's College London	5*A	390	62	93.0
8 Bath	5A	358	76	92.7
=9 Sheffield	5*A	420	54	92.1
=9 St Andrews	5A	470	56	92.1
11 Durham	4C	461	72	89.5
12 Newcastle	5B	369	68	89.3
13 School of Asian Studies	4B	341	80	89.0
14 Nottingham	4A	419	62	88.9
=15 Cardiff	5A	364	60	88.7
=15 Exeter	5B	379	64	88.7
17 Aberystwyth	5*A	321	56	88.5
18 Birmingham	5B	371	64	88.3
19 Hull	5A	304	66	87.8
20 Essex	5*A	315	52	87.2
21 Leeds	4B	371	68	87.0
22 Queen's, Belfast	5A	332	58	86.8
23 Queen Mary	4A	336	64	85.9
24 Edinburgh	4C	418	64	85.5
25 Manchester	5B	413	46	85.3
26 Sussex	4A	349	58	84.9
=27 Bradford	5B	301	60	84.3
=27 Glasgow	5B	389	46	84.3
29 Loughborough	5B	288	60	83.8
30 Keele	5A	300	50	83.4
31 Aberdeen	4A	334	54	83.2
32 Royal Holloway	4B	286	66	82.9
33 University College London	3aA	369		82.8
=34 Liverpool	4A	317	54	82.5
=34 Salford	5A	240	56	82.5
36 Reading	5B	330	48	82.4
37 Strathclyde	5B	362	42	82.1

38 Southampton	4B	364	50	81.9
39 Lancaster	4B	343	48	80.5
40 Kent	3aB	279	66	80.2
41 East Anglia	4B	352	44	79.8
42 Oxford Brookes	3aA	275	60	79.6
43 Ulster	3aB	275	62	79.0
44 Leicester	3aB	305	56	78.7
45 Brunel	4B	274	50	78.2
46 Swansea	3aB	265	60	78.0
47 De Montfort	5B	186	54	77.9
48 Stirling	3aB	321	50	77.7
49 Portsmouth	5C	231	56	77.4
50 Kingston	4A	221	48	76.8
51 Dundee	4B	299	38	76.0
=52 West of England	4C	247	50	74.6
=52 London South Bank	4B	239	42	74.6
=54 Plymouth	3aC	253	48	72.4
=54 Leeds Metropolitan	3aA	229	40	72.4
56 Nottingham Trent	3aC	258	46	72.1
57 Coventry	4C	197	48	72.0
58 UCE Birmingham	3aC	228	50	71.9
59 Manchester Metropolitan	3aC	229	48	71.4
60 Liverpool John Moores	3aD	205	58	70.9
61 Robert Gordon	3aA	267	28	70.8
62 Northumbria	3aD	225	50	69.6
63 Aston		290	58	69.3
64 Westminster	4C	213	32	68.4
65 Greenwich		216	62	67.2
66 Staffordshire	3aC		36	67.1
67 Goldsmiths, University of London		262	54	67.0
68 Huddersfield	3aC	215	28	65.5
69 Lincoln		219	50	64.2
70 Wolverhampton	3aD	212	24	62.1

Average starting salary:	£18,384	Studying and not employed:	21%
Employed in graduate job:	30%	Unemployed:	7%
Employed in graduate job and studying:	5%		
Employed in non-graduate job:	32%	The letters that appear in the Research Quality column indicate the proportion of staff included in the assessment, A showing that almost all staff were included and F showing that hardly any were.	
Employed in non-graduate job and studying:	5%		

Psychology

Only law and medicine had attracted more applications than psychology at the start of 2006, but a 9 per cent increase in 2005 had turned into a 6 per cent decline for the subject that was the phenomenon of the 1990s. Most undergraduate programmes are accredited by the British Psychological Society, which ensures that key topics are

Psychology cont.

covered, but the clinical and biological content of courses still varies considerably. Some universities require maths and/or biology A levels among an average of at least three Bs, but others are much less demanding. The contrast is obvious in the ranking, with 20 universities averaging more than 400 points but three dipping below 200 points.

Cambridge has lengthened its lead at the top of the table, with by far the highest entrance and destinations scores, as well as a 5* research grade. All the top five are considered internationally outstanding for research, as are York, Cardiff, Newcastle, Glasgow, Reading, Birmingham and Bangor. Second-placed Oxford is the only university to approach Cambridge's average entry grades, while Bath, in seventh place, comes closest on graduate destinations.

Cardiff is the top university in Wales and St Andrews is the leader in Scotland. Abertay is the only new university in the top 40, although Plymouth has a grade 5 research rating. East Anglia University College London and the Open University produced the best results in the first national student satisfaction survey.

Employment scores are more bunched than in many other tables, with 21 universities averaging more than 400 points and several more in the 390s. Only three of the ninety-two universities in the table average less than 200 points. Nationally, the unemployment rate is below average for all subjects, but nearly half of all leavers are either in low-level jobs or without work six months after graduation.

- **The British Psychological Society:** www.bps.org.uk

Psychology	Research quality/5	Entry standards	Graduate prospects %	Overall rating
1 Cambridge	5*A	550	84	100.0
2 Oxford	5*A	497	68	94.0
3 University College London	5*B	434	75	92.7
4 Bristol	5*A	414	73	92.5
5 St Andrews	5*A	437	68	92.0
6 Nottingham	5A	451	67	90.8
7 Bath	5B	403	76	90.7
8 York	5*A	475	56	90.0
9 Cardiff	5*A	429	60	89.6
10 Durham	5A	427	61	88.4
11 Newcastle	5*C	441	62	87.7
12 Royal Holloway	5A	394	61	87.3
13 Sheffield	5A	442	53	86.7
14 Exeter	5B	400	61	86.6
15 Warwick	5B	431	57	86.5
16 Surrey	5A	356	62	86.3
17 Southampton	5A	377	59	86.2
=18 Sussex	5A	365	60	86.0
=18 Glasgow	5*C	390	62	86.0
20 Reading	5*B	399	54	85.9
21 Edinburgh	5C	433	59	85.6

22	Loughborough	4B	397	62	85.5
23	Manchester	5B	437	52	85.4
24	Leeds	5C	422	58	85.0
25	Kent	4B	355	65	84.9
26	Birmingham	5*C	403	56	84.8
27	Aberdeen	4B	320	67	84.3
28	Bangor	5*A	312	54	84.1
29	Queen's, Belfast	4A	359	58	83.9
=30	Essex	5A	335	55	83.7
=30	Lancaster	5A	398	47	83.7
32	Swansea	4A	317	62	83.6
33	Aston	5C	328	63	83.2
=34	Dundee	4B	316	62	82.8
=34	Goldsmiths, University of London	4A	300	61	82.8
36	Liverpool	4C	390	56	82.4
37	Abertay	3bB		66	82.2
38	Strathclyde	4B	362	52	81.7
39	City	4A	315	55	81.6
40	Leicester	4B	362	51	81.4
41	Oxford Brookes	3aC	316	64	81.1
42	Hull	3aC	321	62	80.7
43	Stirling	5A	345	42	80.6
44	Brunel	4B	307	53	80.1
45	Thames Valley	1C		71	80.0
46	Keele	4B	326	50	79.9
=47	Plymouth	5C	306	47	78.2
=47	London South Bank	4B	216	57	78.2
=49	Northumbria	4D	323	53	77.9
=49	Portsmouth	3aD	318	56	77.9
51	Nottingham Trent	3aC	332	48	77.3
52	Liverpool Hope	2D	231	67	76.5
53	Hertfordshire	4B	239	47	76.2
54	Greenwich	3bC	212	61	75.8
55	Southampton Solent	2D	240	61	75.2
56	Westminster	3aD	252	53	74.9
57	Lincoln	2D	291	53	74.7
58	De Montfort	3aD	249	51	74.2
59	Derby	3aC	241	47	74.1
60	Manchester Metropolitan	3aD	303	43	73.9
=61	Sheffield Hallam	3bC	325	38	73.4
=61	Central Lancashire	3aE	282	48	73.4
63	Middlesex	3aD	198	54	73.3
64	Staffordshire	3aD	298	41	73.2
=65	Bournemouth		268	54	73.0
=65	Leeds Metropolitan		292	51	73.0
=67	Worcester	2D	219	54	72.6
=67	Ulster	3aD	248	45	72.6

Psychology cont.

	Research quality/5	Entry standards	Graduate prospects %	Overall rating
=67 Winchester	2B	274	43	72.6
70 Sunderland	3bD	243	48	72.5
71 Teesside		236	56	72.4
72 Wolverhampton	3bD	252	45	72.0
73 Liverpool John Moores		228	54	71.6
=74 East London	3aC	178	44	71.2
=74 Luton	2E	200	53	71.2
=76 Chester		261	48	71.1
=76 Roehampton	3aE	229	46	71.1
78 Gloucestershire		236	50	70.8
79 Bradford		236	49	70.6
80 Glasgow Caledonian	4E	315	31	70.4
81 Coventry	2D	261	40	70.3
82 Salford		267	43	70.0
=83 Bolton	3bD	205	43	69.9
=83 UWIC, Cardiff		256	44	69.9
85 Paisley	3aC	242	30	69.5
86 Kingston		208	48	69.4
=87 Huddersfield		245	42	69.0
=87 Canterbury Christ Church		220	45	69.0
89 Queen Margaret College		290	36	68.9
90 West of England		280	36	68.6
91 Northampton		220	38	67.1
92 Buckinghamshire Chilterns UC		188	34	65.0

Average starting salary:	£16,186	Studying and not employed:	17%
Employed in graduate job:	28%	Unemployed:	6%
Employed in graduate job and studying:	6%		
Employed in non-graduate job:	38%	The letters that appear in the Research Quality column indicate the proportion of staff included in the assessment, A showing that almost all staff were included and F showing that hardly any were.	
Employed in non-graduate job and studying:	5%		

Russian and Eastern European Languages

Sheffield had a commanding lead last year in Russian and Eastern European languages, but has dropped four places after losing the benefit of the only perfect score for teaching quality – all teaching scores have been removed this year because of their age. Despite not being the leader in any of the three measures, Cambridge moves up from second place. Second-placed St Andrews has the best graduate employment record, while Oxford, in third, has slightly higher average entry grades than Cambridge.

Unlike the top two, Birmingham, Sheffield, Oxford and Bristol were all rated internationally outstanding for research. Only two new universities feature in the ranking. Portsmouth has a grade 5 research rating, but Northumbria is narrowly ahead by virtue of a better destinations score.

Entry standards are high: half of the universities in the table average over 400 points and only one is under 300. Fewer than 700 students take Russian at degree level, and fewer than half of the universities assessed in England offer Russian as a single-honours degree. Most of the students were learning the language *ab initio*, and there was a high dropout rate from some universities, despite an "excellent rapport" between staff and students. The small numbers make for exaggerated swings in employment prospects: no subject has a higher unemployment rate in this year's *Guide*, but last year's figure was exactly on the average. Almost two thirds were in graduate jobs or postgraduate study within six months of completing courses in 2004.

- **CILT – The National Centre for Languages:** www.cilt.org.uk
- **The Institute of Translation and Interpreting:** www.iti.org.uk

Russian and East European Languages	Research quality/5	Entry standards	Graduate prospects %	Overall rating
1 Cambridge	5A	497	75	100.0
2 St Andrews	4A	445	80	95.7
3 Oxford	5*B	502	55	95.3
4 Bristol	5*A	383	75	95.1
5 Sheffield	5*A	401	65	93.4
6 Nottingham	5A	413	70	93.2
7 Birmingham	5*B	395	70	92.7
8 University College London	5A	396	70	92.1
9 Edinburgh	4A	432	65	90.6
10 Heriot-Watt	4B	469	50	87.6
11 Strathclyde	3aA	436	55	85.7
12 Glasgow	4B	425	45	83.3
13 Leeds	4B	348	55	81.2
14 Bath	5A	328	45	80.8
15 Sussex	4D	361		74.3
16 Northumbria	3bE		60	73.0
17 Portsmouth	5D	280	40	69.3
18 Reading		321	30	62.1

Average starting salary:	£18,051	Studying and not employed:	19%
Employed in graduate job:	40%	Unemployed:	14%
Employed in graduate job and studying:	3%		
Employed in non-graduate job:	24%	The letters that appear in the Research Quality column indicate the proportion of staff included in the assessment, A showing that almost all staff were included and F showing that hardly any were.	
Employed in non-graduate job and studying:	1%		

Social Policy

Scores at the top of the social policy ranking are so tightly bunched that Manchester can leap eight places to the top by virtue of a big improvement in graduate destinations – the 80 per cent of leavers going straight into graduate-level jobs or further study represented

Social Policy cont.

the year's best performance. The London School of Economics, last year's leader, has the highest entry standards, as well as one of the three 5* research grades, and is only a fraction behind. The other research stars are Kent, in fifth place, and Loughborough, two places lower.

Glasgow is the top university in Scotland, Cardiff the leader in Wales. There are eleven new universities in the table, compared with last year's six. Central Lancashire, which shares with Bristol the distinction of the second-best destinations score, is the leading former polytechnic.

Entry standards are comparatively low, with no university averaging 400 points. Although two thirds of entrants come with A levels or their equivalent, some courses cater very largely for mature students. Not all institutions have entry scores but, of those that do, four average less than 200 points. However, the proportion of students getting firsts or 2:1s is also low.

Demand for places in social policy had been dropping, but there was a spectacular recovery in 2005, when applications rose by 21 per cent. The revival did not survive the imminent introduction of top-up fees, with applications down by 6 per cent at the start of 2006. Graduate unemployment is on the average for all subjects, but only about half of all leavers go straight into graduate jobs or postgraduate study.

• **The British Sociological Association:** www.britsoc.co.uk

Social Policy	Research quality/5	Entry standards	Graduate prospects %	Overall rating
1 Manchester	5B	370	80	100.0
2 London School of Economics	5*A	387	65	99.7
3 Bristol	5A	322	75	98.0
4 Goldsmiths, University of London	4A		70	95.9
5 Kent	5*A	269	60	93.9
6 Nottingham	4A	362	60	93.7
7 Loughborough	5*A	298	55	93.6
=8 York	5A	299	60	93.2
=8 Glasgow	4B	375	60	93.2
10 Bath	5B	319	60	92.7
11 Cardiff	5A	344	50	92.2
12 Birmingham	4C	311	70	91.8
13 Sheffield	5B	355	50	91.4
14 Leeds	5A	317	50	91.2
15 Hull	4B	234	70	90.5
16 Newcastle	4B	338	55	90.4
17 Queen's, Belfast	5A	295	50	90.3
18 Central Lancashire	3aD		75	89.6
19 Bangor	3aA		60	89.1
20 Keele	5B		50	88.8
21 Liverpool	4B		55	88.3
22 Stirling	5B		45	86.8

23 London South Bank	4B		50	86.3
24 Southampton	5A	326	30	86.1
25 Nottingham Trent	3aB	205	60	85.1
=26 Edinburgh	4B		45	84.3
=26 Ulster	4C	219	55	84.3
28 Portsmouth	3aB	216	55	84.2
29 Sheffield Hallam	3aC	281	50	84.0
30 Brighton	3bC	240	60	83.8
31 Swansea	3aB	192	55	83.3
32 Salford	3aA	205	45	81.9
=33 Lincoln	3aD	209	50	79.7
=33 Plymouth	4D	255	40	79.7
35 Anglia Ruskin	3aD		50	79.6
36 Bolton	2B	116	60	78.5
37 Roehampton		151	65	78.0
38 Northampton		179	50	75.0
39 Wolverhampton		162	40	71.7

Average starting salary:	£17,862	Studying and not employed:	13%
Employed in graduate job:	37%	Unemployed:	7%
Employed in graduate job and studying:	5%		
Employed in non-graduate job:	34%		
Employed in non-graduate job and studying:	3%		

The letters that appear in the Research Quality column indicate the proportion of staff included in the assessment, A showing that almost all staff were included and F showing that hardly any were.

Social Work

Social work used to be unusual for having more students taking certificate or diploma courses than degrees, but the diploma has now been withdrawn in the quest for an all-graduate profession. The new degree attracted almost double the number of applicants its predecessor managed when it was introduced in 2004, and then produced the biggest increase of any subject (73 per cent) the following year. Another 7 per cent increase at the start of 2006 placed social work among the ten most popular subjects. Extra places at undergraduate level have brought nine more universities into the table and should ensure that entry requirements remain comparable. Up to now, almost two thirds of all students have been selected on qualities or qualifications other than A level.

The table has been among the most volatile in recent years, with Stirling occupying first place and then dropping out entirely because there were too few students taking social work to compile scores at entry or graduation. This year, Lancaster has made the opposite journey, entering the ranking at the top after a year's absence. It has the highest entry grades and is among the top scorers on the other two measures. Bristol, last year's leader, has the only 5* research grade, but drops to fourth with after a drop in graduate employment.

The vocational nature of the subject generally produces good employment figures. The latest survey showed only 4 per cent unemployment six months after graduation, although the proportion finding graduate-level jobs or going straight on to further

Social Work cont.

training is down on last year. Only Hertfordshire reported full employment among its graduates, although De Montfort, Hull and Sheffield Hallam were not far off.

Entry requirements are the lowest of any of the tables in this year's *Guide*: only Lancaster averages more than 350 points and thirteen institutions – a quarter of the table – average less than 200. Robert Gordon is the top new university, and is joined by Nottingham Trent and Middlesex in the top ten. Third-placed Dundee is the leading Scottish university, while Newport, at the bottom of the table, is the only representative from Wales. Oxford Brookes, Coventry and the Open University produced the best results in the first national student satisfaction survey

- **Social Work Careers:** www.socialworkcareers.co.uk
- **The General Social Care Council:** www.gscc.org.uk

Social Work	Research quality/5	Entry standards	Graduate prospects %	Overall rating
1 Lancaster	5A	358	94	100.0
2 Bath	5B	323	96	95.1
3 Dundee	4B	302	94	89.5
4 Bristol	5*C	334	74	88.5
5 Edinburgh	4B		94	85.5
6 Robert Gordon	3aA	253	96	83.9
7 Hull	3aB	243	98	82.0
8 Nottingham Trent	3aB	248	94	81.4
=9 Southampton	3aB		94	80.8
=9 Middlesex	4C		94	80.8
11 Durham	4A		74	79.8
12 Birmingham	4C	248	76	76.2
13 Huddersfield	5C	188	84	75.4
14 Ulster	3bD	252	92	73.9
15 De Montfort	3aD	213	98	73.8
16 Anglia Ruskin	3aD		96	73.5
17 Salford	3aA	208	72	72.9
18 Plymouth	4D	236	78	72.0
19 Brunel	3aD		92	71.8
20 Northumbria	3aB	221	68	71.4
21 Coventry	3bE	259	88	71.3
22 Bradford	4D	183	92	71.2
23 Hertfordshire	3bE		100	69.3
24 Sheffield Hallam		219	98	67.6
25 Kingston		216	96	66.8
26 Sunderland	3aB	194	56	65.5
=27 Staffordshire	3bC	197	72	65.3
=27 Oxford Brookes		225	88	65.3
29 Leeds		287	62	63.6
30 Lincoln		210	84	62.8

	Research Quality			
31 UCE Birmingham		196	88	62.7
=32 Manchester Metropolitan	3aE	174	68	58.8
=32 Liverpool John Moores	3bC	157	62	58.8
=34 Canterbury Christ Church		217	62	57.1
=34 East London	3bD		64	57.1
36 Derby		172	76	57.0
37 Central Lancashire	3aD	140	62	56.8
38 Luton	3aC	171	36	55.2
39 Wolverhampton		184	62	54.1
40 Chichester		201	48	51.6
41 Leeds Metropolitan		156	56	49.8
42 University of Wales, Newport		162	50	48.6

Average starting salary:	£20,703	Studying and not employed:	6%
Employed in graduate job:	65%	Unemployed:	4%
Employed in graduate job and studying:	7%		
Employed in non-graduate job:	16%		
Employed in non-graduate job and studying:	1%		

The letters that appear in the Research Quality column indicate the proportion of staff included in the assessment, A showing that almost all staff were included and F showing that hardly any were.

Sociology

The popular image of sociology may still be stuck in the 1960s, but it remains one of the largest of the social sciences, despite a 5 per cent drop in applications at the start of 2006. There had been an increase of similar proportions the previous year and the 84 institutions in the latest table make it one of the largest in the *Guide*.

Cambridge retains the leadership and widens the gap at the top with the highest entry standards and the best employment record in the table. The London School of Economics jumps to second place from eighteenth after losing the handicap of a relatively low teaching quality score (dropped in common with such scores throughout the *Guide*). Loughborough, in third place, has one of seven 5* research grades in sociology. Of the other research stars, Essex, Manchester, Surrey and Kent, are in the top ten and Goldsmiths is close to it, but a poor graduate employment rate relegates Lancaster to outside the top 30.

Aberdeen has overtaken Edinburgh to become the leading university in Scotland, while Cardiff is best-placed in Wales. Northumbria is the only new university in the top 30, although Sheffield Hallam has one of the best employment rates. The employment scores show wide variations, with 86 per cent of Cambridge graduates going straight into graduate jobs or higher-level courses, but under half doing the same in 54 institutions in the table. Entry qualifications are less variable, with only two universities averaging more than 400 points and eight under 200 points

Other subjects such as criminology, urban studies, women's studies and some communication studies were also covered in the assessments, which included a large number of institutions where sociology is taught as part of a combined studies or modular programme. Although the unemployment rate is no higher than average for all subjects, at 7 per cent, only three subject areas had a lower proportion of "positive

Sociology cont.

destinations" in 2004. More than four in ten of those completing courses were in low-level jobs six months after graduation.

- **The British Sociological Association:** www.britsoc.co.uk

Sociology	Research quality/5	Entry standards	Graduate prospects %	Overall rating
1 Cambridge	5A	489	86	100.0
2 London School of Economics	5A	442	72	94.8
3 Loughborough	5*A	337	68	91.4
4 Bath	5B	338	76	90.8
5 Warwick	5A	385	64	90.7
6 Bristol	5B	369	70	90.5
7 Essex	5*A	333	60	89.3
8 Manchester	5*A	382	52	89.2
9 Surrey	5*A	299	58	87.5
10 Kent	5*A	282	60	87.4
11 Durham	4A	399	54	87.2
12 Aberdeen	5A	321	58	86.8
13 York	5A	371	48	86.3
14 Goldsmiths, University of London	5*A	247	60	86.0
15 Leeds	5A	359	48	85.8
=16 Newcastle	4B	343	60	85.7
=16 Nottingham	4A	371	52	85.7
18 Sussex	4A	341	56	85.5
19 Edinburgh	5A	400	40	85.4
20 Southampton	5A	337	48	85.0
21 Glasgow	4A	385	46	84.7
22 Sheffield	5B	350	48	84.4
=23 Aston	5B	294	54	83.8
=23 Brunel	5A	306	48	83.8
25 Cardiff	5A	329	44	83.7
26 Queen's, Belfast	5A	311	46	83.5
27 Exeter	5B	345	44	83.3
28 Portsmouth	3aB	271	66	83.1
29 Keele	5B	304	48	82.7
=30 Northumbria	3aB	269	64	82.5
=30 Lancaster	5*B	314	40	82.5
32 Stirling	5B	344	40	82.2
33 Birmingham	3aC	366	50	81.6
34 Oxford Brookes	4A	305	44	81.2
35 Strathclyde	3aB	347	46	81.0
=36 Liverpool	4B	293	46	80.4
=36 East London	4B		48	80.4

38 Reading	3aB	326	46	80.3
=39 City	4A	250	44	79.1
=39 Anglia Ruskin	3aD		60	79.1
41 Hull	3aB	252	52	78.9
42 Sheffield Hallam		262	72	78.7
43 Bangor	3aA	238	46	77.6
44 Nottingham Trent	3aB	266	44	77.5
45 Salford	4A	233	38	77.0
46 London South Bank	4B	227	42	76.9
47 Kingston	4A	178	44	76.4
=48 Teesside	3aC	216	50	75.9
=448 Derby	2B	232	54	75.9
50 Paisley	3aC	239	44	75.3
51 Plymouth	4C	229	40	75.1
=52 Liverpool Hope	2D	216	58	75.0
=52 Glasgow Caledonian	3aC	295	34	75.0
=52 West of England	3aB	251	36	75.0
55 Roehampton	3aC	205	46	74.6
56 Middlesex	4C	184	44	74.4
57 Sunderland	3aB	205	40	74.2
58 Ulster	3bD	250	46	74.1
59 Worcester	2C	220	50	73.9
60 Robert Gordon		269	50	73.6
61 Manchester Metropolitan	3aC	229	38	73.5
62 East Anglia		324	40	73.3
63 Central Lancashire	3bC	238	40	73.2
64 Bradford	4D	205	42	73.1
65 Westminster	3aB	186	38	73.0
66 Brighton	3bC	231	40	72.9
67 Napier		263	46	72.4
=68 Northampton	3bD	229	38	71.4
=68 Southampton Solent	2D	211	44	71.4
=68 Greenwich	3aB	195	30	71.4
=68 De Montfort		248	44	71.4
72 Staffordshire	3aD	213	36	71.1
73 Wolverhampton		197	50	70.9
74 Liverpool John Moores		183	50	70.4
75 Leeds Metropolitan		206	46	70.3
76 Bath Spa		212	44	70.0
77 Chester		247	36	69.4
78 UCE Birmingham		207	42	69.3
79 Winchester		270	30	68.8
80 Luton		176	44	68.7
81 Gloucestershire		239	34	68.6
82 Buckinghamshire Chilterns UC		173	42	68.0
83 Coventry		203	36	67.7
84 Canterbury Christ Church		219	32	67.3

Sociology cont.

Average starting salary:	£17,368	Studying and not employed:	14%
Employed in graduate job:	30%	Unemployed:	7%
Employed in graduate job and studying:	4%		
Employed in non-graduate job:	41%	
Employed in non-graduate job and studying:	4%	

The letters that appear in the Research Quality column indicate the proportion of staff included in the assessment, A showing that almost all staff were included and F showing that hardly any were.

Theology and Religious Studies

Oxford and Cambridge swap places at the top of the theology and religious studies table. They have the same destinations score, but Cambridge's lead in entry scores is bigger than Oxford's in research. Oxford is one of four universities with 5* research grades, but it did not enter a full complement of academics for assessment.

Scores in the top half of the table are unusually close. Manchester, for example, has dropped out of the top ten from joint second place last year despite raising its entry standards and recording virtually the same employment score. Manchester has lost the benefit of a perfect teaching quality score (removed this year throughout the *Guide*) but none of its rivals was more than a point behind on that criterion.

Glasgow is the top university in Scotland and holds onto fourth place overall with the best record for graduates going into high-level employment or postgraduate study. Chester, one of this year's new universities, shares with third-placed Durham the next-best employment record.

Manchester, Nottingham and Cardiff are the other universities considered internationally outstanding for research. Winchester is the top new university and is joined by Roehampton in the top 20. Entry qualifications are relatively high. Although only the top three average more than 400 points, none of the 25 institutions with enough students to register a score slips below 200 points.

Theology and religious studies have enjoyed substantial increases in popularity recently, with a 10 per cent rise in applications in 2004 and more than 20 per cent in 2005. Although there had been a drop at the start of 2006, the 3 per cent decline was marginally less than the average for all subjects. By no means all graduates go into the church, but the vocation helps the subjects to the upper reaches of the graduate employment table. Only 5 per cent of graduates are unemployed after six months, while 40 per cent go on to further study.

- **Humbul Humanities Hub:** www.humbul.ac.uk
- **The British Academy Portal:** www.britac.ac.uk/portal/bysection.asp?section=H2

Theology and Religious Studies	Research quality/5	Entry standards	Graduate prospects %	Overall rating
1 Cambridge	5A	482	75	100.0
2 Oxford	5*B	454	75	99.3
3 Durham	5B	424	80	97.8
4 Glasgow	5B	330	90	96.5
5 Nottingham	5*A	398	65	95.6

6 Edinburgh	5A	371	75	95.4
7 Bristol	5B	364	80	95.3
8 Cardiff	5*A	310	75	94.5
9 St Andrews	5A	369	70	93.9
10 Leeds	4A	337	75	92.2
11 King's College London	5A	351	65	91.9
12 Manchester	5*B	329	65	91.4
13 Birmingham	5B	304	70	90.1
14 Sheffield	5A	357	55	89.5
=15 Exeter	5A	323	60	89.4
=15 Aberdeen	5B	318	65	89.4
17 Winchester	4B	285	75	89.0
18 Bangor	4B	308	70	88.7
=19 Lampeter	5C	275	70	87.0
=19 Roehampton	4A	213	75	87.0
21 Lancaster	5A	325	50	86.9
22 Liverpool Hope	4A	221	70	86.0
23 School of Asian Studies	5B	264	60	85.8
24 Chester	3aD	271	80	85.5
25 Bath Spa	4A	233	65	85.2
26 Kent	3aD	291	75	85.0
27 Queen's, Belfast		325	75	83.0
=28 Stirling	5C		50	80.6
=28 Hull	3aD	248	65	80.6
30 Oxford Brookes	1D	271	65	78.9
31 Canterbury Christ Church	3aA	268	40	78.3

Average starting salary:	£19,757	Studying and not employed:	29%
Employed in graduate job:	32%	Unemployed:	5%
Employed in graduate job and studying:	7%		
Employed in non-graduate job:	23%		
Employed in non-graduate job and studying:	4%		

The letters that appear in the Research Quality column indicate the proportion of staff included in the assessment, A showing that almost all staff were included and F showing that hardly any were.

Town and Country Planning and Landscape

Cambridge extends its lead at the top of the town and country planning and landscape studies ranking, with Reading becoming the closest challenger. Cambridge has by far the highest entry standards and one of the top destinations scores. Third-placed Cardiff has the only 5* research grade in the table and comes closest to full employment, with 98 per cent of leavers going straight into graduate-level work of further study. But its average entry score is more than 100 points behind Reading's.

Leeds also managed a 5* research grade, but it has dropped out of the table this year. Only 14 old universities offer degrees in a subject which was once available only at postgraduate level in most institutions. More than 5,000 students now take first degree courses, with almost another 1,000 taking certificate or diploma programmes. The size of departments varies from more than 500 students to less than 150, with about a third of the total postgraduates.

Town and Country Planning and Landscape cont.

Aberdeen is the top university in Scotland, improving from fourteenth place to fifth. Nottingham Trent is the leading new university, just outside the top ten, although Kingston's 96 per cent "positive destinations" represent the second-best score on that measure. Entry standards are moderate: only the top two in the table average more than 400 points, but none is below 200 points.

Fewer than half of the students are awarded firsts or 2:1s, but jobs prospects are good, with unemployment below average at 4 per cent and only one graduate in five in low-level work after six months. In the latest survey, every university reported "positive destinations" for more than half of their graduates and most were over 70 per cent.

- **The Royal Town Planning Institute:** www.rtpi.org.uk
- **The Landscape Institute:** www.landscapeinstitute.org

Town and Country Planning and Landscape	Research quality/5	Entry standards	Graduate prospects %	Overall rating
1 Cambridge	5B	493	94	100.0
2 Reading	5B	415		96.7
3 Cardiff	5*A	304	98	95.6
4 Sheffield	5A	366	82	92.2
5 Aberdeen	5B	341	84	90.1
6 University College London	4C	334	88	86.9
7 Queen's, Belfast	3bA	313	96	86.8
8 Newcastle	5B	286	78	85.9
9 Liverpool	4A	292	76	84.9
10 Manchester	4B	312	76	84.7
11 Nottingham Trent	3aB	248	82	81.3
12 Loughborough	3aB	335	66	81.2
13 West of England	3aB	219	82	79.9
14 Oxford Brookes	4C	264	72	79.4
15 Gloucestershire	4A	248	62	79.2
16 Kingston		251	96	77.4
17 Leeds Metropolitan	3aB	217	64	75.1
18 Dundee	3bD	241	76	74.9
19 Sheffield Hallam	4D	257	62	74.2
20 Northumbria		243	82	73.4
21 Birmingham		350	58	72.3
22 UCE Birmingham	3bE	219	72	71.4
23 Ulster		206	66	67.5
24 Greenwich		214	52	64.2

Average starting salary:	£17,950	Studying and not employed:	14%
Employed in graduate job:	49%	Unemployed:	4%
Employed in graduate job and studying:	12%		
Employed in non-graduate job:	18%	The letters that appear in the Research Quality column indicate the proportion of staff included in the assessment, A showing that almost all staff were included and F showing that hardly any were.	
Employed in non-graduate job and studying:	2%		

Veterinary Medicine

Only medicine itself compares with veterinary medicine for high entry standards: the number of applications has dropped slightly in each of the last three years, but still there were about 20 candidates for each place. This combined with the uncanny closeness of grades for research, plus the virtual guarantee of a job for graduates who choose to practise, make it difficult to separate the seven schools. Nottingham opened a new school in 2006.

Cambridge has moved up from fifth to head the table, thanks to the highest entry qualifications. Second-placed Liverpool, last year's leader, has the best destinations score, with 99 per cent of graduates finding work or going on to further study within six months of completing the course.

In research, all six schools were awarded grade 4 in 1996; in 2001 they had all moved up to grade 5, having entered similar numbers of academics. Bristol and the Royal Veterinary College entered a slightly lower proportion of staff than the rest in the last research assessment exercise.

Bristol, Cambridge and the Royal Veterinary College set applicants the specialist aptitude test also used by a number of medical schools in 2006. Vets' final qualifications are not classified, but between 5 and 15 per cent are awarded a commendation. The five-year courses have to meet the requirements of the Royal College of Veterinary Studies, but they vary in size from 65 to 155 students. Up to 10 per cent drop out, but those who complete the course are in high demand. Only medicine, dentistry and nursing have a lower unemployment rate.

- **The Royal College of Veterinary Surgeons:** www.rcvs.org.uk

Veterinary Medicine	Research quality/5	Entry standards	Graduate prospects %	Overall rating
1 Cambridge	5B	520	97	100.0
2 Liverpool	5B	479	99	98.2
3 Glasgow	5B	486	95	97.1
4 Edinburgh	5B	478	94	96.2
5 Royal Veterinary College	5C	468	98	94.2
6 Bristol	5C	445	88	88.8

Average starting salary:	£22,048	Studying and not employed:	16%
Employed in graduate job:	77%	Unemployed:	3%
Employed in graduate job and studying:	2%		
Employed in non-graduate job:	2%	The letters that appear in the Research Quality column indicate the proportion of staff included in the assessment, A showing that almost all staff were included and F showing that hardly any were.
Employed in non-graduate job and studying:	0%	

Applying to University

Once you have made your decisions about what you want to study and where, you can heave a huge sigh of relief because the really hard part is over. The next stage, making an application, is much easier. However, there are still enough issues and decisions to warrant a closer look at the process and how to go about it.

All applications to UK universities for full-time courses are made through UCAS, the Universities and Colleges Admissions Service. While *The Good University Guide* is only concerned with universities, many colleges of one sort or another also recruit through UCAS and so you will find over 300 institutions listed on the UCAS website. If you are interested in a part-time course you will need to contact universities individually to find out how to apply.

UCAS moved to all electronic applications for entry in 2006, using its online application procedure *Apply*. UCAS works closely with schools, colleges, libraries and the agencies to ensure that all applicants have access to this system. *Apply* is available on the UCAS website (www.ucas.ac.uk) alongside details of all the courses available so you can apply from any computer with access to the web. A big advantage of *Apply* over the old paper application is that it can correct many common errors, such as invalid postcodes or a date of birth that makes you out to be just 7 years old.

At the time of writing, the detailed procedures for 2007 entry had not been finalised, so do check for any changes from what is given here.

Filling in Your Application

The UCAS application may only be a few electronic screens, but it still looks rather daunting. There is no substitute for reading the guidance and then going slowly and carefully through each section, checking back against the guidance as you go. For most applicants, what you (and your referee) say will be all the university uses to make a decision, so it is important to get it right.

If you follow the guidance carefully, most of the application is straight-forward, but on the following pages are a few points about some of the more significant sections.

Address

This looks simple, and it is, but don't just fill in your current address and then forget about it. If your address changes, make sure you tell UCAS immediately. UCAS will automatically notify your university choices of the change. If you don't keep UCAS informed of your change of address you will find letters (which might be offers or a confirmation of a place) go to the wrong place. It is surprisingly common for applicants at a boarding school to put down their school address on the form but then forget to tell UCAS when they go home for the summer. They then find that the letter confirming a place at university goes to the school instead of to them at home.

Examination Results

Make sure you get the details of your examinations to be taken exactly right. If you are taking English Language and Literature, put the full title and not just English, even if everyone in your school or college calls it English. This is important because any mistakes could mean that UCAS cannot match your application with your examination results straightaway in the summer, resulting in a delay in universities making their decisions. Listing the full module details of a BTEC award is also important to avoid confusion over precisely what you have studied.

If you are taking the examinations of another country do not try to give a UK equivalent. Always state exactly what you are doing and let the university decide the equivalence so as to avoid any confusion. If the column headings on the form are inappropriate, then ignore them.

And be honest! Never be tempted to massage your results to make them look a little better. UCAS has some sophisticated fraud-busting techniques and admissions tutors are remarkably good at spotting dodgy applications. If you are found to be giving false or incomplete information, you will be promptly ejected from UCAS and lose any chance of a place at university that year. Even if you manage to slip through all the detection devices, you will probably be asked by the university to present your certificates. Any sign of tampering, or lame excuses about them having been eaten by the dog, will result in a check with the records of the examining board. When the board points out that the ABB on your form was really DDD, you will politely be shown the door.

Personal Statement

This is your chance to say anything you like, in your own words, to persuade admissions tutors that yours is the brightest and best application ever to have crossed their desk. You can write what you like, but the key areas probably include:

- why you want to study your chosen subject
- what particular qualities and experience you can bring to it
- details of any work experience or voluntary activity, especially if it is relevant to your course
- any other evidence of achievement, such as the Duke of Edinburgh award
- details of any sponsorship or placements you have secured or applied for
- your career aspirations
- any wider aspects of life that make you an interesting and well-rounded student

Application Timetable

May – Sept	Research and make choices about universities and courses
1 Sept – 15 Oct	Apply for Cambridge or Oxford or medicine, dentistry or veterinary science/medicine in any university
1 Sept – 15 Jan	All other applications from the UK or elsewhere in the EU (except art and design route B)
1 Sept – 30 June	All other applications from outside the UK or elsewhere in the EU (except art and design route B)
1 Jan – 24 March	Art and design route B
16 Jan – 30 June	Late applications from the UK or elsewhere in the EU considered at universities' discretion
18 Mar – 30 June	UCAS Extra
1 July onwards	Applications go straight into the Clearing procedure

- if your first language is not English, describe any opportunities you have had to use English (such as an English-speaking school or work with a company that uses English).

Remember that for most admissions tutors an awful lot of applications will cross their desk. Many applicants will get advice about how to write the statement and see model examples. The result is a tendency for personal statements to be rather similar and, to a hard-pressed admissions tutor faced with a metre-high pile of UCAS forms, rather dull. Somehow you have to make it personal and stand out from the crowd. On the other hand, avoid being too wacky – not all admissions tutors will share your sense of humour and your form may be read by one who doesn't.

If there is anything about your application that is even slightly unusual, then explain why. If you want to defer your entry to the following year, say why and what you intend to do with your year out. If you are a mature student, explain why you want to enter higher education. In general, the more vocational the course, the more you need to emphasise your commitment to the profession and relevant experience you have gained. Conversely, the more academic the course, the more you need to enthuse about the subject and explain why you want to study it for several years.

As with examinations, be honest. If you say you are interested in philosophy and then get called for interview, you can almost guarantee that some learned professor will ask you about Plato's *Theory of Forms* or Spinoza's *Ethics*. If you can't talk sensibly about philosophy, you will look rather silly and will be unlikely to get an offer. Be specific in what you write. Don't just say you did some voluntary work; describe what you learned through the experience. Don't just say you are interested in reading – after all, students have to be interested in reading as they do a lot of it; describe what you like to read and why.

There is no ideal way to structure your statement, but it is a good idea to use paragraphs or sub-headings to make the presentation clear and easy for an admissions tutor to read. If you want to say more than there is space available, do not send additional papers to UCAS, as they will not automatically be passed on to your chosen universities. If you really can't make it fit, then send any additional material directly to the universities to which you have applied but wait until you have received your application number from UCAS, so that you can include this with your papers and make sure they are matched with the correct application.

Apply will let you paste in your personal statement from another source. It is, therefore, a good idea to prepare it in advance and check it thoroughly before entering it into your application.

Choice of Courses

By the time you fill in your application, you should have your choice of courses ready. You are allowed six, but you don't have to use them all and many applicants don't – the average number of choices used is about five. (Indeed if you only use one choice there is a lower application fee.) If you want to apply for medicine, dentistry or veterinary science/medicine, you are only allowed to use four choices for these courses, though you can use the other two for different subjects if you wish.

Each university will only see details of its own application and so they will not know where else you have applied or whether all the courses in your application are the same.

In all sections of your application, make sure the grammar and punctuation are correct. It is a good idea to show it to someone else as a final check. Don't rely on a spellchecker – it won't pick up the difference between organic chemistry and orgasmic chemistry. When you have finally finished, print out a copy and arrange for your referee (usually someone from your school or college) to add their reference and follow the instructions about ways in which you can pay the fee (£15 for entry in 2005, or £5 if you only use one choice).

Your application can arrive at UCAS any time between 1 September and 15 January (or 15 October if Oxford or Cambridge or any medical, dental or veterinary course is among your choices – see the *Application Timetable* for this and other exceptions). In some circumstances there can be a small advantage in applying early (see below, *Should I Apply Early?*) but generally it will not make any difference. If you apply after the appropriate deadline your application will still be processed by UCAS but universities do not have to consider it. They can, if they wish, reject you on the grounds that they have received enough applications already. However, if you are applying for one of the less competitive courses or are applying from overseas you will probably find your application is treated just like those that arrived on time.

What Happens Next?

The first thing to happen after you have submitted your application to UCAS is the arrival of a Welcome Letter confirming the courses and universities you have chosen. It is important to check this carefully to make sure there is no mistake and keep your application number safe as you will probably need it later. The Welcome Letter will also include your application number and your password for *Track*, the online system for following the progress of your application. You can, if you wish, opt to have all communications sent to you by email rather than the post.

Then there is nothing to do but wait. Universities are increasingly aware that applicants don't like to be kept hanging around so you may find some decisions arriving

---

Should I Apply Early?

Universities are required by UCAS rules to treat all applications received by the appropriate deadline on an equal basis. This means that applying early or late should make no difference, as long as the deadline is met, and in practice this is the case for virtually all applicants. Indeed if you are applying for a low-demand subject you will probably get equal treatment even if your application arrives well after the deadline.

Occasionally a very popular university may experience a sudden increase in applications in very high-demand subjects such as medicine, English or law, which only becomes apparent after it has started making decisions. It will then be faced with a choice of either carrying on making offers in the same way and ending up with an intake way above target, or tightening up its criteria and admitting the right number. Neither of these outcomes is desirable: too many students means large classes and over-worked staff; tightening the criteria means being slightly tougher with some applicants. The university may choose the latter course, in which case a few of the later applicants might be rejected whereas, if they had applied earlier, before the increased number of applications was apparent, they might have received an offer. This situation is very rare, but the conclusion is that applying early never does any harm while applying later to high-demand subjects very occasionally might.

fairly soon. However, if your application arrived at UCAS close to the main deadline it can take several weeks to make its way through UCAS processing and on to your universities. When any decisions do arrive, they will be one of the following:

Unconditional Offer (U): This means you have already met all the entry requirements for the course.

Conditional Offer (C): This means the university will accept you if you meet certain additional requirements, usually specified grades in the examinations you will be taking.

Rejection (R): This means that either you have not got, and are unlikely to get, some key requirement for the course, or that you have lost out in competition with other, better applicants.

If you receive an offer, you will almost certainly be invited to visit the university concerned. This is a good chance to find out much more about the course and university than you can through reading prospectuses and looking at websites. However, bear in mind that the occasion is designed to encourage you to accept the offer as well as to give you the opportunity to find out more. So, just like reading prospectuses, you have to be critical of what you are told and look for evidence for any claims that are made.

Sometimes you may be invited for an interview before a decision is made. This could be the normal practice for that particular course, or it could be because your application is unusual in some way and the university wants to check that you are really suitable (perhaps you are a mature student without the usual formal qualifications). In some cases interviews are not quite what they seem (see below, *When is an Interview Not an Interview?*), but you can never be sure, so treat any interview as a real interview.

When is an Interview Not an Interview?

Interviews come in two forms. Outwardly both look the same, but in fact they have very different purposes. The first type of interview is the 'real' interview, where a genuine attempt is being made to assess your suitability for the course and your performance in the interview will make a difference to your chances of being made an offer. The second type of interview is the 'psychological' interview. It looks like an interview, feels like an interview, but actually doesn't make any difference. The university has already decided to make you an offer and the interview is merely a psychologically clever way of encouraging you to accept the offer. If you travel half way across the country, answer some tough questions and then get made an offer of a place, it makes you feel good, both about yourself and about the university. Hence you are more likely to accept that offer in favour of one which just arrived in the post. At least that is the idea behind the psychological interview.

The problem for you is that it is hard to tell which type of interview you are facing. Generally speaking, interviews for medical and medically related professions and for education are real (though it is still common for 80 per cent or more of interviewees to be made an offer). Interviews at very competitive universities such as Oxford and Cambridge are also usually real, and interviews for applicants who have an unusual background or lack the usual qualifications are generally genuine attempts to assess suitability. However, interviews for less popular courses, such as chemistry or engineering, at anywhere other than the most competitive universities for these subjects are often the psychological type of interview.

If you do get called for interview, then go – you are unlikely to be made an offer if you don't turn up – and be sure that you arrive on time. Prepare yourself in advance, particularly for the obvious questions such as why you want to study the subject and why you want to go to that university. Re-read the copy of your application form to remind yourself what is in your personal statement. And dress smartly. While it is not necessary to look as if you are going to a wedding, an interview is not the time to make a fashion statement.

All being well, particularly if you have chosen your universities carefully, you will get several offers. You can hold on to any offer you receive until all your chosen universities have made their decisions, but then you have to choose which ones you want to accept.

Replies to Offers

You can accept one offer as your firm acceptance (often called your UF choice if the offer was unconditional or your CF choice if it was conditional). If your firm acceptance is CF, then you can accept a second offer as your insurance acceptance (often called your CI choice), but you must decline any others. Most applicants who have more than one conditional offer will accept as CF their first choice university and then a university which has made a lower offer as their CI choice.

You can, in fact, decline all your offers if you wish. Perhaps you have realised that you have made a dreadful mistake in your choice of subject and now wish to look for another subject in UCAS Extra or the Clearing procedure (see below). However, normally you will want to accept one offer as your firm acceptance.

Firm and Insurance Choices on Results Day

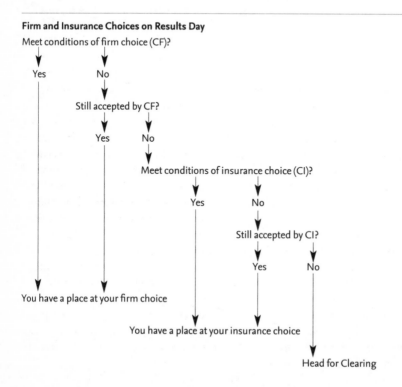

Once you have done that, you and the university are bound together by the rules of UCAS. If you firmly accept an unconditional offer then you have a definite place at that university. If you firmly accept a conditional offer and then meet all the conditions, the university is obliged to accept you and you are obliged to go there. In making your firm acceptance, assuming you have conditional offers, you will have to balance your desire to attend a particular university against your estimate of whether you can meet the conditions. If you expect to get ABB at A level and the offers are all BCC or below, then it is easy: choose the place you want to go. If, however, you think you will get BCC and your offers are ABB, BBB, BCC and CDD, the decision is more difficult, especially if you really want to go to the university that offered ABB.

This is where the insurance acceptance comes in. If you want to, you can just have a firm acceptance and decline the rest. However, most applicants with more than one offer choose an insurance acceptance as well. If you are accepted by your firm choice then that is it, and the insurance choice becomes irrelevant. However, if your firm choice turns you down because you don't meet their conditions, you might still be accepted by your insurance choice, so you get a second chance before heading for Clearing. Obviously, it makes sense to choose a lower offer for your insurance choice so as to maximise your chances of getting at least one of your two choices. However, make sure it is somewhere you would still like to go because, if that is where you are placed, the UCAS rules require you to go there. Remember that in some subjects, such as chemistry or electronic engineering, places in Clearing, even at prestigious universities, are easy to obtain, so you could be better off choosing just a firm choice rather than two choices, one of which you don't really want. In fact, holding an insurance offer just for the sake of it would delay your entry into Clearing. If all this sounds rather complicated, the flowchart above, Firm and Insurance Choices on Results Day may help. Finally, make sure you do reply to your offers. If you don't, and ignore the reminders UCAS will send you, you will be 'declined by default' and lose your offers.

You can track the progress of your application throughout the process using *Track*. Your password will be sent to you with the acknowledgement of your application and the facility will give you an up-to-the-minute summary of where all your applications have got to. There is even a version for wap-enabled mobile phones.

UCAS Extra

If you are unlucky enough not to receive any offers from any of your choices, or you have a change of heart and decide to decline any offers you do have, UCAS Extra comes into play in mid-March. This, in effect, allows you to make a seventh choice of university. If you become eligible for UCAS Extra, UCAS will send you all the details you need, and courses at universities willing to consider UCAS Extra applications will be available on the UCAS website. You can then either use the UCAS website to make an application or contact a university directly. If you are made an offer, either unconditional or conditional, you can firmly accept or decline it just like any offer in the main UCAS scheme. If you don't get an offer (or decide to decline your offer), you can opt to make another UCAS Extra choice and so on, until either you get an offer or you run out of time (the scheme ends in July).

Once you have an offer and accept it, you become unconditional firm (UF) or conditional firm (CF) for that university (there is only one choice at any time in UCAS Extra so there is no question of an insurance choice). You are committed to it in exactly the same way as the main UCAS scheme. In 2005, about 20,000 applicants were eligible for UCAS Extra, about 8,000 applied and 3,400 gained a place.

Results Day

If you accepted an unconditional offer, all you have to do is wait for the start of your course and roll up to register. However, most of you will be anxiously waiting for examination results before you find out whether you have been accepted. If you are taking Scottish Highers or an access course, then your results will usually come out before A levels in England. This can be helpful if you don't get accepted, as you will then have a chance to find a place somewhere else before the scramble for places after A-level results are published.

If you find that your results mean you have met all the conditions of your firm choice, congratulations! You have a place at your chosen university and you can relax, at least for now. Do check carefully though, especially if you have an offer expressed in terms of points rather than grades.

If you are sure you have met all the conditions, you don't have to do anything except to check UCAS *Track* to make absolutely certain that your place has been confirmed. In a day or two you will receive confirmation of your place from UCAS, with a form to sign to confirm that you still want it, and details of when and where to register from your chosen university will follow a little while later. If you are not sure, or just need reassurance, you can ring the university to check, though bear in mind that several thousand others may be doing the same thing, so it may take a little while to get through. If you do ring, make sure you have your UCAS number handy.

Even if you have not met all the conditions, you may still find your place is confirmed and, again, *Track* is the quickest and easiest way to check. The university may be short of applicants that year or the other offer-holders had worse results than you (see below, *What if I Just Miss My Grades?*). If you are just one grade down, your chances will often be quite good; more than that and your chances will be much less.

Clearing

If you find that you don't have a place then you will be eligible for the UCAS Clearing scheme, a way of matching universities without students to students without universities. Essentially, it is up to you to find a university that is prepared to accept you. The best way to do this is to ring a university and tell them what you want to do. Usually, if they have vacancies, they will take your details and either give you a decision straightaway or very soon afterwards. Just keep going until somewhere offers you a place. Here are some points to remember if you end up in this position:

- prepare in advance – unless you are very confident you will get the grades, do some contingency planning before results day. Make a list of possible courses and universities where you might be prepared to go in priority order. This will be easy to check against the Clearing vacancy lists when they are published
- be there – don't go on holiday at the critical time
- if you think you may not have a place, check with your firm and insurance choices as soon as possible
- check the Clearing vacancy lists in newspapers, the UCAS website, or the websites of individual universities to find where there are vacancies in your subject

- think about alternative courses (perhaps a joint course with another subject instead of a single subject course) to maximise the choice available
- start ringing possible universities straight away (places at good universities can be filled very quickly)
- always ring yourself – universities are less impressed by people ringing on your behalf
- if you can't get through, keep trying, but also send an e-mail or fax.

There will be a few vacancies not listed in the official vacancy lists because the universities know they can fill them with speculative callers and do not need the extra calls generated by the vacancy lists. If there is somewhere you really want to go, it might just be worth ringing even if they are not in the lists. However, such vacancies will be taken within hours, at most within a day of A-level results being published.

Some applicants find that their results are much better than they expected and they are qualified for a much better university than the one where they accepted an offer, or for a high-demand course such as medicine for which they never thought they would be accepted. If you find yourself in this position, you can do one of three things:

1   Carry on with your existing choice, as long as you are sure that is still what you want to do.
2   Find an alternative university which is prepared to accept you and then negotiate with the university where you have been placed to be released into the Clearing scheme. The university is not obliged to do this, and will probably try to persuade you not to, but most will eventually give way if it is clear that you have genuinely thought through what you are doing. Once in Clearing your alternative university can accept you.
3   Withdraw completely from UCAS and apply again the following year.

If your results are much worse than you expected, the situation can be more difficult. If there were genuine extenuating circumstances (perhaps you were taken ill during your examinations or there was a bereavement in your family) your school should have told the examining board and university about this already. Neither will be impressed by being told about it after your low grades have been published. If the results are just plain surprising, you may wish to seek a re-mark by the examining board. If this brings to light an error, and your grades go up, the university will review its decision, though if you miss the deadline the university may say it can only accept you for the following year.

What if I Just Miss My Grades?

Suppose you are offered BBC at A level and get BCC: will you still be accepted? This will depend on two main factors. First, did you drop a grade in a critical subject? If you were asked for a B in, say, chemistry and that was the subject where you got a C, this will reduce the chances of your being accepted. Second, what did everyone else with an offer for the course get? If the university has 50 places and 40 get the grades, they will look first for the extra 10 among those who just missed the offer and you will probably be accepted. However, if 60 get the grades, they will probably reject anyone who didn't meet the offer precisely, and you may well not be accepted. There is nothing you can do about this. Universities are financially penalised for admitting the wrong number of students, so they will always want to admit as near as possible to their target number.

Trying to get a place in Clearing is not as difficult as it sounds. There is always a lot of talk about "chaos" and "scrambling", but universities are getting much better at dealing with large numbers of enquiries very quickly. They have a strong interest in signing up good students as they suffer financial penalties if they under-recruit by a large margin. And the range of courses available in Clearing is huge. In 2004, for example, there were a number of vacancies on courses in law and English, two very high-demand subjects. They may not have been precisely the right course or in an ideal part of the country, but they were there and anyone with the right grades who acted quickly could have obtained a place. If you wanted chemistry or engineering you could have chosed from a number of prestigious universities, even with quite low grades in some cases.

Having said that, trying to find a place in Clearing is not much fun for anyone. The best way to avoid it is to be sensible and realistic early on in the application process. If you apply for courses and universities where you have a good chance of being made an offer and accept offers you have a good chance of achieving, then you will probably be able to avoid Clearing altogether. That is much better for both you and the universities.

Do I Apply This Year?

Some students take a year out between finishing at school or college and starting university, often known as a gap year. About 8 per cent of the applicants are accepted for deferred entry to the following year. In general, gap years are a good thing. It is possible to go trekking in Thailand, sailing in the Seychelles, teaching in Tanzania, on an adventure up the Amazon or even do drama in Stratford-upon-Avon. You can go for a few weeks or a full year and some opportunities will enable you to earn money to finance your degree course. If you choose your opportunity carefully, you will develop the kind of maturity and enterprise that will help with your studying and your future career. In particular, being able to demonstrate sustained commitment can be attractive to employers.

There are a number of reputable organisations that can help you organise your gap year. They have ready-made activities, take care of some of the practicalities and have a proper concern for safety and security.

On the other hand, a gap year means it will be one year later before you are in the job market and earning a salary. If your chosen course is a long one, this could be a consideration. In a few subjects it may take you a little while to get back into serious study – mathematics is notorious for being a bit harder to take up again after a year away from study – but most students soon catch up again.

If you are thinking about taking a gap year it is still best to apply during your final year at school or college as a "deferred applicant". When you fill in your application, you should put a D in the "defer entry" column in section 3 of the application. This should mean that you get your university place sorted out before starting your job or travels and so don't have to worry about it during your gap year. Indeed, for the more adventurous travellers, trying to fill in a UCAS form on the back of a Mongolian yak or half way across the Australian desert is not recommended. Also, if things go badly wrong in your examinations and you don't get a place, you do get an opportunity to rethink your career options or resit your exams and still start at university when you planned to.

As a general rule, universities are happy to consider deferred applicants but, if the prospectus does not make a clear statement about the university's policy, it would be sensible to check.

Where to Live

After choice of university and course, the next most important decision is where to live. And here student demand is polarising. Some are seeking premium accommodation with fast internet connection and Sky, perhaps even a great view as standard, whilst others, more cash-strapped, are looking for the bare minimum. There might well be a bewildering number of options on offer; the National Union of Students (NUS) has identified 16 categories, ranging from deluxe en suite accommodation in a hall of residence with all meals provided to lodging in a family house or staying at home. No doubt we could even find a few students who live on houseboats or in caravans, but the majority of first-year undergraduates going away to university choose to live in university-managed accommodation if they can, as the table opposite shows.

Wherever you decide to live, you may well be expected to pay a term's rent in advance. The information in the individual university profiles (see chapter 11) gives you a good idea of the weekly rent you might reckon to pay for basic catered and self-catering university accommodation. As a general rule, student accommodation and travel costs are highest in London and southeast England and least expensive in the Midlands, Wales, Scotland and Northern Ireland.

UNITE Student Experience Report 2006	
Where Students Live	**(%)**
University Hall (en suite)	23
University Hall (not en suite)	23
University house or flat	4
Private house or flat	16
Living with parents	26
Living in own house or flat	8

A recent survey has published the average weekly expenditure, including accommodation, by students in the 24 university towns and cities shown in the table below. This might not seem much of a differential at first glance but it amounts to a huge £2,070 saving over a full academic year if you opt to study at Leicester or Sheffield

Royal Bank of Scotland Student Living Index 2005
Student weekly living costs (£)

	£		£
Leicester	174	Leeds	193
Sheffield	174	Nottingham	193
Glasgow	177	Durham	194
York	178	Edinburgh	195
Dundee	179	Liverpool	196
Birmingham	183	Brighton	197
Coventry	187	Southampton	208
Cambridge	188	Newcastle	211
St Andrews	190	Oxford	212
Belfast	191	Aberdeen	216
Cardiff	192	Bristol	217
Manchester	192	London	243

rather than London. However, this is not quite the whole story, particularly if you are intending to take a term-time job because your average London hourly rate (£8.70) would be much higher than that for Leicester (£5.10) or Sheffield (£5.60).

In addition to an advanced rental payment, you could also be asked to part with a deposit or bond (typically the equivalent of one month's rent) to cover breakages and damage. This could be about £150 (higher in London) in university-owned accommodation and as much as £200 in the private sector. This is returned, less any deductions, at the end of the contract and, at that stage, there is potential for dispute as to what constitutes fair wear and tear! In fact, disputes over the return of deposits is a real and recurring issue, particularly in the private sector, and the 2004 Housing Act (see below) has introduced a National Tenancy Deposit Scheme to protect students from unscrupulous landlords who withhold deposits for no good reason. Under this scheme, deposits will be lodged with an independent body, not the landlord, and this will ensure that deposits are fairly returned with any disputes resolved quickly and cheaply.

University Halls and Houses

Most universities provide places for first-year students in their own accommodation like halls of residence but here boundaries are becoming blurred with universities entering into partnerships with private sector organisations to build and manage student complexes. These initiatives still account for less than 10 per cent of the student bed spaces available, but their growing importance is highlighted by the fact that this figure has more than doubled in the last year. As well as providing halls specifically for individual universities, UNITE plc (www.unite-students.com), the biggest developer, and others offer students secure and flexible accommodation of their own with a wide range of payment options. This style of living can be somewhat more expensive but is purpose-built and of high quality. You might expect as standard for your room to be en suite with internet access, satellite TV and a phone line, and for your shared kitchen to have all mod cons. Nonetheless, we still have a long way to go to match some American universities where the more exotic offerings include in-room movies, bubble-jet tubs and personal trainers. One even invites parents to submit their offspring's favourite recipes to incorporate in their gourmet menus!

University-owned residences continue to be upgraded, often with one eye on the conference business in vacations, and new rooms coming on stream might well be similarly en suite with all mod cons. Paradoxically, at a time when there is much talk about student hardship, even poverty, these more expensive rooms are often in greatest demand. Perhaps students hope to balance the books by saving on food costs. Certainly, an increasing number are looking for the more independent lifestyle offered by self-catering. The universities and other providers have responded to this shift in demand by providing much more flexible eating arrangements rather than the traditional full-board package of accommodation and fifteen or so meals a week. Now many universities offer pay-as-you-eat as well as wholly catered and self-catering facilities in their residences. Halls can be mixed or, more rarely, single sex and might house up to 800 students. They are great places to make friends and be part of the social scene. They are also probably best for support, should you need it in those first few weeks and months away from family and friends. They can also be first-year student ghettos and are often rowdy well into the beginning of the academic year. In many universities you will be guaranteed accommodation if you firmly accept their offer by a given date in the summer, but not necessarily if you come through Clearing. However, private halls might still have some places available at Clearing time. You will generally be expected – and, most probably, will want – to move out to other accommodation at the end of your first year. There are exceptions, particularly in the collegiate universities, and it is quite common at Oxford or Cambridge to live in your college for a further year or two.

You will no doubt be asked to sign an agreement with the university and the average length of the contract is 40 weeks, including the Christmas and Easter vacations. With shorter term-time-only contracts you will be required to move out in the vacations, but there may be storage space to leave your belongings. If not, check if the university has a secure storage facility with a local company. Special arrangements are often made to enable international students to remain in residence in the short vacations. They might also experience life within a UK family home over a weekend or at Christmas under the auspices of www.hostuk.org and similar organisations.

If you possibly can, take full advantage of Open Days to see the accommodation for yourself. UCAS publishes an annual guide to Open Days, Taster Courses and its own Education Conventions. Opting for university accommodation often gives the distinct advantage that it can be arranged at a distance whereas much of the private housing requires you to be on the spot to secure it. The university cannot sign a tenancy agreement on your behalf. The University Accommodation or Housing Office will have literature describing the facilities in detail and many have excellent websites containing invaluable information on student housing provided by both the university and the private sector.

Whilst the largest number of first-year students live in Halls, some prefer smaller, self-catering properties with shared kitchen, toilet, bathroom and possibly a lounge area. Unlike inclusive Hall costs, here you may find that you receive an additional bill for heating and lighting. But at least you are in control of the food bills and you might even be able to engage in a spot of discounted bulk buying with fellow residents and hence stretch the money further. University properties are often in or near the campus itself and so travel costs to and from the university are minimal. As a general rule, the older universities tend to have much more housing stock, but the scene is constantly changing with high rise cranes a regular feature of the university skyline.

Private Sector Accommodation

Some students will head for private sector accommodation because they have to or choose to, and we have already referred to the growth of some private sector building initiatives. UNITE, for example, rents and manages apartment blocks housing more than 30,000 students in 32 university cities, where you could rent for a year – or three years if you like. In addition, there are legions of accommodation agencies and individual landlords in university towns and cities in response to the continuing growth in student numbers. Many have long since abandoned their cottage industry image and competition from some major property developers has created a much greater professionalism. It is illegal for them to levy a joining fee but they may charge a booking or reservation fee on an agreed property, and perhaps a fee for references or for drawing up the Tenancy Agreement. The University Accommodation Service will have an approved list and some are working closely with local councils to develop best practice for student housing in their areas through Student Accommodation Accreditation Schemes. This is timely, given a recent estimate that 14 per cent of full-time students living away from home do so in unsatisfactory conditions. Bear this statistic in mind when undertaking your own search for a roof over your head. These Schemes require the landlord to have mandatory gas and electrical safety certificates and guarantee basic standards of security and safety.

Always take someone with you to view accommodation and do not rush to sign on the dotted line for the first one you see. Try to spend some time in the area, perhaps by staying at a bed and breakfast or a YHA hostel for a few days, preferably when students are in residence. Locations can look – and be – very different in the vacations and after dusk. How safe is the district? It is important, too, to check out public transport and the journey time to and from the university. What is the traffic flow (or chaos!) like at weekday peak times as compared with a quiet Sunday morning? For some students living in private accommodation, travel might mean not only time but also money. A recent survey of travel time between term-time accommodation and the university concluded that students fared best in Wales (86 per cent less than 30 minutes away) and, not surprisingly, worst in London (50 per cent more than 30 minutes away and 17 per cent more than an hour).

Make sure that you aware of any Student Travel Card for local travel and the university or students' union transport system when returning to your accommodation late at night.

Houses in Multiple Occupation

As a result of the 2004 Housing Act, the licensing of Houses in Multiple Occupation (HMOs) in England and Wales, like Scotland and Northern Ireland, will no longer be discretionary. The Act defines an HMO as a house occupied by three or more unrelated residents and so it covers virtually all private houses occupied by students – although it specifically excludes university-run accommodation. Compulsory licensing for those properties most at risk – where there are five or more unrelated residents and the house is three or more stories tall – took effect in 2006. In addition, local authorities can designate whole areas where all HMOs, including smaller houses, will have to be licensed, and there is no doubt that they will look to do this in some university city suburbs with large student populations. This may result in a reduced supply of privately rented properties or the additional costs associated with mandatory licensing being passed on by landlords to students.

It sounds complicated, but licensed HMOs give better property management, greater financial regulation, and added health and safety protection to student tenants so you need to understand all of this if the property that interests you is an HMO. In fact, it's worth asking if your house is covered by an accreditation scheme or code of standards. These codes are models of good practice and act as a checklist of what constitutes decent standards and common sense responsibilities for both owner and student. Now that the Housing Act is law, it is likely that larger properties, even those administered by the universities themselves, will be required to comply with a scheme like the National Code of Standards for Larger Student Developments compiled by the Accreditation Network UK (www.anuk.org.uk).

The Paperwork

Once you have settled on the shared house, flat or bedsit you like, the next thing is to sort out the paperwork. You will almost certainly be asked to sign a Tenancy Agreement or lease offering perhaps an 'Assured Shorthold Tenancy'. This is a binding legal document so read it through carefully before signing. If you do not understand some of the clauses, do not sign but seek clarification, if needs be, from the University Accommodation Office or the Students' Union – they may well have model Tenancy Agreements – or from a local Citizens Advice Bureau or Law Advice Centre. It is much easier to agree terms at this early stage but almost impossible after you have signed and moved in. This is one of those occasions in your life when it pays (literally!) to read the small print. Where you are sharing with other students, beware that a joint tenancy implies joint liability so you might end up being responsible for the deeds and, more importantly, misdeeds of others. The same applies if you are asked to name, say, your parent as a guarantor to pay any charges not covered by you. Never part with money without getting a receipt and keep a copy of all documents. Remember that by law the landlord cannot increase the rent more than once a year unless your agreement contains a rent review clause.

What other paperwork might you expect?

- An Inventory and Schedule of Condition listing everything in the accommodation when you take it over and its condition. If you are given one, check it for accuracy and annotate any changes. If you are not, make one of your own, have it witnessed, send it to the landlord, and keep a copy yourself. Take photographs if necessary to record any initial damage.
- A Rent Book in the unlikely event that rent is payable on a weekly basis.
- A recent Gas Safety Certificate issued by a recognised CORGI engineer.
- A Fire Safety Certificate covering the furnishings.
- A record of current gas/electricity meter readings. If not, take your own readings as soon as you move in.

Water rates are usually included in the rent but clarify this and take meter readings if you are expected to pay separately for water.

You will not have to pay Council Tax if all the residents are full-time students. However, you may need to obtain an Exemption Certificate from the university to offer as proof. If, on the other hand, one of the inmates is not a full-time student then a reduced Council Tax will be levied.

The average length of the contract in private-sector accommodation is likely to be higher (45 weeks and often 52 weeks) than for university-owned property and deposits nearer £200 (higher in London) can be expected. The longer lease is becoming more popular and can, of course, be a distinct advantage for some students. You will not have to make way for conference delegates, can keep your belongings with you, stay to obtain vacation work in the university or nearby, and you might even get a rent discount, especially if you are staying in the property for a further year.

Sharing

Now you cannot choose your family but you can choose your housemates, and you never know someone until you have lived with them. University accommodation officers can vouch for the problems they have to try and sort out as a result of student tenants falling out with each other over the state of the kitchen or the bathroom. Most reading this would be amazed (or would they?) at the depths of squalor to which some students can descend once away from the watchful eyes of parents. A quarter of students smoke –

could you live with one? And what about a serial phone user? It is best to arrange at the outset for individual billing and a number of providers (eg, The Phone Co-op at www.thephone.coop) offer this facility. Or a nocturnal TV addict? It is a legal requirement to have a TV licence. Or a surrogate penguin who warms to the heating system left on all day every day? Remember fuel bills are not usually included in the rent.

Regardless of whether you are applying for university or private halls, always make sure you fill in the application forms as fully as you can. Universities and landlords will try to take your personal preferences and lifestyle into account when grouping tenants together in a flat or on a corridor.

Living at Home
A significant, and growing, number of first-year students, twice as many in London, live at home and the reasons advanced are many and varied. There are clearly pros and cons but one potential disadvantage is to treat university as a nine-to-five job and risk missing the whole university experience. Stay-at-home students are likely to make fewer friends and to feel rather detached from campus activities but there is no evidence that their academic work suffers. As a general rule, the new universities recruit many more local students. This being so, their students are twice as likely to opt for staying at home than those at the old universities.

Another feature of the current scene is "buy to rent" – accommodation bought by parents to house the student member of the family. With mortgage interest rates still low, property prices and rents reasonably steady, and the stock market still nervous some parents are opting to buy a small house or flat, perhaps defraying the expense by charging rent to fellow students. Such properties, if large, are still subject to HMO licensing.

UNITE Student Experience Report 2006	
Reasons for Living at Home	(%)
To save money or cut costs	38
Just want to	20
Cannot afford to live away	16
Near to university of choice	8
To concentrate on my studies	6
For an easy life; to be looked after	3
Parents wanted me to	2
Other reasons	7

However, "buy to rent" is not without its pitfalls, particularly in those university towns where "areas of student housing restraint" are being introduced, where there is increasing competition from national developers of purpose-built student housing, and where the universities, themselves, are upgrading their own residences.

Hostels and Lodgings
Some registered charities run small hostels, especially for students with particular religious affiliations or those who come from specific overseas countries. These are mainly in London and further details can be found in the British Council publication, *Studying and Living in the UK*.

Small numbers of students live in lodgings where they might share a home with the landlord and his family. A study bedroom and some meals are usually provided but other facilities might well be shared. Reports suggest that this integrated accommodation is preferred by some overseas students

We have deliberately devoted a complete chapter to where to live because it is often by far the biggest item of expenditure – rent alone could account for 70 per cent of weekly income. It is also crucially important to success at university so it is well worth giving time and effort to the various accommodation options available, making sure you maintain maximum flexibility within any arrangements. Leaving home, and perhaps your country, is a big move and it will all feel very strange at first. It is reassuring that the other first-year students are in the same boat. The trick is to survive, even thrive, to the Christmas vacation. Most who leave university do so in those first few months simply because they are lonely and feel isolated. If you are warm and well fed this will impact on your happiness and enjoyment and help you to settle in quickly. This, in turn, will have a positive effect on your studies and as a result you are likely to do well. It is false economy to cut corners when it comes to choosing your first accommodation.

Finally, a word on behalf of the neighbours! They were all young once and most welcome students. But whole areas of our major university towns and cities are now dominated by student housing in what has become known as "studentification" This has had some adverse effects, not only on the local people but also on students themselves. Living in such a community invites respect, tolerance and a bit of "give and take" – work on it. Follow the Community Code: "say hello, keep the peace and clean up".

Safety and Security

It is better to be safe than sorry and a few basic precautions could go a long way to securing your wellbeing. Students are seen as rich pickings by some petty criminals who can pretty well guarantee that you have a mobile phone, portable television, CD or DVD player, probably a laptop, digital camera or mp3, and maybe even a bike, a car or some designer gear. All are relatively easy to dispose of in the world they frequent. It is estimated that a third of students become victims of crime, mainly theft and burglary, but many could have been prevented. The trouble is most students are blissfully unaware of crime in our towns and cities until they fall prey to it. This is particularly true of freshers partying in their first few weeks at university who are not "street-wise" about the local area. More often than not student victims are the worse for wear, having taken too much advantage of drinks promotions in a club or pub. The figures speak for themselves; about 20 per cent of student robberies occur in the first six weeks of the academic year.

The table (overleaf) summarises crime rates in those 23 towns and cities (not London) with two or more universities profiled in chapter 12 and focuses on those issues most likely to affect students. You can check on analogous data for other university places by going to www.crimereduction.gov.uk We make no apology for publishing these figures together with the tips which follow on the basis that 'forearmed is forewarned'. They are compiled from official police data and, whilst not perfect, give a much more realistic picture than you might get from scare stories in the press or questionable claims about safety in the odd prospectus. If safety and security are significant factors in your choice of where to study then here are some hard facts for you to consider

Local statistics about crimes solely against students are not available but, after seeking expert advice, we have chosen three as likely to be the most relevant, namely burglary, robbery and assault. The data are rolling averages for the three years to 2005 per 1000 population. Definitions differ somewhat for Scotland and thus figures for the Scottish university cities are listed separately and should not be compared with the others.

These figures are also likely to over-represent crime levels. This is because they are based on resident populations and hence take no account of short-stay visitors and commuters. The likelihood of your becoming a victim are therefore less in real terms than these figures might suggest. However, for the cities listed, this reporting problem is a common issue and hence the relative crime rates are still valid.

Crime Levels in University Cities per 1000 population 2002–05

City	Burglary*	Robbery	Assault**	Total
Canterbury	4.2	0.6	0.5	5.3
Bath	5.5	0.8	0.6	6.9
Southampton	5.2	1.3	0.7	7.1
Brighton	8.0	1.6	0.7	10.3
Oxford	8.7	2.0	0.7	11.4
Cardiff	8.7	1.1	2.0	11.8
Belfast	8.8	1.6	1.5	11.9
Coventry	9.3	2.0	1.3	12.7
Cambridge	9.6	2.1	1.0	12.7
Newcastle	10.8	1.4	0.8	13.0
Sheffield	11.4	1.8	0.8	13.9
Leicester	10.9	3.9	2.2	17.1
Birmingham	10.9	5.3	1.2	17.5
Liverpool	13.6	3.0	3.0	19.5
Leeds	18.4	2.4	0.9	21.8
Bristol	15.9	5.3	1.7	22.9
Manchester	21.5	8.9	3.0	33.5
Nottingham	26.5	6.3	1.0	33.8
Edinburgh	4.6	1.3	0.9	6.8
Dundee	6.1	0.7	0.7	7.5
Aberdeen	7.2	1.1	0.9	9.2
Glasgow	6.3	2.7	3.9	13.0

*domestic housebreaking in Scotland
**serious assault in Scotland

Don't let it happen to you.

- Do carry a personal alarm with you – many men see these as female accessories and somehow not macho. But figures show that male students stand a much higher risk of been attacked in the street.
- Do try to avoid walking home on your own in the dark and make sure you are familiar with any late night transport provided. Keep to well-lit and busy streets, avoid pedestrian underpasses, and use designated safe walking routes where available.
- Do be aware of people crowding around you when using a cash machine and preferably draw out money during the day.
- Do be suspicious of e-mails or phone calls requesting too much personal information and destroy papers carrying bank or credit card details. Identity theft is on the increase.
- Do keep a record somewhere safe of plastic card details and the serial and model numbers of your expensive electrical equipment.
- Do mark your possessions with a UV pen – your student registration number plus the initials of your university is a unique number.
- Do remember dialling *#06# will give you your unique mobile registration (IMEI) number. Make a note and register it at www.immobilise.com. If your phone is then lost or stolen, a quick call to the immobilise hotline (08701 123 123) will result in your handset being blocked on all the networks. Mobiles are by far the most popular items stolen from young people.
- Do try to avoid using your mobile in isolated places. Texting can distract you from what is happening around you. When you are out and about switch your mobile to vibrate mode rather than a ring tone.
- Do consider installing security software on your laptop and always carry it hidden inside a sports bag rather than in its own obvious case. Nowadays, university IT and learning centres are open around the clock and many students could be leaving these places in the middle of the night.
- Do make sure the outside doors are fitted with a "Yale" type lock and five lever mortise deadlock. Fit any vulnerable downstairs windows with key-operated locks. Students in private housing are twice as likely to be burgled than those in halls of residence, not least because their accommodation is often unoccupied for long periods of the day and night. You can give the impression of being at home by using timer switches on lights and radios.
- Do immobilise your car or lock your bike whenever you leave it even for a few minutes. Think about where you park. Stealing from vehicles is still a major problem and you should routinely remove your stereo and sat nav (hot property!) and store it in a safe place.
- Do have adequate personal belongings insurance – over half the students who fall prey to burglars are not insured.
- Do consider secure storage for expensive items if you are leaving these over the vacations. International students might find this service particularly helpful.
- Do get hold of your own free copy of the *Student Survival Guide* from www.good2bsecure.gov.uk or by phoning 0870-241 4680 quoting reference SSG.

None of these simple precautions will cost you much in time or money. In fact, you will find that many universities or their students' unions, often working closely with the local police, distribute personal alarms, UV pens, etc, to new students. Many of the other items mentioned are not expensive so could be added to the birthday presents list! Don't act after the event when you or one of your friends has had something stolen. Imagine how you would feel if weeks of work on your lap-top was lost for ever – we all know of situations where that has actually happened. Better to be safe than sorry?

6 Sport at University

University life offers a unique opportunity to enjoy sport and recreation and the range and quality of sports facilities, clubs and classes available will be a revelation. Not surprisingly, universities encourage all their students to take advantage of them. You may well have already gained an initial idea of what's available from a visit, but a guided tour during Freshers' Week will give you the chance to find out much more. Whether your interest is in continuing an existing involvement in sport or trying an entirely new activity alongside your studies, use your first week or so at university to find out about the full range of opportunities before signing up to specific classes or clubs.

Most universities offer a full range of traditional (British) sports such as football, rugby, netball, badminton, tennis and squash, and Oxford and Cambridge are only two of the many universities at which rowing has a high profile. They also provide less common sports and related activities such as archery, American football, caving, fencing, gliding, hot-air ballooning, motor sports, Pilates, sub-aqua, tai chi, triathlon, ultimate Frisbee and windsurfing. The list is varied and constantly changing in response to students' needs and expectations. In addition, there will be opportunities to take part in a wide range of fitness activities from aerobics to working out in modern, well equipped fitness studios that in many universities are every bit as good as those in the trendiest commercial fitness club – but much better value for money.

Don't worry if you've never played a particular sport or taken part in a particular activity before. There'll be both beginner classes and coaching for those who wish to improve, usually provided either by the staff employed in university sport and recreation departments (they go by various titles) or fellow students. Qualified coaches will run most of the classes in popular activities, such as badminton, golf, squash, aerobics and tai chi, and any equipment you need, such as bows and arrows or racquets and balls, will be readily available. The scale and range of taught recreation programmes varies from one university to another, with some offering over 100 classes a week. They provide an ideal opportunity to grasp the basics of a sport or a range of activities both cheaply and without any long-term commitment.

The other route for getting involved is through Athletic or Sports Union clubs or intra-mural leagues (for simplicity, the rest of this chapter refers simply to Sports Unions). They generally operate under the philosophy of student sport, run for students by students, but increasingly with support from professional staff within the university. Many universities have over 50 student sports clubs, and by joining one (or more) you might even discover a real aptitude for a particular sport and move from beginner to student or full international competitor by the time you graduate.

If you want to take part in the most popular competitive sports, but without committing to regular training and competition for university teams, intra-mural ("within the walls") sport is tailor-made for you. It provides opportunities for regular but relatively casual competition in activities such as badminton, basketball, cricket, football, hockey, netball, squash and tennis. Most intra-mural competitions are available for both men and women, although there will probably also be some for mixed teams, such as in hockey or korfball. Most teams come from a hall of residence, a faculty or department;

though some are groups of friends who may well adopt "off the wall" team names. Teams can be highly competitive or recreational – but are almost certain to be pretty sociable. Some may involve university staff or the occasional graduate as well as students and there's usually around one match a week during term. There may also be a major sports festival in the week just after exams in the summer.

If you aspire to higher things, virtually all universities field a range of representative teams across a wide range of sports. They take part in matches against other universities and often also participate in local leagues and other competitions. So if you're a member of a representative team you can expect to play a couple of matches a week, one against another university and the other against a local sports club. You'll probably also have at least one training and/or coaching session. An increasing number of universities now employ professional coaches (either full- or part-time) for most of their student clubs/teams, often supported by student members with a coaching qualification who will help coach new members. As a result, if you're interested in becoming a coach the cost of getting the necessary qualification – which will obviously look good on your CV – may well be subsidised by the club or Sports Union. The same goes for those interested in umpiring or refereeing.

The best players in any university team are eligible to be selected for the British or one of the home country student international teams to take part in the World Student Games or other international events.

University Sports Facilities

To support all this activity most universities have a good range of high-quality sports facilities – and the range is getting better by the day. There will almost certainly be a sports centre with at least a multi-sports hall and other dry sports facilities including a fitness gym with modern cardio-vascular and resistance machines, one or more exercise studios and facilities such as squash courts. Many also have a pool and specialist facilities such as a martial arts room (dojo) or a climbing wall. Outdoors, you might typically expect a number of grass pitches for different sports – generally of a very high quality – at least one floodlit artificial turf pitch and possibly an athletics track and/or a boat house. Some universities also own or have access to outdoor centres for activities such as water sports, climbing and hill walking. Very few have their own golf course, but many have come to an arrangement with one or more local clubs which allow students to use their courses at a reduced charge.

The Administration of Student Sport

Most student sports clubs are mixed, though some remain either men or women only (netball and cheerleading for example). All of them will be members of a Sports Union – the umbrella body for all the student sports clubs within a particular university. In some it is an integral part of the wider Students' Union, though an increasing number of Sports Unions are integrating with their university's professionally run sports department to provide a "one-stop shop" for all student/university sport. In either case, financial and other support will be provided by the university, most likely through the Sports Union, which will also have policies and procedures for things such as health and safety, monitoring of equipment and the accreditation of coaches, to which all clubs must conform. This helps to ensure that university sport is safe as well as fun. The Sports Union will also control the awarding of university "full colours" and "half-colours" to recognise major individual and club sporting achievement and will normally arrange an annual ball or awards dinner – often one of the highlights of the university sporting calendar.

Most universities (via their sports unions), in turn, are members of the British Universities Sports Association (www.busa.org.uk), the governing body for competitive university student sport. BUSA runs national competitions in 43 sports from athletics to windsurfing and also co-ordinates the British teams for the World University Games and World University Championships. The BUSA sports programme involves some 60,000 students across the UK and 3,200 teams are engaged in BUSA competitions in a typical week. In fact, with over 500 leagues, BUSA runs the biggest sporting programme of its kind in Europe.

BUSA also selects the British Universities teams for events such as the biennial World University Games (WUGs) – the second biggest multi-sport event in the world after the Olympic Games. In 2007 the World University Summer Games is to be held in Bangkok, and the Winter games in Torino. In intervening years (2006, 2008, etc) some 30 other sports not involved in WUGs have separate World University Championships in which UK student teams compete.

The professional association for members of university staff working to deliver sports opportunities from participation to performance is Universities and Colleges Sport (www.ucsport.net). Its website gives more details of university sports facilities and programmes than is possible in this chapter.

Investment in Sport by Universities

Sporting success brings prestige and good publicity to a university and can help to attract students. Not surprisingly, therefore, most take sport seriously. A 2004 survey for Sport England found that English higher education institutions had a combined budget of around £73 million for sport. Many universities have invested heavily in new or upgraded sports facilities, often with significant support from the Lottery Sports Fund, and in the past five years alone the universities listed in the table below have spent over £375 million on sports facilities. One result is that four of Britain's limited stock of 50-metre pools, for example, are on university campuses (at Bath, East Anglia, Loughborough and Stirling) while the two Manchester universities share a further two and a number of others are planning to invest in new 50-metre pools or other high profile training and competition facilities prior to the London 2012 Olympic Games. A significant number host key elements in the UK's network of Institutes of Sport and through them are actively helping sports governing bodies to develop Britain's next crop of Olympians and potential World Champions. Where these facilities exist there are obvious spin-off benefits for students and student teams, not least the opportunity to rub shoulders with elite athletes.

Universities are active supporters of student sport – at all levels – because of the range of benefits it brings to campus life: exercise for students, a chance to let off steam and make friends, not to mention good publicity and "town and gown" relationships for the university. Universities provide and subsidise facilities, they fund professional staff to manage facilities, provide activity programmes (such as recreation classes) and services (such as physiotherapy) and they support student clubs in a range of ways. They also try – with varying degrees of commitment – to ensure that Wednesday afternoons are free from teaching so that students can take part in sport.

The Cost of Sport

Student sport isn't free, but for most students it isn't particularly expensive either, thanks to the subsidies provided by universities and the energetic way in which student clubs seek sponsorship. Most universities offer a range of peak and off-peak membership packages for their indoor sports centre either on a term by term or annual basis, and also offer "pay on entry" for those who don't want to take out a membership. Annual membership ranges from nothing to £200 with an average of about £75 and you'll probably find that membership will be cheaper than paying on entry if you want to use facilities or take part in classes more than once a week.

Student clubs also charge membership fees, but again they should be reasonable. Often, there are two charges: membership of the Sports Union (typically £5–£25) and membership of one or more clubs (typically £25–£50 each). Some sports are inherently more expensive than others, so club fees vary. However, the cost will be evened out to some extent by financial support from the university, so sports which need expensive equipment, such as rowing or gliding, should still be affordable. Intra-mural sport is significantly cheaper and likely to cost only about £1–£2 per session, if anything.

Opportunities for Leadership

With up to 50 or more student sports clubs, there will be lots of opportunities for you to take on committee and leadership positions and learn skills which will add to your employability on graduation. Captaining a team, organising fixtures, handling club finances, finding and servicing sponsors, organising club social events or even just being a committee member may sound mundane, but they are both enjoyable and can add significant value to your CV when going for that all-important first job after graduating. The experience will also develop your self-confidence and basic business skills. Senior student officials – such as Sports Union officers – rub shoulders with the "great and good" in their universities on a regular basis and can learn a lot from seeing how they operate. The few who become full or part-time sabbatical officers also get a year off from their studies to oversee the operation of student sport and usually have responsibility for managing both a sizeable budget and full or part-time staff.

Opportunities for Employment

Most university sports centres need part-time staff and this creates opportunities for students to get valuable work experience and earn some money. Working in a university sports centre is a lot more fun – and healthier – than most of the low paid jobs otherwise on offer, such as bar work. Don't expect to earn a fortune, but pay of around £6–£7 an hour is quite common – and maybe up to £16 an hour for coaching if you have a suitable governing-body qualification. Local clubs and leisure centres may then also be interested in employing you for a few hours each week. Students who take on jobs in university sports centres also gain training in things like first aid, fire safety, risk assessments, manual handling, event management, customer care, and health and safety – all of which can be transferable to other work environments.

Sporting Excellence

The UK has rapidly developed an elite sporting infrastructure in the past few years with a range of sports institutes and initiatives designed to nurture the country's future sports stars. Many of these involve universities, so higher education is an increasingly important engine room for sporting excellence in the UK – not surprising considering that academic and sporting ability often go hand in hand. In addition, most world class sportsmen and women are either in the student age group or only a year or so older. Sixteen of the 31 medallists for Team GB at the Athens Olympics were either current students or university graduates, while Loughborough University students won more medals in the 2006 Commonwealth Games than 32 countries and almost equalled New Zealand's performance. Ways in which universities support sporting excellence include:

- Providing sports scholarships or bursaries: managed by university sport and recreation services, bursaries usually offer a range of "in-kind" forms of support to a selection of talented students. Sporting bursaries and scholarships are highlighted in the grid on pages 212–217, and in the individual university profiles in chapter 11. Loughborough, Bath and Queen's, Belfast are the leaders here.
- Supporting the Talented Athlete Scholarship Scheme (TASS). TASS is currently available only to students at English universities who are eligible to compete for England. It is a government-funded sports scholarship programme delivered through a partnership between universities and national governing bodies of sport. Each scholarship provides around £3,000 worth of high-quality performance sport support. Further details are available at www.tass.gov.uk.
- Supporting academic flexibility (depending upon the university): although universities expect student athletes competing at national level to fulfil their academic commitments, most will offer some flexibility in learning and examination schedules. However, make the necessary arrangements well in advance.
- Providing facilities, services and a high-quality sports performance environment to house a centre of excellence for one or more governing bodies of sport.
- Housing centres of excellence. Aberdeen, Abertay, Bath, Birmingham, Brighton, Bristol, Coventry, Dundee, Durham, East Anglia, Edinburgh, Exeter, Glamorgan, Heriot-Watt, Hertfordshire, Kent, Leeds Metropolitan, Loughborough, Middlesex, NE Wales, Northumbria, Portsmouth, Robert Gordon, St Andrews, St Mark and St John, Stirling, Strathclyde, Teesside, University College London, Ulster, Warwick and Wolverhampton all host at least one centre of excellence linked to a home country Sports Institute.
- Housing one of the multi-sport regional hubs of one of the home country Institutes of Sport

Scoring System for the Table on University Sport and Recreation (pages 188–93)

Different students look for different things from their sport while at university. The table on the following pages therefore contains a mix of factual information (such as the number of sports scholarships) and star rankings, with 5* the best and 1* the worst. Some parts of the table are not applicable (n/a) to some universities. The information in the table includes:

- BUSA Rankings, based on all sports. Teams get points each year for their success in inter-university competitions and BUSA uses them to compile an annual league table. The universities with the highest rankings (eg, Loughborough, Bath and Birmingham) are therefore overall the most successful competitively.
- A star rating for the range of indoor dry sports facilities, such as sports halls, dance studios, squash courts and fitness gyms, derived from the total at-one-time capacity of the facilities. Not surprisingly, the largest universities tend to offer the widest range.
- A star rating for access to the indoor dry facilities: this relates the range of facilities to the number of full time equivalent (FTE) students to give an indication of how busy the facilities are likely to be or, conversely, how easy it may be book a court or access a facility at any given time; 5* facilities are likely to be the easiest and 1* facilities the least easy. However, the star rating does not take account of other factors which may also influence this, such as opening hours or the commitment of facilities to external groups such as governing bodies of sport.
- Similar star ratings for the range of and access to pools and outdoor pitches and courts, such as football, rugby or cricket pitches and tennis or netball courts.
- Whether the university has a boat house and therefore convenient access to suitable water for its rowing club (Y = yes; N = no).
- Whether the university has an athletics track, with an indication of the type of track (Y = 400-metre track; NS = non-standard length track; N = no track).
- The total number of sports scholarships available from the university each year. These totals exclude TASS scholarships, which are provided by the Government. The table gives the total number of scholarships, whose value can vary widely from free access to facilities to a package that includes a range of support services, sports science, sports medicine, nutrition, strength and conditioning, coaching and biomechanics, as well as funding.
- The total number of sports union clubs.
- Whether there is a part-time or full-time Sports Union President. At universities with a full-time sabbatical president, the Sports Union is likely to be larger and more active that those with a part-time one, which in turn are likely to be more active that those with no sabbatical officers at all.
- The opportunity to take part in intra-mural sport, derived from the approximate number of students per 1,000 FTEs who take part. The table is split into indoor leagues (eg, badminton and squash), pitch leagues (eg, football, cricket and rugby) and outdoor court sports (eg, netball and tennis).
- The opportunity to take part in fitness or sports beginner classes, derived from the approximate number of students per 1,000 FTEs who take part in classes each week.

The table is based on a detailed survey of university sport undertaken by UCS in early 2006. The information relates only to the facilities and services that universities provide centrally for all their students and ignores any facilities there may be in halls of residence or colleges. At Oxford and Cambridge, for example, many colleges have facilities that are not reflected in the table.

Universities	BUSA Ranking 2004–2005	Indoor Dry Sports Facilities: range	Indoor Dry Sports Facilities: access	Pools: range	Pools: access	Pitches and Courts: range	Pitches and Courts: access
Aberdeen	30	2*	2*	*	2*	2*	2*
Abertay	70	*	*	n/a	n/a	2*	5*
Aberystwyth	=60	4*	5*	2*	4*	4*	5*
Anglia Ruskin	=94	*	*	n/a	n/a	2*	*
Aston	87	2*	4*	*	4*	*	2*
Bangor	93	4*	5*	n/a	n/a	3*	4*
Bath	2	5*	5*	5*	5*	4*	4*
Bath Spa	=101	n/a	n/a	n/a	n/a	n/a	n/a
Birmingham	3	4*	2*	2*	*	3*	2*
Bolton	86	No further information reported					
Bournemouth	41	3*	4*	n/a	n/a	*	*
Bradford	=101	No further information reported					
Brighton	25	4*	3*	2*	2*	4*	4*
Bristol	11	4*	4*	4*	4*	5*	4*
Brunel	27	4*	4*	n/a	n/a	4*	4*
Cambridge	6	No further information reported					
Canterbury Christ Church	79	*	2*	n/a	n/a	*	2*
Cardiff	21	4*	2*	n/a	n/a	2*	*
Central Lancashire	62	2*	*	n/a	n/a	3*	*
Chester	74	No further information reported					
Chichester	49	No further information reported					
City	99	No further information reported					
Coventry	=60	2*	2*	n/a	n/a	*	*
De Montfort	44	3*	2*	n/a	n/a	5*	4*
Derby	98	No further information reported					
Dundee	53	2*	2*	2*	2*	4*	4*
Durham	5	2*	*	n/a	n/a	3*	3*
East Anglia	56	5*	5*	5*	5*	5*	5*
East London	n/a	*	*	2*	3*	4*	4*
Edinburgh	9	5*	5*	3*	2*	4*	3*
Essex	73	3*	5*	n/a	n/a	2*	4*
Exeter	12	5*	5*	2*	3*	5*	5*
Glamorgan	64	4*	4*	n/a	n/a	2*	*
Glasgow	18	5*	4*	3*	2*	4*	3*
Glasgow Caledonian	71	3*	3*	n/a	n/a	n/a	n/a
Gloucestershire	36	2*	3*	n/a	n/a	*	2*
Goldsmiths, London	=101	2*	4*	n/a	n/a	*	*

Boat house	Althletics track	Sports scholarships	Sports Union clubs	Sabbatical Sports Union president	Indoor intra-mural leagues	Pitch sport intra-mural leagues	Outdoor court intra-mural leagues	Fitness classes	Sports beginner classes
Y	N	20	54	Full time	n/a	3*	*	5*	3*
N	NS	10	22	Full time	4*	n/a	3*	2*	4*
Y	N	0	67	Full time	5*	4*	5*	5*	2*
N	N	11	0	No	2*	n/a	*	*	3*
N	N	0	32	Full time	n/a	n/a	n/a	4*	3*
Y	NS	6	44	Full time	*	n/a	3*	4*	*
N	Y	420	48	Full time	2*	3*	2*	3*	3*
n/a	n/a	n/a	n/a	No	n/a	n/a	n/a	n/a	n/a
Y	Y	33	45	Full time	5*	4*	5*	5*	5*
				No	*	n/a	*	3*	2*
N	N	29	16	No	2*	n/a	4*	3*	4*
Y	NS	0	33	Full time	n/a	n/a	n/a	5*	4*
N	N	6	44	Shared	*	2*	3*	2*	*
Y	N	20	51	Full time	3*	5*	4*	4*	4*
Y	Y	0	52	Shared	3*	*	2*	n/a	n/a
N	NS	0	33	Full time	n/a	3*	n/a	4*	4*
N	N	47	106	Full time	n/a	4*	2*	4*	*
N	NS	20	36	No	*	n/a	*	2*	n/a
					3*	*	2*	4*	3*
N	N	22	16	Full time	2*	2*	n/a	2*	n/a
Y	N	0	33	Full time	n/a	n/a	n/a	*	5*
Y	N	12	46	Full time	3*	2*	*	5*	5*
Y	Y	20	49	Full time	5*	5*	4*	4*	5*
Y	Y	27	46	No	5*	4*	5*	5*	5*
Y	N	No further information reported							
Y	NS	33	61	Full time	4*	5*	*	5*	*
Y	N	12	45	Full time	5*	n/a	5*	5*	2*
Y	Y	31	98	Full time	2*	4*	5*	4*	5*
N	N	19	22	Full time	4*	n/a	4*	3*	5*
Y	Y	27	46	Full time	n/a	n/a	3*	5*	3*
N	N	0	27	Shared	n/a	n/a	n/a	5*	5*
N	N	11	44	Full time	3*	2*	3*	*	n/a
N	N	0	17	Shared	n/a	n/a	2*	*	n/a

Universities	BUSA Ranking 2004–2005	Indoor Dry Sports Facilities: range	Indoor Dry Sports Facilities: access	Pools: range	Pools: access	Pitches and Courts: range	Pitches and Courts: access
Greenwich	75	No further information reported					
Heriot Watt	55	2*	4*	n/a	n/a	4*	5*
Hertfordshire	58	4*	3*	4*	3*	4*	3*
Huddersfield	100	*	*	n/a	n/a	4*	3*
Hull	=67	3*	3*	n/a	n/a	5*	5*
Imperial College	40	5*	5*	5*	5*	5*	5*
Keele	=94	2*	4*	n/a	n/a	4*	4*
Kent	43	3*	3*	n/a	n/a	3*	3*
King's College, London	47	No further information reported					
Kingston	72	*	*	n/a	n/a	3*	2*
Lampeter	=101	*	5*	3*	5*	*	5*
Lancaster	65	3*	5*	3*	4*	3*	4*
Leeds	15	5*	2*	n/a	n/a	5*	3*
Leeds Metropolitan	23	5*	4*	*	*	3*	2*
Leicester	=83	3*	3*	n/a	n/a	4*	5*
Lincoln	77	2*	3*	n/a	n/a	2*	3*
Liverpool	38	3*	2*	4*	4*	2*	2*
Liverpool Hope	76	*	4*	n/a	n/a	*	2*
Liverpool John Moores	52	2*	*	*	*	*	*
London Metropolitan	22	No further information reported					
London School of Economics	51	*	*	n/a	n/a	*	*
London South Bank	49	*	*	n/a	n/a	*	*
Loughborough	1	5*	5*	5*	5*	5*	4*
Luton	=96	*	*	n/a	n/a	3*	3*
Manchester	14	5*	2*	5*	5*	5*	3*
Manchester Metropolitan	26	5*	3*	2*	*	3*	*
Middlesex	63	4*	2*	2*	*	3*	2*
Napier	=80	*	*	n/a	n/a	n/a	n/a
Newcastle	19	3*	2*	4*	3*	3*	3*
Northampton	=83	No further information reported					
Northumbria	10	4*	3*	n/a	n/a	3*	3*
Nottingham	7	5*	3*	4*	2*	5*	4*
Nottingham Trent	29	4*	2*	*	*	3*	2*
Oxford	8	4*	3*	4*	3*	5*	4*
Oxford Brookes	54	5*	5*	*	2*	4*	4*
Paisley	=101	No further information reported					
Plymouth	57	*	*	n/a	n/a	2*	2*

Boat house	Athletics track	Sports scholarships	Sports Union clubs	Sabbatical Sports Union president	Indoor intra-mural leagues	Pitch sport intra-mural leagues	Outdoor court intra-mural leagues	Fitness classes	Sports beginner classes
Y	N	20	4	Full time	4*	3*	*	5*	3*
N	N	19	26	Full time	n/a	2*	*	3*	n/a
N	N	0	20	Shared	n/a	n/a	n/a	2*	n/a
Y	NS	2	41	Full time	n/a	3*	2*	3*	n/a
Y	N	14	140	Shared	4*	5*	2*	4*	3*
N	N	0	35	No	3*	*	4*	4*	4*
Y	N	8	42	Full time	3*	*	4*	4*	5*
N	N	26	28	Shared	n/a	n/a	n/a	2*	n/a
N	N	0	12	Shared	n/a	n/a	n/a	2*	n/a
Y	NS	0	39	Full time	n/a	n/a	n/a	3*	5*
N	N	42	60	Full time	5*	4*	3*	3*	4*
N	Y	21	42	Full time	*	2*	*	2*	n/a
Y	Y	0	32	Shared	4*	5*	4*	5*	n/a
N	N	0	30	Full time	3*	*	3*	3*	2*
N	N	50	45	No	n/a	5*	5*	3*	3*
0	NS	0	22	No	n/a	n/a	n/a	3*	*
0	N	16	26	No	*	3*	n/a	2*	n/a
N	N	2	32	No	3*	2*	n/a	*	3*
N	N	53	18	Full time	*	n/a	n/a	*	n/a
Y	Y	118	53	Full time	5*	5*	5*	2*	2*
N	NS	0	16	Full time	*	*	*	*	*
Y	N	21	35	Full time	2*	3*	2*	3*	n/a
N	N	16	58	Full time	*	2*	n/a	4*	2*
N	N	17	0	No	*	*	n/a	*	2*
N	N	0	40	Full time	n/a	n/a	n/a	n/a	n/a
Y	NS	10	55	Full time	5*	5*	4*	4*	*
N	N	0	17	Full time	*	3*	n/a	*	n/a
Y	N	32	41	Full time	4*	3*	*	2*	2*
Y	N	38	73	Full time	2*	3*	3*	3*	2*
N	Y	16	43	Full time	4*	2*	4*	2*	n/a
Y	Y	6	80	Full time	5*	5*	4*	*	2*
Y	N	0	68	No	*	4*	3*	3*	3*
N	NS	0	49	Full time	No further information reported				

Universities	BUSA Ranking 2004–2005	Indoor Dry Sports Facilities: range	Indoor Dry Sports Facilities: access	Pools: range	Pools: access	Pitches and Courts: range	Pitches and Courts: access
Portsmouth	39	3*	2*	n/a	n/a	2*	2*
Queen Mary, London	69	No further information reported					
Queen's, Belfast	=67	4*	2*	4*	3*	3*	2*
Reading	32	2*	2*	n/a	n/a	5*	5*
Robert Gordon	90	4*	5*	3*	4*	*	*
Roehampton	92	No further information reported					
Royal Holloway	66	*	3*	n/a	n/a	4*	5*
Salford	91	No further information reported					
Sheffield	31	5*	4*	4*	2*	4*	3*
Sheffield Hallam	17	3*	*	n/a	n/a	*	*
SOAS	=101	No further information reported					
Southampton	13	5*	4*	2*	2*	5*	5*
Southampton Solent	42	4*	4*	3*	3*	3*	4*
St Andrews	35	*	4*	n/a	n/a	5*	5*
Staffordshire	89	4*	4*	n/a	n/a	2*	*
Stirling	16	3*	5*	5*	5*	3*	4*
Strathclyde	33	2*	*	*	*	*	*
Sunderland	=80	3*	3*	5*	4*	5*	5*
Surrey	59	4*	5*	n/a	n/a	2*	2*
Sussex	48	2*	2*	n/a	n/a	2*	3*
Swansea	45	3*	3*	5*	5*	2*	2*
Teesside	85	2*	*	n/a	n/a	*	*
Thames Valley	n/a	No further information reported					
Ulster	=59	5*	3*	n/a	n/a	5*	3*
University of the Arts, London	n/a	*	*	n/a	n/a	n/a	n/a
UCE Birmingham	=96	n/a	n/a	n/a	n/a	*	*
University College London	46	2*	*	n/a	n/a	2*	2*
UWCN, Newport	=59	*	5*	n/a	n/a	2*	5*
UWIC, Cardiff	4	3*	5*	3*	4*	3*	5*
Warwick	24	5*	5*	3*	3*	5*	5*
West of England	28	2*	*	n/a	n/a	*	*
Westminster	88	3*	2*	n/a	3*	5*	5*
Winchester	=101	No further information reported					
Wolverhampton	82	5*	4*	*	*	4*	3*
Worcester	37	*	4*	n/a	n/a	*	3*
York	34	3*	3*	n/a	n/a	2*	3*

Boat house	Athletics track	Sports scholarships	Sports Union clubs	Sabbatical Sports Union president	Indoor intra-mural leagues	Pitch sport intra-mural leagues	Outdoor court intra-mural leagues	Fitness classes	Sports beginner classes
N	NS	0	54	Full time	5*	*	5*	3*	n/a
N	N	0	28	Full time	2*	4*	2*	*	3*
Y	N	70	50	Shared	2*	4*	*	4*	4*
Y	N	30	48	Full time	3*	4*	2*	5*	*
Y	N	6	80	Full time	2*	n/a	n/a	5*	n/a
N	N	17	39	Full time	n/a	n/a	n/a	3*	n/a
Y	N	0	13	Shared	n/a	n/a	n/a	*	n/a
N	N	27	47	Full time	3*	3*	5*	4*	n/a
N	N	29	34	Full time	2*	*	3*	4*	n/a
Y	N	19	75	Full time	4*	5*	4*	5*	5*
Y	NS	32	29	Shared	3*	n/a	n/a	2*	4*
N	NS	0	54	Full time	3*	5*	5*	5*	5*
Y	Y	14							
N	Y	50	38	Full time	5*	n/a	5*	5*	4*
Y	N	28	41	Full time	2*	n/a	n/a	3*	*
Y	Y	27	53	Full time	4*	2*	2*	*	*
N	N	6	38	Full time	5*	n/a	4*	5*	4*
N	N	9	34	Full time	4*	*	3*	4*	2*
N	Y	36	36	Full time	n/a	n/a	n/a	2*	2*
Y	N	11	51	Shared	n/a	*	3*	2*	n/a
Y	NS	32	98	Full time	5*	*	4*	5*	*
N	N	0	9	Shared	n/a	2*	2*	*	4*
N	NS	0	53	Shared	2*	*	2*	*	*
Y	NS	32	53	Shared	4*	n/a	n/a	*	n/a
0	N	2	26	Full time	4*	n/a	4*	4*	4*
N	Y	15	19	No	n/a	n/a	n/a	*	n/a
Y	Y	17	73	Full time	5*	4*	5*	3*	5*
N	N	5	40	Full time	*	n/a	*	*	n/a
Y	N	0	16	No	n/a	n/a	5*	*	5*
N	Y	24	24	Shared	2*	n/a	n/a	*	*
0	N	29	28	Full time	3*	3*	2*	2*	*
Y	Y	6	53	Full time	5*	5*	5*	2*	2*

7 Managing Your Money

The head of one university tells the story of a photographer at Graduation asking the student to place a hand on her parent's shoulder, only to hear the riposte from the parent, "Wouldn't it be more appropriate to have a hand in my pocket!" It is an apocryphal tale but one which will ring true for many parents, given the financial support required these days. Going to university can be an expensive family business and student debt, a bit like a house mortgage, has become an accepted fact of life. That said, middle-class students are more likely to view debt from the low-interest student loans available (see p. 195) as an investment – some have even been known to re-invest in ISAs – whereas many working-class students see it as a burden. A recent survey by Barclays Bank shows that, on average, students graduate with a debt of £13,500, most of it in student loans and it is likely that this level of debt will increase under the new system of student funding. But there will be much more generous support for students from low-income families, and all UK and EU students will be able to take out Government loans under very favourable terms to meet the total cost of any tuition fees you might be liable for. This support could also perhaps be supplemented by university bursaries and scholarships or by employer payments as part of their sponsorship packages.

| UNITE Student Experience Report 2006 | |
Sources of student debt	(%)
Student loan	86
Bank overdraft	23
Parental loan	10
Credit card	7
Personal loan	5
Friends	3
Store card	2
Utility bills	1
Car loan	1
Mail order	1
Hire Purchase	1
Family loan	1

You will need to muster all the resources you can lay your hands on unless you are one of that small band who has a regular private income. The vast majority of students have to rely on loans, savings, earnings, overdrafts and the generosity of family and friends. But help is also in hand from the public purse following on radical plans for students starting at universities from now on. These various loans, grants and bursaries are outlined below and are intended to shift the onus of responsibility from parents to students. No longer do you or your family have to make advanced, up-front payments towards any tuition fees.

University Tuition Fees

Nearly all the financial figures quoted in this chapter are for undergraduate entry to full-time university courses in 2006 and you can assume that most will increase for 2007 in line with inflation. You will not be far out in any calculations if you assume an increase of 3 per cent.

Parliament introduced the new system of funding for students entering the English and Northern Irish universities in 2006 and this has had a knock on effect in Scotland and Wales. The dust is settling and if you are planning to go to university in 2007, the situation is now quite clear but still rather complicated. We will try and keep it simple.

Tuition Fees have been introduced in all four countries but not all students will have to pay these and, in any case, you can take out a fees loan to cover them. Let's look at each country in turn.

In England and Northern Ireland, the maximum tuition fee in 2006 for full-time undergraduates was £3,000 a year. This maximum is fixed for the rest of the decade (apart from small increases to take account of inflation) and can only be changed by a vote of the UK Parliament. In theory, this fee can be varied by the individual universities, even for particular courses within the same university, but in practice virtually every university in the first year of the new system opted for a blanket £3,000 and that is likely to be the future pattern. In fact, only four universities charged less than the maximum amount: Leeds Metropolitan, £2,000; Greenwich, £2,500; Northampton, £2,500+ and Thames Valley, £2,700.

Scotland is expected to introduce a fixed tuition fee in 2006 of £1,700 (£2,700 for medicine) but this will only affect students coming to the Scottish universities from the other UK countries, who can defer payment by applying for a student loan administered by their LEA or devolved government. Students ordinarily resident in Scotland and staying there to study will have these fees paid for them by the Student Awards Agency for Scotland (SAAS). However, this is not done automatically – you will still have to apply. Many will also will have to contribute to a Graduate Endowment. Although not a loan, this Graduate Endowment can similarly be paid after you graduate and hence is described below under graduate loans.

The Welsh Assembly has agreed a similar policy to England with effect from 2007 when the Welsh universities will be able to charge variable tuition fees of up to £3,000, perhaps a little more for inflation.

The table *Tuition Fees in the UK by Country* (below) summarises the tuition fee levels. But it is worth reiterating: where you incur these fees you can also take out a fees loan to cover them and this will be paid straight to the university. You can then defer worrying about tuition fees until after you have graduated and are earning sufficient money to start paying the loan back.

Student Loans

All UK students in all four UK countries are eligible for student loans administered by the Student Loans Company (SLC). Any money you borrow is at a nominal interest rate so that, in effect, you pay back no more than you actually borrowed. Interest is, however, added from the time you take out the loan even though you do not have to start paying it off until after you have graduated and are earning more than £15,000. You can, of course, pay it, or parts of it, at any time you like – you don't have to wait until reaching that magical £15,000 salary if you do not want to.

Tuition fees in the UK by country

Country	Level	Type
England	£3,000 max	Variable
Northern Ireland	£3,000 max	Variable
Wales	£3,000 max	Variable
Scotland	£1,700	Fixed
Scotland (Medicine)	£2,700	Fixed

There are two types of loan from the Government: a *fees loan* to cover any tuition fees you have to pay and a *maintenance loan* to help with your day-to-day living costs. The fees loan is not means-tested; every student can have the full amount to cover the tuition fees regardless of family income. If the university levies a fee of £3,000 for your particular course then you can have a fees loan for £3,000 to cover it completely. The situation for a Welsh resident opting to study at a Welsh university is even better. You would get a repayable fees loan of £1,200 and a non-repayable fees grant of £1,800 to cover the £3,000 and neither of them is means-tested.

For Scots staying in Scotland there are no university fees to pay by you and so there is no need to take out a fees loan. But most of you will be expected to contribute a total of £2,216 (2005 figure) to the Graduate Endowment set up to support future generations of students and you can take out a deferred SLC Loan to cover this. If you do, then the normal rules for paying back by instalments after graduation apply.

The *maintenance loan*, on the other hand, is part means-tested. The amount set each year is linked to average student expenditure. The specific factors taken into consideration include your family income, whether or not you plan to live at home and also where you intend to study. It is lowest if you live outside London and decide to stay at home and highest if you go to a university in London and have to find your own accommodation.

The figures in the table *Maintenance Loan Amounts for a New First-Year Student 2006* (below) are based on a course lasting for 30 weeks. This was the maximum amount you could expect to receive as a maintenance loan last year. These will, no doubt, be increased in line with inflation for 2007 entry. But you might well be asking what determines what you, yourself, might get. The good news is that 75 per cent of the loan comes to you regardless of your family circumstances. The remaining 25 per cent depends on the family income, both from you and your parents. If your parents are separated, divorced or widowed then only the income of the parent with whom you normally live will be assessed. However, if that parent has remarried, has a partner of the opposite sex or has entered into a civil partnership, both their incomes will be taken into consideration. Certain allowances are deducted for other dependent siblings, personal pension payments, etc, to arrive at the family *residual income*. Taking the 2006 figures as an example, if this was less than £37,900 then the family would not be expected to make any contribution. Depending on where you were living/studying, you would have received one of the three maximum maintenance loan rates shown. Where the residual income was higher than £37,900 the family would be expected to contribute something towards your living costs up to the maximum given in the table. The higher the residual income the greater the contribution expected.

The rules and regulations are different for Scottish students. For example, their maintenance loan rates are somewhat lower, especially for students going to London, and the proportion assessed on the basis of family income is considerably higher. Full

Maintenance Loan Amounts for a New First-Year Student 2006

	Loan	Family Contribution
Living at home	£3,415 max	£0–£855 max @ £46,030
Living away from home (not London)	£4,405 max	£0–£1,100 max @ £48,350
Living away from home (London)	£6,170 max	£0–£1,540 max @ £52,530

details are available on the SAAS website (www.saas.gov.uk).

If you are a mature student (over 25 or married or have supported yourself for at least three years prior to becoming a student), you will be assessed for the maintenance loan and any other applicable grants on your own income plus that of your spouse or partner (not informal partners in Scotland) where appropriate. Your parents will not be expected to contribute to your living costs. In addition, specific grants are available for students with children or adult dependents and for single parents. Two new financial grants, the Parents' Learning Allowance and the Child Tax Credit, have also been introduced to provide further support for students with a family.

You don't have to take out student loans – although more than 80 per cent of students do – but we recommend that you give the matter serious consideration. They are likely to form a significant part of your income, are essentially interest free and you can always put the money in an interest-bearing account where you might expect a 5 per cent return. But remember only the maintenance loan will come to you; your fees loan will go straight to your university. Your maintenance loan will usually be paid straight into your bank or building society account in three instalments, the first at the start of the academic year.

English and Welsh students must apply for these loans and any grants (see next section) through the Local Education Authority (LEA) where they normally live, Scottish students through the Student Awards Agency for Scotland (SAAS) and those in N Ireland to their Education and Library Board (ELB). You should do so as soon as you have received an offer – even a conditional offer – from a university. Other EU students will usually be sent an application form by the university offering a place. New interactive online enquiry services have been introduced and these include an online application form and entitlement calculator. You can apply online or download an application form by logging onto the appropriate country website. You can also track your application by accessing the online service using a unique ID number.

The arrangements for repaying your student loans are generous and you can put this to the back of your mind until at least the April after you finish your course. And you only have to start thinking about it then if you are in work and your salary is over £15,000 a year. Thereafter, repayments will be deducted through the tax system at the rate of 9 per cent on that part of your income over £15,000 a year so, for example, at a salary of £20,000 before tax your monthly repayment would be:

$$£20,000 - £15,000 = £5,000 \times 9\%$$
$$= £450 \text{ a year or } £37.50 \text{ a month.}$$

Should your income fall below £15,000 then repayments would stop. Unlike a commercial loan, how much you repay each month is determined only by your income, not by how much you owe. In addition, the Government has agreed to write off any loans outstanding after 25 years so most of you could taste freedom before you are 50!

Grants

Unlike the loans outlined above, grants, bursaries and scholarships do not have to be repaid. They are yours to keep and spend as you like. But, that said, they are more difficult to describe because they come in all shapes and sizes and have different names in the various UK countries. To help matters, we will deal with them on a country-by-country basis, starting with England.

England

Here you might be eligible for a maintenance grant from the Government plus a bursary from your university or college. These have been introduced particularly to help students from lower-income homes to come to university and the Government anticipates that about half of new students will be eligible for a full or partial maintenance grant. Bursaries are such a significant topic that we have devoted a whole section to them below. You will also find more information on the bursaries offered by the individual universities in their profiles (see chapter 11) and in the summary grid on pages 212–17. Many, but not all, are dependent on family income, as is the maintenance grant which was set at a maximum of £2,700 a year in 2006. You will receive this maximum support if your family income is £17,500 or less. Between £17,500 and £37,425 you will be eligible for a partial grant, but above £37,425, nothing. To keep your debt manageable, you cannot have a full maintenance loan and a full maintenance grant. The (repayable) loan will be reduced by a £1 for every £1 of grant (not repayable) up to a maximum reduction of £1,200. Like your maintenance loan, this maintenance grant is paid in three instalments, the first at the start of the academic year.

Northern Ireland

The position here is very similar to that in England with both a means-tested maintenance grant and bursaries from the universities all of which do not have to be paid back. However, whilst the grant maximum in England is £2,700 there is a more generous upper limit in Northern Ireland of £3,200 at the same family income threshold of £17,500.

Wales

In Wales, you could be eligible not only for an assembly learning or maintenance grant of up to £2,700 and a bursary from your chosen university but also benefit from the new *National Bursary Scheme* (NBS). The National Assembly will have the option of adding funds to the NBS where it wishes to promote particular aspects of the Welsh economy or culture. These bursaries will be available to every full-time student, regardless of their UK country of origin, but not to Welsh students going to English universities. However, the latter will, of course, be eligible for bursaries offered by their chosen universities. The National Bursaries are means-tested and will be worth a minimum of £300 a year.

Scotland

The maintenance grant in Scotland is called a *Young Students' Bursary* and, like all the other grants mentioned, it is means-tested and does not have to be repaid. This replaces part of your maintenance loan and hence reduces the amount of loan you need to take out. The maximum bursary available is £2,455 if your family annual income is under £17,940. Between this and an income of £31,775 you would receive a partial bursary and beyond £31,775, nothing. There is an additional loan of up to £560 if your family income is £20,225 or less.

As you can see, these maintenance grants have largely been introduced for new full-time students from less affluent homes to help them with the costs of going to university.

Bursaries and Scholarships

The Labour Government is committed to 50 per cent of young people experiencing higher education and wants to ensure individuals are not deterred from coming to universities because of lack of funds. Coupled, therefore, with the introduction of higher tuition fees is an extensive system of support for students from low-income families, including new university bursaries, all designed to encourage wider access to higher education. In developing these, the universities seem not to have made any clear cut distinction between the words "bursary" and "scholarship", but rather to use these interchangeably.

The Office for Fair Access (OFFA)

All of these new arrangements are overseen for England and Wales by a new body, the Office for Fair Access. It required universities to submit Access Agreements by March 2005 outlining what fees they intended to levy and how they planned to widen access. A significant feature of these rather complex documents is a description of the new bursaries and scholarships available from 2006. Some are guaranteed and are based on your personal circumstances whilst others are available through open competition. These are really important to readers of the *Good University Guide*, as OFFA suggests that some 400,000 students are likely to benefit. The Access Agreements contain much other helpful information for would-be university applicants and copies of all of them can be found at www.offa.org.uk. You are strongly encouraged to read those of particular interest to you. Some Access Agreements specifically mention that the university has a Hardship Fund or runs a Job Shop to help you find local employment but you should not assume that this is unique. Most universities have these now but have chosen not to highlight them to OFFA.

We must also emphasise that these bursaries and scholarships are often targeted at specific groups and hence the list is by no means comprehensive. The grid on pages 212–17 summarises this particular Government initiative aimed principally – but not exclusively – at students from low-income families, but universities have always offered a small number of bursaries and scholarships to undergraduates. If you are interested in the full range on offer, you will need to consult the websites of the individual universities. Some have even produced booklets with listings and there are invariably references to university awards in the prospectuses. Even this is not the whole story because there is nothing to stop a university enhancing the offers made in its Access Agreement with OFFA. What it cannot do is lower the offer. So the message has to be "watch this space" and to urge you to look at the relevant prospectuses and websites (including www.ucas.com) when you come to apply to universities. If that turns out to be at Clearing be particularly watchful because there have been suggestions that some universities might reduce fees or increase bursaries in August to fill their places.

Practicalities

We have already referred to the four English universities charging a £2,700 fee or less. These are not required to provide bursaries for students from low-income families but all the others with tuition fees of £3,000 must. The minimum bursary will be £300 a year for those of you receiving the full maintenance grant of £2,700. In other words, your fees are met in full by your maintenance grant and the university bursary, both of which do not have to be re-paid. However, as our grid shows, it could be even better than that because most universities are offering a standard bursary well above this minimum, often also to students in receipt of only a partial maintenance grant. In addition, take a look at the array of other bursaries and scholarships for applicants from local colleges or living in the region, in particular subjects of interest or for high academic or sports achievement at school and so on.

When it comes to application procedures, a number of universities are quite specific and indicate both timing and availability of online applications, including a timetable for notification of decisions. Some universities have gone out of their way to keep it simple and will not require an application at all; entitlement will be calculated by direct reference to your LEA financial assessment without your having to do anything else. On payments, some expect to make these through the Student Loans Company whilst others plan to administer their schemes in-house. There is some indication in some of the Access Agreements about whether the bursary will be made in advance of the academic year or as staged payments during the year. Generally, the information suggests that if your personal circumstances change part-way through the course, for example, through unsatisfactory academic progress or a change in residual family income, then your entitlement will be reviewed. Reduced tuition fees and bursaries will normally apply for any part of the university course spent on placement elsewhere. This might be as part of a sandwich degree, for a year abroad within a modern language degree, or whilst undertaking professional training. Where this is the case, it is detailed in the individual university entries. Foundation year studies also often attract lower fees and/or bursaries. If this all sounds rather vague, we are assured that all the missing detail will be revealed by the end of this year.

All of this argues for a great deal of help and advice and most universities are now providing web-based (see chapter 11, university profiles) or hard copy (see prospectus) information, even help-lines in some cases. In addition, most universities deploy support staff to assist the implementation of these new arrangements and some institutions even provide direct, over-the-counter help. Yet again, we cannot emphasise enough the value of consulting individual university websites for up-to-date information. If all else fails, phone the university; this is particularly the case where you come across inconsistencies or difficulties in understanding or interpreting the bursaries and scholarships information. We have lived in universities most of our lives but still find all of this something of a quagmire, so don't be afraid to ask!

Points to Ponder

- **Is the bursary automatic or conditional?** If it is conditional, when will I know? For those bursaries dependent on family income, you will have a good idea of eligibility when you apply and will know for definite when you get your LEA assessment. For others, you won't know until you get your exam results, well after you have made all the crucial decisions. And if you are doing unusual entry qualifications (especially any not in the UCAS tariff), you may not know until you or your parents have had a debate with the university's Admissions Office!
- **Is the bursary application procedure complex?** Or does it all follow from LEA assessments, postcodes or exam results without your having to do anything?
- **Assess the generosity of the university offer.** Some are ploughing back a large slice of their fee income. Some have tried to grab the headlines with high-value bursaries to the few. Some only offer the minimum bursary of £300.

- **How many applicants will benefit from the large headline sums?** Check both the value of the bursary and the number on offer. Be realistic – but not pessimistic – about your chances.
- **Do you qualify?** If your parents are high-income earners, then you are likely only to be eligible for scholarships linked to your academic achievement and/or a desire to study "shortage" subjects. So if your mum or dad is a successful barrister, forget it unless you are going to get straight AAAs at A level and plan to do physics!
- **Look out for special (unadvertised) offers** when you go to interviews and open days or in Clearing.
- **Some universities offer fee remission rather than a bursary.** This is really a choice between reduced debt in the future versus cash in hand now.

Crossing Borders

This is a year when what UK country you come from and which one you plan to study in could have a marked effect on your pocket. However, both the Scottish Parliament and the Welsh Assembly have flagged their intentions to make sure that Scottish and Welsh students accepting places at English universities are not financially disadvantaged by the introduction of the new funding arrangements.

Nonetheless, there have been concerns about increased migration across borders of would-be undergraduates seeking refuge from higher fees or less generous grants and bursaries. The Welsh and Scottish universities have a long tradition of welcoming scholars from elsewhere and are already net importers of students from the other UK countries. The Scots, already facing a shortfall in recruitment of home-grown medical staff, have a particular concern about the potential for increased numbers coming into their medical schools from south of the border. They have put in place, therefore, preferential financial treatment for students staying in their own country. Conversely, to make sure that there is no significant increase in students coming to Scotland, their universities will charge incomers a tuition fee.

But there is no doubt that the various changes in student financial support beginning in 2006 have had a significant impact on student applications across borders. Whilst applications through UCAS from English students to English universities fell, those to institutions in Scotland and Wales showed increases. Once again, the financial arrangements for those of you planning to study in a UK country other than where you live are rather complicated, but we will attempt a brief overview.

Students based in one UK country who choose to study elsewhere in the UK will pay the tuition fees charged by their chosen university but will be eligible for the usual fees loan to cover these. They are also eligible for the various grants and bursaries described, including the National Bursary Scheme in Wales. Any maintenance loan or grant will still come from the awarding bodies in your own country, although if you go to a Scottish university you may be entitled to a grant of up to £300 from SAAS. In addition, you will need to consult the individual universities of specific interest to you for their bursaries and scholarships.

The fees loan for Scottish students going to Northern Ireland or England, like the fees loans available in the other UK countries, has to be repaid but does not depend at all on family income. It is part alleviated for students from low-income families by the means-tested Students' Outside Scotland Bursary which does not have to be repaid. This operates at the same income thresholds as the Young Students' Bursary (see above) but with a lower maximum award of £2,000 (cf. £2,455). You might also qualify for the same additional loan. However, unlike a Scottish student going to a Scottish university, you will *not* have to pay the Graduate Endowment.

Students from EU countries other than the UK are liable for the standard home (not international) tuition fees but can also be considered for a fee loan and perhaps for some of the bursaries offered by the individual universities, but exchange students, including those on the Socrates Erasmus programme will not be charged fees. You will not have to pay tuition fees in Scotland but, like Scottish students, you will be expected to contribute to the Graduate Endowment. Unless you have been living and studying in the UK for at least three years, you will not be eligible for the maintenance loans and grants outlined above, so you should seek any such financial support available from your own country.

Countdown to 2007

Financial Planning for Student Loans, Grants and Bursaries

You will need funds to live now and to pay back tuition fees later (not Scotland) but you will be entitled to help from the Government and maybe the university. Some things you know now. Nearly all the universities in England, Wales and Northern Ireland will charge tuition fees of about £3,000. The Scottish universities will levy fees on those coming into Scotland from the other UK countries but Scottish students will be exempt. All of you will be eligible for student loans, about half of you for a Government grant; and many also for a university bursary.

THEY = LEA or in some cases **SLC** (England); **LEA** (Wales); **SAAS** (Scotland); **ELB** (Northern Ireland)

March onwards	**YOU** receive or request an application form for Student Support and any Guidance Notes. You can also apply online (see relevant websites above) but make sure you include all the information requested. **YOU** read booklet and return application form (keep a copy).
April/May/June	Within 6 weeks or so, **STUDENT FINANCE DIRECT** will send you a letter confirming details of the financial help to which you are entitled, including how and when it will be paid. Scottish-domiciled students will receive similar information in an award notice from SAAS within three weeks of applying.
May/June	Deadline by which **YOU** must return your Application Form in order to guarantee that **THEY** will have your entitlement ready at the beginning of the academic year.
August/September	**YOU** notify **THEM** if the university you will be attending is not your original first choice university.
September/October	Make sure **YOU** have your SLC or SAAS correspondence with you when you register at the university. **THEY** will confirm your registration to the SLC. If all goes according to plan, within three days the first instalment of your loan and any grant to which you are entitled will be paid into your bank or building society account or, more rarely, for you to collect at university. **YOU** can now start spending your loan and any grant!

As we have said, all of these new funding arrangements for students are far-reaching. They are also likely to prove decidedly complex and confusing to you! We strongly advise you to check out the full story as it affects you by consulting the key country websites for the most up-to-date information. These are:

- England   www.dfes.gov.uk/studentsupport
- Wales   www.studentfinancewales.co.uk
- Scotland   www.saas.gov.uk
- Northern Ireland   www.studentfinanceni.co.uk

In our opinion, you cannot start this monitoring and research too early because there will be much to do. No sooner will you have completed your UCAS application then it will be time to apply for financial support. A timetable for this is summarised in *Countdown to 2007* (across). The fine detail has yet to be published and is not expected to become available until towards the end of 2006. However, it is likely to be very similar to the existing operation.

The table *Financial Support and Family Income* (below) gives, by way of example, a basic summary of your eligibility for the various components of the support package in England.

Financial Support and Family Income for English Domiclied Students

Family Income	Low	Medium	High
Financial Support	Up to £17,500	£17,501–£37,425	Above £37,425
Full Maintenance Grant £2,700	Yes	No	No
Partial Maintenance Grant £1–£2,699	n/a	Yes	No
Full Bursary (1) £300 Minimum	Yes	No	No
Fees Loan £2,000–£3,000	Yes	Yes	Yes
Full Maintenance Loan (2) £3,415–£6,170	Yes	Yes	No
Partial Maintenance Loan (75%) £2,560–£4,630	n/a	n/a	Yes (3)

(1) Assumes that all universities charging more than £2,700 in tuition fees are charging the maximum permitted of £3,000

(2) Students cannot receive a full maintenance grant and a full maintenance loan. The loan is reduced by £1 for every £1 of grant entitlement up to £1,200. So, for example, if you decided to live at home other than in London and go to a local university, the combined maximum you could receive would be £3,415 loan + £2,700 grant = £6,115 − £1,200 = £4,985

(3) If your residual family income is above £37,900 then the family would be expected to contribute towards the remaining 25 per cent until at £52,530 they would be paying the full 25 per cent (£1,540) if you were living away from home and studying at a London university.

Tuition Fees for Overseas Students

Overseas students normally resident in countries outside the EU and EEA pay full-cost tuition fees in all of the UK universities and these are likely to be in the range shown in the table below. In addition, you will not be eligible for the loans and grants described earlier in this chapter. Whilst many overseas students coming to Britain receive financial support from their home countries, it must be emphasised that UK scholarships, whether from the UK government, sponsors or the individual universities themselves are limited. The vast majority are for post-graduate study, although there are one or two schemes for which undergraduates can be considered in exceptional circumstances. Students from overseas are strongly advised, therefore, to make sure they have sufficient funds for the full tuition fees and all necessary living costs before leaving home. Indeed, you will almost certainly be asked to guarantee in writing that you have sufficient funds for the complete duration of your course. Estimates suggest that living costs alone could amount to £6,500 and considerably more in London. It is virtually impossible to arrange financial support once you have left your own country.

Your Likely Expenditure
Living costs

For all students the biggest expenditure items will be the regular living costs, such as accommodation, food and drink, travel and even, perhaps, some clothes. There is much evidence to suggest that most university entrants don't know what it costs to be a student and can seriously underestimate these items by as much as 50 per cent. An increasing number, particularly in London, are staying at home and travel daily to a nearby university and that is probably the cheapest option. Buy only what you need, including the occasional treat, and don't be tempted by "two for the price of one" when you did not even want one in the first place. Local markets are good for fresh fruit and vegetables, charity shops like Oxfam for clothes, and the students' union for stationery. If you are sharing, you might even be able to engage in a spot of discounted bulk food buying with fellow residents and hence stretch the money further. There are travel costs, too, where most students rely on public transport, not just between home and university, perhaps two or three times a year, but also from your accommodation to the university every day. As a general rule, the cost of living is lower the further north and west you choose to study in the UK.

Apparently, a good third of students say they would rather spend more money on socialising than on a better roof over their heads! However, given the importance of day-to-day living, chapter 5 *Where to Live* is devoted to this issue.

Tuition Fees for Overseas Students

Subject	£ Sterling	$ US
Humanities and Social Sciences	£7,600–£8,500	$13,300–$14,900
Sciences and Engineering	£8,300–£10,900	$14,500–$19,100
Clinical Subjects	£19,500–£22,700	$34,100–$39,700

Conversion rate UK£1.00 to US$1.75

Studying costs

Next come costs associated with course work and the essentials: books, stationery, equipment and perhaps fieldwork or electives, here and overseas. After all, you are at university to get a degree! Such additional course work is often compulsory, and whilst you might get some financial support for this it is unlikely to meet the full costs of a language year, medical elective, or archaeological dig overseas or a residential geography field trip away from the university. The recommended reading list might be long and expensive. You would be well advised not to rush out and buy the lot but rather get to know how to use the library at the earliest opportunity. Students' unions often organise second-hand book sales and access to the internet is easy and free via the university network. Are some textbooks you want available through these sources, at the very least to buy at discount prices? Or is it feasible to share books with a fellow student?

Other costs

But university most definitely shouldn't be all work. Again, the students' union will cater for play in all its guises at a fraction of the cost demanded by commercial providers. In fact, university is a great time – perhaps the only time – to pursue the most common or esoteric of interests at a price you can easily afford. However, expenditure on the social scene, whether it be the launderette, cinema or nightclub, drinking or occasional eating out, is still likely to be a significant cost for most students.

Phone bills can be another sizeable item, especially if you ring the old folks at home or that distant loved one for an hour or so every day and they happen to be in Tokyo or San Francisco! Competition for your custom is fierce and the students' union may well be able to advise on the best deals amongst a growing army of call providers. Selecting an appropriate package for your mobile from the many options available will also be important.

Insurance

Most students own desirable items like portable televisions, CD and DVD players, laptops, mobile phones and bikes, and a third of them fall victims of crime. Even so, recent surveys have shown that many students are uninsured or under-insured. Insurance cover is essential and might be possible under existing parental policies at home. If not, there are a number of insurance companies which tailor policies to student belongings and lifestyle. Premiums are usually linked to postal codes, and university residences often provide cheaper cover than private houses. It is worth the precaution of photographing expensive items and keeping serial numbers in a safe place. Some insurance companies offer a special policy for international students to cover goods in transit and emergency travel.

This, then, is a brief look at what you will need money for. Try looking at your own personal situation to draw up an annual expenditure list and return to it on a regular basis throughout the year to see how you are doing. In other words, begin to estimate an annual budget. This is shown in the chart of income and expenditure which appears later in this chapter on page 209.

Your Likely Income
Taking a gap year

One possible source of earnings to consider prior to coming to university is a gap year –

another is sponsorship. Taking a year out is attractive to many students, whether to gain experience, to earn money or both. Circumstances might dictate that the opportunity to spend a year working whilst travelling may not come again and it is much easier to get a temporary work visa when you are young. There are essentially four main possibilities: cultural exchanges and courses, expeditions, volunteering, and structured work placements. These can be here in the UK or overseas and some could require considerable funding by you whilst others would pay a wage. You need to question, therefore, your own motives and means before embarking on a year out. The reasons for taking a gap year seem to be shifting from solely an opportunity for personal development to more one to boost the bank balance ahead of becoming a student. This understandable short-term expediency needs to be carefully measured against the somewhat longer-term but less tangible benefits of a placement, here or overseas, of real service to the community, but perhaps with less monetary reward. The Government wants to encourage voluntary work, particularly for gap year students, and has recently established a charity to develop the range of such opportunities both here and overseas. The various projects offer training, a weekly allowance, help with accommodation and even an accreditation option (see www.russellcommission.org).

These days, university selectors take careful note of extracurricular experience and interests alongside good exam grades and generally support a gap year but utter occasional reservations for those planning to study the mathematical sciences. Employers, too, operating increasingly in a global economy, look more and more to the development of self-reliance and teamwork skills and expertise beyond academic performance and class of degree, skills often developed through a gap year. Work placements might be structured as, for example, with the "Year in Industry Scheme" (www.yini.org.uk) or 'GAP Activity Projects' (www.gap.org.uk), or casual. Both provide invaluable experience to put on your CV. Sponsorship is available mostly to those wishing to study engineering or business and a good source for finding more information is www.everythingyouwantedtoknow.com.

Support from Government sources

We have already described the main loans, grants and bursaries available from public sources but there are others for some students who fit particular circumstances.

The Access to Learning Fund (Financial Contingency Fund in Wales, Hardship Fund in Scotland, Support Funds in N Ireland) is a further source of modest government help to students on university courses and is allocated by the universities themselves to undergraduates in financial difficulties. This may simply be help with day-to-day study and living costs or to meet an unexpected or exceptional cost. The university decides which students need support and what the level of that support will be. Priority groups tend to be older or disadvantaged students and finalists. The Access to Learning Fund is a back-stop and is normally given as a non-repayable grant according to need. It can be available as a one-off sum or in the form of a bursary payable every year.

If you are ineligible for any of the above financial support, you may still be able to apply for a Career Development Loan, available through some major high street banks in partnership with the DfES. Students on a wide range of vocational courses can borrow from £300 to £8,000 at a fixed rate of interest to help you fund up to two years of learning and not pay anything back until you finish your studies.

Part-time work

Some firms, particularly the big supermarket chains, offer continuing part-time employment to their school employees when they go away to university. The last few years have also seen a significant growth in student employment offices on university campuses, no doubt a response, in part, to the introduction of fees and loans. These offices act as agencies introducing employers with work to students seeking work, perhaps even in the university itself, throughout the academic year. They are also guardians of the student interest, abiding by Codes of Practice which regulate such things as minimum wages and maximum hours worked in term (typically 15 hours a week so as to avoid adverse effect on studies). This is necessary because there is growing evidence that part-time work beyond this level lowers academic attainment.

Getting on for half of all first year undergraduates take a job in term-time bringing in an average of £94 for a 14-hour week. Any income you earn by working part-time will not normally affect your entitlement to loans and bursaries. Some students use their expertise to good effect as web designers, tutors or healthcare workers but most do casual work in retail stores, restaurants, bars and call centres. Many organisations are also interested in what students like and how they think and are willing to pay to find out. Others appoint brand managers on campus to promote their goods and services.

UNITE Student Experience Report 2005	
Funds generated for university	(%)
Full-time holiday job	26
Part-time holiday job	20
Long-term savings	15
Part-time school job	15
Gap year to save	13
Monetary gifts	12
Family loan	8
Scholarship	6
Bank loan	4
Other grants and loans	9
No funds	19

Universities, too, frequently involve their students in market research, fundraising amongst their alumni or as ambassadors in schools and colleges.

Most universities have a student employment office run by their careers service or the students' union and they make a welcome contribution to the local economy. This is hardly surprising given the enormous range of skills and knowledge residing in any student community.

Vacation work

Vacations, too, offer an opportunity to earn cash whilst developing skills for that CV. Such work experience can be casual, formalised in a scheme like the "Shell Technology Enterprise Programme" (www.step.org.uk), or even as part of a sponsorship programme.

Banks

Finally, banks are well disposed towards today's university students in the certain knowledge that many will be tomorrow's high-earning professionals. Indeed, there is fierce competition amongst them for your custom so weigh up carefully what they are offering and don't be unduly swayed by the opening gift of discounted driving lessons, an MP3 player or a rail card. Banks are sympathetic to the student cause and will generally permit modest overdrafts on your account to ease cash flow problems without pain. It pays – literally – to shop around for the best offers when transferring or opening your account.

Your Annual Budget

You can now complete your estimated annual budget by listing all your expected income, including any savings you will bring with you to university. See how this compares with your anticipated expenditure in the hope that the balance sheet almost balances or, better still, that you are left with spare cash in the bank for doing what you've always wanted to do. However, budgeting accurately is never an easy process, and we have constructed this simple but realistic annual income and expenditure summary to make monitoring and controlling your finances easier. This is a budget for non-smokers and assumes the latest findings of an average weekly spend of £25 on food and £19 on drink. For the quarter of you who smoke, an additional outlay of almost £20 would be needed – is it worth it?

It can be difficult to predict accurately some variable expenses such as entertainment. Start by identifying bills which must be paid and include in this a small contingency fund. This will leave you with the "flexible" part of your income to take weekly from the bank. Don't be too optimistic in your first budget, and do be aware of how much you actually spend. Budget for university gigs and balls, birthdays and parties, or you may find yourself missing out on the best social events of the year. If there is a big gap between planned budget and actual expenditure, perhaps your spending habits need attention rather than your budgeting. Above all, remember to keep a check on your finances so that money worries do not detract from your studying and from enjoying university life. Clearly, your patterns of expenditure will differ significantly between term-time and vacations and you will need to allow for this.

Survival Tips

- Take out your maximum Student Loans, if only to invest some of it elsewhere
- Check what Grants and Bursaries are available to you
- Sign on with the bank which offers the best long-term benefits
- Find a part-time job and be paid gross if not liable for tax
- Make the most of any student discounts
- Get to know how to use the library at the earliest opportunity
- Use the internet to buy and sell on secure sites
- Opt for the best value telephone landline provider
- Keep an eye open for the best mobile package
- Buy essential books and equipment second-hand
- Shop in local markets, charity shops and the students' union
- Be careful with heating and lighting
- Try and buy in bulk if living in a student house
- Share to save whenever you can, particularly on transport
- Walk or cycle during the day rather than take public transport
- Check to see if your belongings can be covered by your family insurance
- Try drawing up a weekly budget and sticking to it

The information in this chapter was correct at the time of writing (April 2006) but the rules and regulations for student loans, maintenance grants and other supplementary payments (for disabled students, applicants with dependents, single parents, care leavers, and for some essential travel costs) are somewhat complicated and you are urged to consult the relevant country website (see page 203) for the fine detail.

A Typical Budget for a Student Entering University in 2007

Income	£	Expenditure	£
Fees Loan	3,000	Tuition Fees	3,000
Maintenance loan/grant	4,405	Rent	2,350
Bursary	300	Electricity, gas, water	250
Term time/vacation work	3,000	Mobile/internet	350
		Insurance	100
		Food, drink	1,500
		Toiletries	300
		Laundry	100
		Books, stationery	300
		Course costs	100
		Clothes, shoes	400
		Travel, transport	400
		Going out	600
		Home entertainment	200
		Sports, leisure	200
		Holidays, presents	400
		Emergencies	400
Total income	10,705	Total expenses	10,950
		(Deficit)	(245)

In this example, we have assumed that you are studying in England (other than London), you are not living at home, you have taken out a fees loan to cover tuition fees of £3,000, you are in receipt of the maximum maintenance grant/loan of £4,405 and minimum standard bursary of £300. The deficit of £245 is in addition to the two loans from the Student Loans Company which will be carried forward as a debt to be repaid after you graduate.

Bursaries and Scholarships Grid

The grid below summarises the types of bursaries (B) and scholarships (S) available. For a more detailed description of the bursaries and scholarships offered by universities see their individual entry in chapter 11 *University Profiles*.

A number of points need to be borne in mind by the reader when consulting this grid. The information was up to date and accurate at the time of writing (April 2006). However, by then the tuition fee and maintenance grant levels permitted for the 2007–08 academic year had not been confirmed by the Government and accordingly universities were unable to confirm some of the fine detail. It should be noted, however, that the overwhelming majority of universities intend to continue to charge the upper limit for tuition fees set by the Government, ie, £3,000 uprated for inflation of about 3 per cent. Therefore, the figures printed below are indicative rather than absolute and, for the most part, are those for the academic year 2006–07. To obtain exact figures, you should enquire direct to the university using the contact addresses provided in the individual university's profile, or check their websites.

The grid does not provide a definitive summary of all scholarships and bursaries offered by UK universities. Many universities have had scholarships and bursaries schemes for years and this grid does not address those opportunities. Again, consult individual universities for information about all of their scholarships and bursaries.

The new funding arrangements in Scotland and Wales are both separate from and different to those in England and Northern Ireland. These are detailed below. Remember, as with the other UK universities, conditions often apply to these scholarships and you should consult individual institution for detailed information.

Scotland

- Scottish domiciled students: no fees will be payable by eligible students although a "graduate endowment" will be payable after graduation: the 2005–06 level was £2,216.
- Non-Scottish domiciled students fees: £1,700 a year (£2,700 for medicine). Payment of fees can be deferred by applying for a student loan administered by your LEA or devolved government. Students who come from a low-income household in England or Northern Ireland may also qualify for a HE grant of up to £2,700 a year for English students and £3,200 a year for students normally resident in Northern Ireland. This is to cover living expenses and is in addition to their student loan to cover fees.
- The Scottish Executive has announced that English, Welsh and Northern Ireland domiciled students studying in Scottish Universities and from low-income family backgrounds may be entitled to up to £300.

Wales

- Fees for undergraduate courses £3,000. Students living in Wales or a non-UK EU country will be eligible for a Welsh Assembly fee grant of approximately £1,800 a year.
- National Bursary Scheme: the Welsh Assembly government is introducing a National Bursary Scheme from 2007, which provides a bursary of up to £300 a year for students from lower-income families who are studying at Welsh institutions. Currently no details have been published by the Welsh Assembly.

The grid reflects as accurately as possible what is available in all four UK countries, but be aware that different conditions and eligibility prevail depending on residence.

An Explanation of the Headings

- **In receipt of full Maintenance Grant** are Bursaries for students from the lowest income families and these will have a MG (Maintenance Grant) of £2,700 and a mandatory non-repayable bursary of at least £300. But, as the grid shows, this bursary will often be considerably higher than this minimum.

- **In receipt of partial Maintenance Grant** are students from low-income families who, whilst not receiving the full £2,700 MG, will still receive a lower MG and, in addition, at many universities also the bursary shown.

- **Living in region** is defined by the university itself. For most, this will be the city or county where the university is located, but it could be wider than that, particularly for universities in rural areas.

- **Living in specified postcodes** will usually be for students who live in deprived parts of towns and cities where there is little tradition of entry to universities. But the university may also have other good reasons for targeting these districts.

- **Progression from outreach** will be for students who have already been involved in the outreach activities of the university. Most higher education institutions have developed strong links, sometimes called Compacts or Partnerships, with schools and colleges with which they have special arrangements for encouraging their students to apply to universities.

- **Ethnic minorities** are students from black and other ethnic communities where these are under-represented in the university student population.

- **Disabled** because, again, these students are often under-represented in universities.

- **Sport** is seen as an increasingly important factor in widening access to universities. Some, most notably Loughborough, have fine reputations and have long since offered scholarships but here is a new selection to consider.

- **Shortage subjects** are those which the universities find difficult to fill yet ones which are crucial to the UK economy. They tend to be modern languages, the physical sciences and engineering.

- **Academic achievement** is usually defined by the universities in terms of high entry qualifications (A-level grades or points, UCAS tariff scores, etc). But note that many of the scholarships for academic achievement are only open to certain individuals (eg, first generation, ethnic minorities, low-income).

England

Universities	Academic achievement	Shortage subjects	Sport	Disabled	Ethnic minorities	Progressing from outreach	Living in specified postcodes	Living in region	Partial Maintenance Grant (£)	Full Maintenance Grant (£)
Anglia Ruskin †				•B	•B	•B		•B	500 max	800 min
Aston		•B			•B	•B			750 max	750 min
Bath									300–1200	1,500 min
Bath Spa		•S							up to 320	1,150
Birmingham	•S 1,200	•S							800	800
Bolton †						•S 700			Sliding scale to min 50	300
Bournemouth	•S		•S			•B 500			Sliding scale based on level of MG	1,000
Bradford						•S 300			500-900	500-900
Brighton		•B		•B		•B			500 min	1,000 max
Bristol †		•S	•S			•S		•B	700	1,100
Brunel		•S			•S	•S			200	300
Cambridge		•S		•B					700-2,300	3,000
Canterbury Christ Church									500	800
Central Lancashire						•B		•B	1,000	1,000
Chester		•S							450-900	1,350
Chichester									250-999	1,000
City		•S					•S		800	800

Coventry	500	500			•S 1,000	•S	•S 2,000
De Montfort	300	500	•S		•S 1,000		•S 1,000
Derby †	800	200–600					
Durham	3090	600–1,545					•S
East Anglia	540	108–432					•S 1,000
East London †	300				•S 1,000	•B	•S 1,000
Essex	300	Up to 1,500	•B		•B	•S Maths	
Exeter	2,000	50–1,500	•B		•S 1,000		•S
Gloucestershire	500–1110	200–1109	•B		•S		
Goldsmiths, University of London	1,000 max	50 min	•S		•S		•S
Greenwich*	500	500					•S 500
Hertfordshire	1,350	Up to 1,350			•S	•S	•S
Huddersfield †	1,000	500–750					
Hull	1,000	500–1,000		•B			•S 3,000
Imperial College	2,700	100–2,700					•S 4,000
Keele	300	Up to 4,000	•B	•B	•B •B	•S Maths	•B
Kent	1,000	250–1,000		•S	•S		•S
King's College London	1,350	Up to 1,350					
Kingston	300–1,000	300–1,000		•B			
Lancaster	1,000	0–500				•B	•B
Leeds	1,300	0–1,170	•S	•S	•S 1,000		•B
Leeds Metropolitan*	n/a	n/a					
Leicester	1,300–1,500	50–950					•S 1,000
Lincoln	600	Sliding scale based on level of MG	•B 100–300	•S 100–300			•S 500–5,000
Liverpool	1,300	1,000	•B			•S 1500	•B
Liverpool Hope	1,000	400–700	•S	•S			•S

Universities	Full MG (£)	Partial MG (£)	Living in region	Living in specified postcodes	Progressing from outreach	Ethnic minorities	Disabled	Sport	Shortage subjects	Academic achievement
Liverpool John Moores †	1,000	400			•S			•S		•100 S
London Metropolitan	1,000	Up to 975								•S
London School of Economics	2,500	Up to 1,650								
London South Bank †	300									
Loughborough	1,300	200–1,100							•S	•S
Luton †	1,750	300–1,000								
Manchester	1,000	Up to 1,000	•S						•S	•S
Manchester Metropolitan	1,000	Sliding scale % of MG received		•S						
Middlesex	300	300	•S					•S		•S
Newcastle	1,200	600–900			•S					•S
Northampton*	500	500	•B	•B						
Northumbria	550–1300	250	•B	•S			•S			
Nottingham	1,000	1,000	•B		•B		•S		•B	
Nottingham Trent	1,000	200–800		•B	•B					•S
Oxford	3,000	100–2,600								
Oxford Brookes †	1,200	200–1,200		•S	•S					
Plymouth	300		•B		•B					•S 500
Portsmouth	800	Up to 500								

Institution							
Queen Mary, University of London	1,000	800					•S
Reading	1,300	325–1,300		•B			•S 1,000
Roehampton	500	500					
Royal Holloway	500	500					•S
Salford	650	50-650					
SOAS	700	400		•B 400			
Sheffield	650	400		•B		•B	•B
Sheffield Hallam	700	700		•B			•S
Southampton	1,000	Up to 1,000	•B	•B			•S
Southampton Solent	1,000	250-500	•S	•S			
Staffordshire	1,300	500–1,000					
Sunderland	500	500					•S
Surrey	1,000	Up to 1,000		•S		•S	•S
Sussex	1,000			•S	•S		
Teesside	1,300	Up to 500		•S			•S
Thames Valley*	1,000	1,000					
University of the Arts, London †	300		•B	•B			
UCE Birmingham	500	500					
University College London	1,350–2,500	50% of MG value					
Warwick	2,000–3,000	1,000–2,000					
West of England	1,250	750					
Westminster	300	Up to 300					•S
Winchester	800	400		•S			
Wolverhampton	300	More than 300, so that the bursary plus the MG total 3,000		•S			•S

Universities	Academic achievement	Shortage subjects	Sport	Disabled	Ethnic minorities	Progressing from outreach	Living in specified postcodes	Living in region	Partial MG (£)	Full MG (£)
Worcester	•S		•S						700	700
York									600–1,000	1,400

*Greenwich will charge a tuition fee of £2,500 rather than the full £3,000

*Leeds Metropolitan will charge a tuition fee of £2,000 rather than the full £3,000

*Northampton will charge a tuition fee of £2,500-3,000

*Thames Valley will charge a tuition fee of £2,700 rather than the full £3,000

† Information for these universities comes from the 2006 Access Agreements

NORTHERN IRELAND

Universities	Partial MG (£)	Full MG (£)
Queen's Belfast	100-600	1,100
Ulster	min 300	1,000
	on a sliding scale	

WALES

	1,000	200				
Aberystwyth	1,000	200	•S			
Bangor				•S		•S
Cardiff						
Glamorgan				•S		•S
Lampeter			•S	•S		
Newport						
Swansea			•S	•S		•S
UWIC, Cardiff					•B	•S

SCOTLAND

Aberdeen	300					
Abertay	300					
Dundee	300				•B	•S
Edinburgh	300		•S	•B		
Glasgow	300				•B	
Glasgow Caledonian	300		•S			
Heriot-Watt	300		•S	•S		
Napier	300					
Paisley	300					
Robert Gordon	300					
St Andrews	300		•S			
Stirling	300		•S			
Strathclyde	300		•S	•B		

What Parents Need to Know

Many things in university life have changed in recent years and one of them is the increasing role of parents. Nowadays many are actively involved throughout the application process, a constant presence as universities are chosen, forms filled in and open days attended. One important reason for this is that parents are increasingly providing financial backing for their children's higher education. When you are paying for something, it is only natural to take a close interest in what is going on and seek to ensure you are getting value for money. On the whole this is a welcome development. Applying to university and surviving the examinations necessary to get there is a difficult time and young people need all the support they can get.

This chapter is aimed specifically at parents, offering a guide to what they will go through and some practical ways in which they can help. It focuses on areas specific to parents, so if you want to know about the application process in detail or how to choose a university, see the other chapters in this book. While this chapter generally refers to parents, it applies equally to guardians and other carers who may get involved.

Practical Support for Applications

The single most important thing parents can do is relentlessly be positive about higher education. All the evidence is that, for most people, attending university is one of the most enjoyable and fruitful times of their lives.

> **UNITE Student Experience Report 2006**
> 96% of students agree that going to university is worthwhile.
> 89% of students agree that the money they are spending on going to university is a good investment for their future.

It is a time when they try a vast range of new experiences, form lifelong friendships and equip themselves for the world of work. If that isn't enough, the crude economics are telling: on average a graduate will earn much more in their working life than a non-graduate (the Government has estimated that it amounts to £120,000) and is much less likely to be unemployed. We all know of a few people who missed out on university but went on to be high-achievers, such as Richard Branson or the former Prime Minister John Major, but we know their names precisely because there are so few of them. Generally speaking, university is the gateway to success: the more you learn, the more you earn.

Having instilled the value of a university education sufficiently for your offspring to be making an application, it is time to get practical. A good school or college should provide plenty of practical support for their students through the application process (see chapter 4) but there are still some ways in which you can contribute:

- Help to gather all the necessary information. Provide stamps and surf time, and, if you borrowed this book, buy a copy!
- Read up about the things you are interested in, even if they are not at the top of the list of most applicants' priorities. For example, many parents are concerned about the safety of the university environment and many universities have information about this on their websites or in special publications. Don't just assume that big cities are bad and rural

campuses good. Some city universities are in areas of their city with low crime rates; some campus universities may result in some students travelling home late at night to off-campus accommodation.

- Get to know the process and keep a check that UCAS deadlines are met (see chapter 4).
- Provide any information needed for LEA Assessment Forms.
- Offer a taxi service to university open days. Most universities now expect large numbers of parents to roll up for open days (both the big general open days and the specific departmental days held for applicants who have been made an offer) and make special arrangements. Far from being an embarrassing appendage, you will often get taken off for a parents' programme with sessions by university counsellors, safety officers and suchlike. If you have joined in the trip, you can help your son or daughter to be critical about what they have seen and heard. Open days are like prospectuses: they are designed to attract. A university that is unlucky with the weather can't hide the fact that it is a long walk in the rain from the lecture theatres to the Students' Union, but you can be sure that the lecture theatres you see are the most modern and up-to-date.
- If you move house, make sure UCAS is on your 'change of address' list.

A well-organised school and a well-organised student will cover most of this between them, but if either isn't quite on top of things then you can help to make sure that the process runs smoothly.

Advice

Offering advice to your children about their application is a fine and natural thing you will want to do. Parents can be an invaluable source of experience and good sense. If you happen to be a university admissions tutor or the head of recruitment for a large corporation, then you will be particularly well-placed to offer good advice about some (but probably not all) aspects of the process. However, if you are not as close to the heart of it as that, you do need to think carefully before you offer advice. Here are some of the common pitfalls:

- Basing your advice on your own experience of university 25 years ago. Universities and university life have changed since that time and you will almost certainly be out of date.
- Suggesting certain courses will always lead to a good job. Are you sure? See chapter 1 for the facts about graduate employment.
- Suggesting certain universities are good for a particular subject. Again, are you sure? See chapters 2 and 3 for the facts about quality.
- Projecting your own desires onto your offspring. However much you love being a doctor or an advertising executive, it doesn't mean that they want to be, too. Students switching courses routinely comment that they never really wanted to do their initial subject but felt that it was expected by their family.

So advice can be a tough one. You can offer all the usual sound, sensible stuff that kids never want (but always need) to hear. Read the prospectuses, take decisions slowly and carefully, don't apply for Aramaic & Offshore Engineering just because a best friend has done so, that sort of thing. One really helpful thing you can do is test the reasons for decisions. Check out that universities have been chosen for sensible reasons, such as the quality of a course, and not as a result of some dubious gossip. Be careful with specific advice: if you can't be sure you are accurate it may do more harm than good.

Examination Results

It's August. You've come through the application process together. You had a great time accompanying your son or daughter to an open day at your alma mater. They wisely ignored your romantic reminiscences and applied to six other universities instead. You were a rock when the first decision was a rejection and then provided the chocolates when the next one was an offer. Now things are tense as mid-August approaches.

After your important role in extolling the virtues of university life at the start of the process, Results Day is another time when your support can be crucial. The paramount thing is to remain calm and collected yourself. Whatever contortions your digestive system is engaged in there will be enough tension around already without your adding to it. If the right results come in, things are easy: just join in the celebration. But if they don't and disappointment reigns, don't add your own. No doubt you will feel disappointed, but your son or daughter will have enough to deal with already, not least the fact that many of their friends are probably celebrating. Now is the time to be a calm, comforting and constructive presence.

A few practical things are possible. First, be there, not on a Mediterranean beach. Moral support is not quite the same over a long-distance telephone call. Second, prepare for the possibility of Clearing by getting familiar with the procedure. Make sure you know how and when you can get access to the official vacancy lists and what needs to be done. Encourage clear and sensible thinking, so decisions are made carefully, and the first place available is not jumped at. They will have to do the leg-work, of course (universities much prefer to get the applicant on the phone), but sometimes it helps to be able to point them in the right direction. Third, be available as a taxi driver. Some universities run Clearing open days and some courses, even when recruiting in Clearing, will require an interview. Both of these possibilities will require transport.

Preparing to Leave

All being well, come September you will be preparing to drive off to university. In the last couple of weeks the doormat will have been dented by vast quantities of mail: confirmation of a place at university, details of registration, details of university accommodation and so on. Some of this may require forms to be filled in and returned. Assuming the university is not the local one, there is all the preparation for living in a completely different place that may be several hundred miles away. Most students will get on and sort all this out. There are a few ways in which you can make it easier.
- Remember the boring things that are easy to forget, such as checking on insurance (many household insurance policies don't cover possessions taken to university), getting a

---

What a School Should Do

A good school or college will provide a programme of support for its students who are applying for higher education. This will include many or all of the following:
- A library of resources, including university prospectuses and UCAS publications
- A trip to a university open day
- A visit to a higher education fair with stands for many or all universities
- Talks by representatives of one or more universities
- A series of sessions giving advice about the UCAS process and how to fill in the UCAS application
- A member of staff responsible for all this and available to provide assistance.

licence if they have their own television, and arranging passport photographs.
- If they are self-catering, make sure they know a few simple recipes. There are plenty of books aimed at students cooking on a budget and a copy of one might be useful, too.
- Make sure they know how to operate a washing machine (but expect to run yours several times if they come home for a weekend).

The Empty Nest

Finally, all the tension of applications, interviews and examinations is over, the mass of form filling is complete, and you are driving away from a university leaving behind a slightly nervous-looking new student. For them the nervousness will soon evaporate as Freshers Week activities and the course get underway. If necessary, advice centres, tutors and counselling services will be on hand to provide help and support. In fact it may well be that you find the transition harder than they do. A new student is embarking on an exciting adventure that will lead to new experiences and new possibilities. It will be a new beginning for you, too, in some ways, but it will also be an ending and a reminder that time is passing, you are getting older and a new phase of life is beginning. Don't under-estimate how long it will take you to adjust.

Then, just as you are settling into a new routine, discovering new things to do as family life takes up less time, the Christmas vacation arrives and you are all together again. Your son or daughter is the same person, a few months older, back in the same bedroom and abandoning clothes in the same place on the landing. But they will have moved on and grown up in subtle ways. You, too, are the same person but you will have moved on as well, with that spot on the landing reserved for a nice Greek urn you bought on your first autumn holiday for 15 years.

Keeping in touch will help. It probably won't be you who is first to get in touch, but keep the contact going as the distractions of term-time mount. However, regardless of how long the phone calls and e-mails, and how frequent the text messages, you can't say everything that could be said. Indeed, one thing you can be sure of is that you won't get told everything. That is probably just as well – it would only make you worry about them even more. So, however hard you try, the chances are that both of you will behave as though the other hasn't changed a bit. They will expect their bedroom to be exactly as they left it and your routines to be the same as ever; you will expect them to behave just as they used to. You will almost certainly both be wrong and there will be another process of readjustment to go through. And the Greek urn will probably have a pair of dirty socks inside for months.

Ten Dos and Don'ts

Do	be positive about higher education	**Don't**	expect them to follow in your footsteps
Do	get to know the UCAS procedures	**Don't**	offer advice unless you are sure it is accurate
Do	stay calm in anxious times		
Do	be there when they need you	**Don't**	go on holiday in the middle of August or the end of September
Do	expect them to have changed when they come back home		
		Don't	expect them to tell you everything
		Don't	convert their bedroom into your study without asking

Coming from Overseas

It is difficult enough for individuals living in the UK when faced with the bewildering choice amongst the 110 or so universities. How much more so if you live on the other side of the world where, in addition, you will want to consider the varying costs of living and studying in another country. Take, for example, your accommodation. Will this be university-owned or in the private sector? How far is it from the university? Is it secure, safe and warm? Does it have access to an international telephone? Would you have to move out in the vacations? You will need a great deal of information – considerably more than is available within this chapter – but this and other chapters will give you a good start and point you in the right direction.

The Country

The British Isles comprises two sovereign and independent states of the European Union (EU), the United Kingdom (UK) and the Republic of Ireland. Within the UK there are three further countries: England, Scotland and Wales – sometimes collectively called Great Britain – and the province of Northern Ireland. Of the 110 universities covered in *The Times Good University Guide*:

- 87 are in England
- 13 are in Scotland
- 8 are in Wales
- 2 are in Northern Ireland.

In the late 1990s, a Parliament in Scotland and an Assembly in Wales were established, each with devolved powers. These bodies are already having a positive impact on university education in these countries. For example, EU students at Scottish universities do not pay tuition fees, but do have to contribute after graduation to an endowment for future generations of disadvantaged students. In fact, Scottish universities have seen a surge in numbers of overseas applicants, no doubt as a result of such policy changes. Some may also have benefited from Prince William's decision to study at St Andrews!

The Culture

Britain is a multicultural society which has become home to immigrants from the Indian subcontinent, the Middle East, Africa and the West Indies. In recent years, many mainland Europeans have made their homes here, and more are expected from the ten countries (mainly in eastern Europe) who joined the EU in May 2004. Travelling on the London underground, you are likely to hear a host of languages all around you.

The British have a reputation for tolerance and fair play. The media is independent and frequently critical and outspoken, and we strongly believe in justice, law and order. On the whole, British people are polite, often to an extreme that appears insincere. As a result, we tend to use indirect language when making a request or complaint. "Please" and "thank you" are among the first words a child is taught and these phrases are used liberally by everyone you meet. We also have a subtle sense of humour which is sometimes difficult to understand. And another thing (apart from the trains!), we try to keep to time. Lateness for a lecture or a doctor's appointment is considered rude but, oddly enough, you should avoid being the first to arrive as a guest at a social engagement. This might all sound rather strange but you will soon get used to us. Make the effort to get involved in sport, voluntary work or one of the many student societies on campus or perhaps as a mentor or a student representative. Taking part in such activity will improve your command of the language and give you a good insight into British culture. One of the many joys of living and studying in another country is to experience other ways of doing things, so take advantage of any opportunity to meet people. They will be interested in you and your culture and you will be made very welcome.

The Weather

Most students coming to the UK will find the climate different – it is also a major topic of conversation! Given its position west of the European mainland, Britain tends to have low humidity, warm summers and mild winters. Days are long and bright in June but short and grey in December and you will need to bring or buy a range of suitable clothing Although there are four distinct climatic seasons – spring, summer, autumn and winter – the weather is unpredictable and liable to change and change again in the course of a day. Rainfall is highest in and close to the hilly regions in the north and west – typically over 1,200 mm a year – whilst average maximum daily temperatures range from 6 °C in January to 19 °C in July. Snow falls for a short time most winters and there is even a short skiing season in the Scottish Highlands. As a general rule, southeast England is relatively dry and sunny and northwest Scotland wet and cloudy.

Entry and Employment Regulations

There are four main receiving countries for university students in the English-speaking world – Australia, Canada, the UK and the USA – and all have their distinctive characteristics but one thing in common – the need to apply early. All four have restrictions on entry and employment for foreign nationals and, since the attacks on the World Trade Center and the London bombings, reports suggest that visas for students from some countries might be harder to come by or, at very least, subject to greater scrutiny and long delays. Some US universities, for example, are planning to pay the visa fee to counter a perception that students are not welcome. Meanwhile, Australia has closed some of its student recruitment offices overseas to focus on the core Asian market. Developments are also taking place in other parts of the world, with increased competition from the Singapore hub, universities in northern Europe offering courses taught in English, and new opportunities to stay and study in your own home country.

In June 1999 the Prime Minister, Tony Blair, launched a worldwide campaign to encourage more overseas students to come to the UK's universities. A further initiative this year launched a plan to recruit an extra 100,000 international students by 2011. As part of the campaign, the Government made the passage much easier by streamlining visa and entry procedures. In addition, overseas students can now work for up to 20 hours a week during the academic year and full-time in the vacations without the need for a work permit. Similarly, if you are staying in the UK for a year or more, then your spouse and children will be able to take paid employment even if they are here for a shorter period. You can also now apply to remain in the UK after graduation, perhaps for professional training, work experience or a graduate induction programme. This recent package of new measures on immigration and work experience is designed to make the

UK a more attractive place to study. However, an increase in the initial student visa fee, a doubling of the fees for visa extensions and the discontinuation of the right to appeal against being refused a visa have taken some of the shine off this policy. It has led to protests by the universities. The Government also plans to introduce a points system for entry to the UK not unlike the one that has operated in Australia for a number of years. Prospective students will be able to check their eligibility for entry against published criteria and so assess their points score. Universities will also be required to provide a Certificate of Sponsorship to their international student entrants.

In Scotland, the "Fresh Start" initiative has been established to attract inward migration because of a declining population, particularly among young people. Under this scheme, international students can apply for an initial two-year extension to stay on after graduation to live and work. The Scottish Parliament has also developed new scholarships that will allow graduates to combine a year of postgraduate study with work experience.

Table 1 Which Countries Do Overseas Students Come From?

EU Countries		%	Non-EU Countries (Top 25)		%
Greece	7,640	18.5	China*	17,184	24.9
Republic of Ireland	6,268	15.2	Malaysia	7,091	10.3
Germany	5,638	13.7	Hong Kong	6,765	9.8
France	5,497	13.3	India*	2,451	3.6
Spain	2,531	6.1	United States	2,416	3.5
Cyprus	2,379	5.8	Singapore	2,312	3.4
Sweden	1,938	4.7	Norway	2,065	3.0
Italy	1,648	4.0	Nigeria*	2,038	3.0
Belgium	1,341	3.3	Japan	1,897	2.7
Finland	1,235	3.0	Kenya*	1,650	2.4
Portugal	1,057	2.6	Pakistan*	1,350	2.0
The Netherlands	970	2.4	South Korea	1,159	1.7
Denmark	702	1.7	Sri Lanka*	1,153	1.7
Austria	612	1.5	Mauritius	919	1.3
Luxembourg	544	1.3	Oman*	850	1.2
Gibraltar	453	1.1	Taiwan*	841	1.2
Poland	276	0.7	Canada	802	1.2
Czech Republic	125	0.3	Russia*	761	1.1
Hungary	84	0.2	Zimbabwe*	749	1.1
Latvia	64	0.2	Thailand*	686	1.0
Malta	61	0.1	United Arab Emirates*	677	1.0
Lithuania	55	0.1	Bangladesh*	570	0.8
Slovak Republic	45	0.1	Switzerland	557	0.8
Estonia	34	0.1	Ghana*	556	0.8
Slovenia	18	0.0	Saudi Arabia*	528	0.8
All EU students	**41,207**		**All non-EU students**	**68,267**	

* Students from these non-EU countries and the Turkish Republic of North Cyprus require a visa to study in the UK.

In addition to a valid passport, some students – called "visa nationals" – coming to university in Britain will need to obtain a visa from the British Embassy or High Commission before arrival and this could take weeks to arrange. You should apply at least one month, but not more than six months, before coming to the UK. Non-visa nationals do not, as the name implies, require a visa for entry but it might be wise for you to submit your study documents to the British Consulate in your own country just to be on the safe side. In doing so, you can obtain an official entry certificate. Nationals of an EU country, Liechtenstein, Norway and Iceland and now Switzerland are free to travel to the UK without a visa to study or work.

How and When to Apply

Chapter 4 deals with this matter and you should read the information there in conjunction with what follows. If you are applying for a full-time first degree course you will need to fill in a UCAS application form at the UCAS website via the internet at school or perhaps your nearest British Council office.

If you are applying from within an EU country, your application form must be received at UCAS by 15 January, otherwise you will be treated as a late applicant. Different, usually earlier, dates apply for Oxford and Cambridge, and for medical and art and design courses (see details in chapter 4). Prospective students from the ten new EU accession countries (Cyprus, Czech Republic, Estonia, Hungary, Latvia, Lithuania, Malta, Poland, Slovakia and Slovenia) are treated the same as applicants from the other EU member states.

Table 2 What Do Overseas Students Study?

Subject Group	EU Students	Non-EU Students	Total
Business and administrative studies	8,436	18,573	27,009
Engineering and technology	5,049	10,526	15,574
Social, economic and political studies	4,155	5,919	10,074
Computer studies	2,555	6,933	9,488
Creative arts and design	3,514	4,370	7,884
Subjects allied to medicine*	2,608	2,865	5,473
Biological sciences	2,951	2,511	5,462
Legal studies	1,691	3,572	5,263
Languages	3,057	1,896	4,953
Architecture	1,308	1,786	3,094
Medicine and dentistry	726	2,315	3,041
Physical sciences	1,250	1,418	2,668
Librarianship and information science	1,234	1,271	2,505
Humanities	1,280	1,006	2,286
Mathematical sciences	515	1,769	2,283
Education	322	792	1,114
Combined studies	282	419	701
Agriculture	234	187	422
Veterinary science	38	140	178

*Subjects allied to medicine include Pharmacy and Nursing.

If you are applying from a non-EU country, you can submit your application to UCAS at any time between 1 September and 30 June preceding the academic year in which you plan to commence your studies. However, most students apply well before 30 June to make sure that places are still available and to allow plenty of time to make immigration, travel and accommodation arrangements.

British Universities

The UK universities have their origins in the ancient seats of learning at Oxford (1096), Cambridge (1209) and St Andrews (1411). They enjoy a world-wide reputation for the quality of their courses, teaching and research which are rigorously assessed by these independent bodies:

- Higher Education Funding Councils
- Quality Assurance Agency for Higher Education
- Office for Standards in Education.

The appointment of external examiners at each university also guarantees good standards. These, in turn, are reflected in high entry requirements, short and intensive courses of study, and high completion rates, the latter resulting from an infrastructure that offers strong student support. A degree from a British university is a well respected qualification throughout the world, not least because of an increasing emphasis on employability alongside knowledge and skills.

Support for international students is more comprehensive than in most countries and begins long before you arrive in the UK. Most universities have advisers, even offices, in other countries and they are likely to put you in touch with current students or graduates and answer any queries. Then there may well be pre-departure receptions for students and their families and certainly full written pre-arrival information on all aspects of living and studying in Britain. On arrival in the UK, there are often arrangements to meet and greet students at the nearest coach or rail station or airport, a guarantee of warm and comfortable university accommodation, an orientation programme – often lasting several days – to meet friends and to help students adjust to their new surroundings, and courses in the English language for those who need them. But it's not all work. Each university has a students' union which organises social, cultural, religious and sporting clubs and events, including many specifically for overseas students, such as short visits to other European countries. Both the university and its students' union are most likely to have full-time staff whose sole purpose is to look after the welfare of overseas students.

And that's not all! Students receive free medical and subsidised dental and optical treatment under the National Health Service, full access to a professional counselling service and a university careers service network – with an enviable reputation throughout the world – to help you decide what to do on completion of your studies. The fact that degree courses here are more intensive, and thus shorter, than those in many other countries has an obvious financial advantage, not only in study and living costs, but also in the opportunity to enter, or re-enter, the employment market sooner.

Where Overseas Students Study

Most of what follows in this chapter refers to the tables within it. It must be emphasised that these are based solely on the numbers of overseas students attending a particular university and say nothing about the quality of that university. It is very important, therefore, that you cross refer to the main ranking table in chapter 2 and the individual subject tables (chapter 3) which are concerned with quality.

The data are based on overseas students enrolling in all years of first degree courses at UK universities in 2003–04 and are the latest figures available. They exclude those students whose complete study programmes were outside the UK but include the majority of students taking part in European Union exchange programmes such as ERASMUS, TEMPUS and LINGUA at UK universities. Foundation degrees are relatively new and take two years. The traditional first degrees are mostly awarded at Bachelor level (BA, BEng, BSc, etc) and last for three or four years. There are also some so-called "enhanced" first degrees (MEng, MChem, etc) which take four years to complete. Vocational courses like architecture, dentistry and medicine are one or two years longer. Some universities offer one-year courses, including English language tuition, to act as a bridge for overseas students whose qualifications are insufficient for direct entry to a degree course.

The Prime Minister's initiative to recruit an additional 50,000 university students from overseas by 2005 was achieved a year early. The demand is buoyant with significant

Table 3 Where Do Overseas Students Study?

Institution (Top 25)	EU Students	Institution (Top 25)	Non-EU Students
Ulster	1,340	Manchester	2,189
University of the Arts, London	1,069	University of the Arts, London	1,889
Napier	947	Nottingham	1,887
Portsmouth	931	Middlesex	1,716
Brighton	781	Portsmouth	1,471
Edinburgh	778	Leeds	1,448
Westminster	764	Hertfordshire	1,404
Coventry	753	University College London	1,379
Anglia Ruskin	745	Imperial College	1,377
Kingston	725	London School of Economics	1,357
University College London	678	Warwick	1,273
Kent	670	Northumbria	1,257
King's College London	637	Sheffield	1,154
Oxford Brookes	634	Oxford Brookes	1,103
Manchester	616	Liverpool John Moores	1,067
West of England	559	Greenwich	1,000
Manchester Metropolitan	547	Sheffield Hallam	978
Imperial College	546	King's College London	963
Greenwich	542	Luton	962
Middlesex	541	Birmingham	940
Glamorgan	537	Wolverhampton	936
Sussex	532	Westminster	912
Wolverhampton	521	Cardiff	899
Liverpool John Moores	494	Kent	883
Lincoln	494	Edinburgh	883

numbers coming particularly from China and Hong Kong, and India but also from Pakistan, Nigeria, Sri Lanka, Canada and the USA. In many UK universities you could expect to have fellow students from over 100 countries across the world. The British university system is truly a global one and increasingly so with more than one in ten of its student population – a much higher figure than the USA – coming from countries overseas.

Table 1 *Which Countries Do Overseas Students Come From* and Table 2 *What Do Overseas Students Study* give a broad overview of overseas students in Britain. Greece and China are prominent as the major sending countries whereas, to date, very few students have come from the new EU member states except Cyprus. However, most international students, regardless of their country of origin, pursue courses of study which are strongly vocational. Table 3 *Where Do Overseas Students Study* lists those universities with large numbers of overseas students. Ulster owes much of its popularity to its close proximity to the Republic of Ireland. This pattern of distribution largely reflects chosen fields of study. As emphasised earlier, you must satisfy yourself about course and university quality by going back to chapters 2 and 3.

Probably the most useful information is to be found in the series of tables *The Most Popular Subjects and Universities for Overseas Students* which lists the universities by numbers of overseas students in the 25 most popular subjects, each of which has at least 1,000 overseas students. Use this information in conjunction with the tables that measure quality in the earlier chapters. The subjects are listed in order of popularity.

Advice and information on the UK universities are available through the British Council at its worldwide offices, a visit to one of more than 60 university exhibitions overseas and its website (www.educationuk.org), where you can find details of their support services for international students. There is also information on course fees, living costs and English language requirements. UKCOSA, the Council for International Education, is another useful source of advice and information. Its website can be viewed at www.ukcosa.org.uk.

Table 4 The Most Popular Subjects and Universities For Overseas Students

Business Studies	EU	Non-EU	Computer Science	EU	Non-EU
Oxford Brookes	214	380	Middlesex	53	527
Westminster	291	284	Portsmouth	155	295
Northumbria	211	334	Hertfordshire	22	328
Hertfordshire	86	437	Northumbria	38	258
Middlesex	118	404	Manchester	54	231
Luton	117	386	Luton	54	207
Sunderland	79	337	Westminster	56	202
Greenwich	130	267	Sunderland	40	192
Coventry	210	180	Napier	159	58
Lancaster	228	153	Greenwich	26	187
All overseas students	6,376	11,006	**All overseas students**	2,555	6,933

Accounting and Finance

	EU	Non-EU
London School of Economics	34	341
City	68	294
Leeds Metropolitan	6	313
Middlesex	33	180
Lancaster	22	188
Essex	37	144
Warwick	20	148
Hertfordshire	5	151
Oxford Brookes	11	145
Kent	21	134
All overseas students	**690**	**5,807**

Economics

	EU	Non-EU
Manchester	65	366
London School of Economics	38	329
Portsmouth	83	219
University College London	65	229
Anglia Ruskin	257	18
Essex	82	150
Leicester	22	153
Warwick	56	113
Royal Holloway	44	116
Nottingham	32	121
All overseas students	**1,863**	**3,950**

Electrical and Electronic Engineering

	EU	Non-EU
Sheffield	18	272
Imperial College	67	192
Liverpool John Moores	47	192
Manchester	29	189
Surrey	67	148
Birmingham	15	188
Nottingham	15	171
Portsmouth	73	110
Sheffield Hallam	10	168
UCE Birmingham	28	146
All overseas students	**1,381**	**4,618**

Law

	EU	Non-EU
King's College London	143	145
Kent	95	158
Sheffield	44	176
London School of Economics	38	166
Northumbria	13	172
Cardiff	18	164
Nottingham	10	171
Wolverhampton	21	147
Warwick	62	105
Leicester	59	92
All overseas students	**1,691**	**3,572**

Art and Design

	EU	Non-EU
University of the Arts	859	1700
UC Creative Arts	192	269
UCE Birmingham	54	149
Middlesex	70	108
Nottingham Trent	30	117
Kingston	37	72
Brighton	54	51
Wolverhampton	57	43
Goldsmiths	31	67
UWCN, Newport	66	28
All overseas students	**2,346**	**3,477**

Biological Sciences

	EU	Non-EU
Edinburgh	111	78
Imperial College	67	108
University College London	43	71
King's College London	32	73
Aberdeen	68	29
Manchester	29	54
Leeds	26	46
Oxford	26	46
Cambridge	25	44
Glasgow	35	32
All overseas students	**1,359**	**1,561**

Hospitality, Leisure, Recreation, Sport and Tourism

	EU	Non-EU
Thames Valley	44	182
Oxford Brookes	86	93
Brighton	127	39
Queen Margaret	12	146
Surrey	59	90
Leeds Metropolitan	52	60
Kent	30	80
Lincoln	106	4
Bournemouth	46	60
Manchester Metropolitan	27	74
All overseas students	**1,304**	**1,492**

Civil Engineering

	EU	Non-EU
Napier	151	3
East London	81	55
Imperial College	33	102
Portsmouth	69	46
Liverpool	26	68
Nottingham	7	85
Brighton	59	22
Cardiff	33	47
Heriot-Watt	68	10
Dundee	74	4
All overseas students	**1,212**	**1,187**

Medicine

	EU	Non-EU
King's College London	80	150
Manchester	35	142
University College London	54	114
Imperial College	39	108
Edinburgh	35	112
Cambridge	43	96
Glasgow	19	116
Nottingham	17	110
Aberdeen	25	98
Queen Mary	17	97
All overseas students	**626**	**2,079**

Mathematics

	EU	Non-EU
Warwick	37	154
Imperial College	42	145
Manchester	23	137
University College London	27	114
Cambridge	46	80
London School of Economics	19	96
Oxford	30	81
Heriot-Watt	15	89
Queen Mary	7	61
Lancaster	9	48
All overseas students	**515**	**1,769**

Mechanical Engineering

	EU	Non-EU
Imperial College	50	115
Liverpool John Moores	24	103
Manchester	21	94
Sheffield	6	109
Coventry	46	59
Nottingham	16	87
Bath	21	60
Sheffield Hallam	8	67
Hertfordshire	18	54
Newcastle	38	34
All overseas students	**870**	**1,703**

Communication and Media Studies

	EU	Non-EU
Thames Valley	107	84
Westminster	95	93
Liverpool John Moores	30	107
Goldsmiths	33	88
Middlesex	36	58
Sunderland	24	68
Wolverhampton	77	13
Bournemouth	34	51
Glasgow Caledonian	61	14
East London	42	31
All overseas students	**1,143**	**1,113**

Politics

	EU	Non-EU
London School of Economics	84	166
St Andrews	64	104
Sussex	83	40
Kent	86	33
Warwick	51	41
Edinburgh	45	31
Oxford	30	45
Aberdeen	49	20
Aberystwyth	38	30
Essex	33	32
All overseas students	**1,158**	**1,023**

Other Subjects Allied to Medicine

	EU	Non-EU
Queen Margaret	70	57
Cardiff	40	70
Ulster	110	0
Manchester Metropolitan	34	36
Cambridge	25	44
Robert Gordon	49	6
Westminster	32	20
Bangor	47	4
Glamorgan	47	2
Bradford	23	23
All overseas students	**1,095**	**861**

Psychology

	EU	Non-EU
Ulster	109	0
Nottingham	24	85
Bangor	54	28
Middlesex	47	30
Kent	45	23
Goldsmiths	37	26
University College London	26	32
Sussex	37	16
City	31	16
East London	25	21
All overseas students	**1,316**	**845**

Architecture

	EU	Non-EU
Nottingham	21	108
Greenwich	60	53
Oxford Brookes	47	39
East London	38	40
Liverpool	35	40
Manchester Metropolitan	24	46
Dundee	52	11
Cardiff	19	44
Edinburgh	28	35
Westminster	35	26
All overseas students	**826**	**789**

English

	EU	Non-EU
Portsmouth	97	215
Central Lancashire	52	202
Wolverhampton	96	56
Ulster	75	1
Coventry	60	5
Kent	28	36
St Andrews	17	37
Salford	9	31
Edinburgh	21	20
Canterbury Christ Church	37	3
All overseas students	**998**	**1,039**

Nursing

	EU	Non-EU
Dundee	37	411
Glasgow Caledonian	40	94
Ulster	133	1
Luton	19	62
Napier	44	25
Queen's, Belfast	58	2
London South Bank	13	42
Thames Valley	40	6
City	10	31
UCE Birmingham	28	6
All overseas students	**615**	**948**

Pharmacology and Pharmacy

	EU	Non-EU
Robert Gordon	177	29
Sunderland	121	63
Brighton	121	55
Nottingham	5	143
Liverpool John Moores	54	75
Bath	15	67
Bradford	28	47
Manchester	11	56
King's College London	17	47
Portsmouth	10	51
All overseas students	**559**	**633**

Drama, Dance and Cinematic

	EU	Non-EU
UC Creative Arts	89	68
Roehampton	31	36
University of the Arts	33	32
Westminster	44	21
Luton	29	34
Liverpool John Moores	12	31
Kent	31	10
Wolverhampton	24	8
Aberystwyth	24	7
Brunel	19	8
All overseas students	**667**	**455**

General Engineering

	EU	Non-EU
Coventry	158	25
Cambridge	44	138
Napier	105	27
Warwick	18	80
Oxford	18	60
Central Lancashire	15	49
Portsmouth	8	29
Southampton	9	26
Greenwich	7	25
Queen Mary	4	25
All overseas students	**586**	**764**

Education

	EU	Non-EU
Leeds	2	350
Middlesex	30	152
Liverpool Hope	38	5
Chichester	7	23
Greenwich	13	17
Roehampton	11	14
Manchester	1	23
Strathclyde	20	2
Wolverhampton	11	10
Warwick	1	20
All overseas students	**322**	**792**

Aeronautical and Manufacturing Engineering

	EU	Non-EU
Sheffield Hallam	0	115
Kingston	40	67
Imperial College	37	56
Wolverhampton	1	63
Manchester	11	47
Coventry	17	41
Hertfordshire	20	36
Nottingham	4	52
Brunel	22	29
Bristol	13	26
All overseas students	**380**	**876**

Table 5 Percentage of First-Degree-Only Students Who Come From Overseas By Institution

Institution	Overseas Students %	Institution	Overseas Students %
Aberdeen	11.8	East London	16.4
Abertay Dundee	9.2	Edinburgh	11.8
Aberystwyth	7.2	Essex	22.7
Anglia Ruskin	17.1	Exeter	5.4
Aston	10.0	Glamorgan	10.9
Bangor	8.0	Glasgow	6.6
Bath	14.1	Glasgow Caledonian	5.5
Bath Spa	3.4	Gloucestershire	6.1
Birmingham	8.5	Goldsmiths	15.2
Bolton	11.2	Greenwich	16.9
Bournemouth	7.8	Heriot-Watt	17.9
Bradford	17.9	Hertfordshire	14.9
Brighton	13.3	Huddersfield	6.9
Bristol	11.4	Hull	11.3
Brunel	8.1	Imperial College	35.6
Cambridge	12.2	Keele	7.6
Canterbury Christ Church	4.2	Kent	19.1
Cardiff	9.9	King's College London	19.2
Central Lancashire	9.8	Kingston	12.6
Chester	2.3	Lampeter	21.4
Chichester	2.3	Lancaster	12.4
City	22.8	Leeds	9.3
Coventry	15.7	Leeds Metropolitan	9.5
De Montfort	5.6	Leicester	11.9
Derby	5.5	Lincoln	7.8
Dundee	13.6	Liverpool	10.2
Durham	5.3	Liverpool Hope	6.3
East Anglia	10.5	Liverpool John Moores	12.9

Institution	Overseas Students %	Institution	Overseas Students %
London School of Economics	47.1	SOAS	27.4
London South Bank	14.7	Southampton	8.5
Loughborough	6.1	Southampton Solent	8.0
Luton	31.0	St Andrews	21.4
Manchester	14.7	Staffordshire	7.9
Manchester Metropolitan	6.3	Stirling	5.1
Middlesex	21.7	Strathclyde	4.1
Napier	19.5	Sunderland	16.1
Newcastle	9.5	Surrey	18.2
Northampton	5.1	Sussex	13.2
Northumbria	12.7	Swansea	9.2
Nottingham	15.1	Teesside	6.2
Nottingham Trent	4.6	Thames Valley	17.7
Oxford	10.9	Ulster	9.3
Oxford Brookes	19.6	University of the Arts, London	35.8
Paisley	6.9	UCE Birmingham	10.7
Plymouth	8.3	University College London	22.1
Portsmouth	18.4	UWCN, Newport	6.5
Queen Mary	19.4	UWIC, Cardiff	6.5
Queen's, Belfast	7.1	Warwick	18.3
Reading	9.0	West of England	6.6
Robert Gordon	11.9	Westminster	14.9
Roehampton	6.9	Winchester	1.3
Royal Holloway	21.3	Wolverhampton	14.0
Salford	8.7	Worcester	5.0
Sheffield	10.5	York	9.8
Sheffield Hallam	7.2		

10 Oxbridge

Oxbridge (as Oxford and Cambridge are called collectively) is another world when it comes to university admissions. Although part of the UCAS network, the two universities have different deadlines from the rest of the system, and applications are made through UCAS direct to colleges. There is little to choose between them in terms of entrance requirements, but a formidable number of successful applicants have the maximum possible UCAS tariff.

However, that does not mean the talented student should be shy about applying: both have fewer applicants per place than many less prestigious universities, and admission tutors are always looking to extend the range of schools and colleges from which they can recruit. For those with a realistic chance of success, there is little to lose except the possibility of a wasted space on the UCAS application. While a few universities are said to have looked askance at candidates who consider them second best to any other institution, UCAS no longer shows a chosen university the applicant's other choices.

Overall, there are about three applicants to every place at Oxford and Cambridge, but there are big differences between subjects and colleges. As the tables in this chapter show, competition is particularly fierce in subjects such as medicine and English, but those qualified to read metallurgy or classics have a high chance of success. The pattern is similar to that in other universities, although the high degree of selection (and self-selection) that precedes an Oxbridge application means that even in the less popular subjects the field of candidates is likely to be strong.

These two universities' power to intimidate prospective applicants is based partly on myth. Both have done their best to live down the Brideshead Revisited image, but many sixth-formers still fear that they would be out of their depth there, academically and socially. In fact, the state sector produces about half the entrants to Oxford and Cambridge, and the drop-out rate is lower than at many other universities. The "champagne set" is still present and its activities are well publicised, but most students are hard-working high achievers with the same concerns as their counterparts on other campuses. A joint poll by the two universities' student newspapers showed that undergraduates were spending much of their time in the library or worrying about their employment prospects, and relatively little time on the river or in the college bar.

State School Applicants

Student organisations at both universities have put in a great deal of effort trying to encourage applications from state schools, and some colleges have launched their own campaigns. Such has been the determination to convince state school pupils that they will get a fair crack of the whip that a new concern has grown up of possible bias against independent school pupils. In reality, however, the dispersed nature of Oxbridge admissions discounts any conspiracy. Some colleges set relatively low-standard offers to encourage applicants from the state sector, who may reveal their potential at interview. Some admissions tutors may give the edge to candidates from comprehensive schools over those from highly academic independent schools because they consider theirs the greater achievement in the circumstances. Others stick with tried and trusted sources of good students. The independent sector still enjoys a degree of success out of proportion to its share of the school population.

Choosing the Right College

Thorough research to find the right college is therefore very important. Even within colleges, different admissions tutors may have different approaches, so personal contact is essential. The college is likely to be the centre of your social life, as well as your home and study centre for at least a year, so you need to be sure not only that you have a chance of a place, but that you want one at that college. Famously sporty colleges, for example, can be trying for those in search of peace and quiet.

The tables in this chapter give an idea of the relative academic strengths of the colleges, as well as the varying levels of competition for a place in different subjects. But only individual research will suggest which is the right place for you. For example, women may favour one of the few remaining single-sex colleges (St Hilda's at Oxford; New Hall, Newnham and Lucy Cavendish at Cambridge). Men have no such option.

The findings in the Tompkins Table (*below*) are not officially endorsed by Cambridge University itself. However, for the first time this year we are able to publish the "official" Norrington Table from Oxford. Sanctioned or not, both tables give an indication of where the academic powerhouses lie – information which can be as useful to those trying to avoid them as those seeking the ultimate challenge. Although there can be a great deal of movement year by year, both tables tend to be dominated by the rich, old foundations. Both tables are compiled from the degree results of final-year undergraduates. A first is worth five points, a 2:1 four, a 2:2 three, a third one point. The total is divided by the number of candidates to produce each college's average.

In both universities, teaching for most students is based in the colleges. In practice, however, this arrangement holds good in the sciences only for the first year. One-to-one tutorials, which are Oxbridge's traditional strength for undergraduates, are by no means

Cambridge The Tompkins Table 2005

College	2005	2004	College	2005	2004
St Catharine's	1	7	Corpus Christi	16	10
Gonville and Caius	2	5	Trinity Hall	17	12
Trinity	3	3	Churchill	18	19
Christ's	4	2	Selwyn	19	11
Emmanuel	5	1	Magdalene	20	22
Pembroke	6	6	Newnham	21	13
Jesus	7	9	Peterhouse	22	21
Queens'	8	8	Wolfson	23	28
Clare	9	4	Girton	24	25
King's	10	20	New Hall	25	23
Robinson	11	16	Homerton	26	24
St John's	12	14	Lucy Cavendish	27	26
Fitzwilliam	13	15	St Edmund's	28	29
Sidney Sussex	14	18	Hughes Hall	29	27
Downing	15	17			

universal. However, teaching groups remain much smaller than in most universities, and the tutor remains an inspiration for many students.

Both Oxford and Cambridge give applicants the option of leaving the choice of college to the university. For those with no ready source of advice on the colleges, this would seem an attractive solution to an intractable problem, but it is also a risky one: a lower proportion succeeds in this way than by applying to a particular college and, inevitably, you may end up somewhere that you hate.

The Applications Procedure

Both universities have set a deadline of 15 October 2006 for entry in 2007. At the same time as your UCAS application is submitted, an Oxford Application Form or Cambridge Preliminary Application Form (PAF), which your school can obtain direct from the relevant university, must be sent direct to Oxford or Cambridge. You may apply to only one of Oxford or Cambridge in the same admissions year, unless you are seeking an Organ award at both universities. Interviews take place in September for those who have left school or applied early, but in December for the majority. By the end of October, the first group can expect an offer, a rejection or deferral of a decision until January. The main group of applicants to Oxford will receive either a conditional offer or a rejection by Christmas, while in Cambridge the news arrives early in the new year. There are other differences between the two universities, however. Some Cambridge colleges ask candidates to sit the university's Sixth Term Examination Papers. Oxford abolished its entrance examination because of claims that it favoured candidates from independent schools. Applicants are now given conditional offers in the normal way, although they may be asked to sit tests when they are called for interview. Oxford is more likely than Cambridge to make an offer as low as two E grades if it is sure that it wants the applicant, but the practice is no longer common.

Oxford The Norrington Table 2005

College	2005	2004	College	2005	2004
St John's	1	2	Corpus Christi	16	14
Merton	2	1	Pembroke	17	22
Balliol	3	3	Brasenose	18	24
Magdalen	4	5	Mansfield	19	29
University	5	25	Queen's	=20	26
Hertford	6	4	Worcester	=20	12
Exeter	7	13	St Catherine's	22	6
St Anne's	8	17	St Hilda's	23	30
Christ Church	9	20	Lincoln	24	16
Keble	10	21	St Edmund Hall	25	9
Wadham	11	8	St Peter's	26	10
Somerville	12	15	Oriel	27	18
Jesus	13	7	St Hugh's	28	19
Trinity	14	23	Lady Margaret Hall	29	27
New College	15	11	Harris Manchester	30	28

Cambridge Applications and Acceptances by Course

Arts	Applications		Acceptances		% places to Applications	
	2005	2004	2005	2004	2005	2004
Anglo-Saxon, Norse and Celtic	79	57	33	30	41.8	52.6
Archaeology and Anthropology	139	165	60	67	43.2	40.6
Architecture	410	389	44	38	10.7	9.7
Classics	151	124	76	60	50.3	48.3
Classics (4 years)	41	29	11	8	26.8	27.5
English	989	1,000	214	204	21.6	20.4
Geography	276	324	91	97	32.9	29.9
History	855	806	202	198	23.6	24.5
History of Art	105	92	27	22	25.7	23.9
Modern and Medieval Languages	563	648	171	179	30.4	27.6
Music	190	192	67	67	35.3	34.8
Oriental Studies	175	147	53	40	30.3	27.2
Philosophy	314	322	49	54	15.6	16.8
Theology and Religious Studies	134	125	49	52	36.6	41.6
Total Arts	4,421	4,420	1,147	1,116	25.9	25.2

Social Science	2005	2004	2005	2004	2005	2004
Economics	1,001	1,027	170	151	16.9	14.7
Land Economy	247	177	55	34	22.3	19.2
Law	1,281	1,495	222	225	17.3	15.1
Social and Political Sciences	720	663	108	125	15.0	18.9
Total Social Sciences	3,249	3,362	555	535	17.1	15.9

Science and Technology	2005	2004	2005	2004	2005	2004
Computer Science	266	311	68	92	25.6	29.6
Engineering	1,226	1,245	288	281	23.5	22.6
Mathematics	1,042	1,060	243	238	23.3	22.5
Medical Sciences	1,553	1,591	300	282	19.3	17.7
Natural Sciences	1,974	2,002	609	583	30.8	29.1
Veterinary Medicine	379	419	70	59	18.5	14.1
Total Science and Technology	6,440	6,628	1,578	1,535	24.5	23.2
Education	233	272	98	107	42.1	39.3
Total	**14,343**	**14,682**	**3,378**	**3,293**	**23.6**	**22.4**

Note: the dates refer to the year in which the acceptances were made.
Mathematics includes those applying for mathematics, mathematics with computer science, and mathematics with physics.
The tripos course at Cambridge in chemical engineering, linguistics, management studies and manufacturing engineering can only be
taken after Part 1 of another tripos. The entries for these courses are recorded under the first-year subjects taken by the student involved.

Oxford Applications and Acceptances by Course

Arts	Applications		Acceptances		% places to Applications	
	2005	2004	2005	2004	2005	2004
Ancient and Modern History	88	78	20	20	22.7	25.6
Archaeology and Anthropology	62	51	25	22	40.3	43.1
Classical Archaeology and Ancient History	97	86	18	24	18.6	27.9
Classics	262	262	108	114	41.2	43.5
Classics and English	39	30	8	8	20.5	26.7
Classics and Modern Languages	39	34	14	13	35.9	38.2
Economics and Management	634	608	88	84	13.9	13.8
English	1,116	1,098	248	247	22.2	22.5
English and Modern Languages	139	114	21	18	15.1	15.8
European and Middle Eastern Languages	39	25	12	12	30.8	48.0
Fine Art	148	150	21	19	14.2	12.7
Geography	283	247	92	78	32.5	31.6
History of Art	65	39	12	9	18.5	23.1
Law	1,006	1,105	202	211	20.1	19.1
Law with Law Studies in Europe	278	273	27	24	9.7	8.8
Mathematics and Philosophy	84	77	23	22	27.4	28.6
Modern History	809	813	240	243	29.7	29.9
Modern History and Economics	39	43	8	7	20.5	16.3
Modern History and English	79	88	8	12	10.1	13.6
Modern History and Modern Languages	111	96	24	22	21.6	22.9
Modern History and Politics	287	305	53	48	18.5	15.7
Modern Languages	473	409	174	178	36.8	43.5
Modern Languages and Linguistics	63	47	25	14	39.7	29.8
Music	168	146	61	60	36.3	41.1
Oriental Studies	140	110	48	44	34.3	40.0
Philosophy and Modern Languages	62	52	16	17	25.8	32.7
Philosophy and Theology	106	102	22	24	20.8	23.5
Physics and Philosophy	55	42	13	13	23.6	31.0
PPE	1,154	1,107	249	251	21.6	22.7
Theology	134	90	45	39	33.6	43.3
Total Arts	**8,059**	**7,727**	**1,925**	**1,897**	**23.9**	**24.6**

Oxford Applications and Acceptances by Course cont

Sciences	Applications 2005	Applications 2004	Acceptances 2005	Acceptances 2004	% places to Applications 2005	% places to Applications 2004
Biochemistry	237	273	84	87	35.4	31.9
Biological Sciences	223	229	107	90	48.0	39.3
Chemistry	383	319	174	176	45.4	55.2
Computer Science	60	103	20	28	33.3	27.2
Earth Sciences (Geology)	51	55	24	35	47.1	63.6
Engineering Science	387	406	133	135	34.4	33.3
Engineering and Computer Science	21	35	4	2	19.0	5.7
Engineering, Economics and Management	85	92	21	12	24.7	13.0
Engineering and Materials	–	13	–	1	–	7.7
Experimental Psychology	238	251	55	42	23.1	16.7
Human Sciences	103	105	32	36	31.1	34.3
Materials Science and MEM	51	50	28	27	54.9	54.0
Mathematics	592	553	186	178	31.4	32.2
Mathematics and Computer Science	37	60	19	17	51.4	28.3
Mathematics and Statistics	114	105	29	31	25.4	29.5
Medicine	1,025	1,090	154	154	15.0	14.1
Physics	608	519	179	173	29.4	33.3
Physiological Sciences	28	49	11	17	39.3	34.7
PPP	171	201	29	38	17.0	18.9
Total Sciences	**4,414**	**4,508**	**1,289**	**1,279**	**29.2**	**28.4**
Total Arts and Sciences	**12,473**	**12,235**	**3,214**	**3,176**	**25.8**	**25.9**

Note: the dates refer to the year in which the acceptances were made.

For general information about Oxford and Cambridge universities, see each institution's profile in chapter 11.

Oxford College Profiles

Balliol

Balliol College, Oxford OX1 3BJ
01865 277777   admissions@balliol.ox.ac.uk   www.balliol.ox.ac.uk
Undergraduates: 408

Famous as the alma mater of many prominent postwar politicians, including Harold
Macmillan, Denis Healey and Roy Jenkins, the university's last Chancellor, Balliol has
maintained a strong presence in university life and is usually well represented in the
Union. Academic standards are formidably high, as might be expected in the college of
Wycliffe and Adam Smith, notably in the classics and social sciences. PPE in particular is
notoriously oversubscribed. Library facilities are good and include a 24-hour law library.
Balliol began admitting overseas students in the 19th century and has cultivated an
attractively cosmopolitan atmosphere, of which the lively JCR (Junior Common Room) is a
natural focus. Most undergraduates are offered accommodation in college for three years,
while graduate students are usually lodged in the Graduate Centre at Holywell Manor.
Centrally located with a JCR pantry that is open all day, Balliol is convenient as well as
prestigious.

Brasenose

Brasenose College, Oxford OX1 4AJ
01865 277510 (admissions)   admissions@bnc.ox.ac.uk   www.bnc.ox.ac.uk
Undergraduates: 368

Brasenose may not be the most famous Oxford college but it makes up for its discreet
image with a consistently healthy academic performance and an advantageous position in
the centre of town. Brasenose was one of the first colleges to become co-educational in the
1970s, although men still take two thirds of the places. In its defence, the college prospectus
points out that the major undergraduate office, President of the JCR, has been filled as
often by a woman as a man. But BNC, as the college is often known, still has the image of a
rugby haven. Named after the door knocker on the 13th-century Brasenose Hall, the college
has a pleasant, intimate ambience which most find conducive to study. Law, PPE and
modern history are traditional strengths and competition for places in these subjects is
intense. Its library is open 24 hours a day and all undergraduate rooms have internet
connections. Sporting standards are as high as at many much larger colleges and the
college's rowing club is one of the oldest in the university. An annexe, the St Cross
Building, means all undergraduates can live in. Most third years live in the Brasenose
annexe at Frewin Court, just a few minutes' walk away.

Christ Church

Christ Church College, Oxford OX1 1DP
01865 276150   admissions@chch.ox.ac.uk   www.chch.ox.ac.uk
Undergraduates: 408

The college founded by Cardinal Wolsey in 1525 and affectionately known as The House has
come a long way since Evelyn Waugh mythologised its aristocratic excesses in *Brideshead*

Revisited. The social mix is much more varied than most applicants suspect and the college has gone out of its way recently to become something of a champion of political correctness. Academic pressure at Christ Church is reasonably relaxed, although natural high-achievers prosper and the college's history and law teaching is highly regarded. The magnificent 18th-century library is one of the best in Oxford. It is supplemented by a separate law library. Christ Church has its own art gallery, which holds over 2,000 works of mainly Italian Renaissance art. Sport, especially rugby, is an important part of college life. The playing fields are a few minutes' walk away through the Meadows. The river is also close at hand for the aspiring oarsman, and the college has good squash courts. Accommodation for all three years is rated by Christ Church students as excellent and includes flats off Iffley Road as well as a number of beautifully panelled shared sets (double rooms) in college. The modern bar adds to the lustre of a college justly famous for its imposing architecture and cathedral, the smallest in England.

Corpus Christi

Corpus Christi College, Oxford OX1 4JF
01865 276693 (admissions tutor)   admissions.office@ccc.ox.ac.uk   www.ccc.ox.ac.uk
Undergraduates: 237

Corpus, until recently Oxford's smallest college, is naturally overshadowed by its Goliath-like neighbour, Christ Church, but makes the most of its intimacy, friendly atmosphere and exquisite beauty. Like The House it has an exceptional view across the Meadows. Although the college has only around 340 students including postgraduates, it has an admirable library open 24 hours a day. Academic expectations are high and English, PPE and medicine are especially well established. The college is beginning to make the most of ties with its namesake at Cambridge, establishing a joint lectureship in history in 1999. Corpus is able to offer accommodation to all its undergraduates, one of its many attractions to those seeking a smaller community in Oxford.

Exeter

Exeter College, Oxford OX1 3DP
01865 279648 (academic secretary)admissions@exeter.ox.ac.ukwww.exeter.ox.ac.uk
Undergraduates: 327

Exeter is the fourth oldest college in the university and was founded in 1314 by Walter de Stapeldon, Bishop of Exeter. Nestling halfway between the High Street and Broad Street, site of most of the city's bookshops, it could hardly be more central. The college boasts handsome buildings, the exceptional Fellows' garden and attractive accommodation for most undergraduates for all three years of their university careers. Exeter's academic record is strong and the college is usually a high performer in the Norrington Table. It is, however, often accused of being rather dull. Given its glittering roll-call of alumni, which includes Martin Amis, J.R.R. Tolkien, Alan Bennett, Richard Burton, Imogen Stubbs and Tariq Ali, this seems an accusation that on the face of it at least is hard to sustain. College food is not rated highly by students although the bar is popular with students from other colleges. The social scene is livelier than the male/female ratio might suggest.

Harris Manchester

Harris Manchester College, Oxford OX1 3TF
01865 271009 (admissions)   college.office@hmc.ox.ac.uk   www.hmc.ox.ac.uk
Undergraduates: 96

Founded in Manchester in 1786 to provide education for non-Anglican students, Harris Manchester finally settled in Oxford in 1889 after spells in both York and London. A full university college since 1996, its central location with fine buildings and grounds in Holywell Street is very convenient for the Bodleian, although the college itself does have an excellent library. Harris Manchester admits only mature students of mostly 25 years and above to read for both undergraduate and graduate degrees, predominantly in the arts. There are also groups of visiting students from American universities and some men and women training for the ministry. Most of its members live in and all meals are provided, indeed the college encourages its members to dine regularly in hall. The college has few sporting facilities but its students do still manage to represent Harris Manchester in football, cricket, swimming and chess as well as playing on other college or university teams. Other outlets include the college Drama Society and also the chapel, a focal point to many there.

Hertford

Hertford College, Oxford OX1 3BW
01865 279404   admissions@hertford.ox.ac.uk   www.hertford.ox.ac.uk
Undergraduates: 365

Though tracing its roots to the 12th century, Hertford is determinedly modern. It was one of the first colleges to admit women (in 1976). Hertford also helped set the trend towards offers of places conditional on A levels, which paved the way for the abolition of the entrance examination. It is still popular with state school applicants. The college lacks the grandeur of Magdalen, of which it was once an annex, but has its own architectural trademark in the Bridge of Sighs. It is also close to the History Faculty library (Hertford's neighbour), the Bodleian and the King's Arms, perhaps Oxford's most popular pub. Academic pressure at Hertford is not high but the quality of teaching, especially in English, is generally thought admirable. Accommodation is improving, thanks in part to the Abingdon House complex, and the college can now lodge almost all of its undergraduates at any one time. Like most congenial colleges, Hertford is often accused of being claustrophobic and inward-looking – a charge most Hertfordians would ascribe simply to jealousy.

Jesus

Jesus College, Oxford OX1 3DW
01865 279720   undergraduate.admissions@jesus.ox.ac.uk   www.jesus.ox.ac.uk
Undergraduates: 315

Jesus, the only Oxford college to be founded in the reign of Elizabeth I, suffers from something of an unfair reputation for insularity. Its students, whose predecessors include T.E. Lawrence and Harold Wilson, describe it as "friendly but gossipy" and shrug off the legend that all its undergraduates are Welsh. Close to most of Oxford's main facilities, Jesus has three compact quads, the second of which is especially enticing in the summer. Academic standards are high and most subjects are taught in college. Physics, chemistry and engineering are especially strong. Rugby and rowing also tend to be taken seriously. Accommodation is almost universally regarded as excellent and relatively inexpensive. Self-catering flats in north and east Oxford have enabled every graduate to live in throughout his or her Oxford career. The range of accommodation available to undergraduates is similarly good and is available for the full length of any course. The college's Cowley Road development is described by the students' union as "some of the plushest student housing in Oxford".

Keble

Keble College, Oxford OX1 3PG
01865 272711   admissions@keb.ox.ac.uk   www.keble.ox.ac.uk
Undergraduates: 408

Keble, named after John Keble, the leader of the Oxford Movement, was founded in 1870 with the intention of making Oxford education more accessible and the college remains proud of "the legacy of a social conscience". With around 420 undergraduates, Keble is one of the biggest colleges in Oxford, while its uncompromising Victorian Gothic architecture also makes it one of the most distinctive. Once famous for the special privileges it extended to rowers, the college is now academically strong, particularly in the sciences where it benefits from easy access to the Science Area, the Radcliffe Science Library and the Mathematical Institute. At the same time, the college's sporting record remains exemplary, providing a large number of rugby Blues in recent years. Undergraduates are guaranteed accommodation in their first two years and the college can also accommodate most undergraduates in their final year. Its library is open 24 hours a day and all rooms have internet connections. Students who live in must eat in Hall 30 times a year. The Starship Enterprise bar is a particular attraction.

Lady Margaret Hall

Lady Margaret Hall, Oxford OX2 6QA
01865 274310/1   admissions@lmh.ox.ac.uk   www.lmh.ox.ac.uk
Undergraduates: 381

Lady Margaret Hall, Oxford's first college for women, has been co-educational since 1978 and is now equally balanced. For many students, LMH's comparative isolation – the college is three quarters of a mile north of the city centre – is a real advantage, ensuring a clear distinction between college life and university activities, and a refuge from tourists. Although the neo-Georgian architecture is not to everyone's taste, the college's beautiful gardens back onto the Cherwell river, which allows LMH to have its own punt house. The students' union describes academic life at the college as "fairly lax" while commending its record in English, history and law. Accommodation is guaranteed for first and third years and for the great majority of second years. The college's two recent accommodation buildings have the remarkable attraction of private bathrooms in all their rooms. LMH shares most of its sports facilities with Trinity College though it has squash and tennis courts on site. Recently, it has become one of Oxford's dramatic centres.

Lincoln

Lincoln College, Oxford OX1 3DR
01865 279836   admissions@lincoln.ox.ac.uk   www.lincoln.ox.ac.uk
Undergraduates: 274

Small, central Lincoln cultivates a lower profile than many other colleges with comparable assets. The college's 15th-century buildings and beautiful library – a converted Queen Anne church – combine to produce a delightful environment in which to spend three years. Academic standards are high, particularly in arts subjects, although the college's relaxed atmosphere is justly celebrated. Accommodation is provided by the college for all undergraduates throughout their careers and includes rooms above The Mitre, a medieval inn. Students parade around Oxford in sub fusc (formal wear) on Ascension Day while choristers beat the bounds. Graduate students have their own centre a few minutes' walk away in Bear Lane. Lincoln's small size and self-sufficiency have led to the college being accused of insularity. Lincoln's food is outstanding, among the best in the university. Sporting achievement is impressive for a college of this size, in part a reflection of its good facilities.

Magdalen

Magdalen College, Oxford OX1 4AU
01865 276063   admissions@magd.ox.ac.uk   www.magd.ox.ac.uk
Undergraduates: 368

Perhaps the most beautiful college in Oxford or Cambridge, Magdalen is known around the world for its tower, its deer park and its May morning celebrations when students throw themselves off Magdalen Bridge into the river Cherwell. The college has shaken off its public school image to become a truly cosmopolitan place, with a large intake from overseas and an increasing proportion of state school pupils. Magdalen's record in English, history and law is second to none, while its new science park at Sandford is bound to bolster its reputation in the sciences. Library facilities are excellent, especially in history and law. First-year students are accommodated in the Waynflete Building and allocated rooms in subsequent years by ballot. Undergraduates can be housed in college for the full length of their course. Sets in cloisters and in the palatial New Buildings are particularly sought after. Magdalen is also conveniently placed for the wealth of pubs and places to eat in east Oxford. The college bar is one of the best in Oxford and the college is a pluralistic place, proud of its drama society and choir. Enthusiasm on the river and sports field makes up for a traditional lack of athletic prowess.

Mansfield

Mansfield College, Oxford OX1 3TF
01865 270982   admissions@mansfield.ox.ac.uk   www.mansfield.ox.ac.uk
Undergraduates: 205

Mansfield's graduation to full Oxford college status marked the culmination of a long history of development since 1886. Its spacious, attractive site is fairly central, close to the libraries, the shops, the University Parks and the river Cherwell. With just over 200 undergraduates, the community is close-knit, although this can verge on the claustrophobic. The male to female ratio is slightly better than for the university as a whole. Women may prefer the less intimidating atmosphere of Mansfield, perhaps helped by its strong representation of state-school students. First and third years live in college accommodation. Mansfield students share Merton's excellent sports ground and have numerous college teams although it is in drama that its students truly excel. Despite its former theological background, students are not admitted on the basis of religion and can read a wide variety of subjects. Mansfield is home to the Oxford Centre for the Environment, Ethics and Society (OCEES) and also the American Studies Institute, evidence of the strong links between Mansfield and the United States, which is reflected by some 70 visiting students annually.

Merton

Merton College, Oxford OX1 4JD
01865 276329   undergraduateadmissions@admin.merton.ox.ac.uk   www.merton.ox.ac.uk
Undergraduates: 299

Founded in 1264 by Walter de Merton, Bishop of Rochester and Chancellor of England, Merton is one of Oxford's oldest colleges and one of its most prestigious. Quiet and beautiful, with the oldest quad in the university, Merton has high academic expectations of its undergraduates, often reflected in a position at the top of the Norrington Table, as in 2002 and 2003. History, law, English, physics and chemistry all enjoy a formidable track record. The medieval library is the envy of many other colleges. Accommodation is cheap, of a good standard and offered to students for all three years. Merton's food is among the best in the university; formal Hall is served six times a week. No kitchens are provided for students who live in college, however. Merton's many diversions include the Merton Floats, its dramatic society, an excellent Christmas Ball and the peculiar Time Ceremony, which celebrates the return of GMT. Sports facilities are excellent, although participation tends to be more important than the final score.

New College

New College, Oxford OX1 3BN
01865 279551   admissions@new.ox.ac.uk   www.new.ox.ac.uk
Undergraduates: 390

New College is large, old (founded in 1379 by William of Wykeham) and much more relaxed than most expect when first confronting its daunting facade. It is a bustling place, as proud of its excellent music and its bar as of its strength in law, history and PPE. The college has been making particular efforts to increase the proportion of state school students, inviting applications from schools that have never sent candidates to Oxford. The Target Schools Scheme, designed to increase applications from state schools, is well established. Almost all undergraduates will be able to have college accommodation for three years. The college's library facilities are impressive, especially in law, classics and PPE. The sports ground is nearby and includes good tennis courts. Women's sport is particularly strong. A new sports complex, named after Brian Johnston, opened in 1997, at St Cross Road. The sheer beauty of New College remains one of its principal assets and the college gardens are a memorable sight in the summer. In spite of these traditional charms, the college has strong claims to be considered admirably innovative. Music is a feature of college life and the Commemoration Ball, held every three years, is a highlight of Oxford's social calendar.

Oriel

Oriel College, Oxford OX1 4EW
01865 276522   admissions@oriel.ox.ac.uk   www.oriel.ox.ac.uk
Undergraduates: 284

In spite of its reputation as a bastion of muscular privilege, Oriel is a friendly college with a strong sense of identity and has adjusted rapidly to co-educational admissions (women were not admitted until 1985). The students' union describes the college as having "a strong crew spirit" reflecting its traditions on the river. Academic standards are better than legend suggests and the college's well-stocked library is open 24 hours a day. But Oriel's sporting reputation is certainly deserved and its rowing eight is rarely far from the head of the river. Other sports are well catered for, even if their facilities are considerably farther away than the boathouse, which is only a short jog away. Accommodation is of variable quality but Oriel can provide rooms for all three years for those students who require them. Scholars and Exhibitioners chasing firsts in their final year are given priority in the ballot for college rooms. Extensive new accommodation has been completed one mile away off the Cowley Road and at the Island Site on Oriel Street. Oriel also offers a lively drama society, a Shakespearian production taking place each summer in the front quad.

Pembroke

Pembroke College, Oxford OX1 1DW
01865 276412   admissions@pembroke.ox.ac.uk   www.pembroke.ox.ac.uk
Undergraduates: 391

Although its alumni include such extrovert characters as Dr Johnson and Michael Heseltine, Pembroke is one of Oxford's least dynamic colleges. Academic results are solid, and the college has Fellows and lecturers in almost all the major university subjects. Pembroke expects to accommodate all first years and most final-year undergraduates. The Sir Geoffrey Arthur building on the river, ten minutes' walk from the college, offers excellent facilities; in addition to 100 student rooms there is a concert room, computer room and a multigym. College food is reasonable, though some find formal Hall every evening rather too rich a diet. Rugby and rowing are strong, with Pembroke second only to Oriel on the river, and squash and tennis courts are available at the nearby sports ground.

Queen's

Queen's College, Oxford OX1 4AW
01865 279167   admissions@queens.ox.ac.uk   www.queens.ox.ac.uk
Undergraduates: 312

One of the most striking sights of the High Street, Queen's has now shed its exclusive "northern" image to become one of Oxford's liveliest and most attractive colleges. The college's academic record is good, rising in the 2005 Norrington Table. According to the students' union, "the general attitude to work is fairly relaxed and seems to bring good results". Modern languages, chemistry and mathematics are reckoned among the strongest subjects. Queen's does not normally admit undergraduates for the honours school of English language and literature or geography. The library is as beautiful as it is well stocked. All students are offered accommodation, first years being housed in modernist annexes in east Oxford. The college's beer cellar is one of the most popular in the university and the JCR's facilities are also better than average. An annual dinner commemorates a student who is said to have fended off a bear by thrusting a volume of Aristotle into its mouth.

St Anne's

St Anne's College, Oxford OX2 6HS
01865 274825   enquiries@st-annes.ox.ac.uk   www.st-annes.ox.ac.uk
Undergraduates: 412

Architecturally uninspiring (a row of Victorian houses with concrete "stack-a-studies" dropped into their back gardens), St Anne's makes up in community spirit what it lacks in awesome grandeur. One of the largest colleges, it has a high proportion of state school students. A women's college until 1979, its academic standing is growing having climbed to eighth in the Norrington Table in 2005, after being in last place in the middle of the last decade. The library is particularly rich in law, Chinese and medieval history texts. Opening hours are long. Accommodation is guaranteed to all undergraduates and the college is just to the north of the city centre. Three new accommodation blocks contain 150 student rooms, including four for disabled students, while the older rooms have been refurbished.

St Catherine's

St Catherine's College, Oxford OX13UJ
01865 271703   admissions@stcatz.ox.ac.uk   www.stcatz.ox.ac.uk
Undergraduates: 431

Arne Jacobsen's modernist design for "Catz", one of Oxford's youngest undergraduate college and fourth largest, has attracted much attention as the most striking contrast in the university to the lofty spires of Magdalen and New College. Close to the university science area and the pleasantly rural Holywell Great Meadow, St Catherine's is nevertheless only a few minutes' walk from the city centre. Academic standards are especially high in mathematics and physics though the college's scholarly ambitions are far from having been exhausted. The students' union prospectus used to complain that Fellows were "increasingly eager to apply more academic pressure in college". The well-liked Wolfson library is open till 1 am on most days. Rooms are small but tend to be warmer than in other, more venerable colleges. Accommodation is available for first and third years, and plans are underway to extend this to all three years. Squash, tennis and netball courts are all on the main college site. There is an excellent theatre, and the college is host to the Cameron Mackintosh Chair of Contemporary Theatre. Recent incumbents have included Sir Ian McKellen, Alan Ayckbourn and Lord Attenborough. St Catherine's has one of the best JCR facilities in Oxford.

St Edmund Hall

St Edmund Hall College, Oxford OX1 4AR
01865 279008   admissions@seh.ox.ac.uk   www.seh.ox.ac.uk
Undergraduates: 377

St Edmund Hall – "Teddy Hall" – has one of Oxford's smallest college sites but also one of its most populous with 377 undergraduates swarming through its medieval quads. Some two thirds of undergraduates are male, but the college is anxious to shed its image as a home for "hearties", and the authorities have gone out of their way to tone down younger members' rowdier excesses. Nonetheless, the sporting culture is still vigorous and the college usually does well in rugby, football and hockey. Academically, the college has some impressive names among its fellowship as well as a marvellous library, originally a Norman church. The students' union reports that "a laid-back approach (to work) is the norm". Accommodation is reasonable and is guaranteed to first and third years, though most second-year students live out. Its accommodation is being extended and it will soon be able to provide rooms for all three years. The college has two annexes, one near the University Parks, the other in Iffley Road, where many of the rooms have private bathrooms. Hall food is better than average.

St Hilda's

St Hilda's College, Oxford OX4 1DY
01865 286620   college.office@st-hildas.ox.ac.uk   www.sthildas.ox.ac.uk
Undergraduates: 408 (women only)

With Somerville co-educational, St Hilda's is now the last bastion of all-women education in Oxford. How long the university will allow it to remain that way is open to question. In spite of its variable academic record, the college is a distinctive part of the Oxford landscape and is usually well represented in university life. The 50,000-volume library is growing fast and plans for its extension are being considered. St Hilda's also boasts one of the largest ratios of state school to independent undergraduates in Oxford. Accommodation is guaranteed to first years and for one of the remaining two years. The JCR has its own punts, which are available free for college members and their guests. Many of the rooms offer some of the best river views in Oxford. Social facilities are limited but the standard of food is high.

St Hugh's

St Hugh's College, Oxford OX2 6LE
01865 274910   admissions@st-hughs.ox.ac.uk   www.st-hughs.ox.ac.uk
Undergraduates: 388

One of Oxford's lesser-known colleges, St Hugh's was criticised by students in 1987 when it began admitting men. There are now fewer women than men at the college, although the male/female ratio is better balanced than at most Oxford colleges. Like Lady Margaret Hall, St Hugh's is a bicycle ride from the city centre and has a picturesque setting. It is an ideal college for those seeking a place to live and study away from the madding crowd, and is well liked for its pleasantly bohemian atmosphere. Academic pressure remains comparatively low, although the students' union says there are signs that this is changing. St Hugh's guarantees accommodation to undergraduates for all three years, although the standard of rooms is variable. Sport, particularly football, is taken quite seriously. The extensive grounds include a croquet lawn and tennis courts.

St John's

St John's College, Oxford OX1 3JP
01865 277317   admissions@sjc.ox.ac.uk   www.sjc.ox.ac.uk
Undergraduates: 370

St John's is one of Oxford's powerhouses, excelling in almost every field and boasting arguably the most beautiful gardens in the university. Founded in 1555 by a London merchant, it is richly endowed and makes the most of its resources to provide undergraduates with an agreeable and challenging three years. The work ethic is very much part of the St John's ethos, and academic standards are high, with English, chemistry and history among the traditional strengths, though all students benefit from the impressive library. It now has one of the highest number of state school students in Oxford, and the college compensates to some extent by offering generous hardship funds to those in financial difficulty. As might be expected of a wealthy college, the accommodation is excellent and guaranteed for three or four years. St John's has a strong sporting tradition and offers good facilities, but the social scene is limited.

St Peter's

St Peter's College, Oxford OX1 2DL
01865 278863   admissions@spc.ox.ac.uk   www.spc.ox.ac.uk
Undergraduates: 336

Opened as St Peter's Hall in 1929, St Peter's has been an Oxford college since 1961. Its medieval, Georgian and nineteenth-century buildings are in the city centre and close to most of Oxford's main facilities. Though still young, St Peter's is well represented in university life and has pockets of academic excellence, rising to tenth in the Norrington Table in 2004, although it fell back the next year. History tutoring is particularly good. There are no Fellows in classics at the college. Accommodation is offered to students for first and third years and about 60 per cent of second years. Student rooms vary from traditional rooms in college to new purpose-built rooms a few minutes' walk away. The college's facilities are impressive, including one of the university's best JCRs. St Peter's is known as one of Oxford's most vibrant colleges socially. It is strong on acting and journalism and has a recently refurbished bar.

Somerville

Somerville College, Oxford OX2 6HD
01865 270629   secretariat@somerville.ox.ac.uk   www.somerville.ox.ac.uk
Undergraduates: 358

The announcement, early in 1992, that Somerville was to go co-educational sparked an unusually acrimonious and persistent dispute within this most tranquil of colleges. Protests were doomed to failure, however: the first male undergraduates arrived in 1994 and now account for half the students. Lady Thatcher was one of those who flocked to their old college's defence, illustrating the fierce loyalty Somerville inspires. The college's atmosphere appears to have survived the momentous change, although the culture of protest reappeared when a number of students refused to pay the government's tuition fees in 1998. Accommodation, including 30 small flats for students, is of a reasonable standard, and is guaranteed for first years and students sitting public examinations. Sport is strong at Somerville and the women's rowing eight usually finishes near the head of the river. The college's hockey pitches and tennis courts are nearby. The 100,000-volume library is open 24 hours a day and is one of the most beautiful in Oxford.

Trinity

Trinity College, Oxford OX1 3BH
01865 279910   admissions@trinity.ox.ac.uk   www.trinity.ox.ac.uk
Undergraduates: 280

Architecturally impressive and boasting beautiful lawns, Trinity is one of Oxford's least populous colleges. It is ideally located, beside the Bodleian, Blackwell's book shop and the White Horse pub. Cardinal Newman, an alumnus of Trinity, is said to have regarded Trinity's motto as "Drink, drink, drink". Academic pressure varies, as the college darts up and down the unofficial Norrington Table of academic performance. Nonetheless, the college produces its fair share of firsts, especially in arts subjects. Trinity has shaken off its reputation for apathy, though the early gate closing times can leave the college isolated late at night. Members are active in all walks of university life and the college has its own debating and drama societies. The proportion of state school entrants has been rising. Accommodation is of a reasonable standard and undergraduates can live in for three years.

University

University College, Oxford OX1 4BH
01865 276601   admissions@univ.ox.ac.uk   www.univ.ox.ac.uk
Undergraduates: 387

University is the first Oxford college to be able to boast a former student in the Oval Office. Indeed, the college seems certain to benefit from its unique links with former President Clinton, a Rhodes Scholar at University in the late 1960s. The college is probably Oxford's oldest, though highly unlikely to have been founded by King Alfred, as legend claims. Academic expectations are high and the college prospers in most subjects. Physics, PPE and maths are particularly strong. That said, University has fewer claims to be thought a powerhouse in the manner of St John's, arguably its greatest rival. Accommodation is guaranteed to undergraduates for all three years, with third years lodged in an annexe in north Oxford about a mile and a half from the college site on the High Street. The students' union complains that facilities are poor. Sport is strong and University is usually successful on the river, but the college has a reputation for being quiet socially.

Wadham

Wadham College, Oxford OX1 3PN
01865 277947   admissions@wadham.ox.ac.uk   www.wadham.ox.ac.uk
Undergraduates: 392

Founded by Dorothy Wadham in 1609, Wadham is known in about equal measure for its
academic track record – the college generally ranks in the top third in examination
performance – and its leftist politics. The JCR is famously dynamic and politically active,
although the breadth of political opinion is greater than its left-wing stereotype suggests.
And for somewhere supposedly unconcerned with such fripperies, its gardens are
surprisingly beautiful. The somewhat rough-hewn chapel is similarly memorable. The
college has a good 24-hour library. Accommodation is guaranteed for at least two years and
there are many large, shared rooms on offer. Journalism and drama play an important part
in the life of the college, although sport is there for those who want it. The College also
includes the eighteenth-century Holywell Music Room, a historic concert hall.

Worcester

Worcester College, Oxford OX1 2HB
01865 278391   admissions@worc.ox.ac.uk   www.worc.ox.ac.uk
Undergraduates: 417

Worcester is to the west of Oxford what Magdalen is to the east, an open, rural contrast to
the urban rush of the city centre. The college's rather mediocre exterior conceals a
delightful environment, including some characteristically muscular Baroque Hawskmoor
architecture, a garden and a lake. Though academic pressure has been described as
"tastefully restrained", law, theology and engineering are among the college's strengths.
The 24-hour library is strongest in the arts. Accommodation, guaranteed for two years and
provided for the majority of third years, varies in quality from ordinary to conference
standard in the Linbury Building. The ratio of bathrooms to students (one to four) is better
than in many colleges. Sport plays an important part in college life, Worcester having
engaged more success recently in rowing and rugby.

Cambridge College Profiles

Christ's

Christ's College, Cambridge CB2 3BU
01223 334953   admissions@christs.cam.ac.uk   www.christs.cam.ac.uk
Undergraduates: 395

Christ's prides itself on its academic strength, and it is also one of the few colleges
still to offer places on two E grades at A level, meaning that the college is confident
of its ability to identify potential high-flyers at interview and, in effect, prepared to
circumvent A levels as the principal criteria for entry. The college has a 54:46 state-
to-independent ratio and women make up a third of the students. Though the
college has a reputation for being dominated by hard-working natural scientists
and mathematicians, it has had the best results in the university for history and

music over the past five years. The atmosphere has been described as cosy, but some complain of short bar opening hours and a poor relationship between undergraduates and Fellows. Accommodation is guaranteed to all undergraduates in college, some of whom will be allocated rooms in the infamous New Court "Typewriter". The Typewriter houses the excellent New Court theatre, home to Christ's Amateur Dramatics Society and the adventurous student film society, Christ's Films. College sport has flourished in recent years, with teams competing to a good standard. The playing fields (shared with Sidney Sussex) are just over a mile away.

Churchill

Churchill College, Cambridge CB3 0DS
01223 336202   admissions@chu.cam.ac.uk   www.chu.cam.ac.uk
Undergraduates: 440

Founded in 1960 to help meet "the national need for scientists and engineers and to forge links with industry", Churchill has been rising again in the Cambridge league table and still has high standards. Maths, natural sciences, engineering and computer science are traditional strengths, but arts results have been disappointing recently. The college has some of the university's best computer facilities. Deferred entry is encouraged in all subjects. Churchill has a high ratio of state to independent pupils (about 66:34) but one of the lowest proportions of women under-graduates: only one in three. Some are put off by Churchill's unassuming modern architecture and the college's distance from the city centre; others argue that the distance offers much-needed breathing space. One undeniable advantage is Churchill's ability to provide every undergraduate with a room in college for all three years. There are extensive on-site playing fields, and the college does well in rugby, hockey and rowing. The university's only student radio station (broadcasting to Churchill and New Hall) is based here.

Clare

Clare College, Cambridge cB2 1TL
01223 333246   admissions@clare.cam.ac.uk   www.clare.cam.ac.uk
Undergraduates: 440

Though for many Clare's outstanding features are its gardens and harmonious buildings, hard-pressed undergraduates are just as likely to praise the rent and food charges, among the lowest in the university. Accommodation is guaranteed for all three years, either in college or nearby hostels. One of the few colleges which openly encourages applications from "candidates of a good academic standard who have special talents in non-academic fields", Clare tends to feature near the top of the academic tables. Applicants are encouraged to take a gap year. Languages, social and political science and music are especially strong, but science results have been disappointing The ratio of male to female students is better than many colleges, while systematic attempts to raise the proportion of state-educated students has left those from independent schools in a minority. Music thrives. The choir records and tours regularly, and Clare Cellars (comprising the bar and JCR) is rapidly becoming the Cambridge jazz venue as well as providing more contemporary sounds such as drum and bass. Sporting emphasis is on enjoyment as well as competition.

The women's teams have had outstanding success in recent years. The playing fields are little more than a mile away.

Corpus Christi

Corpus Christi College, Cambridge CB2 1RH
01223 338056 admissions@corpus.cam.ac.uk www.corpus.cam.ac.uk
Undergraduates: 250

The only college to have been founded by town residents, Corpus's size inevitably makes it one of the more intimate colleges. It prides itself on being a cohesive community, but some find the focus on college rather than university life excessive. Although small, it is traditionally broad based academically. The kitchen fixed charge is above average but the college is known for a good formal hall. Almost all undergraduates are allocated a room in college or neighbouring hostels. The library is open 24 hours. There is a fairly even social balance: the independent-to-state ratio is about 48:52. The college bar has an enviable atmosphere. The sporting facilities, at Leckhampton (just over a mile away), are among the best in the university and include a swimming pool. The size of the college means that its sporting reputation owes more to enthusiasm than success, however. Drama is also well catered for, and the college owns The Playroom, the university's best small theatre.

Downing

Downing College, Cambridge CB2 1DQ
01223 334826 admissions@dow.cam.ac.uk www.dow.cam.ac.uk
Undergraduates: 410

Downing's imposing neo-Classical quadrangle may look more like a military academy than a Cambridge college but the atmosphere here is anything but martial. Founded in 1800 for the study of law, medicine and natural sciences, these are still the college's strong subjects. Indeed Downing is often called "the law college", although recent results have been better in sciences than arts. A reputation for hard-playing, hard-drinking rugby players and oarsmen is proving hard to shake off. The college claims the best Cambridge boat club. But while sport undoubtedly enjoys a high profile, pressure to conform to the sporty stereotype is never excessive. Downing currently guarantees a place in college accommodation for two out of three years; the completion of a new accommodation block in 2000 allows students to be housed throughout a first degree. The library, opened by Prince Charles in 1993, has won an award for its architecture. There is close to a 50:50 balance between students with state and independent school backgrounds. The student-run bar/party room has improved college social life following three candlelit formal dinners a week.

Emmanuel

Emmanuel College, Cambridge CB2 3AP
01223 334290 admissions@emma.cam.ac.uk www.emma.cam.ac.uk
Undergraduates: 483

Thanks in no small part to its huge and stylish, strikingly modern bar, Emmanuel has something of an insular reputation; although the students are active in university clubs and societies. Traditionally a mid-table college, with no subject bias, Emmanuel has significantly raised its academic profile recently, gaining strength in medicine and social science, but particularly in English, and has been placed in the top 5 in every Tompkins Table since 2003. Deferred entry is greatly encouraged. An almost even state-to-independent ratio contributes to the college's unpretentious atmosphere and nearly half the undergraduates are women. All students are guaranteed accommodation. Second years are housed in college hostels. With self-catering facilities limited, most students eat in Hall. The college offers ten expedition grants to undergraduates every year, and has a large hardship fund. In the summer, the college tennis courts and open-air swimming pool offer a welcome haven from exam pressures. The duck pond is one of the most picturesque spots in Cambridge. The sports grounds are excellent, if some distance away.

Fitzwilliam

Fitzwilliam College, Cambridge CB3 0DG
01223 332030   admissions@fitz.cam.ac.uk   www.fitz.cam.ac.uk
Undergraduates: 474

Based in the city centre until 1963, the college now occupies a large, modern site on the Huntingdon Road. What it may lack in architectural splendour, Fitzwilliam makes up in friendly informality. Around 70 per cent of its undergraduates come from the state sector, and about 40 per cent are women, though the college hopes "significantly to raise this proportion in the coming years". College accommodation is now available for all undergraduates with the completion of the Wilson Building. Fitzwilliam's academic record has been improving, with languages and geography the strongest subjects. Arts are generally stronger than sciences. Applications are also encouraged in archaeology and anthropology, classics, social and political sciences and music. As at Christ's, offers of places are sometimes made on the basis of two Es only at A level. On the extracurricular front, the badminton, hockey and football teams are among the best in the university. The playing fields are a few hundred yards away. The twice termly Ents (college entertainments) are exceptionally popular. Music and drama thrive.

Girton

Girton College, Cambridge CB3 0JG
01223 338972   admissions@girton.cam.ac.uk   www.girton.cam.ac.uk
Undergraduates: 503

The joke about needing a passport to travel to Girton refuses to die. In fact, with the city centre a 15-minute cycle ride away, the college is closer than many hostels at other universities. But if comparative isolation inevitably encourages a strong community spirit, Girtonians still manage to participate in university life at least as much as students at more central colleges and are particularly active in university sports. On the other hand, since Girton stands on a 50-acre site and the majority of second-year students live in Wolfson Court (near the University Library), there is no question of over-crowding: rooms are available for the entire course. Some find that the long corridors remind them of boarding school. Since becoming coeducational in 1979, the college has maintained a balanced admissions policy. Just over half of the undergraduates are from state schools. Girton also has the highest proportion of women Fellows in any mixed college (50 per cent). The onsite sporting facilities, which include a swimming pool, are excellent. The college is active in most sports and particularly strong in football. The formal hall is excellent and popular, but held only once a week.

Gonville and Caius

Gonville and Caius College, Cambridge CB2 1TA
01223 332447   admissions@cai.cam.ac.uk   www.cai.cam.ac.uk
Undergraduates: 543

Gonville and Caius College – to confuse the outsider, the college is usually known as Caius (pronounced "keys") – is among the most beautiful of Cambridge's colleges, as well as one of the most central. It has an excellent academic reputation, especially in medicine and history, though maths and law are also highly rated. Recent results have been better in sciences than arts. Book grants are available to all undergraduates. The library has been refurbished and computer facilities improved. Accommodation is split between the central site on Trinity Street and Harvey Court, a five-minute walk away across the river. Rooms are guaranteed for all first and third years. The majority of second years live in college hostels, none of which is more than a mile away. Undergraduates are obliged to eat in Hall at least 45 times a term, a ruling some find restrictive but which at least ensures that students meet regularly. The college has something of a Home Counties or public school reputation especially for its "It" girls, society high-fliers. In 2002 acceptances for state-school pupils was around 46 per cent. However, Caius is "eager to extend the range of its intake". Caius tends to do well in rowing and hockey, but most sports are fairly relaxed. A lively social scene is helped by the student-run Late Night Bar.

Homerton

Homerton College, Cambridge CB2 2PH
01223 507114   admissions@homerton.cam.ac.uk   www.homerton.cam.ac.uk
Undergraduates: 543

Homerton's origins were in 18th-century London and it moved to Cambridge in 1894. Although still formally an "Approved Society", its students have been university members for a quarter of a century. The college continues to specialise in education, including teacher training – through the BA degree and the postgraduate certificate in education (PGCE) courses offered by the Faculty of Education – but now offers places for many of the other courses offered by the university at both undergraduate and postgraduate level. All first years have rooms in college in new accommodation blocks. In the second year accommodation may be in college or in private rented houses, but final-year students can live in if they wish. There is a 72:28 state–independent split, with men, at the moment, making up no more than 13 per cent of undergraduates. The college's position, a mile from the city centre in its own large grounds, means that the onus is on Homerton students to take the initiative and get involved in university activities. Many do. Homerton is like the other undergraduate colleges in what it offers, and students can take advantage of Formal Hall, sport (there are on-site playing fields), music and drama.

Hughes Hall

Hughes Hall, Mortimer Road, Cambridge CB1 2EW
01223 334898   admissions@hughes.cam.ac.uk   www.hughes.cam.ac.uk
Undergraduates: 80

Hughes Hall admits mature undergraduates over the age of 21 and affiliated students (who already have a good honours degree from another university). The College is the oldest graduate College in the University, founded in 1885 for the training of graduate women teachers. Since then it has become a lively and cosmopolitan community of 450 mature undergraduate and graduate students studying for nearly all the degrees offered by the University. Accommodation within the College is available for all single undergraduates and affiliated students throughout their course. The college is centrally located, with a new accommodation block and attractive gardens.

Jesus

Jesus College, Cambridge CB5 8BL
01223 339495   undergraduate-admissions@jesus.cam.ac.uk   www.jesus.cam.ac.uk
Undergraduates: 503

For those of a sporting inclination Jesus is perhaps the ideal college. Within its spacious grounds there are football, rugby and cricket pitches as well as three squash courts and no less than ten tennis courts, while the Cam is just a few hundred yards away. With these facilities, it is hardly surprising that sports, in particular rowing, rugby and hockey, rate high on many students' agendas. That said, sporting prowess is far from the whole story. The music society thrives, and has extensive practice facilities. Although Jesus lacks a theatre of its own, the college is active in university drama. On the academic front, the Fellows-to-undergraduates ratio is generous and, while philosophy and politics are among the college's strong suits, the balance between arts and sciences is fairly even. There is an excellent and stylish new library. Rooms in college are guaranteed for all first and third-year students. The majority of second years live in college houses directly opposite the college. Over half the undergraduates are state educated and the college is keen to encourage more applications from the state sector. The college grounds – particularly The Chimney walkway to the porter's lodge – are attractive.

King's

King's College, Cambridge CB2 1ST
01223 331417   undergraduate.admissions@kings.cam.ac.uk   www.kings.cam.ac.uk
Undergraduates: 386

The reputation of King's as the most right-on place in the university has become something of an in-joke. It is true that the college has a 70/30 state-to-independent ratio and that it has banned Formal Hall and abandoned May Balls in favour of politically correct June Events. The college is involved in an initiative to increase the number of candidates from socially and educationally disadvantaged backgrounds, and is also keen to encourage applications from ethnic minorities and from women. The students' union is active politically. The college has fewer undergraduates than the grandeur of its buildings might suggest, one result being that accommodation is guaranteed, either in college or in hostels a few hundred yards away. With the highest ratio of Fellows to undergraduates in Cambridge, it is not surprising that King's has been one of the most academically successful colleges, although it has been falling down the Tompkins Table recently. No subjects are especially favoured, but recent results have been better in arts than sciences. Applications are not accepted in veterinary medicine and there are few law students. Sport at King's is anything but competitive. An extremely large bar/JCR is the social focal point, while the world-famous chapel and choir form the heart of an outstanding music scene.

Lucy Cavendish

Lucy Cavendish College, Cambridge CB3 0BU
01223 330280   lcc-admissions@lists.cam.ac.uk   www.lucy-cav.cam.ac.uk
Undergraduates: 118 (women only)

Since its creation in 1965, Lucy Cavendish has given hundreds of women over the age of 21 the opportunity to read for Tripos subjects. A number of its students had already started careers and/or families when they decided to enter higher education. The college seeks to offer financial support to those with family responsibilities, though as yet it has no childcare facilities. Accommodation is provided for all who request it, either in the college's three Victorian houses or in its three modern residential blocks. The college's small size enables all students to get to know one another. Plans to increase the intake are unlikely to alter the intimate and informal atmosphere. Law is still the dominant subject in terms of numbers of students, but veterinary science is also strong and the college welcomes applications in the sciences and other disciplines. All the Fellows are women. For subjects not covered by the Fellowship, there is a well-established network of university teachers.

Magdalene

Magdalene College, Cambridge CB3 0AG
01223 332135   admissions@magd.cam.ac.uk   www.magd.cam.ac.uk
Undergraduates: 337

As the last college to admit women (1988), Magdalene has still to throw off a lingering image as home to hordes of public school hearties. In fact, around 55 per cent of its undergraduates are from the state sector while over a third are women. That said, the sporty emphasis, on rugby and rowing in particular, is undeniable. The nearby playing fields are shared with St John's and the college has its own Eton fives court. Despite finishing closer to the foot of the academic league tables than its Fellows would wish, Magdalene is strong in architecture, law and social and political science. Students are heavily involved in university-wide activities from drama to journalism as well as sport. Accommodation is provided for all undergraduates, either in college or in one of 21 houses and hostels, "mostly on our doorstep". Living in is more expensive than in most colleges. Magdalene is proud of its river frontage, the longest in the university, which is especially memorable in the summer.

New Hall

New Hall, Huntingdon Road, Cambridge CB3 0DF

01223 762229 admissions@newhall.cam.ac.uk www.newhall.cam.ac.uk

Undergraduates: 370 (women only)

One of three remaining all-women colleges, New Hall enjoys a largely erroneous reputation for feminism and academic underachievement not helped by a much-publicised whitewash on University Challenge. Founded in 1954 to increase the number of women in the university, it occupies a modern grey-brick site next door to Fitzwilliam. Students are split 55:45 between state and independent schools. The college lays claim to certain paradoxes. While a rent strike early in the 1990s attested to a degree of political activism, tradition is far from rejected. The following year saw New Hall's first-ever May Ball, an event hosted jointly with Sidney Sussex. Its results regularly place the college near the bottom of the academic league, but it must be remembered that women's results lag behind men's throughout the university. Natural sciences, medicine, economics, and English are New Hall's strongest areas. The college is known for its unusual split-level bar, but many students choose to socialise elsewhere. Sport is a good mixture of high-fliers and enthusiasts, with grounds, shared with Fitzwilliam, half a mile away. The college is particularly proud of its collection of contemporary women's art.

Newnham

Newnham College, Cambridge CB3 9DF

01223 335783 adm@newn.cam.ac.uk www.newn.cam.ac.uk

Undergraduates: 401 (women only)

Newnham has long had to battle with a blue-stocking image. Its entry in the university prospectus used to insist that it "is not a nunnery" and that the atmosphere in this all-women college is no stricter than elsewhere. It even has a "Newnham Nuns" drinking club to make the point. With about a 60:40 state–independent ratio, the college has also successfully cast off a reputation for public school dominance. Newnham is in the perfect location for humanities students, with the lecture halls and libraries of the Sidgwick Site just across the road. The college is, however, keen to encourage applications in engineering, maths and the sciences, and recent results in these subjects have been better than in the arts. All of the Fellows are women. Around 95 per cent of students live in for all three years. This is not to say that ventures into the social, sporting and artistic life of the university are the exception rather than the rule. Newnham students are anything but insular. As well as being blessed with the largest and most beautiful lawns in Cambridge, Newnham has its playing fields on site. The boat club has been notably successful, while the college competes to a high standard in tennis, cricket and a number of minority sports.

Pembroke

Pembroke College, Cambridge CB2 1RF

01223 338154 admissions@pem.cam.ac.uk www.pem.cam.ac.uk

Undergraduates: 400

Another college with a reputation for public school dominance (but with a current state-to-independent ratio of around 50:50), Pembroke's image is changing. Rowing and rugby still feature prominently, but with a female population of about 42 per cent the heartiness is giving way to a more relaxed atmosphere. Around two thirds of all undergraduates live in college, including all first years. The rest are housed in fairly central college hostels, though the standards of these are variable. Academically, Pembroke is considered solid rather than spectacular. Engineering and natural sciences have the largest number of undergraduates, but the subject range is wide with history, classics and English recent strengths. The bar is inevitably the social focal point, but a restriction on advertising means that Pembroke bops attract few students from other colleges. The Pembroke Players generally stage one play a term in the Old Reader, which also doubles as the college cinema, and many Pembroke students are involved in university dramatics. The Old Library is a popular venue for classical concerts. Indeed music is a Pembroke strength. In a city of memorable college gardens, Pembroke's are among the best.

Peterhouse

Peterhouse, Cambridge CB2 1RD
01223 338223 admissions@pet.cam.ac.uk www.pet.cam.ac.uk
Undergraduates: 284

The oldest and among the smallest of the colleges, Peterhouse is another that has had to contend with an image problem. But while by no means as reactionary as its critics would have it, Peterhouse is certainly not overly progressive. There is a 2/1 male-female split, while the state-independent ratio is around 53:47, having seen an increase in state school undergraduates in 2002. The college's diminutive size inevitably makes for an intimate atmosphere. But this does not mean that its undergraduates never venture beyond the college bar. Peterhouse is known above all as "the history college". But while history is indeed a traditional strength and results are excellent, there are in fact no more history students than there are taking natural science or engineering. Academically, the college is generally a mid-table performer, with a better record in arts than sciences, but has recently fallen down the Tompkins Table. The 13th-century candle-lit dining hall provides a fitting setting for what by common consent is the best food in the university. Rents are below average, and undergraduates live in for at least two years, the remainder choosing rooms in college hostels, most within one or two minutes' walk. The sports grounds are shared with Clare and are about a mile away. The college teams have a less than glittering reputation, not surprisingly, given its size.

Queens'

Queens' College, Cambridge CB3 9ET
01223 335540 admissions@quns.cam.ac.uk www.quns.cam.ac.uk
Undergraduates: 490

There is a strong case for claiming that Queens' is the most tightly knit college in the university. With all undergraduates housed in college for the full three years, a large and popular bar (open all day) and outstanding facilities, including Cambridge's first college nursery, it is easy to see why. Queens' also has the distinction of attracting an above-average number of applicants. The state-to-independent ratio is around 47:53, and more than a third of students are female. Though not to all tastes, the mix of architectural styles, ranging from the medieval Old Court to the 1980s Cripps Complex, is as great as any in the university. In addition to three excellent squash courts, the Cripps Complex is also home to Fitzpatrick Hall, a multipurpose venue containing Cambridge's best-equipped college theatre and the hub of Queens' renowned social scene. Friday and Saturday night bops are extremely popular. Queens' has perhaps the foremost college drama society and a thriving cinema. Law, maths, engineering and natural sciences are the leading subjects in a college with an enviable academic record across the board. Apart from squash, Queens' is not especially sporty. The playing fields (one mile away) are shared with Robinson.

Robinson

Robinson College, Cambridge CB3 9AN
01223 339143   undergraduateadmissions@robinson.cam.ac.uk   www.robinson.cam.ac.uk
Undergraduates: 390

Robinson is the youngest college in Cambridge and admitted its first students in 1979. Its unspectacular architecture has earned it the nickname "the car park". On the other hand, having been built with one eye on the conference trade, rooms are more comfortable than most and the majority have their own bathrooms and online links to the university computer network. Almost all students live in college or in houses in the attractive gardens. The college is one of the few with rooms adapted for disabled students. Robinson has sometimes been close to the bottom of the academic tables, but it sat just outside the top ten in 2005. There is no particular subject bias, but recent results have been better in sciences than arts. One in four Fellows are women, the second highest proportion in any mixed college. Its youth and balanced admissions policy (38 per cent are from independent schools, and there is a 44 per cent female intake) ensure that Robinson has one of the more unpretentious atmospheres. The auditorium is the largest of any college and is a popular venue for films, plays and concerts. The college fields (shared with Queens') are home to excellent rugby and hockey sides, and the boat club is also successful.

St Catharine's

St Catharine's College, Cambridge CB2 1RL
01223 338319   undergraduate.admissions@caths.cam.ac.uk   www.caths.cam.ac.uk
Undergraduates: 436

Known to everyone as "Catz", this is a medium-sized, 17th-century college standing opposite Corpus Christi on King's Parade. The principal college site, with its distinctive three-sided main court, though small, provides accommodation for all its first years. The majority of second years live in flats at St Chad's Court, a ten-minute walk away. Catz is not considered one of the leading colleges academically, but its status is improving, having been halfway up the Tompkins Table in 2003. It has a reputation as a friendly place. Geography and law are usually the strongest subjects. More than a third of the students are women, and the split between independent and state school pupils is around 43:57. A new library and JCR have improved the facilities considerably, and there is a strong musical tradition. College social life centres on the large bar, which has been likened, among other things, to a ski chalet or sauna. With a reputation for being sporting rather than sporty, Catz is one of the few colleges that regularly puts out three rugby XVs, and also has a good record in football and hockey. The playing fields are a ten-minute walk away.

St Edmund's College

St Edmund's College, Mount Pleasant, Cambridge CB3 0BN

01223 336250   admissions@st-edmunds.cam.ac.uk   www.st-edmunds.cam.ac.uk

Undergraduates: 100

St Edmund's is primarily a graduate college, with over half its students coming from overseas. Of 350 members, there are 100 mature undergraduates (at least 21 years of age) including affiliated students, who have a prior degree from another university. The College is set in quiet grounds and is conveniently placed to the northwest of the city centre. The College buildings currently house 130 single students, and some of the accommodation has been constructed specifically for students with physical disabilities. In addition there are six maisonettes that are suitable for students with children and three flats for married couples. A new building with an additional 70 student rooms will open in October 2006, and will also include additional teaching, computing and library facilities.

St John's

St John's College, Cambridge CB2 1TP

01223 338685   admissions@joh.cam.ac.uk   www.joh.cam.ac.uk

Undergraduates: 560

Second only to Trinity in size and wealth, St John's has an enviable reputation in most fields and is sometimes resented for it. The wealth translates into excellent accommodation in college for almost all undergraduates throughout their three years, as well as book grants and a new 24-hour library. First years are housed together, which can hinder integration. There is no particular subject bias and St John's has a formidable academic record. English and natural sciences have been recent strengths. A reputation for heartiness persists and the female intake is 40 per cent, slightly below average. The state-to-independent split is about 45:55. The boat club has a powerful reputation, but rugby, hockey and cricket are all traditionally strong. In such a large community, however, all should be able to find their own level. Extensive playing fields shared with Magdalene are a few hundred yards away and the boathouse is extremely good. The college film society organises popular screenings in the Fisher Building, which also contains an art studio and drawing office for architecture and engineering students. Music is dominated by the world-famous choir. Excellent as the facilities are, some students find that the sheer size of St John's can be daunting and this makes it hard to settle into.

Selwyn

Selwyn College, Cambridge CB3 9DQ

01223 335896   admissions@sel.cam.ac.uk   www.sel.cam.ac.uk

Undergraduates: 350

Described by one undergraduate as "the least overtly intellectual college", Selwyn has a down-to-earth and relatively unpressured atmosphere with a regular mid-table performance in the Tompkins Table. Located behind the Sidgwick Site, it is in an ideal position for humanities students, and its academic prowess has traditionally been on the arts side although engineering is an emerging strength. One of the first colleges to go mixed (1976) now approaching half of Selwyn's undergraduates are female. Its state-to-independent ratio stands at about 58:42. Accommodation is provided for all students, either in the college itself or in hostels, all of which are close by. The college has been a leader in IT provision: all college rooms have online connections to the university computer network and there are two well-stocked computer rooms. As well as the usual college groups, the Music Society is especially well supported. The bar is popular if a little "hotel-like". In sport, the novice boat crews have done well in recent years, as have the hockey and badminton sides, but the emphasis is as much on enjoyment as achievement. The grounds are shared with King's and are three quarters of a mile away.

Sidney Sussex

Sidney Sussex College, Cambridge CB2 3HU
01223 338872   admissions@sid.cam.ac.uk   www.sid.cam.ac.uk
Undergraduates: 346

Students at this small, central college are forever the butt of jokes about Sidney being mistaken for the branch of Sainsbury's over the road. Two other, more serious, aspects of life at Sidney stand out: almost every year its undergraduates raise more for the Rag Appeal than any others; while rents are comfortably the lowest in the university (all students are housed either in college or one of 11 nearby hostels). Exam results generally place the college in the middle of the academic leagues. Engineering, geography and law are generally the strongest subjects. Sidney has a good social balance, with a 58:42 state-to-independent ratio, while more than 40 per cent of the undergraduates are women. There is a large student-run bar which is the venue for fortnightly bops, an active drama society (SADCO) and plenty of involvement in university activities. The sports grounds are shared with Christ's and are a 10-minute cycle ride away. Sidneyites are enthusiastic competitors, but the college does not have a reputation for excellence in any individual sports. Sidney's size means that the college is a tight-knit community. Some students find such insularity suffocating rather than supportive.

Trinity

Trinity College, Cambridge CB2 1TQ
01223 338422   admissions@trin.cam.ac.uk   www.trin.cam.ac.uk
Undergraduates: 663

The legend that you can walk from Oxford to Cambridge without ever leaving Trinity land typifies Cambridge undergraduates' views about the college, even if it is not true. Indeed, the college is almost synonymous with size and wealth. Founded by Henry VIII, its endowment is almost as big as the other colleges' put together. However, the view that every Trinity student is an arrogant public schoolboy is less easily sustained. That said, it is true that only about 45 per cent of undergraduates come from state schools and a third of Trinity undergraduates are women, the lowest proportion in any of the mixed colleges. On the other hand, there is little obvious bias in the admissions policy. Being rich, Trinity offers book grants to every student as well as generous travel grants and spacious, reasonably-priced rooms in college for all first and third-year students as well as many second years. The college generally features in the top ten academically. Generally better for sciences than arts, the strongest subjects are engineering, maths and natural sciences. Trinity rarely fails to do well in most sports, with cricket in the forefront. The playing fields are half a mile away.

Trinity Hall

Trinity Hall, Cambridge CB2 1TJ
01223 332535   admissions@trinhall.cam.ac.uk   www.trinhall.cam.ac.uk
Undergraduates: 359

The outstanding performance of its oarsmen has ensured the prevailing view of Trinity Hall as a "boaty" college, but it is also known for its drama, music and bar. The Preston Society is one of the better college drama groups and stages regular productions. Weekly recitals keep the Music Society busy. The small bar is invariably packed. Not surprisingly, many undergraduates rarely feel the need to go elsewhere for their entertainment, although there has been considerable involvement in the students' union recently. The college is strong academically, despite an unusually low position in the recent tables. Law is a traditional speciality and recently results have been excellent in modern languages. The college is strong in the arts, though the natural sciences are well represented. Almost half of the undergraduates are women and around 45 per cent are from state schools. All first years and approximately half the third years live in college, which is situated on the Backs behind Caius. The remainder take rooms either in two large hostels close to the sports ground, or in college accommodation about five minutes' walk away.

Wolfson

Wolfson College, Barton Road, Cambridge CB3 9BB
01223 335900)   ug-admissions@wolfson.cam.ac.uk   www.wolfson.cam.ac.uk
Undergraduates: 90

Wolfson, although primarily a graduate college, has about 90 mature or affiliated undergraduates, about 15 per cent of the total college student population. Wolfson is one of three colleges that admit students for the Graduate Course in Medicine. Its life is enriched by the high proportion (about 50 per cent) of overseas students, from over 70 countries. The relationship between senior and junior members is informal; common rooms, facilities and social activities are equally open to both. The College is situated in west Cambridge, close to the University Library and the arts faculties. The main buildings of Wolfson College were built in the 1970s around attractive garden courts. The College has accommodation for most students who want to live in College. There is also some accommodation for couples.

University Profiles

The following 110 profiles contain valuable information about each university. Each profile includes some standard information, which is described below:

- the telephone number for admission enquiries.
- the e-mail address for admissions and prospectus enquiries.
- the address of the main university website.
- the website of the students' union.

The Times **rankings** These figures are taken from the main League Table. See pages 39–44 for this table and the sources of the data. The headings used match those in the main League Table. Please refer to pages 35–8 for a full explanation of all these measures. This year a new measure, Student Satisfaction has been included. This is a measure of the way students viewed the teaching quality of their university by subject. The National Student Survey canvassed the opinion of 175,000 final year students in early 2005. See page 35 for an explanation of this assessment.

Undergraduates The first figure is for full-time undergraduates. The second figure (in brackets) gives the number of part-time undergraduates. The figures are for 2003–04, and are the most recent provided by HESA.

Postgraduates The first figure is for full-time postgraduates. The second figure (in brackets) gives the number of part-time postgraduates. The figures are for 2003–04, and are the most recent provided by HESA.

Mature students The percentage of First degree acceptances in 2004 who were over 21. The figures were compiled by UCAS.

Overseas students The number of undergraduate overseas students (both EU and non-EU) as a percentage of full-time undergraduates. All figures relate to 2003–04 and are based on HESA data.

Applications per place The number of applicants per place for 2004 as calculated by UCAS.

From state-school sector The number of young full-time undergraduate entrants from state schools or colleges in 2003–04 as a percentage of total young entrants. The figures are published by HESA.

From working-class homes The number of young full-time undergraduate entrants in 2003–04 whose parental occupation is skilled, manual, semi-skilled or unskilled (Social Classes IIIM–V) as a percentage of total young entrants. The figures are published by HESA.

Accommodation The information was obtained through a survey made of all university accommodation services, and their help in compiling this information is gratefully acknowledged.

Comments on campus facilities apply to the universities' own sites only. New universities, in particular, operate "franchised" courses at further education colleges, which are likely to have lower levels of provision. Prospective applicants should check out the library and social facilities before accepting a place away from the parent institution.

Bursaries and Scholarships A summary of the bursary and scholarship schemes to be offered in 2006. This is not comprehensive, so check the details with the individual universities and see chapter 7, *Managing Your Money*. The information was obtained with the assistance of the individual universities and their help is gratefully acknowledged.

Some famous names are missing from our university listings: the Open University, the separate business and medical schools, Birkbeck College and Cranfield University among them. Their omission is no reflection on their quality, simply a function of their particular roles. The *Guide* is based on provision for full-time undergraduates and the factors judged to influence this. The Open University (www.open.ac.uk), though Britain's biggest university, with 75,000 students, could not be included because most of the measures used in our listing do not apply to it. As a non-residential, largely part-time institution, Birkbeck College, London (www.bbk.ac.uk), could also not be compared in many key areas. Although Cranfield (www.cranfield.ac.uk) offers undergraduate degrees on two of its campuses, it is primarily for graduate students. Manchester Business School (www.mbs.ac.uk) and London Business School (www.lbs.ac.uk) were excluded for the same reason. Specialist institutions such as the Royal College of Art (www.rca.ac.uk) and St George's Hospital Medical School (sghms.ac.uk) could not fairly be compared with generalist universities. A number of colleges with degree-awarding powers also do not appear because they have yet to be granted university status. However, at the end of the book, we list higher education colleges with their addresses and websites.

The **University of London** is a federal university composed of a number of institutions. In this profile section, the pages on the University of London (pages 384–85) outline the colleges of the university that are not listed separately in this guide. There are separate entries on the leading undergraduate colleges.

Founded in 1893, the **University of Wales** is also a federal university. Separate profiles can be found for the leading institutions. Other members are North East Wales Institute; Swansea Institute of Higher Education; Trinity College, Carmarthen; and the Royal Welsh College of Music and Drama. The University of Cardiff is no longer a member of the University of Wales. See www.wales.ac.uk.

University of Aberdeen

Aberdeen has been building on a sharply improved performance in the last Research Assessment Exercise, when the number of internationally-rated departments shot up from two to ten. The relatively small French department achieved the only 5* rating, but other top grades were divided among the university's three colleges. These successes, which have been accompanied by consistently good teaching grades, have brought record applications, including a 5 per cent increase, against the trend in Scotland, in 2006.

The university has boosted its external research funds so successfully that it is now in the top 20 in the UK on this measure. Only three subjects were rated less than Highly Satisfactory in the initial round of teaching inspections, and the pattern continued in the audits carried out in the early years of this decade. French, biology, sociology and community-based medicine have top ratings for both teaching and research.

Female students now outnumber the men, but Aberdeen still considers itself a "balanced" university because roughly half of its students study medicine, science or engineering, half the arts or social sciences. Most are not even admitted to a particular department, allowing them to try out three or four subjects before committing themselves at the end of their first or even second year. The modular system, covering almost 600 first-degree programmes, is so flexible that the majority of students change their intended degree before graduation.

Medicine, law and divinity head Aberdeen's traditional strengths – the university established the English-speaking world's first chair in medicine and has produced its share of advances since. The Institute of Medical Sciences, which has brought together all Aberdeen's work in this area, was completed in 2002 with state-of-the-art laboratory facilities.

Biological sciences have developed considerably in recent years, becoming second only to the social sciences in terms of size. Biomedicine is particularly strong, and the university's links with the oil industry show in geology's high reputation. The university is also the main centre for agriculture in Scotland and part of a new European network for the subject.

Today's university is a fusion of two ancient institutions which came together in 1860. With King's College dating back to 1495 and Marischal College following almost a century later, Aberdeen likes to boast that for 250 years it had as many universities as the whole of England. The original King's College buildings are the

King's College,
Aberdeen AB24 3FX
01224 272090/91
sras@abdn.ac.uk
www.abdn.ac.uk
www.ausa.org.uk

ABERDEEN
Edinburgh
Belfast
London
Cardiff

The Times Rankings
Overall Ranking: 36

Student satisfaction:	–	(–)
Research assessment:	=42	(4.7)
Entry standards:	33	(348.5)
Student–staff ratio:	=12	(14.1)
Library/IT spend/student:	16	(£759)
Facilities spend/student:	55	(£211)
Good honours:	32	(65.5%)
Graduate prospects:	28	(70.1%)
Expected completion rate:	66	(81.8%)

focal point of an appealing campus, complete with cobbled main street and some sturdily handsome Georgian buildings, about a mile from the city centre. Medicine is at Foresterhill, a 20-minute walk away, adjoining the Aberdeen Royal Infirmary. Buses link the two sites with the Hillhead residential complex, and there is a free late-night service. The Aberdeen arm of Northern College has now joined the fold and moved to the main campus, restoring the university's original involvement in teacher training, and forming its fifth faculty. More than a third of all students come from the north of Scotland, but taking one in ten from outside Britain ensures a cosmopolitan atmosphere. Students from England and the 120 nationalities from further afield are generally prepared for Aberdeen's remote location and, although the winters are long, the climate is warmer than the uninitiated might expect. As the energy capital of Europe, transport links are good. Students find the city lively and welcoming but expensive, although its prosperity does provide a good selection of part-time jobs from the JobLink service.

Student facilities are good: there are first-class sports facilities and an NHS medical practice on campus. The students' union closed in 2004 but there is a city centre bar and a new students' centre on the King's College campus – The Hub – is due to open in September 2006. The ICT network has over 1,000 computers for student use and the library is well stocked. Its replacement will be the next priority for one of the most successful fundraising campaigns at any British university. The institution's residential stock has been increased in recognition of the limited private market and all new undergraduates are guaranteed a place.

Bursaries and Scholarships

- Scottish domiciled students: no fees will be payable by eligible students although a "graduate endowment" will be payable after graduation. The 2005–06 level was £2,216.
- Non-Scottish domiciled students fees: £1,700 a year (£2,700 for medicine).
- Fees for placement year and year abroad are normally 50% of full-time fee.
- 90 bursaries available in 2006–07.

Contact: http://www.abdn.ac.uk/sras/ undergraduate/bursaries.shtml

Students

Undergraduates:	9,285	(1,125)
Postgraduates:	1,480	(2,125)
Mature students:	20%	
Overseas students:	11.8%	
Applications per place:	5.4	
From state-sector schools:	84.4%	
From working-class homes:	25%	

For detailed information about fees, grants and bursaries and how they work, see chapter 7.

Accommodation

Number of places and costs refer to 2005–06
University-provided places: about 2,171
Percentage catered:41%
Catered costs: £87–£105 a week (38 weeks).
Self-catered costs: £53.50–£75.00 a week (38 weeks).
First-year students are guaranteed accommodation.
International students: as above.
Contact: studentaccomm@abdn.ac.uk

University of Abertay

Scotland's newest university doubled in size during the 1990s and has grown further since up-front tuition fees were abolished for Scottish students. There are now more than 5,500 students, mainly in Dundee but with several hundred in locations as far afield as Malaysia. The former central institution has enjoyed a series of good teaching scores. Published drop-out projections have been high but may have been overestimated in the official statistics. Almost three in ten undergraduates come from socially deprived areas, considerably more than the average for the subjects offered. Practically all the students attended state schools and nearly a third come from working-class homes.

The former Dundee Institute of Technology was made to wait for university status, which only came two years after the polytechnics were promoted. But the institute had already established its academic credentials, with teaching in economics rated more highly than in some of Scotland's elite universities. Subsequent assessments were solid, without living up to that early promise, but economics, engineering and environmental sciences were given the highest possible rating in later inspections.

Research is not being ignored. Abertay is proud of its record in establishing a series of specialist centres, in areas as diverse as wood technology, urban water systems and bioinformatics. The university opened Europe's first research centre dedicated to computer games and digital entertainment and a major new environmental science centre is still being developed. The last research assessments showed a big improvement on 1996, doubling the average score, although only environmental sciences reached any of the top three grades.

Abertay plays to its strengths with a limited range of courses, and is not shy about its achievements. Among them is a high-tech approach that permeates all four of the university's schools. Until recently, its website offered prospective students "better networking than Oxford", and its spending on libraries and computers is the second-highest per student in Britain in our League Table, providing one computer for every four students.

Based mainly in the centre of Dundee, all the university's buildings are within 15 minutes' walk of each other. The imposing Dudhope Castle dominates recruitment literature and houses the Tayside Institute for Health Studies and the Abertay Pain Management Research Centre. Other buildings are more modern and functional. New facilities are gradually being added, notably the £8-million library opened by the Queen and a £6-million student centre,

---

Bell Street, Dundee DD1 1HG
01382 308080
siro@abertay.ac.uk
www.abertay.ac.uk
www.abertayunion.com

The Times Rankings
Overall Ranking: 57

Student satisfaction:	–	(–)
Research assessment:	=92	(2.0)
Entry standards:	90	(226.2)
Student–staff ratio:	=78	(20.6)
Library/IT spend/student:	2	(£1,318)
Facilities spend/student:	101	(£108)
Good honours:	77	(52.6%)
Graduate prospects:	14	(74.3%)
Expected completion rate:	108	(66.9%)

which opened in 2005. A 500-bed student village is next on the list.

Entrance requirements have been rising, although for most courses they are still modest. Degrees are predominantly vocational, with more subjects being added every year. Forensic science, forensic psychobiology, computer arts and sports coaching and development are recent examples. All courses can be taken on a part-time basis, and the aim is for new programmes to offer students the chance to spend at least 30 per cent of their time in industry.

The university's revamped modular degree scheme means that undergraduates take a maximum of eight modules a year. First-year students are assessed by coursework alone in the first semester, with examinations at the end of the year. Students can complete a Certificate of Higher Education after one year, a diploma after two, an ordinary degree after three, or honours in four years.

Dundee has a large student population and is improving as a youth centre where the cost of living is modest. Relatively low student numbers translate into a moderate social scene, particularly at weekends. Around 30 per cent of the undergraduates are over 21 on entry, many living locally. This lifts the pressure on university-owned beds sufficiently to allow all first years to be guaranteed accommodation.

Bursaries and Scholarships

- Scottish domiciled students: no fees will be payable by eligible students although a "graduate endowment" will be payable after graduation. The 2005–06 level was £2,216.
- Non-Scottish domiciled students fees: £1,700 a year.
- Fees for placement year and year abroad are normally 50% of full-time fee.

Contact: www.abertay.ac.uk

Students

Undergraduates:	3,100	(355)
Postgraduates:	345	(310)
Mature students:	29.1%	
Overseas students:	9.2%	
Applications per place:	4.4	
From state-sector schools:	97.7%	
From working-class homes:	31.2%	

For detailed information about fees, grants and bursaries and how they work, see chapter 7.

Accommodation

Number of places and costs refer to 2006–07

University-provided places: 650

Percentage catered: 0%

Self-catered costs: £44.50–£74.00 a week.

New first years are given priority provided conditions are met. Some residential restrictions. Restrictions apply for senior students.

International students: prioritised by distance from Dundee.

Contact: accommo@abertay.ac.uk

Aberystwyth, University of Wales

Although the oldest of the Welsh university colleges, Aberystwyth has long prided itself on a modern outlook. The modular degree system has been running since 1993, covering academic and vocational courses, and the principle of flexibility was established long before that. Uniquely in the UK, every student is offered the opportunity of a year's work experience in commerce, industry or the public sector, either at home or abroad. Students who have taken advantage of the scheme have achieved better than average degrees and enhanced their employment prospects. The mix served Aberystwyth well in the first national student satisfaction survey, winning it a place in the top 20. History, archaeology and geography did particularly well.

Aber is always heavily oversubscribed even though the number of places has increased. Almost a third of the students are from Wales. A new agreement to collaborate with the University of Wales, Bangor, in a range of subjects from business to science emphasises teaching in Welsh. An attractive seaside location does the university no harm when the applications season comes around. The college has expanded significantly in recent years, with a new School of Management and Business as well as a department of Sports and Exercise Science among the additions. A £3.6 million centre for theatre, film and television studies and a purpose-built sports and exercise science centre are among the latest developments on the Penglais campus, which overlooks the town. A new £5 million building for the internationally-acclaimed International Politics Department was due to open in 2006.

More than 90 per cent of the undergraduates come from state schools or colleges – a far higher proportion than the mix of subjects would imply – but less than 30 per cent come from working-class homes and only about half that number hail from areas that send few students to higher education. However, the drop-out rate of 10 per cent is among the lowest in Wales and also better than the funding council's "benchmark" figure for the institution.

The Institute of Rural Sciences allows Aber to claim the widest range of land-related courses in the UK. The institute shares the Llanbadarn campus with information and library studies and a further education college. Teaching ratings were impressive, especially in the arts and social sciences. Offers of places are made on the basis of the UCAS tariff, which not only recognises general studies as full A or AS levels, but also gives credit for Key Skills

---

Old College, King Street,
Aberystwyth, Ceredigion SY23 2AX
01970 622021
ug-admissions@aber.ac.uk
www.aber.ac.uk
http://union.aber.ac.uk

The Times Rankings
Overall Ranking: 46

Student satisfaction:	=8	(15.5)
Research assessment:	50	(4.5)
Entry standards:	50	(299.4)
Student–staff ratio:	=83	(20.8)
Library/IT spend/student:	56	(£540)
Facilities spend/student:	27	(£277)
Good honours:	54	(59.0%)
Graduate prospects:	101	(50.3%)
Expected completion rate:	=33	(89.4%)

qualifications. Celtic studies and politics were rated internationally outstanding in the latest research assessments, while theatre, film and television studies reached the next rung of the ladder. Criminology was added to the degree portfolio in 2006.

Entrance scholarships and bursaries are available in a range of subjects, even though Welsh students have been spared the full impact of top-up fees. Aber boasts one of higher education's most informative websites and also publishes a 12-page guide for parents. There is 24-hour access to the computer network, and the four university libraries are complemented by the National Library of Wales.

The town of Aberystwyth is compact and travel to other parts of the UK slow, so applicants should be sure that they will be happy to spend three years or more in a tight-knit community. Applications have fluctuated over recent years, but were down by almost 10 per cent at the official deadline for entry in 2006. The students' guild is the largest entertainment venue in the region and the arts centre has been extended at a cost of £3.5 million.

The student-produced Alternative Prospectus describes the traditional seaside town of 25,000 people as the "Welsh California". They say it has "plenty of life and vitality, and a certain *je ne sais quoi*". It also offers plenty of out-of-season accommodation to supplement the university's 3,700 places, all of which are now online. Sports facilities are good for the size of institution, with 50 acres of pitches, a swimming pool, a climbing wall and specialist outdoor facilities for water sports.

Bursaries and Scholarships

- Fees for undergraduate courses   £3,000
- Students living in Wales will be eligible for a Welsh Assembly fee grant of approximately £1,800 a year.
- Fees for placement year and year abroad: £1,538 (50%).
- For information on the National Bursary Scheme see page 198, chapter 7.
- Excellence bursaries in specified subjects. £2,000 for students who achieve 300 UCAS points and enrol on courses in Science, European Languages, Welsh and defined Welsh-medium schemes.
- Aberystwyth Bursaries are means-tested awards open to all UK students.
- Accommodation bursaries of £500 for students who make Aberystwyth their firm choice through UCAS by the end on June in the year of application. Bursary is in the form of a reduction of hall fees in their first year and is open to all UK and EU students.

Contact: www.aber.ac.uk/en/prospectus/bursaries

Students

Undergraduates:	6,080	(2,010)
Postgraduates:	870	(1,435)
Mature students:	11.6%	
Overseas students:	7.2%	
Applications per place:	4.2	
From state-sector schools:	93.1%	
From working-class homes:	28.1%	

For detailed information about fees, grants and bursaries and how they work, see chapter 7.

Accommodation

Number of places and costs refer to 2005–06
University-provided places: 3,858
Percentage catered: 26.3%
Catered costs: £71.19–£86.48 a week.
Self-catered costs: £56.11–£75.32 a week.
First years are guaranteed accommodation if conditions are met.
International students: accommodation guaranteed.
Contact: mew@aber.ac.uk
website: www.aber.ac.uk/residential

Anglia Ruskin University

The last university to retain the polytechnic title has finally discarded it in order to avoid confusion among employers and overseas applicants. Having previously rejected a series of alternative names and decided to stay as it was, the former APU has now taken the name of John Ruskin, who founded the Cambridge art school that eventually developed into the university. Since the change, in October 2005, two £8-million developments have opened on the larger of the university's two main sites, in Chelmsford, and more are on the way. A new student centre houses support services as well as the normal union facilities, while the music and arts faculty has new and enhanced teaching and practice facilities.

In addition, the university has acquired Homerton College's school of health studies, in Cambridge, after a long period of partnership. A new Institute of Health and Social Care is among the next developments planned for the 22-acre Rivermead campus in Chelmsford, where an impressive business school opened in 2003 and there is a new sports hall. The total construction bill is expected to reach £55 million over the next few years.

An amalgamation of two well-established higher education colleges made Anglia the first regional polytechnic, but the twin bases in Chelmsford and Cambridge remain distinct. The two very different locations are far enough apart to ensure that there is little contact, although electronic networking and a central administration mean that key academic facilities are available throughout the university.

The regional ideal extends to a network of more than 20 partner colleges in Cambridgeshire, Essex, Norfolk and Suffolk, where 4,000 students take Anglia's courses. One, at Benfleet in Essex, has become a "local campus" of the university. East Anglia has always lagged behind other parts of England for participation in higher education and, although the university has continued to grow, it has sometimes struggled to fill its places. Applications were down at the start of 2006, but by no more than the national average. Over 95 per cent of the students attended state schools or colleges and more than a third are from working-class homes.

Most teaching ratings were solid, rather than spectacular, although there was an improvement in the latter years of assessment. Nursing and theology (a postgraduate subject only) produced the best scores, but the tourism and leisure course added to the low scores in 2001. The last research grades also showed improvement, but only one university submitted a lower

---

Rivermead Campus: Bishop Hall Lane, Chelmsford, Essex CM1 1SQ

Cambridge Campus: East Road Cambridge CB1 1PT

0845-271 3333 (enquiries)

answers@anglia.ac.uk

www.anglia.ac.uk

www.apusu.com

The Times Rankings
Overall Ranking: =87

Student satisfaction:	=60	(14.6)
Research assessment:	=103	(1.5)
Entry standards:	84	(233.4)
Student–staff ratio:	68	(19.6)
Library/IT spend/student:	88	(£444)
Facilities spend/student:	=78	(£161)
Good honours:	59	(56.1%)
Work and further study:	=62	(61.8%)
Expected completion rate:	78	(87.0%)

proportion of academics for assessment, and only English made the top three categories. Management and art and design were the best performers in the first national student satisfaction survey. The introduction of a benchmarking system to take account of the mix of subjects at each university saw Anglia Ruskin tumble down *The Times* League Table and it has not recovered.

The university has a strongly international outlook, providing an unusually large number of exchange opportunities in Malaysia and China, as well as Europe and the United States. Each undergraduate has an adviser to help compile a degree package which looks at the chosen subject from different points of view to maximise future job prospects. Employers play a part in planning courses which are integrated into a modular system extending from degree level to professional programmes, including a modest selection of vocational two-year foundation degrees.

The social scene inevitably varies between the two campuses. Cambridge students enjoy the advantages of a great university city, but have to shrug off the tag of attending the lesser institution. There is limited collaboration with Cambridge University, for example on a new cricket academy and a base for Anglia Ruskin's rowing club. Some students find Chelmsford dull, but the social scene is said to be improving. Neither base is far from London by train.

Bursaries and Scholarships[†]

In receipt of full Maintenance Grant	£800 min
In receipt of partial Maintenance Grant	£500 max
Living in region	Bursary
Living in specified postcodes	Bursary
Progressing from outreach	Bursary
Ethnic minorities	Bursary
Disabled	Bursary

- Tuition fees (2006)   £3,000
- Anglia also plans to target people living in areas remote from higher education institutions.
- Eligibility for bursaries to be assessed using UUK/SLC model bursary scheme (HEBSS).

Contact:
www.anglia.ac.uk/ruskin/en/home/study/ ukstudents/fees.html

[†] Information taken from 2006 Access Agreement

Students

Undergraduates:	9,855	(10,360)
Postgraduates:	705	(3,395)
Mature students:	33.9%	
Overseas students:	17.1%	
Applications per place:	4.3	
From state-sector schools:	96%	
From working-class homes:	36.1%	

For detailed information about fees, grants and bursaries and how they work, see chapter 7.

Accommodation

Number of places and costs refer to 2006–07
University-provided places: Cambridge, about 715 plus 182 nomination rooms; Chelmsford, 531
Percentage catered: 0%
Self-catered costs: Cambridge: £58.00–£83.05 a week; Chelmsford: £60–£76 a week.
Residential restriction at Cambridge campus.
International students: conditions apply.
Contact : Cambaccom@anglia.ac.uk
essexaccom@anglia.ac.uk

Aston University

Aston has always gloried in its role as a tight-knit, vocational, urban university, which has swum against the tide of British higher education over the past decade. Small and lively, set in the heart of Birmingham, it has remained resolutely specialist in science and technology, business and languages, concentrating on the sandwich degrees which have served its graduates so well in the employment market.

Despite some modest growth recently, the university still has only 6,000 undergraduates. This used to make for a bumpy ride financially, with the funding council having to provide special help several times to avoid damaging budget cuts. But now, helped by healthy funding from industry and commerce, Aston is able to invest in its future, boosting staffing in business, engineering and languages and developing the campus. Applications were down by 8 per cent at the start of 2006, although the 29 per cent increase 12 months earlier was bettered by only one old university, and entry grades have risen consistently.

There were much-improved research grades at the end of 2001, with four of the five subject areas judged to be producing work of international quality. Business and management, languages and European studies, general engineering and neurosciences all achieved top scores. Academic restructuring, designed mainly to break down barriers between departments, has since reduced the number of schools to four.

As befits a one-time college of advanced technology, Aston's strengths are on the science side, although the business school is highly rated and accounts for almost half of the students. A £20-million extension to the business school has seen an increase in staff from 80 to over 120. After a bruising introduction to the teaching quality assessments, ratings improved considerably, with maximum points for pharmacy, business and management and good scores for optometry and biological sciences.

There is a wide range of combined honours programmes for those who prefer not to specialise. Four out of five Aston graduates go straight into jobs, spurning the postgraduate courses and training programmes which have become the first port of call for many of their counterparts in the old universities. Often they are returning to the scene of work placements, which have become the norm for 70 per cent of Aston's undergraduates.

The university is flexible about entry requirements for mature students, but average entry grades for school-leavers have now reached 350 points and the

---

Aston Triangle,
Birmingham B4 7ET
0121-359 6313 (admissions
enquiries only)
prospectus@aston.ac.uk
www.aston.ac.uk
www.astonguild.org.uk

The Times Rankings		
Overall Ranking: 13		
Student satisfaction:	=38	(14.9)
Research assessment:	=36	(5.0)
Entry standards:	40	(328.3)
Student–staff ratio:	19	(15.0)
Library/IT spend/student:	9	(£921)
Facilities spend/student:	11	(£356)
Good honours:	22	(69.4%)
Graduate prospects:	9	(76.0%)
Expected completion rate:	27	(90.9%)

rising demand for places is likely to prolong the trend. The drop-out rate has been improving and is now well below the 11 per cent national average for Aston's subjects. Socially, the intake is diverse, with almost 40 per cent of the undergraduates coming from working-class homes.

The 40-acre campus, a ten-minute walk from the centre of Birmingham, is barely recognisable from the university's early days. Carefully landscaped, it has benefited from a £16-million building programme, which has brought all Aston's residential and academic accommodation onto the same site. Almost half of the undergraduates live there, with places guaranteed for first years. New developments in sporting facilities have included the addition of a new gymnasium, while an £8-million Academy of Life Sciences merges research with private practice in eye care and brain imaging. Another £4 million has been spent upgrading the IT and computing network.

Aston was among the pioneers of "smart cards", giving students access to university facilities and enabling them to make purchases on campus, once they have money in their accounts. There is plenty of opportunity to use them in a buzzing social scene, which most students find to their taste. The guild of students

has always been among the most active both socially and politically.

Bursaries and Scholarships

In receipt of full Maintenance Grant	£750 min
In receipt of partial Maintenance Grant	£750 max
Shortage subjects	Bursary

- Tuition fees (2006) £3,000
- Tuition fee for placement year and year abroad is £1,500. However, placement allowances of £1,000 are available to all Aston students on their placement year and allowances and awards worth a total of £1,500 are available to all Aston students on their year abroad. Students on unpaid placement years qualify for an additional award of £500 for that year.
- Subject Awards of £750 a year available for students studying certain subjects of regional and national importance at Aston, including: Full Modern Languages programmes, accredited Engineering and Applied Sciences Programmes, some Biological Sciences Programmes. Subject Awards are not based on family income or academic achievement at A level.
- 12.5% of tuition fee to be earmarked for means-tested bursaries.
- Eligibility for bursaries to be assessed using UUK/SLC model bursary scheme (HEBSS).

Contact: www.aston.ac.uk/fees

Students

Undergraduates:	5,575	(200)
Postgraduates:	645	(1,520)
Mature students:	11.3%	
Overseas students:	10.0%	
Applications per place:	6.9	
From state-sector schools:	91.9%	
From working-class homes:	39.5%	

For detailed information about fees, grants and bursaries and how they work, see chapter 7.

Accommodation

Number of places and costs refer to 2006–07
University-provided places: 2,117
Percentage catered: 0%
Self-catered costs: £59.81–£93.48 a week.
First years are guaranteed accommodation if conditions are met.
International fee-paying students are guaranteed places provided conditions are met.
Contact: accom@aston.ac.uk;
www.aston.ac.uk/accommodation

Bangor, University of Wales

Bangor performed well in the first national student satisfaction survey, winning high praise for its campus and coming out best in England and Wales for student support. Modern languages students were the most satisfied in their subject, as were undergraduates in music. The "small and friendly" nature of the university and the town no doubt helped. Bangor's community focus dates back to a 19th-century campaign which saw local quarrymen putting part of their weekly wages towards the establishment of a college. The department of lifelong learning continues the tradition with courses across North Wales, but the college has also built a worldwide reputation in areas such as environmental studies and ocean sciences.

The last research assessments were an improvement on 1996, although only psychology and Welsh were rated internationally outstanding. Three quarters of the researchers were placed in the top three categories of seven. Teaching assessments were more impressive, with half of the subjects rated as excellent. As well as traditional strengths such as biology and forestry, the list includes social policy, placing Bangor at 19 in *The Times* ranking for the subject. There is a high proportion of small-group teaching and tutorials, as well as one of Britain's largest peer guiding schemes, which sees senior students mentoring new arrivals.

Bangor merged with a nearby teacher training college, Colleg Normal, in 1996, and that site is now part of the university. All departments are within walking distance of each other, apart from ocean sciences, which is two miles away near the Menai Bridge. The university estate is being redeveloped, with more en suite student accommodation on the way and a £5-million environmental sciences building being added, while a £3.5-million Cancer Research Institute is attracting specialists of international repute.

An academic reorganisation brought together a number of different disciplines in a School for Business and Regional Development focused on the needs of the Welsh economy. The theme continues through a combination of private funds and a £5-million European grant to establish a new Management Development Centre on a waterfront site. Another development has seen law taught at Bangor for the first time, capitalising on existing expertise in particular areas of the subject. A suite of degrees introduced in 2004 twin the subject with accounting and finance, business studies, criminal justice, environmental conservation and social policy, as well as offering single honours law. Other recent innovations include

Bangor,
Gwynedd LL57 2DG
01248 382016
admissions@bangor.ac.uk
www.bangor.ac.uk
www.undeb.bangor.ac.uk

The Times Rankings
Overall Ranking: 42

Student satisfaction:	=12	(15.4)
Research assessment:	=42	(4.7)
Entry standards:	53	(285.6)
Student–staff ratio:	=33	(16.6)
Library/IT spend/student:	18	(£748)
Facilities spend/student:	58	(£205)
Good honours:	70	(54.0%)
Graduate prospects:	49	(64.4%)
Expected completion rate:	60	(82.9%)

journalism and media, and chemistry with biomolecular sciences.

Based little more than a stone's throw from Snowdonia with its attractions for sports enthusiasts, Bangor is an expanding centre for Welsh-medium teaching. As well as a single honours degree in Welsh, some courses are only available in Welsh while others are offered in either English or Welsh. Although a majority of students come from outside Wales – there is a strong link with Ireland, for example – more than 10 per cent of the students speak the language and one of the seven halls of residence is Welsh-speaking. The college also has a flourishing international exchange programme, with some unusual partner institutions: Poland and Italy are favourite destinations for linguistics students, while biologists tend to head for Sweden or Norway. All biology, chemistry or engineering degrees carry the option of a year abroad. The university has also cut its fees by £1,000 for students from the world's poorest countries as part of a growing focus on overseas students.

Bangor does better than most traditional universities when judged against access benchmarks. More than nine out of ten students come from state schools or colleges, and three in ten come from working-class homes. Applications were up by 3 per cent in 2006, the third successive increase. There is a strong focus on student support – the pioneering dyslexia unit, for example, offering individual and group support throughout students' courses.

Bursaries and Scholarships

- Fees for undergraduate courses £3,000
- Students living in Wales will be eligible for a Welsh Assembly fee grant of approximately £1,800 a year.
- Fees for placement year and year abroad to be confirmed.
- For information on the National Bursary Scheme see page 198, chapter 7.
- Bursaries for students from low-income families.
- Start-up bursaries for mature students and those entering university from care.
- Scholarships for those who can demonstrate excellence within specific subject areas, eg, music, creative arts, science.
- The value of new bursaries will vary from £500–£3,000.

Contact:
www.bangor.ac.uk/studyatbangor/bursary
www.bangor.ac.uk/studyatbangor/scholps

Students

Undergraduates:	5,630	(2,125)
Postgraduates:	1,045	(715)
Mature students:	18.9%	
Overseas students:	8.0%	
Applications per place:	4.5	
From state-sector schools:	93.1%	
From working-class homes:	30.8%	

For detailed information about fees, grants and bursaries and how they work, see chapter 7.

Accommodation

Number of places and costs refer to 2006–07
University-provided places: 2,045
Percentage catered: 30%
Catered costs: £81.97–£98.84 a week (31-week contract).
Self-catered costs: £50.61–£75.25 a week (37-week contract)
All first-year students are guaranteed places.
International students: as above.
Contact: halls@bangor.ac.uk

University of Bath

Bath has recently completed a £70-million "campus enhancement plan" and the next few years will see the addition of further facilities for science. But, for the moment, it remains a relatively small university of 11,000 students. The extra places will cater to some degree for the burgeoning demand at an institution which enjoys both an attractive location and a high academic reputation. Applications held steady in the first year of top-up fees, despite earlier years' increases resulting in entrance requirements rising by the equivalent of a full grade at A level. Bath's healthy showing in league tables may be one reason for its popularity – it has never been out of the top 20 in *The Times* League Table.

Students like the "small and friendly" image the university projects, and one of the lowest drop-out rates in Britain suggests that they are well supported. The library is one of only two in the country to open 24 hours a day, seven days a week. Few can fail to be impressed by the magnificence of the city's architecture. The modern campus on the edge of Bath, with some undistinguished buildings dating from its origins as a technological university in the 1960s, offers an unfortunate contrast. But the 200-acre site has pleasant grounds and is functional,

with academic, recreational and residential facilities in close proximity. New teaching facilities for chemistry were added in 2003, followed by a £2.8-million physics facility, and 468 new study bedrooms have also been added recently. More lecture theatres and computer laboratories have eased the pressure on teaching space.

A campus in Swindon caters for 1,000 part-time students, bringing higher education to one of the few remaining counties without a university. The development is based in school premises, but there are plans for a large new campus. However, research is Bath's greatest strength, with applied mathematics, mechanical engineering and pharmacy all rated internationally outstanding in the last assessments. Teaching assessments confirmed the university's excellence in science and technology, with biosciences, physics, mathematics and statistics all achieving maximum points. Arts and social science ratings were mixed, but there were successes in management economics and politics, while European languages and area studies scored well in the first national student satisfaction survey.

The latest academic developments have seen the establishment of a School for Health and an Institute for Contemporary Interdisciplinary Arts, both engaged in teaching as well as research. Most courses

---

Claverton Down, Bath BA2 7AY
01225 323019
admissions@bath.ac.uk
www.bath.ac.uk
www.bathstudent.com

The Times Rankings
Overall Ranking: 9

Student satisfaction:	=33	(15.0)
Research assessment:	=10	(5.7)
Entry standards:	14	(403.4)
Student–staff ratio:	=42	(17.3)
Library/IT spend/student:	45	(£597)
Facilities spend/student:	4	(£417)
Good honours:	8	(75.2%)
Graduate prospects:	5	(79.8%)
Expected completion rate:	4	(96.1%)

throughout the university have a practical element, and assessors have praised the university for the work placements it offers. The majority of students take sandwich courses or include a period of study abroad, which helps to produce consistently outstanding graduate employment figures.

The university's other great claim to fame lies in its sports facilities, which were already among the best in Britain before the addition of a £20-million training village, funded with Lottery money. The campus acquired an international-standard swimming pool by this route, to which it has added an indoor running track, a new sports hall and even a simulated bobsleigh start area. There is a strong tradition in competitive sports: the university pioneered sports scholarships more than 20 years ago, and they are now worth up to £12,000 a year for performers of international calibre. There are also courses to do the facilities justice, as recognised in a near-perfect score for teaching quality in sport and leisure in 2001.

Students – a fifth of whom were educated at independent schools – may find the campus quiet at weekends and struggle to afford some of Bath's attractions, but they value its location. When they tire of the beauty of Bath, the nightlife of Bristol is only a few minutes away. The two cities have a combined student population of more than 50,000. The students' union is active and the university has been upgrading its student support services in recent months, for example through the introduction of 64 laptops adapted for use by students with disabilities.

Bursaries and Scholarships
In receipt of full Maintenance Grant £1,500 min
In receipt of partial Maintenance Grant
£300–£1,200

- Tuition fees (2006) £3,000
- Tuition fee for placement year is £600–£1,000. Financial assistance in the form of bursaries will be available for eligible students on their placement year.
- 21% of the additional fee income will be used to assist students from low-income families.
- Eligibility for bursaries of students from Wales, Scotland and Northern Ireland to be decided.
- Eligibility for bursaries to be assessed using UUK/SLC model bursary scheme (HEBSS).

Contact: www.bath.ac.uk/students/scholarships

Students

Undergraduates:	7,515	(1,985)
Postgraduates:	1,330	(3,020)
Mature students:	9.5%	
Overseas students:	14.1%	
Applications per place:	7.9	
From state-sector schools:	76.6%	
From working-class homes:	18.5%	

For detailed information about fees, grants and bursaries and how they work, see chapter 7.

Accommodation
Number of places and costs refer to 2006–07
University-provided places: 3,055
Percentage catered: 0%
Self-catered cost: £65–£88 a week.
First years guaranteed accommodation if conditions are met.
International students: as above. Exchange students are housed on a reciprocal basis.
Contact:
www.bath.ac.uk/accommodation/enquiry/

Bath Spa University

Bath Spa is one of the nine new "teaching-led" universities created since the last edition of the *Guide*. But it is far from new in other respects and not without research strengths. Its Newton Park headquarters four miles outside the World Heritage city is in grounds landscaped by Capability Brown in the 18th century with a handsome Georgian manor house as their centrepiece and owned by the Prince of Wales. A second campus, housing the Bath School of Art and Design, boasts one of the city's famous Georgian crescents surrounded by ornamental gardens. The history of the predecessor colleges goes back 150 years, with some famous alumni including Body Shop founder Anita Roddick and Turner Prize winner Sir Howard Hodgkin.

The new university has been undertaking its biggest-ever building programme to take advantage of a doubling in the number of applications over the past five years. This came to an end in 2006, with the prospect of top-up fees, but the decline was less than the national average. With around 5,000 students, it is still comparatively small, but the range of courses and the number of places have been growing steadily. At Newton Park, the base for all students except those taking art and design subjects, the students' union has practically doubled in size, a new library has added about 120 workstations and £3 million has been spent on an impressive performing arts arena with a 200-seat theatre. A new creative writing centre will be housed in the 14th-century gatehouse, bringing it into student use for the first time.

Bath Spa has been awarding its own degrees since 1992 – much longer than some of the other new arrivals on the university scene. Every subject assessed for teaching quality scored at least 22 points out of 24 and results in the first national student satisfaction survey were good. The university has been designated a Centre for Excellence in Teaching and Learning in the creative industries, bringing significant investment in the Schools of Music and Performing Arts, English and Creative Studies, and Art and Design. English and theology did well in the last research assessments, when the 43 per cent of academics entered for the exercise represented a much larger proportion than at many of the former polytechnics. About a fifth of the students are postgraduates.

Despite a setting that would seem a magnet for overseas students and applicants from independent schools, more than 90 per cent of the home intake is state-educated and three in ten are from

Newton Park
Newton St Loe
Bath BA2 9BN
01225 875875
enquiries@bathspa.ac.uk
www.bathspa.ac.uk/
prospectus/order
www.bathspasu.co.uk

Edinburgh
Belfast
Cardiff
BATH London

The Times Rankings
Overall Ranking: 73

Student Satisfaction:	=8	(15.5)
Research assessment:	=76	(2.5)
Entry standards:	73	(249.2)
Student–staff ratio:	102	(24.2)
Library/IT spend/student:	109	(£337)
Facilities spend/student:	102	(£104)
Good honours:	46	(60.0%)
Graduate prospects:	107	(47.0%)
Expected completion rate:	38	(87.0%)

working-class homes. Two thirds of the students are female, reflecting the arts and social science bias in the curriculum, and 40 per cent are over 25. The latest projected drop-out rate, of 12 per cent, is significantly better than the national average for the university's courses and entry grades. There are about 400 overseas students from a variety of countries, and summer courses targeted at Americans make a valuable contribution to the new university's healthy financial position.

Many students take the first year of their course in further education colleges in the region. Among the options is a range of two-year foundation degrees, the latest of which are in development geography and applied art and design. About 95 per cent of first years attending Bath Spa itself are offered hall places. Students like the "small and friendly" atmosphere, which the university is anxious to retain in spite of the temptation to go for more substantial growth. Sports facilities are not extensive, but the countryside – on and off campus – is a major draw.

Bursaries and Scholarships

In receipt of full Maintenance Grant	£1,150
In receipt of partial Maintenance Grant	up to £320

- Tuition fees (2006) £3,000
- Scholarships worth £1,000 in science-based subjects will not be means-tested.
- 29% of the additional fee income will be used to assist students from low-income families.
- Eligibility for bursaries to be assessed using UUK/SLC model bursary scheme (HEBSS).

Contact: www.bathspa.ac.uk/prospectus/ money-matters/undergraduate/ financial-support

Students

Undergraduates:	3,660	(375)
Postgraduates:	730	(1,060)
Mature students:	22.4%	
Overseas students:	3.4%	
Applications per place:	6.2	
From state-sector schools:	92.1%	
From working-class homes:	29.7%	

For detailed information about fees, grants and bursaries and how they work, see chapter 7.

Accommodation

Number of places and costs refer to 2005–06
University provided places: 850
Percentage catered: 0%
Self-catered costs: £65.00–£89.25 a week
First years are housed in university-managed or accredited accommodation provided requirements are met. Residential restrictions apply.
International students: as above.
Contact: accommodation@bathspa.ac.uk

University of Birmingham

Birmingham set itself the target of becoming the "Oxbridge of the Midlands", which may have been ambitious, but its position in *The Times* ranking is a good starting point. A consultants' report in 2004 found the university had a boring image, but that is being addressed. And, despite offering an unusually wide range of subjects, its teaching and research ratings seldom slip.

Students come to Birmingham from more than 100 countries, but the university enjoys particularly high prestige in its own region. Entry standards are high, averaging the equivalent of more than three Bs at A level. With eight applicants for each place, they are likely to remain so, but aspiring students still flock to the largest open days in Britain each spring. There is also an additional open day for upper sixth-formers in September.

The university's enduring reputation is based on its research, with two thirds of its departments considered nationally or internationally outstanding in the last assessments. A dozen 5* ratings tripled the number awarded in 1996, with languages doing particularly well: French, German, Italian and Russian all reached the top level.

Many of the teaching scores were impressive too, with mathematics, biological sciences and physiotherapy following sociology and electrical and electronic engineering in recording maximum points. Economics only just missed out and there was a string of Excellent verdicts in the early assessments. Physics, biology and European languages fared best in the first national student satisfaction survey.

Birmingham's highly regarded medical school was granted the biggest expansion in Britain when quotas for the subject were reviewed in 1999 and has since added an £11.8-million student facilities building. Engineering has been reorganised, following a year-long review, to promote an interdisciplinary approach, responding to employers' wish for more flexibility. Students can enter either a BA or BSc degree programme, combining Technology with subjects ranging from Latin or modern Greek to the management of floods and other natural disasters.

The 230-acre campus in leafy Edgbaston is dominated by a 300-foot clocktower, which is one of the city's best-known landmarks, and boasts its own station. Dentistry is located in the city, while the Centre for Lifelong Learning and part of the School of Education are in Selly Oak. Most of the halls and university flats are conveniently located in an attractive parkland setting nearby. There are more than 5,000 university-owned beds, following a ten-year programme costing £80 million, and

Edgbaston, Birmingham B15 2TT
0121-414 3374 (general admission enquiries)
prospectus@bham.ac.uk
www.bham.ac.uk
www.bugs.bham.ac.uk

Edinburgh
Belfast
BIRMINGHAM •
Cardiff
London

The Times Rankings
Overall Ranking: 33

Student satisfaction:	=49	(14.8)
Research assessment:	=25	(5.3)
Entry standards:	21	(380.3)
Student–staff ratio:	=40	(17.1)
Library/IT spend/student:	23	(£701)
Facilities spend/student:	52	(£220)
Good honours:	=24	(68.9%)
Graduate prospects:	32	(68.1%)
Expected completion rate:	20	(92.8%)

private sector accommodation is also plentiful.

The campus is less than three miles from the centre of Birmingham, but the area has plenty of shops, pubs and restaurants of its own. With its own nightclub among the facilities on campus, some students do not even stray that far, but the city is acquiring a growing reputation among the young, which is helping to make the university even more popular.

Pressure on teaching space was eased to some extent in 1999 with the creation of the Selly Oak campus, a joint venture with a Free Church college whose education and theology degrees the university had validated for many years. The site is used for part-time degrees and continuing education, as well as the existing college courses, under an agreement that saw the university take over the management of nine partner colleges. The campus is also to house the BBC Drama Village, following the agreement of a strategic alliance with the corporation.

Student facilities are on a par with the best in the country, with many restaurants and bars on campus, and an outdoor pursuits centre on Coniston Water, in the Lake District. Birmingham has always been concerned with the body as well as the mind; compulsory exercise was only abandoned in 1968. The Active Lifestyles Programme, the voluntary modern-day equivalent, attracts 4,000 students to 150 different courses. Tutors with national qualifications run classes from beginner to advanced level. In addition, Birmingham ranks in the top three universities in intervarsity competitions.

Bursaries and Scholarships

In receipt of full Maintenance Grant	£800
In receipt of partial Maintenance Grant	£800
Shortage subjects	Scholarship
Academic achievement	Scholarship £1,200

- Tuition fees (2006)   £3,000
- Tuition fee for placement year will be half the standard tuition fee.
- Scholarship scheme will be means-tested and open only to those students receiving a bursary and having at least 340 UCAS points.
- Part-time employment, paid volunteering and placement opportunities will be created by the university as supplementary income sources.
- Eligibility for bursaries may be assessed using UUK/SLC model bursary scheme (HEBSS).
- Payment will be made in instalments.

Contact: http://www.bham.ac.uk/ prospectus.asp?section=0001000400050002

Students

Undergraduates:	16,180	(3,990)
Postgraduates:	5,570	(6,365)
Mature students:	11.7%	
Overseas students:	8.5%	
Applications per place:	8.2	
From state-sector schools:	80.6%	
From working-class homes:	22.6%	

For detailed information about fees, grants and bursaries and how they work, see chapter 7.

Accommodation

Number of places and costs refer to 2006–07
University-provided places: 4,924
Percentage catered: 53%
Catered costs: £94.57–£128.42.
Self-catered costs: £81.16–£103.05 a week.
All first years are guaranteed accommodation (subject to conditions).
International students: as above
Contact: ugradaccomm@bham.ac.uk
studentaccommodation@contacts.bham.ac.uk
(private sector housing enquiries)

University of Bolton

The largest town in England finally got a university in 2005 after eight years of frustration. The former Bolton Institute was turned down by the Quality Assurance Agency and the Privy Council before eventually winning approval for university status. The switch had an instant impact: Bolton recorded the biggest increase in applications in the UK at the start of 2005, an unprecedented 35 per cent rise. But even that was bettered in 2006, when there was an increase of more than 50 per cent – comfortably the biggest at any university.

The new university traces its roots back as far as 1824 with the foundation of a mechanics institute in the town. Proposals to take the name of North Manchester or West Pennine have been rejected in order to stick with Bolton. There are already more than 9,000 students and there are no plans for dramatic growth, despite the new-found popularity. Based on two town-centre sites, the university sees itself as a regional institution, with three quarters of the students coming from the North West, many through partner colleges. But there is also an international dimension, with long-established links in Malaysia and a regular contingent of overseas students from 70 different countries.

Bolton has set itself the ambitious target of climbing into the top half of the university system within 15 years. Judged on our criteria, it has some way to go, but it is not unusual for brand-new universities to make their debut near the foot of the table. Even in its days as an institute of higher education, it was competitive in categories such as facilities and library spending, but it is dragged down by other indicators. Student satisfaction is not one of these: the university almost made the top ten in rankings of the first national student satisfaction survey. Nursing students were the most satisfied in the country.

Teaching assessments had been variable, but education, nursing and psychology all achieved maximum points and the last seven assessments all produced more than 20 points out of 24. Not surprisingly, research grades were less impressive, but metallurgy and materials reached grade 4 in the last assessments. A centre for research and innovation in materials which opened in 2003 is to be the first of a series of "knowledge exchange zones". Bolton is not one of the new breed of "teaching-only" universities; it has been accredited for research degrees for several years and acquired its new status under the old rules. About 1,700 of the students are postgraduates, taking qualifications up to and including PhDs.

Most development has taken place at the Deane campus, which houses the

Deane Road,
Bolton BL3 5AB
01204 900600
enquiries@bolton.ac.uk
www.bolton.ac.uk
www.bisu.co.uk

university's headquarters. A £6-million four-storey design studio opened in 2004, but there is more work to be done. A new students' union is the top priority, following access problems in the existing building. The 700 reasonably-priced residential places go a long way in an institution with a high proportion of home-based students. Three quarters of the students are over the age of 20 on entry.

The university exceeds all the access measures designed to widen participation in higher education: nearly all the students are state-educated, almost half are from working-class homes and the proportion from areas without a tradition of higher education is twice the national average for Bolton's subjects and entry qualifications. The downside – a big one – is that nearly a third of the students are projected to leave without a qualification: by far the highest proportion in England.

Bursaries and Scholarships[†]

In receipt of full Maintenance Grant	£300
In receipt of partial Maintenance Grant	
	Sliding scale to min £50
Progressing from outreach	Scholarship £700

- Tuition fees (2006) £3,000
- No tuition fee will be charged for year-out placement students.
- 33% of the additional fee income will be earmarked for bursaries and outreach.
- Payment will be made in instalments.

Contact:
www.bolton.ac.uk/studentcentre/recruitment/fees.html

[†] Information taken from 2006 Access Agreement

Students

Undergraduates:	3,270	(2,480)
Postgraduates:	510	(845)
Mature students:	18.2%	
Overseas students:	11.2%	
Applications per place:	7.0	
From state-sector schools:	97.3%	
From working-class homes:	42%	

For detailed information about fees, grants and bursaries and how they work, see chapter 7.

Accommodation

Number of places and costs refer to 2006–07
University-provided places: 700
Percentage catered: 0%
Self-catered costs: £2,280 a year.
All first years are generally accommodated.
International students: accommodation is secured for these students.
Contact: accomm@bolton.ac.uk

University of Bournemouth

Always an institution with an eye for the distinctive, Bournemouth's strategic plan declares that it will "dare to be different and stand out from the crowd". Study boundaries are set by areas of social or economic activity, rather than traditional academic disciplines, because the aim is to be a "pre-eminent vocational university". Thus, there is no Faculty of Arts but there is a School of Services Management.

Bournemouth's forte is in identifying gaps in the higher education market and then filling them with innovative programmes. Degrees in public relations, retail management, scriptwriting and tax law are among the examples. The university also boasts the National Centre of Computer Animation. The mix has been popular with students – the 22 per cent rise in applications at the beginning of 2005 was one of the largest at any university, while the decline in 2006 was less than the national average.

The university claims a number of firsts in its growing portfolio of courses, notably in the area of tourism, media-related programmes and conservation. It was no surprise to find the university among the pioneers of Foundation Degrees – two-year highly vocational courses, which are at the heart of the Government's expansion plans for higher education. Now much expanded, the new courses are being delivered in further education colleges from Somerset to Salisbury, supporting the needs of business in the creative arts, media and tourism.

Many of Bournemouth's courses have an international focus and all students are encouraged to improve their linguistic ability. A majority of undergraduates take sandwich courses, and 70 per cent do work placements. The result is an employment rate which is the university's proudest achievement: four out of five graduates go straight into jobs. The Retail Management degree notched up eight successive years of full employment and is still running at over 90 per cent. Students are offered personal development planning, both online and with trained staff, while 1,400 first-years also take advantage of peer-assisted learning, receiving advice from more experienced undergraduates.

Archaeology, television and video production, media studies and nursing achieved the best teaching grades, while psychology was the star performer in the first national student satisfaction survey. Media courses are a particular strength, with entry requirements well above the university's modest average. State-of-the-art equipment includes a Motion Capture facility for real-time animation, which is used in teaching and available for use by

---

Talbot Campus, Fern Barrow,
Poole, Dorset BH12 5BB
01202 524111
prospectus@
bournemouth.ac.uk
www.bournemouth.ac.uk
www.subu.org.uk

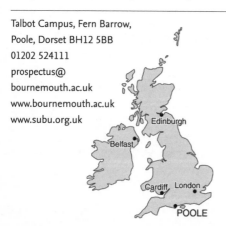

The Times Rankings
Overall Ranking: 69

Student satisfaction:	=75	(14.3)
Research assessment:	=94	(1.9)
Entry standards:	56	(277.0)
Student–staff ratio:	=60	(18.3)
Library/IT spend/student:	108	(£340)
Facilities spend/student:	107	(£87)
Good honours:	=39	(61.7%)
Graduate prospects:	82	(57.2%)
Expected completion rate:	50	(85.1%)

outside companies, and a £3.5-million Centre for Excellence in Media Practice is on the way. Computer animation was the star performer in the 2001 research assessments, which saw much-needed improvement on 1996.

Among the new developments planned is the world's first fully commercial teaching hotel. The 4-star establishment, which has public and private sector backing, is due to take its first students in 2007. New teaching and residential accommodation has been added in recent years, with more to come. A multimillion-pound library opened in 2003. There are now two campuses – the original Talbot site in Poole and a dedicated campus in Bournemouth town centre – with associate colleges in Yeovil, Bournemouth and Poole, Cannington, Salisbury and Weymouth.

The southern seaside location and the subject mix attract more middle-class students than most new universities. Students are discouraged from bringing cars (which are banned within a mile of the town-centre campus) but many still do. The area has plenty to offer students during the summer season. Although it naturally becomes less lively in the winter months, Bournemouth no longer shuts up when the tourists go home. The students' union's Old Fire Station bar is the favourite among many nightlife options.

Bournemouth offers a wide range of accommodation, from 1,400 places in university halls to bed-and-breakfast lets and shared houses.

Bursaries and Scholarships

In receipt of full Maintenance Grant	£1,000
In receipt of partial Maintenance Grant	
	Sliding scale based on level of MG
Progressing from outreach	Bursary £500
Sport	Scholarship
Academic achievement	Scholarship

- Tuition fees (2006) £3,000
- Placement year tuition fee will be around £500.
- Bursary available for eligible students completing written application form prior to enrolment.
- Tuition fee will be all-inclusive, with no extra charges for equipment, field trips, etc.
- Incentive schemes such as discounts for up-front fee payments will be introduced.
- Scholarship scheme to reward academic and vocational merit and success in sport, music and citizenship. No values available to date.
- 27% of additional tuition fee income will be earmarked for bursaries.

Contact: www.bournemouth.ac.uk/ moneymatters

Students				Accommodation
Undergraduates:	9,265	(4,105)		Number of places and costs refer to 2006–07
Postgraduates:	1,515	(990)		University-provided places: about 2,350
Mature students:	21.7%			Percentage catered: about 2%
Overseas students:	7.8%			Catered costs: £77–£97 a week (private hotels).
Applications per place:	5.1			Self-catered costs: £62–£82 a week.
From state-sector schools:	93.2%			The university expects to offer all first years a
From working-class homes:	28.1%			place to live. Residencal restrictions apply.
				International students: guaranteed if conditions

For detailed information about fees, grants and bursaries and how they work, see chapter 7.

are met.
Contact: accommodation@bournemouth.ac.uk

University of Bradford

Plans to merge with the city's main further education college to create an institution spanning GCSE and postgraduate courses were shelved, leaving Bradford to plough a lone furrow as a university of less than 10,000 students. But the university is persevering with alliances with several institutions to help boost participation in a region where it is among the lowest in Europe. A ground-breaking foundation course run with Leeds University, for example, is intended to broaden the intake to clinical sciences and medicine. A BSc in clinical sciences was launched as part of the same initiative.

There are now nine foundation degrees, delivered in collaboration with local further education colleges, in areas such as public sector administration, metallurgy and enterprise in IT. Perhaps the best known is in health and social care, where the university was already expanding opportunities locally, bringing about a fourfold increase in nursing enrolments by young women from South Asian families.

Bradford has carved out a niche for itself with mature students, who now make up a third of all undergraduates. They relish the vocational slant and the accent on sandwich courses, which regularly place Bradford near the top of the graduate employment tables – it was second on this measure in last year's *Times* table. Demand for places has recovered after a difficult period, and the older intake helped propel the university to one of the biggest increases in applications in Britain – almost 30 per cent – at the start of 2005. Admission requirements are modest compared with those in other old universities, especially in engineering, which still accounts for a significant share of the places and where applicants are notoriously thin on the ground.

The relatively small, lively campus is close to the city centre. Health students have their own building a few minutes' walk away, while the highly-rated management school is two miles away in a 14-acre parkland setting. The eventual aim is to develop a health and science quarter, with the School of Health Studies housed in its own building on campus. This is part of a £130-million plan to enhance the academic facilities and create more social space for students, beginning with improved laboratories for chemical and forensic science, more teaching accommodation and a new swimming pool.

Teaching assessments saw sudden and dramatic improvement after 1999, when no subject had been rated as excellent or amassed the 22 points regarded as its equivalent. After that, nursing, pharmacy

Richmond Road
Bradford BD7 1DP
01274 233081
enquiries@bradford.ac.uk
www.bradford.ac.uk
www.ubu.brad.ac.uk

The Times Rankings
Overall Ranking: 47

Student satisfaction:	=33	(15.0)
Research assessment:	=51	(4.4)
Entry standards:	59	(268.2)
Student–staff ratio:	29	(16.1)
Library/IT spend/student:	55	(£542)
Facilities spend/student:	25	(£291)
Good honours:	=47	(59.9%)
Graduate prospects:	=16	(72.7%)
Expected completion rate:	72	(81.2%)

and other health studies all managed 23 points out of 24, while politics and the interdisciplinary human studies programme, which combines psychology, literature and sociology with the study of philosophy, was awarded full marks. The university also did well in the first national student satisfaction survey, with medical science and pharmacy the top scorers.

Research grades improved in the last assessment exercise, with European studies achieving the coveted 5* and archaeology, biomedical sciences, mechanical engineering and politics on the next rung of the ladder. Politics includes the university's best-known offering of peace studies, which has acquired an international reputation. A £6-million Institute of Pharmaceutical Innovation opened in 2003.

Bradford has launched suites of ICT and media studies courses to add to those in e-commerce and internet computing, computer animation and special effects, interactive systems and video games design. Computer-assisted learning is increasing in many subjects, making use of unusually extensive IT provision and a new wireless network. Some courses feature online assessment and the use of laptops in lectures.

More southerners are being attracted to Bradford's status as Britain's cheapest student city. Almost 2,000 places in self-catering halls are reasonably priced. Many have been refurbished and more are promised by 2007. There is particularly good provision for disabled students, who account for 6 per cent of the university population. The university's senior management group includes a Dean of Students to ensure that the student voice is heard in future developments. The students' union operates a late-night "safety bus" for those living within two miles of the campus.

Bursaries and Scholarships

In receipt of full Maintenance Grant £500–£900
In receipt of partial Maintenance Grant
£500–£900
Progressing from outreach   Scholarship £300

- Tuition fees (2006)   £3,000
- Placement year tuition fee will be £600.
- The University offers one bursary scheme which is available to all home and EU students who are eligible for receipt of any level of Higher Education Maintenance Grant. The current yearly bursaries available are as follows: Foundation Year: £500; Year 1: £500; Year 2: £700; Year 3: £900.
- 30% of additional tuition fee income (£955,000 in 2006–07) will be earmarked for bursaries.

Contact: www.bradford.ac.uk/tuitionfees
www.bradford.ac.uk/scholarships

Students

Undergraduates:	6,790	(1,690)
Postgraduates:	1,160	(2,760)
Mature students:	32.6%	
Overseas students:	17.9%	
Applications per place:	4.8	
From state-sector schools:	93.8%	
From working-class homes:	49.2%	

For detailed information about fees, grants and bursaries and how they work, see chapter 7.

Accommodation

Number of places and costs refer to 2005–06
University-provided places: 1,681
Percentage catered: 0%
Self-catered costs: £52.50–£76.50 a week.
All first years are guaranteed accommodation (terms and conditions apply).
International students: all first-year students are guaranteed accommodation.
Contact: halls-of-residence@bradford.ac.uk
www.brad.ac.uk/accommodation
www.unipol.bradford.ac.uk

University of Brighton

Brighton came of age as one of the first new universities to be awarded a medical school. Run jointly with neighbouring Sussex University, the £28.5-million school is training 128 doctors a year and is already proving popular, registering big increases in applications since it opened. Brighton was already heavily engaged in other health subjects such as nursing and midwifery. The medical school's headquarters, on Brighton's Falmer campus, has also provided a new base for applied social sciences such as criminology and applied psychology, which are among the university's most sought-after degrees.

The two universities have been collaborating since Brighton was a polytechnic. There is a joint research building for science policy and management studies, and a joint accord guarantees the offer of a place to all suitably qualified applicants from the Channel Island of Jersey. Brighton does the same for applicants from Sussex and is leading a new Learning Network for the county. Almost a third of undergraduates now come through the accords.

Only two new universities did as well as Brighton in the last Research Assessment Exercise, and only one entered such a high a proportion of its academics. Art and design, biological sciences and European studies were all rated nationally excellent, with some work of top international quality. Teaching ratings were also consistently good, never dropping below 20 points out of 24, with philosophy registering a maximum score. Sports science, physical geography and environmental science achieved the best scores in a generally successful first national student satisfaction survey. The plaudits have not gone unnoticed: applications were rising until top-up fees brought a reversal of fortunes in 2006.

Brighton's strengths in art and design – recognised in the award of national teaching centres in design and creativity – have been at the forefront of the university's rise. But health subjects have grown strongly and the university also has a growing reputation in areas such as sport and hospitality, as well as scoring well in teacher education rankings. The Design Council's national archive is lodged on campus, and the four-year fashion textiles degree offers work placements in the United States, France and Italy, as well as Britain. The Faculty of Management and Information Sciences is now the largest in the university.

Four sites house the five faculties. Art and Design has the prime location opposite the Royal Pavilion, with sports science, service management and the

---

Mithras House, Lewes Road,
Brighton BN2 4AT
01273 642828
admissions@brighton.ac.uk
www.brighton.ac.uk
www.ubsu.net

The Times Rankings
Overall Ranking: 59

Student satisfaction:	=60	(14.6)
Research assessment:	=64	(2.9)
Entry standards:	61	(266.1)
Student–staff ratio:	=56	(18.1)
Library/IT spend/student:	=64	(£512)
Facilities spend/student:	64	(£193)
Good honours:	56	(57.9%)
Graduate prospects:	=44	(65.2%)
Expected completion rate:	=81	(79.8%)

health professions at Eastbourne and the other subjects on the outskirts of Brighton, at Falmer and Moulsecoomb, the university's headquarters. There is also a university centre at Hastings.

Over £100 million has been spent on new facilities and refurbishment since university status arrived in 1992. At Eastbourne there is a new library and extensive sports and leisure facilities, including a sports centre with three gymnasia and a dance studio, a refurbished swimming pool and fitness facilities. Sport-science laboratories and 354 en-suite residential places have been added and improvements made to the learning resources centre, lecture theatres and refectory. The extensive modernisation of the Falmer campus continues, with extra accommodation, a library and a nursing and midwifery centre already added.

The university has a cosmopolitan air, with more overseas students than most of the former polytechnics. Almost a quarter of the full-time undergraduates are over 21 on entry, often attracted by strongly vocational courses and the prospect of three years in "London by the sea". Numerous European links give most courses an international flavour, often allowing a period of study on the Continent. Most undergraduates have a personal tutor who will advise on combinations within the modular degree scheme.

Students have taken to the "managed learning environment", known as Studentcentral, an interactive service providing online access to teaching materials and other information. Most also like Brighton, although the cost of living is high for those not in hall. There is a lively social scene and part-time work is plentiful. Eastbourne is also surprisingly popular, and both towns offer plentiful accommodation to supplement the university's stock.

Bursaries and Scholarships

In receipt of full Maintenance Grant £1,000 max
In receipt of partial Maintenance Grant £500 min

Disabled	Bursary
Academic achievement	Bursary

- Tuition fees (2006) £3,000
- Placement year tuition fee will be £650.
- Merit-based Governors' bursaries available at the end of years 1 and 2 and on the basis of student achievement. Half will be held by students in financial need.
- 5 disabled athletes bursaries worth £1,000.
- 25% of additional fee income will be earmarked for bursaries.

Contact: www.brighton.ac.uk/money
www.brighton.ac.uk/studentlife/money/
2006.php?PageID=560

Students		
Undergraduates:	11,195	(4,425)
Postgraduates:	1,460	(2,555)
Mature students:	27.2%	
Overseas students:	13.3%	
Applications per place:	5.7	
From state-sector schools:	92.5%	
From working-class homes:	25.7%	

For detailed information about fees, grants and bursaries and how they work, see chapter 7.

Accommodation

Number of places and costs refer to 2006–07
University-provided places: 1,950; 300 in private sector university-managed houses or flats.
Percentage catered: 0%
Self-catered costs: £60–£87 a week.
First years guaranteed accommodation if conditions are met. Residential restrictions apply.
International students: as above.
Contact: accommodation@brighton.ac.uk
a.eastbourne@brighton.ac.uk

University of Bristol

Bristol has long been a natural alternative to Oxbridge, favoured particularly by independent schools, whose pupils take at least three in ten places. But the university found itself at the centre of an admissions furore over long-established radical plans to widen its intake. Departments are encouraged to make slightly lower offers to promising applicants from schools with poor records at A level, and some top schools have seen a link in the rejection of highly-qualified applicants. As the most popular university in Britain in terms of applications per place, Bristol has always turned away excellent candidates. Fleeting talk of a boycott by leading independent schools is now a fading memory – there was healthy growth in applications in 2005 and only a small decline when top-up fees arrived in 2006.

The university has found it difficult to attract working-class teenagers, who fear that they would be out of place socially, if not academically. In 2003–04 only about one in seven came from a working-class home – the lowest proportion outside Oxbridge. Tiny numbers are recruited from the schools in the bottom half of the A-level league tables. Bristol believes the controversy was worthwhile if previously untapped sources of bright students can be brought to the surface.

For most applicants, entry standards remain among the highest at any university. A modular course system is now well established, although the majority of students still take single or dual honours degrees.

The city is one of the most attractive in Britain, as well as possessing a vibrant youth culture. It is also prosperous, offering job opportunities to students and graduates alike. The university merges into the centre, its famous Gothic tower dominating the skyline from the junction of two of the main shopping streets. Departments dot the hillside close to the picturesque harbour area.

Bristol has no intention of aping the growth plans of some of its rivals, but there has been modest expansion to 12,000 students and the university has continued to live up to expectations in assessments of teaching and research. A third of the staff assessed for research are in departments considered internationally excellent and three quarters saw their departments reach one of the top two grades. There are 31 Fellows of the Royal Society and similar numbers in other learned societies.

Research is Bristol's traditional strength. The 2001 assessments saw the university's tally of 5* subjects shoot up from one to 15, with another 21 subjects on the next of the seven grades. Only

---

Senate House, Tyndall Avenue,
Bristol BS8 1TH
0117-928 9000
admissions@bris.ac.uk
www.bris.ac.uk
www.ubu.org.uk

Cambridge, Oxford and University College London had more maximum scores. The 33 excellent teaching ratings also represent one of the largest totals in the university system, with veterinary medicine, molecular biosciences, anatomy, electronic engineering and, most recently, education all achieving perfect scores.

Bristol was given the best rating among the small group of universities seeking to demonstrate their creditworthiness to the money markets. A funding appeal which has raised more than £100 million has enabled the university to create new chairs and embark on a number of building projects. The highly-rated chemistry department, for example, moved into a well-appointed new centre in 2000, allowing new medical science laboratories to be constructed in the department's former premises. An impressive sports centre at the heart of the university precinct opened in 2002. Dynamics engineering and neurology opened new buildings in 2004 and a new students' union is among the projects included in investment plans totalling £250 million over the next five years. A £35-million life sciences building is due to begin construction in 2007.

Most students enjoy life in Bristol – a *New Musical Express* poll rated the social life the best at any university in 2004 – although some find the high cost of living a serious drawback, together with security concerns in some parts of the city. The drop-out rate is among the lowest in Britain. The current students' union is less of a social centre than in some universities, but it runs an evening bus service to the halls of residence, and there is a free late-night service for women from the library and the union to their homes.

Bursaries and Scholarships[†]

In receipt of full Maintenance Grant	£1,100
In receipt of partial Maintenance Grant	£700
Living in region	Bursary
Sport	Scholarship
Shortage subjects	Scholarship
Academic achievement	Scholarship

- Tuition fees (2006) £3,000
- Bursaries take the form of a package comprising a cash component, support with course-related costs and a free sports pass.
- 100 scholarships will be available for bursary holders and for non-bursary holders with high academic potential in specified shortage subject areas. Scholarships take the form of a fee remission up to a value of £2,500.
- 12 Vice-Chancellor's scholarships worth £3,000
- Pre-existing bursaries and scholarships will continue to be offered in 2006–07.
- 17% of additional fee income (£987,000 in 2006–07) will be earmarked for bursaries.

Contact: www.bristol.ac.uk/studentfinance

[†] Information taken from 2006 Access Agreement

Students

Undergraduates:	10,940	(3,920)
Postgraduates:	2,695	(5,150)
Mature students:	8.3%	
Overseas students:	11.4%	
Applications per place:	11.2	
From state-sector schools:	65.2%	
From working-class homes:	14.1%	

For detailed information about fees, grants and bursaries and how they work, see chapter 7.

Accommodation

Number of places and costs refer to 2006–07
University-provided places: about 4,500
Percentage catered: 37%
Catered costs: £93–£132 a week.
Self-catered costs: £48–£118 a week.
One offer of accommodation is guaranteed provided conditions are met.
International students: accommodation is guaranteed provided conditions are met.
Contact: Accom-office@bris.ac.uk

Brunel University

Brunel has been celebrating 40 years as a university in 2006 and, in the run-up to this anniversary, invested in a £170-million plan to upgrade and centralise its teaching, research and sporting facilities, as well as making a large number of new academic appointments. For the first time since its early years, the whole university will be located on the main Uxbridge campus, as the last academic school moves into a new health and social care building. The move will see the closure of the old Borough Road College, which will bring its illustrious sporting traditions to the most modern surroundings. The building programme already includes a £6.5-million outdoor sports complex and a £7-million indoor athletics and netball centre, as well as a hugely extended university library. Other developments will see a big increase in residential accommodation, more catering and social amenities and enhanced teaching and research facilities.

There is plenty of scope for development. The university has quadrupled in size, with almost 13,000 students sharing a spacious but hitherto uninspiring main campus that has an isolated feel despite affording easy access to central London.

In recent years, Brunel has introduced more variety into a portfolio of degrees that was once given over almost entirely to sandwich courses. About half of all undergraduates still take four-year degrees with a work placement of six months or a year, but new developments have tended to be conventional three-year arts and social science programmes. There has also been significant growth in courses specialising in new technologies, such as multimedia design, interactive computing and mobile computing. Other innovations include creative music technology, aviation engineering and pilot studies and motorsport engineering.

Work placements and the inclusion in degree courses of skills modules such as oral and written communication, business and computer literacy have helped maintain a consistently good record in the graduate employment market. Many courses are validated by professional institutions.

Teaching assessments were consistently good, with drama, education, sport science and politics producing the best scores. All the assessments since the millennium produced scores of at least 22 points out of 24. The last research assessments also showed further improvement, although only 61 per cent of the academics were entered and design lost its 5* rating. General and mechanical engineering, law, library and information studies and sociology all reached grade 5, and a £14-

Uxbridge, Middlesex UB8 3PH
01895 203214 (admissions office)
admissions@brunel.ac.uk
www.brunel.ac.uk
www.brunelstudents.com

Edinburgh

Belfast

UXBRIDGE
Cardiff   London

The Times Rankings
Overall Ranking: 50

Student satisfaction:	86	(14.0)
Research assessment:	=53	(4.3)
Entry standards:	49	(303.2)
Student–staff ratio:	=54	(18.0)
Library/IT spend/student:	=40	(£608)
Facilities spend/student:	23	(£305)
Good honours:	30	(66.0%)
Graduate prospects:	=51	(63.9%)
Expected completion rate:	=44	(86.4%)

million investment in 60 more research posts should produce further progress. Sporting excellence is also being maintained, with double gold-medal-winning rower James Cracknell and heavyweight boxer Audley Harrison the best-known alumni of recent times.

More than a third of the undergraduates come from working-class homes – significantly more than the national average for the subjects on offer. Efforts to widen access further include plans for England's only school on a university campus, where the 800 sixth-formers will be mentored by Brunel students as part of the Government's academy programme. Brunel was also among the first of the traditional universities to introduce access courses, run in further education colleges, to bring underqualified mature applicants up to the necessary standard for entry. The level of applications to the university has fluctuated as it has raised its entrance requirements, but the university bucked the downward national trend in 2006, recording a 3 per cent increase. The projected total of 12 per cent leaving without a qualification is significantly better than the UK average for Brunel's subjects and entry grades.

Student union facilities are good and students like Brunel's intimacy, although the university did not do well in the first national student satisfaction survey. The residential stock has been increased in recent years and new undergraduates will be guaranteed accommodation on campus in 2007.

Bursaries and Scholarships

In receipt of full Maintenance Grant	£300
In receipt of partial Maintenance Grant	£200
Living in specified postcodes	Scholarship
Progressing from outreach	Scholarship
Ethnic minorities	Scholarship
Academic achievement	Scholarship

- Tuition fees (2006) £3,000
- Placement year tuition fee will be £350–£700.
- 150 scholarships worth up to £3,000 each for students from under-represented groups with a minimum of 280 tariff points.
- 50 scholarships worth up to £2,000 available for late applicants in specific subjects, for first in family, and those who do better than expected in A levels.
- Up to 25 scholarships worth up to £3,000 for high-performing students from partnership schools in low-participation boroughs.
- Payment will be made in instalments.
- Non-tariff scheme entrants: 2 scholarships per academic school of the university each worth up to £3,000 a year in years 2 and 3 for high performance in year 1 (for those in receipt of a minimum of 50% LEA/SLC support).

Contact: www.brunel.ac.uk/ugstudy
www.brunel.ac.uk/courses/ug/fees2006/

Students

Undergraduates:	9,110	(1,070)
Postgraduates:	1,915	(3,030)
Mature students:	22.9%	
Overseas students:	8.1%	
Applications per place:	7.1	
From state-sector schools:	92.2%	
From working-class homes:	37.5%	

For detailed information about fees, grants and bursaries and how they work, see chapter 7.

Accommodation

Number of places and costs refer to 2006–07
University-provided places: 3,541
Percentage catered: 0%
Self-catered costs: £75.04–£92.05 a week.
All new full-time first-year students are eligible for on-campus accommodation.
All new full-time international students are given on-campus accommodation.
Contact: accom-uxb@brunel.ac.uk

University of Buckingham

Britain's only private university describes itself as Britain's smallest and friendliest. And it claimed, even before the advent of top-up fees elsewhere, to be no more expensive than other universities, especially if you are well qualified and local. Buckingham's intensive two-year degrees cut maintenance costs, and a discount scheme reduces the £12,000-a-year fees by more than £4,000 for applicants with the 300 points at A level, or the equivalent. The threshold is reduced to 240 points for those who go to school or live in Buckinghamshire and the surrounding counties of Bedfordshire, Berkshire, Hertfordshire, Northamptonshire and Oxfordshire. In addition, students of 25 or more at the start of their course can apply for bursaries of £1,200 a term and there are two smaller schemes offering full-fee scholarships for local students.

The university, which celebrated its 25th anniversary in 2001, has no ambitions to follow its peers into the mass higher education market: it values the personal approach that comes with having only ten students to each member of staff, when the UK average is 17. One-to-one tutorials, which have all but disappeared outside Oxbridge and are by no means universal there, are common at Buckingham. The average teaching group contains about six students.

The scholarship initiative, which is open to British and foreign students, could bring modest growth and breathe new life into the university. A Conservative-backed experiment of the 1970s, Buckingham had to wait almost ten years for its royal charter, but is now an accepted part of the university system. Although in 1992 it installed Baroness Thatcher as Chancellor, the university has no party political ties. Dr Terence Kealey, a biochemist from Cambridge University, became the latest Vice-Chancellor in April 2001, declaring an ambition for Buckingham to "one day" challenge the cream of American higher education. He has recruited a number of high-profile libertarians, including Chris Woodhead, the former Chief Inspector of Schools.

Buckingham's private status excludes it from the funding council's assessment of teaching and research, making it impossible to place in our league table. However, the university commissioned its own audit of teaching standards from the Quality Assurance Agency, which gave it a clean bill of health in 2004 and is joining the national student satisfaction survey. The university's degrees carry full currency in the academic world and teaching standards are high. Law and business are particularly popular, while education

Hunter Street,
Buckingham MK18 1EG
01280 824081 (admissions)
admissions@
buckingham.ac.uk
www.buckingham.ac.uk
student.union@
buckingham.ac.uk

The Times Rankings
not applicable

courses now have accreditation from the Teacher Training Agency .

The university runs on calendar years, rather than the traditional academic variety, although some courses give the option of entering in July or September. Between October and December, students taking degrees including French are offered a ten-week course in Lille. Degree courses run for two 40-week years, minimising disruptive career breaks for the many mature students. About three quarters of the students are from overseas, but the proportion from Britain has been growing. Students have the option of a three-year degree in the humanities and soon the university is hoping to open the UK's first private medical school, in partnership with Brunel University.

Even before the QAA audit, the two-year degree had been fully assessed by Professor John Clarke, a founder member of the university staff. Although hardly neutral, he concluded that the individual tuition given to Buckingham students, made possible by unusually generous staffing levels, allowed the system to succeed. However, he acknowledged that 'undercapitalisation' has prevented the university achieving as much as it hoped.

Recent additions to the subjects on offer included multimedia journalism and media communications, both paired with English. The university is also focusing on e-commerce, with a Certificate in Internet Technologies and an MSc in e-business. A BSc has been added in business enterprise, complementing a new business advice hub for the locality.

Campus facilities have improved considerably in recent years, although they cannot compare with those available at traditional universities. Buckingham operates on three sites, all within easy walking distance of each other, including a business school which opened in 1996. An academic centre containing computer suites, lecture theatres and student facilities provides a focal point that was missing previously.

The social scene is predictably quiet, given the size of the university and the workload, especially at weekends. A university cinema opened recently and the town is pretty with a good selection of pubs and restaurants. Milton Keynes or Oxford are near, except that Buckingham has no station.

Students

Undergraduates:	510	(30)
Postgraduates:	130	(20)
Mature students:	51.4%	
Overseas students:	70%	
Applications per place:	20.3	
From state-sector schools:	n/a	
From working-class homes:	n/a	

For detailed information about fees, grants and bursaries and how they work, see chapter 7.

Accommodation

Number of places and costs refer to 2006–07

University-provided places: 446

Percentage catered: 0%

Self-catered accommodation: £800–£1,300 a term.

First years are guaranteed accommodation.

International students: same as above.

Contact: admissions@buckingham.ac.uk

University of Cambridge

Until 2001, Cambridge had enjoyed an unbroken run at the top of *The Times* League Table, and even now it is practically inseparable from first-placed Oxford. The university has the best record in the teaching and research assessments. Traditionally supreme in the sciences, where it was ranked best in the world by *The Times Higher Education Supplement* in 2005, the university boasts an array of subjects with top ratings for teaching and research. But the arts and social sciences have also been strengthened. The Centre for Research in the Arts, Social Sciences and Humanities, designed to compete with similar institutes in Australia, Germany and the United States, has been one example, while the Judge Management School is also well established now.

All but one of the subjects assessed in the first rounds of teaching quality assessment were considered excellent and none dropped more than two points out of 24 under the later system. However, Cambridge students did not respond in sufficient numbers for the university to be included in the first national student satisfaction survey. Almost three quarters of the academics entered for research assessment were in subjects rated internationally outstanding, and only three subjects failed to reach the next-highest grade. The tripos system was a forerunner of the currently fashionable modular degree, allowing students to change subjects (within limits) midway through their courses. Students receive a classification for each of the two parts of their tripos degree.

More students now come from state schools than the independent sector – a trend the university is keen to continue – but the proportion of working-class undergraduates remains low, at only 11 per cent. Summer schools, student visits and, in some colleges, sympathetic selection procedures, are helping to attract more applications from comprehensive schools. The appointment of Alison Richard as the first woman to head the university since the Vice-Chancellorship became a permanent post has trained the spotlight on Cambridge once more.

A lively alternative prospectus, available from the students' union, says there is no such thing as Cambridge University, just a collection of colleges. Where applications are concerned, this is true, as it is to some extent socially. Making the right choice of college is crucial, both to maximise the chances of winning a place and to ensure an enjoyable three years if you are successful. Applicants can take pot luck with an open application if they prefer not to opt for a particular college. But, though the statistics show that this route is

---

Kellet Lodge, Tennis Court Road,
Cambridge CB2 1QJ
01223 333308
ucam-undergraduate-
admissions@lists.cam.ac.uk
www.cam.ac.uk
www.cusu.cam.ac.uk

The Times Rankings
Overall Ranking: 2

Student satisfaction:	–	(–)
Research assessment:	1	(6.6)
Entry standards:	1	(525.1)
Student–staff ratio:	4	(11.9)
Library/IT spend/student:	6	(£1,129)
Facilities spend/student:	3	(£425)
Good honours	2	(84.6%)
Graduate prospects:	1	(86.9%)
Expected completion rate:	1	(98.9%)

equally successful, only a minority take it. Most teaching is now university-based, especially in the sciences, and a shift of emphasis towards the centre has been taking place more generally. The trend may accelerate if a £1-billion funding appeal to mark the university's 800th anniversary is successful.

The university's leading place in British higher education was underlined by its success in attracting Microsoft's first research base outside the United States. This is one of a series of technological partnerships with the private sector, several of which benefit undergraduates as well as researchers. Cambridge was also chosen for a Government-sponsored partnership with the Massachusetts Institute of Technology to promote entrepreneurship.

Such is the scale of development that almost £500 million worth of building is either planned or under construction. Although the medical school's facilities are being upgraded at Addenbrooke's Hospital, the university is looking to the outskirts to expand. The West Cambridge site will take a mixture of teaching and research buildings, and there are plans for more on green-belt land further north. In the long term, up to three new colleges could be built but there will be few extra places for undergraduates in the foreseeable future.

For the moment, therefore, entrance requirements will remain the toughest in Britain. With around four applicants for each place – fewer still if you choose your subject carefully – the competition for places appears less intense than at the popular civic universities. The difference is that nine out of ten entrants have at least AAA at A levels. The pressure does not end there: the amount of high-quality work to be crammed into eight-week terms can prove a strain, although the 1 per cent drop-out rate is the lowest in Britain.

Bursaries and Scholarships

In receipt of full Maintenance Grant	£3,000
In receipt of partial Maintenance Grant	
	£700–£2,300
Disabled	Bursary

- Tuition fees (2006) £3,000
- Year abroad tuition fee will be around £1,500.
- Mature students who are Cambridge residents and are recipients of the full MG will be eligible for an enhanced bursary of £5,000. Also bursaries for disabled students and students with dependent children.
- Students from Scotland, Wales and Northern Ireland may be eligible for bursaries, subject to assessment.
- 30% of additional fee income (£7 million in 2010–11) will be earmarked for bursaries.

Contact: www.cam.ac.uk/admissions/ undergraduate/finance/support.html

Students

Undergraduates:	11,910	(4,355)
Postgraduates:	5,380	(3,825)
Mature students:	5.5%	
Overseas students:	12.2%	
Applications per place:	4.3	
From state-sector schools:	56.9%	
From working-class homes:	11.4%	

For detailed information about fees, grants and bursaries and how they work, see chapter 7.

Accommodation

See chapter 10 for information about individual colleges.

Canterbury Christ Church University

This former Church of England college started branching out well before university status arrived in 2005. There is a network of campuses right across Kent, the most populous county in England but, until recently, one of the most sparsely provided with higher education. At the purpose-built campus at Broadstairs, for example, where applications were up by 28 per cent at the start of 2006, the university offers subjects as diverse as commercial music, digital media, business, police studies, computing, nursing and child and youth studies. There is also an imposing country house and one-time convalescent home outside Tunbridge Wells, mainly for postgraduates, and a new site at Chatham, operated partly in conjunction with Greenwich and Kent universities.

The majority of the 14,000 students, however, are at the new university's Canterbury headquarters. The main campus, which dates from 1962, is a few minutes walk from the city centre, but the university has several off-site buildings in other parts of Canterbury. One is being developed as a learning resource centre, with specialist teaching and IT facilities, to open in 2008.

The Church of England link was underlined with the installation of the Archbishop of Canterbury as the university's Chancellor in 2005. Religious studies is available as a single-honours degree or as part of the modular scheme, which cover the arts and humanities, business and science, education and health and social care. The large health and teacher training programmes make the university the largest provider of higher education to the public services in Kent. Canterbury is one of the few Grade 1 providers of teacher training offering the full range of courses from early years to primary, secondary, further and higher education. Every police officer in Kent automatically becomes a Canterbury undergraduate – a programme that attracted the first Skillsmark Award at a university.

Religious studies registered the best teaching quality grades, but all the assessments were good, as were the results from the first national student satisfaction survey. The university college, as it then was, entered an ambitious 34 per cent of academics for the last Research Assessment Exercise, but none of the subject areas reached the top three of the seven grades. This was not an issue when Canterbury sought to shed its college title because it has become one of the new "teaching-led" universities.

More than 95 per cent of the

North Holmes Road,
Canterbury CT1 1QU
01227 767700
admissions
@canterbury.ac.uk
www.canterbury.ac.uk
http://c4online.net/

The Times Rankings
Overall Ranking: 86

Student satisfaction:	=12	(15.4)
Research assessment:	=94	(1.9)
Entry standards:	78	(239.2)
Student–staff ratio:	=81	(20.7)
Library/IT spend/student:	101	(£394)
Facilities spend/student:	108	(£83)
Good honours:	99	(46.5%)
Graduate prospects:	=56	(62.8%)
Expected completion rate:	57	(83.7%)

undergraduates are state-educated and 34 per cent are from working-class homes – both significantly more than the national average for the university's subjects and entry grades. The dropout rate of around 16 per cent is just below the university's benchmark figure. University-wide applications were down by 3.4 per cent at the start of 2006 – precisely the national average – but this came after 15 per cent increases in both of the preceding years.

Recent capital development has been concentrated on the Chatham campus, where 250 computers have been installed in the Rowan Williams Court building. All the campuses are connected by a microwave link, which provides fast access to teaching and learning materials, as well as email. The new Drill Hall Library at Chatham provides 147,000 items, 370 computers and 250 study spaces for Canterbury, Greenwich and Kent students. Social and sports facilities naturally vary between the campuses, although the students' union is present on all of them. Residential accommodation is not plentiful, but first years are given priority.

Bursaries and Scholarships

In receipt of full Maintenance Grant £800
In receipt of partial Maintenance Grant £400–500

- Tuition fees (2006) £3,000
- Bursary of £400 to students from families with income between £32,000–£45,000.
- Eligibility for bursaries to be assessed using UUK/SLC model bursary scheme (HEBSS).

Contact: http://www.canterbury.ac.uk/support/student-support-services/students/finance/flb.asp

Students

Undergraduates:	5,900	(5,180)
Postgraduates:	1,025	(1,845)
Mature students:	22.1%	
Overseas students:	4.2%	
Applications per place:	4.5	
From state-sector schools:	96.0%	
From working-class homes:	33.9%	

For detailed information about fees, grants and bursaries and how they work, see chapter 7.

Accommodation

Number of places and costs refer to 2006–07
University-provided places: 1,148
Percentage catered: 12.8%
Catered costs: £67–£75 a week. Food is purchased on Smart card basis.
Self-catered costs: £80–£91 a week.
Accommodation guaranteed for first years if conditions are met.
International students: as above.
Contact: accommodation@canterbury.ac.uk
http://accommodation.canterbury.ac.uk

University of Cardiff

Cardiff has established itself as the front-runner in Welsh higher education. It has now left the University of Wales, believing that only full independence would enable it to compete with other top universities, although some health courses still lead to degrees from the federal university. After 75 years of partnership, Cardiff has also merged with the University of Wales College of Medicine with the backing of £60 million from the Welsh Assembly and other sources. The new venture has already attracted brain imaging facilities worth £10.8 million.

With more than 22,000 students and 5,000 staff, the university is a match for most rivals in teaching and research. A third of the students come from Wales, but the 3,000 from overseas testify to Cardiff's international reputation. Seven subjects – city and regional planning, civil engineering, education, English, optometry, psychology and theology – were rated internationally outstanding in the latest research assessments. Almost nine out of ten researchers were placed in the top two of the seven categories, one of the best ratios in Britain.

Research income is healthy, too, with industrial collaboration by the Manufacturing Engineering Centre winning a Queen's Anniversary Prize in 2001. Teaching quality is also highly rated. The 21 subjects graded as excellent represent more than half of the university. An overall audit by the Quality Assurance Agency complimented the university on its "powerful academic vision and well-developed and effectively articulated mission to achieve excellence in teaching and research". Student support services, including counselling facilities and the help offered to dyslexics, were among the features singled out for praise.

Humanities and social sciences take the largest share of places. Philosophy, theology, religious studies and English achieved the best scores in the first national student satisfaction survey, although mathematical sciences were close behind. A partial reorganisation has created two "super schools" of biosciences and social sciences, while a new Centre for Lifelong Learning co-ordinates 700 courses, which are offered at 100 regional centres. Many full-time degrees share a common first year, and the introduction of a modular system has made undergraduate study more flexible.

The university enjoys a central location in the Welsh capital, occupying a significant part of the civic complex around Cathays Park. In recent years, more than £200 million has been invested in new buildings and equipment, and extensive refurbishment. The flagship

PO Box 921,
Cardiff CF10 3XQ
029-2087 4839
admissions@cardiff.ac.uk
www.cardiff.ac.uk
www.cardiffstudents.com

The Times Rankings
Overall Ranking: 16

Teaching assessment:	=24	(15.2)
Research assessment:	=22	(5.4)
Entry standards:	23	(371.1)
Student–staff ratio:	=8	(13.0)
Library/IT spend/student:	17	(£758)
Facilities spend/student:	=40	(£238)
Good honours:	26	(68.6%)
Graduate prospects:	15	(73.5%)
Expected completion rate:	13	(94.8%)

projects involved a £30-million centre for engineering, physics and computer science, with facilities comparable with the best in Britain, and a £3.5-million refurbishment of the chemistry department. The latest phase of the programme has seen the opening of a £3.5-million resource centre alongside the business school and a £14-million life sciences building, with optometry and vision sciences.

The medical school is a mile away at Heath Park, where the five healthcare schools share a 53-acre site bordering parkland and fields with the University Hospital of Wales. Between the two campuses the university is building student accommodation containing 511 en suite study bedrooms, adding to the 4,700 beds already available. Two thirds of those are also en suite, and most are within walking distance of lectures. Rents are among the lowest in the UK, according to a National Union of Students survey.

Entry requirements have been rising, despite recent expansion, and the graduate employment record is good. There was a 15 per cent rise in applications for courses beginning in 2005 and another of 6 per cent the following year when top-up fees were introduced in England. One undergraduate in seven comes from an independent school, but still almost a quarter have a working-class background.

The 5 per cent dropout rate is the lowest in Wales and among the lowest in Britain.

The city of Cardiff is popular with students, offering all the attractions of a large conurbation without such high prices as students experience elsewhere. The main residential site at Talybont boasts a "sports village", with three multipurpose sports halls, a fitness suite and outdoor pitches. There is also a city-centre fitness suite and a sports ground that was used as a training facility for the rugby union World Cup.

Bursaries and Scholarships

- Fees for undergraduate courses £3,000
- Students living in Wales will be eligible for a Welsh Assembly fee grant of approximately £1,800 a year.
- Fees for placement year and year abroad £600.
- For information on the National Bursary Scheme see page 198, chapter 7.
- Cardiff University is developing a comprehensive student support package which, subject to final approval, will include both bursaries and scholarships. More information about this will be published on its website in due course.

Contact: www.cardiff.ac.uk/2614

Students

Undergraduates:	13,275	(4,185)
Postgraduates:	3,500	(2,050)
Mature students:	14.1%	
Overseas students:	9.9%	
Applications per place:	7.0	
From state-sector schools:	84.5%	
From working-class homes:	21.8%	

For detailed information about fees, grants and bursaries and how they work, see chapter 7.

Accommodation

Number of places and costs refer to 2005–06
University-provided places: about 5,171
Percentage catered: 5.2%
Catered costs: £65–£71 a week.
Self-catered costs: £46–£71 a week.
All first years are guaranteed accommodation if conditions are met.
Policy for international students: as above
Contact: residences@cardiff.ac.uk

Cardiff, University of Wales Institute (UWIC)

UWIC has an international reputation for sport, but is no slouch in some academic fields either, as the eighth highest-placed new university in *The Times* League Table. The combination has been attracting record numbers of applicants: a 6 per cent increase at the official deadline for courses beginning in 2006 may have owed something to the fees advantage enjoyed by Welsh students, but it followed on from more substantial surges earlier in the decade.

Extra places have been added, but plans for UWIC to become part of a much larger university through a merger with neighbouring Glamorgan or the University of Wales, Newport have been abandoned. Two thirds of UWIC's 9,000 students are Welsh, half of them from Cardiff or the Vale of Glamorgan. Nearly 95 per cent attended state schools and, although little more than a quarter come from working-class homes, the 17 per cent who come from areas sending few students to higher education is slightly ahead of the "benchmark" set according to the mix of courses. The drop-out rate is lower than the average for new universities.

UWIC is one of Britain's leading centres for university sport, with team performances to match some excellent facilities. The Institute has had British university champions in gymnastics, trampolining, athletics, rugby union, rugby league, boxing, squash, archery, weightlifting and judo. More than 240 past or present students are internationals in 28 sports, world and Olympic champions among them. The £7-million National Indoor Athletics Centre is UWIC's pride and joy, but other facilities are also of high quality.

Academically, art and design is the star performer, with teaching in ceramics, fine art and interior architecture rated excellent, and the whole area considered nationally excellent for research. All six teacher training courses are rated excellent for teaching and there have been top scores in several sciences, but less than one academic in five was entered for the last Research Assessment Exercise, leaving UWIC near the bottom of the research table in terms of average grades per member of staff.

Entrance requirements are generally modest, but the menu of largely vocational courses means that many students come with qualifications other than A levels. About a fifth are mature students and there is a relatively high proportion from overseas.

UWIC has four sites, all within three miles of the centre of Cardiff. The

---

Cardiff Institute
Western Avenue,
Cardiff CF5 2YB
029-2041 6070
uwicinfo@uwic.ac.uk
www.uwic.ac.uk
www.uwicsu.co.uk

The Times Rankings
Overall Ranking: 61

Student satisfaction:	=67	(14.5)
Research assessment:	=72	(2.7)
Entry standards:	77	(243.0)
Student–staff ratio:	=78	(20.6)
Library/IT spend/student:	=90	(£439)
Facilities spend/student:	=5	(£395)
Good honours:	81	(50.7%)
Graduate prospects:	85	(57.0%)
Expected completion rate:	62	(82.5%)

Cyncoed campus, which houses education and sport, is the centre of activity, particularly for first-year students. The athletics centre is there, together with a multitude of outdoor facilities and also the Welsh Sports Centre for the Disabled. Student facilities, including the Institute's largest bar, have been upgraded recently. A £2-million learning centre opened in 2005; the IT suite has 250 computers available 24 hours a day.

Howard Gardens is the home of fine art, while the Llandaff campus hosts design, engineering, food science and health courses. A new £3-million student centre is at Llandaff, which includes a dyslexia support unit among a number of advice and representation services, and a learning centre with more than 300 computers opened in 2003. Business, hospitality and tourism are taught at the Colchester Avenue campus.

Students tend to like Cardiff as a city, and UWIC's enterprising union does its best to make their time there as lively as possible. It owns a nightclub and bar in the city centre to add to the campus choices. Before the recent expansion, all first years were guaranteed accommodation, and 90 per cent still live in halls. UWIC is the only university to have been awarded the government's Charter Mark four times, the judges commenting particularly on the level of satisfaction among students. This was not especially evident in the first national satisfaction survey, although teacher training and health-related subjects did well.

Bursaries and Scholarships

- Fees for undergraduate courses £3,000
- Students living in Wales will be eligible for a Welsh Assembly fee grant of approximately £1,800 a year.
- Fees for placement year and year abroad not yet known.
- For information on the National Bursary Scheme see page 198, chapter 7.
- For students living in a designated Wales Communities First area, a bursary of up to £3,000 over 3 years is available to students registered on any of its 3-year full-time undergraduate programmes.
- Subject specific bursaries to be confirmed for 2007.

Contact: www.uwic.ac.uk/advice4applicants/financialsupport.asp

Students		
Undergraduates:	6,100	(1,355)
Postgraduates:	765	(925)
Mature students:	19.7%	
Overseas students:	6.5%	
Applications per place:	4.3	
From state-sector schools:	94.9%	
From working-class homes:	26.6%	

For detailed information about fees, grants and bursaries and how they work, see chapter 7.

Accommodation

Number of places and costs refer to 2006–07
University-provided places: 1,183
Percentage catered: 33%
Catered cost: £93–£104 a week.
Self-catered costs: £66.50–£84.00 a week.
First-year students have no guarantee, terms and conditons apply.
International students: accommodation is reserved, subject to availability and if conditions are met.
Contact: accomm@uwic.ac.uk

University of Central Lancashire

A big university at the heart of England's newest city, Central Lancashire does not dominate Preston to the extent that Cambridge or Durham do their cities, but students account for a sixth of the population during term time. The balance will shift much further in their favour if the university succeeds in its aim of expanding to 50,000 students by the end of the decade. The modern, town-centre campus has seen considerable development, as the university has doubled in size, and still the building continues. A £12-million Lottery-funded sports arena and a "knowledge park" for technology transfer were followed by a new computing and technology building in 2003. Now £6.5 million has been spent on extending and refurbishing the students' union, giving it one of the largest student venues in the country, and new buildings have opened for biology and psychology and health and business.

Amid the expansion, the university has revamped its pioneering credit accumulation and transfer system, allowing undergraduates to mix and match from a menu of more than 3,000 courses. Electives are used to broaden the curriculum, so that up to 11 per cent of students' time is spent on subjects outside their normal range. There is particular encouragement to include a language as part of the package, and more than 2,000 students do so. A growing proportion also take advantage of the numerous international exchange programmes, which are available in all subject areas. The university's website is even available in Chinese.

The former polytechnic has acquired a high reputation in some apparently unlikely fields. American studies, psychology, education and nursing all achieved perfect scores for teaching quality. Journalism, which also scored well, is sufficiently popular to be able to demand the equivalent of three Bs at A level. Astrophysics benefits from two observatories, including one of the largest optical telescopes in Britain. Although its teaching quality score was disappointing, it was one of the successes of the last research assessments. These were a definite improvement on 1996 but, apart from physics and astronomy, only history and law rated in the top three categories. Geography and environmental science, technology and psychology were the top scorers in the national student satisfaction survey.

In its first excursion beyond Preston, the university took in an agricultural college at Newton Rigg, in Cumbria, which is now known as its Penrith campus. A £3.5-million learning resources centre has

Preston PR1 2HE
01772 201201
cenquiries@uclan.ac.uk
www.uclan.ac.uk
www.yourunion.co.uk

The Times Rankings
Overall Ranking: 72

Student satisfaction:	=38	(14.9)
Research assessment:	=86	(2.2)
Entry standards:	69	(252.0)
Student–staff ratio:	98	(22.8)
Library/IT spend/student:	98	(£406)
Facilities spend/student:	31	(£266)
Good honours:	80	(50.8%)
Graduate prospects:	72	(59.6%)
Expected completion rate:	78	(80.2%)

been added and there are plans for an all-weather sports facility, a Centre for Outdoor Management and Training and a new building for the National School of Forestry. UCLan is now involved in plans to bring more higher education to the county, which has never had a university of its own. A campus in Carlisle specialises in business, management and law courses, which are taught in 17th-century buildings which have been upgraded to incorporate up-to-date teaching and learning facilities.

More than a third of Central Lancashire's students come from working-class homes. A high proportion are local people in their twenties or thirties, many of whom come through the well-established lifelong learning networks run in colleges throughout the North West. No fewer than 14 per cent of the university's students are taught in colleges but, unlike some institutions involved in "franchising", Central Lancashire has carried out a thorough review of the quality of its external programmes. Applications have been low for the number of places on offer and, while there have been improvements in recent years, there was a 10 per cent decline at the start of 2006. More than 20 per cent of undergraduates entered through clearing in 2005.

The social scene in Preston may not compare with Manchester or Liverpool, but neither do the security risks and the cost of living is low. Both cities are within easy reach, and the student union's "Feel" club nights have won national recognition. Although still not the most fashionable university, Central Lancashire commands great loyalty among its students.

Rents for the nearly 1,500 places in university accommodation are among the lowest in Britain and the 60-acre Preston Sports Arena is among the best in any higher education institution. Three miles from the main campus, the centre is available to clubs throughout the region but there are reserved periods for students, who can also book at peak times.

Bursaries and Scholarships

In receipt of full Maintenance Grant	£1,000
In receipt of partial Maintenance Grant	£1,000
Living in region	Bursary
Progressing from outreach	Bursary
Shortage subjects	Scholarship

- Tuition fees (2006) £3,000
- Placement year tuition fee will be £600.
- £1,000 scholarship for students in receipt of Maintenance Grant is extended to include all full-time UK undergraduate students who come from homes where the principal earner's gross salary is less than £60,000 a year.
- Harris Bursary Fund is for local students.
- 100 £2,000 Excellence Scholarships in year 1, across a range of subject areas.
- Bursaries do not apply to other EU students

Contact: www.uclan.ac.uk/fees/scholarships.htm

Students

Undergraduates:	15,065	(9,310)
Postgraduates:	850	(1,960)
Mature students:	27.3%	
Overseas students:	9.8%	
Applications per place:	4.2	
From state-sector schools:	96.4%	
From working-class homes:	36.1%	

For detailed information about fees, grants and bursaries and how they work, see chapter 7.

Accommodation

Number of places and costs refer to 2005–06
University-provided places: 1,450
Percentage catered: 0%
Self-catered costs: £45–£75 a week.
The Student Accommodation Service guarantees to help all first years find suitable accommodation either in university-managed housing or in the private sector.
Policy for international students: as above.
Contact: saccommodation@uclan.ac.uk

Chester University

The picturesque Roman city of Chester is one of those places that outsiders probably always expected to have its own university. Indeed, William Gladstone was among the founders of the first Church of England teacher training college there in 1839. Although it took until 2005 for that college to achieve university status, it had been building up a solid reputation recently in a number of subjects beyond education alone. A 45 per cent rise in applications in the year before top-up fees was the biggest at any institution in this *Guide*, and the new university bucked the national trend with a 9 per cent rise in 2006 as well.

The main campus is only a short walk from the centre of Chester, a 32-acre site boasting manicured gardens and a number of new developments. A new sports hall is just the latest in a stream of improvements, which have included a new library and media centre, a large auditorium, a science building, an art and technology centre and a swimming pool. The Warrington campus, which has seven halls of residence, focuses on media courses and has recently acquired state-of-the-art production facilities in collaboration with Granada Television and a new students' union. It is expected to be the focus of future development to accommodate modest increases in student numbers.

Chester was among the top ten universities in the first national student satisfaction survey, with outstanding results in religious studies and theology, history and archaeology, and English. There were good scores, too, in geography and sport, which was one of the top performers in the later rounds of teaching assessment. Maths was the other subject to manage 23 points out of 24. Although research activity has been growing, it has been from a low base: the average grades in the 2001 assessments were in the bottom ten of the universities in this year's *Guide*.

With 10,000 students, including part-timers, Chester is among the biggest of this year's new universities. More than half of the undergraduates are mature students and three quarters are female. Nearly all are state-educated and more than a third have working-class roots. About a third of the undergraduates take combined honours degrees, while single honours often includes a period of extended work experience. There is also a limited range of foundation degrees in health subjects. The 13 per cent projected dropout rate is marginally better than the national average for the university's courses and entry standards.

A student contract of the type that is likely to become commonplace elsewhere in higher education sets out clear

---

Parkgate Road
Chester CH1 4BJ
01244 511000
enquiries@chester.ac.uk
www.chester.ac.uk
www.chestersu.com

Edinburgh
Belfast
CHESTER
London
Cardiff

The Times Rankings
Overall Ranking: 68

Student satisfaction:	=4	(15.6)
Research assessment:	=101	(1.6)
Entry standards:	70	(251.5)
Student–staff ratio:	72	(20.0)
Library/IT spend/student:	89	(£441)
Facilities spend/student:	=56	(£210)
Good honours:	104	(44.9%)
Graduate prospects:	103	(49.3%)
Expected completion rate:	=51	(84.6%)

conditions on the offer of a place, as well as detailing the university's responsibilities. Students promise to "study diligently, and to attend promptly and participate appropriately at lectures, courses, classes, seminars, tutorials, work placements and other activities which form part of the programme." The university undertakes to deliver the student's programme but leaves itself considerable leeway beyond that.

However, Chester offers considerable support and facilities for its students. There are libraries on both sites and extensive sports facilities, especially on the main campus, catering partly for the large physical education progamme. Most first years are offered one of the growing number of hall places, although there is not yet enough university accommodation to make this a guarantee. Student union facilities form the basis of the social scene on both campuses, but Chester has more to offer for those looking further afield.

Bursaries and Scholarships

In receipt of full Maintenance Grant £1,350
In receipt of partial Maintenance Grant
£450–£900

- Tuition fees (2006) £3,000
- Eligibility for bursaries to be assessed using UUK/SLC model bursary scheme (HEBSS).

Contact:
www.chester.ac.uk/undergraduate/fees.html

Students

Undergraduates:	6,175	(3,375)
Postgraduates:	325	(905)
Mature students:	15.6%	
Overseas students:	2.3%	
Applications per place:	6.3	
From state-sector schools:	97.3%	
From working-class homes:	36.2%	

For detailed information about fees, grants and bursaries and how they work, see chapter 7.

Accommodation

Number of places and costs refer to 2006–07
University-provided places: 1,040
Percentage catered: 55%
Catered costs: £74.20–£110.60 a week.
Self-catered costs: £51.45–£73.15 a week.
First years cannot be guaranteed accommodation.
International students: guaranteed accommodation if they apply in good time.
Contact: www.chester.ac.uk/accommodation

University of Chichester

Chichester is the smallest of the nine universities created since the last edition of the *Guide*, despite being an amalgamation of two former teacher training colleges. But it is already one of the top ten in our table in terms of student satisfaction, boasting some of the best scores for teaching in the first national student survey. Indeed, the university has had an extremely creditable debut overall in *The Times* League Table, finishing ahead of most of the former polytechnics, as well as all the remaining newcomers. These achievements came too late to influence applications for courses beginning in 2006, when the prospect of top-up fees saw a 6 per cent decline on the previous year, but they should stand Chichester in good stead in future.

The university traces its history back to 1839, when the college that subsequently bore his name was founded in memory of William Otter, the education-minded Bishop of Chichester. It became a teacher training college for women, who still account for two thirds of the places. Two further stages preceded university status – 20 years as the West Sussex Institute of Higher Education, following an amalgamation with the nearby Bognor Regis College of Education, and then seven as University College Chichester.

The Chichester campus – now the larger of two – continues to carry the Bishop Otter name, signifying a continuing link with the Church of England.

There are six schools divided between the two sites, all of them in the arts, social science or education. Degree subjects range from adventure education to humanistic counselling, fine art and theology. The PE teacher training course is the largest in the country – the university now trains one in five PE teachers in England – and highly rated by Ofsted. Media studies achieved full marks in the best of Chichester's teaching assessments and, while the university was less successful in the Research Assessment Exercise, it entered a larger proportion of its academics than any of its peer group. The Mathematics Centre, at Bognor, has an international reputation, working with over 30 countries as well as teaching the university's own students. It has become a focal point for curriculum development in Britain and elsewhere.

Almost all the students are state-educated, but the proportions from working-class homes and areas of low participation in higher education are both below the national average for the university's courses and entry grades. However, the projected dropout rate is significantly better than that benchmark. Four out of ten students are 21 or more on

Bishop Otter Campus
College Lane
Chichester
W. Sussex PO19 6PE
01243 816002
admissions@chi.ac.uk
www.ucc.ac.uk
www.chisu.org

The Times Rankings
Overall Ranking: 64

Student satisfaction:	=4	(15.6)
Research assessment:	=90	(2.1)
Entry standards:	80	(238.9)
Student–staff ratio:	90	(21.6)
Library/IT spend/student:	85	(£452)
Facilities spend/student:	=96	(£126)
Good honours:	100	(46.3%)
Graduate prospects:	46	(65.0%)
Expected completion rate:	46	(86.2%)

entry. The university runs summer taster sessions and has a series of partnerships with schools in the Channel Islands and Sussex to encourage a broader intake. Courses are also run in collaboration with Isle of Wight College, where fees are pegged at £1,200, and with the Academy of Play and Child Psychotherapy, in Uckfield, East Sussex.

Both of the university's campuses are within ten minutes' walk of the sea and the 520 residential places are roughly equally divided between them. There is a university bus service linking the two and student union bars on each. Sports facilities are good and competitive teams surprisingly successful for such a small university. The small cathedral city of Chichester is best known as a yachting venue, while Bognor's days as a leading holiday resort are well in the past, but both offer a good supply of private housing and some student-oriented bars.

Bursaries and Scholarships

In receipt of full Maintenance Grant £1,000
In receipt of partial Maintenance Grant
£250–£999

- Tuition fees (2006) £3,000
- Eligibility for bursaries to be assessed using UUK/SLC model bursary scheme (HEBSS).

Contact: http://chi.ac.uk/applying/chichesterbursaries.cfm

Students

Undergraduates:	2,615	(635)
Postgraduates:	285	(1,545)
Mature students:	19.3%	
Overseas students:	2.3%	
Applications per place:	5.3	
From state-sector schools:	97.3%	
From working-class homes:	28.5%	

For detailed information about fees, grants and bursaries and how they work, see chapter 7.

Accommodation

Number of places and costs refer to 2006–07
University-provided places: 662
Percentage catered: 67%
Catered costs: £87.30–£116.70 a week.
Self-catered costs: £70.00–£95.20 a week.
First years are accommodated on a first come-first served basis.
International students: as above.
Contact: accommodation@chi.ac.uk

City University

Once a college of advanced technology, a third of City students now study business, a third health subjects and the remaining third law, computing, engineering, journalism, and the arts. But the university has maintained its links with business, industry and the professions, reaping the benefits with consistently good graduate employment figures. Courses have a practical edge, and many of the staff hold professional, as well as academic, qualifications.

The university is still comparatively small despite steady growth in the last five years, which has seen student numbers pass 13,000, including large contingents of postgraduates and part-timers. Numbers doubled during the 1990s, partly due to the incorporation of a nursing and midwifery college at nearby St Bartholomew's Hospital and the Charterhouse College of Radiography. Applications were up by almost 16 per cent at the start of 2005 and there was another small increase a year later.

Development has taken place at the university's headquarters, on the borders of the City of London, but the most ambitious project has been a new £42-million home for the business school, in the financial district of the City of London. Opened in 2002, the new building, spread over eight floors, has doubled the school's usable space, enabling it to expand its academic activity and executive programmes. Another £20 million has gone into an impressive new building for the School of Social Sciences.

Cass Business School is, not surprisingly, one of City's great strengths. It was the first Western university to forge links with the Bank of China, running an Executive MBA programme in Shanghai as the first step to a wider role in business education throughout southeast Asia.

The university had already boosted its legal provision by incorporating the Inns of Court School of Law in 2001. The City Law School, which includes the university's original department, offers London's only "one-stop shop" for legal training, from undergraduate to professional courses. City is also working with Queen Mary, University of London, in a range of subjects, starting with medicine and other health subjects, journalism and engineering. The two universities jointly host a national centre for teaching and learning in nursing and midwifery.

City has a particularly high reputation in music, where it is associated with the Guildhall School of Music and Drama, with its teaching rated as excellent and research internationally outstanding. The subject achieved the university's only 5* rating in the 2001 Research Assessment

---

Northampton Square,
London EC1V 0HB
0207-040 5060
ugadmissions@city.ac.uk
www.city.ac.uk
www.cusuonline.org

The Times Rankings
Overall Ranking: 53

Student Satisfaction:	–	(–)
Research assessment:	=51	(4.4)
Entry standards:	43	(314.7)
Student–staff ratio:	93	(22.3)
Library/IT spend/student:	=90	(£439)
Facilities spend/student:	=82	(£154)
Good honours:	=47	(59.9%)
Graduate prospects:	12	(74.7%)
Expected completion rate:	53	(84.5%)

Exercise, but arts policy, business, information science, law and optometry all reached the next grade.

Early teaching assessments were disappointing. The university's response was to establish an educational development unit to enhance the quality of teaching and launch a review of the effectiveness of personal tutoring. Scores improved dramatically, with business and management, maths and statistics, and health leading the way.

Recent additions to the portfolio of degrees include environmental engineering and Anglo-American law, while the journalism department is well regarded. There is also a flourishing sub-degree programme for adults, which ranges from sitcom writing to e-business. The changes have maintained City's position among the most popular universities in London, with nine applications per undergraduate place.

Official performance indicators for higher education have brought mixed news: the drop-out rate has been falling but 15 per cent is still high for a traditional university. City has a good record among its peers for widening participation in higher education, with four in ten undergraduates from working-class homes. Students tend to be more concerned about their inability to afford the attractions of a trendy part of London.

Most fall back on the extended students' union, but this is usually shut at weekends for lack of demand for its facilities.

Bursaries and Scholarships

In receipt of full Maintenance Grant	£1,000
Living in specified postcodes	Scholarship
Shortage subjects	Scholarship

- Tuition fees (2006) £3,000
- Placement year tuition fee will be £1,000. Fees for part-time students will be on a sliding scale. Fees for Foundation year will be £1,500.
- Scholarships for able students from low-income backgrounds in subject areas as follows: law (£800), business (£750) and engineering (£1,000).
- 15% of additional fee income will be earmarked for bursaries; 2% for scholarships.

Contact:
www.city.ac.uk/ugrad/finance/index.html
www.city.ac.uk/ugrad/finance/additional.html

Students		
Undergraduates:	6,760	(6,980)
Postgraduates:	3,385	(5,240)
Mature students:	22.5%	
Overseas students:	22.8%	
Applications per place:	7.6	
From state-sector schools:	85.2%	
From working-class homes:	40.0%	

For detailed information about fees, grants and bursaries and how they work, see chapter 7.

Accommodation

Number of places and costs refer to 2005–06
University-provided places: 1,190
Percentage catered: 0%
Self-catered costs: £89–£105 a week.
Accommodation is guaranteed for first years if conditions are met. Residential restrictions apply.
International students: preference is given to new overseas students.
Contact: accomm@city.ac.uk
www.city.ac.uk/accommodation

Coventry University

Coventry's origins go back to the foundation of the College of Design in 1843 and its links with the motor industry of the Midlands were reflected in its earlier title of Lanchester Polytechnic, named after a leading engineering figure. The campus of the university is close to the city centre, with all its departments within walking distance of each other. There has been an ambitious building plan after a decade in which student numbers doubled, reaching 20,000 in 2004 with 17,000 in Coventry itself. A new library, media and arts centre, technology park and enhanced student facilities, including additional accommodation and a second students' union building, are transforming the university.

The university's financial base is sound, its income more than doubling in the 1990s, but its recruitment targets have not always been met. Although some class sizes have increased, students have been benefiting from an innovative approach to computer-assisted learning, supported by an expanded computer network and the £20-million showpiece library, almost entirely naturally ventilated and lit. The old library has been renovated for nursing, midwifery, social work and health sciences staff. The university was chosen to house national centres of excellence in teaching for e-learning in health and social care, as well as in transport and product design. Degrees in automotive engineering and design courses have been developed in collaboration with the motor industry, both in Coventry and further afield.

A £7-million arts centre and the conversion of a former working men's club provides much needed space for the students' union with dedicated facilities for mature and international students. A £3.6-million centrally-located sports complex opened in 2004. The university put £50,000 into sports scholarships for 56 students that year.

Its predominantly vocational curriculum has a strong sense of direction, and its IT and engineering courses have proved particularly popular with overseas students. A rough balance is maintained between arts, technology, business and health studies in order to preserve an all-round educational environment. The majority of students exercise their right to take "free choice modules" that cover the full range of university provision, with IT skills and languages particularly popular. Coventry has been building up its portfolio of courses, having introduced eye-catching degrees in subjects such as disaster management, forensic chemistry, criminology and boat design. The vocational slant of its courses ensures that

---

Priory Street,
Coventry CV1 5FB
024-7688 7688
info.reg@coventry.ac.uk
www.coventry.ac.uk
www.cusu.org

The Times Rankings
Overall Ranking: =76

Student satisfaction:	=53	(14.7)
Research assessment:	=90	(2.1)
Entry standards:	89	(228.8)
Student–staff ratio:	=78	(20.6)
Library/IT spend/student:	60	(£527)
Facilities spend/student:	39	(£239)
Good honours:	=64	(55.2%)
Graduate prospects:	=65	(61.4%)
Expected completion rate:	83	(79.4%)

the university always enjoys a healthy graduate employment rate.

Teaching ratings were good, with history and politics, economics, health subjects and mathematics achieving near-perfect scores, following early successes for geography and mechanical engineering. Social work was the biggest success in the first national student satisfaction survey. Research grades improved considerably in the 2001 assessment exercise, but only design, materials and politics reached any of the top three categories. Design benefits from a revolutionary £1.6-million digital modelling workshop, sponsored by the Bugatti Trust, which provides full-scale vehicle modelling facilities for undergraduates as well as researchers.

Among recent initiatives to improve the student experience have been the introduction of tangible rewards for excellent teaching and further development of electronic learning. More than 40 per cent of the undergraduates have working-class backgrounds and the projected dropout rate is better than the benchmark figure for the university, which takes account of entry qualifications and the mix of subjects. A 7 per cent increase in applications at the start of 2006 was another positive sign.

More than most universities, Coventry is a creature of its city, and the civic-minded approach of the university has created many town–gown links. The main buildings open out from the ruins of the bombed cathedral, as university and public facilities mingle in the city. Student residences are within easy walking distance of the campus and city centre. Students welcome the relatively low cost of living in Coventry, and, as at most new universities, the student body encompasses a wide range of ages.

Bursaries and Scholarships

In receipt of full Maintenance Grant	£500
In receipt of partial Maintenance Grant	£500
Progressing from outreach	Scholarship £1,000
Sport	Scholarship
Academic achievement	Scholarship £2,000

- Tuition fees (2006) £3,000
- Placement year tuition fee will be 50% of the standard fee. Foundation year fee £2,000.
- £750 bursary for those with residual income up to £10,000 higher than the qualifying amount for Maintenance Grant eligibility.
- Creative or Performing Arts, Academic, STAR, Sports, and Enterprise scholarships worth £2,000; Phoenix scholarships worth £1,000.
- Achievement Scholarships for continuing students with an average academic performance of at least 70% in previous complete stage of study, worth £1,000.
- 75% of estimated additional fee income to be earmarked for bursaries and scholarships by 2010–11.

Contact: www.coventry.ac.uk/studentfinance

Students

Undergraduates:	10,640	(4,820)
Postgraduates:	1,395	(1,605)
Mature students:	29.6%	
Overseas students:	15.7%	
Applications per place:	4.3	
From state-sector schools:	94.4%	
From working-class homes:	41.1%	

For detailed information about fees, grants and bursaries and how they work, see chapter 7.

Accommodation

Number of places and costs refer to 2005–06
University-provided places: 2,357
Percentage catered: 25.5%
Catered costs: £86 a week (10 meals).
Self-catered costs: £47.00–£79.50 a week.
First-year students are guaranteed an offer of accommodation provided conditons are met.
International students: given priority for university-owned accommodation.
Contact: accomm.ss@coventry.ac.uk
www.coventry.ac.uk/accommodation

De Montfort University

Like the 13th-century Earl of Leicester, after whom the university is named, De Montfort had a fiefdom of sorts: in this case a network of campuses in a 50-mile radius. Based on what was Leicester Polytechnic, the new university spread ever outwards, making it the biggest in the region. But DMU is now putting £50 million into consolidating a more manageable estate. The Milton Keynes outpost closed in 2003, following the transfer of campuses in Lincolnshire to Lincoln University, and the Bedford campus has now been sold to Luton University.

There will soon be only two campuses, both in Leicester, following the relocation of health and life sciences to the university's headquarters. Another 12 colleges are associates, linked into the university's network and offering its courses. A formal agreement commits the colleges, which stretch from North Oxfordshire to Grantham, to work with each other as well as with De Montfort.

The university has an uncompromisingly vocational emphasis in its courses, but has also invested in research. The approach paid off in the 2001 Research Assessment Exercise, when DMU registered the highest proportion of subjects of any new university in the top three categories. Politics and English were only one grade off the top of the seven-point scale, while the total of 11 subjects on the next grade was easily the highest among the former polytechnics.

Teaching ratings improved after a patchy start, with politics and international studies achieving full marks and the sport and leisure courses only one mark short of the maximum. The professional accounting courses were awarded "premier" status in a worldwide accreditation scheme and the university has been chosen to house a national teaching centre for drama, dance and theatre studies. English, history and archaeology achieved the best scores in the national student satisfaction survey.

De Montfort's range of programmes has been expanding and student enrolments are healthy. Among the new degrees is a BSc in Public and Community health, which will tackle issues such increases in sexually-transmitted diseases and obesity. The drop-out rate improved considerably in the last set of statistics: at 16 per cent, it was no higher than the national average for the university's courses and entry grades. The university is abandoning semesters and going back to a three-term year, partly because it believes the prospect of imminent assessment encouraged some students to give up at Christmas in their first year. De Montfort

---

The Gateway,
Leicester LE1 9BH
0645 454647 (Enquiry Centre)
enquiry@dmu.ac.uk
www.dmu.ac.uk
www.mydsu.com

The Times Rankings
Overall Ranking: =99

Student satisfaction:	=71	(14.4)
Research assessment:	60	(3.1)
Entry standards:	81	(237.7)
Student–staff ratio:	=81	(20.7)
Library/IT spend/student:	73	(£489)
Facilities spend/student:	=99	(£123)
Good honours:	109	(38.5%)
Graduate prospects:	67	(61.0%)
Expected completion rate:	80	(80%)

has a proud record for widening access to higher education with 42 per cent of students coming from working-class homes. It was one of the first to set up an employment agency to help students find part-time work during their course of study, as well as find careers upon graduation. Strong links with local business and industry manifest themselves in courses such as the BSc in media production, produced in conjunction with the BBC, and in the provision of facilities such as a new telematics laboratory sponsored by Orange, the mobile telephone company.

Over £100 million is being spent on the main campus area in Leicester, some of it by the city council and local businesses. The investment includes a £9-million campus centre, which opened in September 2003, incorporating a new students' union, music venue and other facilities. Part of the ring road is being diverted to allow the university to open up the 15th-century Magazine Gateway building, which will become the focal point of a university quarter with public open spaces and new links to the city centre.

Accommodation difficulties have been addressed, with five new halls of residence opening in 2003. All first years, apart from locals, are now guaranteed a residential place.

Bursaries and Scholarships

In receipt of full Maintenance Grant	£300
In receipt of partial Maintenance Grant	£500
Living in region	Scholarship
Progressing from outreach	Scholarship £1,000
Sport	Scholarship £1,000
Academic achievement	Scholarship £1,000

- Tuition fees (2006)   £3,000
- £1,000 Access scholarships for those in designated schools and colleges who are first generation university entrants with 280 UCAS Tariff points.
- £1,000 Academic Scholarship for students with at least 280 UCAS points.
- £1,000 Sports Scholarship.
- £1,000 Opportunities Scholarship for students entering DMU with an Access qualification. Details to be finalised.
- 23% of additional fee income to be earmarked for bursaries and scholarships.
- Eligibility for bursaries to be assessed using UUK/SLC model bursary scheme (HEBSS).
- Bursary for students receiving partial MG may be higher than the bursary for students receiving full MG to assist the many students not qualifying for full MG but still perceived as being in great need of financial assistance.
- Payment will be made in instalments.

Contact: www.dmu.ac.uk/funding

Students

Undergraduates:	14,305	(4,405)
Postgraduates:	1,040	(3,190)
Mature students:	20.0%	
Overseas students:	5.6%	
Applications per place:	4.7	
From state-sector schools:	95.9%	
From working-class homes:	40.5%	

For detailed information about fees, grants and bursaries and how they work, see chapter 7.

Accommodation

Number of places and costs refer to 2006–07
University-provided places: 2,801
Percentage catered: 0%
Self-catered costs: £61.00–£83.00 a week.
First years are guaranteed accommodation.
Residential and age restrictions apply.
International students: guaranteed accommodation.
Contact: studenthousing@dmu.ac.uk

University of Derby

Derby sees itself as a prototype for the modern university, providing courses at all levels from the age of 16 into retirement. Although not as extensive as the original plans for spanning further and higher education in the same institution, a merger with High Peak College and the subsequent creation of the University of Derby College Buxton have stayed true to the model. While accepting that Derby will never scale the heights in league tables such as ours, the university set itself the target of becoming the pre-eminent university of its type by 2020. Its yardsticks are student satisfaction, employability and cost-effectiveness.

As the only higher education college promoted to university status with the polytechnics, Derby had to run to keep up with its peers in its early days. Student numbers doubled in four years, the residential stock increased fivefold and extra teaching space was built. The pace of expansion inevitably imposed strains, and at one time Derby was the only university with two Unsatisfactory verdicts in the teaching assessments. Although still not spectacular, scores improved subsequently. Indeed, a failure in pharmacy turned into maximum points on re-inspection after provision was rationalised. Business and theology also scored well, as did biosciences and other health subjects before them.

The university takes pride in its record for widening access: almost all the undergraduates are state-educated and four in ten are from working-class homes. The 20 per cent projected dropout rate is lower than in previous years and slightly better than the national average for the subjects and entry qualifications found at Derby.

Development is still continuing, with an £8-million art and design campus due to open in 2007, bringing together courses presently spread around three different sites. The college already has a new home in the centre of Buxton, where the purchase of the Devonshire Royal Hospital for a nominal fee has provided an ideal centre for courses in tourism and hospitality management, as well as further education programmes. The landmark building, which has a bigger dome than St Paul's Cathedral, will house a 4-star training hotel and health spa, in addition to academic facilities.

There are three main sites in and around Derby. The Kedleston Road campus, two miles north of the city centre, is the largest, catering for most of the main subjects as well as the students' union headquarters and multi-faith centre. The Mickleover campus, which specialises in education and health, is also in a

---

Kedleston Road,
Derby DE22 1GB
01332 622289
admissions@derby.ac.uk
www.derby.ac.uk
www.udsu-online.co.uk

Edinburgh
Belfast
DERBY
London
Cardiff

The Times Rankings
Overall Ranking: 105

Student satisfaction:	=71	(14.4)
Research assessment:	=103	(1.5)
Entry standards:	95	(218.3)
Student–staff ratio:	=94	(22.5)
Library/IT spend/student:	48	(£585)
Facilities spend/student:	92	(£137)
Good honours:	98	(47.0%)
Graduate prospects:	91	(55.6%)
Expected completion rate:	100	(72.5%)

suburban location, while art and design have had smaller, more central sites.

Courses are modular and a foundation programme allows students to begin work at a partner college before transferring to the university. Distance learning is a growth area either online or through Derby's nine regional centres. Prospective students can even sample a virtual open evening. Business and management is by far the biggest academic area, but work placements are encouraged in all subjects. The accent on employability continues with an eight-week course on key skills such as CV preparation and interview technique. Derby has also been in the forefront of the adoption of new teaching methods, pioneering the use of interactive video for a national scheme. A variety of courses, from foundation degrees to postgraduate qualifications, are available online.

The university has spent £30 million in five years to maintain its guarantee of accommodation for all first years. Students seem to appreciate the university's efforts because Derby comes out well in its own satisfaction surveys, if not particularly in the national equivalent. There was a 6 per cent increase in applications at the start of 2005, but a 14 per cent decline the following year continued a trend from earlier in the decade.

Bursaries and Scholarships[†]

In receipt of full Maintenance Grant	£800
In receipt of partial Maintenance Grant	
	£200–£600

- Tuition fees (2006) £3,000
- Placement year tuition fee will be £1,500 but no bursary will be available for that year.
- 28% of additional fee income to be earmarked for bursaries.
- Payment will be made in instalments.
- Additional support to be announced.

Contact: www.derby.ac.uk/
   C1_fees.asp?MenuID=1&ContentID=1

[†] Information taken from 2006 Access Agreement

Students

Undergraduates:	8,595	(2,675)
Postgraduates:	650	(1,915)
Mature students:	28.2%	
Overseas students:	5.5%	
Applications per place:	5.3	
From state-sector schools:	97.0%	
From working-class homes:	40.6%	

For detailed information about fees, grants and bursaries and how they work, see chapter 7.

Accommodation

Number of places and costs refer to 2006–07
University-provided places: 2,500
Percentage catered: 0%
Self-catered costs: £38.99–£74.97.
First-year students are guaranteed accommodation.
Policy for international students: as above.
Contact: www.derby.ac.uk/residential/
Derby Student Residences Limited –
www.dsrl.co.uk/index.php?node=550

University of Dundee

Dundee describes itself as "Scotland's most enterprising university" and, while there would be other claimants to that title, it has certainly been among the liveliest in recent years. A long series of good quality ratings and the acquisition of education, nursing and art colleges, which doubled its size and greatly increased its scope, have been complemented by high-profile research successes, especially in medicine and the life sciences. The message appears to be getting through to prospective students: applications have shot up by 88 per cent in the five years that Sir Alan Langlands has been Principal.

The university now has more than 18,000 students, including a healthy number from overseas, and is looking outwards to achieve the "critical mass" which experts regard as essential to break into the higher education elite. Dundee has been appointing professors at the rate of one a month for the last three years and has embarked on a £200-million campus redevelopment designed by the leading architect Sir Terry Farrell. Almost £40 million of this is being spent on wireless-networked student residences.

Best-known for the life sciences, where research into cancer and diabetes is recognised as world-class, the university has already opened new buildings for interdisciplinary research, applied computing and clinical research. The main library is being extended and the Faculty of Education and Social Work will have new premises in 2007.

Set in 20 acres of parkland, the medical school is the one of the few components of the university outside the compact city-centre campus – some of the nursing and midwifery students are 35 miles away in Kirkcaldy, while education and social work are waiting to move from the former Northern College campus, two miles outside the centre.

Biochemistry is the flagship department, moving into the £13-million Wellcome Trust Building in 1997. Its academics were the first in Britain to be invited to take part in Japan's Human Frontier science programme and are now the most-quoted researchers in their field. Medicine and the biological sciences won Dundee's other 5* research ratings, while six more subjects were on the next rung of the research assessment ladder, leaving half of the university's researchers in departments rated in the top two categories.

Teaching ratings were almost uniformly impressive, with only philosophy judged less than Highly Satisfactory. Vocational degrees predominate, helping to produce the

Nethergate,
Dundee DD1 4HN
01382 344160
srs@dundee.ac.uk
www.dundee.ac.uk
www.dusa.dundee.ac.uk

The Times Rankings
Overall Ranking: 44

Student satisfaction:	–	(–)
Research assessment:	=34	(5.1)
Entry standards:	38	(340.0)
Student–staff ratio:	=22	(15.7)
Library/IT spend/student:	=67	(£503)
Facilities spend/student:	=69	(£179)
Good honours:	=39	(61.7%)
Graduate prospects:	20	(71.9%)
Expected completion rate:	58	(83.1%)

university's consistently good graduate employment record. The university sends more graduates into the professions than any other institution in Scotland and only Oxbridge graduates came out ahead of Dundee's in a national survey of starting salaries. All degrees include a career planning module and an internship option, and students are now provided with their own personal development website. Among the new courses introduced recently are forensic anthropology, sports biomedicine and innovative product design. The highly-rated design courses are taught at the former Duncan of Jordanstone College of Art.

There has been an emphasis on opportunities for women ever since Dundee's separation from St Andrews University in 1967, and the addition of teacher training has increased the female majority. Two thirds of Dundee's students are from Scotland and nearly one in ten from Northern Ireland. One in five come from areas with little tradition of higher education and almost a quarter are from working-class homes. They enjoy a welcoming atmosphere and a cost of living which is lower than in most university cities. Private accommodation is plentiful for those who are not housed by the university. New students even have their own website. The city is profiting from recent regeneration programmes and becoming more fashionable. Spectacular mountain and coastal scenery are close at hand, but social life tends to be concentrated on the students' union, which is one of the largest and most active in Scotland.

Bursaries and Scholarships

- Scottish domiciled students: no fees will be payable by eligible students although a "graduate endowment" will be payable after graduation: the 2005–06 level was £2,216.
- Non-Scottish domiciled students fees: £1,700 a year (£2,700 for medicine).
- Fees for placement year and year abroad are normally 50% of full-time fee.
- Chancellor's Scholarships worth £1,000 a year to UK students who enter at Level 2. Scholarship holders will normally receive a maximum of £3,000 over 3 years.
- Subject scholarships and bursaries available in many subjects.

Contact: www.dundee.ac.uk/prospectus/ undergrad/general/bursaries.htm

Students		
Undergraduates:	8,910	(3,975)
Postgraduates:	1,035	(3,470)
Mature students:	20.9%	
Overseas students:	13.6%	
Applications per place:	6.5	
From state-sector schools:	92.5%	
From working-class homes:	25.0%	

For detailed information about fees, grants and bursaries and how they work, see chapter 7.

Accommodation
Number of places and costs refer to 2006–07
University-provided places: 1,807
Percentage catered: 0%
Self-catered costs: £63.35–£98.84 a week.
Entrant students guaranteed accommodation if conditions are met.
International students: guaranteed accommodation if conditions are met.
Contact: residences@dundee.ac.uk
www.studentvillage.dundee.ac.uk

University of Durham

Long established as a leading alternative to Oxford and Cambridge, Durham even delays selection to accommodate those applying to the ancient universities. A collegiate structure and picturesque setting add to the Oxbridge feel, attracting a largely middle-class student body. However, although a third of undergraduates come from independent schools, the university is attracting more applicants from non-traditional backgrounds. Those who receive offers without interview are invited to a special open day to see if Durham is the university for them. Since around 80 per cent come from outside the North East of England, most are seeing the small cathedral city for the first time. The proportion of regional students is much higher at the Stockton campus.

Applications are made to one of the 15 colleges, all of which are mixed since the decision of St Mary's to abandon its women-only tradition from 2004. The newest, Josephine Butler College – a self-catering college with around 400 bedrooms – will accept its first intake of students in 2006. Colleges range in size from 300 to 900 students and are the focal point of social life, although all teaching is done in central departments. There are significant differences in atmosphere and student profile, ranging from the historic University College, in Durham Castle, to modern buildings on the outskirts of the city.

Winning a place is far from easy – entrance requirements are among the highest in Britain – but the dropout rate of less than 4 per cent is also among the lowest in any university. Six subjects (chemistry, applied mathematics, geography, law, English and history) reached the pinnacle of the last research assessment exercise, and 14 others were considered nationally outstanding. Most of the teaching ratings also produced high scores. Biological sciences, physics and chemistry are particularly strong on the science side; history, philosophy, economics and theology among the stars of the arts. A £3-million grant to establish a centre for fundamental physics should place Durham at the forefront of world research on the structure of the universe.

Durham is generally quite traditional. Wherever possible, teaching takes place in small groups and most assessment is by written examination. However, the establishment of the Queen's Campus, in Stockton-on-Tees, broke the mould of tradition. Initially a joint venture with Teesside University, Stockton is now Durham's own venture into community education. Entry standards are 288 points at A level, compared with an average of 329

University Office,
Old Elvet, Durham DH1 3HP
0191-374 2000
admissions.office@
durham.ac.uk
www.durham.ac.uk
www.dsu.org.uk

The Times Rankings
Overall Ranking: 10

Student satisfaction:	=12	(15.4)
Research assessment:	=10	(5.7)
Entry standards:	5	(454.9)
Student–staff ratio:	=87	(21.2)
Library/IT spend/student:	19	(£747)
Facilities spend/student:	17	(£326)
Good honours:	11	(74.6%)
Graduate prospects:	18	(72.4%)
Expected completion rate:	=10	(95.1%)

for the main university, and subjects such as business, primary education and psychology have helped broaden the university's intake.

The Stockton campus has also seen the fulfilment of Durham's long-held ambition to restore the medical education it lost when Newcastle University went its own way more than 35 years ago. In another joint project, this time with Newcastle, 95 students will do the first two years of their training on Teesside, concentrating on community medicine before transferring to Newcastle to complete their training. Medicine has added to the 200-plus undergraduate study programmes. Undergraduates are also offered a variety of generalist "free elective" modules, such as environmental economics and personal language learning. The aim is to make Durham graduates even more employable.

The university dominates the city of Durham to an extent which sometimes causes resentment, but adds considerably to the local economy. For those looking for nightlife, or just a change of scene, Newcastle is a short train journey away. Sports facilities are excellent, and Durham is among the premier universities in national competitions. It came fifth in the national student championships in 2005 and won the rowing title for the second year in a row. Among the alumni are the former England cricket captain, Nasser Hussain, Ashes hero Andrew Strauss and rugby World Cup winner, Will Greenwood. The university runs Centres of Excellence in cricket and fencing, and has plans to build on its existing strengths in rowing, rugby and hockey.

Bursaries and Scholarships

In receipt of full Maintenance Grant £3,090
In receipt of partial Maintenance Grant
£600–£1,545

- Tuition fees (2006) £3,000
- Placement year tuition fee will be £1,500. Fees for Foundation year will be £1,200.
- Durham Grant Scheme worth up to £12,000 in non-repayable support over and above any statutory support from the government, available to UK domiciled, home, full-time undergraduates and PGCE students. Means testing carried out by Local Education Authorities. All eligible students will receive support.
- 30% of additional fee income to be earmarked for Durham Grant Scheme.

Contact:
www.durham.ac.uk/studying/student-finance

Students

Undergraduates:	10,950	(360)
Postgraduates:	2,405	(2,470)
Mature students:	6.3%	
Overseas students:	5.3%	
Applications per place:	7.4	
From state-sector schools:	63.8%	
From working-class homes:	15.8%	

For detailed information about fees, grants and bursaries and how they work, see chapter 7.

Accommodation

Number of places and costs refer to 2006–07
University-provided places: 6,373
Percentage catered: 70%
Catered costs: £3,945 (3 terms, Durham)
Self-catered costs: £2,823 (3 terms, Stockton).
All full-time students become a member of one of the university's colleges or societies.
International students: all first years and final years are offered accommodation.
Contact: admissions@durham.ac.uk

University of East Anglia

Best known for its star-studded creative writing course and extensive art collections, UEA was one of the big winners in the first national student satisfaction survey, finishing in the top four universities. Psychology, law and the creative arts produced outstanding results, but most subjects showed high levels of satisfaction. Students appear to like the scale of this relatively small campus university, as well as the quality of its courses, although the message is yet to get through to sixth-formers. Applications were down by 9 per cent in 2006.

The university is engaged in an ambitious building programme, which has allowed its residential stock to keep pace with the expansion in student numbers and has added extensive new sports facilities. Other recent developments on the 320-acre site on the outskirts of Norwich have included 560 more en suite student bedrooms, a new health centre, the extension and refurbishment of the central library, catering facilities and students' union, as well as research and teaching facilities. The work has allowed the expansion of specialist provision for students with disabilities and other learning and health difficulties. Health studies have been among UEA's fastest-developing areas. The university was awarded one of the first new medical schools for 20 years, and has since added pharmacy and speech and language therapy degree courses.

Some of the broad subject combinations that the university pioneered from its origins in the 1960s are still highly regarded in the academic world. Development studies and environmental sciences are two such areas. With successive 5* ratings for research and an excellent teaching grade, environmental sciences is the flagship school. The Climatic Research Unit is among the leaders in the investigation of global warming, and UEA also hosts the Government-funded Tyndall Centre for Climate Change Research, which brings together scientists, economists, social scientists and engineers in nine institutions. History and film studies added to the 5* research grades in 2001.

Philosophy and politics joined American studies as the top performers in the teaching assessments. Like the English degrees, one of which includes creative writing, American studies is heavily oversubscribed. With authors Michele Roberts and Patricia Duncker taking up where Andrew Motion, the Poet Laureate, and the late Malcolm Bradbury left off, the attraction of creative writing for both undergraduates and postgraduates remains undimmed. Art history is another

---

University Plain
Norwich NR4 7TJ
01603 592216
admissions@uea.ac.uk
www.uea.ac.uk
www.stu.uea.ac.uk

Edinburgh
Belfast
NORWICH•
London
Cardiff

The Times Rankings
Overall Ranking: 23

Student satisfaction:	=4	(15.6)
Research assessment:	=22	(5.4)
Entry standards:	26	(365.3)
Student–staff ratio:	=38	(17.0)
Library/IT spend/student:	44	(£604)
Facilities spend/student:	13	(£353)
Good honours:	28	(66.9%)
Graduate prospects:	76	(58.8%)
Expected completion rate:	=41	(86.7%)

strong subject, aided by the presence of the Sainsbury Centre for the Visual Arts, perhaps the greatest resource of its type on any British campus. The centre, which has been refurbished and extended, houses a priceless collection of modern and tribal art, in a building designed by Lord (Norman) Foster.

Almost nine out of ten undergraduates come from state schools or colleges, but only just over one in five has a working-class background. Since 1999, most have had the opportunity of work experience as part of their course. An academic adviser guides students on their options under the modular course system and monitors their progress right through to graduation.

Projected dropout rates have fluctuated in recent years. Almost 13 per cent of students who started courses in 2002 are expected to leave without the qualification they originally sought. Most UEA students come from outside the region, although there is an unusually large contingent of mature students for a traditional university, who tend to be more local. The university also runs a programme of over 200 evening and day courses across Norfolk and Suffolk.

The number of university-owned beds has increased considerably, ensuring that most first years can still be guaranteed accommodation. Sporting facilities are excellent: a £17.5-million sports park, with an Olympic-size swimming pool and climbing wall, opened in 2000, and the university was chosen as the base for the English Institute of Sport in the East, developing a sports science network for the region.

The university is situated in parkland, formerly a golf course, with easy access to the medieval city of Norwich, which can boast a pub for every day of the year. Rail links to London are improving, while Norwich airport offers flights through Amsterdam to worldwide connections.

Bursaries and Scholarships

In receipt of full Maintenance Grant	£540
In receipt of partial Maintenance Grant	
	£108–£432

- Tuition fees (2006) £3,000
- Placement year and year abroad tuition fee will be 50% of the standard, non-variable tuition fee – around £600.
- Scholarships of between £500 and £4,000 for students achieving the highest grades. Scholarships available for high achieving EU students.
- 16% of additional fee income to be earmarked for bursaries.
- Eligibility for bursaries to be assessed using UUK/SLC model bursary scheme (HEBSS).

Contact: www.uea.ac.uk/admissions/finance

Students

Undergraduates:	7,400	(4,300)
Postgraduates:	2,170	(1,385)
Mature students:	18.6%	
Overseas students:	10.5%	
Applications per place:	5.5	
From state-sector schools:	88.0%	
From working-class homes:	21.4%	

For detailed information about fees, grants and bursaries and how they work, see chapter 7.

Accommodation

Number of places and costs refer to 2006–07
University-provided places: 3,400
Percentage catered: 0%
Self-catered costs: £53.48–£87.01 a week.
First years guaranteed accommodation provided conditions are met. Residential restrictions.
International students; overseas for fees students are guaranteed accommodation if conditions are met.
Contact: accom@uea.ac.uk
www.uea.ac.uk/accom

University of East London

East London's £40-million Docklands campus, which opened in 1999, offered a new lease of life to a university which had struggled to recapture the sparkle it had as a pioneering polytechnic. The last phase is due to open in September 2006, with student residences and recreational facilities side by side with academic buildings in a prize-winning waterside development for more than 7,000 students. The campus helped attract big increases in applications to UEL in the two years before top-up fees and the university bucked the national trend with another 7 per cent rise in 2006.

The capital's first new campus for 50 years, which borders on London City Airport, has given the university a new focal point, with its modern version of traditional university features like cloisters and squares. Students of fashion, fine art, graphic design, product design, media and cultural studies were first into the futuristic premises near the Thames, which also houses a technology centre promoting links with local business and industry. UEL's highly-rated School of Architecture and the Visual Arts moved to the site in 2004 and were joined by electrical and manufacturing engineering in 2005.

The university's original campus in Stratford is also being redeveloped, with a new Learning Resource Centre, student residences and facilities for part-time and evening courses. The London Foot Hospital, housing the university's podiatric students, was due to open in 2006, with student residences and a computer centre next on the development plan. The Barking campus closed in 2005, replaced by a lifelong learning centre run in partnership with the neighbouring further education college and local council.

With research in media studies judged to be nationally outstanding and sociology and art and design on the next grade, UEL was among the leading new universities in the last research assessments. However, teaching assessments were patchy, despite a requirement for all new lecturers to take a teaching qualification if they do not already have one. Psychology, English and architecture did well, but communication and media studies and electrical and electronic engineering both registered unusually low scores. Electrical and electronic engineering did better in a more recent assessment, when environmental sciences and law were also highly rated. Teacher training courses, too, were given good marks by the Office for Standards in Education.

UEL's mission is more concerned with extending access to higher education than competing with the elite universities. Barely more than half of the new first year

Romford Road,
London E15 4LZ
020-8223 2835
admiss@uel.ac.uk
www.uel.ac.uk
www.uelsu.net

The Times Rankings
Overall Ranking: 93

Student satisfaction:	–	(–)
Research assessment:	=76	(2.5)
Entry standards:	107	(191.7)
Student–staff ratio:	86	(21.0)
Library/IT spend/student:	36	(£614)
Facilities spend/student:	1	(£487)
Good honours:	108	(39.6%)
Graduate prospects:	=88	(55.8%)
Expected completion rate:	107	(67.0%)

intake now arrive with A levels and a majority are over 21 on entry – many choosing to start courses in February, as 800 students did in 2005. Most degrees are vocational and employers are closely involved in course planning. The university has pioneered a work-based learning initiative, offering accredited placements with local employers.

More than four out of ten UEL students come from working-class homes, many from the area's large ethnic minority population. A successful mentoring scheme for black and Asian students has become a model for other institutions. A Widening Participation Unit provides advice and guidance sessions for people considering returning to education. The university is also strong on provision for disabled students, who can share their experiences with others worldwide through the new Rix Centre for Innovation and Learning Disability. The projected dropout rate has been improving, but still more than a quarter of those who began degrees in 2002 were not expected to complete the course they started. Graduate employment rates have also been relatively poor, but the university is working to improve both retention and employability through its innovative Skillzone programme.

University-owned accommodation is still not plentiful for the number of students, despite new building, but it represents good value for London. Because many choose to live at home, all first years who request accommodation are housed. The social mix means that UEL has not been the place to look for the archetypal partying student lifestyle, although the new campus is beginning to change this. A new students' union facility, housed in a restored Victorian building, opened in 2003. There are some sports facilities on both campuses.

Bursaries and Scholarships[†]

In receipt of full Maintenance Grant	£300
Sport	Scholarship £1,000
Academic achievement	Scholarship £1,000

- Tuition fees (2006) £3,000
- Bursary also available to all EU students.
- 200 Achievement Scholarships a year for academic, sporting and performance arts achievement.
- 50 Refugee Scholarships to cover the difference between home and overseas fees.
- In kind benefits include books, equipment, fees for field trips (package valued at £750 over three years).

Contact: www.uel.ac.uk/students/being_student/money.htm

[†] Information taken from 2006 Access Agreement

Students

Undergraduates:	7,930	(2,915)
Postgraduates:	1,570	(2,760)
Mature students:	54.5%	
Overseas students:	16.4%	
Applications per place:	4.3	
From state-sector schools:	96.5%	
From working-class homes:	41.7%	

For detailed information about fees, grants and bursaries and how they work, see chapter 7.

Accommodation

Number of places and costs refer to 2006–07
University-provided places: 1,500
Percentage catered: 0%
Self-catered costs: £75–£88 a week (39 weeks)
First years are guaranteed accommodation if conditions are met.
International students: as above.
Docklands Campus 020-8223 5093/4
Barking Halls of Residence 020-8223 2409/2909
dlres@uel.ac.uk

University of Edinburgh

Edinburgh retains a special status in Scotland, where the university is regarded as the nearest thing to Oxbridge north of the border. The university dropped out of our top ten for the first time in 2004, but soon regained its previous position, overtaking St Andrews to become the top university in Scotland.

Like Oxbridge, Edinburgh has been trying to widen its intake, especially since the arrival of Professor Tim O'Shea as Principal, the first non-Scot to hold the office in modern times. More than £1 million is going into access bursaries of £1,000 a year, with hopes of increasing the number beyond the initial 100 awards. Other measures include an eight-week summer school for teenagers from local area schools and a mentoring programme. The university has always attracted a high proportion of middle-class candidates – many from England – and is a favourite in independent schools, whose students take about a third of the places. New selection guidelines aim to look more broadly at candidates' potential, reducing minimum entry requirements and placing more weight on references and personal statements. The measures appeared to have an instant impact, with big increases in applications in 2004 and 2005, followed by another 9 per cent rise in 2006, when

several Scottish universities experienced a decline. There are plans for a 40 per cent increase in overseas students, who already number more than 2,000, testifying to Edinburgh's worldwide reputation.

The university raised a £40-million investment bond to ensure long-term financial stability, and carried out limited restructuring, abandoning some subjects and cutting staff, but making investment in new buildings and extra posts in selected areas. First to go were degree courses in agriculture, which transferred to Aberdeen. The university has also stepped up its fundraising activities, which have already produced a new Medical Research Centre. A second review was launched early in 2005.

The incorporation of Moray House, whose Holyrood site houses education, made Edinburgh the largest university in Scotland, now with more than 21,000 students. Yet, despite the new approach to selection, entry standards remain high, whether in A levels or Highers. The university's buildings are scattered around the city, but most border the historic Old Town. The science and engineering campus is two miles to the south.

The last research assessments showed a big improvement on a disappointing outcome in 1996, when only two subjects reached the top grade. This time, nine were awarded the coveted 5* and another

---

Old College, South Bridge,
Edinburgh EH8 9YL
0131-650 4360
rals.enquiries@ed.ac.uk
www.ed.ac.uk
www.eusa.ed.ac.uk

The Times Rankings
Overall Ranking: 11

Student satisfaction:	–	(–)
Research assessment:	=16	(5.6)
Entry standards:	10	(414.8)
Student–staff ratio:	=14	(14.2)
Library/IT spend/student:	10	(£890)
Facilities spend/student:	44	(£233)
Good honours:	5	(77.7%)
Graduate prospects:	=23	(70.7%)
Expected completion rate:	25	(91.9%)

19 achieved grade 5, accounting for three quarters of those entered for the exercise. The 15 subjects rated as Excellent for teaching already amounted to the biggest haul in Scotland. Despite having to settle for Highly Satisfactory in its teaching assessment, medicine is a traditional strength and the law faculty is the largest north of the border. The university enjoys a reputation for high quality across the board.

Departments organise visiting days in October for those thinking of applying and in the spring for those holding offers. There is also an annual open day in June. New students join one of three Colleges, which are divided into 21 Schools, and generally take three subjects in both their first and second years. Every student has a Director of Studies to help them narrow down the selection of a final degree and give personal advice when necessary.

Considerable sums have been spent making the university more accessible to the 1,200 disabled students, who can also call on the services of a disability office. All students are issued with a smart card for access to university facilities, which can be loaded with money to pay for a variety of goods and services. The students' union operates on several sites and sports facilities are excellent.

The city is a treasure-trove of cultural and recreational opportunities, even away from the Festival period. Most students thrive on Edinburgh life, even though the cost of living can make it difficult to do it justice. Some scientists complain of isolation, although there is a regular bus link with George Square. The plentiful stock of residential accommodation was increased in 2003 with the addition of 526 rooms, which are not only en suite, but come with their own television.

Bursaries and Scholarships

- Scottish domiciled students: no fees will be payable by eligible students although a "graduate endowment" will be payable after graduation: the 2005–06 level was £2,216.
- Non-Scottish domiciled students fees: £1,700 a year (£2,700 for medicine).
- Fees for placement year and year abroad are normally 50% of full-time fee.
- Over 125 Entrance Bursaries of between £1,000–£2,500 for students from schools or colleges in the UK whose financial or personal circumstances might prevent them from entering higher education.
- Industrial Scholarships within the Schools of Engineering & Electronics, Informatics and Chemistry of £1,000. Opportunities to undertake a paid work placement over the summer months are also available.

Contact: www.scholarships.ed.ac.uk
www.scholarships.ed.ac.uk/bursaries

Students		
Undergraduates:	15,745	(1,040)
Postgraduates:	3,685	(2,540)
Mature students:	12.1%	
Overseas students:	11.8%	
Applications per place:	9.0	
From state-sector schools:	65.3%	
From working-class homes:	15.3%	

For detailed information about fees, grants and bursaries and how they work, see chapter 7.

Accommodation

Number of places and costs refer to 2006–07
University-provided places: about 5,800
Percentage catered: about 32%
Catered costs: £125–£150 a week
Self-catered costs: £80–£94 a week.
First years are guaranteed an offer of accommodation providing conditions are met. Residential restrictions apply.
International students: accommodation guaranteed if conditions are met.
Contact: www.accom.ed.ac.uk

University of Essex

Essex has long since moved out of the shadow of its radical past, acquiring a reputation for high-quality research, especially in the social sciences. It did well in the last research assessments and was in the top 10 in our last league table for teaching. There were some good results, too, in the first national student satisfaction survey – notably in languages and history – although Essex did not do quite as well as some universities of similar size. There are still fewer than 9,000 students, a quarter of whom are postgraduates.

Law was top-rated in the early teaching quality assessments and sociology is among the leading departments in Britain, attracting a series of prestigious research projects as well as a high score for teaching. Both sociology and government achieved their second successive 5* grades in the latest research assessments, with economics joining them on the top grade. With eight subjects on grade 5, three quarters of the researchers are in departments where most work is judged to be of international quality.

The sciences have been growing in strength, and the biological sciences department is one of the university's largest. Electronic engineering recorded a perfect score for teaching quality to add to an improved research rating, and bio-sciences almost repeated the feat. Computer science is also strong and a BSc in computer games and internet technology shows Essex keeping pace with changing demands in graduate employment. The last four teaching assessments – for sports science, economics, philosophy and politics – all produced full marks.

But improvements in the university's academic performance could not disguise the fact that the glass and concrete campus, set in 200 acres of parkland on the outskirts of Colchester, was showing distinct signs of a quarter of a century's wear and tear. The university has been carrying out a programme of refurbishment at the same time as expanding student facilities. Teaching and administration blocks, which cluster around a network of squares, are gradually being transformed and extra catering and residential facilities added.

The University Quays development added a further 750 en suite bedrooms in 2004. All accommodation is now networked to the university IT system. The library has been extended to provide 1,100 reader spaces and is open for over 84 hours a week. A new Networks Centre for computer science and electronic systems engineering features a powered floor system for robotics and an iDorm laboratory. A £4.3-million building

---

Wivenhoe Park, Colchester,
Essex CO4 3SQ
01206 873666
admit@essex.ac.uk
www.essex.ac.uk
www.essexstudent.com

Edinburgh
Belfast
COLCHESTER
Cardiff
London

The Times Rankings
Overall Ranking: 30

Student satisfaction:	=24	(15.2)
Research assessment:	=16	(5.6)
Entry standards:	46	(308.7)
Student–staff ratio:	18	(14.6)
Library/IT spend/student:	=31	(£643)
Facilities spend/student:	21	(£307)
Good honours:	63	(55.4%)
Graduate prospects:	=56	(62.8%)
Expected completion rate:	48	(85.7%)

containing a 1,000-seat lecture theatre which can be divided into smaller units, or used for exhibitions and conferences is also opening soon.

The incorporation of the East 15 acting school, in Loughton, has enhanced the university's provision in theatre studies, and was the university's first venture beyond Colchester. However, a £75-million campus offering courses in business, health, education and the arts is now being developed in partnership with South East Essex College. And Essex is collaborating with the University of East Anglia on plans for a campus in Ipswich. Students also take the university's degrees at Writtle College in Chelmsford.

Essex champions academic breadth, and in each of the four schools of study, undergraduates follow a common first year before specialising. They may take four or five different subjects before committing themselves to a particular degree. Essex's student population is also unusually diverse for a traditional university, with high proportions of mature and overseas students. More than a quarter of the undergraduates are from working-class homes and 95 per cent went to state schools or colleges – a significantly higher proportion than the subject mix would suggest.

Social and sporting facilities are good, the more so following an extension of the Sports Centre and the refurbishment of the student union bars. There are now four bars, a nightclub and numerous cafés on campus. Some 40 acres of land are devoted to sports facilities, used extensively by individual students and over 40 university sports clubs. The campus can be bleak in winter, but there is a strong community atmosphere.

Bursaries and Scholarships

In receipt of full Maintenance Grant	£300–£400
In receipt of partial Maintenance Grant	
	Up to £1,500
Shortage subjects	Scholarship
Sport	Scholarship

- Tuition fees (2006) £3,000
- Placement year and year abroad tuition fee will be £1,500.
- Different criteria for the Essex Bursary (Colchester and Loughton campuses) and the Southend Bursary (Southend campus).
- For students in receipt of partial MG the Essex Bursary is intended to bridge the gap between the MG and the tuition fee with a bursary.
- Maths scholarship.
- Foundation year tuition fee will be £1,200.
- 25% of additional fee income to be earmarked for bursaries.

Contact:

www.essex.ac.uk/newfundingarrangements

Students

Undergraduates:	5,930	(1,680)
Postgraduates:	1,875	(1,030)
Mature students:	14.9%	
Overseas students:	22.7%	
Applications per place:	6.2	
From state-sector schools:	94.5%	
From working-class homes:	28.1%	

For detailed information about fees, grants and bursaries and how they work, see chapter 7.

Accommodation

Number of places and costs refer to 2005–06
University-provided places: 3,996
Percentage catered: 0%
Self-catered costs: £52.50–£78.68 a week.
New undergraduates are guaranteed accommodation if conditions are met.
International students: new students are guaranteed accommodation if conditions are met; priority given to students in 2nd and 3rd year.
Contact: admit@essex.ac.uk

University of Exeter

Exeter is one of Britain's most popular universities in terms of first-choice applications, not only in its traditional strong suit, the arts, but increasingly in the sciences and social sciences. Almost 30 per cent of the undergraduates come from independent schools – a much higher proportion than the national average for the subjects Exeter offers, although the proportion dropped significantly in the last statistics. Professor Steve Smith, the Vice-Chancellor, has put broadening the social mix at the top of his agenda, particularly targeting schools and colleges in the rural South West.

Location is partly responsible for the relatively rarified social mix. There is no large industrialised centre of population to draw on and, however lively, cathedral cities in the South West are not what every teenager is looking for. Applications were down by 10 per cent at the start of 2006. However, the academic reputation is strong and there have been exciting developments recently. Chief among them was the opening of the £65-million Tremough campus at Penryn, in Cornwall. A distinctive range of new degrees in English, geography, conservation biology and environmental fields has begun to tempt students further west, as well as catering for Cornish demand. The

Camborne School of Mines, now a department of the university, is also based there, as is the Combined Universities in Cornwall (in which Exeter's partners are Falmouth College of Arts, Plymouth University and further education colleges in the county).

The other big development was the opening of Peninsula Medical School, in association with Plymouth University, in 2002. Recruitment has been strong and Peninsula was the only successful bidder for a new dental school in 2006.

Exeter was the subject of national controversy after deciding to close the chemistry and music departments as part of a rationalisation exercise ahead of the next research assessment exercise. The last assessments were an improvement on 1996: only German was considered internationally outstanding, but another 18 areas reached the next highest grade. However, the university decided that research funding was too low in other subjects to keep all the more expensive departments open. Physics and the biosciences are among the beneficiaries in the first phase of a £140 million investment programme to accompany the restructuring.

Arabic and Islamic studies have benefited from support from the Middle East. A longstanding international focus is exemplified by the popular European Law

---

Northcote House
The Queen's Drive, Exeter EX4 4QJ
01392 263035
admissions@exeter.ac.uk
www.exeter.ac.uk
http://xnet.ex.ac.uk

degree. All students are offered tuition in foreign languages and even some three-year degrees include the option of a year abroad. Language degrees scored well in the teaching assessments, with German achieving a perfect score, as did education and archaeology.

English literature, drama, law, psychology and history are among the most heavily subscribed courses in their fields, and successful applicants appear not to be disappointed. Exeter was among the leading universities in the first national student satisfaction survey, securing particularly good scores in history and archaeology, English, philosophy and religious studies, physics and combined studies. Flexible combined honours, previously available only from the second year, will be open to first-year students from 2007. Career management skills are built into degree programmes and students can gain work experience through the university's employability and business project programmes. Web-based learning is used in all academic areas.

The main Streatham Campus, close to the centre of Exeter, is one of the most attractive in the country, with a lively campus social scene. The highly-rated schools of education, sport and health studies are a mile away in the former St Luke's College. Some £38 million is being invested in residential accommodation.

The guild of students had a £1-million revamp in 2005, adding a nightclub, and there has been a substantial investment in sports facilities, including a high-quality tennis centre.

Bursaries and Scholarships

In receipt of full Maintenance Grant	£2,000
In receipt of partial Maintenance Grant	
	£50–£1,500
Living in region	Bursary
Progressing from outreach	Bursary
Sport	Scholarship £1,000
Academic achievement	Scholarship

- Tuition fees (2006) £3,000
- Placement year tuition fee will be £1,500.
- 22% of additional fee income to be earmarked for bursaries, rising to 24% in 2010–11.
- 25 Jubilee and Millhayes Science Scholarships worth £2,000–£3,000 a year for students in biosciences, physics, engineering, computer science, mathematics and BSc geography.
- Ten Vice-Chancellor's Excellence Scholarships worth £5,000 a year are available for students who, in addition to academic excellence, demonstrate commitment to at least one of the following areas: volunteering, leadership, entrepreneurship, music, the arts or sport.
- Local Access to Exeter scheme designed to attract first generation applicants and those facing major obstacles.
- Access to Exeter bursary scheme: up to £2,000.

Contact: www.ex.ac.uk/bursaries
www.ex.ac.uk/scholarships

Students

Undergraduates:	8,025	(1,755)
Postgraduates:	2,295	(2,060)
Mature students:	10.3%	
Overseas students:	5.4%	
Applications per place:	8.0	
From state-sector schools:	71.2%	
From working-class homes:	16.6%	

For detailed information about fees, grants and bursaries and how they work, see chapter 7.

Accommodation

Number of places and costs refer to 2006–07

University-provided places: 3,939

Percentage catered: 45%

Catered costs: £90.37–£142.10 a week (31 weeks).

Self-catered costs: £60.34–£95.69 a week (40 or 51 weeks).

Unaccompanied first years are guaranteed accommodation provided conditions are met .

International students: as above.

Contact: accommodation@exeter.ac.uk

University of Glamorgan

Glamorgan's plans to establish one of the largest universities in Britain, by merging with nearby UWIC, have been shelved. But the university is by no means small: there are 21,000 students, 18,000 of them on the Treforest campus, 20 minutes by train from Cardiff overlooking the market town of Pontypridd. Collaborative linking programmes operate in five overseas centres, while in Wales a growing number of further education colleges offer the university's courses. Four have become associate colleges, guaranteeing places on degree courses if students fulfil set conditions.

Originally based in a large country house, Glamorgan now has purpose-built premises for the science and technology departments. There has also been a £5-million refurbishment of teaching accommodation for mathematics and computing. The law, nursing and midwifery schools are in Glyntaff, a short walk from the campus. They are housed in new buildings and specially restored tramsheds, a reminder of the industrial past of the area. The Institute of Chiropractic is the only university-based centre for training chiropractors in the UK, while the new Film Academy for Wales is another unique development, built on a successful range of film-related courses.

Glamorgan is committed to retaining its vocational slant, tailoring a diploma in management to the needs of the Driver and Vehicle Licensing Agency, for example. The business school is the largest in Wales, and the university was among the first providers of the two-year foundation degree, focusing on human resources management and marketing, business and accounting. The range of courses has since expanded rapidly, covering subjects as diverse as turf management and product design, with a strong representation of two-year foundation degrees.

The vocational approach pays dividends for graduate employment, which is consistently good, although the dropout rate has been the highest among the university institutions in Wales. The funding council expected a quarter of the students starting degree courses in 2002 not to complete their course in the normal period, although doubts about the accuracy of the figures led to Glamorgan's omission from the latest completion statistics. The intake is more socially diverse than elsewhere in Wales. Four out of ten undergraduates come from working-class homes and more than a quarter are from areas with no tradition of higher education – one of the highest figures at any UK university. The 13 per cent increase in applications by the official deadline for courses starting in 2006 was

---

Llantwit Road, Treforest,
Pontypridd,
Mid Glamorgan CF37 1DL
01443 480480
enquiries@glam.ac.uk
www.glam.ac.uk
www.glamsu.com

The Times Rankings
Overall Ranking: =74

Student Satisfaction:	=30	(15.1)
Research assessment:	=82	(2.4)
Entry standards:	96	(215.1)
Student–staff ratio:	65	(19.2)
Library/IT spend/student:	70	(£496)
Facilities spend/student:	38	(£245)
Good honours:	87	(49.7%)
Graduate prospects:	81	(57.6%)
Expected completion rate:	97	(73.7%)

the biggest in Wales.

Glamorgan was one of the top scorers among the former polytechnics in teaching quality assessments: 12 subjects were rated as Excellent at degree level, and there have also been awards for the remaining further education course provision. The university also did well in the first national student satisfaction survey, especially in health subjects and the creative arts. The success of the English and creative writing programmes is reflected in the establishment at the university of the National Centre for Writing, which opened in 2002. The School of Technology has been designated a centre of excellence for Wales, while three National Partnership awards testify to high standards in course design and delivery.

Many of the 9,000 full-time undergraduates live around Pontypridd, while others choose Cardiff, which is both livelier than Pontypridd and a better source of accommodation. However, the campus has been developing, with the addition of a recreation centre and an extension to the students' union, which is the focus of social life. Its bars are the only part of the university where smoking is allowed.

The sports facilities are good enough for Glamorgan to have been awarded the 2001 British University Games and to become one of six centres of excellence in cricket. The university is successful in student competitions, especially in rugby, and offers a number of sports bursaries for students with international potential. But there is also a wide range of health and fitness classes for those with lower aspirations.

Bursaries and Scholarships

- Fees for undergraduate courses £3,000.
- Students living in Wales will be eligible for a Welsh Assembly fee grant of approximately £1,800 a year.
- Fees for placement year and year abroad £1500.
- For information on the National Bursary Scheme see page 198, chapter 7.
- Entry scholarships £500 for 3 years for students who have achieved 240 or more UCAS points prior to starting course.
- Successful Completion of Year scholarships in year 2 and 3 for successful completion of year 1 at the first attempt.
- Residential Allowance of £250 for 3 years for students whose home address is more than 45 miles away by road if student is under 21 at start of the course.
- Law Entry Scholarship of £300 a year for three years .

Contact: www.glam.ac.uk/money

Students		
Undergraduates:	9,740	(7,510)
Postgraduates:	980	(2,365)
Mature students:	27.1%	
Overseas students:	10.9%	
Applications per place:	3.9	
From state-sector schools:	98.6%	
From working-class homes:	42.7%	

For detailed information about fees, grants and bursaries and how they work, see chapter 7.

Accommodation

Number of places and costs refer to 2006–07
University-provided places: 1,108
Percentage catered: 6%
Catered costs: £83–£94 a week.
Self-catered costs: £58–£72 a week (37 weeks).
First-year students are offered accommodation.
Local restrictions apply.
International students are guaranteed accommodation.
Contact: accom@glam.ac.uk

University of Glasgow

Glasgow enjoys the rare distinction of having been established by Papal Bull, and began its existence in the Chapter House of Glasgow Cathedral in 1451. Since 1871 it has been based next to Kelvingrove Park in the city's fashionable west end on the Gilmorehill campus, with its many listed buildings. The last major addition, to house the prestigious medical school, opened in 2002, while a £15-million cancer research centre is due to open in late 2006.

The university took in St Andrew's College to form a new faculty of education, which has been based on the Park campus, between Gilmorehill and the city centre, since summer 2002. The campus, formerly the Queen's College, was acquired from Glasgow Caledonian University, and provides the extra teaching accommodation needed to locate the education faculty close to the main campus. The Vet School and outdoor sports facilities are located at Garscube, a few miles away, while the innovative Crichton College campus in Dumfries is taking higher education to southwest Scotland with three-year degrees.

More distinctively Scottish than its rivals in Edinburgh or St Andrews, almost half of the students come from within 30 miles of Glasgow and three quarters are from north of the border. There was a high proportion of home-based students long before the city became fashionable, but the university also attracts students from some 80 countries.

Glasgow has adopted an increasingly outward-looking style in recent years, marked by two Queen's Anniversary prizes for opening up artistic, scientific and cultural resources and taking computing to local communities. A 'synergy' agreement with neighbouring Strathclyde University has led to the development of teaching and research partnerships, the latest establishing a single department of naval architecture and marine engineering. Not that Glasgow is a stranger to innovation: it was the first university to have a school of engineering, for example. The huge science faculty – the biggest outside London – is strong, having received top ratings for teaching in six subjects. Applications for science degrees reflect this quality, having risen by 25 per cent since the mid-1990s. Overall, a 6.6 per cent increase in applications for courses starting in 2005 was one of the highest in Scotland, a total repeated a year later. Among other sources, the university has seen a steady flow of applicants from schools taking part in the university's access scheme.

The last research assessments were an improvement on a disappointing set of

---

University Avenue,
Glasgow G12 8QQ
0141-339 8855 (main switchboard)
sras@gla.ac.uk
www.gla.ac.uk
www.glasgowstudent.net

GLASGOW

Edinburgh

Belfast

London

Cardiff

The Times Rankings
Overall Ranking: =28

Student Satisfaction:	–	(–)
Research assessment:	=30	(5.2)
Entry standards:	17	(392.6)
Student–staff ratio:	11	(13.6)
Library/IT spend/student:	24	(£688)
Facilities spend/student:	53	(£219)
Good honours:	=20	(69.6%)
Graduate prospects:	38	(66.3%)
Expected completion rate:	47	(85.8%)

results in 1996, with arts and social sciences leading the way. Four subjects were rated internationally outstanding – English, European studies, psychology and sports science – a further 19 achieving grade 5 and 95 per cent of researchers were in the top three categories. The university has opened an office in California's Silicon Valley in order to make the most of its research successes.

Overseas recruitment has remained strong, especially in engineering. Glasgow is also taking an active role in the Universitas 21 worldwide group of universities, involving partnerships on five continents. But the home market has not been overlooked: the Century 21 Club has enrolled 20 firms to sponsor under-graduates at £1,000 a year, as part of an arrangement to forge closer links with local business. Another ten scholarships for students from poor backgrounds commemorate the life of Donald Dewar, Scotland's late First Minister. The scheme is the first of a number of memorials planned for one of the university's best-known graduates.

Over a fifth of the students are from working-class homes, one in six from an area without a tradition of higher education. Most like the combination of campus and city life, with the relatively low cost of living an added attraction, but the dropout rate of 14 per cent is above the average for the subjects on offer and entry qualifications. Undergraduates have the choice of two student unions, plus a sports union supporting 50 different clubs and activities.

Bursaries and Scholarships
- Scottish domiciled students: no fees will be payable by eligible students although a "graduate endowment" will be payable after graduation: the 2005–06 level was £2,216.
- Non-Scottish domiciled students fees: £1,700 a year (£2,700 for medicine).
- Fees for placement year and year abroad are normally 50% of full-time fee.
- 13 Wider Access Bursaries are available which are £500 for 4 years.
- Donald Dewar Bursary valued at £500 for 3 years.

Contact:
www.gla.ac.uk/services/registry/students/studentfinance/index.html

Students		
Undergraduates:	14,925	(4,460)
Postgraduates:	2,640	(2,725)
Mature students:	14.7%	
Overseas students:	6.6%	
Applications per place:	6.6	
From state-sector schools:	87.8%	
From working-class homes:	22.8%	

For detailed information about fees, grants and bursaries and how they work, see chapter 7.

Accommodation
Number of places and costs refer to 2006–07
University-provided places: 3,344
Percentage catered: 7%
Catered costs: £92.05–£102.06 a week.
Self-catered costs: £68.46–£84.63
First years are guaranteed accommodation if conditions are met. Local restrictions apply. International students: first years are guaranteed accommodation if conditions are met.
Contact: accom@gla.ac.uk

Glasgow Caledonian University

Glasgow Caledonian has spent more than £70 million transforming previously mediocre facilities into a single campus that does justice to a modern university of more than 14,000 students. Only Edinburgh and Glasgow universities are bigger north of the border. Over 80 per cent of the buildings are new or have been upgraded, and improvements are still being made. The health building brings together teaching and research facilities and includes a virtual hospital, where students can hone their clinical and interpersonal skills. The new learning centre, which will bring all library and computing centres together for the first time, opened in 2006.

With the accent firmly on widening participation in higher education, the university will always struggle in league tables such as ours, but it is well-regarded by employers and applications have been healthy, with little change in the two years since a big increase in 2004.

Caledonian is in the top four UK universities for attracting students from areas without a tradition of higher education, and more than a third of its undergraduates come from working-class homes. The university has argued forcefully that extending access should be rewarded more generously if such students are to receive the support they need to make a success of higher education.

Previous performance indicators suggested that one undergraduate in six would fail to complete the degree they embarked upon, but the university was omitted from the latest completion statistics because of doubts about the accuracy of projections for Caledonian. The university had already introduced a series of measures designed to improve retention. Telltale signs are monitored, such as non-attendance at lectures, and better academic, social and financial support offered to those at risk of dropping out.

Consolidated on its city-centre campus, Caledonian's original two sites have now been reduced to one with the sale of the Park Campus, in the west end of the city, to Glasgow University. Leisure facilities have been improved with a new building for the health faculty, opened by Thabo Mbeki, who named it in honour of his father. Physiotherapy was the only subject since chemistry's success in 1993 to be rated Excellent for teaching, and Caledonian now boasts among the most extensive health programmes in Britain.

A string of other subjects (mainly on the science side) are considered Highly Satisfactory. Business is the other big area, the Caledonian Business School boasting

---

City Campus, 70 Cowcaddens Road,
Glasgow G4 0BA
0141-331 3000
admissions@gcal.ac.uk
www.caledonian.ac.uk
www.caledonianstudent.com
GLASGOW
Edinburgh
Belfast
London
Cardiff

Student satisfaction:	–	(–)
Research assessment:	=76	(2.5)
Entry standards:	47	(306.1)
Student–staff ratio:	=48	(17.6)
Library/IT spend/student:	=78	(£473)
Facilities spend/student:	106	(£91)
Good honours:	55	(58.3%)
Graduate prospects:	=77	(57.9%)
Expected completion rate:	=67	(81.6%)

more undergraduates than any other institution in Scotland, with over 1,000 in each year group. The university pioneered subjects such as entrepreneurial studies and risk management – the only university in the country to do so – and offers highly specialist degrees, such as tourism management, fashion marketing, leisure management and consumer protection.

Degrees in all areas are strongly vocational, and are complemented by a wide portfolio of professional courses. A high proportion of students choose sandwich courses, and the university operates on a modular system. The REAL@Caledonian online student facility combines enhanced learning technology with a informal cyber-café atmosphere.

The legacy of Queen's College, which catered mainly for women, has ensured that the proportion of female students is the highest of any university in Britain. Sports and social facilities have been among the priorities in the building programme. Some students find that the high proportion of their peers living at home detracts from the social scene, but Glasgow is a very lively city with a large student population.

Bursaries and Scholarships
- Scottish domiciled students: no fees will be payable by eligible students although a "graduate endowment" will be payable after graduation: the 2005–06 level was £2,216.
- Non-Scottish domiciled students fees: £1,700 a year.
- Fees for placement year and year abroad are normally 50% of full-time fee.
- The University administers hardship and childcare funds to which UK undergraduate students in need may apply.

Contact: www.gcal.ac.uk

Students

Undergraduates:	10,650	(2,840)
Postgraduates:	925	(1,385)
Mature students:	32.6%	
Overseas students:	5.5%	
Applications per place:	6.1	
From state-sector schools:	98.1%	
From working-class homes:	37.7%	

For detailed information about fees, grants and bursaries and how they work, see chapter 7.

Accommodation
Number of places and costs refer to 2005–06
University-provided places: 660
Percentage catered: 0%
Self-catered costs: £70.40–£81.20 a week.
Students under 19 living outside the Glasgow area have priority for accommodation.
International students: non-EU students given priority if conditions are met.
Contact: accommodation@gcal.ac.uk

University of Gloucestershire

One of the more recent additions to the list of English universities, Gloucestershire was also the first for more than a century to have formal links with the Church of England. Although its religious origins have been played down in recent years and students of all faiths are welcomed, the university will maintain an association that includes church appointees on its governing body and Lord Carey, the former Archbishop of Canterbury, as the first Chancellor. This did not prevent it dropping theology, its top-rated subject with good scores for both teaching and research, at undergraduate level, although a degree in religion, philosophy and ethics was introduced in 2006. Theology had been one of 14 degrees to go in a curriculum review that expanded leisure and tourism, social work and journalism.

Before university status in 2001, Cheltenham and Gloucester College of Higher Education had been the product of a merger between a church college and the higher education wing of a college of arts and technology. Teaching ratings were good enough to satisfy the assessors, without being spectacular, and the last research grades suggested that Gloucestershire would not be out of place in the university system. More than 40 per cent of academics were entered for the 2001 Research Assessment Exercise – a figure exceeded by only four former polytechnics – and the average score per member of staff placed the new university seventh among that group for research. English and theology both achieved grade 4, denoting national excellence in virtually all of the work submitted.

After considerable expansion during the 1990s, there are now almost 10,000 students, including 3,200 part-timers, and 1,000 academic and support staff. The main subject areas are business, management, law and IT, the arts, media and design, humanities, the environment, teacher education, leisure and tourism, social sciences and sport. The university prides itself on a good range of work placements, which include British Aerospace and Disneyworld.

The main campus is on the attractive site of the former College of St Paul and St Mary, a one-time botanical garden a mile outside Cheltenham, and there has been considerable development of the Gloucester campus, on the site of a former domestic science college which became part of the university in 2002. Although middle-class Cheltenham is a world away from more working-class Gloucester socially, the two centres are only seven miles apart and students are not as isolated as they are in some split-site

---

The Park Campus, PO Box 220,
The Park, Cheltenham GL50 2QF
01242 543477 (prospectus)
admissions@glos.ac.uk
www.glos.ac.uk
www.ugsu.org

The Times Rankings
Overall Ranking: =78

Student satisfaction:	=53	(14.7)
Research assessment:	=61	(3.0)
Entry standards:	87	(229.4)
Student–staff ratio:	59	(18.2)
Library/IT spend/student:	96	(£419)
Facilities spend/student:	37	(£247)
Good honours:	105	(43.9%)
Graduate prospects:	93	(54.5%)
Expected completion rate:	71	(81.3%)

institutions. There are also two smaller sites in Cheltenham: Pittville for art and design, and Francis Close Hall for a range of subjects, including tourism. The latter will also house a national centre of excellence in the teaching of geography, environment and related disciplines. A free bus service links all four sites and also serves Cheltenham railway station.

Gloucestershire's intake is as diverse as its locations, with 95 per cent of undergraduates from state schools and 30 per cent from working-class homes. The projected dropout rate has improved markedly and, at 14 per cent, is better than the national average for the subjects offered and the students' entry qualifications. The new and well-equipped sport-oriented Oxstalls campus, in Gloucester, where participation in higher education has always been low, will focus particularly on access initiatives.

The university's sports facilities include a swimming pool, sports hall and tennis courts, but are not extensive for a university of 10,000 students. Likewise accommodation, with around 1,400 beds, although the university assures its students that it has access to enough private sector places to meet all their needs. First years are given priority in the allocation of hall places and "enhancement of the student experience" is one of the priorities in the university's strategic plan.

Although Cheltenham and Gloucester are not clubbers' paradises, neither is dull and facilities are improving.

Bursaries and Scholarships

In receipt of full Maintenance Grant	£500–£1,110
In receipt of partial Maintenance Grant	£200–£1,109
Living in region	Bursary
Progressing from outreach	Bursary
Sport	Scholarships

- Tuition fees (2006) £3,000
- Placement year tuition fee will be £1,000.
- Top-up bursaries of 30% of MG for students from county and bordering counties.
- £200 start-up payment for all full-time students on entry to first year of course.
- 10% annual rebate of fees for successful completion of each year of study issued as cash at the beginning of the next academic year.
- 30% of additional fee income to be earmarked for bursaries.
- Top-up bursaries paid in instalments; other amounts paid at the start of term.
- Eligibility for bursaries to be assessed using UUK/SLC model bursary scheme (HEBSS).

Contact: www.glos.ac.uk/2007

Students

Undergraduates:	5,990	(1,975)
Postgraduates:	570	(915)
Mature students:	22.2%	
Overseas students:	6.1%	
Applications per place:	4.5	
From state-sector schools:	95.5%	
From working-class homes:	30.4%	

For detailed information about fees, grants and bursaries and how they work, see chapter 7.

Accommodation

Number of places and costs refer to 2006–07
University-provided places: about 1,325
Percentage catered: 0%
Self-catered costs: £68–£89 a week.
First-year undergraduates have priority for halls.
International students: first-year undergraduates are guaranteed accommodation if conditions are met.

Contact: accommodation@glos.ac.uk

Goldsmiths, University of London

Dubbed the "campus of cool", Goldsmiths describes itself as Britain's leading creative university because of the range of excellence it encompasses in the arts. The nickname, which does no harm in recruiting students, comes from the inclusion of Goldsmiths alongside MTV, Apple and the Tate among 50 "cool brandleaders" identified by the Brand Council in 2004. Alumni include Mary Quant and Damien Hirst among many other famous names, such as Malcolm McLaren and Linton Kwesi Johnson. Graduates of the college won the Turner Prize no fewer than five times during the 1990s and have been much in evidence since.

There is another side to Goldsmiths, however, in its tradition of community-based courses, which predates the college's membership of the University of London. Evening classes are still as popular as conventional degree courses and many subjects can be studied from basic to postgraduate levels. A history of providing educational opportunities for women is reflected in one of the largest proportions of female students in the British university system – over two thirds at the last count.

Determinedly integrated into their southeast London locality, the college precincts have a cosmopolitan atmosphere. Nearly half of all undergraduates are over 21 on entry (more than a third of them over 30), many coming from the area's ethnic minorities, and there is a growing proportion of overseas students. The age profile helped boost applications by more than 20 per cent when the official deadline passed for courses beginning in 2005

The older premises have been likened to a grammar school, with their long corridors of classrooms. But the Rutherford Information Services Building won an award from the Royal Institute of British Architects, and a Grade II listed former baths building has been converted to provide more space for research and art studios. The new Ben Pimlott Building, which features a dramatic metal "scribble" by the acclaimed architect Will Alsop, contains state-of-the-art facilities and two multidisciplinary centres for interaction between the arts and social sciences.

Although dominated by the arts, Goldsmiths' portfolio of subjects stretches through the social sciences as far as computing and psychology. Both media and communications and sociology were rated internationally outstanding in the last research rankings, which were a spectacular success for the college.

Lewisham Way, New Cross,
London SE14 6NW
020-7919 7766
admissions@gold.ac.uk
www.goldsmiths.ac.uk
www.gcsu.org.uk

The Times Rankings
Overall Ranking: 45

Student satisfaction:	=17	(15.3)
Research assessment:	=25	(5.3)
Entry standards:	51	(295.5)
Student–staff ratio:	73	(20.1)
Library/IT spend/student:	59	(£530)
Facilities spend/student:	=73	(£173)
Good honours:	42	(60.9%)
Employment prospects:	80	(57.8%)
Expected completion rate:	63	(82.4%)

Anthropology, art and design, music and English and comparative literature were close behind, leaving more than a third of the academics entered for assessment in the top two of seven categories. The research grades helped transform Goldsmiths' financial position, allowing more investment in teaching. Teaching quality scores were generally good though not spectacular, but psychology and history produced outstanding results in the first national student satisfaction survey. Employment prospects are good, especially for an institution with such a high proportion of students taking performing arts subjects, where a period of unemployment after graduation is commonplace. Indeed, on postgraduate courses, recent success rates have been among the best in Britain.

Student politics has survived at Goldsmiths to an extent not seen at many universities – the union building was given the name Tiananmen – while a college in which Alex James, from Blur, and Graham Coxon are just two of a number of successful rock alumni cannot fail to have a thriving music scene. The union has a strong tradition in volunteering and an award-winning newspaper. The surrounding area has enjoyed a mini-boom as a prime location for loft apartments. Although sky-high prices put them way beyond the reach of the student housing market, there are plenty of more reasonably-priced options in the vicinity. Most first years are allocated one of the 1,000 residential places within walking distance of the campus and overseas students can be housed throughout their course. Sports enthusiasts have been less well provided for, but a new gym was due to open in 2006. There is a swimming pool and indoor complex in Deptford, the main pitches are eight miles away.

Bursaries and Scholarships

In receipt of full Maintenance Grant	£1,000 max
In receipt of partial Maintenance Grant	£50 min
Living in Region	Scholarship
Progressing from outreach	Scholarship
Academic achievement	Scholarship

- Tuition fees 2006   £3,000
- Part-time tuition fee will be £1,500.
- A minimum 20% of additional fee income will be earmarked for bursaries.

Contact: www.goldsmiths.ac.uk/ undergraduate-funding

Students

Undergraduates:	3,420	(1,185)
Postgraduates:	1,555	(1,030)
Mature students:	30.0%	
Overseas students:	15.2%	
Applications per place:	6.2	
From state-sector schools:	91.4%	
From working-class homes:	28.3%	

For detailed information about fees, grants and bursaries and how they work, see chapter 7.

Accommodation

Number of places and costs refer to 2005–06
University-provided places: 971 (college halls)
Percentage catered: 0%
Self-catered costs: £76–£98 a week.
New full-time students living outside Travelcard Zone 6 get priority.
International students: non-EU students are guaranteed a place, subject to conditions.
Contact: accommodation@gold.ac.uk
020-7919 7130
www.goldsmiths.ac.uk/accommodation

University of Greenwich

As one of three universities charging British and EU undergraduates less than £3,000 a year, Greenwich kept as close an eye as any on recruitment in the first year of top-up fees. Having consulted its students, the university plumped for £2,500, with students on foundation degrees or Higher National Diplomas paying only £1,500. The aim is to strike a balance between affordability for the maximum number of students and the need to invest in the university. Greenwich was starting from a position of strength, having enjoyed increases of 9 per cent and 15 per cent in the last two years of lower fees.

The university's move, completed in 2002, into the former Royal Naval College buildings designed by Sir Christopher Wren provided a campus worthy of one of the most desirable titles in the higher education world. Its name has always conjured up images of history and science in equal measure. Following a £45.8-million programme of restoration and conversion the Maritime Greenwich campus is now a World Heritage site.

Wren's baroque masterpiece is now being used, with the former Dreadnought Hospital, to teach over half the university's students humanities, business, law, computing, maritime studies and maths. A former nurses' home nearby has been converted into a hall of residence and conference centre, one of three halls providing 760 beds close to the campus. Another 600 rooms became available in 2004.

Now under the leadership of Baroness Blackstone, the former Higher Education Minister, Greenwich has dropped the soubriquet of "regional university" but still draws primarily from southeast London and Kent, a populous county with only one university of its own. The latest investment is in the Medway campus, centred on the former HMS Pembroke naval base at Chatham, which is being developed in partnership with the University of Kent. Some £20 million is going into one of the first new schools of pharmacy for 20 years, as well as the School of Science, the Medway School of Engineering and the Natural Resources Institute, nursing and some business courses. A joint learning resources centre serves Chatham Maritime and the University of Kent's neighbouring premises. Another shared facility will provide improved teaching facilities and expanded student services, as the campus moves towards its target of 6,000 students.

Other departments are situated at Avery Hill, a Victorian mansion on the outskirts of southeast London, where work has started on a new multipurpose sports hall

---

Old Royal Naval College, Park Row,
Greenwich, London SE10 9LS
0800 005 006
courseinfo@greenwich.ac.uk
www.gre.ac.uk
www.suug.co.uk

The Times Rankings
Overall Ranking: 106

Student satisfaction:	=83	(14.2)
Research assessment:	=76	(2.5)
Entry standards:	103	(200.6)
Student–staff ratio:	105	(25.8)
Library/IT spend/student:	74	(£482)
Facilities spend/student:	86	(£149)
Good honours:	96	(47.5%)
Graduate prospects:	58	(62.7%)
Expected completion rate:	102	(71.9%)

and lecture theatre. The campus is home to a student village of 1,300 rooms, as well as teaching accommodation for health and social care, the social sciences, and the large education faculty, which is one of the few to offer both primary and secondary teacher training courses. Architecture, landscape and construction students have also transferred to Avery Hill from Dartford.

Most teaching assessments were favourable, with pharmacy and pharmacology, town planning, sociology and nursing the star performers. However, Greenwich was near the bottom of rankings from the first national student satisfaction survey, although physics came out well. The university achieved some respectable results in the last research assessment exercise, with computing, German and materials leading the way, although less than a third of the academic staff entered. A fifth of its income is from research and consultancy – the largest proportion at any former polytechnic Strong links with institutions in Europe and further afield provide a steady flow of overseas students – mainly from China, India and Greece – as well as exchange opportunities for those at Greenwich. Seven associated colleges in Kent and London teach the university's courses.

A commitment to extending access to higher education has led to low entrance requirements in many subjects and a relatively high proportion of mature students. More than 95 per cent of students are state-educated, almost half coming from working-class homes. Both figures are significantly higher than the benchmark, which takes account of the subject mix and entrance qualifications. The downside is a projected dropout rate of 25 per cent, which is among the highest in England.

Bursaries and Scholarships

In receipt of full Maintenance Grant	£500
In receipt of partial Maintenance Grant	£500
Academic achievement	Scholarship £500
	More than 300 points

- Tuition fee (2006) £2,500
- Placement year tuition fee and year abroad fee will be £600.
- Bursary of £500 a year for UK students with UCAS tariff scores in excess of 300 (excluding AS levels), as well as mature full-time student cash bursaries of £500 a year for UK students over the age of 25 on 1 September of year of entry, who qualify for means-tested government grants.

Contact:
www.gre.ac.uk/students/finance/tuition-fees/
2006-2007/faqs.htm

Students

Undergraduates:	10,695	(4,195)
Postgraduates:	2,000	(3,420)
Mature students:	34.7%	
Overseas students:	16.9%	
Applications per place:	6.2	
From state-sector schools:	96.0%	
From working-class homes:	45.8%	

For detailed information about fees, grants and bursaries and how they work, see chapter 7.

Accommodation

Number of places and costs refer to 2006–07
University-provided places: 2,300
Percentage catered: 0%
Self-catered costs: £70.49–£140.42 a week.
First years are guaranteed a place.
International students: new students get priority.
Contact: http://accommodation.gre.ac.uk
accommodation-AH@gre.ac.uk (Avery Hill)
accommodation-GM@gre.ac.uk (Greenwich)
accommodation-ME@gre.ac.uk (Medway)

Heriot-Watt University

Concentration on technology, languages and business is fitting for a university which commemorates James Watt, the pioneer of steam power, and George Heriot, financier to King James VI. Still evolving 40 years after attaining university status, in many ways Heriot-Watt is Scotland's most unconventional university. The main campus, on the outskirts of Edinburgh, was completed only in 1992, and is among the most modern in Britain. Still small in terms of full-time students – there are only 6,300 on campus – the primarily technological university is aiming to double its numbers over 20 years. It already has 10,000 students taking distance learning courses and expects to add more. The new Interactive University launched with Scottish Enterprise will help higher education institutions throughout Scotland to market and deliver degrees around the world

For many years, Heriot-Watt's main claim to fame outside the academic community lay in its degree in brewing and distilling. But the university has a wide variety of vocational programmes, as well as more conventional degrees. Research in petroleum engineering is rated internationally outstanding, while modern languages are a more unexpected strength. Actuarial mathematics and statistics is one of only two centres in the UK, and photonics and optoelectronics is highly regarded. The new School of the Built Environment integrates civil and building engineering and surveying, with the former School of Planning and Housing at Edinburgh College of Art.

Only electrical and electronic engineering achieved the maximum score for teaching under the original assessment system, although there was a succession of Highly Satisfactory ratings. However, computer sciences and chemical, electrical and electronic, mechanical and petroleum engineering all achieved the top Commendable grades in 2002.

Science, engineering, management and languages are located on the main campus at Riccarton, which saw £100 million of investment in the 1990s. The university has also been investing in people: a five-year programme has seen £3.7 million worth of new appointments. There is a postgraduate campus in the Orkneys, but in the current decade the focus has been on the Borders, where higher education provision has always been scarce. The Scottish Borders Campus is situated in Galashiels, 35 miles south of Edinburgh, where the university took over and upgraded the Scottish College of Textiles. There are plans to develop a new campus in the town by linking with Borders College, supplementing this with

---

Riccarton,
Edinburgh EH14 4AS
0131-451 3376/77/78
admissions@hw.ac.uk
www.hw.ac.uk
www.hwusa.org

EDINBURGH
Belfast
London
Cardiff

The Times Rankings
Overall Ranking: 48

Student satisfaction:	–	(–)
Research assessment:	=42	(4.7)
Entry standards:	27	(362.7)
Student–staff ratio:	=42	(17.3)
Library/IT spend/student:	61	(£525)
Facilities spend/student:	30	(£268)
Good honours:	43	(60.5%)
Graduate prospects:	=77	(57.9%)
Expected completion rate:	74	(80.9%)

community centres throughout the region.

The university has long been a leader in the use of information technology for teaching, thanks partly to a huge research and development programme. Heriot-Watt is also one of the most commercially diversified universities in Britain, with the share of private research funding consistently among the highest in the UK per member of academic staff. About 45 per cent of Heriot-Watt's income, more than £35 million, comes from research, training and commercial services.

The subject mix also serves graduates well: Heriot-Watt is seldom far from the top of the employment league tables. But the new acquisitions have altered the student profile, with the proportion of women creeping up to 38 per cent. The latest projected dropout rate, at almost 17 per cent, is higher than the average for other universities offering the same subjects. Over a quarter of the students are from overseas, a proportion that has risen sharply in recent years and one that produces a cosmopolitan atmosphere on campus. Around 55 per cent are from Scotland, and 20 per cent from other parts of Britain.

Heriot-Watt has an attractive parkland setting, with the students' union at its heart and halls of residence conveniently placed. Students at Riccarton have complained that the six-mile journey to the city centre leaves them isolated, but transport links have improved. Sports enthusiasts are well provided for, and representative teams do well. Hearts, one of Edinburgh's two SPL clubs, have chosen the campus as the site for their sports academy, which will be used by students and local people as well as the young professionals. Music also thrives: there is a professional musician-in-residence and a number of scholarships, as well as a varied programme of events.

Bursaries and Scholarships

- Scottish domiciled students: no fees will be payable by eligible students although a "graduate endowment" will be payable after graduation: the 2005–06 level was £2,216.
- Non-Scottish domiciled students fees: £1,700 a year.
- Fees for placement year and year abroad are normally 50% of full-time fee.
- A number of scholarships of £500 a year for four/five years of study are available, with preference given to study of subjects in Science and Engineering.
- Scholarships in Engineering and Physical Sciences of £500 a year for up to 5 years are offered for female students.
- The Alumni Fund scholarships at £500 a year for four to five years for UK/EU students.
- Annual music scholarships for instrumentalists and singers applying for a course.

Contact: www.undergraduate.hw.ac.uk

Students		
Undergraduates:	5,040	(305)
Postgraduates:	1,415	(2,010)
Mature students:	24.1%	
Overseas students:	17.9%	
Applications per place:	5.0	
From state-sector schools:	91.5%	
From working-class homes:	29.4%	

For detailed information about fees, grants and bursaries and how they work, see chapter 7.

Accommodation

Number of places and costs refer to 2005–06
University places provided: 1,619
Percentage catered: 19%
Catered costs: £84.50–£90.00 a week.
Self-catered costs: £51–£73 a week.
All new first years are guaranteed accommodation provided conditions are met.
International students: as above.
Contact : AO@hw.ac.uk

University of Hertfordshire

Hertfordshire opened a purpose-built £120-million campus in September 2003 close to the existing Hatfield headquarters, bringing the university together for the first time and promising outstanding facilities. The de Havilland campus, named after the aircraft manufacturer which once occupied the site, houses business, education and the humanities. It has a 24-hour resources centre, £15-million sports complex and 1,600 networked, en suite residential places. The two sites are linked by cycle-ways, footpaths and shuttle buses. The blaze of publicity that accompanied the opening contributed to the biggest rise in applications (22 per cent) at any UK university. That was a hard act to follow but there was another rise of 12.5 per cent at the start of 2005.

As Hatfield Polytechnic, the university's reputation was built on engineering and computer science, but health subjects now account for by far the largest share of places. An innovative degree in Paramedic Science is Britain's first, and the university is still hoping for a medical school, although its last bid was unsuccessful. The announcement of a £500-million hospital and cancer centre in Hatfield should strengthen the university's case, as should the launches of a new School of Pharmacy and a postgraduate medical school. The latter is a collaboration with Cranfield and Luton universities and the Bedfordshire and Hertfordshire health authority. Art and design is also growing, particularly the multimedia courses. In 2005, the university launched a new School of Film, Music and New Media. The College Lane campus includes the largest art gallery in the eastern region, which mounts regular public exhibitions. A new 460-seat auditorium will enhance the cultural programme. An Automotive Centre has upgraded teaching facilities for that branch of engineering, as well as boosting interaction with industry.

Average grades for A-level entrants rose under the previous Vice-Chancellor, who called for a "tougher and more rigorous" academic style and declared a desire to propel Hertfordshire up the league tables. Professor Tim Wilson, the present incumbent, retains this ambition but is also trying to widen the university's base through collaboration with local further education colleges. The intake is more diverse than expected, given the location and subject mix: 97 per cent of undergraduates are state-educated and 40 per cent come from working-class homes. A 18 per cent drop-out rate is better than the national average for the subject mix and entry grades, but still more than a quarter of students do not complete the course they entered in the expected time.

College Lane, Hatfield,
Herts AL10 9AB
01707 284800
admissions@herts.ac.uk
www.herts.ac.uk
www.uhsu.herts.ac.uk

The Times Rankings
Overall Ranking: 85

Student satisfaction:	=75	(14.3)
Research assessment:	=76	(2.5)
Entry standards:	91	(225.4)
Student–staff ratio:	=56	(18.1)
Library/IT spend/student:	62	(£522)
Facilities spend/student:	=78	(£161)
Good honours:	86	(49.9%)
Graduate prospects:	=47	(64.8%)
Expected completion rate:	75	(80.7%)

Many students include work placements in their degrees, the close links with employers sometimes bringing in valuable research and consultancy contracts, and contributing to a consistently good graduate employment record.

Environmental studies and philosophy achieved the best scores for teaching quality, with business and management, psychology and nursing close behind. Grades in the last research assessment exercise showed considerable improvement on 1996, with history rated nationally outstanding and computing, nursing, physics and psychology all in the next category.

Even before the opening of the new campus, students were well served in terms of information technology. The award-winning library and resource centre on the main campus is Britain's biggest, offering 24-hour access to hundreds of computer workstations. A second centre on the de Havilland campus provides another 1,100 workstations. The StudyNet information system has been a leader in its field, giving all staff and students their own storage space. Students can use it for study, revision or communication, as well as to access university information.

Bursaries and Scholarships

In receipt of full Maintenance Grant	£1,350
In receipt of partial Maintenance Grant	up to £1,350
Sport	Scholarships
Shortage subjects	Scholarship
Academic achievement	Scholarship

- Tuition fees (2006) £3,000
- £500 scholarship towards first year tuition fees to all students successfully completing the Edexcel Diploma in Foundation Studies at this university and continuing on to degree study in the Schools of Art and Design or Film, Music and Media.
- Chancellor's Scholarship (£2,500) is a one-off payment in the first year of study for students who achieve a good academic standard – around 360 UCAS points – and enter to study a full-time undergraduate degree.
- Science and Engineering Scholarships (worth up to £3,000) on certain science and engineering degrees available to every student who achieves a minimum academic standard – around 280 UCAS points.
- Scholarships are automatically awarded to students who meet the stated academic standard required when they join the University.
- Sports Scholarship Fund and Talented Athlete Support Fund offer different levels of financial and practical support to encourage the development of sporting excellence.

Contact: www.herts.ac.uk/

Students

Undergraduates:	14,850	(3,595)
Postgraduates:	2,250	(2,165)
Mature students:	14.9%	
Overseas students:	12.3%	
Applications per place:	4.5	
From state-sector schools:	96.8%	
From working-class homes:	39.5%	

For detailed information about fees, grants and bursaries and how they work, see chapter 7.

Accommodation

Number of places and costs refer to 2006–07
University-provided places: 3,400
Percentage catered: 0%
Self-catered costs: £58–£89 a week.
First years are guaranteed accommodation if conditions are met.
International students: as above.
Contact: Accommodation@herts.ac.uk

University of Huddersfield

Official performance indicators for higher education have shown Huddersfield living up to its mission to help produce a more diverse student population, and it has opened satellite centres in Barnsley and Oldham to widen participation further. Four out of ten full-time students are from working-class homes and almost a quarter are from areas without a strong tradition of higher education. The downside of this open access approach is that 20 per cent are not expected to complete their degrees – a lower proportion than in previous years but still marginally more than the funding council's benchmark for the university, which takes account of the courses on offer. Nevertheless, Huddersfield achieved the highest possible score in an audit by the Quality Assurance Agency in 2004.

Imaginative conversion and new buildings have finally allowed the university to come together on one town-centre campus. The university capitalised on Huddersfield's industrial past to ease the strain on facilities that were struggling to cope with expansion which reached 13 per cent a year at its peak. Canalside, a refurbished mill complex, has provided new space for mathematics and computing, and education occupies another mill site – this time a £4-million

recreation of the original. The university is even creating "pocket parks" and a landscaped area along the reopened Narrow Canal to provide additional green space. Human and health sciences have also acquired new premises, and an additional £4 million has been spent on a new students' union, allowing drama courses to take over the existing union complex. The new union, opened by Huddersfield's Chancellor, *Star Trek* actor Patrick Stewart, includes alcohol-free social areas to encourage participation by those overseas students and ethnic minorities who would otherwise avoid the facilities.

A tradition of vocational education dates back to 1841, and the university has a long-established reputation in areas such as textile design and engineering. But there are less obvious gems such as music and social work, both of which were rated excellent for teaching and nationally outstanding for research. Electrical and electronic engineering achieved the best score in assessments of teaching quality. The university's own satisfaction surveys suggest that students value the friendliness and helpfulness of staff, and Huddersfield did well in the national survey, which showed particularly high levels of satisfaction in politics and history.

The university adopted a much more selective approach to the last research

---

Queensgate, Huddersfield,
West Yorkshire HD1 3DH
01484 422288
admissions@hud.ac.uk
www.hud.ac.uk
www.huddersfield
student.com

The Times Rankings
Overall Ranking: =90

Student satisfaction:	=33	(15.0)
Research assessment:	=82	(2.4)
Entry standards:	86	(232.3)
Student–staff ratio:	=74	(20.2)
Library/IT spend/student:	99	(£401)
Facilities spend/student:	=96	(£126)
Good honours:	95	(47.6%)
Graduate prospects:	=83	(57.1%)
Expected completion rate:	88	(77.9%)

assessments, entering half the number of academics it did in 1996. History matched social work and music's grade 5, with mechanical engineering in the next category. A flourishing relationship with industry produces more private income than is achieved in many larger institutions, as well as influencing courses.

The most popular courses are in human and health sciences. Many arts and social science courses have a vocational slant. Politics, for example, includes a six-week work placement, which often takes students to the House of Commons. A third of the students in all subjects take sandwich courses, one of the highest proportions in Britain, and more than 4,000 have some element of work experience. The approach pays off with consistently good graduate employment figures and rises of more than 12 per cent in applications for 2004 courses and nearly twice that a year later.

Additional accommodation is available at Ashenhurst, just over a mile from the campus, but most residential accommodation is now concentrated in the Storthes Hall Park student village. Despite recent developments, the 1,712 residential places are not enough to guarantee accommodation to first years but private housing is cheap and plentiful in Huddersfield. Students are also encouraged to follow a structured fitness programme at the upgraded campus sports centre. Town–gown relations are good and the cost of living low. Most students like the town's friendly atmosphere, although they tend to base their social life on the students' union. It is not far to Leeds for those in search of serious clubbing.

Bursaries and Scholarships

In receipt of full Maintenance Grant   £1,000
In receipt of partial Maintenance Grant
                                           £500–£750

- Tuition fees 2006   £3,000
- No fee to be charged for placement year. Foundation year tuition fee will be £1,200.
- Bursaries open to all EU students.
- 27% of additional fee income to be earmarked for bursaries.

Contact: www.hud.ac.uk/news/05_01/
fees_for_2006.htm

Students

Undergraduates:	9,500	(5,540)
Postgraduates:	1,095	(2,565)
Mature students:	21.6%	
Overseas students:	6.9%	
Applications per place:	5.1	
From state-sector schools:	98%	
From working-class homes:	39.1%	

For detailed information about fees, grants and bursaries and how they work, see chapter 7.

Accommodation

Number of places and costs refer to 2006–07
University-provided places: 1,712 in privately-owned halls
Percentage catered: 0%
Self-catered costs: £57.95–£89.95 a week.
First years are guaranteed accommodation provided conditions are met.
International students: as above.
Contact: info@campusdigs.com;
www.campusdigs.com

University of Hull

Students at Hull are among the most satisfied in the country, according to the first national survey of their views. Physics and politics, English, history, archaeology, philosophy and theology, did particularly well, but most departments produced creditable scores. The university and the city have always commanded loyalty among students, who appreciate the modest cost of living and ready availability of accommodation. But the quality of courses is also high: electronic engineering, drama and Iberian languages all achieved perfect scores in teaching assessments, with politics and theology close behind.

Nursing recorded an unusually low score, but the criticisms were addressed, and new facilities provided. A long-standing focus on Europe shows in the wide range of languages available at degree level, with the purpose-built Language Institute heavily used by students of all subjects. Strength in politics – confirmed by one of three grade 5 assessments for research, as well as the teaching quality success – is reflected in a steady flow of graduates into the House of Commons. But the university was criticised for deciding in 2004 to close mathematics following poor recruitment to the honours degree.

No subject was rated internationally outstanding in the last research assessments, but law and geography joined politics in the next category. Social work collected a Queen's Anniversary Prize and was also rated excellent for teaching. An Institute for Learning tries to put research findings into practice, developing training courses for lecturers and encouraging the university's interest in lifelong learning.

After years of relative stability, Hull has been expanding rapidly, both on its spacious home campus and through mergers. First it added nursing to its portfolio of courses with the acquisition of the former Humberside College of Health, then it took in University College Scarborough in 2000 and finally the university bought the adjacent campus of the former Humberside University, turning it into the Faculty of Health. There are now more than 16,000 students, including part-timers. Applications were up 14 per cent – one of England's biggest rises – at the start of 2004, although they were down fractionally a year later.

The main academic development has been the establishment of a medical school in conjunction with York University. Hull's patient development, in collaboration with the local health authority, of a postgraduate medical school was rewarded with the award of a traditional school housed in a landmark

---

Cottingham Road, Hull HU6 7RX
0870-126 2000
admissions@admin.hull.ac.uk
www.hull.ac.uk
www.hullstudent.com

The Times Rankings
Overall Ranking: 49

Student satisfaction:	=17	(15.3)
Research assessment:	=53	(4.3)
Entry standards:	54	(283.7)
Student–staff ratio:	=63	(18.6)
Library/IT spend/student:	93	(£434)
Facilities spend/student:	71	(£177)
Good honours:	=49	(59.2%)
Graduate prospects:	50	(64.3%)
Expected completion rate:	=41	(86.7%)

building on the former college campus. The original 94-acre main campus has also seen considerable development, with new buildings for languages and chemistry, a Graduate Research Institute and a state-of-the-art sport, health and exercise science laboratory. The campus, with its art gallery and highly automated library, is less than three miles from the centre of Hull.

The Scarborough campus has also seen investment in new laboratories for music technology and digital arts. Hull has always maintained a roughly equal balance between science and technology and the arts and social sciences, believing that this promotes a harmonious atmosphere, but the Scarborough campus has tipped the scales towards the arts.

Only one traditional university in England has a higher proportion of state-educated students than Hull's 93 per cent. Almost three in ten are from working-class homes and the projected drop-out rate of less than 12 per cent is still below the funding council's benchmark for the subjects offered. In an effort to broaden its intake further, the university is offering conditional places to local 16-year-olds if they take part in a Science Experience Programme. Many of the youngsters have been attending a university science club once a month since the age of 11 or 12, and have access to the library and computer facilities. The initiative, which has drawn

praise from Tony Blair, should help to raise participation in higher education in an area where it has traditionally been low. Student leisure facilities, which were always good but becoming crowded, have been upgraded as part of the campus building programme. The students' union, which was rated the best in Britain in one survey, has been refurbished and opened the popular Asylum nightclub. New football pitches have been added recently on campus and the Sports and Fitness Centre has been attracting praise.

Bursaries and Scholarships

In receipt of full Maintenance Grant	£1,000
In receipt of partial Maintenance Grant	
	£500–£1,000
Living in specified postcodes	Bursary
Academic achievement	Scholarship £3,000

- Tuition fees (2006) £3,000
- Foundation year and placement year tuition fee will be £1,500.

Contact: www.hull.ac.uk/money

Students

Undergraduates:	9,875	(7,050)
Postgraduates:	1,835	(2,475)
Mature students:	26.8%	
Overseas students:	11.3%	
Applications per place:	4.5	
From state-sector schools:	92.8%	
From working-class homes:	28.5%	

For detailed information about fees, grants and bursaries and how they work, see chapter 7.

Accommodation

Number of places and costs refer to 2006-07
University-provided places: 2,597 (owned stock); 250 (leased/associated stock)
Percentage catered: 41%
Catered costs: £82.76–£105.18 (31 weeks).
Self-catered costs: £60.53–£80.59 a week (31–50 weeks).
Unaccompanied first years are guaranteed accommodation if conditions are met.
International students: as above.
Contact: rooms@hull.ac.uk

Imperial College of Science, Technology and Medicine

After years of running Oxford close in *The Times* League Table rankings, London's specialist college of science, engineering and medicine briefly moved ahead in 2000 but is now back in third place. Over 5,000 academic staff include Nobel prizewinners and 61 Fellows of the Royal Society. Three quarters of the academics entered in the latest research assessment exercise were in departments considered internationally outstanding – the highest proportion in any university – and almost all were in one of the top two categories.

Teaching scores were up to the same high standard, with electrical and electronic engineering and materials science achieving maximum points. Physics, mathematics and medicine also did well. Imperial is not recommended for academic slouches, but tough entrance requirements ensure that they are a rare breed in any case. The projected dropout rate of 3.7 per cent is one of the lowest in the country. Such is the level of competition that applications had been dropping, although there was a 10 per cent increase when the official deadline passed for courses beginning in 2004. Even though many of the subjects struggle for candidates elsewhere, entrants average

better than an A and two Bs at A level. More than a third of the undergraduates are from independent schools – one of the highest proportions at any university.

Engineering courses last four years and lead to an MEng degree. Almost all branches of engineering achieved the coveted 5* rating for research. The college has been expanding its range of European exchanges, with a variety of prestigious technological institutions available for courses such as the MSc in physics.

Medicine was the main area of development in the 1990s: mergers with the St Mary's, Charing Cross and Westminster, and Royal Postgraduate teaching hospitals producing one of the biggest faculties of medicine in the country. Top ratings for research in clinical medicine are a source of pride, particularly given its size. Further mergers in 2000 brought in the Kennedy Institute of Rheumatology and Wye College, in Ashford, Kent, which is to become a research centre and its courses transferred to the University of Kent.

Imperial celebrates its centenary in 2007 and has announced its intention to leave the University of London to trade on a reputation that puts it among the top 20 universities in *The Times Higher Education Supplement's* world rankings. It has been redeveloping and expanding facilities on its main campus, in the heart of South

---

Exhibition Road,
South Kensington,
London SW7 2AZ
020-7594 8014
admissions@ic.ac.uk
www.ic.ac.uk
www.union.ic.ac.uk

The Times Rankings
Overall Ranking: 3

Student satisfaction:	=71	(14.4)
Research assessment:	=3	(6.4)
Entry standards:	3	(468.2)
Student–staff ratio:	2	(9.4)
Library/IT spend/student:	3	(£1,230)
Facilities spend/student:	2	(£481)
Good honours:	10	(75.0%)
Graduate prospects:	2	(83.8%)
Expected completion rate:	5	(96.0%)

Kensington's museum district, most recently with the construction of a new sports centre and halls of residence complex. The growing Tanaka Business School, rated excellent for teaching, is Imperial's main concession to the academic world beyond science and technology.

The Undergraduate Research Opportunities Programme provides opportunities for "hands-on" experience of the research activities of college staff and postgraduates. A voluntary scheme open to all undergraduates, it is especially popular in the summer vacation, when students can be paid bursaries and international undergraduates can participate without needing a work permit. There is also a vacation placement scheme during the summer for undergraduates to acquire work experience.

Imperial's specialisms have the effect of making it the most male-dominated university institution in Britain, although the number of female students doubled during the 1990s and now stands at more than a third. The imbalance shows in a social scene which many students find limited, despite the impressive selection of clubs and societies on offer. Outdoor sports facilities are remote, but Wednesday afternoons are left free to encourage students to make the effort to exercise.

Bursaries and Scholarships

In receipt of full Maintenance Grant	£2,700
In receipt of partial Maintenance Grant	£100–£2,700
Academic achievement	Scholarship £4,000

- Tuition fees (2006) £3,000
- Home students only eligible for awards.
- Scholarships of £4,000 each year for up to four years for excellent academic performance (3 As at A level or equivalent) to students receiving full MG and who accept firmly a place through UCAS by May prior to admission.
- Additionally, Student Opportunities Fund disbursed according to financial or educational disadvantage.
- 29% of additional fee income to be earmarked for bursaries.
- Eligibility for bursaries to be assessed using UUK/SLC model bursary scheme (HEBSS).

Contact: www.imperial.ac.uk/bursaries
www.imperial.ac.uk/sfo

Students

Undergraduates:	7,425	(0)
Postgraduates:	3,270	(1,345)
Mature students:	4.3%	
Overseas students:	35.6%	
Applications per place:	5.7	
From state-sector schools:	59.6%	
From working-class homes:	17.9%	

For detailed information about fees, grants and bursaries and how they work, see chapter 7.

Accommodation

Number of places and costs refer to 2005–06
University-provided places: 3,100
Percentage catered: 10%
Catered costs: £97–£132 a week.
Self-catered costs: £58–£144 a week.
First years are guaranteed accommodation provided conditions are met.
International students: undergraduates, as above.
Contact: student.accom@imperial.ac.uk

University of Keele

The broad foundation course and four-year degree that made Keele's name is a fading memory, but the university remains committed to breadth of study and has set itself the target of being the leading interdisciplinary institution in Britain. Nine out of ten students take more than one subject for their degree, usually taking a subsidiary from the other side of the arts–science divide in the first year, and the range of options is still widening. Among the more outlandish combinations are astrophysics and criminology, or music technology and environmental management. Most programmes provide the opportunity of a semester abroad, which the university would like a quarter of all undergraduates to take.

American studies, education, politics and philosophy all produced perfect scores in teaching assessments, but the many dual honours programmes – especially those featuring politics or music – and international relations are the university's traditional strengths. Law is the only subject to be rated internationally outstanding for research, but seven more reached grade 5 in the last assessments. The improvement on the exercise in 1996 helped propel Keele up our League Table – it jumped 13 places in 2004, but slipped back a little subsequently.

Science subjects have been gaining ground: biosciences and physics both scored well for teaching quality. However, it is in health subjects that the main development has been focused. First degrees in physiotherapy, medicines management and nursing and midwifery were added to the well-established postgraduate medical school. Now collaboration with Manchester University has brought undergraduate medicine to Keele. Initially, students have been spending their first two years in Manchester, with the choice of completing their training there or moving to the Potteries. But, since 2003, it has been possible to take an entire medical degree at Keele, which will eventually train more than 600 student doctors each year. New buildings have been springing up at the North Staffordshire Hospital site, while a second undergraduate medical school (UGMS2) has opened on the main campus. The most recent addition to the thriving medical portfolio is the introduction of a BSc in Osteopathy, in collaboration with the College of Osteopaths.

All Keele's courses are modular, with the academic year divided into two 15-week semesters, with breaks at Christmas and Easter. The university remains small by modern standards – less than 6,000 full-time students – despite 75 per cent growth during the 1990s. The proportion

---

Keele, Staffordshire ST5 5BG
01782 584005
undergraduate@keele.ac.uk
www.keele.ac.uk
www.kusu.net

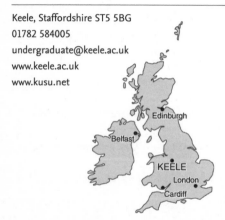

The Times Rankings
Overall Ranking: 52

Student satisfaction:	=38	(14.9)
Research assessment:	=48	(4.6)
Entry standards:	45	(309.3)
Student–staff ratio:	=42	(17.3)
Library/IT spend/student:	94	(£431)
Facilities spend/student:	103	(£100)
Good honours:	73	(53.2%)
Graduate prospects:	=47	(64.8%)
Expected completion rate:	=30	(90.0%)

of postgraduates has also been growing, with a third of the students now taking higher degrees. The university's objective, following an institutional review, is to move gradually to 10,000 students. With applications up by more than a quarter at the beginning of 2005, finding suitable candidates should not be a problem.

Keele has a good record for retaining students, although the projected dropout rate rose to 10 per cent in the last official statistics. Nine out of ten undergraduates are state-educated, a figure exceeded by only two traditional universities in England, and a quarter come from working-class homes. Keele has been proactive in trying to broaden its intake, targeting 12 and 13-year-olds with a special website, as well as running masterclasses in local schools and hosting a summer school at the university.

The attractive 617-acre campus near the M6 outside Stoke-on-Trent is the largest in England. Nearly half of all undergraduates live on campus, which inevitably dominates the social scene as well as providing part-time employment for hundreds of students. The students' union has been refurbished recently, and further improvements are planned under a five-year restructuring. Sports facilities are good for those seeking a more active lifestyle. The cost of living is also relatively low in the Potteries.

Bursaries and Scholarships

In receipt of full Maintenance Grant	£300
In receipt of partial Maintenance Grant	Up to £4,000
Living in region	Bursary
Living in specified postcodes	Bursary
Progressing from outreach	Bursary
Ethnic minorities	Bursary
Shortage subjects	Scholarship (Maths)
Academic achievement	Bursary

- Tuition fees (2006) £3,000
- 20% of additional fee income to be earmarked for bursaries.
- Target groups for non-mandatory bursaries: rural, black and ethnic minorities, postcode and first generation students
- Limited number of non-mandatory bursaries. Application for a bursary does not guarantee an award: bursaries are competitive and are assessed on carefully-defined criteria.
- Additionally, medical education bursaries, work-based bursaries, study abroad bursaries, widening participation mentoring bursaries and contingency bursaries.
- Partial Maintenance Grant bursary higher than full Maintenance Grant to assist the many students not qualifying for full Maintenance Grant but still perceived as being in great need of financial assistance.
- In kind benefit is a reduction in accommodation costs worth £500.

Contact: www.keele.ac.uk/undergraduate/bursaries/index.htm

Students

Undergraduates:	5,390	(3,200)
Postgraduates:	1,095	(2,110)
Mature students:	13.3%	
Overseas students:	7.6%	
Applications per place:	5.7	
From state-sector schools:	91.3%	
From working-class homes:	25.6%	

For detailed information about fees, grants and bursaries and how they work, see chapter 7.

Accommodation

Number of places and costs refer to 2006–07
University-provided places: 3,200
Percentage catered: 0%
Self-catered costs: £56–£87 a week.
First years are guaranteed accommodation on campus if conditions are met.
International students: guaranteed accommodation for the duration of their course.
Contact: hpb93@keele.ac.uk

University of Kent

Kent has capitalised sensibly on its position near the Channel ports, specialising in international programmes, as well as the flexible degree structures that have been the hallmark of most 1960s universities. Interdisciplinary study is encouraged, and many courses include the option of a year spent elsewhere in Europe or in the United States. The process should accelerate with the establishment of the Transmanche University with four counterparts in northern France, which will take its first undergraduates in 2006. The project, backed by both governments, will involve joint courses at a variety of levels and research collaboration. Almost a quarter of Kent's undergraduates take a language for at least part of their degree, and European studies are among the most popular subject combinations.

The university is broadening its horizons at home as well, however, assuming a regional role. Access courses throughout the county allow students to upgrade their qualifications to university standard, but the main focus is on the Medway towns, where Kent is involved in ambitious projects with Greenwich University and Mid-Kent College. The Chatham Maritime campus, based in the old dockyard is intended to cater for 6,000 students by 2010, with a new School of Pharmacy among the main features of a £50-million development. The first intake of pharmacists was 50 per cent larger than planned and the school is eventually expected to take 430 students. Mid-Kent's degree courses will transfer to the university, while further education programmes continue under the aegis of the college.

The original low-rise campus, set in 300 acres of parkland overlooking Canterbury, is tidy rather than architecturally distinguished. The student centre has a nightclub big enough to attract big-name bands, as well as a theatre, cinema and bars. A university centre serves 1,400 part-time students in Tonbridge, and a series of associate colleges also offer university courses. Entry grades are variable, with offers pitched according to the UCAS points tariff, although those taking A levels are expected to pass at least three subjects (one of which may be general studies). A period of declining applications has been reversed in the last four years, with a 22 per cent increase at the start of 2005, partly thanks to the Medway development.

Kent is strongest in the social sciences, although biosciences, philosophy and drama, dance and theatre studies took pride of place in the teaching assessments, each registering a maximum score. The university takes teaching standards seriously, encouraging all academics to

---

Canterbury, Kent CT2 7NZ
01227 827272
recruitment@ukc.ac.uk
www.kent.ac.uk
www.kentunion.co.uk

Edinburgh
Belfast
Cardiff   London
CANTERBURY

The Times Rankings
Overall Ranking: =34

Student satisfaction:	=17	(15.3)
Research assessment:	=40	(4.8)
Entry standards:	42	(316.4)
Student–staff ratio:	21	(15.4)
Library/IT spend/student:	30	(£648)
Facilities spend/student:	65	(£189)
Good honours:	45	(60.3%)
Graduate prospects:	37	(66.6%)
Expected completion rate:	40	(86.8%)

take a Postgraduate Certificate in Higher Education. Social policy and statistics were rated internationally outstanding in the last research assessments, which showed marked improvement on the disappointing grades in 1996.

Kent has been trying to build up its science departments, among which computing is particularly well regarded. Health subjects, biology and electronic engineering did best, together with arts and design, in a generally successful first round of the national student satisfaction survey. But still two thirds of the students take arts or social sciences. Graduates of all disciplines fare well in the employment market – a jobless rate below 4 per cent is impressive for an arts-dominated institution.

The university has a more mixed intake than many in the south of England: nine out of ten undergraduates are from state schools and almost a quarter come from working-class homes. Significant numbers of American and European students give the university a cosmopolitan feel and campus security is good, but some complain that Canterbury itself is expensive and limited socially.

Students are attached to one of four colleges, although they do not select it themselves. The colleges act as the focus of social life, and include academic as well as residential facilities. They provide accommodation for all first years. Among £100 million of completed or planned capital developments has been an expansion of sports facilities and the addition of 500 rooms at the Parkwood student village.

Bursaries and Scholarships

In receipt of full Maintenance Grant	£1,000
In receipt of partial Maintenance Grant	£250–£1,000
Progressing from outreach	Scholarship
Sport	Scholarship £1,000
Academic achievement	Scholarship

- Tuition fees (2006) £3,000
- Foundation year tuition fee will be £1,250. Placement year and year abroad tuition fees will be approximately £750.
- 46 Regional School and College Scholarships worth £1,000.
- Sports Scholarships worth £500–£5,000 for excellence and commitment to sport.
- 10 Music Scholarships worth £1,000 for excellence and commitment to music.
- A condition of holding a bursary is attendance at a student support programme, eg, financial counselling.
- Eligibility for bursaries to be assessed using UUK/SLC model bursary scheme (HEBSS).
- Payment will be made in instalments.

Contact:

www.kent.ac.uk/recruitment/UG_Funding

Students

Undergraduates:	8,870	(3,495)
Postgraduates:	1,145	(1,090)
Mature students:	15.8%	
Overseas students:	19.1%	
Applications per place:	4.7	
From state-sector schools:	89.4%	
From working-class homes:	24.3%	

For detailed information about fees, grants and bursaries and how they work, see chapter 7.

Accommodation

Number of places and costs refer to 2006–07
University-provided places: 3,981
Percentage catered: 33%
Catered costs: £84.70–£118.93 a week.
Self-catered costs: £71.89–£101.22 a week.
First years are guaranteed accommodation provided conditions are met.
International students: guaranteed accommodation provided conditions are met.
Contact: accomm@ukc.ac.uk
www.kent.ac.uk/hospitality

King's College London

The second largest of London University's colleges, King's is now concentrated on three campuses close to the Thames. Most departments are within walking distance of each other, on the original Strand site or the new Waterloo campus, with medicine and dentistry based not far away at London Bridge as well as at Denmark Hill, in south London. Likewise the St Thomas' Hospital campus. Students seem to like the outcome: King's registered a 13 per cent increase in applications for courses beginning in 2004 and topped that the following year. An institutional audit by the Quality Assurance Agency gave King's the highest mark, stressing the excellence of the student support services. Medical subjects have been the main growth point. Two nursing schools were amalgamated, building on the college's longstanding BSc in nursing studies, while a merger with the United Medical and Dental Schools of Guy's and St Thomas's Hospitals made King's a major centre for medical and dental education. Among almost 600 students training to become doctors or dentists are mature students on a new course designed to provide more variety in the medical profession.

A £400-million transformation of the college estate is still in progress. So far, it has produced two well-equipped sites, with 2,800 health and life sciences students occupying the largest university building in London, near Waterloo Station, while biomedical sciences, medicine and dentistry have acquired purpose-built facilities on the Guy's Campus. There is to be further development of the St Thomas' site for medical education and hospital use following the opening of the new and ground-breaking Evelina Children's Hospital.

Another property deal has created the largest new university library in Britain since World War II at the former Public Record Office in Chancery Lane. A donation by a graduate of £4 million has underwritten the spectacular new Maughan Library with 1,400 networked reader places. The first phase of restoration at the Strand was completed by Easter 2006. Refurbishment of half of the campus's main Georgian building, at a cost of £20 million, will provide new teaching facilities, wireless internet access, social and catering facilities.

Once known primarily for science, King's now excels in a wide range of subjects in nine schools of study, including such unusual features as Britain's only department devoted entirely to Portuguese – one of four language departments rated internationally outstanding in the latest research

---

Strand, London WC2R 2LS
020-7848 2929
ceu@kcl.ac.uk
www.kcl.ac.uk
www.kclsu.org

The Times Rankings
Overall Ranking: 17

Student satisfaction:	=30	(15.1)
Research assessment:	=18	(5.5)
Entry standards:	16	(393.7)
Student–staff ratio:	5	(12.0)
Library/IT spend/student:	8	(£954)
Facilities spend/student:	81	(£156)
Good honours:	17	(70.7%)
Graduate prospects:	4	(81.1%)
Expected completion rate:	19	(92.9%)

assessments. War studies, developmental biology, dentistry, history, philosophy and psychiatry completed the college's impressive haul of 5* grades and won a Queen's Anniversary Prize in 2002. Almost one in three of those entered for the exercise were in starred departments. A further 14 departments achieved a 5 grade.

Classics, dentistry, war studies and philosophy are all top-rated for teaching. Clinical psychology, nursing, midwifery, health Visiting and physiotherapy did well in a major review in 2005 while law, history, archaeology and physics were the strongest areas in the first national student satisfaction survey. Throughout the college, scientists remain in a majority, and are now offered a wide range of interdisciplinary combinations, such as war studies and philosophy, or French and mathematics. But the famous chemistry department is to cease teaching undergraduates.

King's was one of the two founding colleges of London University, and the full extent of the college's ambitions is clear from its mission statement, which includes having all its departments rated excellent for both teaching and research. The college was among the first to follow the example of American universities by submitting to a credit rating, which took account of its academic and financial standing. The "AA minus" result was better than many big cities have achieved.

King's is also a solid bet for a good degree for those who satisfy its demanding entry requirements, with over 70 per cent reaching the first or 2:1 classification. Every student is allocated a personal tutor, and much of the teaching is in small groups. There are more than 2,500 residential places, and the college also has access to 522 places in the intercollegiate halls of London University. Some of the outdoor sports facilities are rather dispersed, but are accessible by train.

Bursaries and Scholarships

In receipt of full Maintenance Grant	£1,350
In receipt of partial Maintenance Grant	Up to £1,350

- Tuition fees (2006)   £3,000
- Bursary is to be calculated on the basis of 50% of the student's MG for 2006–07 and is expected to continue in 2007–08.
- King's scholarships: 40 to be offered at £1,800 to all new undergraduates.
- 25% of additional fee income to be earmarked for bursaries.
- Eligibility for bursaries to be assessed using LEA means-testing process.

Contact: www.kcl.ac.uk/funding

Students

Undergraduates:	12,040	(2,835)
Postgraduates:	3,125	(3,310)
Mature students:	16.8%	
Overseas students:	19.2%	
Applications per place:	8.4	
From state-sector schools:	67.3%	
From working-class homes:	21.0%	

For detailed information about fees, grants and bursaries and how they work, see chapter 7.

Accommodation

Number of places and costs refer to 2006–07
University-provided places: 2,545; 522 intercollegiate
Percentage catered: 18%; 100% intercollegiate
Catered costs: £98–£122 a week
Self-catered costs: £59.29–£105.42 (40 weeks).
New full-time students are guaranteed one year in accommodation if conditions are met.
International students: priority for those who have not previously lived or studied in the UK.
Contact: 020-7848 2759; www.kcl.ac.uk/accomm

Kingston University

Having established itself as one of the leading new universities, with nearly 20,000 students, Kingston is hoping for a location to match. The university is planning to take over the headquarters of Surrey County Council, in the town centre, to provide a focal point and give it more flexibility. But it is not waiting for the go-ahead to pursue new developments. A six-floor quadrangle building containing teaching and IT areas is scheduled to open at Penrhyn Road, the current main campus, in September 2007, when library extensions are also due to be operational on the other two main sites. There has also been further development of a joint faculty with St George's Hospital Medical School.

No department scored less than 20 points out of 24 in the final rounds of teaching assessment. The university has been reducing what had been surprisingly large numbers recruited through clearing, bucking the trend among the few former polytechnics by registering regular increases in applications. A 17 per cent rise for courses beginning in 2004 was bettered by only one university in England and the same was true of the impressive 27 per cent rise registered at the start of 2005. However, the first national student satisfaction survey brought disappointing results, which have contributed to a fall in our League Table.

For the moment, the university has four campuses in southwest London: two close to Kingston town centre, another two miles away at Kingston Hill and the fourth in Roehampton Vale, where a a site once used as an aerospace factory is now occupied by a new technology block. A flight simulator and the university's own Learjet continue the tradition and a foundation degree in aeronautical engineering is ministers' favourite example of the two-year course. An unusually extensive, 1,600-terminal computer network links them all. Information technology plays an important role in student life, with the university's Blackboard system giving 24-hour online access to lecture notes and presentations, as well as chat rooms and bulletin boards.

Over the last decade Kingston has invested more than £65 million in new buildings, which include facilities such as a 300-seat lecture theatre and a high-tech learning resources centre. At the Penrhyn Road campus, recent development has featured a £9.8-million science building which has provided additional laboratory space with an electron microscope for the biomedical sciences and spectrometers for pharmaceutical subjects. Earlier phases provided state-of-the-art computing facilities and increased library space.

Kingston upon Thames,
Surrey KT1 1LQ
020-8547 2000
admissions-info@
kingston.ac.uk
www.kingston.ac.uk
www.kingston.ac.uk/guild

The Times Rankings
Overall Ranking: 89

Student satisfaction:	=75	(14.3)
Research assessment:	=72	(2.7)
Entry standards:	101	(207.2)
Student–staff ratio:	=76	(20.4)
Library/IT spend/student:	54	(£547)
Facilities spend/student:	=82	(£154)
Good honours:	83	(50.4%)
Graduate prospects:	40	(66.1%)
Expected completion rate:	73	(81.0%)

Research grades in the last assessment exercise showed improvement, with European studies, history and history of art scoring well, but teaching scores have shown Kingston's real strength. The School of Life Sciences joined building and mechanical, aeronautical and manufacturing engineering in recording perfect scores, following on from some good performances under the original quality system. Politics and nursing also produced good results. Nursing is part of the Faculty of Health and Social Care Sciences, the successful collaboration with St George's Hospital Medical School, which recently added pharmacy to its portfolio of courses.

More than a third of Kingston's places go to mature students and a similar proportion to those from working-class families – both groups with low completion rates nationally. The latest projected dropout rate is 17 per cent, but this is less than the national average for the subjects on offer. To make the university more responsive to its students, it provides a "one-stop shop", which deals with student issues ranging from careers and accommodation to complaints and internal discipline, while the Dean of Students is a member of the university executive. Such responsiveness and the accessibility of staff were singled out for praise in a quality audit. Over £20 million has been spent on halls of residence in recent years, most recently with extensions and refurbishment of the two largest halls, which now have almost 1,400 beds. Students like the location, on the fringe of London, although complaints about the high cost of living are common.

Bursaries and Scholarships

In receipt of full Maintenance Grant £300–£1,000
In receipt of partial Maintenance Grant
£300–£1,000
Progressing from outreach   Bursary

- Tuition fees (2006)   £3,000
- Placement year fee will be 50% of the standard, non-variable tuition fee, currently £600. Fees for year abroad will be around £1,500.
- University Compact Scheme provides £300 for 150 (rising to 500) new entrants.
- Variable Fees Fund, a discretionary hardship fund, is available to students not receiving MG.
- 25% of additional fee income to be earmarked for bursaries.
- Eligibility for bursaries to be assessed using UUK/SLC model bursary scheme (HEBSS).

Contact:
www.kingston.ac.uk/undergraduate/money/bursary.htm

Students

Undergraduates:	13,500	(1,820)
Postgraduates:	1,345	(3,050)
Mature students:	27.3%	
Overseas students:	12.6%	
Applications per place:	5.4	
From state-sector schools:	94.4%	
From working-class homes:	37.5%	

For detailed information about fees, grants and bursaries and how they work, see chapter 7.

Accommodation

Number of places and costs refer to 2006–07
University-provided places: 2,437
Percentage catered: 0%
Self-catered costs: £81.50–£97.25 a week.
First years are offered places provided requirements are met. Residential restrictions apply.
International students: as above.
Contact: Accommodation@kingston.ac.uk

Lampeter, University of Wales

In the whole of England and Wales, only Oxford and Cambridge were awarding degrees before Lampeter. Yet only Buckingham University is smaller today. In fact, Lampeter claims to be the smallest publicly-funded university in Europe, making a virtue of its size by stressing its friendly atmosphere and intimate teaching style. There has been pressure from the Welsh Assembly for closer collaboration between the Principality's small higher education institutions and some administrative tasks are already carried out jointly with Trinity College, Carmarthen. But the students seem to like Lampeter as it is: it was among the leading institutions in the first national student satisfaction survey.

Based on an ancient castle and modelled on an Oxbridge college, St David's College (as it was originally known) was established to train young men for the Anglican ministry. That title receded into the small print, as the University of Wales allowed its member institutions to drop their college titles. But the original quadrangle remains and the chapel is in daily use.

There have been significant changes in the last few years – notably a big expansion in distance learning and the introduction of such subjects as anthropology, IT,

management, and film and media studies. There are now 300 course combinations available in the joint honours programme. Victorian studies and medieval studies are unusual constructs, while Chinese studies, creative writing and media production are among the new arrivals. However, there is no immediate aim to go beyond 2,000 students, itself almost double the numbers taken a decade ago.

Lampeter remains arts-dominated: even IT leads to a BA, and the Bachelor of Divinity is the only other undergraduate degree. Lampeter is best known for theology, one of the two top-rated research departments, the other being English. The small campus includes a mosque for the growing number of Muslim students attracted by a well-endowed programme of Islamic studies. But students are opting increasingly for broad courses such as medieval studies, which includes archaeology, classics and theology, as well as history, English and Welsh. Media studies, which benefits from a well-equipped media centre for film and television students, is also growing in popularity. The university won a Queen's Anniversary Prize for a degree in voluntary sector studies, developed from a series of sub-degree courses.

Modular degrees have been introduced, but degrees are still divided into two parts, with the first year designed to ensure

---

College Street, Lampeter,
Ceredigion SA48 7ED
01570 422351
admissions@lampeter.ac.uk
www.lamp.ac.uk
www.lamp.ac.uk/su

The Times Rankings
Overall Ranking: 66

Student satisfaction:	2	(15.8)
Research assessment:	=42	(4.7)
Entry standards:	76	(245.5)
Student–staff ratio:	103	(24.6)
Library/IT spend/student:	103	(£383)
Facilities spend/student:	91	(£142)
Good honours:	=52	(59.1%)
Graduate prospects:	=96	(52.1%)
Expected completion rate:	90	(76.4%)

breadth of study. Most courses now include the option of a January start. Undergraduates are encouraged to try a new language, such as Arabic, Greek or Welsh. Part two normally takes a further two years, although philosophy takes three. Lampeter is deep in Welsh-speaking rural West Wales, and both the university and the students' union have strong bilingual policies. The university is also taking Welsh to a wider audience, with the only university course teaching the language over the internet.

Although only four hours from London and two from Cardiff, Lampeter's geographical position could be a problem for the unprepared. The town has only 4,000 inhabitants, with among the lowest crime rates in Britain, and the nearest station is more than 20 miles away at Carmarthen. A high proportion of the students run cars. The students' union is the centre of social life – not surprising when the university's guide to the town lists its attractions as "cafés, pubs, a curry house and a French patisserie". Most students have made a deliberate choice to avoid the bright lights, and many would like to remain in the area after graduation, although jobs are scarce. The location helps to produce a relatively high proportion of students from areas with little tradition of higher education and, more surprisingly, almost 45 per cent from working-class homes. The college's size can make for big fluctuations in the various published indicators. The projected dropout rate, for example, had dipped below 10 per cent in the official statistics published in 2004, but was back above 20 per cent in 2005.

Bursaries and Scholarships
- Fees for undergraduate courses £3,000.
- Students living in Wales will be eligible for a Welsh Assembly fee grant of approximately £1,800 a year.
- Fees for year abroad not yet known.
- For information on the National Bursary Scheme see page 198, chapter 7.
- 10 University scholarships of up to £2,000 for students from England.
- 10 University scholarships of up to £2,000 for students from Wales (5 of these for students from Community First areas).
- 9 Departmental scholarships of up to £1,000 for students aged 18–21.
- 9 Departmental scholarships of up to £1,000 for students aged 21 and over.

Contact: www.lamp.ac.uk/scholarships

Students		
Undergraduates:	920	(5,655)
Postgraduates:	180	(1,005)
Mature students:	30.5%	
Overseas students:	21.9%	
Applications per place:	3.4	
From state-sector schools:	97.0%	
From working-class homes:	45.3%	

For detailed information about fees, grants and bursaries and how they work, see chapter 7.

Accommodation
Number of places and costs refer to 2006–07
University-provided places: around 500
Percentage catered: 0%
Self-catered costs: £52.30–£62.30 a week.
First years are guaranteed accommodation.
International students: as above.
Contact: p.thomas@lampeter.ac.uk
www.lamp.ac.uk/accommodation/index.htm

Lancaster University

Having celebrated its 40th birthday, Lancaster has almost completed a £180-million makeover for its campus to give it a more modern feel and increase its capacity by up to 50 per cent. Still a relatively small institution, the aim is to establish itself in the leading group of research universities and help improve the local economy. An assessment by investment analysts, who examined educational and financial issues, gave Lancaster a good rating. The process placed Lancaster among the top dozen universities for research and in the top 20 for teaching, as well as pronouncing it financially sound and capable of competing for students and research funds nationally and internationally. Official assessments place the university higher still: its last research grades were in the top ten and teaching ratings were consistently excellent. Lancaster also made the top ten in the first national student satisfaction survey, with particularly good results in history, religious studies, languages, computer science, politics and physics.

Results from the 2001 Research Assessment Exercise were an improvement on an already strong performance five years earlier. Business and management, physics, sociology and statistics were all rated internationally outstanding and, with another ten subjects achieving grade 5, more than 70 per cent of the academics were in departments placed in the top two categories.

A £25-million environment centre shared with the Natural Environment Research Council opened in 2003, reinforcing the university's strength in environmental science. A £15-million centre of excellence in information communication technology, Infolab 21, was launched in 2005, providing a new research, computing and communications centre on campus. It will act as a technology transfer and incubation facility and house a training facility for high-tech businesses. The highly-rated Management School is also acquiring a £9.5-million extension.

Social work, which has a dozen applications for every place, attracted one of a number of glowing reports for teaching. Education, philosophy and religious studies, psychology and music, art and theatre studies all achieved maximum scores. Nevertheless, Lancaster is not just a ratings factory. The university has a longstanding tradition of provision for students with special needs, for example.

Lancaster is another of the campus universities of the 1960s which has always traded on its flexible degree structure.

Bailrigg, Lancaster LA1 4YW
01524 65201
ugadmissions@lancaster.ac.uk
www.lancaster.ac.uk
www.lusu.co.uk

Most undergraduates can broaden their first-year studies by taking a second or third subject. The final choice of degree comes only at the end of that year. Combined degree programmes, with 200 courses to choose from, are especially popular.

The dropout rate, at less than 6 per cent, is much lower than the average for the subjects on offer. Lancaster also exceeds expectations for the recruitment of students from state schools, but the proportion from working-class homes and disadvantaged areas are both marginally below the benchmark for the university's courses.

The previously uninspiring campus has benefited from recent developments, which have included refurbished lecture theatres, sports facilities and residences. The university is a ten-minute bus ride from Lancaster, three miles away. Students join one of nine residential colleges, which become the centre of most students' social life. Most house between 800 and 900 students in self-catering accommodation. Some 3,400 new and updated residential places came on stream in 2005. The development has enabled Cartmel and Lonsdale colleges to transfer to the New Alexandra Park area of the campus with enhanced social facilities.

The campus has a reputation for being one of the safest in the UK. Sports facilities are good and conveniently placed. For those who want the outdoor life, the Lake District is within easy reach. Road and rail communications are good but, while Manchester and Liverpool are within easy reach, some students still find the immediate location more isolated than they expected.

Bursaries and Scholarships

In receipt of full Maintenance Grant	£1,000
In receipt of partial Maintenance Grant	£0–£500
Shortage subjects	Bursary
Academic achievement	Scholarship
• Tuition fees (2006)	£3,000

- Bursaries will be potentially available to UK students.
- Subject awards worth £1,000 a year available to all UK and EU students taking selected subjects in science, modern languages and engineering.
- Scholarships worth £1,000 a year potentially available to UK students taking non-subject award subjects.
- Scholarships and subjects awards are in addition to any bursaries awarded to students.
- Student employment scheme.
- Eligibility for bursaries is on basis of LEA financial assessments.
- Eligibility for bursaries to be assessed using UUK/SLC model bursary scheme (HEBSS).

Contact: www.lancs.ac.uk/users/ studentsupport/finance
www.lancs.ac.uk/ugfinance

Students

Undergraduates:	8,170	(6,195)
Postgraduates:	1,665	(1,640)
Mature students:	9.0%	
Overseas students:	12.4%	
Applications per place:	5.6	
From state-sector schools:	89.0%	
From working-class homes:	22.3%	

For detailed information about fees, grants and bursaries and how they work, see chapter 7.

Accommodation

Number of places and costs refer to 2005–06
University-provided places: 6,300
Percentage catered: 0%
Self-catered costs: £50.00–£76.50 a week.
First years are usually accommodated but insurance, clearing and very late applicants are not guaranteed places.
International students are guaranteed accommodation throughout their studies.
Contact: CRO@lancaster.ac.uk

University of Leeds

The rise of Leeds as a clubbing mecca to rival Manchester has added to the attractions of a university which has long been one of the giants of the higher education system. It was the most popular university in Britain in 2003 and 2004, and was second only to the newly-merged Manchester University in 2005. The university plans to invest £172 million in new buildings and bring in more than 100 senior academics over the next five years in order to break into the top 50 universities in the world. It is currently on the verge of the top 100 in *The Times Higher Education Supplement*'s world rankings.

An unusually wide range of degrees gives applicants more than 700 undergraduate programmes to choose from, with over 1,300 academic staff teaching 32,000 students.

The university occupies a 140-acre site, two thirds of which is designated a conservation area, within walking distance of the city centre. The buildings are a mixture of Victorian and modern, the latest of which have extended the library, provided more space for biology and moved the business school into new £10-million premises.

The university had begun to spread its wings by merging with Bretton Hall College, near Wakefield, with its sculpture park and established reputation in the performing and visual arts. But it has already been decided to close the campus in 2007 and bring the new Faculty of Performing Arts and Cultural Industries back to Leeds, where there will be a £1.5-million development including a theatre, performance design studio and rehearsal space. Nine other colleges in various parts of the county offer Leeds courses, but handle their own admissions.

Further afield, Leeds is also part of a "worldwide network" which brings together four American and four British universities to collaborate initially on research, postgraduate degree programmes and continuing professional development. There was already a thriving European programme involving more than 100 Continental partners and a flow of students in both directions. A free-standing language unit caters for casual learners as well as specialists.

Leeds has followed the fashion for modular courses, enabling its students to take full advantage of a growing range of interdisciplinary degrees. Almost a quarter now take dual honours or combinations such as communications, women's studies or international studies. The university has been chosen to house a national centre of excellence in interdisciplinary teaching and another in assessment and

---

Leeds, West Yorkshire LS2 9JT
0113-233 2332
admissions@leeds.ac.uk
www.leeds.ac.uk
www.luuonline.com

The Times Rankings
Overall Ranking: =34

Student satisfaction:	=49	(14.8)
Research assessment:	=25	(5.3)
Entry standards:	22	(374.7)
Student–staff ratio:	=52	(17.9)
Library/IT spend/student:	34	(£635)
Facilities spend/student:	63	(£196)
Good honours:	=15	(71.5%)
Graduate prospects:	=26	(70.2%)
Expected completion rate:	26	(91.7%)

learning in medical practice settings. Business and management is also increasingly popular, the business school having moved into the former Leeds Grammar School site.

Electrical and mechanical engineering, English, food science, Italian and town planning were all rated internationally outstanding for research in 2001, when Leeds had among the largest number of academics in the national assessment exercise. Teaching ratings were generally good, with education, philosophy, physics and healthcare studies awarded maximum points. Medicine, pharmacy and English were the top performers in the first national student satisfaction survey.

Student facilities are generally first rate. Leeds teams regularly excel in competition and the university hosts one of five centres of cricketing excellence. The 8,000 computer workstations are among the most at any university and the library one of the biggest. It all contributes towards an 8 per cent dropout rate, which is lower than the national average for the university's courses and entry grades. Nearly a quarter of the undergraduates come from independent schools, and there is a low proportion of working-class students – less the one in five. The already large students' union, famous for its long bar and big-name rock concerts, has been extended to cope with the latest phase in the university's expansion. A £4-million upgrade provided a new venue, more shops and catering facilities. Town–gown relations are generally good.

Bursaries and Scholarships

In receipt of full Maintenance Grant	£1,300
In receipt of partial Maintenance Grant	£0–£1,170
Living in specified postcodes	Scholarship
Progressing from outreach	Scholarship

- Tuition fees (2006) £3,000
- Foundation year tuition fee , £1,200; place-ment year and year abroad tuition fees £800.
- Targeted scholarship scheme to attract first generation students from low socio-economic groups including those on access programmes such as Access to Leeds. Available to students receiving full Maintenance Grant and is in addition to bursary. Worth £3,000.
- Targeted scholarship scheme (around 40 available) to attract students from low income backgrounds (defined as £33,500 a year or less) who also demonstrate academic excellence. This scheme is in addition to the bursary. Worth £1,000 a year.
- Targeted scholarship scheme to attract students from low socio-economic groups in the Barnsley, Rotherham and Doncaster areas of South Yorkshire. The scholarship is instead of the bursary. Worth £3,000 a year.
- £8.7 million of additional fee income to be earmarked for bursaries by 2010–11.

Contact: http://scholarships.leeds.ac.uk

Students

Undergraduates:	21,995	(3,530)
Postgraduates:	6,090	(3,550)
Mature students:	8.8%	
Overseas students:	9.3%	
Applications per place:	7.6	
From state-sector schools:	76.3%	
From working-class homes:	19.6%	

For detailed information about fees, grants and bursaries and how they work, see chapter 7.

Accommodation

Number of places and costs refer to 2005–06
University-provided places: 7,863
Percentage catered: 26%
Catered costs: £72.58–£109.68 a week.
Self-catered costs: £31.25–£85.00 a week.
Single first years are guaranteed a place providing conditions are met.
International students: guaranteed to full fee-paying undergraduates if conditions are met.
Contact: accom@adm.leeds.ac.uk
www.unipol.leeds.ac.uk

Leeds Metropolitan University

Leeds Met took the bold step of becoming the first university to set fees below the £3,000-a-year maximum allowed in 2006, and at £2,000 it is the cheapest at which to take a full-time degree. Professor Simon Lee, the Vice-Chancellor, admitted that some of his colleagues considered him 'crazy' because students might think the university's degrees were of lower quality than its competitors', but the move made a mark in a crowded market. The rate inevitably limited the scope for bursaries for students from poor backgrounds, but was bound to attract middle-class students, who would not qualify for bursaries.

The university already had a reputation for widening participation in higher education: it is one of the largest providers of foundation degrees and has more than 41,000 students since the incorporation of a large further education college in Harrogate. Partnerships with colleges in Leeds and Bradford have produced a 'comprehensive' post-school institution, in which students can take courses from diplomas to doctorates. Four out of ten of its students come from the Yorkshire and Humberside region, and over half are over 21 on entry. More than nine out of ten are state-educated and a third come from working-class homes.

Applications were up by more than 11 per cent when the official deadline passed for courses beginning in 2005. More than 3,500 students come from 120 countries outside the UK. Just over half are taking conventional full-time degrees, such is the popularity of sandwich and part-time courses. The projected dropout rate of 15 per cent is significantly below the official benchmark. As part of its efforts to widen access, LMU runs a course for sixth-formers from the region, awarding UCAS points for those who complete successfully. There is also a wide range of summer schools, including one for Asian women and one for Afro-Caribbean boys. Even before the advent of top-up fees, the university offered a range of scholarships for students from non-traditional backgrounds.

There are two campuses in Leeds: the main site close to the city centre and Beckett Park, a former teacher training college three miles away in 100 acres of park and woodlands. The latter boasts outstanding sports facilities, including the £2-million Carnegie Regional Tennis Centre, as well as teaching accommodation for education, informatics, law and business. Over 7,000 students take part in some form of sporting activity, and there is a range of £1,000 sports scholarships. The city campus is the subject of a £100 million

---

City Campus, Leeds,
West Yorkshire LS1 3HE
0113-283 3113
course-enquiries@lmu.ac.uk
www.lmu.ac.uk
www.lmusu.org.uk

development programme, beginning with the opening in 2005 of a new film school. A futuristic lecture theatre complex is planned next to Leeds Civic Hall, with a new headquarters for the business school wrapped around it. Before that, the former BBC building will reopen as Old Broadcasting House, described as a 'meeting place' for the arts, enterprise and students.

Business, management and economics achieved the best scores for teaching quality. Education and the large School of Health Sciences, with its 1,200 students, were close behind. Only 12 subjects were entered for the last research assessment exercise, with librarianship and information management the only one to reach the top three categories of seven. However, an institutional audit by the Quality Assurance Agency in 2004 praised the university for "placing the student experience at the heart of the enterprise". Students are included on the committees that design and manage courses, but the impact was not obvious in a relatively disappointing set of results from the first national student satisfaction survey.

There is a growing emphasis on educational technology, which was enhanced by a £20-million learning resources centre. More than 400 computers, audio-visual presentation studios and study areas are available all hours. Contacts with small and medium-sized businesses, which won a Queen's Anniversary Prize, have been carefully fostered as part of the university's successful attempts to maintain a good record in graduate employment. Most undergraduate courses are determinedly vocational, although the modular system gives students considerable control over the content of their degree. Like its older neighbour, Leeds Met is benefiting from the city's growing reputation for nightlife, but it is making its own contribution with a famously lively entertainments scene.

Bursaries and Scholarships

- Tuition Fees (2006)   £2,000
- Leeds Met Bursary Scheme will continue to offer discretionary hardship awards of about £2,000 over 3 years to 15–20 students each year.

Contact: http://helpzone.leedsmet.ac.uk/

Students		
Undergraduates:	15,295	(8,960)
Postgraduates:	1,510	(2,815)
Mature students:	18.3%	
Overseas students:	9.5%	
Applications per place:	4.7	
From state-sector schools:	92.8%	
From working-class homes:	31.7%	

For detailed information about fees, grants and bursaries and how they work, see chapter 7.

Accommodation

Number of places and costs refer to 2006–07
University-provided places: 3,200
Percentage catered: 0%
Self-catered costs: £58–£113 a week.
First years with Conditional Firm or Unconditional Firm offers have priority.
International students: guaranteed accommodation if conditions are met.
Contact: accommodation@leedsmet.ac.uk

University of Leicester

Leicester is beginning to take off, after many years living in the shadow of the big city universities. A string of excellent assessments for teaching and research have coincided with a £300-million campus development programme – one of the biggest in Britain – that has produced a buzz around the university. It was in the top two in the first national student satisfaction, with the best teaching score among the conventional universities, and was shortlisted for *The Times Higher Education Supplement*'s University of the Year in 2005.

Rising demand for places (reversed in 2006) has led to many subjects raising their entrance requirements.

Though the university celebrated its 80th anniversary in 2001, it is only now approaching the size of most of its traditional counterparts after growing by more than 60 per cent in recent years. Less than half of the 18,500 registered students are full-time campus-based undergraduates, but Leicester has the largest number of taught postgraduates in Britain and more than 6,000 distance learners, many of them overseas. Professor Robert Burgess, the Vice-Chancellor, is focusing on strengthening research and has scaled down the university's initial enthusiasm for two-year foundation degrees. But efforts continue to broaden Leicester's intake, for example through a summer school for local teenagers. Almost nine out of ten undergraduates come from state schools and approaching a quarter come from working-class homes. The 4 per cent drop-out rate is one of the lowest in Britain.

Teaching ratings were generally good: the last dozen assessments all produced at least 22 points out of 24, with archaeology, ancient history, economics, education, museum studies and psychology recording full marks. The university is a leader in space science, with Europe's largest university-based space research facility, including the £52-million National Space Centre, and was heavily involved in the Beagle 2 mission to Mars. By contrast, the university has also been chosen to promote good teaching practice in archaeology.

The medical school registered one of the best teaching quality scores for the subject. It has developed a new style of medical degree with Warwick University, allowing graduates in the health and life sciences to qualify in four years. The school has among the most modern facilities in Britain, and the siting of a medically-based interdisciplinary research centre at the university was another indication of growing strength. Genetics, which won the university a second Queen's Anniversary Prize in 2002, achieved the only 5* rating in the last research assessments. But a dozen

University Road,
Leicester LE1 7RH
0116-252 5281
admissions@le.ac.uk
www.le.ac.uk
www.leicesterstudent.org

The Times Rankings
Overall Ranking: =18

Student satisfaction:	3	(15.7)
Research assessment:	=36	(5.0)
Entry standards:	30	(351.9)
Student–staff ratio:	=40	(17.1)
Library/IT spend/student:	51	(£570)
Facilities spend/student:	=5	(£395)
Good honours:	36	(64.3%)
Graduate prospects:	39	(66.2%)
Expected completion rate:	6	(95.6%)

subjects in the next category enabled Leicester to outperform a clutch of civic universities in terms of average grades per member of staff.

Other than clinical medicine at the city's three hospitals, all teaching and much residential accommodation is concentrated in a leafy suburb a mile from the city centre. Its location, adjacent to one of Leicester's main parks, is an attraction to students. A new biomedical sciences building opened in 2004 and a £25-million library extension, doubling its size and expanding its capacity to 1,500 seats, is scheduled for completion in 2007. The Richard Attenborough Centre has given Leicester a particular reputation for catering for disabled students.

Among a number of areas to have been refurbished recently is the students' union, which has spruced up its main bar areas and runs one of the most popular university nightclubs, the Venue. Extensive residential accommodation includes a £20-million 600-bed en suite development, with another 580 rooms due to be refurbished by September 2006. First years are guaranteed a residential place and many second and third-year students also live in hall, although the majority choose to live in the reasonably-priced private accommodation available nearby. The main sports facilities are conveniently located; in 2005–06, students paid £50 a year to use them.

Bursaries and Scholarships

In receipt of full MG	£1,300–£1,500
In receipt of partial MG	£50–£950
Academic achievement	Scholarship £1000

- Tuition fees (2006) £3,000
- Bursaries will be available to UK students only.
- £1,000 scholarship to students in most subject areas who gain at least ABB at A level or equivalent.
- Eligibility for bursaries to be assessed using UUK/SLC model bursary scheme (HEBSS).
- In kind benefits include loan of laptop computers, free local bus pass for term 1, allowance for food from university catering, print card and bookshop allowance (package valued at £1,200).
- Hardship Fund of £100,000 a year.

Contact: www.le.ac.uk/fees

Students

Undergraduates:	8,320	(1,625)
Postgraduates:	2,075	(4,205)
Mature students:	19.3%	
Overseas students:	11.9%	
Applications per place:	6.1	
From state-sector schools:	87.2%	
From working-class homes:	24.5%	

For detailed information about fees, grants and bursaries and how they work, see chapter 7.

Accommodation

Number of places and costs refer to 2005–06
University-provided places: 4,326
Percentage catered: 28%
Catered costs: £97.23 a week (30 weeks).
Self-catered costs: £56.14 (39 weeks).
First-year students are offered a guarantee of accommodation provided conditions are met. International students: as above, with priority to those returning.
Contact: accommodation@le.ac.uk
www.le.ac.uk/accommodation

University of Lincoln

The opening, ten years ago, of an impressive purpose-built campus alongside a marina in the centre of Lincoln brought about the most dramatic transformation of any university in recent times. Humberside University, as it then was, even gave its new location pride of place in its title. Five years later it went a step further, selling the previous headquarters campus and securing the approval of the Privy Council to become plain Lincoln University. While not moving out of Hull entirely, the university is concentrating its activities on a much smaller city-centre site.

The switch has paid undoubted dividends, helping to attract high-quality academics. The number of professors has grown from eight to almost 60 in three years. Student applications increased for five years in a row, until a big drop at the start of 2006 with the introduction of top-up fees. Rising entry grades in a number of the more popular courses may have put some applicants off.

New science laboratories and sports facilities brought the cost of the development in Lincoln to more than £75 million and another £30 million has been committed to complete the campus. A new building for architecture, media and communications opened in 2003, while the conversion of a derelict warehouse on the edge of the campus into a £5-million library was nominated for a Civic Trust award. The campus now has just over 1,000 beds and another conversion – this time of a former engine shed – will provide a new student centre and entertainment venue from the summer of 2006.

Despite the change of name, the university remains effectively two institutions 40 miles apart, although a broadband telecommunications network links the sites – part of the impressive IT provision, which runs to 1,200 computers. A further rationalisation of courses has left Hull with health and social care, applied computing, art and design and management, with £4 million being invested over five years in a site that now takes 2,000 students.

Lincoln initially concentrated on social sciences, accentuating the university's bias in favour of the arts, but has been building up a wider range of courses. The School of Architecture, for example, now has over 400 students. Following the acquisition of former art and design and agriculture colleges from De Montfort University in 2001, the university now has more than 8,000 students in and around Lincoln. Art and design is based in the former college campus in the city centre, while agriculture and equine studies are at

---

Brayford Pool, Lincoln LN6 7TS
01522 882000
marketing@lincoln.ac.uk
www.lincoln.ac.uk
www.lincolnsu.com

The Times Rankings
Overall Ranking: 104

Student satisfaction:	=67	(14.5)
Research assessment:	=99	(1.7)
Entry standards:	74	(249.2)
Student–staff ratio:	107	(26.4)
Library/IT spend/student:	57	(£538)
Facilities spend/student:	80	(£159)
Good honours:	89	(49.3%)
Graduate prospects:	108	(45.0%)
Expected completion rate:	70	(81.4%)

Riseholme Park, a 1,000-acre site ten minutes outside Lincoln.

Poor performances in both teaching and research assessments account for Lincoln's low position in *The Times* ranking, although results improved in the later years of the cycle. Education achieved maximum points for teaching quality and two recent institutional audits have been complimentary. Only 21 per cent of the academics were entered for the last research ratings, when no subjects reached the top three categories of seven, but twice as many academics are now engaged in research and the income from this activity is much increased.

All students take the Effective Learning Programme, which uses computer packages backed up by weekly seminars to develop necessary study skills and produce a detailed portfolio of all their work. Research into teaching and learning methods has been aided by a £1-million fund provided by BP. Some degrees can be taken as work-based programmes, with credit awarded for relevant aspects of the jobs.

Lincoln was the first university to win a Charter Mark for exceptional service, but the student experience inevitably differs between sites. More than a third of the undergraduates come from working-class homes and, although the projected dropout rate is 18 per cent, that is no more than the average for the subjects on offer, given the entry standards. Lincoln is adapting to its new student population with new bars and clubs, but will always be quieter than Hull, where a lively waterfront area means the city is no longer known just for the low cost of living.

Bursaries and Scholarships

In receipt of full Maintenance Grant	£600
In receipt of partial Maintenance Grant	
	Sliding scale based on level of MG
Living in region	Bursary £100–£300
Progressing from outreach	Scholarship £100–£300
Academic achievement	Scholarship £500–£5,000

- Tuition fees (2006) £3,000
- Placement year and year abroad tuition fee will be £1,500.
- A minimum of £2.65 million of additional fee income earmarked for bursaries for those in receipt of Maintenance Grant.
- Eligibility for bursaries to be assessed using UUK/SLC model bursary scheme (HEBSS).
- All students receive automatic scholarships if they meet entry requirements.

Contact: www.lincoln.ac.uk/fees

Students

Undergraduates:	7,885	(3,795)
Postgraduates:	445	(1,040)
Mature students:	23.9%	
Overseas students:	7.8%	
Applications per place:	3.6	
From state-sector schools:	97.3%	
From working-class homes:	34.2%	

For detailed information about fees, grants and bursaries and how they work, see chapter 7.

Accommodation

Number of places and costs refer to 2006–07
University-provided places: Lincoln, 1,037; Hull, 200
Percentage catered:0%
Self-catered costs: £85–£78 a week.
Students living more than 25 miles away have priority.
International students are given detailed information and assistance.
Contact:www.lincoln.ac.uk/home/accommodation/index.htm

University of Liverpool

Liverpool is investing £200 million to improve its 100-acre precinct for a student population that has reached 22,000 and will continue to grow despite another drop in new applications at the official deadline for courses starting in 2006. The programme has seen an extended and renovated sports centre, new buildings for biosciences and cancer research, and a management school with courses from first degree to MBA. A new small animal teaching hospital will open in 2007, bringing all veterinary science clinical teaching onto one site. A £50-million fundraising drive aims to establish world-class centres of excellence in management, law, medicine, engineering, veterinary science and architecture.

The university is continuing to modernise its portfolio of courses while preserving a well-established reputation for research. Liverpool is among the top 15 recipients of research funds, with outside income increasing dramatically in recent years. And there has been substantial investment in new educational technology, helping to cope with the demands of extra undergraduates. The main library has been extended and is now open 24 hours and the top-rated medical school has also been expanded. Full-time numbers are almost exactly balanced between the sexes.

A series of excellent ratings in the early teaching assessments took time to repeat, but philosophy, veterinary science, medicine and physics all achieved perfect scores. Physiology, mechanical engineering and English recorded 5* ratings for research in the last assessments, when more than half of the academics entered for research assessment were in departments placed in one of the top two categories. There has been considerable investment in the recruitment of world-renowned academics in advance of the next assessments in 2008. Liverpool could have done better in the first national student satisfaction survey, but geography and environmental science, English and maths all scored well.

The university prides itself on strength across the board and is opening a new university in China in 2006. The university is popular with international students, 93 per cent of whom say they would recommend Liverpool to their friends. Most undergraduate courses are divided into modules totalling 120 credits over a two-semester year, with examinations at the end of each semester which count towards the final degree. New courses include graduate-entry dentistry, avionic systems with pilot studies, and wireless communications with 3G technology.

Liverpool was among the first traditional universities to run access

Liverpool L69 3BX
0151-794 5928
ugrecruitment@liv.ac.uk
www.liv.ac.uk
www.liverpoolguild.org.uk

The Times Rankings
Overall Ranking: 39

Student satisfaction:	=38	(14.9)
Research assessment:	=30	(5.2)
Entry standards:	31	(351.2)
Student–staff ratio:	=27	(16.0)
Library/IT spend/student:	72	(£491)
Facilities spend/student:	=82	(£154)
Good honours:	37	(61.8%)
Graduate prospects:	=16	(72.7%)
Expected completion rate:	21	(92.7%)

courses for adults without traditional academic qualifications, but the projected dropout rate of 6 per cent is still below the national average for the courses and entry grades. Even before the introduction of top-up fees, the university was awarding record numbers of scholarships and bursaries to widen opportunities further. They include five in memory of the Hillsborough disaster victims and 30 in memory of John Lennon, mainly for Merseyside residents. Other access initiatives include a week-long summer school and the opening of a purpose-built children's centre to help mature students and staff, with 68 subsidised places. The proportion of state-educated students is higher than at the other civic universities and a quarter of the undergraduates are from working-class homes.

Both the university and the city have a loyal following among students, and Liverpool's status as Capital of Culture for 2008 should add to the attractions. The 3,364 places in halls of residence, self-catering flats and houses are more than enough to guarantee accommodation to all first years. The suburban setting of the main halls complex and the focus of social life on the guild of students means that there is less integration than at some other civic universities, but there is no shortage of nightlife.

Bursaries and Scholarships

In receipt of full Maintenance Grant	£1,300
In receipt of partial Maintenance Grant	£1,000
Living in region	Bursary
Living in specified postcodes	Bursary
Shortage subjects	Scholarship £1,500
Academic achievement	Bursary

- Tuition fees (2006) £3,000
- Placement year tuition fee will be £600; foundation year fee will be £1,200. These students are eligible for bursaries.
- Bursaries will be available to UK/EU students only, subject to means-testing.
- Targeted attainment scholarships in chemistry, physics, engineering, computer science, earth and ocean sciences.
- Eligibility for bursaries to be assessed using UUK/SLC model bursary scheme (HEBSS).

Contact:
www.liv.ac.uk/study/undergraduate/fees_and_financing1.htm#Scholarships_and_Bursaries

Students

Undergraduates:	13,315	(3,655)
Postgraduates:	2,035	(2,650)
Mature students:	14.5%	
Overseas students:	10.2%	
Applications per place:	6.9	
From state-sector schools:	85.1%	
From working-class homes:	25.3%	

For detailed information about fees, grants and bursaries and how they work, see chapter 7.

Accommodation

Number of places and costs refer to 2006–07
University-provided places: 3,364
Percentage catered: 62%
Catered costs: £94.99–£107.94 a week.
Self-catered costs: £66.99–£72.94 a week.
First-year students are guaranteed accommodation if requirements are met.
International students: as above.
Contact: accommodation@liverpool.ac.uk
www.liv.ac.uk/accommodation

Liverpool Hope University

Liverpool Hope is a unique ecumenical institution formed from the merger of two Catholic and one Church of England teacher training colleges in 1980. The two churches' leading figures on Merseyside described the union as a "sign of hope", unintentionally providing the title for one of the nine new universities created in 2005. It describes itself as "teaching led, research informed and mission focused". There is an accent on extending higher education to people of all ages who might not otherwise experience university, which breeds particular resentment about league tables. The university's website carries complimentary quotes from external examiners in a section entitled "what league tables won't tell you".

The Times League Table criteria do Hope no favours. Only two universities had a lower average grade in the last Research Assessment Exercise, for example, but the university is in the top 30 for student satisfaction. Management did particularly well in the first national satisfaction survey, as it did in the earlier assessment of teaching quality, where the subject scored full marks. Only theology, easily the top scorer for research, came close to matching this achievement.

University status appears to have provided a bigger boost in applications than at any of the other newcomers to the guide. At the start of 2006, the demand for places had increased by over 11 per cent, despite the prospect of top-up fees. There had been an even bigger increase in 2005, when applications were rising nationally. Most students opt for combined subject degrees, choosing after the first year whether to give them equal weight or to go for a major/minor arrangement. Gaming technology and Irish studies is one of the more unusual combinations suggested, environmental management and dance another. Subjects are grouped into four "deaneries": arts and humanities, education, business and computing, and sciences and social sciences.

Some 70 per cent of the students are over 20 on entry and female undergraduates outnumber their male counterparts by more than two to one. Hope comfortably exceeds all of the official benchmarks for widening participation in higher education. Almost all the undergraduates attended state schools or colleges, more than four out of ten are from working-class families and almost a third are from areas with little tradition of higher education – a figure matched by only two universities in England. This is partly the result of the Network of Hope, which brings university courses to sixth-form colleges across the North West of England, in areas where

Hope Park,
Liverpool L16 9JD
0151-291 3000
admission@hope.ac.uk
www.hope.ac.uk
www.hopesu.co.uk

Edinburgh
Belfast
LIVERPOOL
London
Cardiff

The Times Rankings
Overall Ranking: =96

Student satisfaction:	=24	(15.2)
Research assessment:	107	(1.3)
Entry standards:	99	(208.0)
Student–staff ratio:	106	(26.0)
Library/IT spend/student:	97	(£407)
Facilities spend/student:	104	(£97))
Good honours:	=90	48.8%
Graduate prospects	29	69.5%
Expected completion rate:	93	76.0%

there is limited higher education. Combined honours, foundation degrees and postgraduate teacher training courses are taught in Bury, Wigan and Blackburn. The downside of the university's access agenda is a projected dropout rate of more than 23 per cent, significantly more than the national average for the courses and entry qualifications.

The university's own premises are now concentrated on two sites in Liverpool, with a residential outdoor education centre set in 20 acres of woodland in the heart of Snowdonia, North Wales. The main campus is in the suburb of Childwall, three miles from the city centre, while the performing arts are based at the more central Everton campus, which also boasts a £15-million headquarters for community education activities. The £5-million main library, on the Hope campus, has 250,000 items and 700 study spaces, with electronic access from other sites.

Sports facilities have been improving and there are student union bars on both campuses. The university has a range of residential accommodation, some of it provided by a private firm, and is able to guarantee places for first years and all overseas students.

Bursaries and Scholarships

In receipt of full Maintenance Grant	£1,000
In receipt of partial Maintenance Grant	£400–£700
Living in region	Scholarship
Progressing from outreach	Scholarship
Academic achievement	Scholarship

- Tuition fees (2006) £3,000
- 200 Scholarships of £2,000 a year for 360 UCAS points or higher at A2 or equivalent.
- 150 Scholarships of £1,000 a year for 360 UCAS points or equivalent at AS and A2 combined or equivalent.
- 200 Scholarships of £500 a year for region/outreach work.
- There are also annual Deans awards for on-course achievement and 30 Graduate Scholarships worth £5,000 for the best graduates from 2009.

Contact: www.hope.ac.uk/students/ studentfunds/

Students

Undergraduates:	4,840	(1,210)
Postgraduates:	865	(995)
Mature students:	23.8%	
Overseas students:	6.3%	
Applications per place:	4.7	
From state-sector schools:	97.6%	
From working-class homes:	42.4%	

For detailed information about fees, grants and bursaries and how they work, see chapter 7.

Accommodation

Number of places and costs refer to 2006–07
University-provided places: 3,100
Percentage catered: 10%
Catered costs: £81–£117 a week.
Self-catered costs: £55–£127 a week.
First years are guaranteed accommodation provided requirements are met.
International students: as above.
Contact: accommodation@hope.ac.uk

Liverpool John Moores University

Naming itself after a football pools millionaire was just the start for one of the most innovative of the new universities. JMU was once accused of marketing itself more as a fun factory than a seat of learning, but the former polytechnic prefers to portray itself as "forward-thinking". Among the initiatives to its credit was the launching of Britain's first student charter, which became a template for others. It also launched the first degree in criminal justice and the first distance learning degree in astronomy. Now it is investing £60 million in its campus to keep pace with the requirements of the top-up fees era. Facilities for science, technology and the environment have been upgraded and an Art and Design Academy is due to open in 2008, when Liverpool becomes the European City of Culture.

Before university status had even been confirmed, it set about transforming itself into a huge, futuristic multimedia institution. The two learning resource centres serving different academic areas and a state-of-the-art media centre are open all hours. Many lectures have been replaced by computer-based teaching, freeing academic staff for face-to-face tutorials. Student numbers increased substantially in the early years of the decade and applications held steady in 2006, against the national trend.

Mainly concentrated in an area between Liverpool's two cathedrals, the university is now one of Britain's biggest with more than 21,000 students. Arts and science courses occupy separate sites within easy reach of the city centre, with the IM Marsh campus three miles away in the suburbs for education and community studies. JMU has retained a local commitment, with more than 60 per cent of the students drawn from the Merseyside area, some attracted by the range of diploma courses which still supplement the largely vocational degree programme. A "learning federation" embracing four further education colleges in St Helens, Southport and Liverpool itself adds to the regional flavour.

A growing research reputation is a source of particular pride, and is reflected in an unusually large number of postgraduates for a new university. JMU was one of only two new universities to have a subject rated internationally outstanding in the latest research assessment exercise. Sports science made the step up from a grade 5 in 1996 and has now been marked out as a national teaching centre. General engineering succeeded in holding onto grade 5 and

---

Roscoe Court, 4 Rodney Street,
Liverpool L1 2TZ
0151-231 5090
recruitment@livjm.ac.uk
www.livjm.ac.uk
www.l-s-u.com

The Times Rankings
Overall Ranking: 83

Student satisfaction:	=38	(14.9)
Research assessment:	75	(2.6)
Entry standards:	100	(207.4)
Student–staff ratio:	51	(17.8)
Library/IT spend/student:	=78	(£473)
Facilities spend/student:	=82	(£154)
Good honours:	93	(47.9%)
Graduate prospects:	68	(60.6%)
Expected completion rate:	91	(76.2%)

four more subjects reached the next category. Astronomy has a growing reputation, with a part share in a telescope in the Canary Islands. The International Centre for Digital Content, a partnership with Mersey Television, is developing a range of new courses, including masters programmes in computer games design and e-commerce. A £1.6-million maritime centre features the UK's most advanced 360-degree shiphandling simulator.

The impressive range of courses in hospitality, leisure, sport and tourism achieved a perfect score for teaching quality, as did physics and the healing and human development courses in the School of Health. JMU is one of the most popular of the new universities, judged in terms of applications per place. The university's efforts to extend access to higher education are successful: there are more state-educated undergraduates than average for the subjects offered and almost a quarter come from areas where participation in higher education is low. Work-based degrees, which give students credit towards their final awards for experience in the workplace and encourage them to build study projects around their job, should attract even more non-traditional students. However, the projected dropout rate of almost 23 per cent is higher than the funding council's benchmark for the university.

Facilities for conventional under-graduates have been improving. The conversion of a city-centre hotel was one of a number of residential projects which have allowed the university to guarantee a place for young entrants from outside Merseyside. In addition to the university's own accommodation, a number of private halls, with around 3,500 beds, have been developed in collaboration with JMU.

Bursaries and Scholarships[†]

In receipt of full Maintenance Grant	£1,000
In receipt of partial Maintenance Grant	£400
Progressing from outreach	Scholarship
Sport	Scholarship
Academic achievement	Scholarship 100 awards

- Tuition fees (2006) £3,000
- Placement year tuition fee will be £1,500.
- Bursaries will be available to UK students only; scholarships open to UK and EC students.
- Scholarships worth £1,000 except for 6 awards of £10,000 to outstanding, academically-gifted applicants.

Contact: www.ljmu.ac.uk/

[†] Information taken from 2006 Access Agreement

Students

Undergraduates:	14,215	(5,060)
Postgraduates:	1,090	(2,465)
Mature students:	18.9%	
Overseas students:	12.9%	
Applications per place:	5.0	
From state-sector schools:	94.3%	
From working-class homes:	35.0%	

For detailed information about fees, grants and bursaries and how they work, see chapter 7.

Accommodation

Number of places and costs refer to 2006–07
University-provided places: 3,000; 15,000 through Liverpool Student Homes.
Percentage catered: 0%
Self-catered costs: £58.50–£85.95 a week.
First-year students are guaranteed a place in university accommodation.
International students: as above
Contact: accommodation@ljmu.ac.uk;
www.ljmu.ac.uk/accommodation

University of London

The federal university is Britain's biggest by far. If some of the most prestigious members have considered going their own way and their autonomy increased, they are bound together by the London degree, which enjoys a high reputation worldwide. The colleges are responsible both for the university's academic strength and its apparently precarious financial position. London students have access to some joint residential accommodation, sporting facilities and the University of London Union. But most identify with their college, which is their social and academic base.

The following colleges – some of which have dropped the word "college" from their title to underline their university status – have separate entries, and each also appears within the main university League Table.

Goldsmiths, University of London
Imperial College of Science, Technology
   and Medicine
King's College London
London School of Economics and Political
   Science
Queen Mary
Royal Holloway
School of Oriental and African Studies
University College London

Many of London's teaching hospitals have now merged with colleges of the university:

Imperial College of Science, Technology and Medicine now incorporates St Mary's, Charing Cross and Westminster teaching hospitals.

King's College now incorporates Guys and St Thomas's (the United Medical and Dental Schools of Guys and St Thomas's).

Queen Mary now incorporates St Bartholomew's and the Royal London School of Medicine and Dentistry.

University College now incorporates the Royal Free Hospital Medical School and the Eastman Dental Hospital.

In addition, the School of Slavonic and Eastern European Studies is now part of University College, and Wye College (in Ashford, Kent, and offering degrees in agriculture, rural affairs and environmental studies) is now part of Imperial College.

Senate House, Malet Street,
London WC1E 7HU
020-7636 8000
enquiries@eisa.lon.ac.uk
www.lon.ac.uk
www.ulucube.com

Enquiries: to individual colleges, institutes or schools.

Colleges not listed separately

Birkbeck College
Malet Street, London WC1E 7HX
020-7631 6000
enquiries@bbk.ac.uk
www.bbk.ac.uk
12,085 undergraduates, mainly part-time.
Apply direct, not through UCAS.

Courtauld Institute of Art
Somerset House,
London WC2R 0RN
020-7848 2645
ugadmissions@courtauld.ac.uk
www.courtauld.ac.uk
125 undergraduates. History of art degree.

Heythrop College
Kensington Square,
London W8 5HQ
020-7795 6600
enquiries@heythrop.ac.uk
www.heythrop.ac.uk
130 undergraduates. Degrees in theology
and philosophy.

Institute of Education
20 Bedford Way,
London WC1H 0AL
020-7612 6000
info@ioe.ac.uk
www.ioe.ac.uk
165 (mainly) postgraduate education
courses.

London Business School
Regent's Park.
London NW1 4SA
020-7262 5050
help@london.edu
www.lbs.ac.uk
Postgraduate MBA and other courses.

London School of Hygiene and Tropical Medicine
Keppel Street,
London WC1E 7HT
020-7636 8636
registry@lshtm.ac.uk
www.lshtm.ac.uk
Postgraduate medical courses.

Royal Academy of Music
Marylebone Road,
London NW1 5HT
020-7873 7373
registry@ram.ac.uk
www.ram.ac.uk
340 undergraduates. Degrees in music.

Royal Veterinary College
Royal College Street,
London NW1 0TU
020-7468 5149
registry@rvc.ac.uk
www.rvc.ac.uk
935 undergraduates. Degrees in veterinary
medicine.

St George's, University of London
Cranmer Terrace,
London SW17 0RE
020-8672 9944
www.sgul.ac.uk
2,845 undergraduates. Degrees in
medicine.

School of Pharmacy
29–39 Brunswick Square,
London WC1N lAX
020-7753 5831
registry@pharmacy.ac.uk
www.pharmacy.ac.uk
675 undergraduates. Degrees in pharmacy.

London Metropolitan University

London Met made its debut in our guide three years ago, perilously close to the bottom of *The Times* League Table. It has not appeared since because it has blocked the release of data from the Higher Education Statistics Agency. Initially, senior officials argued that using figures relating to the two universities from which London Met was formed – London Guildhall and North London – would create a misleading impression of the new institution. This objection no longer applies, but still the university is the only one in Britain that chooses to keep its performance secret. Other published statistics do not suggest that its position in this year's table would have been substantially different: it was bottom of rankings compiled from the first national student satisfaction survey, for example.

London specialises in extending the boundaries of higher education to bring in groups who are under-represented at traditional universities. Since the merger, it has developed 240 new degree courses, which it describes as both intellectual and vocational, and which allow students to study citizenship, ethics or enterprise alongside their main subject. Many prepare students for professional qualifications and give credit for work experience or volunteering.

With 33,000 students and more than 2,000 academic staff, including part-timers, it has become the biggest single institution in the capital. However, applications have been uneven: a 29 per cent rise in applications in 2005 was one of the biggest in England, but it followed a decline in demand for full-time places which returned in 2006, when other London institutions saw increases. The university had its grant for 2005–06 reduced for failing to hit its enrolment targets. Fortunately, many students come through other routes and overseas recruitment has remained healthy. London Met has more undergraduates from other EU countries than any university and has among the most from the rest of the world.

The 29 departments at the predecessor universities have been whittled down to 14, with the loss of up to 6 per cent of posts over five years, but the management expects the process to produce a more viable institution. Sites remain centred on the City of London and north London's Holloway Road. Both universities had been refurbishing and reorganising their premises in the years before the merger. Since then, a new graduate school, designed by Daniel Libeskind, has opened, and a science centre followed in 2006.

31 Jewry Street, London EC3N 2EY
020-7320 1616
166–220 Holloway Road
London N7 8DB
020-7753 3355
admissions@londonmet.ac.uk
www.londonmet.ac.uk
www.londonmetsu.org.uk

The Times Rankings
London Metropolitan blocked the release of data from the Higher Education Statistics Agency and so we cannot give any ranking information.

The business school is one of the largest in Britain, many students coming from City firms to join part-time degrees or professional courses. Among a variety of craft subjects, the silversmithing and jewellery courses are the largest in Britain, with facilities to match, while those in furniture restoration and conservation were the first of their kind in Europe.

Courses are also directed at the local community. More than a third of the students are Afro-Caribbean and the proportion of mature students is the highest in England. The projected drop-out rate is high, at nearly a quarter, but it has been falling and is now less than the national average for the university's subjects and entry grades. One of London Met's first objectives was to improve student retention: student support services, from admission to careers advice, have been remodelled and there is a particular emphasis on academic and pastoral counselling on entry and at other key points of courses.

Quality assessments were patchy at the two predecessor universities. Economics and business studies scored well for teaching quality at Guildhall, while business and management achieved the only perfect score at North London. Research grades were generally low in the last assessments, but London Met has a long-term strategy to bring about improvement. Fewer than 100 Guildhall academics were entered for the latest research assessment exercise, and only German reached the top three grades. American studies was the only subject to make the top three grades at North London, but, in contrast to 1996, none of the 17 entries finished in the bottom two categories.

Residential accommodation is limited, but many of London Met's students live at home. Sports facilities are not extensive either, although competitive teams are successful. However, the social scene is lively, particularly in north London.

Bursaries and Scholarships

In receipt of full Maintenance Grant	£1,000
In receipt of partial Maintenance Grant	up to £975
Academic achievement	Scholarship

- Tuition fees (2006) £3,000
- Discretionary hardship fund available.
- Scholarships for academic achievement to be announced.
- Employment services to help find suitable employment for students.

Contact: www.londonmet.ac.uk/advice

Students

Undergraduates:	15,525	(8,145)
Postgraduates:	2,835	(4,270)
Mature students:	44.6%	
Overseas students:	n/a	
Applications per place:	6.6	
From state-sector schools:	96.4%	
From working-class homes:	43.0%	

For detailed information about fees, grants and bursaries and how they work, see chapter 7.

Accommodation

Number of places and costs refer to 2006–07
University-provided places: 1,300
Percentage catered: 15%
Catered costs: £103 a week.
Self-catered costs: £77–£98 a week.
First years are guaranteed a place if conditions are met. Disabled students have priority. International students: given priority.
Contact: accommodation@londonmet.ac.uk

London School of Economics and Political Science

Always one of the big names of British higher education, the LSE was second only to Harvard University in *The Times Higher Education Supplement*'s world rankings for social science in 2005. Now it is planning 20 per cent more places, having seized the chance to tackle a longstanding shortage of teaching space by acquiring former government buildings near the school's Aldwych headquarters.

The LSE took on a new lease of life under Professor Anthony Giddens, the academic face of Tony Blair's Third Way, as big names arrived from a variety of other top universities. Sir Howard Davies, his equally high-profile successor, is building on that progress, having made the move into academic life from the Financial Services Authority. The cosmopolitan feel that derives from the highest proportion of overseas students at any publicly-funded university will continue and many of the new places will be for postgraduates, but there will be some increase in UK undergraduate places.

The LSE has produced 29 heads of state and 13 Nobel prizewinners in economics, literature and peace – including George Bernard Shaw, Bertrand Russell, Friedrich von Hayek and Amartya Sen. The nationals of more than 150 countries take up half of the places. Only the much larger Manchester University had more applications from overseas at undergraduate level at the start of 2005. Its international character not only gives the LSE global prestige but also an unusual degree of financial independence. Less than a fifth of its income is from the Higher Education Funding Council.

Only Oxford and Cambridge have higher entry standards. A third of British undergraduates are from independent schools – one of the highest ratios in the country and higher than the funding council's benchmark figure, although still significantly less than it was five years ago. Efforts are being made to attract a broader intake with Saturday classes and summer schools. The projected dropout rate of 4 per cent is among the lowest at any university.

Areas of study range more broadly than the name suggests. Law, management and history are among the subjects top-rated for teaching, and there is even a small contingent of scientists. Business, economics, psychology and mathematics all produced good results recently. Only Cambridge outperformed the LSE in the last research assessments, which saw half of the school's subjects rated internationally outstanding. The school entered the highest proportion of its academics, at

Houghton Street,
London WC2A 2AE
020-7955 7124
UG-admissions@lse.ac.uk
www.lse.ac.uk
www.lsesu.com

Edinburgh
Belfast
Cardiff
LONDON

The Times Rankings
Overall Ranking: 4

Student satisfaction:	=30	(15.1)
Research assessment:	=3	(6.4)
Entry standards:	4	(466.9)
Student–staff ratio:	10	(13.4)
Library/IT spend/student:	7	(£1,106)
Facilities spend/student:	66	(£186)
Good honours:	12	(74.4%)
Graduate prospects:	3	(81.5%)
Expected completion rate:	=7	(95.5%)

97 per cent, of any university and just one subject (statistics) slipped below the top two grades.

The LSE does not hide its light under a bushel: it describes itself as "the world's leading social science institution for teaching and research". A pan-European survey also showed the school's students to be more active in student associations, more entrepreneurial and more open to opportunities to work abroad than those at other leading universities. The students' union claims to be the only one in Britain to hold weekly general meetings at which every student may attend and vote, while the 120 student societies cover an unusually wide range of interests.

Improvements were being made to the campus long before the opportunity arose to expand. A £30-million Norman Foster-designed redevelopment of the Lionel Robbins Building now houses a much-improved library. The move was a welcome one since the number of books borrowed by LSE students is more than four times the national average, according to a recent survey. Additional buildings have been acquired, routes between buildings are being pedestrianised and a new student services centre has opened.

Partying is not the prime attraction of the LSE for most applicants, who tend to be serious about their subject, but London's top nightspots are on the doorstep for those who can afford them. The 3,650 residential places for 7,500 full-time students offer a good chance of avoiding central London's notoriously high private sector rents.

Bursaries and Scholarships

In receipt of full Maintenance Grant	£2,500
In receipt of partial Maintenance Grant	up to £1,650

- Tuition fees (2006) £3,000
- Students from low-income families and disabled students have access to hardship funds and accommodation awards and LSE Discretionary Bursaries.
- A Job Shop provides part-time employment opportunities for students.
- 25% of additional fee income to be earmarked for bursaries.

Contact: www.lse.ac.uk/financialSupportOffice/

Students

Undergraduates:	3,630	(180)
Postgraduates:	3,625	(1,135)
Mature students:	4.3%	
Overseas students:	47.1%	
Applications per place:	12.5	
From state-sector schools:	64.3%	
From working-class homes:	17.3%	

For detailed information about fees, grants and bursaries and how they work, see chapter 7.

Accommodation

Number of places and costs are approximate and refer to 2006–07
University-provided places: 3,650
Percentage catered: about 36%
Catered costs: from £57–£89 a week.
Self-catered costs: from £66–£92 a week.
First years are guaranteed an offer of accommodation.
Policy for international students: same as above.
Contact: accommodation@lse.ac.uk
to apply online: www.lse.ac.uk/accommodation

London South Bank University

London South Bank ensured that there was no confusion about its location by adding the capital's name to its title in 2003, but there has been no change of direction. Once marketed as "the university without ivory towers", its mission statement underlines the point with an emphasis on wealth creation and the labour market. Links with the local community are such that 70 per cent of students are from the area, many coming from south London's wide range of ethnic minorities. Of nearly 18,000 students, over a third are part-time and half of the undergraduates are on sandwich courses.

Applications soared by more than 30 per cent at the start of 2005 and rose again in 2006, despite the introduction of top-up fees. The proportion of mature entrants is among the highest in Britain, encouraged by initiatives such as the summer school for local people to upgrade their qualifications. The Fast Track to Higher Education programme has been expanded to include numeracy, communication and study skills, as well as the original mathematics. The courses, some of which are tailored to the needs of mature students and some for younger students, start at the end of June and are limited to 15 hours a week so as not to affect students' benefit entitlement.

South Bank has stayed closer than most of the new universities to the technological and vocational brief given to the original polytechnics. Until the recent explosion in demand for health subjects, engineering was second only to business studies in terms of size. Diploma and degree courses run in parallel so that students can move up or down if they are better suited to another level of study. There have been some good teaching assessments, but the university did not quite match the general improvement in scores seen elsewhere in the later stages of subject review. Education, hospitality and town planning produced the best scores, but politics and health subjects also did well.

No subjects reached the top two categories in the last research assessments, but more than four out of ten researchers were in departments on the next rung of the ladder. Computer science, electronic engineering, town planning, social policy and English led the way. The results were considerably better than those in 1996 even though a higher proportion of academics entered. Specialist facilities such as the Centre for Explosion and Fire Research show that the vocational theme carries through into research.

The main campus is in Southwark, near the Elephant and Castle, and not far from the South Bank arts complex. The nine-

---

103 Borough Road,
London SE1 0AA
020-7815 7815
via website
www.lsbu.ac.uk
www.lsbsu.org

The Times Rankings
Overall Ranking: 101

Student satisfaction:	–	(–)
Research assessment:	=64	(2.9)
Entry standards:	106	(192.3)
Student–staff ratio:	=69	(19.7)
Library/IT spend/student:	=75	(£478)
Facilities spend/student:	105	(£96)
Good honours:	=75	(52.9%)
Graduate prospects:	42	(65.8%)
Expected completion rate:	101	(72.0%)

storey Keyworth Centre, which opened in 2003, has upgraded much of the teaching accommodation and provided a new focal point for the university. Further development of the site is planned, but some projects will have to wait for planning permission. The faculty of the built environment was the latest to be brought onto the site, moving from its own premises three miles away. Some health students are based on the other side of London, in hospitals in Romford and Leytonstone, where there are limited learning resources, supplementing those in Southwark. The university now trains 40 per cent of London's nurses.

The social scene suffers from the fact that the large numbers of mature students are more likely to spend their leisure time with their family or local community than their fellow-students. The capital's attractions are on the doorstep but, with almost half of the students coming from working-class homes, many cannot afford them. The projected dropout rate has slipped back to a quarter after a big improvement in 2004.

A new hall of residence means that London South Bank now has residential places within ten minutes' walk of the main campus. There are not enough to guarantee places for all first years, but the 2,000 overseas students are all given places if they want them. Sports facilities improved considerably with the extension of the campus sports centre and the launch in 2004 of the Academy of Sport, Physical Activity and Well-being. Representative teams have been quite successful in recent years and sports bursaries of £3,000 are available for elite performers.

Bursaries and Scholarships
In receipt of full Maintenance Grant £300

- Tuition fees (2006) £3,000
- Placement year tuition fee is around £600.
- Full-time H/EC undergraduates may be entitled to an annual grant from the university of £500 in year 1 and £750 in years 2 and 3, plus a graduation bonus of £250.
- 20%–30% of additional fee income to be earmarked for bursaries.
- Some payments to be in kind.

Contact: www.lsbu.ac.uk/fees

Students

Undergraduates:	8,380	(7,970)
Postgraduates:	1,495	(3,110)
Mature students:	52.4%	
Overseas students:	14.7%	
Applications per place:	5.1	
From state-sector schools:	97.0%	
From working-class homes:	40.5%	

For detailed information about fees, grants and bursaries and how they work, see chapter 7.

Accommodation
Number of places and costs refer to 2006–07
University-provided places: 900
Percentage catered: 0%
Self-catered costs: £78–£96 a week.
First-year UK students are not guaranteed accommodation, but high priority is given to those who live furthest away.
International students: first years are guaranteed accommodation if conditions are met.
Contact: accommodation@lsbu.ac.uk

Loughborough University

Loughborough has the most satisfied students of any conventional university, according to the first national survey, but the message may not be getting through to sixth-formers because applications for courses starting in 2006 were down by 13 per cent at the official deadline. The university will surely benefit eventually from outstanding testimonies from its students, particularly in physics, which produced the highest score in the entire survey. It also boasts the most satisfied students in seven other areas: computer science; architecture, building and planning; civil and chemical engineering; management; media studies; communication and information studies; and medical science and pharmacy.

Still best known for its successes on the sports field, Loughborough has enhanced its academic reputation recently, consistently finishing well up *The Times* rankings and rivalling Oxbridge in its teaching ratings, which averaged no less than 22 points out of 24. The best results came in information science and human sciences. The Office for Standards in Education also rates Loughborough in its top category for teacher training in physical education, design and science. The built environment, sociology and sports science reached the top rung of the research

assessment ladder in 2001, when almost half of the academics entered for assessment were in the top two categories.

Loughborough merged with the neighbouring colleges of education and art and design, giving a more balanced mix between arts and science, and making the university less male-dominated. The university remains a major centre of engineering with more than 2,800 students in a £20-million integrated engineering complex. Aeronautical, automotive and civil engineering are particularly strong, although art and design, business and sports science now all have more students than any single branch of the discipline.

The original 216-acre campus has benefited from a construction programme which included a large student union extension and a new business school, as well as the gradual refurbishment of residential accommodation. The 4,725 rooms now all have telephone and internet connections. The size of the campus has been increased by 75 per cent following the purchase of the adjacent Holywell Park site. This will become the focus for research and collaboration with industry, including a £59-million BAE-sponsored Systems Engineering Innovation Centre. The university prides itself on a close relationship with industry, which accounts for its record haul of four

---

Ashby Road, Loughborough,
Leicestershire LE11 3TU
01509 222498/9
prospectus-enquiries@lboro.ac.uk
www.lboro.ac.uk
www.lufbra.net

The Times Rankings
Overall Ranking: 6

Student satisfaction:	1	(16.1)
Research assessment:	=34	(5.1)
Entry standards:	29	(362.5)
Student–staff ratio:	62	(18.5)
Library/IT spend/student:	27	(£667)
Facilities spend/student:	12	(£355)
Good honours:	35	(64.7%)
Graduate prospects:	=23	(70.7%)
Expected completion rate:	22	(92.5%)

Queen's Anniversary Prizes. Arts facilities are improving with the upgrading of the Cope Auditorium to serve the campus and local community.

Most subjects are available either as three-year full-time or four-to-five-year sandwich courses, which includes a year in industry. This has helped to give graduates an outstanding employment record, as well a dropout rate of less than 6 per cent, which is particularly low for the subjects Loughborough offers. The university is a leader in the use of computer-assisted assessment, offering students the chance to gauge their own progress online.

Loughborough remains pre-eminent in British university sport, both in terms of facilities and performance. Representative teams have a record second to none and the programme of sports scholarships is the largest in the university system. The heavily-oversubscribed School of Sport and Exercise Science moved into new premises in 2002, and in recent years the campus has acquired a 50-metre swimming pool, national academies for cricket and tennis, a gymnastics centre and a high-performance training centre for athletics. It also opened the UK's only centre for disability sport in 2005.

Social activity is concentrated on the students' union. The small town of Loughborough, a mile away, is never going to be a clubber's paradise, but both

Leicester and Nottingham are within easy reach.

Bursaries and Scholarships

In receipt of full Maintenance Grant	£1,300
In receipt of partial Maintenance Grant	
	£200–£1,100
Shortage subjects	Scholarship
Academic achievement	Scholarship

- Tuition fees (2006) £3,000
- Placement year tuition fee will be approximately £650.
- The value of the bursaries is doubled for mature students.
- Non-means-tested, merit-based entry scholarships for certain science and engineering programmes, worth £1,000.
- £3.2 million of additional fee income to be earmarked for bursaries by 2010–11.
- Eligibility conditions apply for bursaries and scholarships.
- Bursary awards are normally a year except year abroad/placement year.
- Eligibility for bursaries may be assessed using UUK/SLC model bursary scheme (HEBSS).

Contact: www.lboro.ac.uk/admin/ar/studentfinance/uguk/

Students		
Undergraduates:	10,370	(200)
Postgraduates:	2,840	(2,270)
Mature students:	6.0%	
Overseas students:	6.1%	
Applications per place:	6.3	
From state-sector schools:	85.2%	
From working-class homes:	24.8%	

For detailed information about fees, grants and bursaries and how they work, see chapter 7.

Accommodation

Number of places and costs refer to 2006–07
University-provided places: 4,725
Percentage catered: 56%
Catered costs: £91.90–£134.30 a week.
Self-catered costs: £57.20–£123.60 a week.
First years guaranteed accommodation if conditions met.
International students: guaranteed accommodation for two years of their course.
Contact: SAS@lboro.ac.uk

University of Luton

Luton's teaching ratings have been described by no less an authority than Charles Clarke, former Education Secretary, as "bloody brilliant" and recent figures showed that it wins more research contracts per pound of state funding than any other university. But Luton struggles with an unglamorous image. The solution may lie partly in a change of name, following the purchase of De Montfort University's Bedford sites, which give the university the opportunity to rebrand itself as the sole higher education institution in the county. The initiative will also expand the range of courses, which have been overwhelmingly vocational since the university withdrew from several of the remaining academic areas.

Applications were increasing until a 7 per cent decline at the start of 2006 with the introduction of top-up fees. Never a polytechnic, Luton had to break all records for expansion to meet the criteria for promotion a year after the other new universities were created. The dash was worth it because tough obstacles were placed in the way of other ambitious colleges subsequently, but the strains showed in the more exalted company the institution was keeping. After initially poor assessments, however, the university recorded a series of good scores for teaching. Health subjects and nursing produced the best results, and research grades improved in the last assessments, although only history and tourism reached the top three categories.

Luton is indignant that it is so often the butt of jokes about the expansion of higher education. The first official measure of graduate prospects showed the university to have the lowest unemployment rate of all. Developments costing some £80 million have transformed the main campus, and in the later rounds of teaching assessment Luton outperformed most traditional universities.

Although there are partner colleges in Bedford, Dunstable and Milton Keynes, most of the university is concentrated in Luton town centre. The borough council is considering making the Park Square campus the centre of a refurbished "cultural quarter". The campus, which is in the midst of the shopping area, has acquired an impressive learning resources centre, languages centre and extensive residential accommodation in recent years. Media arts was the most recent beneficiary in a £5-million move that gave the students access to digital facilities. There is an attractive management centre and conference venue at Putteridge Bury, a neo-Elizabethan mansion three miles

---

Park Square,
Luton, Bedfordshire LU1 3JU
01582 489262
admissions@luton.ac.uk
www.luton.ac.uk
www.ulsu.co.uk

The Times Rankings
Overall Ranking: 108

Student satisfaction:	85	(14.1)
Research assessment:	98	(1.8)
Entry standards:	108	(185.7)
Student–staff ratio:	99	(23.2)
Library/IT spend/student:	42	(£606)
Facilities spend/student:	47	(£229)
Good honours:	92	(48.4%)
Graduate prospects:	109	(41.7%)
Expected completion rate:	95	(74.8%)

outside Luton, but a graduate business school in Aylesbury was short-lived. Its courses have been transferred to the main campus.

Nursing and midwifery students in the growing Faculty of Health and Social Sciences, are scattered more widely, with Stoke Mandeville Hospital and Wycombe General Hospital the centres in Buckinghamshire, while Bedford, and Luton and Dunstable Hospitals provide the equivalent for Bedfordshire.

The university's commitment to open access is reflected in a high proportion of mature students, many of whom take access courses to bring them up to degree or diploma standard, while about a third of the school-leavers arrive through the clearing system. Luton claims to have the second most diverse intake in Britain, with almost one student in three coming from an ethnic minority and a similar proportion arriving without traditional academic qualifications. The projected dropout rate has been improving but, at almost a quarter, it remains significantly higher than the national average for the subjects on offer.

Courses are strongly job-related. English studies, for example, covers text production, website construction and computer conferencing skills, as well as more traditional English language teaching. The university also makes the most of its high-tech facilities for assessment. More than 10,000 students in disciplines from accountancy to biology are subject to computer-assisted assessment.

Luton, although not known for its social scene, has its share of pubs, clubs and restaurants. London is only half an hour away by train for those seeking something livelier. With approximately 1,000 residential places there is now enough accommodation to guarantee a place for all first years. The university's sports facilities are limited, but students have access to top-class provision at the Vauxhall sports centre.

Bursaries and Scholarships[†]

In receipt of full Maintenance Grant	£1,750
In receipt of partial Maintenance Grant	£300–£1,000

- Tuition fees (2006) £3,000
- 40% of additional fee income to be earmarked for bursaries.
- Eligibility for bursaries will be assessed using UUK/SLC model bursary scheme (HEBSS).

Contact:
www.luton.ac.uk/livingandstudying/fees-2006

[†] Information taken from 2006 Access Agreement

Students

Undergraduates:	5,775	(4,365)
Postgraduates:	1,055	(855)
Mature students:	46.4%	
Overseas students:	31.0%	
Applications per place:	4.5	
From state-sector schools:	98.9%	
From working-class homes:	44.8%	

For detailed information about fees, grants and bursaries and how they work, see chapter 7.

Accommodation

Number of places and costs refer to 2006–07
University-provided places: about 1,000
Percentage catered: 0%
Self-catered costs: £74–£69 a week.
Policy for first-year students: all first years are guaranteed a place provided conditions are met.
International students: as above.
Contact: www.luton.ac.uk/livingandstudying/accomodation
accommodation@luton.ac.uk

University of Manchester

Always among the giants of British higher education, with 22 Nobel prizewinners to its credit, Manchester became larger and more powerful in 2004 through a merger with neighbouring UMIST. The largest conventional university in Britain has kept its familiar name, but is now headed by a Vice-Chancellor from the other side of the world. Professor Alan Gilbert arrived from the University of Melbourne shortly before the new institution was formed.

Some departments were already administered jointly with UMIST and the two institutions only separated fully in 1993, so the new institution hopes to avoid some of the problems associated with other university mergers. An unprecedented £350-million capital fund is helping to smooth over any difficulties and a raft of new professors are being appointed. The aim is not only to break into higher education's "golden triangle" of Oxford, Cambridge and London, but to make Manchester one of the top 25 universities in the world by 2015. By then, the aim is to have at least five Nobel laureates on the staff. The first joined in 2006 and at least one more is said to be on the way.

Manchester celebrated its 150th anniversary with its best ratings to date, and was already going from strength to strength before the merger. Seven of the last dozen subjects to be assessed achieved maximum points for teaching quality – a record that none of its rivals can match – while the 12 subject areas judged internationally outstanding for research in 2001 trebled the haul five years earlier. The successful departments were spread equally between the arts and sciences, representing a quarter of the academics entered for assessment. Altogether, three quarters of the entrants were in subjects placed in the top two categories.

The university has been climbing *The Times* rankings, as well as reclaiming its place as the university with the largest number of applicants. The demand for places has been increasing, and held steady in 2006 against the national trend. One of the priorities in the new institution's founding strategy is to broaden the undergraduate intake, with a particular focus on increasing recruitment from the city and its surrounding area. However, in addition to the normal bursary package for British students, Manchester is aiming eventually to have 750 awards for students from educationally-deprived backgrounds in developing countries.

UMIST's legacy is a strong reputation among academics and employers alike in its specialist areas of engineering, science and management. Two thirds of its

---

Oxford Road, Manchester M13 9PL
0161-275 2077
ug.prospectus@manchester.ac.uk
www.manchester.ac.uk
www.umsu.
manchester.ac.uk

The Times Rankings
Overall Ranking: 26

Student satisfaction:	=60	(14.6)
Research assessment:	=10	(5.7)
Entry standards:	15	(396.3)
Student–staff ratio:	=14	(14.2)
Library/IT spend/student:	12	(£819)
Facilities spend/student:	32	(£263)
Good honours:	18	(70.0%)
Graduate prospects:	36	(66.8%)
Expected completion rate:	=23	(92.3%)

academics reached one of the top two out of seven categories in the last research assessments. Materials technology and health subjects were both 5* rated. Teaching ratings, too, were good, especially in engineering, and its graduates enjoyed a consistently excellent employment record. Surveys of employers frequently placed UMIST among their favourite recruiting grounds, helping to produce an unrivalled network of industrial sponsorship.

The merger has produced the largest engineering school in the UK, with a £20-million budget and 1,200 students. There already was a federal business school, which is certain to be among the strengths of the new institution, as should the medical school, which was rewarded for impressive teaching ratings with extra places in collaboration with Keele University. A new teaching block caters for the additional 230 places a year.

The city's famed youth culture and the university's position at the heart of a huge student precinct already help to ensure keen competition for places – and hence high entry standards in most subjects. Sports facilities, which were already first rate, have improved still further since the city hosted the Commonwealth Games. Students get discount rates at the aquatics centre opened for the games on campus, for example. The city's reputation for violent crime may be overstated, but the students' union runs late-night minibuses, self-defence classes, and regular safety campaigns. Students tend to be fiercely loyal both to the university and their adopted city.

Bursaries and Scholarships

In receipt of full Maintenance Grant	£1,000
In receipt of partial Maintenance Grant	up to £1,000
Living in region	Scholarship
Living in specified postcodes	Scholarship
Shortage subjects	Scholarship
Academic achievement	Scholarship

- Tuition fees (2006) £3,000
- The Manchester Advantage Scholarship : £5,000 a year for all UK students who attain 3s at A level and have an annual household income of £17,500 or less. Subject specific.
- The Manchester Success Scholarship : £1,000 a year for all UK students who attain 3 As at A level irrespective of household family income. This scholarship is subject specific.
- The Manchester Achievement Scholarship : £2,000 a year for students from the Manchester region who have successfully participated in the University's Manchester Access Programme.
- The President's Award : 10 awards worth £10,000 a year for the most outstanding students from the UK.

Contact: www.manchester.ac.uk/ undergraduate/money/scholarshipsand bursaries/universityscholarships/

Students

Undergraduates:	23,455	(4,960)
Postgraduates:	6,080	(4,625)
Mature students:	8.9%	
Overseas students:	14.7%	
Applications per place:	7.7	
From state-sector schools:	79.6%	
From working-class homes:	21.0%	

For detailed information about fees, grants and bursaries and how they work, see chapter 7.

Accommodation

Number of places and costs refer to 2005–06.
University-provided places: 9,100
Percentage catered: 29%
Catered costs: £80–£112 a week (39 weeks).
Self-catered costs: £50–£82 a week (39 weeks).
All unaccompanied students are guaranteed accommodation if conditions are met.
International students paying overseas fees are guaranteed accommodation.
Contact: Accommodation@manchester.ac.uk
www.manchester.ac.uk/accommodation

Manchester Metropolitan University

With over 31,000 students, including almost 9,000 part-timers, Manchester Metropolitan is neck and neck with its newly-merged neighbour for the title of the largest conventional higher education institution in Britain. But the giant institution boasts quality as well as quantity, as it demonstrated in 2001 with one of the first 5* ratings for research at a new university. Sports science was the area rated internationally outstanding, while seven other subjects were rated in the top three of seven categories.

Although the former polytechnic has not been able to sustain the lead it held briefly over Manchester University in applications, still only a handful of institutions are more popular. There was another 10 per cent increase in the demand for places in 2005. Although this progress was not sustained when top-up fees arrived a year later, the 36,000 applications still amounted to the university's second-highest total ever. Longstanding commitments to extending access are being continued: even among the full-time undergraduates, a third are over 25 and a higher proportion still are from working-class homes. Nearly 95 per cent of the undergraduates went to state

schools and 18 per cent come from areas without a tradition of higher education. Almost 1,000 courses cover more than 70 subjects, with the menu of programmes including a growing range of two-year foundation degrees.

The university features in *The Times* top 20 for materials technology, librarianship and drama, dance and cinematics. Only mechanical engineering was rated as excellent in the first rounds of assessment, but scores improved subsequently and included near-perfect results for business, drama and philosophy. The university takes teaching seriously: small groups are used whenever possible and staff are encouraged to take a three-year MA in teaching, which has been running since 1992. Many courses also involve work placements. Geography and mechanical engineering did particularly well in the first national student satisfaction survey.

Education courses have also fared well in the Teacher Training Agency's performance indicators, especially for primary training. The university trains more teachers than any other and has launched a Centre for Urban Education to develop its expertise further. Some 800 trainees and other students taking contemporary arts and sports science are at the former Crewe and Alsager College campuses, 40 miles south of Manchester and now rebranded as MMU Cheshire.

All Saints Building,
Oxford Road, Manchester M15 6BH
0161-247 1035/6/7/8
prospectus@mmu.ac.uk
www.mmu.ac.uk
www.mmunion.co.uk

The Times Rankings
Overall Ranking: =96

Student satisfaction:	=71	(14.4)
Research assessment:	=64	(2.9)
Entry standards:	68	(261.5)
Student–staff ratio:	=94	(22.5)
Library/IT spend/student:	81	(£467)
Facilities spend/student:	95	(£131)
Good honours:	97	(47.2%)
Graduate prospects:	=83	(57.1%)
Expected completion rate:	85	(78.8%)

The remaining education students are based at Didsbury, five miles out of the centre of Manchester, with those taking community studies. A single Institute of Education covers both centres.

The Crewe and Alsager campuses are six miles apart, but free transport is provided between the two. Although the rural location inevitably makes for a quieter life than in Manchester, Alsager has an arts centre with two theatres, a dance studio and an art gallery, as well as extensive sports facilities, while the Crewe campus has its own nightclub. Eventually, the university intends to develop Crewe as its Cheshire base, adding sports facilities and residential accommodation, as well as more lecture theatres.

There are five sites in Manchester, stretching from leafy Didsbury to the extensive All Saints campus, close to the city centre and Manchester University. The large business school has its own site right in the centre, while health courses – including the recently-incorporated Manchester School of Physiotherapy – are not far away on the Elizabeth Gaskell campus, and clothing, food and hospitality courses are another mile out. Overseas links have expanded rapidly in recent years, offering exchange opportunities in Europe and farther afield, as well as establishing teaching bases abroad.

More than half of the students come from the Manchester area, easing the pressure on accommodation in a city of nearly 70,000 students. Some 85 per cent of hall places are reserved for first years, with priority going to the disabled and those who live furthest from the university. The city's attractions do no harm to recruitment levels, but much depends on where the course is based. Didsbury may offer the best of both worlds, with swift access to the city centre and a peaceful environment, but students at Crewe and Alsager can feel isolated. Some potential applicants are daunted by the sheer size of the university, but individual courses and sites usually provide a social circle.

Bursaries and Scholarships

In receipt of full Maintenance Grant £1,000
In receipt of partial Maintenance Grant
  Sliding scale based on level of Maintenance Grant

- Tuition fees (2006) £3,000
- Tuition fees for placement year and year abroad are £600 (2006).
- 33% of additional fee income to be earmarked for bursaries and access work.
- Eligibility for bursaries will be assessed using UUK/SLC model bursary scheme (HEBSS).

Contact: www.mmu.ac.uk/courses/bursaries

Students

Undergraduates:	21,735	(4,510)
Postgraduates:	2,450	(4,500)
Mature students:	19.1%	
Overseas students:	6.3%	
Applications per place:	5.3	
From state-sector schools:	94.9%	
From working-class homes:	36.3%	

For detailed information about fees, grants and bursaries and how they work, see chapter 7.

Accommodation

Number of places and costs refer to 2006–07
University-provided places: 5,100; 8,200 (privately-owned halls).
Percentage catered: 6%; 4% (privately-owned halls)
Catered costs: £76 a week.
Self-catered costs: £61.00–£84.50.
All new full-time students will be offered halls if requirements are met.
International students: as above.
Contact: accommodation@mmu.ac.uk

Middlesex University

Middlesex has been changing the character of its intake, reorganising its courses and becoming more international, and now physical changes are on the way. A £100-million building programme will concentrate the university on three sites in north London. The new package may help encourage a revival in recruitment among home students, which has been patchy in recent years. The university missed its targets in 2005, despite a healthy increase in applications, and demand for places was down by 8 per cent at the start of 2006.

Overseas, however, there have been no such problems. Middlesex has more foreign undergraduates than any UK university, making up a quarter of its intake. A longstanding commitment to Europe sees more than 1,000 students arriving from the Continent and even more come from further afield. There is a network of 11 regional offices, in North and South America, Africa and Asia, producing a student population drawn from 130 countries. Its successes in the overseas market won a Queen's Award for Enterprise in 2003 and the university has now opened its own campus in Dubai.

Now almost 25,000 strong, including part-timers, the university aims to carry on growing. A network of partner colleges at home and abroad participates in exchanges and/or offers Middlesex qualifications. The university has reorganised its schools, having already pulled out of engineering almost entirely, to focus on its strengths in business, computing and the arts.

The highly flexible course system allows students to start many courses in January if they prefer not to wait until autumn, and offers the option of an extra five-week session in July and August to try out new subjects or add to their credits. An experiment bringing forward the start of the academic year to early September has been abandoned, with the result that the first assessments have reverted to after Christmas.

Nine out of ten students take vocational courses, many at postgraduate or sub-degree level. The business school is the biggest subject area, but almost half of the undergraduates are on multidisciplinary programmes. About 42 per cent are over 21 on entry and half of the full-timers come from London.

Almost all of the British students are from state schools and 44 per cent of them are from working-class homes, but the dropout rate of more than a quarter is significantly worse than the national average for the university's subjects and entry qualifications. Even before the introduction of top-up fees, Middlesex was attempting to attract better-qualified

---

White Hart Lane,
Tottenham, London N17 8HR
020-8362 5898
admissions@mdx.ac.uk
www.mdx.ac.uk
www.musu.mdx.ac.uk

The Times Rankings
Overall Ranking: =96

Student satisfaction:	87	(13.8)
Research assessment:	=72	(2.7)
Entry standards:	104	(200.0)
Student–staff ratio:	97	(22.6)
Library/IT spend/student:	22	(£726)
Facilities spend/student:	18	(£322)
Good honours:	82	(50.5%)
Graduate prospects:	=88	(55.8%)
Expected completion rate:	=98	(73.3%)

students by offering £1,000-a-year scholarships for UK entrants with 300 UCAS points (the equivalent of three Bs).

For some time, the university has been reducing the number of campuses dotted around London's North Circular Road. The five remaining locations include a picturesque country estate at Trent Park and a business school campus at Hendon that includes a Real tennis court and a new library. The Tottenham site was to have been the new focal point of the university, but ambitious building plans were shelved to the annoyance of some local councillors and MPs.

Nurses and other health students are based in four London teaching hospitals and on a campus at Archway which is shared with the University College and Royal Free Hospital medical schools. There is also a joint degree in veterinary nursing run with the Royal Veterinary College.

Teaching ratings have improved considerably and Middlesex did well in the first of the new institutional audits in 2003. Philosophy secured the university's best teaching score and also registered one of Middlesex's two grade 5 assessments for research, denoting nationally outstanding work and some of international excellence. History of art was the other top scorer.

The number of residential places is planned to double in the next few years from the current 1,916 beds. Sports facilities have been improving, with a £250,000 refurbishment of facilities on the Enfield campus and the development of an Institute for Sport at Archway.

Bursaries and Scholarships

In receipt of full Maintenance Grant	£300
Living in region	Scholarship
Sport	Scholarship
Academic achievement	Scholarship

- Tuition fees (2006)   £3,000
- Academic scholarships worth £1,000 to students entering with greater than 300 UCAS points at A2 or equivalent.
- Chancellors Scholarships for achievement in sporting, cultural or community/cultural areas, worth £500–£1,000.
- Middlesex First scholarships: 5 x £30,000 to full-time UK UG students. Conditions apply.
- Future Gold: Sports Scholarships 2 x £30,000 for those showing real Olympic potential for 2012.
- North London First: 5 x £1,000 for each of the 4 main North London Boroughs – supporting academic achievement, community and cultural contribution.
- 12% of additional fee income to be earmarked for bursaries and access.

Contact:
www.mdx.ac.uk/apply/funding/index.htm

Students

Undergraduates:	13,150	(3,515)
Postgraduates:	2,905	(2,550)
Mature students:	28.7%	
Overseas students:	21.7%	
Applications per place:	7.2	
From state-sector schools:	99%	
From working-class homes:	44%	

For detailed information about fees, grants and bursaries and how they work, see chapter 7.

Accommodation

Number of places and costs refer to 2005–06
University-provided places: 1,916
Percentage catered: 0%
Self-catered costs: £73.57–£87.71 a week.
Full-year international students have priority; age and residential restrictions apply. International students are guaranteed a room provided requirements are met.
Contact: accomm@mdx.ac.uk

Napier University

Napier was Scotland's first and largest polytechnic, and has been pioneering again with the appointment of the first woman to lead a university north of the border. Professor Joan Stringer moved from neighbouring Queen Margaret University College with the declared aim of making Napier 'one of the leading modern universities in the United Kingdom'. Already an institution of more than 14,000 students, 3,000 of whom are part-timers, it has been developing the facilities to make that possible. Numbers have continued to rise thanks to increased recruitment on the Continent and a better ratio of applications to acceptances, despite a decline in applications seen at most Scottish universities in recent years. A drop in applications in 2005 was reversed a year later, against the national trend.

Two new libraries, a purpose-built music centre and refurbishment of the science laboratories underlined Napier's ambitions, with a £5-million computing centre completing the first phase of the university's development plan in 2001. The second is more ambitious, centring on a £30-million centre, opened in 2004, for the biggest business school in Scotland. The university has launched a £50-million fundraising scheme, with the first £10 million intended to meet part of the cost of the business school. It has given itself a more leisurely period to raise the rest, setting a target date of 2050. A £1-million donation from a Hong Kong businessman got the fund off to a good start, suggesting that success might be achieved somewhat sooner.

Napier has been held up as a model to other universities trying to reduce wastage rates. There is a student mentoring scheme, "bridging programmes" offering pre-term introductions to staff and information on facilities, and summer top-up courses in a variety of subjects. The 21 per cent dropout rate projected for students who began courses in 2003 was a big improvement on the previous year, but still more than the UK average for the subjects on offer. Only two years earlier, Napier had the lowest dropout rate among the new universities in Scotland.

The university is named after John Napier, the inventor of logarithms. The tower where he was born still sits among the concrete blocks of the Merchiston site, in the student district of Edinburgh, where the new computer centre is based. The other main sites are Sighthill, a 1960s development in the west of the city, which is to be used by a number of support departments now that the business school has transferred, and nearby Craiglockhart, a one-time military hospital, where the

---

10 Colinton Road,
Edinburgh EH10 5DT
0500 353570
info@napier.ac.uk
www.napier.ac.uk
www.napierstudents.
com

EDINBURGH

Belfast

London
Cardiff

The Times Rankings
Overall Ranking: =78

Student satisfaction:	–	(–)
Research assessment:	=84	(2.3)
Entry standards:	65	(263.8)
Student–staff ratio:	46	(17.4)
Library/IT spend/student:	=64	(£512)
Facilities spend/student:	=87	(£147)
Good honours:	=49	(59.2%)
Graduate prospects:	=77	(57.9%)
Expected completion rate:	103	(70.2%)

new school has been built. It features a glass atrium housing a cyber café and two spherical lecture theatres with a total of 600 seats.

Ambitious plans for a Scottish Centre for Creative Industries Institute to be built at Craighouse, in the south of Edinburgh, have been shelved. But the campus will still bring together the creative subjects for which Napier is popular. A university bus service links the main sites, but there are several teaching outposts where lectures may be scheduled – notably in the Faculty of Health and Life Sciences, the biggest in the university and one of the largest providers of nursing education in Scotland.

Napier failed to register a single Excellent rating before the Scottish system of assessing teaching quality completed its first round of ratings in 1998, despite a string of Highly Satisfactory grades. However, computing and accounting achieved the highest possible scores in repeat assessments under the new quality regime operated in Scotland between 2000 and 2002.

Most of the avowedly vocational courses include a work placement, and the close relationship with industry and commerce helps to produce consistently good graduate employment figures. The modular course system allows movement between courses at all levels and has

allowed students the option of starting courses in February, rather than September. Links with a network of partner colleges encourage progression from further to higher education, and off-campus courses that already give access to Napier degrees as far afield as Aberdeen will now be extended to China, where the university was hoping to open its own campus and is working with a number of institutions.

The dispersed nature of the university does nothing for the social scene, although Edinburgh is hardly dull. Despite improvements, some students find life too quiet in the evenings and at weekends.

Bursaries and Scholarships

- Scottish domiciled students: no fees will be payable by eligible students although a "graduate endowment" will be payable after graduation: the 2005–06 level was £2,216.
- Non-Scottish domiciled students fees: £1,700 a year.
- Fees for placement year and year abroad are normally 50% of full-time fee.

Contact: www.napier.ac.uk/studentfunding/

Students

Undergraduates:	9,290	(2,180)
Postgraduates:	1,145	(1,425)
Mature students:	47.9%	
Overseas students:	19.5%	
Applications per place:	3.4	
From state-sector schools:	94.8%	
From working-class homes:	35.4%	

For detailed information about fees, grants and bursaries and how they work, see chapter 7.

Accommodation

Number of places and costs refer to 2006–07
University-provided places: 918
Percentage catered: 0%
Self-catered costs: £67.50–£71.85 a week.
First years are guaranteed a place provided requirements are met. Residential restrictions apply.
International students are housed if requirements are met, but there is no guarantee.
Contact: accommodation@napier.ac.uk

University of Newcastle

Major universities in big cities seem to take it in turns to be fashionable – Manchester gave way to Nottingham, and recently it has been Newcastle in the spotlight. Although applications dipped slightly in 2005 and 2006, the longer-term trend has been consistently upwards. A further 800 places have been added in recent years and the university has invested £7.5 million in campus facilities. Science and engineering laboratories are being upgraded, disabled access improved and thousands of students provided with internet connections in university flats and halls of residence.

Originally Durham University's medical school, Newcastle's excellence in that area was confirmed by maximum points for teaching in medicine, anatomy and physiology, pharmacology and pharmacy, reviewed jointly with molecular biosciences, psychology and its department of speech. Dentistry only just missed out on the same score. The medical school's reputation was confirmed by its selection as a national centre to disseminate best teaching practice in medicine. The school is growing larger in a partnership with Durham, with about a third of trainees spending their first two years at Durham's Stockton campus.

Newcastle has also been chosen to house a national centre of teaching excellence in music, which will provide new rehearsal rooms, sound studios and instruments.

Other academic developments include the creation of nine new research institutes, housed in new buildings costing over £30 million. New courses have included Britain's first degree in folk and traditional music, complementing a course in pop and contemporary music, and a four-year business and accounting degree, in conjunction with PricewaterhouseCoopers, which provides a fast-track to professional qualifications. Newcastle already had a number of unusual features for a traditional university, such as a fine art degree which attracts up to 15 applicants per place. It also has a longstanding reputation for agriculture, which recorded good scores for both teaching and research with the benefit of two farms in Northumberland.

Research grades improved in the last assessments, with biological sciences, clinical laboratory sciences, music and psychology all rated internationally outstanding. Six out of ten academics entered for the exercise were in departments placed in the top two categories.

The campus is spacious and varied, occupying 45 acres close to the main shopping area, civic centre, Northumbria

---

Kensington Terrace,
Newcastle upon Tyne NE1 7RU
0191-222 5594
admissions-enquiries@
ncl.ac.uk
www.ncl.ac.uk
www.unionsociety.co.uk

The Times Rankings
Overall Ranking: 25

Student satisfaction:	=38	(14.9)
Research assessment:	=30	(5.2)
Entry standards:	18	(384.6)
Student–staff ratio:	=36	(16.9)
Library/IT spend/student:	14	(£774)
Facilities spend/student:	19	(£312)
Good honours:	31	(65.8%)
Graduate prospects:	33	(68.0%)
Expected completion rate:	18	(93.0%)

University and Newcastle United's ground. Half of the buildings date from the 1960s onwards. The university also boasts a theatre, an art gallery and three museums, which it hopes to bring together in a "cultural quarter" for the city.

The university expanded dramatically in the 1990s, and now has more than 16,000 full-time students. It has become popular with independent schools, whose applicants take almost a third of the places, but the university has stepped up its contacts with local state schools in order to broaden its intake. The 300 students recruited through the programme have been doing at least as well as those with higher entry grades. Alumni and other friends of the university have raised £6 million in two years to add to the bursaries available for students from less affluent backgrounds. Official performance indicators reveal a healthy 93 per cent completion rate – better than anticipated, given the subject mix.

Few students regret choosing Newcastle for a degree, even if southerners can find the winter temperatures a shock. The city's nightlife is legendary – eighth best in the world, according to one survey – and the university topped a student poll based on computer facilities and student services, as well as the social scene. The cost of living is reasonable and town–gown relations better than in many cities.

Sport is a particular strength, Newcastle claiming to be one of the top ten universities both in terms of performance and facilities. A £5.5-million sports centre opened on the campus in 2005, supplementing the two existing centres, which have refurbished fitness suites, massage clinics and all the normal indoor services. The main outdoor pitches are two miles from the university. Over £30,000 is awarded annually in sports bursaries for elite athletes.

Bursaries and Scholarships

In receipt of full Maintenance Grant £1,200
In receipt of partial Maintenance Grant
£600–£900
Academic achievement Scholarship
Progressing from outreach Scholarship
- Tuition fees (2006) £3,000
- Placement year tuition fee will be £750 (25% of the tuition fee).
- Excellence Scholarship scheme, open to all based on achievement. About 229 scholarships a year in all subjects based on various performance-related criteria. Value £500 or£1,000.
- Partners Scholarship. About 36 First Year scholarships for students entering from the Partners Programme. Value £500 or £1,000.
- Eligibility for bursaries will be assessed using UUK/SLC model bursary scheme (HEBSS).
- Payment to be made in instalments.

Contact: www.ncl.ac.uk/undergraduate/finance

Students

Undergraduates:	12,700	(235)
Postgraduates:	3,230	(2,165)
Mature students:	11.0%	
Overseas students:	9.5%	
Applications per place:	3.4	
From state-sector schools:	68.6%	
From working-class homes:	20.9%	

For detailed information about fees, grants and bursaries and how they work, see chapter 7.

Accommodation

Number of places and costs refer to 2006–07
University-provided places: 4,380
Percentage catered: 35%
Catered costs: £80.64–£99.75 a week.
Self-catered costs: £54.74–£79.75 a week.
All single undergraduates are guaranteed a room in university-managed accommodation provided requirements are met. Local restrictions apply.
International students: as above.

Contact: accommodation-enquiries@ncl.ac.uk

University of Wales, Newport

Newport recorded the biggest increase in applications anywhere in the UK in 2005, an almost unprecedented 38 per cent, and followed up with another 12 per cent rise at the start of 2006. All subjects have been experiencing increased demand for places, including areas such as computing, which are in decline nationally. A change of name from college to university was thought to be one reason for last year's boom, but students have also been attracted by a range of new courses in areas such as creative sound and music, cinema studies and scriptwriting, computer games design and internet technologies.

Full membership of the University of Wales had already encouraged more students to consider Newport and the college had embarked on an ambitious expansion strategy. A futuristic riverside campus that will practically double the number of students, will house the School of Art, Media and Design initially. At the same time, the university will pursue closer links with the University of Wales Institute Cardiff, which was already a partner in a number of subjects.

Art, media and design was awarded a grade 5 rating for research in the last assessments, but other research and teaching ratings have been disappointing.

However, both students and employers appear enthusiastic. Newport finished in the top ten in England and Wales in the first national student satisfaction survey, with the best results anywhere in finance and accounting. A poll of local employers was just as positive.

Just one academic in ten was entered for the latest research assessment exercise, the lowest proportion in the university system. As a result, only one university finished below Newport for average grades per member of staff. Business and management was the most successful area in a series of undistinguished teaching assessments, but an overall audit by the Quality Assurance Agency in 2004 was positive. Estyn, the Welsh schools inspectorate, gave the best grades in Wales to the teacher-training courses, which also showed high levels of student satisfaction.

The university, which was previously Gwent College of Higher Education, now has 9,000 students from 44 different countries. Virtually all the full-time undergraduates come from state schools and there is a higher proportion from working-class homes than at any other university institution in Wales. However, the projected dropout rate of 23 per cent is still marginally higher than the benchmark set according to the subject mix. Newport operates a number of access schemes, including one offering students

---

Caerleon Campus,
Newport, South Wales NP18 3YG
01633 432432
admissions@newport.ac.uk
www.newport.ac.uk
www.newportunion.com/

The Times Rankings
Overall Ranking: =80

Student satisfaction:	=53	(14.7)
Research assessment:	=61	(3.0)
Entry standards:	97	(216.8)
Student–staff ratio:	=69	(19.7)
Library/IT spend/student:	87	(£449)
Facilities spend/student:	33	(£255)
Good honours:	69	(54.2%)
Graduate prospects:	92	(55.0%)
Expected completion rate:	92	(76.1%)

at local schools and colleges guaranteed places if they fulfil certain criteria.

The university is actively involved with a range of local businesses. It was rated the number one university in Wales for enterprise education by the Knowledge Exploitation Fund. Among its innovations is the Corus to Campus project for redundant steelworkers (previously employed by Corus), and it is also a leading player in the Community University of the Valleys. The college also hosts the International Film School Wales.

There are currently two campuses, the smaller of which focuses on engineering and computing, business and professional and social studies. The Caerleon campus is further out, with impressive views, and caters for humanities, science, education and art, media and design. It also contains the student village of 660 self-catered study bedrooms and a new building for fashion and other subjects is under construction. Free buses link the two existing sites, which are officially among the safest in Britain: the college was the first educational establishment to pass an industry-standard security inspection.

A new sports centre at Caerleon has transformed facilities that previously compared unfavourably with those of other universities. The city of Newport has established a reputation for producing successful rock bands, but students in search of serious cultural or clubbing activity gravitate to nearby Cardiff.

Bursaries and Scholarships
- Fees for undergraduate courses £3,000.
- Students living in Wales will be eligible for a Welsh Assembly fee grant of approximately £1,800 a year.
- Fees for year abroad not yet known.
- For information on the National Bursary Scheme see page 196, chapter 7.

Contact: www.newport.ac.uk/funding/index.htm

Students		
Undergraduates:	2,570	(4,660)
Postgraduates:	370	(1,460)
Mature students:	33.2%	
Overseas students:	6.5%	
Applications per place:	3.5	
From state-sector schools:	98.4%	
From working-class homes:	42.1%	

For detailed information about fees, grants and bursaries and how they work, see chapter 7.

Accommodation
Number of places and costs refer to 2005–06
University-provided places: 661
Percentage catered: 0%
Self-catered costs: £49–£60 a week.
First years guaranteed accommodation if requirements met.
International students: same as above.
Contact: accommodation@newport.ac.uk

University of Northampton

Northampton had a university in the thirteenth century, but it took until 2005 to get it back after Henry III dissolved the original version – allegedly because his bishops thought it posed a threat to Oxford. More than 100 places separate the two universities in *The Times* League Table, but Northampton will hope to narrow that gap somewhat in years to come. It has already registered good results in the first national student satisfaction survey, particularly in geography and environmental science and in finance and accounting.

The modern university has its origins in teacher training and, as Nene College of Higher Education, lobbied unsuccessfully to become a polytechnic. The later campaign, to establish a university in one of the few counties without one, eventually bore fruit, but only after almost a decade. By then, it had incorporated vocational courses for the leather industry, occupational therapy, nursing and midwifery. All remain in a surprisingly broad portfolio of more than 100 degree and diploma courses.

The university has two sites: an 80-acre campus on the edge of Northampton, where £73 million has been spent on improvements in recent years, and the smaller but more central St George's

Avenue campus, which specialises in art and design, media, technology and the performing arts. Both sites have new halls of residence, and the main Park Campus has also seen several new teaching developments, a management centre and a research centre. Another £80 million of investment is planned over the next ten years. In the first phase, new arts facilities at St George's will form the centrepiece of the town's "cultural mile", while an innovative student centre on the Park Campus will provide administrative and support services both during and outside office hours.

Student numbers have been steady for several years, but are expected to rise from the current 9,500 to about 12,000 by 2010. Applications were up slightly at the start of 2006, against the national trend, perhaps boosted by the fact that tuition fees were set £500 below the £3,000 maximum. Business is the most popular area, but health subjects are not far behind. Art and design produced the best teaching quality score, while English and history were highly rated in the 2001 Research Assessment Exercise.

Northampton takes its mission to widen participation in higher education seriously: almost all the undergraduates attended state schools or colleges, while nearly 38 per cent come from working-class homes. However, the latest official

Park Campus, Boughton Green Road,
Northampton NN2 7AL
01604 735500
study@northampton.ac.uk
www.northampton.ac.uk
www.ucnu.org

The Times Rankings
Overall Ranking: 103

Student satisfaction:	=53	(14.7)
Research assessment:	=99	(1.7)
Entry standards:	94	(219.0)
Student–staff ratio:	92	(22.2)
Library/IT spend/student:	105	(£371)
Facilities spend/student:	93	(£135)
Good honours:	71	(53.7%)
Graduate prospects:	98	(51.8%)
Expected completion rate:	77	(80.5%)

figures suggested that almost 19 per cent of those who began courses in 2002 will fail to complete in the expected time. Some of the courses – such as podiatry and furniture design and manufacture – recruit from all over Britain (and farther afield) but in other subjects most of the students are from the region. As a result, the 1,700 residential places are enough to guarantee accommodation for all first years who make Northampton their first choice.

Sports enthusiasts have a Premier League rugby club and the home of the British Grand Prix on their doorstep, as well as a more modest football club and first-class cricket. The university has its own sports hall and outdoor pitches, but is not especially well provided with facilities. The town of Northampton has a number of student-oriented bars, but the two campuses' union bars remain the hub of the social scene.

Bursaries and Scholarships

In receipt of full Maintenance Grant	£500
In receipt of partial Maintenance Grant	£500
Living in region	Bursary
Living in specified postcodes	Bursary

- Tuition fees (2006) £2,500–£3,000
- Regional/post code bursaries worth £500 (but not in addition to Maintenance Grant bursary)

Contact: www.northampton.ac.uk/ prospectivestudents

Students

Undergraduates:	7,340	(2,580)
Postgraduates:	275	(1,060)
Mature students:	23.4%	
Overseas students:	5.1%	
Applications per place:	5.0	
From state-sector schools:	98.3%	
From working-class homes:	37.4%	

For detailed information about fees, grants and bursaries and how they work, see chapter 7.

Accommodation

Number of places and costs refer to 2006–07
University-provided places: 1,600
Percentage catered: 0%
Self-catered costs: £35.12–£72.82 a week.
First years are guaranteed accommodation provided requirements are met.
International students: as above.
Contact:
www.northampton.ac.uk/stu/accom/infor.htm

University of Northumbria

Always among the leading new universities in *The Times* League Table, Northumbria out-performed the rest of its peer group in 2005. With 24,000 students, including more than 7,000 part-timers, the former polytechnic has begun to benefit fully from its high grades and Newcastle's reputation as an exciting student city. It remains predominantly a local institution, with more than half of the students from the North of England. Although applications were down slightly at the start of 2006, the drop was less than the national average and followed several years of increases.

Entry grades for those with A levels are among the highest in the new universities, but more than half of the students are admitted with other qualifications or on the strength of relevant work experience. Free one-day taster courses run between January and July to give local people an idea of what a university course would be like. There is also a network of feeder colleges encouraging applications from adults without traditional academic qualifications.

The latest official figures show some success for the university's attempts to widen access: the recruitment of one in five students from areas with little tradition of higher education was significantly better than average for the courses on offer, while the 31 per cent from working-class homes was just above expectations. The projected dropout rate has been rising, but remains below the benchmark for Northumbria's courses and entry grades.

The last big leap in numbers came with the incorporation of a large college of health studies in 1995. Health subjects have now overtaken business studies in terms of student numbers and have been highly successful in teaching assessments: nursing achieved Northumbria's first maximum score and, like modern languages and physics, health subjects managed 23 points out of 24. Education also managed maximum points and followed up with a glowing report from the Office for Standards in Education. The university is in the top category for primary training and secondary design and technology. It has also been chosen to run a national centre of excellence in assessment, building on Northumbria's attempts to give students more constructive feedback and teaching them how to assess themselves as future professionals. The university was not especially successful in the first national survey of student satisfaction, but history and politics did well.

A spectacular extension of the main city centre campus is under way, with the

---

Ellison Terrace,
Newcastle upon Tyne NE1 8ST
0191-227 4777
rg.admissions@unn.ac.uk
www.unn.ac.uk
www.mynsu.co.uk

The Times Rankings
Overall Ranking: 58

Student satisfaction:	=53	(14.7)
Research assessment:	=82	(2.3)
Entry standards:	58	(272.1)
Student–staff ratio:	=76	(20.4)
Library/IT spend/student:	25	(£673)
Facilities spend/student:	36	(£250)
Good honours:	72	(53.3%)
Graduate prospects:	55	(63.3%)
Expected completion rate:	65	(82.0%)

first phase due to open in September 2007. Design, business and law will move to the new seven-acre site, which will be linked to the existing campus by bridge and walkway across the city's central motorway. The space vacated by the three schools will make way for extensive refurbishment and pedestrianisation. The majority of subjects will continue to be based there, with health, education and community studies on the Coach Lane campus on the outskirts of the city, where £18 million has been spent upgrading facilities. Coach Lane now incorporates a learning resources centre with a fully integrated library, a clinical skills centre and new sports facilities, as well as teaching and seminar rooms.

Northumbria's best-known feature is its School of Design with its renowned fashion courses, but 20 subjects have achieved the equivalent of the old Excellent grade for teaching. Research ratings improved in 2001 but still three subject areas finished in the last category but one. Only psychology and art and design reached the top three grades. Many degrees are available as sandwich courses, with placements of up to a year in business or industry. Law and business studies have the highest entrance requirements.

All new first years are offered places in university accommodation if they apply "in good time", while others are assisted by the accommodation office. Two large residential developments with en suite rooms opened in September 2005, bringing the total stock to 3,250 places, and there is a plentiful supply of privately rented flats and houses.

Bursaries and Scholarships

In receipt of full Maintenance Grant	£550–1,300
In receipt of partial Maintenance Grant	£250
Living in region	Bursary
Living in specified postcodes	Scholarship
Ethnic minorities	Scholarship
Disabled	Scholarship

- Tuition fees (2006) £3,000
- Placement year tuition fee will be £750.
- Targeted Scholarships worth £250, £500 and £1,000 to be offered.
- 33% of additional fee income to be earmarked for bursaries.
- Eligibility for bursaries will be assessed using UUK/SLC model bursary scheme (HEBSS).

Contact:
http://northumbria.ac.uk/brochure/studfees/

Students		
Undergraduates:	14,980	(4,955)
Postgraduates:	2,150	(2,980)
Mature students:	21.6%	
Overseas students:	12.10%	
Applications per place:	4.2	
From state-sector schools:	90.1%	
From working-class homes:	31.2%	

For detailed information about fees, grants and bursaries and how they work, see chapter 7.

Accommodation
Number of places and costs refer to 2006-07
University-provided places: 3,250
Percentage catered: 8%
Catered costs: £88 a week.
Self-catered costs: £60–85 a week.
All new students can be offered housing.
International students: full-year first years can be guaranteed accommodation provided requirements are met.
Contact:
rc.accommodation@northumbria.ac.uk

University of Nottingham

For many years Nottingham has been among the institutions with the stiffest competition for each place, and a striking new campus and extra courses made it even more fashionable. At the start of 2006, it was still the most popular UK destination for overseas students, but overall applications were down by 14 per cent – the second successive big decline. The university believes that its high entry standards are putting off some potential applicants, but extensive media coverage of crime in the city will not have helped.

The university boasts one of the most attractive campuses in Britain, and has risen up the pecking order of higher education. In less than 20 years, it went from being a solid civic university to a prime alternative to Oxbridge. Constantly among the top 15 universities in *The Times* League Table, it seldom stands still. A £30-million fundraising target was hit a year ahead of schedule and a series of projects have benefited.

The lifting of restrictions on student recruitment allowed the university to make room for 750 more students, but new undergraduates' average A-level grades have not dropped. Once in, they tend to stay the course – the dropout rate of less than 4 per cent is among the best in the country. But the university is trying to broaden an intake which has more independent school students and fewer from working-class homes than the national average for the subjects offered. There is a well-established summer school for state-school teenagers and a bursary scheme for Nottinghamshire students with no history of higher education in their families.

The 30-acre Jubilee campus, which cost £50 million and includes 750 residential places, is barely a mile away from the original parkland site. Futuristic buildings clustered around an artificial lake house the schools of management and finance, computer science and education. An additional building for the fast-growing business school was added in 2004 and a new sports hall opened the following year. The medical school is also close to University Park, but the biosciences and the new veterinary school are at Sutton Bonnington, ten miles south of the city.

Nottingham describes itself as "research-led", with work carried out at the university winning two Nobel Prizes in 2003. Professor Peter Mansfield, who won the prize for medicine for research leading to the development of the MRI scanner, has spent almost all his academic career there. The university's record-breaking research contracts place it among the top four universities for private funding. However, the last research assessments

---

University Park,
Nottingham NG7 2RD
0115-951 5151
undergraduate-enquiries@
nottingham.ac.uk
www.nottingham.ac.uk
www.students-union.
nottingham.ac.uk

Edinburgh
Belfast
NOTTINGHAM
London
Cardiff

The Times Rankings
Overall Ranking: 14

Student satisfaction:	=38	(14.9)
Research assessment:	=25	(5.3)
Entry standards:	9	(429.1)
Student–staff ratio:	=30	(16.2)
Library/IT spend/student:	13	(£799)
Facilities spend/student:	15	(£332)
Good honours:	7	(75.3%)
Graduate prospects:	22	(71.0%)
Expected completion rate:	9	(95.2%)

were disappointing by the university's high standards, with only five subjects awarded the coveted 5* rating – American studies, German, Iberian languages, music and theology – with 26 more subjects on the next assessment grade.

The university has devoted about £70 million to a research recruitment initiative in advance of the next assessments. It set out to fill 20 research chairs and will be investing in the equipment and support posts to accompany them. Recent developments include a £7-million biomedical sciences building on the main campus and a £10-million graduate-entry outpost for the medical school in Derby.

Most teaching assessments were excellent, with classics, economics and politics joining psychology and manufacturing engineering leading the way. Health subjects and agriculture were the top scorers in the first national student satisfaction survey.

Nottingham has long-standing links with the Far East, which provides the majority of its 5,000 overseas students, and has a Chinese physicist, Professor Fujia Yang, as its Chancellor. The university has had a branch in Malaysia since 2000 and launched a new venture in Ningbo, China, in 2004. Purpose-built campuses with echoes of the Nottingham's distinctive clock tower opened in Ningbo and near Kuala Lumpur in September 2005.

Students will have the opportunity to move between the three countries.

Both main campuses are within three miles of the centre of Nottingham, with a good selection of student-friendly clubs. However, halls of residence and the students' union tend to be the centre of social life for students in both locations. Sports facilities are excellent and expanding.

Bursaries and Scholarships

In receipt of full Maintenance Grant	£1,000
In receipt of partial Maintenance Grant	£1,000
Living in Region	Bursary
Progressing from outreach	Bursary
Shortage subjects	Bursary

- Tuition fees (2006) £3,000
- Placement year tuition fee and year abroad tuition fee is 50% full time fee.
- Additional bursaries worth £250–£1,000 for students with residual income of £32,000–£42,500, ie, just above threshold for partial Maintenance Grant.
- Further bursaries for target groups. Students in receipt of core bursary receive the full bursary for placement years and year abroad.
- £2.5 million of additional fee income to be earmarked for bursaries.

Contact: www.nottingham.ac.uk/prospectuses/ undergrad/introduction/finance/

Students

Undergraduates:	18,635	(5,440)
Postgraduates:	4,735	(3,880)
Mature students:	8.8%	
Overseas students:	15.1%	
Applications per place:	7.7	
From state-sector schools:	67.4%	
From working-class homes:	16.1%	

For detailed information about fees, grants and bursaries and how they work, see chapter 7.

Accommodation

Number of places and costs refer to 2006–07
University-provided places: 7,400
Percentage catered: 58%
Catered costs: £92.50–£146.50 a week.
Self-catered costs: £64.75–£99.00 a week.
First years are guaranteed accommodation if conditions are met.
International students: undergraduates guaranteed for 3 years if conditions are met.
Contact: ugaccommodation@nottingham.ac.uk
www.nottingham.ac.uk/nh

Nottingham Trent University

Consistently among the leading new universities in *The Times* League Table, as well as being one of the biggest, Nottingham Trent has demonstrated high quality in an unusually wide range of disciplines. Best known for fashion and other creative arts, which have the largest number of students, it also recorded maximum scores in teaching assessments for physics and biosciences. The law school is one of Britain's largest, offering legal practice courses for both solicitors and barristers, and there is even a commercial farm and equestrian centre on a campus devoted to land-based studies.

Nottingham Trent has the highest entry grades of any new university and an employment record which regularly sees more than 95 per cent of graduates in work or further study within six months. It helps that the university has the third highest number of year-long placements in the UK through its working partnerships with more than 6,000 businesses and private sector organisations. Almost a third of the undergraduates come from working-class homes and over nine out of ten attended state schools or colleges, but the projected drop-out rate had risen to 15 per cent in the latest official statistics.

An ambitious research programme was amply rewarded in the last assessments, when Nottingham Trent had four subjects judged nationally outstanding, with much of their work considered internationally excellent. Only two other new universities matched the achievements of drama, dance and the performing arts, English, media studies and health subjects.

An annual opinion survey shows that most of the students are satisfied, although the university did not do particularly well in the first national satisfaction survey. Helped by the popularity of Nottingham as a student centre, applications grew steadily through the 1990s and the early years of this decade, but – possibly because of perceptions of crime levels in the city – this came to an abrupt halt in 2006, when demand for places slumped by 18 per cent.

There are now more than 25,000 students, including a large contingent of part-timers. The extensive main city site originally housed Nottingham University, but now boasts a mixture of Victorian and modern buildings. The schools of Biomedical and Natural Sciences, Computing and Informatics, Education and Arts, Communication and Culture are five miles away on the Clifton campus. The last addition to the estate came from a merger with Brackenhurst College, an agricultural college 14 miles from Nottingham, where there an equestrian centre with a purpose-built indoor riding

---

Burton Street,
Nottingham NG1 4BU
0115-941 8418
marketing@ntu.ac.uk
www.ntu.ac.uk
www.trentstudents.org

Edinburgh
Belfast
NOTTINGHAM
London
Cardiff

The Times Rankings
Overall Ranking: 60

Student satisfaction:	=60	(14.6)
Research assessment:	=67	(2.8)
Entry standards:	57	(275.9)
Student–staff ratio:	89	(21.4)
Library/IT spend/student:	38	(£611)
Facilities spend/student:	89	(£145)
Good honours:	=61	(55.8%)
Graduate prospects:	=53	(63.4%)
Expected completion rate:	54	(84.1%)

area. Another 300 residential places and a new access road will open in 2006, adding to £3 million of upgraded teaching facilities.

Improvements to the original campuses have seen improvements to art and design facilities on the city campus, as well as refurbishment of the Boots Library and the students' union. Computing and informatics have a new building on the Clifton campus and the university has launched a bus service linking Clifton and the city.

Teaching ratings were variable, but showed improvement towards the end of the cycle of assessment, with politics achieving the best score. The university was responsible for the largest programme of foundation degrees when the two-year qualification was launched. They attracted only 200 applicants at the start of 2006, but subjects ranged from forensic science to wildlife conservation.

The student body is diverse, with large numbers of mature and overseas students. The university's residential stock has been increasing, with a £10-million development with 446 beds opening on the City campus in 2004. It still is not sufficient to house all first years, but new students are guaranteed "university-allocated" accommodation, which may be in the private sector. Social life varies between campuses, but all have access to the city's lively cultural and clubbing scene. A late-night bus service links the main campuses and the city's new tram system serves the university.

Bursaries and Scholarships

In receipt of full Maintenance Grant	£1,000
In receipt of partial Maintenance Grant	
	£200–£800
Living in specified postcodes	Bursary
Academic achievement	Scholarship

- Tuition fees (2006) £3,000
- Placement year tuition fee £600 (2006–07).
- Discretionary Hardship Fund available.
- Scholarship scheme will offer 25 competitive scholarships of £2,000 a year based on academic performance during the first year of study. Only students receiving full MG will be eligible.
- Eligibility for bursaries will be assessed using UUK/SLC model bursary scheme (HEBSS).

Contact: www.ntu.ac.uk/prospective_students/ bursaries/index.html

---

Students

Undergraduates:	16,400	(4,990)
Postgraduates:	2,090	(3,245)
Mature students:	15.1%	
Overseas students:	4.6%	
Applications per place:	5.4	
From state-sector schools:	91.5%	
From working-class homes:	31.1%	

For detailed information about fees, grants and bursaries and how they work, see chapter 7.

Accommodation

Number of places and costs refer to 2006–07
University-provided places: 3,800
Percentage catered: 0%
Self-catered costs: £61.36–£89.04 (40–48 weeks).
First years are guaranteed accommodation, subject to terms and conditions.
International students: guaranteed accommodation, subject to terms and conditions.
Contact: www.ntu.ac.uk/accommodation

University of Oxford

After eight years of league table frustration, Oxford finally toppled Cambridge from top place in *The Times* rankings in 2002, and has maintained its grip ever since. The university also appeared in fourth place in world rankings published by *The Times Higher Education Supplement* in 2005. With a new Chancellor and Vice-Chancellor well established, Oxford has been discussing far-reaching organisational changes designed to safeguard its supremacy and compete more effectively on the international stage. That may mean more research students and marginally fewer UK undergraduates, as well as changes in the relationship between the university and its fiercely independent colleges.

Oxford is the oldest and probably the most famous university in the English-speaking world, and it remains almost inseparable from Cambridge in terms of overall quality. Like Cambridge, it attracts world-class academics and takes its share of the brightest students. The pair are head and shoulders above the other non-specialist universities in *The Times* ranking and in the view of most experts.

Yet Oxford briefly slipped to third place in our table, partly because of comparatively low central spending on facilities such as careers and sport. The college structure, which produces an enviable student environment, acted as a handicap. However, a fairer reflection of overall spending, endorsed by the Higher Education Statistics Agency, together with a change in the scoring system to make allowance for the mix of subjects in each university, had a dramatic effect.

Applications held steady for 2006 despite top-up fees, following increases in the three previous years. But the university is still struggling to broaden its intake and shake of allegations of social elitism. The steady increases in demand for places (which are concentrated in the more job-oriented subjects) are at least partly due to more systematic attempts to get the message through to teenagers that Oxford is open to all who can meet the exacting entrance requirements. Sudent visits to comprehensive schools have been supplemented by summer schools, recruitment fairs and colleges' own initiatives, as well as tireless public statements of intent by the university.

For all the university's efforts to shed its "Brideshead Revisited" stereotype, however, official figures still show 46 per cent of Oxford's students coming from independent schools – the largest proportion at any university. Only 11 per cent come from working-class homes, despite the introduction of £2,000 bursaries for all undergraduates who are

University Offices, Wellington Square,
Oxford OX1 2JD
01865 270207
undergraduate.admissions@
admin.ox.ac.uk
www.ox.ac.uk
www.ousu.org

The Times Rankings
Overall Ranking: 1

Student satisfaction:	–	(–)
Research assessment:	2	(6.5)
Entry standards:	2	(511.7)
Student–staff ratio:	=8	(13.0)
Library/IT spend/student:	1	(£1,656)
Facilities spend/student:	7	(£364)
Good honours:	1	(88.4%)
Graduate prospects:	11	(74.8%)
Expected completion rate:	2	(97.7%)

eligible for full fee remission – well before the advent of top-up fees. Still higher bursaries from 2006 may help broaden the mix. Only two in 100 students drop out, a proportion bettered only by Cambridge.

Selection is in the hands of the 30 undergraduate colleges, which vary considerably in their approach to this issue and others. Sound advice on academic strengths and social factors is essential for applicants to give themselves the best chance of winning a place and finding a setting in which they can thrive. Only a minority of candidates opt to go straight into the admissions pool without expressing a preference for a particular college. The choice is particularly important for arts and social science students, whose world-famous individual or small group tuition is based in college. Science and technology, which have benefited from Oxford's phenomenally successful fundraising efforts, are taught mainly in central facilities. All subjects operate on eight-week terms and assess students entirely on final examinations – a system some find too pressurised.

Recent developments include the successful management school, made possible by a £20-million donation from the controversial Syrian businessman Wafic Said, which opened in 2001. An even bigger project has seen the addition of a £60-million chemistry building to house the western world's largest chemistry department, as well as new premises for economics. A £21-million social sciences library followed in 2004.

There was never much doubt about the strength of Oxford's research but, with 25 out of 46 subject areas rated internationally outstanding and 96 per cent of those entered for assessment placed in the top two categories, the latest grades confirmed the university's high standing. The university had the largest number of top-rated researchers and also attracts the biggest amount of research income, at about £200 million. Most teaching assessments were similarly impressive.

Bursaries and Scholarships

In receipt of full Maintenance Grant

£3,000–£4,000

In receipt of partial Maintenance Grant

£100–£3,000

- Tuition fees (2006)   £3,000
- Tuition fee for year abroad is £1,500 (2006).
- Additional one-off award of £400–£1,000 in first year for students from low-income families.
- Existing bursary schemes, scholarship schemes and hardship funds to run in parallel until 2008–09.
- 36% of additional fee income to be earmarked for bursaries by 2009–10.

Contact: www.oxfordopportunity.com

Students		
Undergraduates:	11,490	(3,820)
Postgraduates:	5,445	(1,420)
Mature students:	3.6%	
Overseas students:	10.9%	
Applications per place:	4.1	
From state-sector schools:	53.8%	
From working-class homes:	11.5%	

Accommodation

See chapter 10 for information about individual colleges.

For detailed information about fees, grants and bursaries and how they work, see chapter 7.

Oxford Brookes University

Now firmly established as a leading new university in *The Times* League Table, Oxford Brookes was one of a handful of former polytechnics to have a subject rated internationally outstanding in the last research assessments. That the 5* rating in history placed the department ahead of its world-renowned neighbour can only have added to the sense of achievement. English and French reached the next grade, although the biggest entry in any new university, representing 41 per cent of the academic staff, meant that overall results were unusually variable.

Applications were down by 8 per cent at the start of 2006, but this followed successive big rises in the years before top-up fees were introduced. The university's location has always been an advantage in student recruitment, but the quality of provision is the real draw. Its departments feature near the top of *The Times* rankings for several subjects, including a second place for land and property management. Town planning and economics achieved perfect scores for teaching, while social work, philosophy, theology and religious studies did best in the first national student satisfaction survey.

The university was chosen to house national centres for the teaching of business and undergraduate research in 2005, having previously won a similar accolade in hospitality, leisure and tourism. Its first two-year foundation degree was in this area and is helping to maintain the university's consistently excellent record for graduate employment. Further foundation degrees have been added, most recently in communication at work. Oxford Brookes is also partnering Warwick University in the Government's academy for gifted and talented schoolchildren.

More than a quarter of the undergraduates come from independent schools – by far the highest proportion among the new universities and twice the national average for the university's subjects and entry grades. Yet the 42 per cent share of places going to students from working-class homes comfortably exceeds this benchmark. The university has been trying to attract more students from state schools and targeted areas in Oxfordshire.

Brookes made a leap in size in 2000, taking in Westminster College, a merger which added 2,000 students, mainly in teacher training and the humanities, and forming a £2.5-million Institute of Education. The new arrivals joined an institution that is challenging the traditional universities on their own ground, but retaining a substantial part-

---

Headington Campus,
Headington, Oxford OX3 0BP
01865 484848
query@brookes.ac.uk
www.brookes.ac.uk
www.thesu.com

The Times Rankings
Overall Ranking: 54

Student satisfaction:	=49	(14.8)
Research assessment:	=67	(2.8)
Entry standards:	55	(282.6)
Student–staff ratio:	=30	(16.2)
Library/IT spend/student:	102	(£393)
Facilities spend/student:	22	(£306)
Good honours:	66	(55.1%)
Graduate prospects:	34	(67.6%)
Expected completion rate:	=81	(79.8%)

time programme and recruiting large numbers of mature students.

As a polytechnic, Oxford pioneered the modular degree system that has swept British higher education. After more than 20 years' experience, the scheme now offers in excess of 2,000 modules in an undergraduate programme which can pair subjects as diverse as history and physical sciences, or catering management and history of art. Each subject has compulsory modules in the first year and a list of others that are acceptable later in the course. Students are encouraged to take some subjects outside their main area of study, and there is a range of possible exit points. They can qualify for a Certificate in Higher Education after eight modules. The university switched over to semesters of 12 teaching weeks in 2004.

There are four main sites, two of which are only a mile from the city centre and linked to each other by a footbridge. The original Gipsy Lane site was becoming overcrowded when the chance came to acquire the late Robert Maxwell's 15-acre estate at neighbouring Headington Hill. Computing and business are five miles away at Wheatley. The Harcourt Hill campus at Botley focuses on teacher education, human development and learning.

A swimming pool and 18-hole golf course have been added to the already impressive sports facilities. Representative teams have a good record, the cricketers now combining with Oxford University to take on county teams. The social scene on campus is not the liveliest and Oxford can be expensive, but there is enough going on to satisfy most students. The university has increased its accommodation stock to 3,700 residential places but, while most first years are offered a place, allocation is based on how far from Oxford a student lives.

Bursaries and Scholarships

In receipt of full Maintenance Grant	£1,230
In receipt of partial Maintenance Grant	£200–£1,230
Progressing from outreach	Scholarship

- Tuition fees (2006) £3,000
- Scholarship scheme to be announced.
- Hardship fund available of £750,000.

Contact: www.brookes.ac.uk/studentfinance

Students		
Undergraduates:	10,135	(2,720)
Postgraduates:	2,030	(3,050)
Mature students:	24.8%	
Overseas students:	19.6%	
Applications per place:	6.4	
From state-sector schools:	72.8%	
From working-class homes:	41.8%	

For detailed information about fees, grants and bursaries and how they work, see chapter 7.

Accommodation

Number of places and costs refer to 2006–07
University-provided places: 3,700
Percentage catered: 23%
Catered costs: £3,800–£4,400 a year.
Self-catered costs: £2,800–£4,800 a year.
All accommodation is allocated to first years by distance from Oxford Brookes.
International students: as above.
Contact: accomm@brookes.ac.uk

University of Paisley

In common with several Scottish universities, Paisley saw the demand for places drop in 2005 and 2006, but it was already on a high plateau after surges in popularity in the early years of the decade. Students flocked to a new range of degrees in subjects such as computer animation, commercial music, computer games technology, sports studies and music technology. The demand for places on the education and media campus in Ayr grew by 50 per cent in a year.

The university is proud of its record in attracting under-represented groups onto courses. Its proportion of students from areas without a tradition of higher education is the highest in Britain, at 36 per cent, and the 43 per cent share of places going to working-class students is exceeded by only a handful of universities. The projected dropout rate has been improving but is still well above average for the university's subjects and entry qualifications. Paisley introduced a range of measures to address the problem, including a personal tutor system, strengthened counselling support and attendance monitoring. Access measures are continuing, with hundreds of youngsters aged 14 and 15 attending the "University Experience" and sampling a week of student life.

Only seven miles from Glasgow, Paisley is Scotland's largest town. The university has more than 11,500 students, including the many part-timers, a high proportion coming from the Glasgow area. Student numbers have grown rapidly in recent years, but staffing levels compare favourably with most new universities. Courses are strongly vocational, with business, multimedia and health subjects by far the most popular choices. There are close links with business and industry, notably with the computer giant IBM and Motorola. All students are offered hands-on computer training, and there is a postgraduate course available in information technology for those who want to move into the industry without a first degree in computing. Paisley was the first UK university approved by Microsoft, Macromedia and Cisco, and has the status of Microsoft Academic Professional Development Centre. A new games development laboratory, supported by Sony, is the latest development in a £300,000 package of investment in multimedia and games facilities.

A majority of subjects were rated Highly Satisfactory for teaching quality. Under the new assessment system, accounting and finance have achieved good results. The university pioneered credit transfer in Scotland, giving credit for non-academic achievement, and its

---

Paisley,
Renfrewshire PA1 2BE
0141-848 3000
info @paisley.ac.uk
www.paisley.ac.uk
www.upsa.org.uk

The Times Rankings
Overall Ranking: 102

Student satisfaction:	–	(–)
Research assessment:	=101	(1.6)
Entry standards:	62	(265.3)
Student–staff ratio:	=74	(20.2)
Library/IT spend/student:	=20	(£729)
Facilities spend/student:	=56	(£210)
Good honours:	101	(45.8%)
Graduate prospects:	=96	(52.1%)
Expected completion rate:	104	(69.1%)

modular course system covers day, evening and weekend classes. Most students either take sandwich degrees or have work placements built into their courses, and earn an average of £10,000 in the process, but the impact on graduate employment has not been as great as in some other universities. Research grades improved in the last assessments, with accountancy achieving the only grade 5 in any new university in Scotland, but still the majority of entrants were placed in the bottom three grades.

The university has invested over £9 million in student facilities in recent years. The main campus, covering 20 acres in the middle of Paisley, has seen substantial development, including a new library and learning resource centre. The campus in Ayr, acquired through a 1993 merger with a former teacher training college, has seen the establishment of a management centre in an 18th-century mansion. A third campus in Dumfries is operated in partnership with Glasgow University and a local college. The venture now has over 400 students, and a new teaching centre is increasing the range of courses available for the under-provided southwest of Scotland.

The two main centres could hardly be more different, Paisley industrial and seaside Ayr smaller both as a campus and a town, and social life varies accordingly.

The university has been investing heavily in improved leisure facilities, with a new students' union already open in Ayr and a £5-million town-centre union building now added in Paisley. Sports provision has also been improving: £1.5 million was spent upgrading Paisley's indoor and outdoor facilities.

Bursaries and Scholarships

- Scottish domiciled students: no fees will be payable by eligible students although a "graduate endowment" will be payable after graduation: the 2005–06 level was £2,216.
- Non-Scottish domiciled students fees: £1,700 a year.
- Fees for placement year and year abroad are normally 50% of full-time fee.
- University Hardship Fund available.

Contact: www.paisley.ac.uk

Students

Undergraduates:	6,085	(3,330)
Postgraduates:	435	(1,600)
Mature students:	43.1%	
Overseas students:	6.9%	
Applications per place:	3.8	
From state-sector schools:	98.4%	
From working-class homes:	43.1%	

For detailed information about fees, grants and bursaries and how they work, see chapter 7.

Accommodation

Number of places and costs refer to 2005–06
University-provided places: 545 (plus 112 at Ayr)
Percentage catered: 0%
Self-catered costs: £50 a week.
First years can apply for accommodation if conditions are met. Local restrictions.
International students: single non-EU students are guaranteed accommodation. Terms and conditions apply.
Contact: www.paisley.ac.uk/facilities

University of Plymouth

One of the first new universities to be awarded a medical school (in collaboration with Exeter University), Plymouth has been carrying out major restructuring. Roland Levinsky, the Vice-Chancellor lured from Imperial College London, set a target of making Plymouth one of Britain's top research universities within 15 years, while still serving the region through teaching. The most controversial element of his plans involved the transfer to Plymouth of courses from the Seale-Hayne agricultural campus, near Newton Abbot, and the arts and humanities programme based in Exeter. Education courses from the Exmouth campus are also transferring to the main North Hill campus in 2008.

The plans were part of an academic reorganisation which divided the university into six faculties and included a big programme of capital investment. It has seen the opening of a £30-million headquarters and a second teaching building for the Peninsula Medical School. The library has been extended and upgraded, with 24-hour study facilities, and the students' union has also been refurbished. A £30-million arts complex is due to open in 2007, housing the Faculty of Arts and the Plymouth Arts Centre, and providing the focal point for a "cultural quarter" around the university.

The Peninsula Medical School has quickly established itself with applicants and was the only successful bidder for a new dental school in 2006. With campuses in Plymouth, Exeter, Truro and Taunton, along with teaching facilities in Bristol, the university's Faculty of Health and Social Work is the largest provider of nurse, midwifery and health professional education and training in the southwest. The new medical school sees a variety of health professionals training side by side.

As a polytechnic, its title laid claim to the whole of the southwest of England, but although the university chose to name itself after its Plymouth base, it maintains a strong regional role. It is a partner in the Combined Universities in Cornwall (CUC) initiative, which aims to increase the provision of further and higher education in one of the few counties without its own university. Plymouth has also established a unique relationship with its 18 partner colleges, which spread from Cornwall to Somerset, through a faculty devoted entirely to serving their 5,300 students taking university courses. They have become the University of Plymouth Colleges, sharing £2 million in capital investment.

The intake reflects Plymouth's position as the working-class hub of the southwest, with nine out of ten students state-educated and almost a third from the

Plymouth,
Devon PL4 8AA
01752 232232
admissions@
plymouth.ac.uk
www.plymouth.ac.uk
www.upsu.com

The Times Rankings
Overall Ranking: 55

Student satisfaction:	=38	(14.9)
Research assessment:	=57	(3.2)
Entry standards:	67	(262.7)
Student–staff ratio:	=48	(17.6)
Library/IT spend/student:	71	(£493)
Facilities spend/student:	=42	(£235)
Good honours:	60	(56.0%)
Graduate prospects:	=86	(56.4%)
Expected completion rate:	56	(83.9%)

Edinburgh
Belfast
London
Cardiff
PLYMOUTH

poorest social classes. The dropout rate is among the best in the new universities. Although the university is still best known for marine studies, its top teaching scores came in civil engineering, building, psychology, nursing, and hospitality, each of which narrowly missed out on full marks. Plymouth was chosen to house no fewer than four national teaching centres: in health and social care placements, experiential learning in environmental and natural sciences, institutional partnerships and education for sustainable development.

The university also has a longstanding commitment to research. More than a third of the academics were entered for the last research assessment exercise, with computer science, psychology and art history all rated nationally outstanding with significant work of international excellence. But it hit the headlines for introducing a degree in surfing, which it insisted was rigorous as well as vocational. The first graduates all found related employment and the course continues to be oversubscribed. Plymouth has since followed it with a degree in applied marine sports science, in collaboration with the neighbouring College of St Mark and St John.

Plymouth offers a lively social scene, with excellent and recently-upgraded facilities for water sports as well as a thriving nightlife. An £850,000 fitness centre has improved the sports facilities, while a range of sports scholarships and bursaries will help support high-fliers. A £15-million scheme has also seen the construction of a 1,300-bed student village.

Bursaries and Scholarships

In receipt of full Maintenance Grant	£300
Living in region	Bursary
Progressing from outreach	Bursary
Academic achievement	Scholarship £500

- Tuition fees (2006) £3,000
- Fees for placement year £600.
- Regional bursaries from £500 for targeted students in receipt of EMA, and Access qualifications. Regional outreach bursary of £1,500 linked to compact scheme. Progression award of £500 for students progressing from partner college foundation degrees. Scholarships worth £300–£1,500. Automatic £500 subject specific scholarship.
- Discretionary Hardship Fund available.
- One-off awards of £500 to target groups: first-generation students and those from low-income families living in the South West region.
- £1,500 relocation award to mature students.
- Additional support for mature and disabled students.
- Eligibility for bursaries will be assessed using UUK/SLC model bursary scheme (HEBSS).

Contact: www.plymouth.ac.uk/ugfees

Students

Undergraduates:	16,610	(6,965)
Postgraduates:	1,095	(3,750)
Mature students:	26.3%	
Overseas students:	8.3%	
Applications per place:	4.6	
From state-sector schools:	92.4%	
From working-class homes:	29.3%	

For detailed information about fees, grants and bursaries and how they work, see chapter 7.

Accommodation

Number of places and costs refer to 2005–06
University-provided places: 1,983
Percentage catered: 0%
Self-catered costs: £50–£88 a week.
First years are guaranteed accommodation.
International students: accommodation is guaranteed providing conditions are met.
Contact: Plymouth:
accommodation@plymouth.ac.uk
Exeter: accomexe@plymouth.ac.uk
Exmouth: accomexm@plymouth.ac.uk

University of Portsmouth

Portsmouth has always been among the leaders of its generation of universities. Strength in teaching has been recognised with the award of two national centres of excellence and four subjects reached grade 5 of the last research assessments: biomedical and biomolecular studies, cosmology, European studies and Slavonic studies. No former polytechnic managed more, and three grade 4s in that exercise left 45 per cent of the researchers in the top three of the seven categories. Every faculty was involved in research, and the 38 per cent of academics entered for the assessment was among the most in the former polytechnics.

Graduate employment is healthy, especially for a university where a high proportion of the students take arts subjects. Languages are Portsmouth's greatest strength – one student in five takes a language course of some sort – and the facilities rival those of many traditional universities. About 1,000 Portsmouth students go abroad for part of their course, and at least as many come from the Continent. French achieved a near perfect teaching score and its research was rated internationally outstanding. However, it is in health subjects that the university now has a national teaching centre, reflecting the broader range of subjects available in recent years. The new School of Professionals Complementary to Dentistry is one example of this. A £4-million building houses the first new dental education facility in England for 50 years. Other additions to the portfolio of degree courses include subjects as diverse as criminology, water sports science and money-market modelling.

Teaching assessments were variable, but there was a marked improvement in later years of the cycle. Pharmacy recorded a maximum score, while education and politics, radiography and psychology all came close. Portsmouth academics have won National Teaching Fellowships in three of the last five years and, in addition to the health centre, the university is to lead on the development of teaching on foundation degrees.

The main Guildhall campus, dotted around the city centre, is undergoing extensive redevelopment with the establishment of a University Quarter. Earlier developments provided some distinctive buildings, including the aluminium-clad St Michael's Centre and the eco-friendly Portland Building, with its solar panels. The business school has moved into a new £12-million building on the main campus, and an equally expensive library extension is due to be complete by the summer of 2006.

Winston Churchill Avenue,
Portsmouth PO1 2UP
023-9284 8484
admissions@port.ac.uk
www.port.ac.uk
www.upsu.net

Edinburgh
Belfast
Cardiff London
PORTSMOUTH

The Times Rankings
Overall Ranking: =76

Student satisfaction:	=60	(14.6)
Research assessment:	=57	(3.2)
Entry standards:	75	(247.8)
Student–staff ratio:	66	(19.3)
Library/IT spend/student:	92	(£438)
Facilities spend/student:	=87	(£147)
Good honours:	103	(45.5%)
Graduate prospects:	=44	(65.2%)
Expected completion rate:	79	(80.1%)

Facilities for design, including workshops for metalworking, woodworking and ceramics, have been upgraded recently. A £6.5-million student centre caters for the multicultural population of the university with alcohol-free areas, an international students' bar and a family area for students with children. Modernised sport, exercise and fitness facilities at St Paul's include resistance and cardiovascular training gyms, dance studios and a sports hall. Facilities for media studies and art and design have been refurbished and extended.

Teaching in all subjects is now concentrated on the Guildhall campus, while much of the residential stock is a mile away at Langstone. Applications dropped by almost 9 per cent in 2006 with the arrival of top-up fees, but they had increased by two thirds over the four previous years, which Portsmouth claimed to be the biggest sustained rise at any university. More than a quarter of the undergraduates come from working-class homes, although this is still less than the national average for the subjects and entry qualifications. However, 94 per cent attended state schools or colleges. Efforts are being made to broaden the intake still further through an award-winning membership club that introduces teenagers to higher education through workshops, holiday courses and access to university facilities. The projected dropout rate of 19 per cent is marginally higher than the university's benchmark.

Portsmouth has a larger working-class population and more deprivation than some applicants may realise. But the city also has a vibrant student pub and club scene to supplement a popular students' union. The cost of living is not as high as at many southern universities, and the sea is close at hand. Hall places are offered to 90 per cent of first years and the university runs "secure a home" days at the beginning of September to help the remaining new arrivals with house-hunting.

Bursaries and Scholarships

In receipt of full Maintenance Grant	£800
In receipt of partial Maintenance Grant	Up to £500

- Tuition fees (2006) £3,000
- Placement year tuition fee will be £600.
- Bursary scheme not available to EU students.
- 21% of additional fee income to be earmarked for bursaries.
- Eligibility for bursaries will be assessed using UUK/SLC model bursary scheme (HEBSS).

Contact: www.port.ac.uk/money

Students

Undergraduates:	13,165	(2,895)
Postgraduates:	1,845	(2,660)
Mature students:	14.2%	
Overseas students:	18.4%	
Applications per place:	5.8	
From state-sector schools:	94.1%	
From working-class homes:	28.6%	

For detailed information about fees, grants and bursaries and how they work, see chapter 7.

Accommodation

Number of places and costs refer to 2006–07
University-provided places: about 2,944
Percentage catered: 24.8%
Catered costs: £82–£105 a week (36 weeks).
Self-catered costs: £67–£106 a week (36 weeks).
First years are guaranteed accommodation, subject to terms and conditions.
International students: as above.
Contact: Student.housing@port.ac.uk

Queen Mary, University of London

More than £150 million has been spent developing London University's East End base into a broadly-based institution of 11,000 students. Professor Adrian Smith, Queen Mary's Principal, believes it has "punched below its weight" at times, and is trying to put that right with a higher profile and impressive new facilities. Queen Mary is ranked among the top universities in the world for the arts and humanities by *The Times Higher Education Supplement* and now has the capital's most extensive self-contained campus. A new state-of-the-art learning resource centre with 24-hour access opened in 2003 and a new student village with almost 2,000 en suite rooms followed in 2004. Added to a new £44-million home for Barts and The London, Queen Mary's School of Medicine and Dentistry, the scale of development is unprecedented. More residences and an arts quarter are due for completion in 2006.

The modern setting is a far cry from the People's Palace, which first used the site to bring education to the Victorian masses, but there is still a community programme as well as conventional teaching and research. The arts-based Westfield College and scientific Queen Mary came together in 1989, but it took time to mould the new institution and overcome financial difficulties. The sale of Westfield's Hampstead base released the necessary capital to begin to modernise the Mile End Road campus. The new Medical and Dental School is not far away, in Whitechapel. The striking new headquarters, complete with an innovative science centre for schoolchildren, is now fully operational.

Already London University's fourth largest unit, Queen Mary is expected to carry on growing. It is one of London's designated points of expansion in the sciences, although its strength is more obvious on the arts side, which boasts a clutch of high-profile academics. Applications rose by more than 7 per cent in 2006, despite top-up fees. There has been consistent success in attracting overseas students, who make full use of a unit specialising in English as a foreign language. A strategic alliance with City University covers teaching and research initiatives in areas such as engineering, health and history.

Teaching ratings improved after a patchy start. Dentistry produced the only perfect score, with politics and modern languages close behind. English, history and archaeology produced the best results in the first national student satisfaction survey, but the Quality Assurance Agency

---

Mile End Road,
London E1 4NS
020-7882 5511/5533
admissions@qmw.ac.uk
www.qmw.ac.uk
www.qmsu.org

Edinburgh
Belfast
Cardiff
LONDON

The Times Rankings
Overall Ranking: 41

Student satisfaction:	=38	(14.9)
Research assessment:	=36	(5.0)
Entry standards:	44	(314.1)
Student–staff ratio:	=6	(12.1)
Library/IT spend/student:	=31	(£643)
Facilities spend/student:	=73	(£173)
Good honours:	57	(57.6%)
Graduate prospects:	21	(71.6%)
Expected completion rate:	=30	(90.0%)

had already given the college a good overall report in its first institutional audit. Iberian and Latin American languages, law and linguistics were the only subjects rated internationally outstanding for research in the 2001 assessments, but another 13 reached grade 5, leaving almost half of the researchers in the top two categories of seven. The proportion of academics entered for the exercise, at nine out of ten, was among the highest at any university.

The majority of undergraduates take at least one course in departments other than their own, under the modular course system. Most degrees are organised in units to allow maximum flexibility. Interdisciplinary study has always been encouraged: for example, medics can choose selected modules in English and drama. The medical school is to house a national teaching centre for clinical and communications skills. There is a flourishing exchange programme, which includes universities in the United States and Japan, as well as Europe. Each student has an adviser to guide them through the possibilities. Language students can use the University of London Institute, in Paris, while students at Beijing's University of Posts and Telecommunications can take double degrees (awarded by their own institution and Queen Mary) without leaving China.

Queen Mary attracts a socially diverse intake: almost a third of the under-graduates come from the two lowest socio-economic classes, many of them from local ethnic groups. Social life centres on the campus, which features an award-winning student nightclub, but the West End is easily accessible by tube. Students welcome the relatively low prices (for the capital) in East London, which has more to offer than many expect when they apply.

Bursaries and Scholarships

In receipt of full Maintenance Grant	£1,000
In receipt of partial Maintenance Grant	£800
Academic achievement	Scholarship

- Tuition fees (2006) £3,000
- £4,000 for students receiving full Maintenance Grant and achieving 3 A grades at A level.
- Eligibility for bursaries will be assessed using UUK/SLC model bursary scheme (HEBSS).

Contact: www.qmul.ac.uk/undergraduate/ feesfinance

Students

Undergraduates:	7,525	(395)
Postgraduates:	1,545	(910)
Mature students:	19.6%	
Overseas students:	19.4%	
Applications per place:	6.8	
From state-sector schools:	85.1%	
From working-class homes:	30.5%	

For detailed information about fees, grants and bursaries and how they work, see chapter 7.

Accommodation

Number of places and costs refer to 2006–07
University-provided places: 2,539
Percentage catered: 8.6%
Catered costs: £106.05–£121.10 a week.
Self-catered costs: £79.03–£107.03 a week.
First years given priority, if terms and conditions are met. Residential restrictions apply.
International students given highest priority and extended deadlines.
Contact: residences@qmul.ac.uk

Queen's University, Belfast

Generally regarded as Northern Ireland's premier university, Queen's is investing £200 million in new staff and improved facilities to improve its research performance and regain the international standing it enjoyed before the Troubles. Research grades improved in the last assessment exercise: although mechanical engineering was again the only subject rated internationally outstanding, 15 of the 40 subject areas reached the next grade. An expensive recruitment programme across all five faculties is designed to reap more rewards in 2008.

The university's vision for the future also includes improvements in student facilities. A £45-million student village will replace the existing tower block residences with three-storey self-catering "villas". A new student centre is bringing services together at the heart of the campus and the students' union is being refurbished. Queen's enjoyed big increases in applications at the end of the 1990s, as more of the province's students decided to stay at home. Although the trend has been reversed in the last two years, the demand for places remains healthy with 10 per cent more young people going into higher education in Northern Ireland than in England. Queen's was one of four university colleges for the whole of Ireland

in the 19th century, and still draws students from all over the island. The aim now is to revive demand from mainland Britain and increase overseas students.

Teaching assessments showed the university's all-round strength. Half of the subjects assessed under the original quality system were rated excellent, and none of the 18 areas inspected after 1996–97 yielded less than 21 points out of 24. Dentistry, economics, electronic engineering, pharmacy and psychology all achieved maximum points, as did education at St Mary's and Stranmillis colleges (both associated with Queen's). The university did well in the first national student satisfaction survey, particularly in maths and languages.

The university district, which is among the most attractive in Belfast, is one of the city's main cultural and recreational areas. Queen's runs a highly successful arts festival each November, opened a new art gallery in 2001 and has the only full-time university cinema in the UK – one of the best in Ireland. Another £2 million has been invested in arts facilities recently, the lion's share of the cash going into a new studio theatre. More teaching accommodation has been added, with better access for the disabled, and the university's great hall has had a £2.5-million refurbishment, courtesy of the university's own foundation.

University Road,
Belfast BT7 1NN
028-9024 5133
admissions@qub.ac.uk
www.qub.ac.uk
www.qubsu.org

Queen's has been spreading its wings in recent years. As well as its partnership with St Mary's and Stranmillis colleges, the university has established a campus in Armagh City, which now has 400 students. There is a smaller outreach centre in Omagh, Co. Tyrone. Other teaching and research premises are located at the Royal Victoria Hospital, Belfast City Hospital, and the Marine Biology Station in Portaferry on Strangford Lough.

Courses at Queen's are modular and semesters have been introduced. Students are encouraged to take language programmes from a unique "virtual" language laboratory, which provides online tuition from any computer in the university. IT facilities are good: Queen's was the first institution to meet the national target of providing at least one computer workstation for every five undergraduate students. An unusually large proportion of graduates go on to further study, which does Queen's no harm in the employment league.

Strictly non-denominational teaching is enshrined in a charter which has guaranteed student representation and equal rights for women since 1908. The charter even precluded the teaching of theology – this is done through a network of four associated colleges.

Nightlife has returned to the city centre, but the social scene is still concentrated on the students' union and the surrounding area. Sports facilities, which include a university hut in the Mourne mountains, are of a high standard and are being expanded. A rugby academy opened in 2002 and there are plans to do the same for Gaelic football. There is plenty of reasonably-priced private housing for those not in hall, although there have been tensions between students and residents of the most popular area.

Bursaries and Scholarships

In receipt of full Maintenance Grant	£1,100
In receipt of partial Maintenance Grant	
	£100–£600

- Tuition fees (2006) £3,000
- Tuition fee for Foundation year is currently £2,000. Tuition fee for placement year and year abroad is currently £600.
- Part of the bursary (£100) paid in kind for sports facilities and buying books.
- 20% of additional fee income earmarked to be for bursaries.
- Access agreement approved by DEL in consultation with OFFA.

Contact: www.qub.ac.uk/2007entry

Students

Undergraduates:	12,595	(5,740)
Postgraduates:	2,050	(3,295)
Mature students:	13.4%	
Overseas students:	7.1%	
Applications per place:	5.3	
From state-sector schools:	99.6%	
From working-class homes:	36.0%	

For detailed information about fees, grants and bursaries and how they work, see chapter 7.

Accommodation

Number of places and costs refer to 2005–06
University-provided places: 2,000
Percentage catered: 0%
Self-catered costs: £50–£70 a week.
First-year students have priority.
International students are given priority.
Contact: accommodation@qub.ac.uk

University of Reading

Assessments in both teaching and research have demonstrated an all-round strength that may have surprised those who knew Reading primarily for its highly-regarded agricultural and environmental courses. The university achieved a series of good grades in the arts and social sciences, with perfect teaching scores in nursing, physics, philosophy and psychology. Drama had already achieved this feat. There were good results, too, in the first national student satisfaction survey, when physical geography and environmental science, history and archaeology were the top performers.

Several of the successes came in subjects added when the university took in Bulmershe College, which provided a second campus near the original 320-acre parkland site on the outskirts of Reading. Facilities for meteorology, management, agriculture, archaeology and psychology were upgraded in the 1990s. More halls of residence have been added recently as part of a £275-million investment plan. The School of Pharmacy opened in 2005 and a new student services centre should be operational in 2007.

Reading was the only university established between the two world wars, having been Oxford's extension college for the first part of the last century, but the attractive main campus now has a modern feel. There are also 2,000 acres of university-owned farmland on the Downs, near Reading, for teaching and research in agricultural and plant sciences. The university's location, a bus ride away from Heathrow Airport, and an international reputation in key areas for developing countries have always ensured a healthy flow of overseas students. However, overall applications for full-time degrees were down by over 17 per cent at the start of 2006, making Reading one of the biggest casualties of top-up fees.

Almost one student in five is from an independent school and the proportion from areas without a tradition of higher education is among the lowest in the country, but the university is close to national averages for its subjects when its location is taken into account. The retention rate exceeds expectations, with a less than 10 per cent of undergraduates who started courses in 2002 expected to leave without a qualification.

All undergraduates take Career Management Skills modules that contribute five credits towards their degree classification. The online system, which has 200 web pages of advice, exercises and information, has been bought by 30 other universities and colleges. Sessions are delivered jointly by academics and careers advisors, with input from alumni and leading employers.

Whiteknights, PO Box 217,
Reading RG6 6AH
0118-987 5123
information@reading.ac.uk
www.reading.ac.uk
www.rusu.co.uk

The Times Rankings
Overall Ranking: 31

Student satisfaction:	=12	(15.4)
Research assessment:	=25	(5.3)
Entry standards:	37	(341.5)
Student–staff ratio:	26	(15.9)
Library/IT spend/student:	=46	(£587)
Facilities spend/student:	=50	(£223)
Good honours:	34	(64.8%)
Graduate prospects:	75	(58.9%)
Expected completion rate:	29	(90.2%)

Reading has been trying to break down the barriers between the arts and sciences, notably in a joint initiative with the Open University to develop standardised course materials to help under-qualified students cope with physics degrees. Arts and social science students are encouraged to broaden their horizons by taking three subjects from the modular course scheme in the first year of their degree.

Successes in the last research assessment exercise were well spread. Archaeology, English, environmental science, Italian and psychology were all rated internationally outstanding, with 58 per cent of the academics entered for assessment placed in the top two categories of seven.

The town may not be the most fashionable, but it has plenty of nightlife and an award-winning shopping centre. London is easily accessible by train, but the cost of living is on par with the capital. More than 4,500 residential places include a landscaped student village, while first-rate sports facilities include accessible rowing and sailing boathouses. Representative teams have a good record in inter-university competitions.

Students praise the social scene, although the high proportion from the South East means that many go home at the weekends. The large students' union had a £500,000 refit to improve and extend its popular main venue, and additional refurbishment is planned in 2006. It has been voted among the best in Britain, but students who live in town often avoid the trek back out to the campus.

Bursaries and Scholarships

In receipt of full Maintenance Grant	£1,300
In receipt of partial Maintenance Grant	£325–£1,300
Progressing from outreach	Bursary

- Tuition fees (2006)   £3,000
- Placement year and year abroad tuition fee will be 25% fee.
- Students from Scotland and Wales eligible for bursaries.
- Pre-application, pre-entry bursaries to target groups.
- Outreach schools to nominate candidates for Vice-Chancellor's Bursary scheme worth £2,000 over 3 years.
- Up to 2 bursaries may be held by each student.
- Hardship Funds available.
- More than 25% of additional fee income to be earmarked for bursaries.
- Eligibility for bursaries will be assessed using UUK/SLC model bursary scheme (HEBSS).

Contact: www.rdg.ac.uk/studentfinance/

Students

Undergraduates:	8,130	(1,845)
Postgraduates:	2,260	(2,315)
Mature students:	12.2%	
Overseas students:	9.0%	
Applications per place:	7.6	
From state-sector schools:	81.8%	
From working-class homes:	23.7%	

For detailed information about fees, grants and bursaries and how they work, see chapter 7.

Accommodation

Number of places and costs refer to 2005–06
University-provided places: about 4,600
Percentage catered: 41%
Catered costs: £100–£133 (30 weeks).
Self-catered costs: £54–£102 (30–39 weeks).
First-year undergraduate students are guaranteed a place if conditions are met.
International students: given priority if conditions are met.
Contact: accommodation@reading.ac.uk

The Robert Gordon University

So close are links with the North Sea oil and gas industries that Robert Gordon has dubbed itself the Energy University, but nursing and the health sciences are now equally important. A new mission statement has switched the emphasis of the university from vocational to professional education, while the creative industries are also a growth area.

There is a full portfolio of courses in business, health, design and engineering. Flexible programmes, with credit accumulation and transfer, make for easy movement in and out of the university for an often mobile local workforce. Work placements, lasting up to a year, are the norm, helping an employment record that has been the best in Scotland for four years and consistently one of the UK's best.

Efforts to extend access beyond the normal higher education catchment have produced a diverse student population, with more than a third of the undergraduates coming from working-class homes and almost a fifth from areas sending few students to higher education. The projected dropout rate of 17 per cent has been improving but is still higher than the UK average for RGU's subjects and entry qualifications.

Only two of the subjects assessed in the main rounds of teaching assessment were rated Excellent, but a majority of the rest were considered Highly Satisfactory. Only 120 academic staff were entered for the latest research assessment exercise and none of the subjects featured in the top three of the seven categories. But the university has committed itself to winning international recognition for applied research in the current decade.

There are now about 140 degrees to choose from. There was serious consideration of a merger with Aberdeen University in 2002. Although this was eventually abandoned, there will be continued collaboration between the two institutions. RGU's finances are now described as "sound as a pound", and the most secure of any new university in Scotland. Students from the city's two institutions mix easily, and there is healthy academic rivalry in some areas, despite the obvious differences between the universities. Named after an 18th-century philanthropist, Robert Gordon has two sites around the city and an attractive field study centre at Cromarty, in the Highlands. The historic Schoolhill site adjoins Aberdeen art gallery, while Garthdee, where 70 per cent of undergraduates are taught, overlooks the River Dee and has had a £70-million face-lift. Sir Norman Foster designed the business school, while other recent developments made room for art,

---

Schoolhill,
Aberdeen AB10 1FR
01224 262105
admissions@rgu.ac.uk
www.rgu.ac.uk
www.rgunion.co.uk

ABERDEEN
Edinburgh
Belfast
London
Cardiff

The Times Rankings
Overall Ranking: 56

Student satisfaction:	–	(–)
Research assessment:	=94	(1.9)
Entry standards:	48	(305.9)
Student–staff ratio:	=63	(18.6)
Library/IT spend/student:	66	(£510)
Facilities spend/student:	90	(£143)
Good honours:	68	(54.4%)
Graduate prospects:	10	(75.9%)
Expected completion rate:	76	(80.6%)

architecture and the faculty of health and social care (with 3,000 students).

Like most new universities, especially in Scotland, RGU recruits most of its students locally, 60 per cent of them female. However, overseas recruitment has been growing sharply, with 30 per cent increases in 2004 and 2005, and the overall demand for places has been stronger than at most universities north of the border. The Scottish Executive has provided £500,000 in European funding to help more people from disadvantaged communities to take courses. The university already offers four-week intensive access programmes in mathematics, engineering, chemistry and computing during August and September for applicants who narrowly miss the entry requirements to top up their qualifications. If they prefer, prospective students may take access units in these subjects by distance learning, using study packs and with the support of an assigned tutor. The scheme, which runs all year round, is recommended for aspiring students without traditional academic backgrounds.

The university is pinning many of its hopes on new technology. A virtual campus was launched with an online course in e-business for postgraduates, again with European funding, which also enables management undergraduates to receive course materials via an intranet, and other degree and short courses are available.

Aberdeen is a long way to go for English students, but train and air links are excellent, and the city regularly features in the top ten for quality of life. In addition, an £11-million sports and leisure centre opened in 2005, providing a centre for excellence for the region in hockey and several other sports. Although private accommodation can be expensive, low prices in the students' union partially compensate, and there are enough residential places to guarantee accommodation to first years from outside the local area.

Bursaries and Scholarships

- Scottish domiciled students: no fees will be payable by eligible students although a "graduate endowment" will be payable after graduation: the 2005–06 level was £2,216.
- Non-Scottish domiciled students fees: £1,700 a year.
- Fees for placement year and year abroad are normally 50% of full-time fee.

Contact:
http://www.rgu.ac.uk/stud_finance/general/page.cfm?pge=33079

Students		
Undergraduates:	6,520	(2,375)
Postgraduates:	935	(2,565)
Mature students:	27.3%	
Overseas students:	11.9%	
Applications per place:	4.2	
From state-sector schools:	94.0%	
From working-class homes:	37.5%	

For detailed information about fees, grants and bursaries and how they work, see chapter 7.

Accommodation

Number of places and costs refer to 2006–07
University-provided places: 1,216
Percentage catered: 0%
Self-catered costs: £66–£80 a week.
All first-year students are eligible to apply for student accommodation. Residential restrictions apply.
International students: accommodation guaranteed.
Contact: accommodation@rgu.ac.uk
www.rgu.ac.uk/accommodation

Roehampton University

Four years after entering a federation with Surrey University, the former Roehampton Institute became a university in its own right in 2004. The two institutions will continue to collaborate on research projects and joint programmes, but undergraduates entering in 2007 will receive Roehampton University degrees.

The new university comprises four distinctive colleges, which still maintain some of the traditional ethos of their religious foundations: the Anglican Whitelands, the Roman Catholic Digby Stuart, the Methodist Southlands, and the Froebel, which follows the teachings of the humanist Frederick Froebel. Students do not have to be any of these denominations to study at the university, which also has a Jewish resource centre and two Muslim prayer rooms. All four colleges occupy a 26-hectare campus, with stunning parkland and lakes, on or adjacent to Roehampton Lane. Whitelands moved from Putney in 2004 to the 18th-century mansion, Parkstead House, overlooking Richmond Park, which also houses the school of human and life sciences and is at the heart of the new five-hectare south campus. The buildings have been refurbished with IT facilities, student accommodation, laboratories and teaching space. A new dance and PE building also

opened on the main campus in 2005. The institute had already spent £20 million relocating Southlands, providing a new site for the social sciences. Current projects include a new £4-million facility for the school of arts, which will open in September 2006, and a new teaching centre for human rights, social justice and citizenship education.

The colleges all have their own bars and other leisure facilities, although they are open to all members of the university. In line with the university's origins, education remains the largest subject area, accounting for more than a quarter of the students, with others taking combined studies programmes in arts; business, social sciences and computing; and human and life sciences. There are over 1,500 subject combinations to choose from, including film studies and biological anthropology, or dance and theology.

Dance was rated internationally outstanding in the latest research assessments, with anthropology and history both in the next-highest category. With 45 per cent of the academics entered for assessment – a higher figure than at any of the former polytechnics – Roehampton outperformed all of its new peer group in terms of average grades per member of staff. The Quality Assurance Agency has complimented Roehampton

---

Erasmus House, Roehampton Lane,
London SW15 5PU
020-8392 3232
enquiries@
roehampton.ac.uk
www.roehampton.ac.uk
www.roehampton
student.com

Edinburgh

Belfast

Cardiff

LONDON

on the accessibility of academic staff to students and the positive ways in which they responded to student needs. However, the results from the first national student satisfaction survey were disappointing.

Teaching grades were respectable, rather than spectacular. Despite the predominance of arts students, biological sciences produced the best score, with psychology and linguistics close behind. A Work and Study Scheme gives local employees credit towards their degree for relevant tasks performed in the workplace. The programme is designed to help employers recruit and retain key staff, as well as helping those who cannot afford to study full time.

Roehampton has been enjoying record intakes at the same time as increasing its entry scores. There was another 6 per cent increase at the start of 2006, against the national trend. Nine out of ten undergraduates were educated in state schools and more than a third come from working-class homes. The projected dropout rate has been coming down, but the latest figures suggest that 17 per cent of undergraduates will leave without a qualification.

About 80 per cent of first years who want a hall place are offered one, with priority going to those who make Roehampton their first preference. Two new residences opened in 2005, adding 300 places to the residential stock. Rents are not cheap for those who miss out on a place or prefer the private sector, but students like the proximity of central London and the lively and attractive suburbs around Roehampton.

Bursaries and Scholarships

In receipt of full Maintenance Grant	£500
In receipt of partial Maintenance Grant	£500
Academic achievement	Scholarship £1,000

- Tuition fees (2006) £3,000
- Year abroad tuition fee will be 50% standard tuition fee.
- £1000 scholarship for each year of study to full time UK and EU students who achieve 320 UCAS points from any 18 unit qualification. All students meeting the criteria will receive the scholarship automatically without the need to apply. The scholarship will be paid directly into successful students' bank accounts and is not repayable.
- 13% of additional fee income to be earmarked for bursaries.
- Eligibility for bursaries will be assessed using UUK/SLC model bursary scheme (HEBSS).

Contact: www.roehampton.ac.uk/ug/finance.asp

Students			Accommodation
Undergraduates:	5,450	(1,000)	Number of places and costs refer to 2006–07
Postgraduates:	705	(885)	University-provided places: 1,600
Mature students:	26.9%		Percentage catered: 12.5%
Overseas students:	6.9%		Catered costs: £105 a week.
Applications per place:	3.8		Self-catered costs: £85–£90 a week.
From state-sector schools:	93.3%		First-year students are given priority if
From working-class homes:	34.5%		conditions are met. Local restrictions apply.

International students: some reserved places.

For detailed information about fees, grants and bursaries and how they work, see chapter 7.

Contact: y.douglas@roehampton.ac.uk
www.roehampton.ac.uk/accommodation/oncamp.asp

Royal Holloway, University of London

London University's "campus in the country" occupies 135 acres of woodland between Windsor Castle and Heathrow. The 600-bed Founder's Building, modelled on a French chateau and opened by Queen Victoria, is one of Britain's most remarkable university buildings. The merger with Bedford College, and the sale of Bedford's valuable site in Regent's Park, enabled Royal Holloway to embark on a major building programme, which has since been extended with a £100-million building programme. Recent projects have included a major new auditorium, extensions to the School of Management and other academic buildings, an extension to the main library and new student residences, which have been praised for their comfort and eco-friendly features.

Other developments include an expanded academic staff, better student services and a portfolio of scholarships and bursaries that pre-dated top-up fees. One offers free places or reduced fees to those who stay on for a postgraduate degree. The conversion of the huge Victorian boilerhouse into a performance space for drama, the launch of a new department of health and social care, and the establishment of formal links with institutions such as New York, Sydney and Yale universities, demonstrate that progress has not just been a matter of bricks and mortar. Closer to home, another link allows music students to take lessons at the Royal College of Music.

Both partners in the merger which formed the college were originally for women only, their legacy commemorated in the Bedford Centre for the History of Women. The arts and humanities still account for most of the top ratings, but the gender balance in the student population is now roughly equal. French, German, geography and music were considered internationally outstanding in the latest research assessments, when three quarters of the academics entered for assessment were in departments rated in the top two of seven categories. The successes placed Royal Holloway in the top dozen research institutions and have helped cement a place in the top 20 of *The Times* League Table.

Royal Holloway is not just about the arts: the college offers a science foundation year at further education colleges in the region, and the balance of disciplines is gradually shifting. Psychology and biological sciences registered perfect scores in teaching assessments. All the sciences were judged nationally outstanding for research in

---

University of London, Egham Hill,
Egham, Surrey TW20 0EX
01784 443883
undergrad-office@
rhul.ac.uk
www.rhul.ac.uk
www.su.rhul.ac.uk

The Times Rankings
Overall Ranking: 12

Student satisfaction:	=8	(15.5)
Research assessment:	=10	(5.7)
Entry standards:	34	(345.3)
Student–staff ratio:	=12	(14.1)
Library/IT spend/student:	53	(£549)
Facilities spend/student:	20	(£311)
Good honours:	29	(66.5%)
Graduate prospects:	35	(67.3%)
Expected completion rate:	=15	(93.8%)

2001 and physics produced the best results in the first national student satisfaction survey. All 18 departments encourage interdisciplinary work, which is facilitated by a modular course structure with examinations at the end of every year. An Advanced Skills Programme, covering information technology, communication skills and foreign languages, further encourages breadth of study.

Immediate expansion plans centre on the college's areas of excellence and on distance learning. In 2003, Royal Holloway launched e-degrees in classics, history, business management and an MA in information security to add to its University of London external programme. It is spearheading the development of the University of London Institute in Paris, allowing students to spend part of their course in France.

The college still draws almost a quarter of its undergraduates from independent schools, although the proportion coming from working-class homes has been rising. However, the ethnic mix is above average and the projected dropout rate of 6 per cent is among the best in Britain.

Almost 2,500 students are in halls of residence, many of them in the Founder's Building itself. The college's green belt location at Egham, Surrey, 35 minutes from the centre of London by rail, ensures that social life is concentrated on an extended students' union. However, the West End is close for those determined to seek the high life. A high proportion of students come from London and the Home Counties, and the campus can seem empty at weekends.

Bursaries and Scholarships

In receipt of full Maintenance Grant	£500
In receipt of partial Maintenance Grant	£500
Academic achievement	Scholarship

- Tuition fees (2006) £3,000
- Scholarships of £500 for all in receipt of Maintenance Grant and with more than 320 UCAS tariff points. Competitive Thomas Holloway Scholarships of £3,500 for "outstanding" students receiving Maintenance Grant. Competitive Bedford Scholarships of £1,000 for "outstanding" students.
- 19% of additional fee income to be earmarked for bursaries.

Contact: www.rhul.ac.uk/prospective-students/

Students

Undergraduates:	4,750	(920)
Postgraduates:	1,165	(765)
Mature students:	13.6%	
Overseas students:	21.3%	
Applications per place:	6.7	
From state-sector schools:	77.6%	
From working-class homes:	23.2%	

For detailed information about fees, grants and bursaries and how they work, see chapter 7.

Accommodation

Number of places and costs refer to 2006–07
University-provided places: 2,466
Percentage catered: 44%
Catered costs: £62–£103 a week.
Self-catered costs: £55–£105 a week.
First years are guaranteed accommodation provided conditions are met.
International students: as above.
Contact: Accommodation-Office@rhul.ac.uk

University of St Andrews

As the oldest Scottish university and the third oldest in Britain, St Andrews has long been both well known and fashionable among a mainly middle-class clientele. There was a 44 per cent surge in applications whenPrince William chose to study there – by far the biggest rise at any university. That kind of increase was unsustainable, but a 20 per cent rise in 2005 was followed by another of 11 per cent at the official deadline for courses beginning in 2006. There are now about eight applications for every place.

With some 40 per cent of the students coming from south of the border, St Andrews has earned the nickname of Scotland's English university. But another 30 per cent come from 90 countries farther afield, giving the university a cosmopolitan feel. Fee concessions and exchange schemes have boosted applications, particularly in the United States, which provides nearly a quarter of first-year students on its own.

Peer assessments have shown that there is top quality behind the prestige. St Andrews has the best teaching and research grades in Scotland, and only Oxford and Cambridge can match the 2.4 per cent dropout rate, which is by far the lowest in Scotland. Uniquely, every subject assessed has been rated either Excellent or Highly Satisfactory for teaching, demonstrating quality across the board. Psychology and English were the only starred research departments, but 15 subjects on the next rung of the ladder put the university into the top ten in terms of the average per member of staff.

St Andrews was one of the universities criticised by its funding council for the narrowness of its intake when performance indicators were introduced. More than a third of the undergraduates come from independent schools, when the UK average for the university's courses and entry scores is just over one in five. A dedicated Access Centre has had some success in trying to broaden the intake. The proportion from working-class homes has been rising and is now higher than at Edinburgh, putting the university within reach of its benchmark for the first time. A successful fundraising campaign is building up a bank of £3,000-a-year scholarships for students from poor homes.

The town of St Andrews is steeped in history, as well as being the centre of the golfing world. The university at its heart accounts for about a third of the 18,000 inhabitants. There are close relations between town and gown, both cultural and social. New students ("bejants" and "bejantines") acquire third and fourth-year "parents" to ease them into university life,

College Gate, North Street,
St Andrews KY16 9AJ
01334 462150
admissions@
st-andrews.ac.uk
www.st-andrews.ac.uk
www.yourunion.net

The Times Rankings
Overall Ranking: =18

Student satisfaction:	–	(–)
Research assessment:	=10	(5.7)
Entry standards:	9	(430.5)
Student–staff ratio:	16	(14.3)
Library/IT spend/student:	=46	(£587)
Facilities spend/student:	61	(£200)
Good honours:	9	(75.1%)
Graduate prospects:	43	(65.7%)
Expected completion rate:	3	(97.6%)

and on Raisin Monday give their academic guardians a bottle of wine in return for a receipt in Latin, which can be written on anything. Another unusual feature is that all humanities students are awarded an MA rather than a BA.

Many of the main buildings date from the 15th and 16th centuries, but sciences are taught at the modern North Haugh site a few streets away. Everything is within walking distance, but bicycles are common. Although small, St Andrews offers a wide range of courses. The university's reputation has always rested primarily on the humanities, which acquired a £1.3-million research centre recently. An £8-million headquarters for the School of International Relations is due to open in September 2006. St Andrews has the largest mediaeval history department in Britain and has now added film studies. But a full range of physical sciences is offered, with sophisticated lasers and the largest optical telescope in Britain. New buildings for computer science and management opened in 2005.

An academic partnership with Dundee University is being developed in order to expand teaching and research in areas of common interest. A joint degree in electronics and optoelectronics was the first project, followed by shared teaching in medical education and health sciences, and the launch of a course pooling St Andrews' excellence in art history and Dundee's flair for design.

Students do not come to St Andrews for the nightclubs, but there is no shortage of parties in a tight-knit community. More than half of all students live in halls of residence and the sports facilities are excellent.

Bursaries and Scholarships

- Scottish domiciled students: no fees will be payable by eligible students although a "graduate endowment" will be payable after graduation: the 2005–06 level was £2,216.
- Non-Scottish domiciled students fees: £1,700 a year (£2,700 for medicine).
- Fees for placement year and year abroad are normally 50% of full-time fee.
- Subject-based entrance scholarships are awarded on academic merit, made in the year of entry only, worth from £250–£1,000.
- Scholarships awarded on the basis of financial need are available to UK and EU students and range in value from £1,000 in the year of entry to £3,000 a year for each year of the undergraduate course.
- Some scholarships are available only to students domiciled in Scotland, others are open to any EU citizen, and some have no geographical restrictions.

Contact: http://scholarships.
st-andrews.ac.uk/Scholarships/
WelcomeScholarships.jsp

Students

Undergraduates:	5,870	(470)
Postgraduates:	1,165	(440)
Mature students:	6.6%	
Overseas students:	21.4%	
Applications per place:	8.1	
From state-sector schools:	65.1%	
From working-class homes:	17.7%	

For detailed information about fees, grants and bursaries and how they work, see chapter 7.

Accommodation

Number of places and costs refer to 2006–07
University-provided places: 3,480
Percentage catered: 47%
Catered costs: £109.93–£155.28 a week.
Self-catered costs: £50.97–£111.94 a week.
Accommodation guaranteed for single entrant undergraduates if conditions are met.
Policy for international students: as above.
Contact: studacc@st-andrews.ac.uk

University of Salford

In the last five years, Salford has begun to slip below some of the new universities in *The Times* League Table. But consistently good graduate employment rates, carefully-targeted courses and an emphasis on the university's location close to the centre of Manchester appeal to students. Applications were up by more than 10 per cent in 2005, although the trend did not survive the introduction of top-up fees. There had been a 6 per cent decline at the start of 2006.

A merger with University College Salford, with which there were already close links, provided a second opportunity to forge a new type of higher education institution. The main victim of higher education budget cuts in the early 1980s, Salford bounced back as the prototype decentralised, customer-oriented university. The next model, which was ahead of its time, was the comprehensive post-school institution. A decade on, however, no further education courses remain, although Salford is an enthusiast for two-year foundation degrees.

Instead, the university stresses its business links and the modern portfolio of courses. Assessment grades have been variable, but the projected dropout rate of 16 per cent is now less than the national average for the subjects and students'

qualifications. Salford takes large numbers from under-represented groups: over a third of the undergraduates come from working-class homes and more than one in five from areas sending few students to higher education.

Teaching quality grades improved ratings in the latter years of the cycle. The university averaged 21 points out of 24 from 1996 onwards, with perfect scores for politics and biological sciences. Business and health subjects are now big recruiters. The university's growing involvement in health has seen the establishment of a national centre for prosthetics and orthotics, and a high reputation for the treatment of sports injuries. Another innovation was the launch of Europe's first nursing course for deaf students, as part of the Government's "Making a Difference" strategy. There is also a degree in traditional Chinese medicine, with an acupuncture clinic.

Engineering is the university's traditional strength, attracting many of the 3,000 overseas students. Two thirds of courses offer work placements, half of them abroad and almost all counting towards degree classifications. The tradition of sandwich courses always serves Salford well in terms of graduate employment. A business enterprise support programme helps students set up their own businesses, providing

---

Salford, Greater Manchester M5 4WT
0161-295 4545
course-enquiries@salford.ac.uk
www.salford.ac.uk
www.salfordstudents.com

The Times Rankings
Overall Ranking: 65

Student satisfaction:	=67	(14.5)
Research assessment:	=53	(4.3)
Entry standards:	72	(249.3)
Student–staff ratio:	=52	(17.9)
Library/IT spend/student:	84	(£454)
Facilities spend/student:	=42	(£235)
Good honours:	=75	(52.9%)
Graduate prospects:	=86	(56.4%)
Expected completion rate:	84	(78.9%)

entrepreneurship training and business skills, as well as a business mentor. Online degrees have been introduced and the university has also made headlines with more unusual innovations, such as degrees in business economics with gambling studies, not to mention the appointment of Britain's first Professor of Pop Music.

Salford's extended range of courses meant that fewer than 40 per cent of the academics were entered for the latest research assessment exercise, when the built environment and information management were the only areas considered internationally outstanding. European studies – another longstanding strength – again reached the second rung of the ladder and will benefit from a new £1-million languages centre. The university remains committed to research: it has established 13 interdisciplinary research centres and a graduate school. It also led the way in formally recognising interaction with business and industry as of equal importance to teaching and research.

The modern landscaped campus, a haven of lawns and shrubberies along the River Irwell, is less than two miles from Manchester city centre and has a mainline railway station. The university also has its own TV and radio stations, as part of a partnership with Granada. Salford has spent £68 million on improvements,

including £16 million on a new building to bring health courses onto the main campus from nearby Eccles. Another £100 million is pledged to capital projects over the next ten years, starting with new premises for health-related studies and further development of the Adelphi arts and cultural quarter. Students like the friendly atmosphere and most of the residential places are either on campus or in a student village 15 minutes' walk away. This is important in an area where security is a big issue, one which the university has been addressing with the police and local authority.

Bursaries and Scholarships

In receipt of full Maintenance Grant   £650
In receipt of partial Maintenance Grant
                                      £50–£650

- Tuition fees (2006)   £3,000
- Fee remission is offered for all placements.
- Additional bursaries available for UK and EU students receiving Maintenance Grant to cover higher course-related costs on specific programmes up to £2,600.
- Bursaries available to students on international placements consisting of fee remission and £500 a semester abroad.
- Eligibility for bursaries will be assessed using UUK/SLC model bursary scheme (HEBSS).

Contact: www.salford.ac.uk/study/fees

Students

Undergraduates:	12,545	(3,000)
Postgraduates:	1,445	(2,410)
Mature students:	29.1%	
Overseas students:	8.7%	
Applications per place:	4.7	
From state-sector schools:	96.0%	
From working-class homes:	36.5%	

For detailed information about fees, grants and bursaries and how they work, see chapter 7.

Accommodation

Number of places and costs refer to 2006–07
University-provided places: 3,248
Percentage catered: pre-pay accounts are available for all halls.
Catered costs: £51.03–£71.74.
Self-catered costs: £49.21–£68.39.
First years are guaranteed accommodation (terms and conditions apply).
International students: as above.
Contact: c.saunders@salford.ac.uk
www.salford.ac.uk/crservice/accommod

School of Oriental and African Studies, London

As the major national centre for the study of Africa and Asia, SOAS has a global reputation in subjects relating to two thirds of the world's population. Originally only a specialist Oriental college, the school has always worked closely with the Foreign Office, whose staff attend its extensive range of language courses and briefings. The library, with nearly one million volumes, periodicals and audiovisual materials in 400 languages, attracts scholars from around the world. It is in the top 50 in the *Times Higher Education Supplement*'s world rankings of universities.

Students come from over 100 countries, although more than 80 per cent of undergraduates are British. However, the school has a much wider portfolio of courses than its name would suggest, with 400 degree combinations on offer. Degrees are available in familiar subjects such as law, music, history or the social sciences, but with a different emphasis.

Student recruitment is on the rise, especially among independent school candidates, who account for almost a third of the British undergraduates. An increase of 33 per cent was one of the largest at any university in 2005, and this was followed by another rise of nearly 18 per cent as top-up fees arrived. The numbers taking first degrees have risen significantly in past decade, accounting for more than half of the 3,500 students. But now the growth area is postgraduate courses, which have helped to tackle a financial deficit. In addition, more than 1,500 students are now taking distance learning courses, mainly outside the UK.

Postgraduates are attracted by a research record which saw history rated internationally outstanding in the last assessments. Seven of the 11 subject areas were placed in the top two categories. Teaching assessments have also been good, a maximum score for history of art leading the way, with East and South Asian studies close behind. The final assessments produced solid results in politics and economics.

Nearly all students take advantage of the unique opportunities for learning one of the wide range of languages on offer: 40 non-European languages are available. There is also an option of spending one, two or three terms of a degree course in one of the school's many partner universities in Africa or Asia. The school has been chosen to house a national teaching centre for languages. Over two thirds of those graduating recently achieved firsts or upper-second class degrees, while the 12 percent dropout rate

---

Thornhaugh Street,
Russell Square, London WC1H 0XG
020-7898 4034
study@soas.ac.uk
www.soas.ac.uk
www.soasunion.org

Edinburgh
Belfast
Cardiff
LONDON

The Times Rankings
Overall Ranking: =18

Student satisfaction:	=60	(14.6)
Research assessment:	=18	(5.5)
Entry standards:	39	(328.6)
Student–staff ratio:	3	(9.8)
Library/IT spend/student:	5	(£1,143)
Facilities spend/student:	72	(£175)
Good honours:	6	(75.9%)
Graduate prospects:	13	(74.5%)
Expected completion rate:	36	(87.4%)

is almost exactly the UK average for the subjects and entry qualifications at SOAS. About one in five of the British undergraduates comes from a working-class home.

SOAS is located in Bloomsbury, but in 2001 opened a second campus at Vernon Square, Islington. Less than a mile from the main Russell Square site, and adjacent to the student residences, it provides student-orientated facilities such as an internet café. The centrepiece of the main campus is an airy, modern building with gallery space as well as teaching accommodation, a gift from the Sultan of Brunei. There is no separate students' union building, although the students do have their own bar and catering facilities. The well-equipped and under-used University of London Union is close at hand, with swimming pool, gym and bars. The West End is also on the doorstep.

The 772 residential places, which accommodate first-year students, are within 15 minutes' walk of the school. Another 115 places are planned in flats in Vernon Square. However, the school has few of its own sports facilities and the outdoor pitches are remote, with no time set aside from lectures. The ethnic and national mix has led to inevitable tensions at times, but SOAS is small enough for most students to know each other, at least by sight, and the normal atmosphere is

friendly. Students tend to be highly committed – not surprising since many will return to positions of influence in developing countries.

Bursaries and Scholarships

In receipt of full Maintenance Grant	£700
In receipt of partial Maintenance Grant	£400
Progressing from outreach	Bursary £400

- Tuition fees (2006) £3,000
- 18% of additional fee income to be earmarked for bursaries.

Contact: www.soas.ac.uk/undergraduate

Students

Undergraduates:	2,160	(55)
Postgraduates:	1,290	(830)
Mature students:	25.3%	
Overseas students:	27.4%	
Applications per place:	5.7	
From state-sector schools:	71.0%	
From working-class homes:	21.3%	

For detailed information about fees, grants and bursaries and how they work, see chapter 7.

Accommodation

Number of places and costs refer to 2005–06
University-provided places: 772 (Shaftesbury Student Housing); 119 (intercollegiate)
Percentage catered: 10%
Catered costs: £108.01–£132.44 a week.
Self-catered costs: £108.01 a week.
First years cannot be guaranteed accommodation.
International students: as above, although they are a high priority.
Contact: student@shaftesburyhousing.org.uk

University of Sheffield

Sheffield slipped out of the top 20 in *the Times* League Table after losing the benefit of some of the best grades in the early rounds of teaching assessment, but its stock remains high both in the academic world and among students. Student numbers have risen by 14 per cent over the last three years, to 16,000 full-time undergraduates, and there has been a corresponding increase in academic staff across all seven faculties. A major new learning facility, the £23-million Information Commons, will open in 2007, providing 1,300 study spaces linked to the campus network, and 110,000 books and periodicals.

Only one subject (medicine) scored fewer than 20 points out of 24 for teaching quality, while three quarters of the staff assessed for the last research assessment exercise were placed in the top two categories. Nine starred departments were spread around medicine, science, engineering and social science. The star performers have been electrical and electronic engineering, the biosciences, politics and Russian, each of which achieved maximum scores for both teaching and research. The university is to house national teaching centres for the arts and social sciences and for enterprise learning. The medical school was allocated more places after a re-inspection found improvements, and it is now the most popular in Britain in terms of applications per place and the best performer in the first national student satisfaction survey. Only medicine and dentistry remain outside the modular course system, which operates on semesters.

Research excellence, which takes pride of place in Sheffield's mission statement, has boosted the university's facilities: £100 million for biological and physical sciences, medicine, engineering and social sciences, and £15 million on an advanced manufacturing research centre in which Boeing is the senior partner, which forms the hub of a technology park. The university is the lead institution for systems engineering, smart materials and stem-cell technology in a research network of European, American and Chinese universities. Sheffield has always enjoyed a high ratio of applications to places, despite expanding through much of the 1990s. Although there was a rare dip in the demand for places in 2003, this was reversed in 2004 and had turned into an 8 per cent increase at the start of 2005.

The academic buildings are concentrated in an area about a mile from the city centre on the affluent west side of Sheffield, with most university flats and halls of residence a little further into the suburbs. Recent developments mean that

---

Western Bank,
Sheffield S10 2TN
0114-222 8027
ug.admissions@
sheffield.ac.uk
www.sheffield.ac.uk
www.shef.ac.uk/union

The Times Rankings
Overall Ranking: 24

Student satisfaction:	=24	(15.2)
Research assessment:	=18	(5.5)
Entry standards:	13	(405.3)
Student–staff ratio:	=22	(15.7)
Library/IT spend/student:	37	(£613)
Facilities spend/student:	46	(£231)
Good honours:	14	(72.4%)
Graduate prospects:	31	(68.6%)
Expected completion rate:	28	(90.4%)

the main university precinct now stretches into an almost unbroken mile-long "campus". The former Jessop Hospital, an imposing building at the heart of the campus, has been purchased by the university for use by academic departments, while another new site adjacent to the engineering departments will house high-tech multidisciplinary facilities.

The intake is more diverse than at most leading universities – 83 per cent come from state schools or colleges – and almost one undergraduate in five comes from a working-class home. A famously lively social scene is based on the student union's recently extended facilities – voted best in Britain in 2004 – but also takes full advantage of the city's burgeoning club life. In addition to its own popular facilities, the union owns a pub in the western suburb where most students live. Town–gown relations are much better and the crime rate lower than in most big cities.

Residential accommodation is plentiful, with most of the 5,234 university-owned places within walking distance of lectures, and private housing reasonably priced. First years from outside Sheffield are guaranteed accommodation. The main halls of residence are being replaced by a student village in a phased programme, which is due for completion in 2009. The university's excellent sports facilities have been the subject of a £6-million makeover, which includes a 150-station fitness centre and a third Astroturf pitch specifically for soccer and rugby. Top-notch facilities were built by the city for the 1991 World Student Games and a £25-million regional centre for the English Institute of Sport opened in 2003.

Bursaries and Scholarships

In receipt of full Maintenance Grant	£650
In receipt of partial Maintenance Grant	£400
Progressing from outreach	Bursary
Sport	Bursary
Shortage subjects	Bursary
Academic achievement	Bursary

- Tuition fees (2006) £3,000
- Additional bursaries for students receiving full or partial Maintenance Grant with outstanding entry grades; amounts vary according to number of A grade A levels achieved and according to subject to be studied. Worth £250–£1,550.
- Bursaries linked to outreach schemes. Worth £100–£800.
- 14% additional fee income to be earmarked for bursaries.

Contact: www.shef.ac.uk/bursaries/

Students

Undergraduates:	16,455	(2,280)
Postgraduates:	4,860	(2,505)
Mature students:	8.8%	
Overseas students:	10.5%	
Applications per place:	7.1	
From state-sector schools:	83.1%	
From working-class homes:	19.8%	

For detailed information about fees, grants and bursaries and how they work, see chapter 7.

Accommodation

Number of places and costs refer to 2006–07
University-provided places: 5,234
Percentage catered: 54%
Catered costs: £86.05–£126.07 a week.
Self-catered costs: £60.20–£99.26 a week.
First years are guaranteed accommodation (terms and conditions apply). Residential restrictions apply.
International students: as above.
Contact: studentoffice@sheffield.ac.uk
www.shef.ac.uk/housing

Sheffield Hallam University

Sheffield Hallam has long been among the leading new universities in *The Times* League Table. Teaching grades improved steadily after a disappointing start, with physics, psychology and hospitality, sport, leisure and tourism recording perfect scores. Physics has since been dropped as an undergraduate subject, but a new science learning centre is among a series of developments in this area.

The university has been undergoing a physical transformation designed to alter its image and cater for an even bigger student population. Its main site is in the heart of Sheffield and when the Faculty of Arts, Technology, Engineering and Sciences sets up home bordering the city's cultural industries quarter, there will be only two campuses.

Development has been continuing apace, with £140 million earmarked for capital projects over the next decade. They will support key areas for the university, including creative and digital disciplines, health and social care. An atrium provides social space for staff and students; and innovative library developments take pride of place on both campuses. Business and management courses, which account for easily the biggest share of places, have their own city-centre headquarters. The Collegiate Crescent campus, a former teacher training college, houses education, health and community studies, while art and design are currently further away in a former art college. The students' union has taken over the spectacular but ill-fated National Centre for Popular Music, with facilities described by the former higher education minister Kim Howells as the best he had seen.

While most of the development has been on the main campus, adjoining the main bus and rail stations, the latest stage has seen the opening of a new social centre on the Collegiate Crescent site. The £14-million development that opened in 2005 has allowed the Faculty of Health and Wellbeing to almost double in size, as extra provision is made for nursing, radiotherapy, physiotherapy and social work. The Centre for Sport and Exercise Science, with its £6-million research facility, won glowing praise from inspectors, and is one of Europe's largest centres of its kind, with more than 2,000 students.

Research in art and design, history and materials were all rated nationally outstanding with significant work of international standard in the last research assessments. Sheffield Hallam traces its origins in art and design back to the 1840s and celebrated the centenary of education and teacher training in 2005. It is now one of the largest of the new universities, with

---

City Campus, Sheffield S1 1WB
0114-225 5555
undergraduate-admissions@
shu.ac.uk
www.shu.ac.uk
www.hallamunion.com

Edinburgh
Belfast
SHEFFIELD
London
Cardiff

The Times Rankings
Overall Ranking: =80

Student satisfaction:	=75	(14.3)
Research assessment:	=61	(3.0)
Entry standards:	64	(264.3)
Student–staff ratio:	104	(24.9)
Library/IT spend/student:	86	(£451)
Facilities spend/student:	45	(£232)
Good honours:	74	(53.0%)
Graduate prospects:	=65	(61.4%)
Expected completion rate:	=44	(86.4%)

high proportions of part-time and mature students, and more than 1,000 students taught on franchised courses in further education colleges. Business and industry are closely involved in the development of more than 650 courses, with almost half of the students taking sandwich course placements with employers. The university is to house two national teaching centres, one for fostering employability and the other promoting autonomous learning. It is also a partner in a third, led by Coventry University, on e-learning in the professions. A "virtual campus" offers students e-mail accounts and cheap equipment to access the growing volume of online courses, assignments and discussion groups provided by the university, even when they are at home or on work placements.

Almost a third of undergraduates come from working-class homes, the majority of them from areas that send few students to higher education. The dropout rate is among the lowest in the new universities and is significantly better than the national average for the subjects offered and the students' entry qualifications.

Such is Sheffield Hallam's size that it is not possible to guarantee all first years university-owned accommodation, although the large local intake means that many live at home. Sports facilities are supplemented by those provided by the city for the World Student Games. The impressive swimming complex, for example, is on the university's doorstep.

Bursaries and Scholarships

In receipt of full Maintenance Grant	£700
In receipt of partial Maintenance Grant	£700
Progressing from outreach	Bursary
Academic achievement	Scholarship

- Tuition fees (2006) £3,000
- Placement year tuition fee will be around £600.
- Partnership Bursaries of £300 for students progressing from partner schools and colleges.
- Discretionary scholarships worth up to £1,000.
- Eligibility for bursaries will be assessed using UUK/SLC model bursary scheme (HEBSS).

Contact: www.shu.ac.uk/courses/ug/money.html
www.shu.ac.uk/scholarships
www.shu.ac.uk/guides/studentfinance/sfso

Students

Undergraduates:	16,425	(4,120)
Postgraduates:	1,995	(4,910)
Mature students:	19.1%	
Overseas students:	7.2%	
Applications per place:	4.9	
From state-sector schools:	95.3%	
From working-class homes:	30.9%	

For detailed information about fees, grants and bursaries and how they work, see chapter 7.

Accommodation

Number of places and costs refer to 2005–06
University-provided places: 3,958
Percentage catered: 10%
Catered costs: £84.25 a week (39 weeks).
Self-catered costs: £57.17–£91.00 a week (39–44 weeks).
All first years offered accommodation.
International students: as above, providing conditions are met.
Contact: accommodation@shu.ac.uk

University of Southampton

Southampton celebrated its 50th anniversary in 2002, but it has really taken off in the course of the last decade. During that time, student numbers have doubled, and the university has opened two new campuses of its own, as well as acquiring two others in college mergers. Its 2001 research grades were among the top ten in Britain, while the last five teaching assessments all produced perfect scores. Applications had been rising faster than the national average until a dip at the start of 2006, with the prospect of top-up fees.

Although the proportions of students from working-class homes and areas with little tradition of university education are lower than the national average for the subjects offered, the funding council concluded that this was largely a matter of location. Students act as ambassadors, associates and mentors in local schools and colleges, as part of the university's effort to broaden its intake. A range of foundation degrees offers flexible ways of learning for students without a family tradition of higher education.

The proportion of income derived from research at Southampton is among the highest in Britain. The 2001 assessments saw the number of subjects rated internationally outstanding shoot up from two to eight, including all branches of engineering. Physics, computer science, European studies, law and music were the other top-scorers. Economics, education and politics, philosophy and archaeology achieved the five late maximums for teaching.

The medical school, too, enhanced its reputation with a maximum score for teaching quality in a set of assessments that saw more variation than most. The school features a common core curriculum for the pre-registration programmes of over 3,000 medical, nursing and other health students from entry to internship. Southampton registered the top scores for medicine and computer science in the first national student satisfaction survey. The main Highfield campus, in an attractive location two miles from the city centre, has been the focus of recent development to cater for the expansion in numbers. Nursing, chemistry, electronics and computer science have all benefited, and there is a new commercial services centre and an e-science centre as well as an extended library and a graduate centre for social sciences. A new student services centre provides learning support and other advisory facilities – all of which will be backed up online for students in other areas of the university.

The Waterside Campus, in the city's revitalised dock area, houses the National

Highfield,
Southampton SO17 1BJ
023-8059 5000
prospenq@soton.ac.uk
www.soton.ac.uk
www.susu.org

The Times Rankings
Overall Ranking: 23

Student satisfaction:	=38	(14.9)
Research assessment:	=7	(5.8)
Entry standards:	19	(386.5)
Student–staff ratio:	=27	(16.0)
Library/IT spend/student:	=20	(£729)
Facilities spend/student:	35	(£252)
Good honours:	23	(69.2%)
Graduate prospects:	25	(70.3%)
Expected completion rate:	=23	(92.3%)

Oceanography Centre, Southampton. A £49-million joint project with the Natural Environment Research Council, it is considered Europe's finest, encompassing teaching, research and knowledge transfer facilities. The Avenue campus, near the main site, is home to most of the arts departments. Clinical medicine is based at Southampton General Hospital, where a new research centre is due to open in December 2006.

The incorporation of Winchester School of Art complemented the university's Continental outlook with its own well-established European links. The school has added conservation and museum studies to its portfolio since taking in the renowned Textile Conservation Centre. But the takeover of the former La Sainte Union campus near the city centre to create Southampton New College did not go to plan. The college continues to offer opportunities for students from different backgrounds to the norm for a university where entry requirements are high and a fifth of the successful candidates come from independent schools, but the curriculum has been scaled down and the original site sold.

Social facilities for students have been expanded and refurbished, with the addition of a popular new nightclub. Sports facilities were upgraded, with the opening in 2004 of an £8.4-million indoor sports complex and swimming pool next to the students' union. This was followed by a £4.5-million development of the outdoor facilities, with grass and synthetic pitches, a new pavilion, bar and meeting rooms. Further residential accommodation, including three renovated halls, will open in 2006.

Bursaries and Scholarships

In receipt of full Maintenance Grant	£1,000
In receipt of partial Maintenance Grant	up to £1,000
Living in region	Bursary
Progressing from outreach	Bursary
Academic achievement	Scholarship

- Tuition fees (2006) £3,000
- Tuition fees for year abroad are £1,500.
- Competitive Hampshire and Isle of Wight Bursaries available to 150 first-generation students from low-income families in the region, especially those in partner schools and colleges. Worth £1,000.
- All BM6 (Bachelor of Medicine widening access programme) bursaries worth £1,000.
- Academic scholarships worth £1,000–£2,000; details to be finalised.
- 22% of additional fee income to be earmarked for bursaries.
- Eligibility for bursaries will be assessed using UUK/SLC model bursary scheme (HEBSS).

Contact: www.soton.ac.uk/study/feesand funding/

Students

Undergraduates:	13,275	(2,755)
Postgraduates:	3,420	(3,805)
Mature students:	16.1%	
Overseas students:	8.5%	
Applications per place:	7.6	
From state-sector schools:	80.0%	
From working-class homes:	20.0%	

For detailed information about fees, grants and bursaries and how they work, see chapter 7.

Accommodation

Number of places and costs refer to 2006–07
University-provided places: 5,200
Percentage catered: 20%
Catered costs: £96.88–£129.36 a week.
Self-catered costs: £62.44–£139.95 a week.
All first years are offered accommodation if conditions met.
International students: single fee-paying non-EU students are guaranteed accommodation.
Contact: accommodation@soton.ac.uk
www.accommodation.soton.ac.uk

Southampton Solent University

The largest of the nine new universities created since the last edition of the *Guide*, Southampton Solent also has the broadest range of programmes, stretching from foundation-year courses for those without the qualifications to begin degrees, to PhDs. The 10,000 students embrace civil and mechanical engineering, as well as media, arts and business, with a separate maritime centre capitalising on the coastal location. The subject mix explains why the former Southampton Institute is now one of the few universities with a majority of male students.

An accent on vocational courses produces consistently good graduate employment rates. Innovative degrees include yacht and powercraft design, computer and video games, and comedy writing and performance. A Graduate Enterprise Centre provides advice and rent-free offices for those hoping to start their own businesses, while the Warsash Maritime Centre is an internationally-renowned training and research facility for the shipping and offshore oil industries.

Teaching quality assessments went well, with the exception of a poor result in art and design in 1999, but research grades were low in the last assessments. The new university will continue to play to its strengths in applied research and teaching, although this is not reflected in staffing levels that are among the least generous in our table. The response rate in the first national student satisfaction survey was too low to publish results, but applications were healthy until the prospect of top-up fees brought an 11 per cent drop at the start of 2006. Solent set fees of less than £2,000 for HNDs and foundation degrees, but even this appeared to have little impact.

Demand for places remains strong, however, in marine-based courses. The university is higher education's premier yachting institution, with a world champion student team that has won the national championships four times in six years. Three new boats will support courses at the Watersports Centre, some of which are targeted on disadvantaged young people in the area. The centre now boasts seven powerboats, nine dinghies and three keelboats.

Almost a third of the students come from Hampshire and a similar proportion have working-class roots. There is a special link with the Channel Island of Guernsey, which has no higher education of its own. Colleges on the island (and in various parts of the south of England) bring students for taster courses and provide evidence of academic potential that can lead to entry on criteria other than A level. Solent's 17 per cent projected dropout rate

---

East Park Terrace,
Southampton SO14 0YN
023-8031 9000
enquiries@solent.ac.uk
www.solent.ac.uk
www.sisuonline.co.uk

Edinburgh
Belfast
Cardiff London
SOUTHAMPTON

The Times Rankings
Overall Ranking: 107

Teaching assessment:	–	(–)
Research assessment:	108	(0.9)
Entry standards:	92	(224.6)
Student–staff ratio:	109	(30.2)
Library/IT spend/student:	43	(£605)
Facilities spend/student:	26	(£283)
Good honours:	=106	(41.6%)
Graduate prospects:	105	(47.9%)
Expected completion rate:	86	(78.6%)

is hardly low, but is less than the national average for the university's subjects and entry grades. About 10 per cent come from overseas, while 100 are enrolled on research degrees.

The main campus has few architectural pretensions, but is conveniently based in the city centre within walking distance of the station. Recent investment has included a new Centre for Professional Development in Broadcasting and Multimedia Production, which includes an online editing suite, digital television studio and gallery, for use by undergraduates as well as community groups and professionals. Media, arts and society courses now attract almost as many students as the consistently popular business school.

Students like the location, close to the city's growing complement of bars and nightclubs, as well as to the main shopping area. There are more than 2,300 hall places close to the campus, most of which are allocated to first years and almost half of which are en suite. A landlord accreditation scheme helps to guarantee standards of accommodation for those who rely on the private sector. Away from the water, there is the usual range of sports facilities, with a sports hall and fitness suite on campus.

Bursaries and Scholarships

In receipt of full Maintenance Grant	£1000
In receipt of partial Maintenance Grant	£250–£500
Living in region	Scholarship
Progressing from outreach	Scholarship

- Tuition fees (2006)   £3,000
- Sandwich year out tuition fee is half the annual tuition fee.
- Local scholarships of £250 for students domiciled in Hants. and the Isle of Wight.
- Accommodation voucher worth £250 for use in halls of residence. This will also be available to those who are only marginally above the threshold for bursaries.
- Eligibility for bursaries will be assessed using UUK/SLC model bursary scheme.
- Various bursaries and scholarships will be available for students who are from local regions, the Channel Islands, overseas and the students on the University's STAND (Solent Talented Athlete Network Development) programme, as well as the University's Alumni.

Contact: www.solent.ac.uk/fees/info.aspx
www.solent.ac.uk/scholarships/
   scholarships_home.aspx
www.solent.ac.uk/welfare/finance/
   funding_advice.aspx

Students

Undergraduates:	8,560	(1,835)
Postgraduates:	300	(550)
Mature students:	21.5%	
Overseas students:	8.0%	
Applications per place:	3.5	
From state-sector schools:	85.4%	
From working-class homes:	31.7%	

For detailed information about fees, grants and bursaries and how they work, see chapter 7.

Accommodation

Number of places and costs refer to 2006–07
University-provided places: 2,340 (85% are offered to first years)
Percentage catered: 0%
Self-catered costs: £68.25–£91.00 a week.
First years are guaranteed accommodation if conditions met.
International students: accommodation guaranteed.
Contact: Accommodation@solent.ac.uk

Staffordshire University

Staffordshire describes itself as a "university in the community" but it is increasingly reliant on overseas students, taught both at home and abroad. There are 5,000 students taking Staffordshire courses outside Britain, almost half of them located around the Pacific Rim, as well as a growing cohort of foreign students in the university's domestic campuses. There are more than 12,000 UK students and the demand for places held steady with the arrival of top-up fees, but previous recruiting difficulties encouraged a growing focus on other countries.

The university is based on two main sites: the headquarters in Stoke and the other 12 miles away in Stafford. The rural Stafford site features the purpose-built Octagon Centre, in which lecture theatres, offices and walkways surround one of the largest university computing facilities in Europe. A £2.4-million New Technologies Centre, opened in 2003, has helped develop popular courses such as film production technology. Health, engineering and technology are all based at Stafford, while Stoke specialises in the arts, sciences and social sciences. The business school, which acquired a new headquarters in Stoke in 1995, straddles the two campuses in an attempt to foster links with the private sector.

However, a new campus in Lichfield gives a glimpse of the future for Staffordshire. An integrated further and higher education centre, developed in partnership with Tamworth and Lichfield College, is the first purpose-built institution of its kind. The main aim is to act as a resource centre for local businesses. The School of Health has branches in Telford, Shrewsbury and Oswestry, but franchised courses spread the university's net much further afield. Staffordshire courses are taken in China, Malaysia, Singapore, Hong Kong, Pakistan, India, Sri Lanka, Greece, Spain and France.

The university also runs courses for more than 1,000 students at further education colleges in its own region, as well as offering incentives for local people to apply. A priority applications scheme guarantees a place to under-21s from Staffordshire, Shropshire or Cheshire as long as they meet the minimum requirements for their chosen course, while mature students are guaranteed at least an interview if they join one of the range of access courses. Even before the advent of top-up fees, the university was offering £500 awards to disadvantaged students from Shropshire, Cheshire and Staffordshire. The policy has been working – more than a third of the students are from the local area and a new programme, run in conjunction with Keele University,

College Road,
Stoke-on-Trent ST4 2DE
01782 294000
admissions@staffs.ac.uk
www.staffs.ac.uk
www.staffsunion.com

Edinburgh
Belfast
STOKE-ON-TRENT
London
Cardiff

The Times Rankings
Overall Ranking: =74

Student satisfaction:	=49	(14.8)
Research assessment:	=86	(2.2)
Entry standards:	82	(235.8)
Student–staff ratio:	=56	(18.1)
Library/IT spend/student:	26	(£671)
Facilities spend/student:	67	(£183)
Good honours:	94	(47.7%)
Graduate prospects:	95	(54.3%)
Expected completion rate:	89	(77.2%)

aims to increase the numbers further. A range of courses, including two-year foundation degrees for teaching assistants, care managers and e-business specialists, are tailored to the needs of the area and graduates will be encouraged to help develop the local economy. Many courses are available with a January start, a particularly popular arrangement with overseas students who take English language courses before beginning a degree.

Economics registered Staffordshire's best score for teaching quality, while geography and environmental science produced the best results in the first national student satisfaction survey. The university learnt the lesson of the 1996 research assessments, when almost two thirds of the academics were entered but nearly all were placed in the bottom three categories. In the last exercise, the proportion of entries was halved and, although no subjects reached the top two grades, media studies and art and design were in the next category.

With 97 per cent of its undergraduates state-educated and more than a third coming from working-class homes, Staffordshire comfortably exceeds all the benchmarks set by the funding council for widening access to higher education. There is good provision for the 700 disabled students. However, the projected dropout rate of 21 per cent is higher than average for the university's courses and entry qualifications.

Stoke is not the liveliest city of its size, but the campus is close to the railway station, within easy reach of the centre and has a buzzing union. Stafford is much the more attractive setting and offers the best chance of a residential place, but the town is quiet and the campus is a mile and a half outside it. Sports facilities are good, especially in Stafford, where there is a new £1.4-million sports centre and all-weather pitches. Sports scholarships and good coaching have helped attract some outstanding athletes, who have access to a sports performance centre to help with training schedules, psychological support and dietary assessments.

Bursaries and Scholarships

In receipt of full Maintenance Grant	£1,300
In receipt of partial Maintenance Grant	£500–£1,000
• Tuition fees (2006)	£3,000

Contact:
www.staffs.ac.uk/marketingservices/cost

Students

Undergraduates:	8,950	(3,285)
Postgraduates:	735	(1,895)
Mature students:	23.3%	
Overseas students:	7.9%	
Applications per place:	4.4	
From state-sector schools:	97.3%	
From working-class homes:	36.8%	

For detailed information about fees, grants and bursaries and how they work, see chapter 7.

Accommodation

Number of places and costs refer to 2006–07
University-provided places: 1,215 (Stoke); 776 (Stafford)
Percentage catered: 0%
Self-catered accommodation: £52.50–£79.00 a week.
First years have priority, if conditions met.
International students: have priority , if conditions are met.
Contact: Accommodation_stoke@staffs.ac.uk
Accommodation_stafford@staffs.ac.uk

University of Stirling

One of the most beautiful campuses in Britain features low-level, modern buildings in a loch-side setting beneath the Ochil Hills on the former Airthrey Estate, two miles from the centre of Stirling. Even after a 20 per cent expansion over four years, largely due to the incorporation of three nursing colleges at Falkirk, Inverness and Stornoway, in Lewis, the university remains a relatively small institution of 9,000 students. Stirling also has probably the most popular Chancellor: spurning the usual dignitaries, the university chose actress Diana Rigg for the post.

Although highly rated in some research fields, there were no starred departments in the last research assessments. However, ten out of the 22 subject areas reached grade 5, denoting national excellence and significant work of international standard. Excellent teaching ratings for economics, sociology, theology, business studies, psychology and English show Stirling's strength in the arts and social sciences. Among the sciences, only environmental science matched this feat, its success reflected in a new School of Biological and Environmental Sciences, with substantially refurbished facilities for both teaching and research. Sports studies are particularly popular, as are film and media studies, which acquired a £40,000 high-tech

newsroom in 2004. International exchanges are common, with many students going to American, Asian and European universities each year.

Stirling was the British pioneer of the semester system, which has now become so popular in other universities. The academic year is divided into two 15-week terms, with short mid-semester breaks. Students have the option of starting courses in February, rather than September. Successful completion of six semesters will bring a general degree; eight semesters, honours. The emphasis on breadth is such that there are no barriers to movement between faculties. Undergraduates can switch the whole direction of their studies, in consultation with their academic adviser, as their interests develop. The modular scheme allows students to speed up their progress on a Summer Academic Programme, which squeezes a full semester's teaching into July and August. Full-time students are not allowed to use the programme to reduce the length of their course, but part-timers can use it to make rapid progress.

The level of competition for places has been unpredictable: there was a 3 per cent decline at the start of 2006, but the 8 per cent increase in applications at the start of 2005 was one of the largest in Scotland. The intake is surprisingly diverse, with 95 per cent of undergraduates state-educated

---

Stirling FK9 4LA
01786 467044
admissions@stir.ac.uk
www.stir.ac.uk
www.susaonline.org.uk

The Times Rankings
Overall Ranking: 37

Student satisfaction:	–	(–)
Research assessment:	=40	(4.8)
Entry standards:	36	(341.8)
Student–staff ratio:	20	(15.3)
Library/IT spend/student:	35	(£634)
Facilities spend/student:	=40	(£238)
Good honours:	27	(67.3%)
Graduate prospects:	=88	(55.8%)
Expected completion rate:	49	(85.5%)

and more than a quarter coming from working-class homes. Large numbers come from areas that send few students to higher education, and even before fee differentials encouraged more Scots to stay at home to study, 70 per cent of Stirling's students were from north of the border. Sports facilities are excellent and still improving. The national tennis and swimming centres are both based on the campus, the latter in a new Olympic-sized pool, and there is even a nine-hole golf course. A new golf centre opened in 2004, adding three target greens and a practice area to the existing driving range and indoor facilities. Following the addition of new artificial pitches a few months earlier, it brought Stirling's spending on sport to more than £10 million in five years. Sports bursaries worth between £900 and £2,000, according to performance, are open to overseas students, as well as Britons. The campus also houses the new headquarters of the Scottish Institute of Sport.

Students appreciate the individual attention a small, campus university can offer, although some find the atmosphere claustrophobic. The original campus buildings are now being refurbished, while applied social science was the latest to acquire new premises in 2003. Stirling is not the top choice of nightclubbers, but the students' union has been named the best in Scotland and there is a lively social programme. The £6.3-million refurbishment of the MacRobert Arts Centre has transformed the cultural programme on campus, while the surrounding scenery offers its own attractions for walkers.

For nurses and midwives, the Highland campus is based in the grounds of Raigmore Hospital in Inverness, with purpose-built teaching accommodation and student flats. The Western Isles campus is located in Stornoway, where the teaching accommodation is an integral part of the recently-built Lewis Hospital.

Bursaries and Scholarships

- Scottish domiciled students: no fees will be payable by eligible students although a "graduate endowment" will be payable after graduation: the 2005–06 level was £2,216.
- Non-Scottish domiciled students fees: £1,700 a year.
- Fees for placement year and year abroad are normally 50% of full-time fee.
- Hardship fund available.
- Scholarships are available in six core sports: canoeing, golf, squash, swimming, tennis and triathlon.
- Academic scholarships are available.

Contact: www.siss.stir.ac.uk/finance/default.htm www.external.stir.ac.uk/undergrad/ financial_info/index.php.

Students

Undergraduates:	5,870	(1,060)
Postgraduates:	785	(1,005)
Mature students:	15.5%	
Overseas students:	5.1%	
Applications per place:	6.9	
From state-sector schools:	94.3%	
From working-class homes:	28.4%	

For detailed information about fees, grants and bursaries and how they work, see chapter 7.

Accommodation

Number of places and costs refer to 2005–06
University-provided places: 2,840
Percentage catered: 0%
Self-catered costs: £56–£73 a week.
All first years are guaranteed suitable housing arranged by the University.
International students: as above.
Contact: Accommodation@stir.ac.uk

University of Strathclyde

Even as Anderson's Institution in the 18th century, Strathclyde concentrated on "useful learning". Some Glaswegians still refer to it as "the tech". But if the nickname does less than justice to the current portfolio of courses, the university has never shrunk from its technological and vocational emphasis. Strathclyde aims to offer courses that are both innovatory and relevant to industry and commerce – hence product design and innovation, or international business with modern languages.

Traditional science degrees have continued to prosper, however, with a series of top ratings. All but two of the 26 subjects assessed under Scotland's original system of grading teaching quality were considered Excellent or Highly Satisfactory. The university is in *The Times* top ten for general engineering, pharmacy and other health subjects. Its careers service is also rated among the best, having four times won a Government charter mark for customer service. No department reached the top grade of the last research assessments, but ten of the 33 subject areas reached the next rung of the ladder, accounting for 90 per cent of those entered.

Strathclyde's main strength, however, is in the top-rated business school, which is one of the largest in Europe and the only one in Scotland to be accredited by the European Quality Improvement System. Business studies students follow an "integrative studies" programme, which is designed to place them in a realistic business environment from day one and involves work with a range of major companies. The scheme is now being piloted in other faculties. The engineering faculty is also the largest in Scotland, and has linked with Glasgow University to provide a joint department of naval architecture and marine engineering.

European focus is evident throughout the university, which has encouraged all departments to adapt their courses to the needs of the single market. Many students combine business or engineering with European studies or languages to give themselves an edge in the job market. Mature students account for a fifth of the places and have a special organisation to look after their interests. With over 20,000 students, including part-timers, Strathclyde is the third-largest university in Scotland, but its numbers swell to 60,000 including short courses and distance learning programmes.

Strathclyde actively promotes wider access, comfortably exceeding national averages for state-educated students, the share of places going to applicants from working-class homes and those from areas

---

16 Richmond Street, Glasgow G1 1XQ
0141-548 2813
j.gibson@mis.strath.ac.uk
www.strath.ac.uk
www.strathstudents.com

GLASGOW
Edinburgh
Belfast
London
Cardiff

The Times Rankings
Overall Ranking: 40

Student satisfaction:	–	(–)
Research assessment:	=42	(4.7)
Entry standards:	20	(381.9)
Student–staff ratio:	=54	(18.0)
Library/IT spend/student:	50	(£572)
Facilities spend/student:	76	(£167)
Good honours:	=24	(68.9%)
Graduate prospects:	30	(69.3%)
Expected completion rate:	59	(83.0%)

sending few students to higher education. Its efforts are underpinned by fundraising for a scholarship programme to aid students from poor homes.

The main John Anderson campus is in the centre of Glasgow, behind George Square and near Queen Street station. Apart from the Edwardian headquarters, the buildings are mostly modern. The site of a former maternity hospital in the centre of the campus will eventually provide extra teaching accommodation, but a £73-million refurbishment programme is taking priority. Strathclyde has a second campus on the west side of the city, acquired from a merger with Jordanhill College of Education, Scotland's largest teacher training institution, in 1993. The 67-acre parkland site houses the faculty of education, which is breaking new ground with Scotland's first part-time teacher training degree and also offers courses in speech and language pathology, community arts, social work, sport and outdoor education. The university plans to sell the site and move the courses onto the main campus, but this is unlikely to take place before the end of the decade.

The university is losing its image as a "nine-to-five" institution, thanks to a student village on the main campus, complete with pub, which has increased the number of residential places. Over 1,400 of these are on campus, all with network access, and another 500 are nearby. The Millennium Student project has delivered full network access from every study bedroom on campus and it is planned to make extensive high-speed dial-up facilities into the University network available for all students in the Glasgow area. The ten-floor union building attracts students from all over Glasgow with its reputation for hard-drinking revelry. For those with more sophisticated tastes, there are several theatres and the city's own variety of cultural venues.

Bursaries and Scholarships

- Scottish domiciled students: no fees will be payable by eligible students although a "graduate endowment" will be payable after graduation: the 2005–06 level was £2,216.
- Non-Scottish domiciled students fees: £1,700 a year.
- Fees for placement year and year abroad are normally 50% of full-time fee.
- Bursaries up to £1,000 are available to top sportsmen and women.

Contact: www.strath.ac.uk/feenews

Students		
Undergraduates:	11,565	(3,565)
Postgraduates:	3,040	(6,235)
Mature students:	18.5%	
Overseas students:	4.1%	
Applications per place:	5.5	
From state-sector schools:	93.2%	
From working-class homes:	29.8%	

For detailed information about fees, grants and bursaries and how they work, see chapter 7.

Accommodation

Number of places and costs refer to 2005–06
University-provided places: 1,973
Percentage catered: 7%
Catered costs: £75 a week.
Self-catered costs: £53–£79 a week.
First years are offered accommodation.
Residential restrictions apply.
International students: as above.
Contact:
student.accommodation@mis.strath.ac.uk

University of Sunderland

The university doubled in size in four years, and has taken advantage of urban regeneration programmes in one of Britain's newest cities to expand its facilities to create among the newest university campuses. The main campus, in the city centre, now has a well-appointed science complex and a new design centre. The Sir Tom Cowie campus at St Peter's, an award-winning 24-acre site by the banks of the Wear, initially housed the business school and the informatics centre. To these is being added a £20-million arts, design and media centre, the first phase of which opened in 2003. An £8.5-million redevelopment programme is under way, adding a central facility for students to access a wide range of services.

Developments have been planned with an eye to history, for example incorporating a working heritage centre for the glass industry at the heart of the new campus, which is built around a 7th-century abbey described as one of Britain's first universities. The glass and ceramics design degree carries on a Sunderland tradition – the National Glass Centre was one of the features of the new campus – while the courses in automotive design and manufacture serve the region's new industrial base. The large pharmacy department is another strength and the well-equipped School of Computing and Technology is one of the largest in the UK with over 3,000 students.

Teaching assessments improved after a poor start. The biosciences recorded the university's only perfect scores, but nursing and anatomy and physiology came close to joining them. The last research assessments were more impressive, registering a big improvement on 1996 and representing the best performance in any new university in terms of average grades per member of staff. Although no subjects reached the top two grades, the 44 per cent of academics entered for assessment was the most in any former polytechnic, and art and design, English and history all managed grade 4. The successes made the university particularly resentful of the government's plans to concentrate research funding further.

Sunderland is making the most of the opportunity to link up with the multinational companies that have arrived on its doorstep. A new Institute for Automotive and Manufacturing Advanced Practice has a team of 40 researchers and consultants working with local businesses, while nearby Nissan played an important role in designing a course in automotive product development. The Sony media centre is another example, providing students with excellent television and video production facilities.

Langham Tower, Ryhope Road,
Sunderland SR2 7EE
0191-515 3000
student-helpline@
sunderland.ac.uk
www.sunderland.ac.uk
www.sunderlandsu.co.uk

The Times Rankings
Overall Ranking: 92

Student satisfaction:	=75	(14.3)
Research assessment:	=67	(2.8)
Entry standards:	83	(233.5)
Student–staff ratio:	47	(17.5)
Library/IT spend/student:	104	(£378)
Facilities spend/student:	=59	(£203)
Good honours:	78	(51.7%)
Graduate prospects:	64	(61.5%)
Expected completion rate:	106	(68.3%)

The university has a determinedly local focus, aiming to double the number of students coming from an area which has little tradition of sending students to higher education. Almost a third now come from "low participation neighbourhoods" – by far the largest proportion at any English university and more than twice the national average for the subjects on offer. A pioneering access scheme offers places to mature students without A levels, as long as they reach the required levels of literacy, numeracy and other basic skills. The Learning North East initiative, based on Sunderland's successful pilot for the University for Industry, even offers free taster courses to take at home.

Nearly 40 per cent of the undergraduates have a working-class background and the proportion from areas of low participation in higher education is the highest in England, but the downside of Sunderland's access efforts is a projected dropout rate of more than a quarter – significantly more than the official benchmark for the courses and entry grades. Provision for disabled students is excellent, with award-winning information produced for those with disabilities, trained support staff in every academic school as well as in the libraries and special modules to help dyslexics. The campus also houses the North East Regional Access Centre, which assesses the learning support requirements of students with disabilities and specific learning difficulties. There is special provision among the 2,200 residential places.

Sunderland itself is fiercely proud of its identity and has the advantage of a coastal location but, despite the city title, with the exception of the impressive new football ground, it has the leisure facilities of a medium-sized town. Those in search of big cultural events or serious nightlife head for Newcastle, which is less than half an hour away by Metro.

Bursaries and Scholarships

In receipt of full Maintenance Grant	£500
In receipt of partial Maintenance Grant	£500
Academic achievement	Scholarship

- Tuition fees (2006) £3,000
- Placement year tuition fee will be £250.
- Progression Scholarships to all students progressing from year one to year two and year two to year three, etc, of a course, worth £1,000.
- Foundation Degree and HND Scholarships: Foundation Degree and HND students receive an extra £500 a year on top of the above.

Contact:
www.welcome.sunderland.ac.uk/fees.asp

Students

Undergraduates:	7,650	(7,495)
Postgraduates:	1,855	(845)
Mature students:	22.8%	
Overseas students:	16.1%	
Applications per place:	4.8	
From state-sector schools:	98.3%	
From working-class homes:	39.0%	

For detailed information about fees, grants and bursaries and how they work, see chapter 7.

Accommodation

Number of places and costs refer to 2006–07
University-provided places: 1,579 beds in halls; 129 (Managed Houses/Head Tenancy scheme).
Percentage catered: 0%
Self-catered costs: £52.15–£114.70 a week.
First-year students are guaranteed a room in hall.
International students: as above.
Contact: residentialservices@sunderland.ac.uk
www.sunderland.ac.uk/residential services

University of Surrey

Surrey has been one of the success stories of the university world, remaining true to the technological legacy of its predecessor institution (Battersea Polytechnic Institute) while building a strong research base and a degree of financial independence envied by its peers. Even some of the arts degrees carry a BSc and are highly vocational: four out of five undergraduates in all subjects undertake work experience. Placements of one (or two half) years, often taken abroad, mean that most degrees last four years. The format and the subject balance combine to keep Surrey at the head of the graduate employment league, as well as producing a healthy research income. Indeed, it has taken to describing itself as the "University for Jobs" to ram the point home. Recent expansion in healthcare, human sciences and performing arts has added to the traditional strengths in science and engineering. The mix has been proving popular: there was only a small decline at the start of 2006, when most universities outside the big cities saw a sharp drop in the demand for places.

All students are encouraged to enrol for a course at the European language centre, and a growing number of degrees, including a new range in engineering, have a language component. The cosmopolitan feel is enhanced by one of the largest proportions of overseas students at any university – a feat which won Surrey a Queen's Award for Export Achievement. The 2,700 foreign students come from 140 different countries.

Combined subjects did well in a generally disappointing first round of the national student satisfaction survey. But teaching assessments were impressive, with near-perfect scores for economics, education, physics and astronomy, and electrical and electronic engineering, one of Surrey's three top-rated research areas. Health and sociology also won 5* research grades, leaving a third of the researchers in departments considered internationally outstanding – a proportion bettered by only four universities in Britain. Six out of ten reached one of the top two grades. Another indication of the university's research strength lies in the growing proportion of income derived from sources other than Government grants: up from 10 per cent to about 70 per cent in little over a decade. The Surrey Research Park is one of only three science parks still owned, funded and managed by the university that opened it, helping Surrey to amass one of the highest proportions of private funding at any British university.

Both the proportions of undergraduates from working-class homes and from areas without a tradition of higher education are lower than the benchmark

---

Guildford, Surrey GU2 7XH
01483 879305
admissions@surrey.ac.uk
www.surrey.ac.uk
www.ussu.co.uk

Edinburgh
Belfast
Cardiff London
GUILDFORD

The Times Rankings
Overall Ranking: 38

Student satisfaction:	=75	(14.3)
Research assessment:	=22	(5.4)
Entry standards:	41	(325.5)
Student–staff ratio:	35	(16.8)
Library/IT spend/student:	52	(£550)
Facilities spend/student:	28	(£275)
Good honours:	=52	(59.1%)
Graduate prospects:	7	(79.5%)
Expected completion rate:	35	(88.5%)

figures, which take account of the subject mix and entry standards. But the statistics agency has acknowledged that the explanation lies in the university's location. The projected dropout rate has risen but, at less than 11 per cent, is still better than the national average.

The compact campus is a ten-minute walk from the centre of Guildford. Most of the buildings date from the late 1960s, but the new business school and the gleaming European Institute of Health and Medical Sciences offer a striking contrast. Shaped like a giant ship's prow, the steel and glass building houses the large nursing and midwifery departments. A £12-million management building and an Advanced Technology Institute opened in September 2002. The campus includes two lakes, playing fields and enough residential accommodation to enable all first-years and most final-year students to live in. A second campus, adjacent to the Stag Hill headquarters, is now being developed. A postgraduate medical school is intended to be the first stage in the development of a health campus, which will also contain more residential places for students and staff, as well as other academic buildings, leisure and sporting facilities.

Guildford has plenty of cultural and recreational facilities, but riotous nightclubs are not encouraged. The campus, inevitably, is the centre of social life, and has seen recent improvements to leisure facilities. The proximity of London is an attraction to many students, but also helps account for the high cost of living, which is not mitigated by the allowances available in the capital.

Bursaries and Scholarships

In receipt of full Maintenance Grant	£1,000
In receipt of partial Maintenance Grant	Up to £1,000
Living in specified postcodes	Scholarship
Shortage subjects	Scholarship
Academic achievement	Scholarship

- Tuition fees (2006) £3,000
- Placement year tuition fee will be 15% of full-time fee; foundation year fee will be set at the standard (non-variable) rate, currently £1,200.
- Scholarships for students with outstanding A levels (3 grade As) worth £1,000. A-level requirement may be relaxed for students from low participation areas and/or studying shortage subjects.
- Scholarships for academic progression based on excellent performance (first class) on university course. Worth £1,000 each year.
- Extended programme award of £1,500 for final year of, eg, MEng courses.
- Value of bursaries doubled for students also in receipt of scholarship.
- 33% of additional fee income to be earmarked for bursaries.

Contact: www.surrey.ac.uk/undergraduate/discover/invest.htm

Students

Undergraduates:	7,065	(3,385)
Postgraduates:	2,640	(4,145)
Mature students:	21.3%	
Overseas students:	18.2%	
Applications per place:	4.8	
From state-sector schools:	87.6%	
From working-class homes:	26.0%	

For detailed information about fees, grants and bursaries and how they work, see chapter 7.

Accommodation

Number of places and costs refer to 2006–07
University-provided places: 4,081
Percentage catered: 0%
Self-catered costs: £51.45–£90.30 a week.
All first years are guaranteed a place.
International students designated overseas for fees are guaranteed accommodation
Contact:
www.surrey.ac.uk/Accommodation/index.html

University of Sussex

Sussex's all-round academic reputation has seldom been higher. The university appeared in the top 100 in *The Times Higher Education Supplement*'s world rankings and was higher still for the arts and social sciences. Sir Harry Kroto won the 1996 Nobel Prize for Chemistry and Professor Anthony Leggett took the 2003 Physics prize for work carried out at Sussex. Although no subject was considered internationally outstanding in the latest research assessment exercise, more than half were placed in the next category. No subject dropped below grade 4, despite a high proportion of academics entered for assessment. The university now generates more than a third of its income from private sources, largely in research contracts. Philosophy and sociology scored maximum points for teaching quality, with politics and international relations, mathematics and American studies – a long-established strength – the best of the rest.

The 23 per cent rise in applications at the beginning of 2005 was one of the largest at an old university and Sussex was one of the few outside the big cities to register an increase at the start of 2006. The demand for places in social work practically doubled, environmental science was up by 81 per cent and even physics saw a 35 per cent increase. With the university filling more places with post-graduates in recent years, the result has been increasing competition for degree places. Sussex's success was said to be due partly to targeting schools in London and the South East, as well as to innovations such as weekly campus tours for prospective applicants and drop-in arrangements for mature students. A revised portfolio of arts subjects seems to have helped, but a similar exercise for the sciences in 2006 has caused bitter controversy.

The interdisciplinary approach that has always been Sussex's trademark has been re-examined to adapt this 1960s concept for the 21st century. The 11 schools have been reduced to five and students are being offered a clearer framework so that they are fully aware of the combinations available to them. Student support is being improved through a revamped personal tutor system and a 50 per cent increase in the number of student advisors. Arts and social science students are still in the majority, but the life sciences are not far behind. Sussex is committed to taking candidates with no family tradition of higher education and has much larger numbers of mature students than most of its peer group of institutions. However, the proportion of working-class students and the share of places going to those

Falmer,
Brighton BN1 9RH
01273 678416
UG.Admissions@sussex.ac.uk
www.sussex.ac.uk
www.ussu.info.dnsupdate.net

Edinburgh

Belfast

Cardiff   London

BRIGHTON

The Times Rankings
Overall Ranking: 27

Student satisfaction:	=53	(14.7)
Research assessment:	=18	(5.5)
Entry standards:	25	(365.7)
Student–staff ratio:	=6	(12.1)
Library/IT spend/student:	29	(£650)
Facilities spend/student:	24	(£296)
Good honours:	=15	(71.5%)
Graduate prospects:	74	(59.0%)
Expected completion rate:	=33	(89.4%)

from areas with little tradition of higher education are both lower than the funding council's benchmark figures. The projected dropout rate has improved and, at 10.6 per cent, is now significantly better than the national average for the subjects on offer. And a survey of graduates five years after leaving Sussex showed an enviable employment record.

The university is based in an 18th-century park at Falmer, close to the South Downs and four miles from the centre of Brighton. Sir Basil Spence's original buildings have been supplemented by new developments. The library has been extended and the language centre recently refurbished. Relations with neighbouring Brighton University are good. The two institutions succeeded in a joint bid for a medical school, which opened in 2003 and has since recorded big increases in applications. The Brighton and Sussex Medical School is split between the Royal Sussex County Hospital and the two universities' Falmer campuses.

Undergraduates can take a year abroad in many subjects. Some courses offer joint qualifications with Continental universities, and those returning from a year abroad are given priority, with first years, for the 2,995 residential places on campus, and more accommodation is being built. Sports facilities are good, and the university has launched initiatives in basketball and hockey to entice top performers.

Sussex has always attracted overseas students in large numbers and has seen big increases recently, but a high proportion of the remainder are from the London area, where many return at weekends. As a result, the well-appointed campus can be quiet, although there is no shortage of social events, and Brighton has plenty to offer.

Bursaries and Scholarships

In receipt of full Maintenance Grant	£1,000
Living in specified postcodes	Scholarship
Ethnic minorities	Scholarship

- Tuition fees (2006) £3,000
- Placement year and year abroad tuition fee is half the annual tuition fee.
- 200 Chancellor's Scholarships available to first generation students from low-income families or experiencing educational or social disadvantage. Also open to students who make a significant contribution to the community. Worth £1,000 (80% earmarked for applicants under 21 years of age).
- 20% of additional fee income to be earmarked for bursaries.
- Eligibility for bursaries will be assessed using UUK/SLC model bursary scheme (HEBSS).

Contact: www.sussex.ac.uk/scolarships_and_bursaries.html

www.sussex.ac.uk/scolarships_and_bursaries/ug/uk/chancellors.php

---

Students

Undergraduates:	6,440	(2,340)
Postgraduates:	1,965	(1,250)
Mature students:	18.7%	
Overseas students:	13.2%	
Applications per place:	6.5	
From state-sector schools:	84.7%	
From working-class homes:	17.9%	

For detailed information about fees, grants and bursaries and how they work, see chapter 7.

Accommodation

Number of places and costs refer to 2006–07
University-provided places: 2,995
Percentage catered: 0%
Self-catered costs: £46–£94 a week.
First-year students are guaranteed accommodation if conditions are met.
International students: given priority providing conditions are met.
Contact: housing@sussex.ac.uk

Swansea, University of Wales

Swansea is the largest institution within the University of Wales. Its attractive coastal location and accessibility to students from outside Wales already made the university a natural alternative to the Welsh capital for thousands of applicants – so much so that in 2005 in a poll of 10,000 students, Swansea won the *Times Higher Education Supplement*'s inaugural award for the best student experience in the UK. A plan to rationalise departments, which led to the abandonment of five subjects, caused unrest among academics and students. But applications have continued to rise, culminating in a 10 per cent increase at the start of 2006.

A wide variety of new courses have been introduced, as part of a development plan stressing language combinations. There are now more than 500 degree courses in the modular scheme, and undergraduates are encouraged to stray outside their specialist area in their first year. Swansea takes its European interests seriously, with links to more than 90 Continental institutions. The new law school offers options in European and international law, while science students, as well as those on arts courses, can undertake some of their studies abroad.

Swansea has won European funding for some of its projects, including Graduate Opportunities Wales, which steers students towards small firms through industrial placements and vacation jobs. The most important academic development, however, has come with the opening of the Swansea Clinical School, more than 30 years after the first attempt to secure approval for a medical school. The university already had a postgraduate school, but collaboration with University of Wales College of Medicine and Swansea NHS Trust saw the Welsh Assembly back plans for 50 undergraduates to begin training in 2001. The "fast track" pro-gramme will allow 70 graduates to qualify as doctors in four years rather than five.

About half of the subjects assessed for teaching quality received Excellent ratings. Swansea counts physical sciences, management and languages among its strengths, and all branches of engineering are highly rated. Civil engineering was the only top-rated subject in the latest research assessments, but a third of the researchers were placed in one of the top two grades. Geography and environmental science, English sports science produced the best scores in a generally successful national student satisfaction survey.

For all its concentration on international activities, Swansea has not forgotten its local responsibilities. A Community University of the Valleys offers part-time courses for mature

---

Singleton Park,
Swansea SA2 8PP
01792 295111
admissions@swansea.ac.uk
www.swan.ac.uk
www.swansea-union.co.uk

The Times Rankings
Overall Ranking: 43

Student satisfaction:	=17	(15.3)
Research assessment:	=48	(4.6)
Entry standards:	52	(288.1)
Student–staff ratio:	=36	(16.9)
Library/IT spend/student:	63	(£520)
Facilities spend/student:	49	(£225)
Good honours:	58	(56.8%)
Graduate prospects:	69	(60.5%)
Expected completion rate:	32	(89.6%)

students as part of the effort to regenerate the area. Compacts with schools in the region encourage students in areas of economic disadvantage to aspire to higher education.

The immediate locality is far from depressing, however. The coastal campus two miles from the centre of Swansea offers ready access to the excellent beaches of the Gower Peninsula, and the university occupies an attractive parkland site overlooking the sea. Apart from Singleton Abbey, the neo-Gothic mansion which houses the administration, most of the buildings are modern. The latest for undergraduates is the £4.3-million Digital Technium Building, which houses the new media and communication studies department, but expensive research institutes for telecommunications and life science are on the way. The city has a reasonable range of leisure facilities, but the campus itself is the focus of social life.

Swansea makes a particular effort to cater for disabled students. There are facilities for the blind, deaf and wheelchair-bound, coordinated through a £250,000 assessment and training centre. Other access measures have been reasonably successful: almost 30 per cent of the undergraduates come from working-class homes, while the 18 per cent from areas sending few students to higher education and the 92 per cent share of places going to applicants from state schools and colleges are both higher than the funding council's benchmark for the institution. The projected dropout rate is a respectable 10 per cent.

Sports facilities are good and representative teams successful. An Olympic-sized swimming pool opened in 2002 and a new athletics track, all-weather pitches and gym are all helping to attract top performers. The 1,800 computers available for student use represent one of the best ratios at any university.

Bursaries and Scholarships

- Fees for undergraduate courses £3,000
- Students living in Wales will be eligible for a Welsh Assembly fee grant of approximately £1,800 a year.
- Fees for placement year and year abroad £1,500.
- For information on the National Bursary Scheme see page 198, chapter 7.
- Each year the university offers 10 undergraduate entrance scholarships for students with outstanding sporting talent. Each scholarship is worth £1,000 a year and is renewable for three years.
- A number of the university's departments and Schools have also set aside funds or have been given grants to reward academic achievement or help students make ends meet. These awards range from £400 to £1,100.

Contact: www.swansea.ac.uk/scholarships/

Students

Undergraduates:	8,070	(3,365)
Postgraduates:	1,350	(1,300)
Mature students:	14.7%	
Overseas students:	9.2%	
Applications per place:	4.6	
From state-sector schools:	92.6%	
From working-class homes:	28.0%	

For detailed information about fees, grants and bursaries and how they work, see chapter 7.

Accommodation

Number of places and costs refer to 2006–07

University-provided places: about 3,050

Percentage catered: 20%

Catered costs: £76–£98 a week.

Self-catered costs: £45–£76 a week.

First-year students are offered accommodation if conditions are met.

International students: guaranteed for 2 years, but students from outside EU will usually get 3 years if required.

Contact: accommodation@swansea.ac.uk

University of Teesside

Teesside has always described itself as the Opportunity University, stressing its open access and customer-oriented approach. But its latest mission statement adds the rider of "pursuing excellence" to suggest that there will be no compromise on quality. Teesside has long been among the leading new universities for the proportion of leavers going into graduate-level jobs or further training and teaching ratings improved sharply in the later years of assessment. Official performance indicators also show the university well ahead of the access benchmarks calculated by the funding council. Few English institutions draw a larger proportion of undergraduates from areas of low participation in higher education, while more than four students in every ten come from working-class homes. The projected dropout has improved, partly because of a European-funded programme on supporting non-traditional students, and is now below the national average for the courses and entry qualifications.

Although Middlesbrough has never been considered a fashionable student destination, the demand for places had been growing at a time when some new universities were having recruitment problems. It was the only university in the northeast of England to register an increase at the start of 2006. There are now more than 20,000 students, half of them taking part-time courses and nearly 40 per cent over 21 on entry. Teesside is particularly strong in niche markets such as computer games design and animation, sport and exercise, and forensic science.

More than 1,000 students are taking Teesside courses at local further education colleges, which are also involved in the growing range of full-time and part-time two-year foundation degrees. In the long term, up to a quarter of the university's students are expected to take their courses off campus, and the university is opening higher education centres attached to further education colleges in Hartlepool and Darlington.

The colleges are the focus of the Passport scheme, which offers help and guidance to students considering going to university. However, the university's best-known access initiative targets a much younger age group. The prize-winning Meteor scheme gives primary school-children a taste of higher education, even offering them the use of a cyber café in the centre of Middlesbrough. University students act as mentors and can earn some useful extra cash and gain experience of working in schools.

Teesside was close to the top 20 in rankings from the first national student satisfaction survey, with English and law

Borough Road,
Middlesbrough TS1 3BA
01642 218121
reg@tees.ac.uk
www.tees.ac.uk
www.utu.org.uk

The Times Rankings
Overall Ranking: 95

Student satisfaction:	=33	(15.0)
Research assessment:	=94	(1.9)
Entry standards:	93	(224.3)
Student–staff ratio:	=83	(20.8)
Library/IT spend/student:	106	(£366)
Facilities spend/student:	98	(£125)
Good honours:	102	(45.7%)
Graduate prospects:	61	(61.9%)
Expected completion rate:	94	(75.2%)

recording the best scores. Design, computer science, nursing and health subjects all did well in teaching assessments. The 6,000 health students are now by far the largest group in the university. The last research grades were an improvement on 1996, with history rated as outstanding, but the overall results still left Teesside among the bottom ten universities. It has since announced a £1.5-million research investment plan.

Over £70 million has been spent in recent years on the town-centre campus. The latest addition is the Olympia Building, which combines indoor sports facilities with teaching and research space for sports science. Before that came an £8-million School of Health, the upgrading of computer science and IT facilities and a state-of-the-art learning resource centre to replace the main library. An £11-million Institute of Digital Innovation and a £7-million Centre for Creative Technologies are due to open in September 2007 to support computing, media and design students. Computer provision is generous, with 1,700 PCs available. The new facilities are being used to provide degrees in subjects such as computer games design, animation and digital visual effects.

Middlesbrough has more nightlife than sceptics might imagine, and the booming student population has attracted new pubs, cafés and student-orientated shops in and around the Southfield Road area. The cost of living is another attraction: university rents are the lowest in the country and the lively students' union, which has twice won the title of students' union of the year, claims to sell some of Britain's cheapest beer. Outdoor sports facilities include a £1.5-million watersports centre on the River Tees, which is shared with Durham University.

Bursaries and Scholarships

In receipt of full Maintenance Grant	£1,300
In receipt of partial Maintenance Grant	up to £500
Progressing from outreach	Scholarship
Academic achievement	Scholarship

- Tuition fees (2006) £3,000
- Placement year tuition fee is around £750.
- Scholarships of £1,000 a year to be allocated on the basis of academic performance to all students who meet the criteria.
- Students whose residual family income is in the upper income threshold for Maintenance Grant will receive a £500 Welcome grant in year 1 only.
- 31% of additional fee income to be earmarked for bursaries.

Contact: www.tees.ac.uk/funding
www.tees.ac.uk/sections/fulltime/fees.cfm

Students

Undergraduates:	8,380	(10,410)
Postgraduates:	770	(1,590)
Mature students:	31.7%	
Overseas students:	6.2%	
Applications per place:	4.1	
From state-sector schools:	98.1%	
From working-class homes:	41.4%	

For detailed information about fees, grants and bursaries and how they work, see chapter 7.

Accommodation

Number of places and costs refer to 2005–06
University-provided places: 1,276
Percentage catered: 0%
Self-catered costs: £32.90–£56.98 a week.
All university-managed accommodation is exclusively for first years (conditions apply).
International students: guaranteed accommodation if designated overseas for fees (terms and conditions apply).
Contact: 01642 342255;
accommodation@tees.ac.uk

Thames Valley University

Having survived a tumultuous period in which the university's academic standards were criticised, the Vice-Chancellor resigned and demand for places collapsed, Thames Valley has embarked on a new future as a much larger institution spanning further and higher education. A merger with Reading College, at the start of 2004, has produced a university of 45,000 students where almost a third of the places are on further education courses and there is even a sixth-form academy. Relaunched as the New Thames Valley University in 2005, half of its students are over 30 years old, 60 per cent female and the same proportion part-time.

A new campus in Brentford, West London, will open fully in September 2006, with 850 residential places as well as extensive teaching accommodation for the largest healthcare faculty in Britain. One of the two campuses in Reading is being completely redeveloped and £9.5 million is being invested in improving the original campus at Ealing. Another £3 million has already been spent on the Slough campus, with more to come.

It is all a far cry from the end of the 1990s, when barely 30 degrees were left. Although the aftermath of that period has left the university rooted to the bottom of The Times League Table, the university is virtually unrecognisable from those dark days. The finances are under control, a quality audit has produced a clean bill of health, and even before the merger, there were plans for renewed growth. Applications increased by more than a quarter in 2005, but even a decision to become one of three universities setting top-up fees at less than £3,000 a year could not prevent a 13 per cent drop at the start of 2006.

Courses are now concentrated in four faculties – arts, music and design; health and human sciences; professional studies; and technology. Many further education programmes are being extended into degrees or professional qualifications. Among the casualties of the reorganisation, however, were the two top-rated subjects: sociology and linguistics, which also achieved one of the few grade 5 research assessments in the new universities in 1996.

Amid the reconstruction, new honours degrees have been launched in areas such as video production, 3D design, entrepreneurship and web and e-business computing. The portfolio of two-year foundation degrees is growing, with employers such as Compaq, Ealing Studios and the Savoy Hotel Group helping to provide courses. Some are run in conjunction with Stratford-upon-Avon College – one of a number of partner

St Mary's Road, Ealing,
London W5 5RF
020-8579 5000
learning.advice@tvu.ac.uk
www.tvu.ac.uk
www.tvusu.org.uk

The Times Rankings
Overall Ranking: 109

Student satisfaction:	–	(–)
Research assessment:	109	(0.5)
Entry standards:	102	(202.5)
Student–staff ratio:	101	(23.7)
Library/IT spend/student:	100	(£398)
Facilities spend/student:	109	(£57)
Good honours:	=90	(48.8%)
Graduate prospects:	=70	(60.1%)
Expected completion rate:	105	(68.6%)

institutions. The university also has 17 outreach centres in and around Reading, at Southall and even Heathrow Airport.

TVU achieved university status only a year after becoming a polytechnic in a merger between two well-established higher education colleges. A policy of open access results in 30 per cent of the undergraduates coming from working-class homes, but also puts the university at a disadvantage in rankings such as ours. Hospitality, leisure and tourism achieved a good score in the final round of teaching assessment, but linguistics and sociology were the only other subjects to manage 22 points out of 24 for teaching quality. TVU also has the worst research record in the university system, having entered fewer than one academic in five for the latest assessments.

Some of the vocational courses have a strong reputation: the school of tourism, hospitality and leisure management, for example, is recognised by the Académie Culinaire de France for its culinary arts programmes. Nursing courses, too, are popular and well regarded. However, Thames Valley remains in a cluster of new universities with projected dropout rates of around 25 per cent.

The town-centre sites in Ealing, Reading and Slough are linked by a free bus service. The business-oriented campus in Slough consists mainly of 1960s buildings, but has been enhanced by an award-winning learning resources centre designed by Sir Richard Rogers. The busier Ealing base was suffering from overcrowding before retrenchment took place. Almost half of the students are from London or Berkshire, despite an unexpectedly large contingent of overseas students.

Residential accommodation is growing from a low base, but students who rely on private housing find the cost of living high. The Slough campus boasts an impressive gym, but otherwise sports facilities are limited.

Bursaries and Scholarships

In receipt of full Maintenance Grant	£1,000
In receipt of partial Maintenance Grant	£1,000

- Tuition fees (2006) £2,700
- Placement year tuition fee will be £1,385.
- All students not receiving Maintenance Grant will receive a bursary of £500.

Contact: www.tvu.ac.uk/prospective/ Undergraduate/Fees.jsp

Students

Undergraduates:	7,805	(7,600)
Postgraduates:	500	(1,360)
Mature students:	42.7%	
Overseas students:	17.7%	
Applications per place:	4.4	
From state-sector schools:	99.0%	
From working-class homes:	30.6%	

For detailed information about fees, grants and bursaries and how they work, see chapter 7.

Accommodation

Number of places and costs refer to 2006–07
University-provided places: about 900
Percentage catered: 0%
Self-catered costs: £83–£100 a week.
First years are guaranteed accommodation if conditions are met.
International students: same as above.
Contact: uas@tvu.ac.uk

University of Ulster

Ulster remains one of the most popular universities in Britain, despite a small drop in applications at the official deadline for courses beginning in 2006. The university – the only one in Britain with a charter stipulating that there should be courses below degree level – would like to expand but is constrained by Government policy. UU has had to pull out of its most ambitious project: the proposed "peaceline campus" linking Belfast's two communities after years of on/off negotiations. But there are plans to improve and expand all four main sites, at a cost of £200 million, during the current decade.

With more Irish students now choosing to stay in the Province to study, there is plenty of scope for expansion, despite the fact that UU already has more than 20,000 students. The main sites in and near Belfast have never been busier, while Magee attracts students from both sides of the border. High technology brings together the university for teaching purposes, but the sites are 80 miles apart at their farthest point and very different in character. Jordanstown, seven miles outside Belfast, has the most students, concentrating on engineering, health and social science. Numbers are being limited to prevent overcrowding and more

building is planned. The isolated original university campus, at Coleraine, follows the style of the 1960s, and is the most traditional in outlook, with a focus on science and the humanities. There is a new £11-million Centre for Molecular Biosciences, and further building is in the pipeline. The small Belfast site has always specialised in art and design, but a £30-million redevelopment will see its range of subjects expand.

Current development is focusing mainly on the Magee campus in Londonderry, although Jordanstown has acquired improved library and computing facilities. Once the poor relation of the university, confined to adult education, Magee is now a thriving centre. Over the next two years, student numbers are expected to grow to about 7,500, including part-timers, with new schools of performing arts, computing and electronics, as well as improved provision for education, nursing and Irish studies. The Institute for Legal and Professional Studies will allow graduates to train as barristers and solicitors. The historic Foyle Arts Centre has become part of the university and a postgraduate medical school is planned

Although often overshadowed by Queen's University, Ulster's community consciousness has worked to its advantage. Almost half the students come from

---

Cromore Road, Coleraine,
Co. Londonderry BT52 1SA
08700-400 700
online@ulst.ac.uk
www.ulster.ac.uk
www.uusu.org

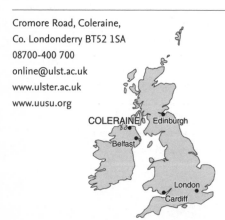

COLERAINE · Edinburgh
Belfast
London
Cardiff

The Times Rankings
Overall Ranking: 51

Student satisfaction:	=38	(14.9)
Research assessment:	56	(3.8)
Entry standards:	66	(262.9)
Student–staff ratio:	67	(19.5)
Library/IT spend/student:	49	(£584)
Facilities spend/student:	48	(£227)
Good honours:	41	(61.5%)
Graduate prospects:	=53	(63.4%)
Expected completion rate:	61	(82.6%)

working-class homes – far more than the UK average – and the student profile mirrors the religious balance in the wider population. Mature students are well catered for, with access courses for those who lack the necessary entry qualifications, a nursery and three playgroups in the university. There has never been a big representation from mainland Britain, but its contingent of international students include those from the Republic of Ireland as well as further afield. The Campus One programme provides an alternative mode of study, with a range of courses available online to students all over the world.

Teaching ratings were mainly sound, rather than spectacular, although business and management registered maximum points. Research is not Ulster's principal strength, but grades improved in the latest assessments, with Celtic studies and biomedical sciences rated internationally outstanding. Sociology and social policy did best in the first national student satisfaction survey.

As with any split-site university, the student experience varies according to the location. Some courses offer lectures on more than one campus, but for the most part students are based on a single site throughout their university life. With more than half of the students living with their parents or at their own home, the university is not always the focus of social life. The exception is Coleraine, a classic campus university, where there are fewer home-based students, although many gravitate towards the nearby seaside towns of Portrush and Portstewart.

Bursaries and Scholarships

In receipt of full Maintenance Grant £1,000
In receipt of partial Maintenance Grant min £300 on a sliding scale

- Tuition fees (2006) £3,000
- Tuition fee for placement year and year abroad will be around £1,500.

Contact: www.ulster.ac.uk/newstudentfinance/

Students		
Undergraduates:	15,410	(4,750)
Postgraduates:	1,970	(4,070)
Mature students:	17.8%	
Overseas students:	9.3%	
Applications per place:	6.7	
From state-sector schools:	99.9%	
From working-class homes:	48.0%	

For detailed information about fees, grants and bursaries and how they work, see chapter 7.

Accommodation

Number of places and costs refer to 2006–07
University-provided places: 2,613
Percentage catered: 0%
Self-catered accommodation: £40–£80 a week.
First-year students are guaranteed accommodation if conditions are met.
International students: same as above.
Contact: accommodation@ulster.ac.uk

University of the Arts, London

The London Institute resisted the temptation to apply for university status after it was formed in 1986 because the art, design, fashion and media colleges that had come together for administrative purposes were world-famous in their own right. But a change of rules governing university titles and the arrival as rector of Sir Michael Bichard, previously Permanent Secretary at the Department for Education and Skills, prompted a rethink. As a result, University of the Arts, London was born in 2004, and is already becoming a powerful "brand" in its own right.

The five component colleges, which continue to use their own names and enjoy considerable autonomy, are Camberwell College of Arts, Central St Martins College of Art and Design, Chelsea College of Art and Design, London College of Fashion and London College of Communication (formerly the London College of Printing). Together, they boast a total of about 18,000 students spread around 16 sites around central London, representing the biggest concentration of art, design and creative arts in Europe.

Teaching and research grades for the Institute barely did justice to the eminence of the colleges. Although Camberwell and what was then the College of Printing achieved near-perfect scores for teaching quality in art and design, the other colleges' grades in this category and those for business and management, materials technology and media studies were strong but not spectacular. Chelsea and London College of Fashion have jointly been awarded a national teaching centre for the arts, focusing on practice-based teaching and learning. But the university was close to the bottom of rankings from the first national student satisfaction survey.

However, assessors liked the heavy use of often eminent visiting lecturers, the close links with industry and the broad range of courses, which stretch from further education to postgraduate. Pioneering enterprise centres offer vital business and legal support to graduates.

A number of two-year foundation degrees have been introduced, including one in interactive games production and another in fashion styling and photography. The mix is going down well with applicants both at home and abroad: demand for places was up by almost 5 per cent at the start of 2006, following two much bigger rises in the years before top-up fees. The 12 per cent dropout rate is also good for the subjects on offer, and the proportion of undergraduates from working-class homes has now reached the national average. The university has been

---

65 Davies Street
London W1K 5DA
020-7514 6000
prospectus@linst.ac.uk
www.linst.ac.uk
www.lisu.org

Edinburgh
Belfast
Cardiff
LONDON

The Times Rankings
Overall Ranking: 84

Student satisfaction:	88	(13.7)
Research assessment:	=42	(4.7)
Entry standards:	35	(345.1)
Student–staff ratio:	108	(26.6)
Library/IT spend/student:	95	(£421)
Facilities spend/student:	=99	(£123)
Good honours:	67	(54.6%)
Graduate prospects:	106	(47.5%)
Expected completion rate:	39	(86.9%)

running weekend classes and summer schools in an attempt to broaden the intake.

Big changes were already under way before the change of title was agreed: a £70-million development programme has produced prestigious new premises for Chelsea College next door to the Tate Gallery, on Millbank, with extensive workshop facilities, studios and an impressive new library. Another £32 million has been spent on new headquarters for the College of Communication at the Elephant and Castle, south of the Thames, where a newly-built Special Archives and Collections Centre will include the archives of the late filmmaker Stanley Kubrick. The college now has Film Academy status.

A new £2-million information technology system links all the sites, and there are plans to devote a similar sum to a ground-breaking centre for fashion enterprise. There was a series of mergers and property moves during the Institute's 18-year existence, but the basic structure of the new university is expected to remain stable for the foreseeable future.

The colleges vary considerably in character and facilities, although a single students' union serves them all. The university is not overprovided with residential accommodation, although there are 11 residences spread around the colleges, providing 1,700 beds. House-hunting workshops help those who have to rely on what is inevitably an expensive private housing market.

Bursaries and Scholarships†

In receipt of full Maintenance Grant	£300
Living in region	Bursary
Living in specified postcodes	Bursary

- Tuition fees (2006) £3,000
- Bursaries will be available to UK students only.
- Bursary of £1,000 is available on application by first-generation students receiving full or partial Maintenance Grant living in specified postcodes.
- 12.5% of additional fee income to be earmarked for bursaries.

Contact: www.arts.ac.uk/tuition-fees.htm

† Information taken from 2006 Access Agreement

Students

Undergraduates:	9,790	(515)
Postgraduates:	1,245	(715)
Mature students:	39.4%	
Overseas students:	35.8%	
Applications per place:	4.5	
From state-sector schools:	94.9%	
From working-class homes:	27.0%	

For detailed information about fees, grants and bursaries and how they work, see chapter 7.

Accommodation

Number of places and costs refer to 2006–07
University-provided places: about 1,751
Percentage catered: 0%
Self-catered costs: £68.50–£164.00 a week.
First-year students are offered accommodation if conditions are met. Priority for disabled students.
International students: guaranteed if conditions met.
Contact: accommodation@arts.ac.uk;
www.arts.ac.uk/housing/

UCE Birmingham

Central England has been dropped from UCE Birmingham's title in a rebranding exercise that has also dispensed with the slogan "the responsive university", but the institution still emphasises its willingness to act on students' wishes as well as serving the needs of the Second City. The annual satisfaction survey goes to half of the student body, in a model that helped inform the new national equivalent. The results are taken seriously: more than £1 million was spent on library stock after one survey, and a more recent exercise has led to the introduction of internet tutorials in engineering and new help with research for undergraduates in law and social science. The long-standing initiative is just one of the activities of the influential Centre for Research into Quality, which is headed by one of the university's most senior academics.

The university has a proud record of extending access to higher education: around 40 per cent of its students come from working-class homes and 97 per cent attended state schools. Nearly 16 per cent drop out, but this is less than the national average for the university's courses and entry grades. About half of the full-time students come from the West Midlands, many from ethnic minorities. UCE also has one of the largest programmes of part-time courses in Britain, making it the biggest provider of higher education in the region. Students also enter through the network of 15 associated further education colleges, which run foundation and access programmes. Demand for places was up by 13 per cent in 2005 but down by more than 8 per cent when top-up fees arrived a year later.

One of the university's best-known features is its Conservatoire, housed in part of Birmingham's smart convention centre. Courses from opera to world music have given it a reputation for innovation, which was recognised in an excellent rating for teaching. Most other teaching ratings were mediocre, however, although the teacher education courses consistently produce among the best scores in the Teacher Training Agency's performance indicators. Those for secondary teachers were bettered only by Oxford and Cambridge in 2005.

Art and design, education and health subjects registered the best scores for teaching quality. The university has been building up its portfolio of high-tech courses with degrees in communications and network engineering, electronic commerce, electronic systems and mechanical engineering systems. The last research assessments showed improvement on 1996, but only art and design reached any of the top three grades.

Perry Barr,
Birmingham B42 2SU
0121-331 5595
recruitment@uce.ac.uk
www.uce.ac.uk
www.unionofstudents.com

The Times Rankings
Overall Ranking: 63

Student satisfaction:	=83	(14.2)
Research assessment:	=86	(2.2)
Entry standards:	79	(242.2)
Student–staff ratio:	=33	(16.6)
Library/IT spend/student:	58	(£536)
Facilities spend/student:	16	(£327)
Good honours:	44	(60.4%)
Graduate prospects:	60	(62.1%)
Expected completion rate:	=67	(81.6%)

Edinburgh
Belfast
BIRMINGHAM •
Cardiff
London

However, income from research contracts has always been healthy.

Seven campuses straggle across the city, but the majority of students are concentrated on the modern Perry Barr site three miles north of the city centre. The large teacher training centre moved there from the southern suburb of Edgbaston in 2001, and the university bought an adjacent 43-acre site to improve sporting provision, which was poorly positioned and inadequate for 25,000 students. The pavilion has added £4.5 million of sports and conference facilities. The Conservatoire library and those at Perry Barr and the Westbourne campus have been refurbished and a New Technology Institute opened.

A £21-million development was already providing new teaching facilities for the Faculty of Health and Community Care and the Royal Centre for Defence Medicine. UCE has also joined with the Birmingham Children's Hospital to provide training for staff, from consultants to domestics, in the care of sick children.

The Institute of Art and Design, refurbished at a cost of £20 million, spreads further south to Bourneville, where it occupies part of the Cadbury village. It is the largest in Britain, and includes a school of jewellery in the city centre. The recent relocation of engineering and computing to the city's Millennium Point high-tech development provided a new focus for the university. Facilities in the £114-million Lottery-funded centre are open to the public.

University-owned accommodation is only guaranteed for some first years. But the high proportion of locally-based mature students and the relatively cheap and plentiful private sector housing make this less of a problem. Students have been critical of the union facilities, but a new complex was due to open on the Westbourne campus in the summer of 2006 and the city's youth scene is highly rated.

Bursaries and Scholarships

In receipt of full Maintenance Grant	£500
In receipt of partial Maintenance Grant	£500

- Tuition fees (2006) £3,000
- 11% of additional fee income to be earmarked for bursaries.
- Eligibility for bursaries to be assessed using UUK/SLC model bursary scheme (HEBSS).

Contact: www.uce.ac.uk/web2/ prospective_students/newfinance.html

Students

Undergraduates:	12,310	(7,050)
Postgraduates:	1,430	(2,585)
Mature students:	23.6%	
Overseas students:	10.7%	
Applications per place:	5.6	
From state-sector schools:	97.0%	
From working-class homes:	39.4%	

For detailed information about fees, grants and bursaries and how they work, see chapter 7.

Accommodation

Number of places and costs refer to 2006–07
University-provided places: 2,146
Percentage catered: 6.3%
Catered costs: £73–£77 a week.
Self-catered costs: £55–£90 a week.
First years guaranteed accommodation provided conditions are met. Residential restrictions apply.
International students: accommodation guaranteed.
Contact: Accommodation@uce.ac.uk

University College London

Such is the breadth and quality of provision at University College (UCL) that it can fairly describe itself not only as a "university within a university" but also as one of the top multi-faculty institutions in England. Its position in *The Times* rankings has regularly confirmed this, and in 2005 it even overtook Oxford and Cambridge for the amount of research support it was allocated by the funding council. UCL's excellence is built on a history of pioneering subjects that have become commonplace in higher education: modern languages, geography and fine arts among them.

The institution is now emerging from a difficult period, in which it ran up a £12-million deficit and saw the unexpected departure of the Provost and the rejection of a proposed merger with Imperial College London. Under Professor Malcolm Grant, who took over in 2003, the largest-ever fundraising effort at a UK university has begun, a reorganisation of staffing has taken place and there have been two years of surpluses.

Already comfortably the largest of London University's colleges, UCL took in a number of specialist schools and institutes at the end of the 1990s. Most were medical or dental and, in combination with the Royal Free Hospital School of Medicine, UCL's medical school is now a large and formidable unit. Its credentials have been strengthened still further with the announcement that UCL is to be the new home of the National Institute of Medical Research. The various acquisitions mean that there are now outposts in several parts of central and north London, but the main activity remains centred on the original impressive Bloomsbury site.

Anatomy, archaeology, several branches of engineering, modern languages and pharmacology are among the areas rated internationally outstanding for research. One academic in three was in a top-rated department in the last assessments but, although almost nine out of ten were in the top two categories, the results did not quite match the high benchmark set in 1996. Economics, health-related subjects, history of art and organismal biosciences all recorded maximum points for teaching, but most subjects scored well. A growing number of degrees take four years, and most are organised on a modular basis.

Many of UCL's students are from overseas, including more than 2,000 from other EU countries, reflecting the college's high international standing. The proportion is likely to rise further in the coming years. Suitably qualified British applicants are interviewed whenever

---

Gower Street,
London WC1E 6BT
020-7679 2000
contact through website
www.ucl.ac.uk
www.uclu.org

Edinburgh
Belfast
Cardiff
LONDON

The Times Rankings
Overall Ranking: 5

Student satisfaction:	=17	(15.3)
Research assessment:	=5	(6.0)
Entry standards:	11	(410.8)
Student–staff ratio:	1	(8.4)
Library/IT spend/student:	4	(£1,152)
Facilities spend/student:	75	(£172)
Good honours:	13	(73.6%)
Graduate prospects:	8	(78.1%)
Expected completion rate:	17	(93.4%)

possible before being offered a place and, once accepted, first-year students in many subjects are given peer tutoring by more experienced colleagues to help them adapt to degree study. The college stresses its commitment to teaching in small groups, especially in the second and subsequent years of degree courses. The approach seems to work: almost three quarters leave with a first or upper second. Although the projected dropout rate had risen sharply in the latest figures, at 6.6 per cent it is still marginally lower than the national average for the courses and entry grades.

UCL is conscious of its traditions as a college founded to expand access to higher education, but the 40 per cent share of places going to independent school students is one of the highest in Britain. Less than one undergraduate in five has a working-class background and just 6.5 per cent come from an area without a tradition of higher education. Concerted attempts are being made to broaden the intake with three summer schools for state school sixth-formers and increased contact with local schools and further education colleges.

The academic pace can be frantic but, close to the West End and with its own theatre and recreational facilities, there is no shortage of leisure options. Students also have immediate access to London University's underused central students' union facilities. Residential accommodation is plentiful and of a good standard. Indoor sports facilities are close at hand, but the main outdoor pitches, though good enough to attract professional football clubs, are a coach ride away in Hertfordshire.

Bursaries and Scholarships

In receipt of full Maintenance Grant

£1,350–£2,500

In receipt of partial Maintenance Grant

50% of Maintenance Grant value

- Tuition fees (2006) £3,000
- All students in receipt of Maintenance Grant to receive a bursary calculated at 50% of its value but enhanced to £1,500–£2,500 for those from families with lowest residual income.
- For students on longer undergraduate courses, eg, with a year abroad or MEng and MSci degrees the bursary will be doubled or valued at 100% Maintenance Grant, whichever is the higher, for the final year.
- Hardship Fund available.

Contact: www.ucl.ac.uk/prospective-students/ undergraduate-study/fees-and-costs/ sources-of-funding/bursaries/index.shtml

Students		
Undergraduates:	11,195	(740)
Postgraduates:	5,350	(2,955)
Mature students:	11.6%	
Overseas students:	22.1%	
Applications per place:	8.9	
From state-sector schools:	59.3%	
From working-class homes:	17.3%	

For detailed information about fees, grants and bursaries and how they work, see chapter 7.

Accommodation

Number of places and costs refer to 2006–07

University-provided places: 4,156 (including 500 intercollegiate places)

Percentage catered: 30%

Catered costs: £94.15–£134.12 a week.

Self-catered costs: £63.56–£128.24 a week.

First years are guaranteed accommodation if conditons are met.

International students: for undergraduates, as above.

Contact: Residences@ucl.ac.uk

University of Warwick

The most successful of the first wave of new universities, Warwick was derided by many in its early years for its close links with business and industry. Few are critical today. Tony Blair described the university as "at the cutting edge of what has to happen in the future" and even brought Bill Clinton there on his last overseas engagement as US President. Both teaching and research are very highly rated, but the university's mission statement still stresses the extension of access to higher education, continuing education and community links.

There is a smaller proportion of independent school students than at most of the leading universities – less than a quarter – but this does not translate into large numbers of working-class under-graduates. The share of places going to students from the lowest social classes and the representation from areas sending few young people to higher education are both lower than the national average for Warwick's subjects and entry qualifi-cations. But the mix helps to produce one of the lowest dropout rates in Britain. Graduates have contributed more than £2 million to a scholarship scheme, which made 105 awards in 2004.

Warwick's teaching assessments were outstanding, with seven maximum scores, but the students did not respond in sufficient numbers to take part in the first national student satisfaction survey. Nevertheless, the university has been awarded a national teaching centre in theatrical performance, in partnership with the Royal Shakespeare Company, and is collaborating with Oxford Brookes University on another centre to "reinvent" undergraduate research. Six subjects were rated internationally outstanding for research – business, economics, English, theatre studies and applied mathematics and statistics. Nine out of ten academics entered for assessment were placed in the top two categories, preserving Warwick's place among the top five research universities. The overall standard of the 29 departments brought Warwick a top European award, while the science park, one of the first in Britain, is among the most successful.

While other leading universities were trying to cover the whole range of academic disciplines, Warwick pursued a selective policy. Without the expense of medicine, dentistry or veterinary science to bear, the university invested shrewdly in business, science and engineering. How-ever, the temptation of medicine has proved too much to bear, and the university has gone into partnership with Leicester University to establish a new kind of course for graduates in biological

---

Coventry CV4 7AL
02476 523723
ugadmissions@
admin.warwick.ac.uk
www.warwick.ac.uk
www.sunion.warwick.ac.uk/
portal

The Times Rankings
Overall Ranking: 8

Student satisfaction:	–	(–)
Research assessment:	=5	(6.0)
Entry standards:	6	(447.6)
Student–staff ratio:	32	(16.4)
Library/IT spend/student:	11	(£853)
Facilities spend/student:	=59	(£203)
Good honours:	4	(78.2%)
Graduate prospects:	=26	(70.2%)
Expected completion rate:	12	(94.9%)

sciences. There are now 330 students in the medical school, which opened in 2000, and numbers are growing.

Another deviation has seen the university embracing the Government's two-year foundation degrees. One of the few leading universities to offer the vocational programmes, Warwick is running three courses in education and community enterprise, the latter taught by a local further education college.

Such is the demand for places on conventional degree courses, that many departments stick rigidly to offers averaging more than an A and two Bs at A level. Applications have been buoyant: there was virtually no change in the total either in 2005 or at the start of 2006, when many universities suffered from the introduction of top-up fees. Warwick has been building up its numbers in science and engineering, as other universities have struggled to fill their places. The business school has also been growing rapidly, with a new £15-million extension now complete, while computer science has acquired new, upgraded facilities.

Some £335 million has been spent on the campus, which has often resembled a building site. However, students have welcomed larger union facilities, a number of academic buildings have been improved and the Arts Centre (the second largest in Britain) has been refurbished with a £33-million lottery grant. The 720-acre campus is three miles south of Coventry, where many students choose to live, and three times as far from Warwick. University accommodation is plentiful. The sports facilities are both extensive and conveniently placed on campus, where there is a new sports centre with 25-metre swimming pool and a range of other facilities.

Bursaries and Scholarships

In receipt of full Maintenance Grant
  £2,000–£3,000
In receipt of partial Maintenance Grant
  £1,000–£2,000

- Tuition fees (2006)   £3,000
- Placement year tuition fee and year abroad tuition fee is 50% full time fee.
- 170 means-tested Philanthropic Scholarships available on application.
- Work/study scheme devised to provide participating students with 5 hours paid work a week, worth £1,000 a year.
- 26% of additional fee income to be earmarked for bursaries.
- Bursary for students receiving partial Maintenance Grant may be higher than the bursary for students receiving full Maintenance Grant to assist the many students not qualifying for full Maintenance Grant but still perceived as being in great need of financial assistance.

Contact: www.warwick.ac.uk/go/WUAP

Students

Undergraduates:	10,080	(9,880)
Postgraduates:	3,115	(6,075)
Mature students:	10.0%	
Overseas students:	18.3%	
Applications per place:	8.8	
From state-sector schools:	76.5%	
From working-class homes:	18.6%	

For detailed information about fees, grants and bursaries and how they work, see chapter 7.

Accommodation

Number of places and costs refer to 2006–07
University-provided places: 5,791 (on campus); 1,650 (head leasing)
Percentage catered: 0%
Self-catered costs: £60–£97 a week.
All first-year undergraduates are guaranteed accommodation (terms and conditions apply). International students designated for overseas fees have guaranteed campus accommodation (terms and conditions apply).
Contact: accommodation@warwick.ac.uk

University of the West of England, Bristol

West of England (UWE) surprised the university world by attracting Sir Howard Newby, chief executive of the Higher Education Funding Council for England, to be its vice-chancellor. But UWE boasted the best teaching quality record in the new universities and has always been regarded among the leaders in its peer group. Perfect scores for education and in the joint assessment for biology and biomedical sciences represented the best results, but every subject assessed since 1995 was given at least 20 out of 24 points. Business and management, the university's biggest subject area with 3,300 students, and economics also scored well at the end of the cycle of assessments.

This record and a popular location had been proving highly attractive to students. Applications rose by more than 16 per cent in 2005, but top-up fees brought a drop of nearly 9 per cent at the start of 2006. The university did find itself in trouble, however, with the funding council for missing its benchmarks for extending access to under-represented groups in higher education. One undergraduate in seven attends a fee-paying school, a proportion exceeded by only one other new university. More than a quarter of places now go to working-class students, but both this and the proportion of students from areas without a history of higher education are still well below the national average for the subjects offered.

The projected dropout rate has been coming down, but it is still more than 15 per cent. More than half of the students come from the West Country and there are close links with local business and industry. A network of 15 colleges stretches into Somerset and Wiltshire, offering UWE programmes. Hartpury College, near Gloucester, has become an associate faculty of the university, specialising in agriculture, equine studies and other land-based courses.

A tradition of vocational education regularly helps the university to a healthy graduate employment record. The entrance system credits vocational qualifications and practical experience equally with traditional academic results. Law received a commendation from the Legal Practice Board and the degree in Architecture and Planning won a similar accolade from the Royal Town Planning Institute for bringing together the two disciplines in one joint-honours course giving dual professional qualifications. Industrial links are paying off in a variety of ways, with the university offering a number of employer bursary schemes in addition to its own.

Frenchay Campus,
Coldharbour Lane, Bristol BS16 1QY
0117-344 3333
Admissions@uwe.ac.uk
www.uwe.ac.uk
www.uwesu.net

The Times Rankings
Overall Ranking: 67

Student satisfaction:	=67	(14.5)
Research assessment:	=67	(2.8)
Entry standards:	60	(266.5)
Student–staff ratio:	71	(19.8)
Library/IT spend/student:	=67	(£503)
Facilities spend/student:	=50	(£223)
Good honours:	=64	(55.2%)
Graduate prospects:	=70	(60.1%)
Expected completion rate:	55	(84.0%)

Among the new universities, only Oxford Brookes entered a larger proportion of academics than UWE's 40 per cent in the 2001 Research Assessment Exercise. The results were an improvement on 1996, with accounting and finance rated nationally outstanding with much work of international standards. However, the scale of the entry also produced more low grades than the university would have wished.

There are four sites in Bristol itself, mainly around the north of the city, with regional centres in Bath, and Swindon concentrating on the growth area of nursing. Only Bower Ashton, which houses art, media and design, is in the south. The main campus at Frenchay, close to Bristol Parkway station but four miles out of the city centre, has by far the largest number of students and includes the Centre for Student Affairs, which brings together the various non-academic services. The St Matthias site (for social sciences and humanities) and Glenside (for midwifery, nursing, physiotherapy and radiography) are more attractive but less lively. Education has moved from the Redland campus, near the city centre, to a £16-million headquarters at Frenchay.

Bristol is a hugely popular student centre: an attractive and lively city, but not cheap. University accommodation has become more plentiful in recent years, with almost 4,500 places available and more on the way. Sports facilities have been a bone of contention for students, but in September 2006 there will be a new sports complex as part of a £200-million investment programme, which is one of the largest in UK higher education.

Bursaries and Scholarships

In receipt of full Maintenance Grant	£1,250
In receipt of partial Maintenance Grant	£750

- Tuition fees (2006) £3,000
- Placement year tuition fees and year abroad tuition fees are £500.
- 44% of additional fee income to be earmarked for bursaries.
- Eligibility for bursaries will be assessed using UUK/SLC model bursary scheme (HEBSS).

Contact: www.uwe.ac.uk/money

Students

Undergraduates:	16,765	(5,220)
Postgraduates:	1,945	(2,590)
Mature students:	22.3%	
Overseas students:	6.6%	
Applications per place:	4.5	
From state-sector schools:	87.2%	
From working-class homes:	28.2%	

For detailed information about fees, grants and bursaries and how they work, see chapter 7.

Accommodation

Number of places and costs refer to 2006–07
University-provided places: 4,337
Percentage catered: 0%
Self-catered costs: £46–£90 a week.
First-year students are guaranteed accommodation provided requirements are met.
International students are offered accommodation where possible.
Contact: SAS@uwe.ac.uk

University of Westminster

Westminster has recently completed a £110-million modernisation of its four sites, which has been going on since the 1990s. Having started with the £33-million transformation of the former Harrow College, in north London, in what was Europe's largest university construction project, the university moved on to an even more costly redevelopment of one of the three central sites, opposite Madame Tussauds. The large business school acquired a "cloistered environment" in a £9.5-million scheme which creates more space for teaching and research. Now the New Cavendish Street site, near the BT Tower, has been the subject of a redevelopment worth £30 million. The last stage saw a new teaching, research and administration building named after the Vice-Chancellor, Dr Geoffrey Copland.

The greenfield Harrow campus boasts a high-tech information resources centre with new facilities for the highly-rated media studies courses. Computing and design are also based on a site designed for 7,500 students. The West End sites provide the perfect catchment area for part-time students, who account for almost half of the 22,000 places. Only the Open University has more. By no means all the students are Londoners, however: nearly 15 per cent come from abroad – among the highest proportions among the new universities. Westminster courses are also taught in nine overseas countries, from Oman to the United States, a characteristic which won the university a Queen's Award for Enterprise.

The historic headquarters building, near Broadcasting House, houses social sciences and languages. French and Chinese scored particularly well in teaching assessments, and Westminster claims to offer the largest number of languages of any British university. Science and health courses are concentrated on the Cavendish campus. The university's growing interest in health covers degrees from the British College of Naturopathy and Osteopathy and a range of courses in complementary medicine, including a BSc in acupuncture. There are degrees in herbal medicine, homeopathy and nutritional therapy, and a diploma in the traditional Chinese massage technique of Qigong.

Westminster gained a series of good teaching quality scores. Psychology and tourism lead the way with maximum points, with media studies, Chinese, community care and primary health all on the next rung of the ladder. The university weaves work-related skills into its degree programmes.

Westminster's haul of four subjects on grade 5 in the last assessment exercise was the best of any new university, although

309 Regent Street,
London W1B 2UW
020-7911 5000
admissions@wmin.ac.uk
www.wmin.ac.uk
www.uwsu.com

Edinburgh
Belfast
Cardiff
LONDON

The Times Rankings
Overall Ranking: 94

Student satisfaction:	=75	(14.3)
Research assessment:	=67	(2.8)
Entry standards:	98	(217.8)
Student–staff ratio:	=48	(17.6)
Library/IT spend/student:	83	(£457)
Facilities spend/student:	=69	(£179)
Good honours:	=61	(55.8%)
Graduate prospects:	=99	(50.9%)
Expected completion rate:	96	(74.4%)

the decision to enter fewer than 30 per cent of academics limited both the funding rewards and the impact on the university's ranking. Asian studies, law, linguistics and media studies were all rated nationally outstanding with much work of international quality.

More than four out of ten undergraduates are from working-class homes – a much higher proportion than the national average for the subjects offered. The university also exceeds its benchmark for the admission of students from state schools and colleges, although the central London location reduces the share of places going to students from areas without a tradition of higher education. The dropout rate had been improving, but was more than one in five in the last projections.

Westminster's students, like those at all the London universities, complain of the high cost of living, particularly for accommodation. The university has added considerably to its residential stock in recent years, but there is no way round the capital's inflated housing market at some stage. The Harrow campus is lively socially, but those based on the other sites tend to be spread around the capital. Sports facilities are also dispersed, with playing fields and a boathouse in Chiswick, west London.

Bursaries and Scholarships

In receipt of full Maintenance Grant	£300
In receipt of partial Maintenance Grant	up to £300
Academic achievement	Scholarship

- Tuition fees (2006) £3,000
- There will be no tuition fee for any placement year.
- Bursaries are open to non-UK EU students.
- Scholarship fund will support academic excellence in under-represented groups and students progressing from foundation level.
- 15% of additional fee income to be earmarked for bursaries.
- Eligibility for bursaries will be assessed using UUK/SLC model bursary scheme (HEBSS).

Contact: www.wmin.ac.uk/funding

Students

Undergraduates:	10,755	(7,305)
Postgraduates:	3,175	(5,380)
Mature students:	34.5%	
Overseas students:	14.9%	
Applications per place:	5.0	
From state-sector schools:	95.5%	
From working-class homes:	43.0%	

For detailed information about fees, grants and bursaries and how they work, see chapter 7.

Accommodation

Number of places and costs refer to 2006–07
University-provided places: 1,235
Percentage catered: 0%
Self-catered costs: £68.60–£95.90 a week.
First-year students have priority. Residential restrictions apply.
International students: as above.
Contact: www.wmin.ac.uk/accommodation

University of Winchester

Winchester celebrated the arrival of university status in 2005 by making the shortlist for the *Times Higher Education Supplement*'s inaugural award of University of the Year. It was quite an achievement for an institution that still has only 3,000 full-time students and which was a university college for only a year, but a place among the top 20 universities in the first national student satisfaction survey suggested that the accolade was deserved. Education and English produced particularly good scores and Winchester bucked the national trend with an increase in applications of almost 5 per cent at the start of 2006.

The new university traces its history as an Anglican foundation back to 1840 and has occupied its King Alfred campus since 1862. The compact site is on a wooded hillside overlooking the cathedral city of Winchester, ten minutes walk away, and with views of the surrounding country-side. A second centre, which opened in 2003, occupies a large 18th-century rectory and concentrates on lifelong learning. It offers foundation degrees in community and performing arts, cultural studies, education and social sciences.

Known as King Alfred's College until 2004, the university is still best-known for teacher training, which accounts for about a third of the places. It is one of the largest providers of primary school training in England, but courses on the main campus also span business, arts and social sciences. Degrees range from choreography and dance, through the creative industries, business, media and teacher training to ethics and spirituality. The later teaching quality assessments were excellent, with maximum scores in archaeology and education, and a near-miss in theology and religious studies. Winchester also outscored many of the former polytechnics in the last Research Assessment Exercise, when an impressive 40 per cent of the academics were entered and both history and theology reached the fifth of the seven categories.

The university is particularly proud of its low dropout rate. At 11 per cent, the last official projection was below the national average for the subjects and entry grades, but the university puts the actual figure lower still. Almost all the British students are state-educated and 30 per cent are from working-class homes. Male undergraduates are heavily outnumbered and there are about 150 overseas students from a range of countries. Winchester students can take advantage of exchange schemes with American universities in Maine, Oregon and Wisconsin.

The main campus is well equipped, with its own theatre, sports hall and

West Hill, Winchester
Hampshire SO22 4NR
01962 841515
course.enquiries@
winchester.ac.uk
www.winchester.ac.uk
www.winchester
students.co.uk

Edinburgh
Belfast
Cardiff London
WINCHESTER

The Times Rankings
Overall Ranking: 62

Student satisfaction:	=12	(15.4)
Research assessment:	=76	(2.5)
Entry standards:	63	(264.4)
Student–staff ratio:	91	(21.9)
Library/IT spend/student:	77	(£476)
Facilities spend/student:	77	(£164)
Good honours:	=49	(59.2%)
Graduate prospects:	104	(48.3%)
Expected completion rate:	=41	(86.7%)

fitness suite. Outdoor pitches and a modern sports pavilion are not far away. A four-storey University Centre, costing £9 million, will open in 2007. It will transform the students' union, adding a nightclub, cinema, catering facilities, a bookshop and a supermarket. An award-winning extension to the library made room for 200,000 books, 450 study spaces and 150 computers.

A £12-million student village provides nearly 1,000 residential places – enough to guarantee accommodation for all first years, as well as those from overseas. Like most of the newest universities, Winchester makes a virtue of its small size. Professor Joy Carter, the new vice-chancellor, will be anxious not to endanger this in the process of capitalising on the institution's enhanced status. Students value the close-knit atmosphere and find the city livelier than its staid image might suggest, with a number of bars catering to their tastes. London is only an hour away by train and Southampton less than half that for those who hanker after the attractions of a bigger city.

Bursaries and Scholarships

In receipt of full Maintenance Grant	£800
In receipt of partial Maintenance Grant	£400
Partner colleges	Scholarship

- Tuition fees (2006) £3,000
- Winchester Scholarship: maintenance award to all full-time undergraduates: year 1 £200; year 2, £300; year 3, £400; year 4 (if on 4-year course), £400.
- Winchester Teacher Education Scholarship: a bursary of £1,800 for those in year 4 of their teaching course.
- Winchester Partnership Colleges Scholarships: £100 for those students who come from a University of Winchester Partnership College.
- Winchester Compact Scholarships: £200 for those students who are compact applicants to the University of Winchester.
- King Alfred Scholarship of £2,000 is available to students from social care institutions.
- 37% of additional fee income to be earmarked for bursaries.
- Eligibility for bursaries will be assessed using UUK/SLC model bursary scheme (HEBSS).

Contact: www.winchester.ac.uk/

Students

Undergraduates:	3,315	(1,115)
Postgraduates:	110	(1,095)
Mature students:	16.5%	
Overseas students:	1.3%	
Applications per place:	3.8	
From state-sector schools:	97.6%	
From working-class homes:	30.1%	

For detailed information about fees, grants and bursaries and how they work, see chapter 7.

Accommodation

Number of places and costs refer to 2005–06
University-provided places: 956
Percentage catered: 21%
Catered costs: £96.39 a week (30 weeks).
Self-catered costs: £72.87–£84.91 a week (40 weeks).
First years are guaranteed accommodation if conditions are met.
International fee-paying students are guaranteed places provided conditions are met.
Contact: housing@winchester.ac.uk

University of Wolverhampton

Wolverhampton is the only university in Britain where a majority of undergraduates come from the three poorest socio-economic groups. This represents twice the proportion at some new universities and almost five times that at Oxford and Cambridge. Almost all the students are from state schools and more than a quarter come from areas of low participation in higher education. The figures accurately reflect the priority the university gives to extending access to higher education. The latest drop-out rate has been estimated at 15 per cent, but this has not prevented the university being awarded a national teaching centre focusing on retention, progression and achievement in a diverse student body.

Almost a quarter of the 23,000 students are from ethnic minorities, and more than a third live with their parents. More than half of the students come from the region. With roots in the 19th-century arts, crafts and technical colleges, Wolverhampton naturally leans towards vocational courses. The university pioneered the high street "higher education shop" and more recently, a dedicated Student Finance Support Unit and Student Gateway Service, bringing all student support together in one convenient location. Big outreach programmes take courses into the workplace. The four campuses each have their own learning centres and are linked by a free bus service. Two are in the city, but sport and performance are based in Walsall. The original site is in the heart of the city centre, with the Wolves football ground nearby. A purpose-built campus in Telford focuses on business and engineering for a county with no higher education institution of its own.

The university is in the midst of a multimillion-pound infrastructure investment programme known as "New Horizons", which is due to be completed by 2008. The first phase of the project saw the completion of the £26-million development of the City Campus, including the flagship Millennium City Building and extension of the Harrison Learning Centre. The former, now housing some 1,300 students and 200 staff, includes over 10,000 square metres of new teaching space, incorporating a 300-seat lecture theatre, dedicated psychology labs, social learning space, cyber café, exhibition hall and refectory. A Lottery-supported sports hall offering elite training facilities for judo, a Sports Science and Medicine Centre and a 350-bed student village have opened on the Walsall campus. A new technology centre opened at Wolverhampton in 2005, with more than 600 computers and specialist IT, engineering, design and media facilities. At Telford a

---

Wulfruna Street,
Wolverhampton WV1 1SB
01902 321000
admissions@wlv.ac.uk
www.wlv.ac.uk
www.wolvesunion.org

The Times Rankings
Overall Ranking: =99

Student satisfaction:	=53	(14.7)
Research assessment:	=92	(2.0)
Entry standards:	105	(199.5)
Student–staff ratio:	=94	(22.5)
Library/IT spend/student:	69	(£499)
Facilities spend/student:	=8	(£362)
Good honours:	85	(50.0%)
Graduate prospects:	=99	(50.9%)
Expected completion rate:	=98	(73.3%)

complementary development – the E-Innovation Centre – has also opened.

Teaching assessments improved after a poor start, with philosophy achieving a perfect score and business and education only one point behind. Teacher training courses are rated in the top four in the country by Ofsted and Wolverhampton academics have been awarded three National Teaching Fellowships by the Higher Education Academy.

Wolverhampton claims a number of firsts for its academic programmes, pioneering interactive multimedia communication degrees, as well as offering the only one in British sign language and one of the first in virtual reality design and manufacturing. It was the first university to be registered under the British Standard for the quality of its all-round provision. The university was also the first to open a student employment bureau with an online jobs vacancy service that has since been adopted by a number of other institutions.

Research ratings are among the lowest in the university system, however, with less than one academic in five entered for assessment and no subjects in the top two of the seven categories. History and Spanish achieved the best results in the last assessments.

Social facilities vary considerably between sites, although they are close enough for students to come together for big events. Wolverhampton claims the fastest growing nightlife in the UK, although the basis of comparison is unclear, but there is no doubt that the cost of living is reasonable. The art gallery was refurbished in 2000 and the cultural attractions of Birmingham are now only a metro tramride away.

Bursaries and Scholarships

In receipt of full Maintenance Grant	£300
In receipt of partial Maintenance Grant	
More than £300, so that the bursary plus the Maintenance Grant total £3,000	
Sport	Scholarship
Academic Achievement	Scholarship

- Tuition fees (2006) £3,000
- Placement year tuition fee is approximately £600.
- Regional fee discount scheme to be introduced giving a £1,000 discount on first year fees only to Aimhigher applicants from the region.
- For students in receipt of partial Maintenance Grant it is intended to bridge the gap between the Maintenance Grant and the tuition fee with a bursary.
- Scholarships up to £3,000 for pre-entry academic or sporting achievements.
- Eligibility for bursaries will be assessed using UUK/SLC model bursary scheme (HEBSS).

Contact: www.wlv.ac.uk/money4students

Students

Undergraduates:	12,510	(7,415)
Postgraduates:	1,100	(2,965)
Mature students:	27.4%	
Overseas students:	14.0%	
Applications per place:	4.2	
From state-sector schools:	98.9%	
From working-class homes:	48.5%	

For detailed information about fees, grants and bursaries and how they work, see chapter 7.

Accommodation

Number of places and costs refer to 2006–07
University-provided places: 2,048
Percentage catered: 0%
Self-catered accommodation: £2,024–£2,875 (a year).
First-year students are offered accommodation provided requirements are met. Residential restrictions apply.
International students: same as above.
Contact: residences@wlv.ac.uk

University of Worcester

Worcester has the most ambitious development plans of all the new universities created since the last edition of the *Guide*. It is spending £90 million on a second campus in the city centre and another £50 million on a unique library and history centre which will be the first joint public and university library in Britain. The aim is to cater for an additional 4,000 students over the next six years. Numbers expanded in each of the last five years before university status arrived and applications have been rising accordingly. Even with top-up fees in prospect in 2006, demand for places grew by another 8 per cent.

First as a post-war emergency teacher training college and later as a university college, the institution has always been the only provider of higher education in Hereford and Worcester. The university remains strong in education and also in nursing and midwifery – a mix that explains an overwhelmingly female student population. Jacqui Smith, the Schools Minister, trained as a teacher there. But the six academic departments include applied sciences, geography and archaeology, a business school and arts, humanities and social sciences. Degrees range from animal biology to sports coaching and computing.

Education secured the best scores in an otherwise sound but unspectacular set of teaching assessments. Research grades were less impressive, although there are pockets of excellence such as the National Pollen and Aerobiology Research Unit, which produces all Britain's pollen forecasts. The first national student satisfaction survey was generally complimentary, with sports science returning the best results. Over 40 per cent of the undergraduates come from working-class homes, well above the national average for the university's subjects and entry grades. However, the projected dropout rate of 18 per cent is also higher than the national benchmark for the subject mix.

The existing campus occupies a parkland site ten minutes walk from the city centre. Recent improvements have included a £1-million digital arts centre and drama studio, and there is a well-appointed sports centre, which also provides employment opportunities for students. Sport plays an important part in university life: competitive teams are successful and the facilities for casual participants are extensive. A mobile 3-D motion analysis laboratory has been used by the England Cricket Board. Sports scholarships are offered in partnership with Worcestershire County Cricket Club and Worcester Wolves Basketball Club.

Henwick Grove
Worcester WR2 6AJ
01905 855000
admissions@worc.ac.uk
www.worcester.ac.uk
www.worcsu.com

The Times Rankings
Overall Ranking: 82

Teaching assessment:	=17	(15.3)
Research assessment:	106	(1.4)
Entry standards:	85	(233.1)
Student–staff ratio:	85	(20.9)
Library/IT spend/student:	107	(£355)
Facilities spend/student:	54	(£216)
Good honours:	=106	(41.8%)
Graduate prospects:	73	(59.4%)
Expected completion rate:	=67	(81.6%)

The new campus, which is being developed with the aid of a £10-million Government grant in conjunction with the regional development authority on the site of the old Worcester Royal Infirmary, is due to open in 2008. It will include teaching, residential and conference facilities, as well as the new library and learning centre. There are also a number of partner colleges around the region offering university courses.

The current campus contains three halls of residence with a total of around 575 rooms, most of which are allocated to first-years. Social life revolves around the students' union, which also has a "job pod" to help members find work experience and part-time jobs. The cathedral city is not large, but is safer than many university locations and has its share of pubs and clubs that cater for a growing student clientele.

Bursaries and Scholarships

In receipt of full Maintenance Grant	£700
In receipt of partial Maintenance Grant	£700
Sport	Scholarship
Academic Achievement	Scholarship

- Tuition fees (2006) £3,000
- All eligible UK and EU students liable to pay the £3,000 fee will be receive a non-repayable Special Support Bursary of £500 a year.
- 50 scholarships of £1,000 will be awarded to students after their first year of study to reward academic achievement.

Contact: www.worcester.ac.uk/finance

Students

Undergraduates:	3,410	(2,750)
Postgraduates:	370	(1,025)
Mature students:	27.7%	
Overseas students:	5.0%	
Applications per place:	4.0	
From state-sector schools:	95.0%	
From working-class homes:	40.5%	

For detailed information about fees, grants and bursaries and how they work, see chapter 7.

Accommodation

Number of places and costs refer to 2006–07
University-provided places: 575
Percentage catered: 0%
Self-catered costs: £50–£75 a week
All first-year students are accommodated.
International students are accommodated provided requirements are met.
Contact: www.worcester.ac.uk/cms/
template.cfm?name=accommodation

University of York

York is another university to have demonstrated in successive *Times* rankings and academic assessments that comparative youth is no bar to excellence. No university had a better record for teaching quality. Of the subjects assessed after 1995 half – archaeology, economics, education, electrical and electronic engineering, biosciences, philosophy, physics, politics and psychology – achieved perfect scores. The university is increas-ingly recognised as a permanent fixture in the top rank of British higher education.

Like Warwick, a contemporary that has been running neck and neck in the *Times* ranking, York has chosen its subjects carefully. There are still only 10,000 students, with no veterinary science, dentistry or law. This will change if the university is able to develop the nearby Heslington East site, which will make room for 50 per cent more students and a new range of subjects. These may include business, finance and law, and a new department of theatre, film and television.

The existing subjects are offered in a variety of unusual combinations, many including a language component. Among the more recent additions have been nursing and midwifery, which grew out of the incorporation of the former North Yorkshire College of Health Studies. Since 2003, there has also been a medical degree, which saw applications grow by 50 per cent in the first year and another 20 per cent at the start of 2005. A joint initiative with Hull, the school will have a strong focus on learning in community settings.

Successive increases in the demand for undergraduate places came to at least a temporary halt at the start of 2006 with the introduction of top-up fees, when there was a 5 per cent drop. However, there are nine applications to each place in most subjects, so entrance requirements are still high. Although nearly eight out of ten undergraduates are state educated, less than 17 per cent come from working-class homes. The 5 per cent dropout rate is among the lowest in Britain. The proportion of local students may rise with the establishment of the Higher York programme, linking the university with the city's further and higher education colleges.

Unlike most universities, York concentrated on science and technology in expanding its entry during the 1990s, balancing an initial bias towards the arts and social sciences. The university won a Queen's Anniversary Prize for its work in computer science, which is rated internationally outstanding for research as well as excellent for teaching and was among the top performers in the first national student satisfaction survey.

Heslington,
York YO10 5DD
01904 433533
admissions@york.ac.uk
www.york.ac.uk
www.yusu.org

The Times Rankings
Overall Ranking: 15

Student satisfaction:	=8	(15.5)
Research assessment:	=7	(5.8)
Entry standards:	7	(435.9)
Student–staff ratio:	=24	(15.8)
Library/IT spend/student:	28	(£653)
Facilities spend/student:	62	(£199)
Good honours:	19	(69.9%)
Graduate prospects:	41	(66.0%)
Expected completion rate:	=10	(95.1%)

Psychology and English were the other starred research departments in the last assessments, which placed 84 per cent of the academics in the top two of seven categories, while physics produced the best results in the satisfaction survey.

Since 1990, York has been reviewing its courses every three years and external audits have also been complimentary. Every student has a supervisor responsible for their academic and personal welfare. Existing courses include language and computer literacy training, and the programme has expanded to include courses on personal effectiveness, financial management, active citizenship and introduction to accounting. The business community is involved at every level. Undergraduates can also take the "York Award", comprising a range of courses, work placements and voluntary activities which aim to prepare students for the world of work. Over 400 students work as volunteer teaching assistants in local schools.

The university is set in 200 acres of parkland, a mile outside the picturesque city centre. Students join one of seven colleges, which mix academic and social roles. Most departments have their headquarters in one of the colleges, but the student community is a deliberate mixture of disciplines, years and sexes. Nursing apart, only archaeology and medieval studies are located off campus, sharing a medieval building in the centre of the city.

Social life on campus is lively. There are two newspapers, television and radio stations, as well as several magazines, to keep students abreast of campus issues. Sports facilities are good, and have been improved further with the opening of a new sports pavilion. Playing fields are on campus and the River Ouse fosters a strong rowing tradition. Cultural events abound in the city, which is also famous for a high concentration of pubs. The club scene has improved, but students still head for Leeds for the top names.

Bursaries and Scholarships

In receipt of full Maintenance Grant	£1,400
In receipt of partial Maintenance Grant	£600–£1,000

- Tuition fees (2006) £3,000
- Placement year and year abroad tuition fee will be 50% of the standard, non-variable tuition fee – around £600.
- Bursaries available to Home students from England, Scotland and Northern Ireland and Wales. EU students are not eligible.
- Bursaries for the Hull-York Medical School are under consideration.
- 19% of additional fee income to be earmarked for bursaries.

Contact: www.york.ac.uk/studentmoney/

Students

Undergraduates:	7,090	(1,390)
Postgraduates:	2,450	(1,460)
Mature students:	10.2%	
Overseas students:	9.8%	
Applications per place:	9.0	
From state-sector schools:	78.7%	
From working-class homes:	16.6%	

For detailed information about fees, grants and bursaries and how they work, see chapter 7.

Accommodation

Number of places and costs refer to 2006–07
University-provided places: 3,830
Percentage catered: 0%
Self-catered costs: £61.39–£80.92 a week.
First-year single undergraduates are provided with accommodation if terms and conditions are met.
International students: as above for non-EU students.
Contact: accommodation@york.ac.uk
www.york.ac.uk/admin/accom

12 University Cities

One glance at their glossy prospectuses shows that universities today are well aware that students look almost as carefully at their future surroundings as at their chosen courses. Those set in rolling countryside, or a lively city, flaunt their advantages. The lecture room and library are only part of the story, and students are not going to achieve peak performance if they are tied for three or four years to a place they do not like. These pages offer a brief guide to the main student centres. All have at least two universities.

Fashions change quickly among students, and a popular city can soon lose its attractions. London, for example, used to be a magnet for students, but some of the capital's universities have struggled to fill their places recently because of the high cost of living. Manchester, by contrast, with its student community of nearly 70,000, has become a popular draw while Newcastle is also challenging for the position of the students' favourite city.

Cost of living variations between cities tend to be the result of differences in the cost of services, including accommodation, transport and entertainment, rather than differences in the price of goods in shops which tend to be similar across the UK. The weekly magazine *The Grocer* (www.thegrocer.co.uk/) produces "The Grocer 33", a weekly shopping basket survey that provides price information throughout eight regions across the country. It tracks price variations on 33 staple foods across the major supermarket chains within the regions. And it shows that, in the supermarkets at least, food prices are not subject to significant regional variation.

See pages 180–1 for some information on the level of crime in major university cities.

The following pages profile:

Aberdeen	Glasgow
Bath	Leeds
Belfast	Leicester
Birmingham	Liverpool
Brighton	London
Bristol	Manchester
Cambridge	Newcastle
Canterbury	Nottingham
Cardiff	Oxford
Coventry	Sheffield
Dundee	Southampton
Edinburgh	

Aberdeen

Known as the Granite City, Aberdeen is Scotland's third largest city and home to Scotland's third oldest university, yet it is still compact enough to get around on foot. The city is close to the Grampian Mountains and beautiful beaches, as well as being a bustling social and commercial centre. The expansion of oil-related industries in the 1980s pushed up living costs, but the low local rate of unemployment means that part-time jobs are a real possibility for students. Social life tends to be focused on the existing student facilities, to which all students have access. The Hub, a new student centre, opens on the King's College campus at Aberdeen University in September 2006.

Getting Around

Local bus services are plentiful and student passes are available. However, short distances mean that walking or cycling are reliable alternatives. Aberdeen is 490 miles from London. Direct rail services link Aberdeen and London, including a sleeper service. The journey takes around 8 hours. Aberdeen is served by its own airport (Dyce).

Attractions for Students

Sport: Sports enthusiasts are well catered for with swimming pools, the largest bowling alley in Scotland, 11 golf courses and a Premier League football team. The hinterland offers opportunities for skiing, sailing, windsurfing, hill climbing, canoeing and most other outdoor activities.

Culture and nightlife: There are three cinemas showing all the usual latest releases. His Majesty's Theatre plays host to drama, ballet, opera and musicals whilst the Aberdeen Arts Centre, the Music Hall and the Exhibition and Conference Centre are the venues for other major musical events. The Lemon Tree and the Beach Ballroom cater for the student market. There is an enviable selection of eating establishments, pubs and clubs. The City Art Gallery has an excellent collection of fine and applied art, and the Arts Centre has a small gallery for contemporary arts and crafts. The Maritime Museum, Marischal Museum, Provost Skene's House and Stratosphere hands-on science museum are all worth a visit.

Shopping: The most recently completed indoor shopping centre is the Academy, with a range of bars, cafés and specialist shopping.

Population: 212,000
Student population: 17,000

Proximity to the city centre:
University of Aberdeen: King's College about 1 mile north of the city, Aberdeen Royal Infirmary is a 10-minute journey by bus.
The Robert Gordon University: based at Garthdee, about 2 miles south of the city, with a smaller site in the city centre.

For more information:
Aberdeen Visitor Information Centre
23 Union Street
Aberdeen AB11 5BP
01224 288828

Aberdeen.information@visitscotland.com
www.visitscotland.com
www.aberdeencity.gov.uk
www.aberdeen-grampian.com

Bath

With natural hot springs and Georgian architecture, Bath is a small, but beautiful city. It has been designated a World Heritage Site by UNESCO and includes the newly-opened Thermae Bath Spa. The universities lie to the east and west of the city. Bath has a cosmopolitan atmosphere and there is plenty on offer to students; however, many find a lively alternative to the nightlife in Bristol, just nine miles away.

Getting Around

There is a reliable network of buses. The city boundaries are made up of walkways and cycle paths, which are pleasant and user friendly. The River Avon runs through the centre of Bath and it is possible to hire punts and canoes from the Victorian Boating Station 10 minutes from the city centre. Bristol International Airport is 21 miles away and an express coach service connects it to Bristol Temple Meads train station. There are frequent rail services from Bath to London taking around 1 hour 30 minutes.

Attractions for Students

Sport: Bath Rugby Club is considered one of the finest in the world; its grounds are near Pulteney Bridge. Cricket is played close to the city centre. Bath City Football Club is located south of the river. There are 10 golf courses in the local area and the University Sports Training Village has a 50-metre pool. Walking, cycling and tennis are all popular.

Culture and Nightlife: Bath is steeped in history and has a range of museums from the American Museum to the Jane Austen Centre. The main art gallery is the Victoria, with various exhibitions as well as its own collection. The Theatre Royal hosts big-name productions; a more alternative selection is at the Ustinov Studio and the Rondo. There is a multi-screen cinema, the ABC; independent films show at the Little Theatre Cinema. Bath has a bustling nightlife with over 150 restaurants and pubs, bars and a good standard of live entertainment. Moles on George Street is a renowned venue for gigs and quality club nights while the Comedy Cavern in the same area has a national reputation. Bath hosts an International Music Festival in early summer.

Shopping: Pulteney Bridge unusually has shops built into its structure. Independent craft can be found on Walcot and Broad Streets. Southgate and Stall Street make up the bulk of the shopping area with familiar names, while Milsom Street houses the famous department store, Jolly's. Try Shire's Yard for designer wear.

Population: 84,000
Student Population: 11,000

Proximity to city centre:
University of Bath: main campus 1 mile from the centre.
Bath Spa University: the main Newton Park campus 4 miles from the centre.

For more information:
Bath Tourist Information Centre
Abbey Chambers
Abbey Church Yard
Bath BA1 1LY
01225 477228

tourism@bathtourism.co.uk
www.visitbath.co.uk
www.bath.co.uk
www.itchybath.co.uk

Belfast

Belfast is Northern Ireland's largest city, and both the cultural and political capital. Recently, the peace process has stimulated applications from the mainland. Queen's campus is within Belfast's Golden Mile of pubs, clubs, café bars, restaurants and entertainment venues. Student life tends to concentrate here, for the Golden Mile provides part-time jobs as well as recreation.

Getting Around
There is a reliable and reasonably priced integrated bus and rail network run by Trans-link. Travel cards are available. Cycling is possible but the weather puts many off. Ferry services operate out of Belfast and Larne. Flights to London take about 1 hour. There are flights from Belfast International and City Airport to many major centres. Both airports operate regular bus transfers to the city centre. Cross-border train services run from Belfast to Dublin and back up to 8 times daily.

Attractions for Students
Sport: Belfast Giants ice hockey team is based in the Odyssey Arena. Ulster rugby is played at Ravenhill Stadium. There are 11 golf courses and centres within the city boundary. The Millennium National Cycling Network, incorporating a newly completed 20-mile route in the greater Belfast area, serves cycling enthusiasts. Ten-pin bowling is offered at two venues and the Dundonald International Ice Bowl is one of Northern Ireland's principal leisure and entertainment facilities with an Olympic-size ice rink. There are five leisure centres within Belfast with pools. The Belfast City Marathon in May is a major sporting event.

Culture and nightlife: Belfast has over 400 bars and restaurants and many theatres, galleries and cinemas. Major concerts are staged at the Waterfront Hall and the Odyssey. Clubs and live music are part of the scene, whether impromptu folk music sessions in the pubs or big name concerts at the Queen's Union. Odyssey (the £100-million Landmark Millennium Project) features Ireland's largest all-seater indoor venue, the Arena; W5, Ireland's interactive discovery centre; the Pavilion, a develop-ment of restaurants, bars, nightclubs and the Sheridan Imax. The free monthly *Whatabout? Guide* details entertainment in the city. In October, Queen's hosts Ireland's largest arts festival.

Shopping: High street names and designer labels are amply represented. Go to Lisburn Road for designer names and Donegall Pass is the antiques sector. Northern Irish crafts are also on offer in abundance.

Population: 297,300
Student population: 33,000

Proximity to the city centre:
Queen's University: main campus, a half mile south
University of Ulster: only about 850 of the student population are based in Belfast, but many of those who study at Jordanstown (7 miles) live in the city

For more information:
Belfast Welcome Centre
47 Donegall Place
Belfast BT1 5AD
028-9024 6609

info@belfastvisitor.com
www.gotobelfast.com
www.belfast.net
www.belfastcity.gov.uk

Birmingham

Massive investment and bold cultural initiatives have transformed the cityscape and underpinned Birmingham's flowering as a major European city. The brutalism of 1960s town planning is giving way to new skyscraper hotels, pedestrianised squares and rejuvenated historic areas. Among the most recent developments are The Water's Edge at Brindleyplace, the Mailbox and Millennium Point, the region's landmark project. The Bullring complex is home to five retail markets. A further £5-billion investment is planned and Birmingham aims to continue its transformation as a vibrant, dynamic modern city.

Getting Around
Birmingham is at the centre of the UK motorway system, and is connected to 500 destinations via the national coach network. Rail links are excellent and a journey to London takes 1 hour 30 minutes. Birmingham International Airport, 8 miles from the city centre, is a major hub with destinations throughout the UK, Europe, North America and Asia. Buses, trains and trams provide a comprehensive network of local transport.

Attractions for Students
Sport: The National Indoor Arena hosts many national sporting events. There are Premiership and Championship football teams, and Test and County cricket is played at Edgbaston. Ten-pin bowling, golf, go-carting, ice-skating, squash, tennis and swimming are all on offer.

Culture and nightlife: Birmingham has one of the liveliest club scenes in the country as well as bars, music venues and restaurants, including over 50 different restaurants within the famous 'Balti Triangle'. Birmingham Royal Ballet is based at the Hippodrome, whilst Symphony Hall is the home of the City of Birmingham Symphony Orchestra. There are numerous theatres and galleries including Star City, a new leisure complex housing a 30-screen cinema. The Waterhall Gallery of Modern Art is Birmingham's newest venue for contemporary art, with the stylish Ikon Gallery displaying the best of international and British art. Birmingham Museum and Art Gallery is famous for its collection of Pre-Raphaelite works. The National Exhibition Centre stages major exhibitions and pop concerts.

Shopping: Usual high street stores and many designer shops can been found in the city centre. Students may prefer browsing in the Victorian arcades. The markets are good. More exclusive boutique shopping is found at the Mailbox with Harvey Nicholls and many designer labels. There are more than 500 jewellery businesses in the Jewellery Quarter.

Population: 977,000
Student population: 42,000

Proximity to the city centre:
Aston University: campus a 10-minute walk
Birmingham University: campus 3 miles southwest at Edgbaston
UCE Birmingham: 9 sites; the main site is at Perry Barr, 3 miles north

For more information:
Marketing Birmingham
Millennium Point, Level L2
Curzon Street, Birmingham B4 7XG
0121-202 5116 (fax)

info@marketingbirmingham.com
www.birmingham.org.uk
www.birmingham.gov.uk
www.itchybirmingham.co.uk
http://icbirmingham.icnetwork.co.uk

Brighton

Located 50 miles south of the capital, the overwhelming majority of Brighton's students come from the London area, contributing to its reputation as "London by the Sea". The similarity to the capital manifests itself not only in Brighton's variety and vitality, helped by large numbers of international students, but also in high prices and frenetic pace. Relaxed places, such as the North Laine, do exist, if you know where to look for them. The variety of nightlife in the city means that Brighton's students' unions are less well used than those at other universities, but they do benefit from easy accessibility compared with those in the city centre.

Getting Around

Brighton is compact and easy to get around on foot. Bus services are plentiful and there is a flat rate fare in the central area. There is a network of cycle lanes. Car parking is at a premium but there is a park-and-ride system. Trains to London take 50 minutes. London Gatwick Airport is 25 miles away with international links.

Attractions for Students

Sport: The Brighton Bears basketball team is based at the Brighton Centre; Brighton and Hove Albion plays football at Withdean Stadium and Sussex County Cricket Club has its ground in the area.

The marina contains a leisure complex with a health club and bowling alley. The city has 2 golf courses, 3 swimming pools, 24 cricket pitches, more than 60 tennis courts and around 70 football pitches.

Culture and nightlife: The city has 19 cinema screens, and 5 major theatres. The Brighton Centre plays host to the large pop and rock tours, whilst the Dome is home to the Brighton Philharmonic Orchestra. There are 10 museums. The Royal Pavilion epitomises Regency Brighton. The Victorian Brighton Pier is packed with traditional seaside amusements. The new-look Beachfront area buzzes with bars, cafés, clubs, basketball and volleyball, artists' and fishing quarters. England's largest arts extravaganza, the Brighton Festival, is in May and the London to Brighton Veteran Car Run takes place in November. Arguably the clubbing capital of the south coast, Brighton attracts big name DJs from all over the country.

Shopping: North Laine with its Saturday flea market is popular with students, while the Lanes provides trendy and expensive shops. Churchill Square has all the High Street favourites under one roof. The Marina contains a factory outlet-shopping village.

Population: 248,000
Student population: 31,000

Proximity to the city centre:
University of Brighton: 1 site in Eastbourne and 3 in and around Brighton
University of Sussex: about 4 miles northeast in Falmer

For more information:
Brighton Visitor Information Centre
10 Bartholomew Square
Brighton BN1 1JS
0906-711 2255 (calls cost 50p a minute)

brighton-tourism@brighton-hove.gov.uk
www.visitbrighton.com
www.brighton-hove.gov.uk
www.itchybrighton.co.uk

Bristol

The largest city in southwest England, Bristol is perennially popular as a student destination. It has benefited from National Lottery funding and other grants to finance major regeneration projects and the city now buzzes with activity at the waterfront bars, restaurants, museums and art galleries. The thriving local economy means high prices and generally expensive accommodation. Bristol is on the whole welcoming to students although pubs in the city centre tend to be more segregated.

Getting Around

Travel by car is not easy with parking both difficult and expensive. However, several park-and-rides in the city offer a cheaper alternative. Walking and cycling are preferable and the cycle tracks are good. There is an extensive and reasonably priced bus network. Travel cards are available. The Studentlink bus service operates during the week. London is 1 hour 30 minutes away by train. National Express operates coach links to many UK destinations. Bristol International Airport now serves many destinations. Bristol's waterfront attractions are served by ferry services.

Attractions for Students

Sport: Bristol has two football clubs, City and Rovers, and Gloucestershire County Cricket Club. Tennis, swimming, ice-skating, golf, rowing and sailing are all available. Bristol Climbing Centre offers indoor climbing while the Avon Gorge is a popular venue for outdoor climbing.

Culture and nightlife: The city is well provided with cinemas, both multiscreens and independents, plus an IMAX. The Bristol Old Vic theatre company is based at the Theatre Royal, whilst the Hippodrome is the venue for musicals, ballet and opera. The Colston Hall is host to comedy, rock, pop and orchestral concerts and exhibitions. The Arnolfini and the Harbourside Watershed Media Centre offer lively programmes of exhibitions, films and theatre. At-Bristol includes three interactive and hands-on attractions. The British Empire and Commonwealth Museum opened in 2002. Bristol has an excellent range of pubs and clubs from the traditional to stylish late night bars. A vibrant scene can be found at the Harbourside, Corn Street and Whiteladies Road.

Shopping: Broadmead (currently being expanded), the Mall Galleries and the Mall at Cribbs Causeway have all the high street names. Park Street is useful for music and second-hand clothing. Clifton Village has many specialist shops, but can be expensive. St Nicholas Markets, established in 1743, has stalls selling a range of food, second-hand books, old clothes, CDs and a range of unusual goods.

Population: 381,000
Student population: 34,000

Proximity to the city centre:
University of Bristol: campus in Cotham area, close to the city centre
University of the West of England at Bristol: 5 campuses; the main purpose-built Frenchay Campus lies about 4 miles north

For more information:
Destination Bristol
53 Queen Square
Bristol BS1 4LH
0906-7112 191 (calls cost 50p a minute)

ticharbourside@destinationbristol.co.uk
www.visitbristol.co.uk
www.venue.co.uk
www.itchybristol.co.uk

Cambridge

Cambridge is a town-sized city easy to navigate on foot or bike and students and tourists throng its streets. The city has also become the centre of the hi-tech "Silicon Fen" industries. Despite the bustle, the atmosphere in a small city of such beauty can feel cloistered or even stifling, especially to those from larger and livelier places. The gulf between new and old universities is nowhere wider than in Cambridge. Nonetheless, the two universities' students do mix, and those at Anglia enjoy access to a wide range of social events, which is fortunate because the university rather than the town is the main host. Town–gown relations are generally good.

Getting Around

Walking and cycling are the most popular modes of transport as much of the city is flat and easily accessible. Buses are fairly reliable, but expensive. However, travel cards are available. Cars are not recommended in the centre. London is 60 miles away, and trains take about an hour. London Stansted International Airport is 30 minutes away by train.

Attractions for Students

Sport: For sports enthusiasts there are two football teams based in the city, Cambridge United and Cambridge City, and the usual range of football, cricket, climbing and swimming is available, although many sports facilities are based within the university.

Culture and nightlife: The Cambridge Corn Exchange is the largest arts and entertainment venue and hosts a full range of events. The Junction is popular for bands, dance and experimental theatre whilst the ADC Theatre is owned by a student society and managed by the university. The Arts Picture House shows foreign and cult classics and hosts the two-week Cambridge Film Festival in July. Cambridge has a good array of pubs but few clubs. The Strawberry Fair is held each June, and the Cambridge Folk Festival in July. The Fitzwilliam Museum offers free admission to its exhibitions of paintings and ceramics. Kettles Yard Gallery is very popular with those who enjoy modern art and sculpture. An excellent way to see the sights of Cambridge is to hire a punt, rowing boat or canoe and travel along The Backs at a leisurely pace or to go upriver to Grantchester. There are also daily walking tours of the City and University from the Visitor Information Centre, on Wheeler Street.

Shopping: Shopping is located in the market place, the Grafton Centre and Lion Yard City Centre shopping arcade.

Population: 109,000
Student population: 30,000

Proximity to the city centre:
Cambridge University: ancient buildings form the city centre
Anglia Ruskin: campus 10 minute walk; its other campus is 40 miles away in Chelmsford

For more information:
Visit Cambridge Visitor Information Centre
The Old Library
Wheeler Street
Cambridge CB2 3QB
0871 226 8006

www.visitcambridge.org
www.cambridge.gov.uk
www.itchycambridge.co.uk

Canterbury

Canterbury is a medieval walled city and the quaint streets, its cathedral and ruins such as St. Augustine's Abbey and the Church of St. Martin collectively form a UNESCO World Heritage Site. Located within easy distance of continental Europe, Canterbury's bustling, cosmopolitan atmosphere is popular with students. Whitstable and Herne Bay, where many students choose to live, are nearby. The Kent Downs to the south and the coastline of the east make very attractive surroundings.

Getting Around

Canterbury is pedestrian-friendly. Traffic is encouraged to stay out of the centre during the day and there is a cost-effective park-and-ride service. The city is ideal for cycling, with plenty of paths. Buses are reasonably priced and frequent, and they also provide services to Whitstable and Herne Bay. London is 55 miles away, taking 1 hour 30 minutes by train. The Eurostar to the Continent is easily accessible from Ashford International, with a train service from Canterbury West. Gatwick Airport is a 1-hour drive. A ferry from Dover to Calais takes about 1 hour 15 minutes.

Attractions for Students

Sport: Canterbury RFC won the Kent Cup in 2005 and is based at Merton Lane. Kent County Cricket Club plays on the St Lawrence ground. Walking and cycling are very popular, with many trails along the East Kent coastline. Badminton, tennis and squash are played throughout the city. Water sports are available at Whitstable.

Culture and Nightlife: The narrow streets are full of cafés and bars with a good selection for dining out. There are a number of clubs in the city, however, not all musical tastes are catered for. Canterbury museums range from a recreation of medieval England in the Canterbury Tales, to the underground Roman Museum at Longmarket. The Dane John Gardens, a Green Heritage Site, is a weekend concert venue with music from brass bands to rock. There are two main theatres: the Gulbenkian at the University of Kent, including Cinema 3, and the more traditional Marlowe Theatre. There are the usual walking tours and river punts as an alternative way to see the city.

Shopping: Canterbury has a good range of high-street shops and three department stores. Whitefriars Shopping Centre is a multimillion-pound development. Boutiques can be found on St. Dunstan's Street, the Borough, Palace Street and Northgate. There is a farmers' market six days a week.

Population: 135,000
Student Population: 28,000

Proximity to the city centre:
University of Kent: campus a short bus ride from the city centre
Canterbury Christ Church University: main campus in the city centre

For more information:
Canterbury Information Centre
12/13 Sun Street
The Buttermarket
Canterbury CT1 2HX
01227 378 100

canterburyinformation@canterbury.gov.uk
www.canterbury.co.uk
www.canterbury.gov.uk

Cardiff

There is much to be proud of in this prosperous and attractive city. It is bounded by an historic waterfront area on one side and beautiful countryside on the other, with good public transport links. Cardiff has all the cultural and commercial facilities one would expect in the home of the National Assembly for Wales, whilst the cost of living is lower than in most capital cities. Recent huge regeneration projects have resulted in the Cardiff Bay waterfront development (including The Pierhead) and the Millennium Stadium. This facelift has really put Cardiff on the map as a forward-looking, modern European city.

Getting Around

Within the city, public transport is efficient and reasonable. Most students use the bus service but cycling and walking are popular. The UWIC bus service links all the sites and the city. London is 154 miles away, and trains take under 2 hours. There are direct flights from Cardiff International Airport to a number of destinations.

Attractions for Students

Sport: Famous for rugby, the Millennium Stadium, the largest covered stadium in Europe, is the also venue for international football fixtures. Other sports catered for in the city include squash, ice-skating, golf, swimming and football.

Culture and nightlife: A range of cinemas and theatres includes the Chapter Arts Centre with two cinemas, three theatres, a visual arts centre plus café and bars. Cardiff has a vibrant nightlife with bars and pubs for all tastes. The city also hosts an annual Mardi Gras in September, now one of the biggest festivals of its kind in the UK. The magnificent Millennium Centre, a multipurpose cultural and entertainment venue, and the new home for the Welsh National Opera was completed in 2004. The Atlantic Wharf entertainment complex offers a 12-screen cinema, bowling alley, nightclub, bars and restaurant. Admission to the National Museum and Gallery, which houses the largest collection of impressionist painting in Europe outside of Paris, is free. St David's Hall is the national concert hall of Wales, and the BBC National Orchestra of Wales is based in Cardiff. Two comedy venues, Jongleurs and the Glee Club are also in the city.

Shopping: The Edwardian arcades of the Capitol Centre offer a variety of unusual shops and cafés. The main shopping areas are Queen Street and the St David's Centre with the full range of high street and designer names.

Population: 305,000
Student population: 25,000

Proximity to the city centre:
Cardiff University: buildings all round the city centre
Cardiff, University of Wales Institute: 4 main teaching campuses situated around the city centre

For more information:
Cardiff Visitor Centre
The Old Library, The Hayes
Cardiff CF10 1NE
029-2022 7281

visitor@thecardiffinitiative.co.uk
www.visitcardiff.info
www.cardiff.gov.uk
www.itchycardiff.co.uk

Coventry

A prosperous medieval town, modern Coventry's success was based on motor manufacture and engineering. Its current image is currently undergoing a major makeover. The Phoenix Initiative is a multimillion-pound scheme to revitalise one area of the city with a series of public squares and gardens alongside cafés, bars and shops. Town–gown relations are generally relaxed, and entertainment is in plentiful supply. Students from the two universities rarely cross paths. Warwick's tend to stay on campus and prefer Kenilworth and Leamington Spa for off-campus accommodation. Coventry's students make the most of the city centre, which complements their own sports centre and students' union.

Getting around

There is a good bus service with special student rates between the city and Warwick University. The area is good for cycling and walking. London is 86 miles away, and trains take 1 hour 15 minutes; Birmingham is less than 30 minutes away. Birmingham International Airport is 20 minutes by train. Coventry airport also provides passenger flights to many European destinations.

Attractions for students

Sport: Coventry City Football Club is now playing at the new Coventry Arena. This huge complex has a large concert facility, conference space and banqueting hall. Coventry Rugby Club has also moved to its new ground at the Butts Arena. Coventry Sports Centre includes a 50-meter Olympic standard pool. Speedway is available in the city and there is an ice rink.

Culture and nightlife: Cinema lovers are well catered for between the Odeon Cineplex, the Film Theatre, and the Showcase Cinema. The Belgrade Theatre offers musicals, pantomime and traditional theatre whilst the Warwick Arts Centre plays host to popular music, dance, classical concerts and opera. It is also home to the Mead Gallery, exhibiting paintings, art, sculpture, craft and photography. The Museum of British Road Transport holds the largest collection of British cars in the world. The Toy Museum and the Herbert Art Gallery and Museum are also worth a visit. The Cathedral quarter links old and new Coventry and has been revived with a range of pubs, cafés and restaurants. Spon Street houses reconstructed medieval buildings and the Heritage Museum.

Shopping: Coventry has a traditional indoor market. The West Orchards Shopping Centre houses all the usual high street names, whilst out-of-town shopping is provided at the Central Six Retail Park.

Population: 301,000
Student population: 26,000

Proximity to the city centre:
Coventry University: purpose-built campus in the city centre
University of Warwick: modern campus about 3 miles from the city centre

For more information:
Coventry Tourist Information Centre
4 Priory Row
Coventry CV1 5EX
024-7622 7264/6

tic@coventry.gov.uk
www.coventry.gov.uk
www.visitcoventry.co.uk

Dundee

Called the "City of Discovery", Dundee has been cleaned up and relaunched in recent years and enjoys a cost of living estimated at 12 per cent lower than the UK average. Jute and jam may have disappeared, but the city is still home to DC Thomson, publishers of the *Press and Journal*, *The Beano* and *The Dandy*. It certainly benefits from its location on the Firth of Tay, with the Highlands within easy reach for outdoor pursuits.

Getting around

There is a decent local public transport network. The Students' Association at the University of Dundee runs a free nightbus for students within the city boundary. The city is on the main East Coast route with direct services to Newcastle, York and London, 430 miles away, taking around 6 hours 30 minutes. Trains to Edinburgh and Glasgow each take about an hour. Dundee Airport has daily flights to London City Airport and a new service to Manchester. Major airports are at Aberdeen, Edinburgh and Glasgow.

Attractions for Students

Sport: Dundee is home to two SPL football clubs. Golfers are spoiled for choice. A running and cycling track is available at the Caird Park. Keen skiers and snowboarders have easy access to Scotland's slopes and Dundee is ideally placed for river fishing and canoeing enthusiasts. The Olympia Leisure Centre hosts a range of activities, including a climbing wall and leisure pool, while Dundee Ice Arena features an Olympic-size ice rink and is a venue for curling and ice hockey.

Culture and nightlife: The Dundee Contemporary Arts Centre is a popular venue for exhibitions, film and theatre. The Repertory Theatre, the Caird Hall, Marryat Hall complex and the Whitehall Theatre offer venues for concerts and dance. The Odeon Multiplex and UGC Cinemas boast 15 screens between them. Discovery Point is home to Scott of the Antarctic's vessel, *Discovery*, as well as the 19th-century frigate, *Unicorn*. The Verdant Works is a living museum depicting a working jute mill. The McManus Galleries host an exhibition of history, art and natural history, whilst the Barrack Street Museum's natural history exhibition includes a 40-foot whale skeleton. The Mills Observatory is the only full-time public observatory in the UK. "Sensation" brings science to life with interactive exhibits.

Shopping: Shopping is centred on the Wellgate and the recently revamped Overgate Centres. Cheap and cheerful furniture is often found at the Dens Road Market. City Quay factory outlets provide designer labels at cheap prices.

Population: 142,000
Student population: 12,000

Proximity to the city centre:
University of Dundee: main campus in city centre
University of Abertay: campus in city centre

For more information:
Visit Scotland Angus and Dundee
21 Castle Street
Dundee DD1 3AA
01382 527527

enquiries@angusanddundee.co.uk
www.visitscotland.com
www.dundeecity.gov.uk
www.angusanddundee.co.uk

Edinburgh

An elegant and cultured capital city, historic Edinburgh, visually spectacular, vibrant and cosmopolitan, is one of the most sought-after cities by students. Now the home of the Scottish Parliament, Edinburgh is enjoying a prosperous time. The compact city centre has an enviable range of pubs, bars and nightclubs, many with extended hours of opening. Students make up a good proportion of the population, and are generally welcomed. Areas such as Marchmont and the New Town are popular, but the city is expensive for accommodation. Shopping and entertainment costs are comparable with other major UK cities.

Getting Around

Edinburgh's seven hills make cycling hard work, but the city centre is easy to walk around. The local bus service is comprehensive. Bus lanes and cycle paths exist. Travel cards are available, though more expensive than in some cities. The National Express coach network links to many destinations. London is 373 miles away, and trains take 4 hours 30 minutes. Trains to Glasgow are frequent and the journey takes about 50 minutes. Edinburgh Airport is 6 miles west, providing national and international flights.

Attractions for Students

Sport: Murrayfield Stadium is home to Scottish Rugby Union and the city supports two football clubs, Hibs and Hearts, as well as an American football squad, ice hockey and basketball. There are three major golf courses, an Olympic-size swimming pool, a sports stadium and the largest artificial ski slope in Europe.

Culture and nightlife: Edinburgh offers six commercial cinemas and three independents. Theatres are plentiful. The world famous Edinburgh Festival takes place every August. The city is home to a wealth of art galleries, including the Queen's Gallery at Holyroodhouse, and museums as well as the Castle and botanical gardens. The recently developed dockland area of Leith is alive with bars, restaurants and clubs.

Shopping: Princes Street is the main shopping area in the city with most national chains as well as Edinburgh institutions, such as Jenners. George Street, Rose Street, the Grassmarket, the Royal Mile and the Stockbridge area of the city have more unusual shops. Ocean Terminal, a new shopping and leisure complex is situated on the waterfront at Leith.

Population: 450,000
Student Population: 37,000

Proximity to the city centre:
University of Edinburgh: in the centre, with science and engineering 2 miles south
Heriot-Watt University: campus 7 miles west of the city centre
Napier University: 2 miles south of the city centre

For more information:
VisitScotland
Ocean Point One, 94 Ocean Drive
Leith, Edinburgh EH6 6JH
0845-225 5121

info@visitscotland.com
www.edinburgh.org
www.edinburghguide.com
www.itchyedinburgh.co.uk

Glasgow

Glasgow is Scotland's largest city, and one of Britain's liveliest. Glasgow has campaigned vigorously and successfully to change its "mean city" image. Home of Charles Rennie Mackintosh and the Glasgow School of Art, it is Scotland's cultural capital. Scotland's opera, ballet and national orchestra are based in the city, which also boasts a profusion of art galleries, museums and theatres. Students find the locals generally very friendly. The three universities are within easy reach of one another and many students live in the attractive West End, though the area's desirability has led to an increase in prices over recent years.

Getting Around

There is a good cheap local bus service and a reliable underground. Few cycle because of the hills and heavy traffic. London is 392 miles away, and trains take 5 hours. Glasgow International Airport, 7 miles to the west of the city, receives national and international flights including transatlantic flights as well as budget flights. Coaches depart from Buchanan Street Bus Station to all major UK cities.

Attractions for Students

Sport: Two famous football clubs, Rangers and Celtic, are based in the city and the range of participative sports includes football, rugby, sailing and skiing on the city's two dry ski slopes. The Trossachs and Loch Lomond are within easy reach, and rail and ferry links make the nearby islands such as Arran and Bute accessible.

Culture and nightlife: Glasgow boasts a variety of theatres and performing and visual arts venues. Glaswegians are famously fond of their pubs, and the city's club scene rivals those of London and Manchester. Live music is very popular and numerous venues range from the SECC to the Barrowlands. The city is home to a great variety of classical music concerts, and has many cinemas, including four multiscreens and two independents. The Glasgow Science Centre features a Science Mall and an IMAX cinema. Glasgow's medieval roots can be explored in the Cathedral and Provand's Lordship. Glasgow has 35 museums and art galleries, including the famous Burrell Collection, most without an entry fee. The main Kelvingrove Museum reopens in 2006 after a major refurbishment.

Shopping: A plethora of designer shops in the Buchanan Galleries, Princes Square and the Merchant City cater for the label-conscious Glaswegian. The Barras street market offers variety for the cash-strapped student.

Population: 609,000
Student population: 45,000

Proximity to the city centre:
University of Glasgow: 3 miles from the centre in the West End
Glasgow Caledonian University: situated in the city centre
Strathclyde University: main campus in the city centre

For more information:
VisitScotland
Glasgow Information Centre
11 George Square, Glasgow G2 1DY
0141-204 4400

enquiries@seeglasgow.com
www.seeglasgow.com
www.glasgow.gov.uk
www.itchyglasgow.co.uk

Leeds

Leeds is a sophisticated commercial centre with more law and accountancy firms than anywhere outside London. The city itself is friendly and lively, and the cost of living is generally low. The two universities live and work together in the city centre, and there is much interchange between their students' unions. Students who live out also tend to live in the same area, making a compact student enclave. Property rental prices are low, helped by the surplus accommodation in the city.

Getting Around
Buses provide a cheap and efficient method of transport and a very reasonably priced student Metrocard is available. Cycling is possible, but unpopular because of the hills and heavy traffic. London is 190 miles away, and trains take 3 hours. Leeds-Bradford International Airport is 8 miles north.

Attractions for Students
Sport: Leeds United plays at Elland Road and two international sporting venues, Yorkshire County Cricket Club and Leeds Rugby League Club, are both located in Headingley. There are 160 tennis courts in the city's parks as well as pitches for rugby, football, cricket and hockey. The city has an Olympic-sized swimming pool and a skateboard park. The Yorkshire Dales, North Yorks Moors and the Vale of York are within easy reach of Leeds.

Culture and nightlife: Music lovers are well provided for with chamber music, jazz, classical and rock at live venues across the city. The gas-lit Hyde Park Picture House offers a unique cinema experience. The City Art Gallery houses the new Henry Moore Centre for the Study of Sculpture. The Abbey House Museum and the Royal Armouries are just two of Leeds' museums. There is a dazzling array of clubs. The recently developed Waterfront is now a dining quarter and restaurants, cafés and bars also surround the Millennium Square.

Shopping: Excellent shopping facilities exist in the Corn Exchange, Granary Wharf and the Victoria Quarter with Harvey Nicholls. Many designer shops and major retail outlets thrive in the heart of the city centre.

Population: 715,000
Student population: 38,000

Proximity to the city centre:
University of Leeds: compact redbrick campus a mile away
Leeds Metropolitan University: high-rise campus near the city centre; Beckett Park campus 3 miles away

For more information:
Gateway Yorkshire, Regional Travel and Tourism Centre, The Arcade,
Leeds City Station, Leeds LS1 1PL
0113-242 5242

tourinfo@leeds.gov.uk
www.leeds.gov.uk
www.leedsguide.co.uk
www.itchyleeds.co.uk

Leicester

Leicester is a compact and friendly place, rich in green spaces. Students find the city ideally sized and its central location means that it attracts students from all over the UK. Student social life tends to be spread evenly all over the city centre. A strong ethnic diversity has contributed to a cosmopolitan and cultured atmosphere and the strength of the local economy recently has resulted in much new development. Life in the city is inexpensive, and the fresh food market, the largest outdoor market in Europe, helps stretch tight student budgets. Accommodation is still not too hard to find and the rents are among the lowest in the country.

Getting Around
There is a good cheap bus service and travel cards are available. Leicester has miles of cycleways. London is 93 miles away, and trains take 1 hour 15 minutes. The nearest airports are Nottingham East Midlands (less than half an hour away) and Birmingham. Road links are good and Leicester is well served by the coach network.

Attractions for Students
Sport: Leicester has a selection of sports and leisure centres, including swimming, tennis, rugby, golf and squash. Leicester City Football Club, Leicestershire County Cricket Club and the Leicester Tigers Rugby Club are based here. Nearby Rutland Water is popular for a range of water sports.

Culture and nightlife: Leicester is bursting with bars, clubs, pubs and restaurants. The city attracts big name bands, DJs and classical music performances. Jazz can be found at the Y Theatre and new bands play at pubs such as the Charlotte. The Haymarket Theatre, the Phoenix Arts Complex and De Montfort Hall, which hosts major concerts, are the big venues. Leicester enjoys a number of annual festivals reflecting the city's cultural diversity, such as the Caribbean Carnival and the Diwali Festival of Light. The annual Comedy Festival is held in the city each February. The New Walk Museum, the Jewry Wall Museum, the Abbey Pumping Station and the National Space Centre are the main visitor attractions.

Shopping: The Shires and Haymarket shopping centres have all the usual high-street names. The arcades of St Martins Square, Silver Street and the Leicester Lanes offer more individuality in shopping. Belgrave Road, also known as the Golden Mile, offers jewellery shops and saris.

Population: 280,000
Student population: 30,000

Proximity to the city centre:
De Montfort University: one campus in the city centre, another nearby at Scraptoft
University of Leicester: campus about 1 mile away

For more information:
Leicester Tourist Information
7–9 Every Street
Town Hall Square
Leicester LE1 6AG
0906-294 1113 (calls cost 25p a minute)

info@goleicestershire.com
www.goleicestershire.com

Liverpool

Liverpool has always been a vibrant city and a centre of cultural wealth and diversity. The announcement that it is to be European Capital of Culture 2008 is already having a huge impact on the city and it is currently enjoying a period of investment and development with the help of funding from central Government and the EU. The Albert Dock development is evidence of great progress. Liverpool is a friendly and economical base for students, with excellent opportunities for part-time work and one of the lowest costs of living in the UK. Students tend to live and socialise around the central Smithdown Road area because of the cheap rents, but the Kensington area is also popular.

Getting Around

Merseyrail (the Metro) supplements an efficient bus service. JMU operates a free shuttle bus between its sites. Cycling is possible but not popular. London is 197 miles away, and trains take 3 hours. National Express coaches operate to many destinations. Flights from Liverpool Airport are expanding, and there are flights to many European cities. Manchester International Airport is less than an hour away for other destinations.

Attractions for Students

Sport: Home to both Liverpool and Everton Football Clubs, it also offers Rugby Union, golf, cricket, gymnastics and basketball. Rugby League teams such as St Helens, Widnes and Wigan play nearby. Water sports enthusiasts are catered for close to the Albert Docks and climbing is available at the Awesome Walls centre. Aintree Race Course, home of the Grand National, has a visitor centre.

Culture and nightlife: Liverpool has a reputation as a lively city and there are about 130 clubs and hundreds of bars and pubs. The city has many cinemas and numerous theatres including the Liverpool Empire and the Everyman. The Philharmonic Hall is the venue for classical concerts. National Museums Liverpool represents the eight museums and galleries in and around the city. Tate Liverpool is famous for its modern art exhibitions and the Maritime Museum gives an account of Liverpool's seafaring history. The Waterfront and the redeveloped Albert Dock with its shops, cafés and bars are popular as are the new Fact Centre art house cinema and multimedia gallery in the developing Ropeworks.

Shopping: As well as the usual high-street stores, Cavern Walks caters for those who like designer gear. St John's Centre and Bold Street are popular with bargain hunters.

Population: 439,000
Student population: 32,000

Proximity to the city centre:
University of Liverpool: modern campus in the city centre
Liverpool John Moores University: two main sites on opposite sides of the city centre
Liverpool Hope University: the main campus is at Hope Park, with another site at Everton.

For more information:
Liverpool Tourist Information Centre
Queen's Square Centre, Queen Square
Liverpool L1 1RG
0845-601 1125

info@visitliverpool.com
www.visitliverpool.com
www.itchyliverpool.co.uk
www.liverpool.gov.uk

London

London is by far the largest city in the UK and it has universities located both in the centre of the city, University College London and the University of Westminster, and well away from the centre, Kingston, Greenwich and Brunel. Check carefully the location of any London university that you are considering.

Whether you are interested in parks or pubs, theatres or cinemas, shopping or sightseeing, museums or art galleries, dancing non-stop throughout the weekend or eating every cuisine under the sun, London can meet your requirements. The city will also present you with a fairly hefty bill for most of the above, and for travel between them. That said, the diligent hunter will find bargains, but the temptation to spend is everywhere.

Whatever bargains can be found, accommodation will be a major expense for every student. Even if rents away from the smart areas of the city centre are slightly less astronomical, travel to and from college can easily eat away any savings made although efforts by ULU (the University of London's Students' Union) mean most students can get money off bus and underground fares. The capital city's hectic pace can overwhelm as easily as it excites, and loneliness can be a problem in a city where you might be living miles away from your college. Nevertheless,

London is justly renowned as one of the most exciting cities in the world and, for those who can strike a balance between making the most of life and avoiding spending their way to bankruptcy, it is the ideal place to be a student.

Getting Around

London is well served by an extensive bus, railway and underground network with special price deals available for students. In many areas the roads are very busy, making cycling a hazardous occupation. The main airports serving London are Heathrow, Gatwick, Stansted and Luton.

Attractions for Students

London is such a large city with so many attractions that a description of particular activities is not given. There are many guidebooks to London.

Population: 7.2 million
Student population: 306,000

Twelve separate universities. The University of London is a loose affiliation of almost 50 colleges and other institutions.

For more information:
www.london.gov.uk
www.londontown.com
www.timeout.com/london
www.londonnet.co.uk
www.londontheatre.co.uk
www.tate.org.uk/modern
www.tfl.gov.uk
www.itchylondon.co.uk
http://uk.visitlondon.com

Manchester

Manchester is a thriving, prosperous northern hub and considers itself the commercial and cultural capital of the North of England. The city is also probably the most fashionable student location in Britain. The success of the 2002 Commonwealth Games and the worldwide fascination with Manchester United Football Club enhance its reputation for glitz and glamour.

Getting Around
The city is well served by bus, train and tram, and the lack of hills means that cycling is a viable alternative. Road and rail links are good. Manchester is 184 miles from London, and trains take 2 hours 30 minutes. National Express coaches travel to many destinations. Manchester International Airport is 10 miles south of the city and has a full range of international flights.

Attractions for Students
Sport: Both Manchester United and Manchester City football clubs are based here, as well as the Lancashire County Cricket Club. There are extensive sporting facilities, including the National Cycling Centre and Manchester Aquatics Centre. It also has the country's largest martial arts club, and is home to the English Wrestling Association and the British Mountaineering Council.

Culture and nightlife: Manchester boasts over 400 pubs, clubs and café bars in the city centre, and many bands have originated on the Manchester scene. It also boasts one of the largest Chinatowns in Britain, a 'Curry Mile' in Rusholme, and a 'Gay Village' in the city centre. There are numerous cinemas including the Cornerhouse with its three screens, café and gallery. Manchester is home to the Royal Exchange Theatre Company, BBC Philharmonic Orchestra and the Hallé Orchestra, housed in the new Bridgewater Hall. The Lowry Centre, consisting of an arts centre and theatres, and the Imperial War Museum North are both on the waterside at Salford Quays.

Shopping: The compact city centre contains an extensive shopping area, a magnet for the region. As well as all the high-street stores, there are trendy designer shops and boutiques.

Population: 410,000
Student population: 68,000

Proximity to the city centre:
University of Manchester: city-centre campus
Manchester Metropolitan University: city-centre campus plus sites in south Manchester, Crewe and Alsager
University of Salford: campus in Salford, 1 mile from the city centre

For more information:
Manchester Visitor Centre, Town Hall Extension, Lloyd Street, Manchester M60 2LA
0871 222 8223

touristinformation@marketing-manchester.co.uk
www.visitmanchester.com
www.manchesteronline.co.uk
www.itchymanchester.co.uk

Newcastle

Newcastle is known as a very friendly, lively city. Students enjoy living in Newcastle with its vibrant nightlife, excellent shopping facilities and one of the lowest costs of living in the north. Bars and pubs in the city centre are cheap and welcoming to students at weekends and on special student nights. The addition of CCTV has made it a safer place after dark, as has the redevelopment of the Quayside area.

Getting Around

Newcastle's Metro connects the city centre with Gateshead, Sunderland, the coast, Newcastle Airport and the railway station. There is also a good bus network. London is 274 miles away, and trains take 3 hours. Newcastle Airport is 6 miles north of the city. There is a daily ferry from the International Ferry Terminal at North Shields (7 miles) to Amsterdam, and other services to Bergen and Gothenburg.

Attractions for Students

Sport: Newcastle United Football Club is based at St James's Park. Rugby, basketball and ice hockey are all played, and the Great North Run is hosted by Newcastle every year. Athletics are at Gateshead's International Stadium across the river. Newcastle is fully equipped with swimming pools, gyms and cycle paths.

Culture and nightlife: A commercial cinema with nine screens is at the Gate, with the independent Tyneside Cinema showing cult and art films. The Metro Radio Arena plays host to major music tours in addition to basketball and ice hockey. The City Hall, Journal Tyne Theatre and Foundation complement a range of smaller venues. Four theatres and five art galleries provide a range of cultural activities. The Discovery Museum is the largest museum complex in the region; the Centre for Life is a virtual reality journey through life. The Gateshead Millennium Bridge for pedestrians and cyclists now links the Quayside area, with its many pubs, clubs, restaurants and hotels, to Gateshead Quays and BALTIC, the Centre for Contemporary Art. Above the Quays, Norman Forster's SAGE Gateshead offers a wide range of musical events from jazz and world music to performances from the great orchestras. The Hoppings, a traditional fair, arrives on the Town Moor for ten days annually at the end of June. Many sites on Hadrian's Wall in North East England are within easy reach.

Shopping: Shoppers can spend their money in Eldon Square or Monument Mall, or can visit the area around the City Library where designer label shops are located. The famous Metro Centre, a vast covered shopping centre, is across the river in Gateshead.

Population: 260,000
Student population: 31,000

Proximity to the city centre:
University of Newcastle: campus in the city centre
University of Northumbria: 2 sites in the city centre, another site 3 miles outside

For more information:
Tourist Information Centre
132 Grainger Street
Newcastle NE1 5AF
0191-277 8000

tourist.info@newcastle.gov.uk
www.newcastle.gov.uk
www.visitnewcastle.co.uk
www.visitnewcastlegateshead.com

Nottingham

Nottingham is probably still most famous for the legendary Robin Hood, whose redistribution of income policy would be welcome to most of the city's students. The locals are generally friendly to students, and many choose to settle here after graduation. The distance between the two universities means that their students tend not to fraternise and live out in different areas. Lenton is favoured by students at the older university and Forest Fields by those at Nottingham Trent. Accommodation takes some finding, but it is not over priced.

Getting Around

Buses are reasonable, and a new tram network opened in spring 2004. Cycle lanes and relatively flat terrain make cycling popular. Nottingham is easily accessible by road, rail and air. London is 122 miles away, and trains take 1 hour 45 minutes. The nearest airport is Nottingham East Midlands.

Attractions for Students

Sport: The National Ice Centre has two Olympic-sized rinks, whilst the National Watersport Centre at Holme Pierrepoint offers white-water rafting in addition to rowing, canoeing and water skiing. Test and county cricket are played at Trent Bridge. Nottingham is equipped with ample leisure centres and swimming pools. The nearby Peak District National Park offers excellent walking and climbing.

Culture and nightlife: Nottingham has a thriving nightlife, from venues such as Rock City, the Rescue Rooms and the Marcus Garvey Centre catering for most musical tastes, to a good selection of clubs. Certain venues may be expensive, but there are plenty of student nights. Theatre is provided at the Theatre Royal and the Nottingham Playhouse and concerts at the Concert Hall. There is no shortage of cinemas, including the Savoy with its double seats and the recently opened UGC at the Cornerhouse. The Broadway Arts Cinema caters for more esoteric tastes. Nottingham offers a host of pubs – including the 'oldest pub in the world', The Trip to Jerusalem, dating back to 1189. The redeveloped canal side area has three bars and a comedy club. The Galleries of Justice is an award-winning museum of the history of crime, punishment and British justice throughout the ages. The annual Goose Fair is a three-day event held in October on the Forest Recreation Ground. Many of the 400 caves lying under the city are open for tours.

Shopping: The small and compact city centre offers the full range of high-street brands and designer names. Nottingham was ranked fourth in The Experian UK retail rankings.

Population: 267,000
Student population: 39,000

Proximity to the city centre:
University of Nottingham: campus about 4 miles from the city centre
Nottingham Trent University: 1 city centre campus; 2 other sites about 4 miles from the city centre

For more information:
City Information Centre, 1–4 Smithy Row, Nottingham NG1 2BY
0115-915 5330

enquiries@experiencenottinghamshire.com
www.experiencenottinghamshire.com
www.leftlion.co.uk
www.nottinghamcity.gov.uk
www.itchynottingham.co.uk

Oxford

The city is beautiful, ancient and expensive. Medium-sized, it has a cosmopolitan and youthful atmosphere. A thriving nightlife and dynamic music scene have added to the buzz of the place. Its historical architecture is world famous and attracts many tourists each year. High costs are probably one reason why student social life tends to be concentrated in college bars and in the Brookes' Students' Union. Contact between the two universities is minimal, though probably greatest in the cosmopolitan Cowley Road area where many students look for non-collegiate, and often overpriced, accommodation.

Getting Around

Most students use bikes, and cycle lanes and cycle parking are abundant. Local buses are inexpensive and services are good. Cars are actively discouraged in the city centre. London is 59 miles away, and trains take 1 hour. Coaches run to London 24 hours a day. There are special coach links to Heathrow (half hourly) and Gatwick (hourly) airports.

Attractions for Students

Sport: The city has a range of swimming pools and leisure centres, an ice rink and an athletics track. Many of the Oxford colleges have their own sports facilities; Oxford Brookes has a pool at Westminster College as well as its own sports provisions. The river provides opportunities for rowing. Rugby, football, basketball and ice hockey are all played.

Culture and nightlife: A number of famous bands has come out of Oxford in recent years, and there are now several venues for live music with gig nights for up and coming bands. Bars, clubs and restaurants are proliferating and a varied club scene with special student nights is attracting students to the city centre. Oxford has two cinemas, plus the Phoenix and the Ultimate Picture Palace. The Oxford Playhouse is the main theatre. The New Theatre is a venue for concerts. The Museum of the History of Science, the Ashmolean, the University Museum of Natural History and the adjacent Pitt Rivers are examples of the many museums. The Oxford Art Weeks takes place in May and June each year. There are walking tours of Oxford and the colleges, which provide an interesting and informed view of the city. The tours leave Oxford Information Centre daily at 11am and 2pm.

Shopping: Cornmarket and Queen Streets are popular shopping areas, as are the Westgate and Clarendon Centres and the traditional Covered Market. Book lovers are spoilt for choice.

Population: 142,000
Student population: 28,000

Proximity to the city centre:

Oxford University: the colleges are an integral part of the city, with most of the undergraduate colleges being in or near to the city centre
Oxford Brookes University: two campuses in Headington, 2 miles from the centre; Wheatley, 6 miles east; and Botley, 3 miles west

For more information:
Oxford Information Centre
15–16 Broad Street, Oxford OX1 3AS
01865 726871

tic@oxford.gov.uk
www.visitoxford.org
www.oxford.gov.uk
www.dailyinfo.co.uk
www.itchyoxford.co.uk

Sheffield

The rejuvenation of the city has put Sheffield back on the map, with the multimillion-pound remodelling of the city centre a major contributory factor. Known for its friendliness, it has long been a popular city with students, a high proportion of whom choose to stay, or return, and settle here. Students live throughout the city, rather than in isolated enclaves, demonstrating just how easy it is to get around. Rents and the cost of living are generally reasonable.

Getting Around

The Supertram serves both universities, the city centre and a number of the main venues and buses are reliable but not cheap. Cycling is only for the fit or the determined as Sheffield is built on hills. London is just over 160 miles away with frequent train services taking about 2 hours 30 minutes. The nearest airports are Manchester, Nottingham East Midlands and Robin Hood Airport at Doncaster. Coaches serve many UK destinations.

Attractions for Students

Sport: Sheffield has two climbing centres; a ski village for skiing and snowboarding; an Olympic-size swimming pool and the world's deepest diving pool. Ice hockey (Sheffield Steelers) and basketball (Sheffield Sharks) are both based at the Arena. There are two football teams, Sheffield Wednesday and Sheffield United, and Rugby League. The National Ice Centre opened in 2003. One third of Sheffield is within the Peak District National Park, a Mecca for hill walking and rock climbing enthusiasts.

Culture and nightlife: Sheffield has more than 30 cinema screens, including those at the acclaimed independent Showroom Cinema. Two main theatres, the Crucible and Lyceum, along with the smaller Studio theatre provide the largest theatre complex outside London's South Bank. The Hallam FM Arena and Sheffield City Hall are just two of the venues hosting major concerts whilst the Leadmill, Boardwalk and Octagon Centre put on regular gigs. Sheffield has a reputation for a vibrant music scene and legendary clubs. The Millennium Galleries house major exhibitions from the V & A and the Tate. Magna, the science adventure centre, celebrates the natural elements of earth, air, fire and water. Kelham Island Museum provides an insight into Sheffield's steel and cutlery industries.

Shopping: All the high-street brands (and more) can be found in the city centre with the Devonshire Quarter being a particular favourite for independent designers. Ecclesall Road offers a range of boutiques whilst the Meadowhall complex is one of the largest shopping malls in Europe.

Population: 513,000
Student population: 48,000

Proximity to the city centre:
University of Sheffield: campus about half a mile west of the city centre
Sheffield Hallam University: campuses in the city centre and approx 1 mile southwest of the city centre.

For more information:
Sheffield Tourism
Blades Enterprise Centre
John Street
Sheffield S2 4SW
0114-221 1900

visitor@sheffield.gov.uk
www.sheffieldtourism.co.uk
www.itchysheffield.co.uk

Southampton

Southampton is known for its waterfront and maritime heritage. Situated close to the New Forest and areas of outstanding natural beauty, it is one of the UK's greenest cities. A development of £160 million is planned for the city centre, creating an entertainment arena, luxury hotel and a City Plaza. A lively place to study with plenty on offer is made affordable by the availability of part-time work.

Getting Around

The city has an excellent student Uni-Link bus service that connects the campuses and a free City Link service from the train station to several key areas. London is 78 miles away and 1 hour 15 minutes by train. The coach station is near to the city centre. Southampton International Airport is to the north, with flights to UK and European destinations. Red Funnel Ferries provide a regular service from Southampton Town Quay to the Isle of Wight (Cowes).

Attractions for Students

Sport: Water sports are everywhere from yachting on the Solent to ocean racing, power boating and windsurfing. In September the city hosts its annual boat show, the largest in Europe. The Quays includes the Eddie Read Swimming and Diving Complex and there is a good sports centre at Bassett. Southampton FC has its home at Friends Provident St. Mary's Stadium, and Hampshire County Cricket Club is at the Rose Bowl. The city has a dry ski slope, tennis courts and all-weather pitches.

Culture and Nightlife: There is a wide range of traditional pubs and trendy bars. Multiscreen cinemas are the Odeon at Leisureworld and UGC at Ocean Village. The Harbour Lights Picturehouse is the independent cinema. The Mayflower Theatre has ballet, panto, opera and comedy. A more alternative programme is at the Nuffield on the Highfield campus. The Turner Sims Concert Hall is a leading venue for jazz, folk and classical music and the Southampton Guildhall is the large music venue. The main galleries are the John Hansard Gallery and the City Art Gallery. The Millais features the work of young artists. Southampton has a huge dance venue, the Ikon Diva and a number of rock and alternative clubs. Homelands is hosted at Winchester to the north of the city.

Shopping: West Quay is a £300-million shopping development with all the usual brands. The antiques quarter is located at Old Northern Road, and traditional and specialist shopping is at Bedford Place.

Population: 221,000
Student Population: 30,000

Proximity to the city centre:
University of Southampton: main campus at Highfield, close to city centre. School of Art is 12 miles north at Winchester.
Southampton Solent University: at East Park Terrace in the city centre.

For more information:
Southampton Tourist Information Centre
9 Civic Centre Road
Southampton SO14 7FJ
023 8083 3333

tourist.information@southampton.gov.uk
www.visit-southampton.co.uk
www.southampton.gov.uk

Colleges of Higher Education

This listing gives contact details for higher education institutions not mentioned elsewhere within the book. All the institutions of the University of London which do not have their own entry are listed under the main entry for the University of London. All the institutions listed below offer degree course, some providing a wide range of courses while others are specialist colleges with a limited range of courses and a small intake. Those marked with a * are members of SCOP (the Standing Conference of Principals; www.scop.ac.uk).

The Arts Institute at Bournemouth*
Wallisdown, Poole, Dorset BH12 5HH
01202 533011
courseoffice@aib.ac.uk
www.aib.ac.uk

Bell College
Almada Street, Hamilton ML3 0JB
01698 283100
inform@bell.ac.uk
www.bell.ac.uk

Birmingham College of Food, Tourism and Creative Studies*
Summer Row, Birmingham B3 1JB
0121 604 1000
marketing@bcftcs.ac.uk
www.bcftcs.ac.uk

Bishop Grosseteste College, Lincoln*
Newport, Lincoln LN1 3DY
01522 527347
info@bgc.ac.uk
www.bgc.ac.uk

Buckinghamshire Chilterns University College*
Queen Alexandra Road, High Wycombe,
Buckinghamshire HP11 2JZ
01494 522141
marketing@bcuc.ac.uk
www.bcuc.ac.uk

Central School of Speech and Drama*
Embassy Theatre, 64 Eton Avenue,
London NW3 3HY
020-7722 8183
enquiries@cssd.ac.uk
www.cssd.ac.uk

Conservatoire for Drama and Dance
c/o London Contemporary Dance School
The Place, 17 Duke's Road,
London WC1H 9PY
020-7121 1000
info@theplace.org.uk
www.theplace.org.uk
and **Royal Academy of Dramatic Arts**
62–64 Gower Street, London WC1E 6ED
020 7636 7076
www.rada.org.uk

Cumbria Institute of the Arts*
Brampton Road, Carlisle,
Cumbria CA3 9AY
01228 400300
info@cumbria.ac.uk
www.cumbria.ac.uk
Cumbria Institute of the Arts and St Martin's College have entered into a joint project to amalgamate to create a new University of Cumbria from August 2007.

Dartington College of Arts*
Hartington Hall Estate
Totnes, Devon TQ9 6EJ
01803 862224
enquiries@dartington.ac.uk
www.dartington.ac.uk

Edge Hill College*
St Helens Road,
Ormskirk, Lancs L39 4QP
01695 575171
enquiries@edgehill.ac.uk
www.edgehill.ac.uk

Edinburgh College of Art
Lauriston Place, Edinburgh EH3 9DF
0131-221 6000
registration@eca.ac.uk
www.eca.ac.uk

Glasgow School of Art
167 Renfrew Street,
Glasgow G3 6RQ
0141-353 4500
registry@gsa.ac.uk
www.gsa.ac.uk

Harper Adams University College*
Edgmond, Newport,
Shropshire TF10 8NB
01952 820280
admissions@harper-adams.ac.uk
www.harper-adams.ac.uk

Newman College of Higher Education*
Genners Lane, Bartley Green,
Birmingham B32 3NT
0121-476 1181
registry@newman.ac.uk
www.newman.ac.uk

North East Wales Institute
Plas Coch Campus, Mold Road,
Wrexham, N. Wales LL11 2AW
01978 290666
admissions@newi.ac.uk
www.newi.ac.uk

Northern School of Contemporary Dance
98 Chapeltown Road
Leeds LS7 4BH
0113-219 3000
admissions@nscd.ac.uk
www.nscd.ac.uk

Norwich School of Art and Design*
St George Street, Norwich NR3 1BB
01603 610561
info@nsad.ac.uk
www.nsad.ac.uk

Queen Margaret University College
Clerwood Terrace
Edinburgh EH12 8TS
0131-317 3247
admissions@qmuc.ac.uk
www.qmuc.ac.uk

Ravensbourne College of Design and Communication*
Walden Road
Chislehurst, Kent BR7 5SN
020-8289 4900
info@rave.ac.uk
www.rave.ac.uk

Rose Bruford College*
Lamorbey Park Campus, Burnt Oak Lane,
Sidcup, Kent DA15 9DF
020-8308 2600
enquiries@bruford.ac.uk
www.bruford.ac.uk

Royal Agricultural College*
Stroud Road, Cirencester,
Gloucestershire GL7 6JS
01285 652531
admissions@rac.ac.uk
www.royagcol.ac.uk

Royal College of Art
Kensington Gore, London SW7 2EU
020-7590 4444
admissions@rca.ac.uk
www.rca.ac.uk

Royal College of Music
Prince Consort Road, London SW7 2BS
020-7589 3643
info@rcm.ac.uk
www.rcm.ac.uk

Royal College of Nursing*
FREEPOST, 23Lon20336,
London W1E 0DW
020-7647 3700
distance.learning@rcn.org.uk
www.rcn.org.uk

Royal Northern College of Music
124 Oxford Road
Manchester M13 9RD
0161-907 5200
info@rncm.ac.uk
www.rncm.ac.uk

Royal Scottish Academy of Music and Drama
100 Renfrew Street,
Glasgow G2 3DB
0141-332 8901
registry@rsamd.ac.uk
www.rsamd.ac.uk

Royal Welsh College of Music and Drama
Castle Grounds,
Cathays Park,
Cardiff CF10 3ER
029-2034 2854
music.admissions@rwcmd.ac.uk
drama.admissions@rwcmd.ac.uk
www.rwcmd.ac.uk

The College of St Mark and St John*
Derriford Road,
Plymouth
Devon PL6 8BH
01752 636890
admissions@marjon.ac.uk
www.marjon.ac.uk

St Martin's College*
Bowerham Road
Lancaster LA1 3JD
01524 384384
admissions@ucsm.ac.uk
www.ucsm.ac.uk
St Martin's College and Cumbria Institute of the Arts
have entered into a joint project to amalgamate to create
a new University of Cumbria from August 2007.

St Mary's College*
Waldegrave Road,
Twickenham,
Middlesex TW1 4SX
020-8240 4000
enquiry@smuc.ac.uk
www.smuc.ac.uk

St Mary's University College
191 Falls Road
Belfast BT12 6FE
028-9032 7678
admis@stmarys-belfast.ac.uk
stmarys-belfast.ac.uk

Stranmillis University College
Stranmillis Road
Belfast BT9 5DY
028-9038 1271
registry@stran.ac.uk
www.stran.ac.uk

Swansea Institute of Higher Education
Mount Pleasant, Swansea SA1 6ED
01792 481085
enquiry@sihe.ac.uk
www.sihe.ac.uk

Trinity and All Saints College*
Brownberrie Lane, Horsforth,
Leeds LS18 5HD
0113-283 7100
admissions@tasc.ac.uk
www.tasc.ac.uk

Trinity College Carmarthen
College Road, Carmarthen
Wales SA31 3EP
01267 676767
registry@trinity-cnm.ac.uk
www.trinity-cm.ac.uk

Trinity College of Music
King Charles Court, Old Royal Naval Court,
Greenwich, London SE10 9JF
0208-305 4444
info@tcm.ac.uk
www.tcm.ac.uk

University College for the Creative Arts*
info@ucreate.ac.uk
www.ucreate.ac.uk
New Dover Road, Canterbury, Kent CT1 3AN
01227 817302
Ashley Road, Epson, Surrey KT18 5BE
01372 728881
Falkner Road, Farnham, Surrey GU9 7DS
01252 722441
Oakwood Park, Maidstone, Kent ME16 8AG
01622 620000
Fort Pitt, Rochester, Kent ME1 1DZ
01634 888702

University College Falmouth*
Woodlane Campus, Falmouth,
Cornwall TR11 4RH
01326 211077
admissions@falmouth.ac.uk
www.falmouth.ac.uk

University of the Highlands and Islands
UHI Millennium Institute, Caledonia House,
63 Academy Street, Inverness IV1 1LU
01463 279000
eo@uhi.ac.uk
www.uhi.ac.uk

Wimbledon School of Art*
Merton Hall Road
London SW19 3QA
020-8408 5000
info@wimbledon.ac.uk
www.wimbledon.ac.uk

Writtle College*
Chelmsford
Essex CM1 3RR
01245 424200
info@writtle.ac.uk
www.writtle.ac.uk

York St John University College*
Lord Mayor's Walk,
York YO31 7EX
01904 716960
admissions@yorksj.ac.uk
www.yorksj.ac.uk

Internet Resources

Abbreviations

EEA European Economic Area
ELB Education and Library Board (Northern Ireland)
EU European Union
FTE Full-Time Equivalent
HE Higher Education
LEA Local Education Authority
SLC Student Loans Company
TQA Teaching Quality Assessment (later called Subject Reviews)

General

DEL Department for Employment and Learning (Northern Ireland)
www.delni.gov.uk
DfES Department for Education and Skills
www.dfes.gov.uk
HEFCE Higher Education Funding Council for England
www.hefce.ac.uk
HEFCW Higher Education Funding Council for Wales (Education and Learning Wales)
www.elwa.ac.uk
HESA Higher Education Statistics Agency
www.hesa.ac.uk
Mayfield University Consultants
www.mayfield-uc.org.uk
NUS National Union of Students
www.nusonline.co.uk
OFSTED Office for Standards in Education
www.ofsted.gov.uk
QAA Quality Assurance Agency for Higher Education
www.qaa.ac.uk
RAE Research Assessment Exercise
www.hero.ac.uk/rae
SCOP Standing Conference of Principals
www.scop.ac.uk
SFC Scottish Funding Council
www.sfc.ac.uk
UniversitiesUK (formerly The Committee of Vice-Chancellors and Principals)
www.universitiesuk.ac.uk

Applying to University

Aimhigher
www.aimhigher.ac.uk
BBC
www.bbc.co.uk/dna/h2g2/A626762
www.bbc.co.uk/radio1/onelife/education
www.bbc.co.uk/ouch/lifefiles/student
BUSA British Universities Sports Association
www.busa.org.uk
Course Discover Database
www.coursediscoveronline.co.uk_
Foundation Degrees
www.foundationdegree.org.uk
HERO Higher Education and Research Opportunities in the United Kingdom
www.hero.ac.uk
NISS National Information Services and Systems
www.hero.ac.uk/niss
SKILL National Bureau for Students with Disabilities
www.skill.org.uk
UCAS Universities and Colleges Admissions Service for the UK
www.ucas.com
UCS University and College Sport
www.ucsport.net
UK Course Finder
www.ukcoursefinder.co.uk
UK Sport
www.uksport.gov.uk
Uni4me
www.uni4me.co.uk
University Open Days
www.opendays.com
University Options
www.universityoptions.co.uk
University of Wolverhampton UK Sensitive Maps
Universities and HE Colleges
www.scit.wlv.ac.uk/ukinfo/ac/
  index.php?refs1196=(none)
Unofficial Guides
www.unofficial-guides.com
Woody's Web-Watch
www.woodyswebwatch.com

Managing Your Money
CDL Career Development Loans
www.lifelonglearning.co.uk/cdl/index.htm
DfES Higher Education Student Support
www.dfes.gov.uk/studentsupport
Department of Health
Financial Support for Healthcare Students
www.dh.gov.uk
EGAS Educational Grants Advisory Service
www.egas-online.org.uk
HMRC HM Revenue and Customs
www.hmrc.gov.uk/students
Moneyfacts
www.moneyfacts.co.uk
Need 2 Know
www.need2know.co.uk
SAAS Student Awards Agency for Scotland
www.saas.gov.uk
SLC Student Loans Company Limited
www.slc.co.uk
Student Finance Direct
www.studentsupportdirect.co.uk
Student Finance Northern Ireland
www.studentfinanceni.co.uk
Student Finance Wales
www.studentfinancewales.co.uk
Support 4 Learning
www.support4learning.org.uk/money
UNIAID
www.uniaid.org.uk

Gap Year
CSV Community Service Volunteers
www.csv.org.uk
FCO Foreign and Commonwealth Office
Know Before You Go Campaign
www.fco.gov.uk/travel
GAP Activity Projects
www.gap.org.uk
Gap Year Company Ltd
www.gapyear.com
Millennium Volunteers
www.mvonline.gov.uk
Project Trust
www.projecttrust.org.uk

Raleigh International
www.raleigh.org.uk
Russell Commission
www.russellcommission.org
Timebank (volunteering)
www.timebank.org.uk
Volunteering England
www.volunteering.org.uk
Volunteering/Voluntary and Community Sector
www.dfes.gov.uk/volunteering
Worldwide Volunteering
http://wwv.org.uk
Year in Industry
www.yini.org.uk
Year Out Group
www.yearoutgroup.org

Coming From Overseas
The British Council
www.britishcouncil.org
English UK
www.englishuk.com
DfES Student Support EU students
www.dfes.gov.uk/studentsupport/eustudents
DfES International Students
www.dfes.gov.uk/international-students
Education UK (British Council course search)
www.educationuk.org
Education UK (Scholarships Database)
www.educationuk.org/scholarships
Embassy World
www.embassyworld.com
FCO Foreign and Commonwealth Office
Visa Information
www.i-uk.com
www.ukvisas.gov.uk
Sources of Funding for International Students (British Council)
www.britishcouncil.org/learning-funding-your-studies.htm
UKCOSA Council for International Education
www.ukcosa.org.uk
UK NARIC National Recognition Information Centre
www.naric.org.uk

Studying Abroad
ACU Association of Commonwealth
Universities
www.acu.ac.uk
The European Choice
www.eurochoice.org.uk
Fulbright Commission
www.fulbright.co.uk
Leonardo Da Vinci Programme
http://europa.eu.int/comm/education/program
mes/leonardo/leonardo_en.html
see also
European Training for the UK
www.leonardo.org.uk
Socrates/Erasmus Education and Training
http://europa.eu.int/comm/education/program
mes/socrates/erasmus/erasmus_en.html
UKSEC UK Socrates-Erasmus Council
www.erasmus.ac.uk
Study Abroad
www.studyabroad.com

Work Experience and Graduate Employment
Activate
www.activate.co.uk/
AGCAS Association of Graduate Careers
Advisory Services
www.agcas.org.uk
The Big Choice
www.thebigchoice.com
BUNAC
http://validate.bunac.org.uk
Graduate Prospects
www.prospects.ac.uk
Graduate Careers in Ireland
www.gradireland.com
**National Association of Student Employment
Services**
www.nases.org.uk

National Council for Work Experience
www.work-experience.org.
Shell STEP
www.step.org.uk
SummerJobs.com
www.summerjobs.com
**Training and Development Agency for
Schools**
www.tda.gov.uk
Vacation Work Publications
www.vacationwork.co.uk
Where to Live
BBC
www.bbc.co.uk/radio1/onelife/housing
Student Accommodation
www.thestudentvillage.com
Directgov Public Services
www.direct.gov.uk
DWP Department for Work and Pensions
Housing Benefit
www.dwp.gov.uk/lifeevent/benefits/
housing_benefit.asp
Council Tax
www.dwp.gov.uk/lifeevent/benefits/
council_tax_benefit.asp
CAB Citizens Advice Bureau
www.citizensadvice.org.uk
www.adviceguide.org.uk
The Letting Centre
www.letlink.co.uk
Traveline Public Transport Information
www.traveline.org.uk
Safety
www.good2bsecure.gov.uk
www.crimereduction.gov.uk/studentcrime1.htm
www.immobilise.com
www.suzylamplugh.org
UNITE
www.unite-students.com

Index